The Crouching Beast

The Crouching Beast

*A United States Army Lieutenant's
Account of the Battle for
Hamburger Hill, May 1969*

FRANK BOCCIA

McFarland & Company, Inc., Publishers
Jefferson, North Carolina, and London

LIBRARY OF CONGRESS CATALOGUING-IN-PUBLICATION DATA

Boccia, Frank.
The crouching beast : a United States Army lieutenant's account of the Battle for Hamburger Hill, May 1969 / Frank Boccia.
     p.   cm.
Includes index.

ISBN 978-0-7864-7439-4
softcover : acid free paper ∞

1. Boccia, Frank. 2. Hamburger Hill, Battle of, Vietnam, 1969.
3. Vietnam War, 1961–1975 — Personal narratives, American. 4. United States. Army — Biography. 5. Soldiers — United States — Biography. I. Title.
DS557.8.A54B63 2013   959.704'342 — dc23   2013017741

BRITISH LIBRARY CATALOGUING DATA ARE AVAILABLE

© 2013 Frank Boccia. All rights reserved

No part of this book may be reproduced or transmitted in any form or by any means, electronic or mechanical, including photocopying or recording, or by any information storage and retrieval system, without permission in writing from the publisher.

Cover photograph: WO Searcey, Genna's seatmate, guiding in a Ghost Rider bringing in the first of the Alpha Company troops, at 1500 hours, April 26, 1969. Genna was badly wounded, and Searcey killed, during the NVA attack that night (photograph by Pat Lynch)

Manufactured in the United States of America

McFarland & Company, Inc., Publishers
Box 611, Jefferson, North Carolina 28640
www.mcfarlandpub.com

Table of Contents

Acknowledgments vii
Preface 1
Author's Note 5

1. The Mountains of Viet Nam   9
2. Firebase Helen   20
3. The First Patrol   33
4. Mud Is the Universal Constant   48
5. The Poor Guys in Korea   60
6. The Tiger Dines   67
7. Black Jack   74
8. Firebase Barbara   84
9. Firebase Brick   95
10. Firebase Rakkasan: Abbot's Tale   106
11. March Madness   116
12. Dickson's Shining Moment   126
13. Father Haney's Lament   133
14. Dennis Helms, Bravo One Six Romeo   141
15. The Banana Tree   149
16. The Rao Trang   159
17. Zeus Frowns   171
18. The Crater   178
19. Death Dance of the Ghost Riders   189
20. Welcome to the 6th NVA Regimental HQ   206
21. The Body Bags   222
22. Rescued by the Gnome   233

Table of Contents

23. Black Jack's Seminar   242
24. Firebase Airborne   257
25. Sergeant Samuel Wright RA   267
26. Palace Guard   276
27. The Broken Strap   287
28. The Ordeal of Bravo Four Six   296
29. The Clearing   308
30. The Book of Myles Westman   325
31. Feeling Our Way   338
32. Sanguis Agni   350
33. Logan's Run   365
34. The Bamboo Corridor   376
35. Charlie's Ridge   387
36. Fratricide   401
37. The Number Seventeen   413
38. The Stain   422
39. The Storm   434
40. The Naked Beast   447

Epilogue   451
Glossary   455
Index   459

Acknowledgments

The list of people who have helped with this manuscript is long. The most obvious ones are those who have taken the time to provide accounts of their actions and perceptions during the six months covered in the book: My brother officers Jerry Wolosenko and Charles Denholm; Joel Trautman and Dan Bresnahan, who not only gave testimony to what occurred with Alpha Company but was invaluable in helping me with the discrepancies and omissions of the after-action report. Gerald "Bob" Harkins, now president of the Hamburger Hill chapter of the Rakkasans, and Mike Smith have been extremely helpful and supporting. Luther "Lee" Sanders, then CO of Delta, and of course, General Honeycutt, who has made me aware of many events that took place out of my ken during the battle.

I am grateful to Tom Lough, then CO of the 326th Engineers, and several of the pilots of the Ghost Rider squadron who inserted us into Hill 1485, for their insights and information: Chris Genna, Gene Franck, Luis Molinar, Pat Lynch; all these people helped enormously.

And, of course, the men of First Platoon, who have provided both inspiration and information throughout the years. I am grateful to them all, but I must single out Dennis and Beverley Helms, and John and Linda Snyder, for their unrelenting and steadfast support, encouragement and care over the decades. They are four special people.

Preface

The battle of Dong Ap took place over 11 days, from the 10th to the 20th of May 1969. From a military historian's perspective, compared to the great battles of the American Civil War and the two world wars, the battle was modest in its scope. Initially, it involved five infantry battalions totaling over 2,000 men, as well as airmen, support artillery, engineers and medical corps personnel from other commands. Fewer than 100 Americans died, among some 500 or so casualties; a minuscule number, compared to the Somme, when 20,000 British soldiers died in less than half an hour, or Cold Harbor, or Saipan.

And yet it caused a firestorm of criticism, and earned its sobriquet Hamburger Hill. For those of us who were there, the number of casualties was irrelevant. What mattered was that they were ours, Rakkasans primarily. What mattered to me was that so many of them were mine; men of First Platoon, Bravo Company, 3rd of the 187th. They and many others left their blood on the mountain called by the locals Dong Ap Bia—the Mountain of the Crouching Beast.

Casualties were staggering. Alpha Company, the lightest hit of the four companies of the battalion, took over 30 percent casualties; Bravo, just over 50 percent. Charlie lost 60 percent, after replacements—their original roster suffered over 75 percent—and Delta a mind-numbing 75 percent including replacements. When the battalion CP dead and wounded were added, the total represented 60 percent of the entire unit. This is stunning. The two wars in which unit casualties had been the highest, the American Civil War and the First World War, had rarely seen units suffer as much as 50 percent dead and wounded. At the battle of the Somme, which by all accounts represents the nadir in military tactics and is the bloodiest, most sickening example of carnage and destruction the modern world has ever seen on a battlefield, a unit that took 50 percent casualties was classified as *destroyed*. Such a unit would normally be disbanded.

Three of the four company commanders were wounded, two seriously. Of the 14 original platoon leaders, only four made it through the battle, and two of them were lightly wounded; three of the five replacement platoon leaders were also wounded or killed. Three of the four FOs—forward observers—went down; the battalion CO, Lt Col Honeycutt, was wounded twice. NCOs, senior and junior, were also disproportionate casualties: Bravo Company alone lost a first sergeant, two platoon sergeants and nine squad leaders.

The enemy suffered even greater loss. Some 600 dead were buried on the hill itself, in mass graves bulldozed into the flanks of the mountain, but the testimony of the Montagnard tribe that formed the support battalion for the NVA 29th Regiment, who took the brunt of the action, indicates that more than 1,000 died and hundreds more were wounded.

The politicians, predictably, were not long in making their opinions known. Ted Kennedy, then still a new and junior senator, denounced the action on the floor; scathing editorials were written, in which the stupidity of the generals was excoriated, particularly so when it was announced, a few weeks later, that we were abandoning the hill we had purchased so dearly.

But no war in our history has been as badly reported and as thoroughly misunderstood as the war in Viet Nam, and this is but an example of that. The fact is that we never set out to capture Hill 937; it wasn't even mentioned in our briefings before the operation. Contrary to published reports, it does not dominate the A Shau valley; there are too many intervening ridges and hills, and the valley floor can't be seen from its summit. Even on the second day, the 11th, when I was told to move my platoon up the southwestern flank of the hill, it was with the purpose of establishing a battalion CP on top. We had no interest in the hill as a topographical feature, and the only other thing we heard initially was a vague and unsubstantiated reference to a possible NVA supply complex there.

No, we didn't care about the hill. We were there to seek out, find, engage and kill the enemy—the North Vietnamese Army. We didn't expect them to hold and fight; they seldom did, in the face of as many troops as we had. And when they did hold, and not disappear over the Laotian border, only two kilometers distant, we moved in on them and mauled them until they broke.

There was a reason they held their ground. Dong Ap Bia was one of the most heavily fortified hills in all of Viet Nam. It was a perfect defensive position; the ridges leading to its summit were long, narrow and steep-sided, making maneuvering impossible. Laos, as mentioned, was only a couple of kilometers distant, and across its borders were replacements, resupply, medical facilities and a safe avenue of retreat. Other supply areas were within a few kilometers, and so were other regiments, poised to strike our firebases and flanks—as they did on Firebase Airborne, the evening of the 12th.

The ridge Bravo Company followed, the central of the three western approaches to the hilltop, led eventually to a small clearing; it was a true razorback ridge, no more than a meter or so wide as it approached the crest, and the flanks were not only deep and steep, but choked with dense triple-canopy vegetation. Movement along those ridge flanks was impossible. So in order to reach the top, we had to go through the clearing, about 20 meters wide and perhaps 30 deep, dominated by two small knolls at its eastern end, and by the mountain summit and other, higher ridges on either side.

It was full of bunkers, spider holes and automatic weapons positions, and guarded by claymores, shape charges, trip wired grenades and direct RPG fire. I have never seen or heard or read of a more perfect — and deadly — defensive position.

So a good part of this book deals with what we went through to breach that clearing, over the 11 days in May. But I begin it much earlier than that, months before May; in mid–December, and it starts not in the A Shau but on a firebase many kilometers to the east called Helen, high on a ridge overlooking the imperial capital of Hue and, not coincidentally, a sprawling base camp called Evans, the home of the Third Brigade of the 101st Airborne Division.

It is not that anything of historical significance took place during those intervening months; there were no major battles, and for my platoon, at any rate, no meaningful contact until late April, on Dong Ngai. And when I do begin to recount the battle, my perspective is, by necessity, narrowly focused. The story as I wrote it is not a history, although I emphasize that it is accurate; I have had access to, along with my memory (excellent in my youth), my diary, kept on almost a daily basis; my notebook used while in the field; my letters home; after-action reports; oral and written accounts from other participants, and the research of others who wrote about the battle. But in the main, what I write about is what I saw and experienced directly.

It is not a history, but a drama; real, about real events and real people, but a drama. Its protagonists are for the most part the men of First Platoon; I write about them because I know of no other group of men whose story deserves to be told more than theirs. I try to present them as they are; neither cartoon heroes nor unthinking automatons, but human beings of almost incredible resource, resiliency and resolve. They are your neighbors and employees, sons and husbands, students and teachers. And they did extraordinary things. What they showed, collectively, was that the human spirit has no limits.

I wasn't born in the United States; I wasn't even a citizen as the time of the battle. Faced with the choice of returning to my native Italy when I graduated from college, and living a safe and comfortable life, or staying in the states and facing the draft and uncertainty, without hesitation, I enlisted for the army and OCS.

I grew up playing baseball and basketball, trading baseball cards, drinking beer on a Friday night with buddies and dating girls on Saturday in the family car, but I didn't become truly American until I knew these men. They are your neighbors, and they are the bedrock of this nation.

To come to know the men of my platoon, as I hope you will in the following pages, was the greatest privilege of all the many that I was blessed with as a young man. To know these men was to come to know America, and America at its finest.

I want the reader to know them as I did, or as close to that as my skill as a writer can effect. You will see, in the months before Dong Ap Bia, a great change; but you will note that the change was most pronounced and complete in me. I was a much better man and officer after leading these men, and that was their doing, not mine.

I make no apologies for the language I use; it is that of the soldier, and I will not change it. No, it is not the diction I use in my living room or in the office, but then that would be as out of place in a platoon CP as the profanity would be back home. I have tried to keep the dialogue as realistic and true to events as I can recall. As I said, these men are not plaster saints or cartoon characters.

Every May since 1999, the Rakkasans have gathered at Fort Campbell, in Kentucky, to commemorate the events of 1969. It is a solemn time, as we honor our dead; it is a joyous time, as we celebrate being reunited with our comrades. Above all, it is a time for remembrance. And more: It is a time for quiet pride, for we know what we did, and how much it cost.

Our unit — the 3/187th — is now the most highly decorated battalion in the history of the United States Army, and we have been in existence only since World War II. Two of those unit awards — The Valorous Unit Award and the Presidential Unit Citation — were earned in a 26 day period, for actions on Dong Ngai and Dong Ap Bia. This is wholly unprecedented; no other unit has ever been so recognized. And it is by chance that I was in the middle of both actions. I say this not to aggrandize myself — as you will see, I had little choice in the matter — but to point out that what I write about is truly historical.

A word about Weldon Honeycutt: He was a lieutenant colonel then, our battalion commander, and was called Black Jack. Because I end my account with the last day of the battle, on May 20th, I say nothing about him after the event. I should. As he is portrayed (accurately), he will seem harsh and even brutal; egocentric and demanding. He was, and probably still is, all those things. He rarely praised and often excoriated With me, in particular, he was seldom anything but abusive and scathing. I had no reason to love him.

But then, I wasn't paid to love or even like him. I was paid to follow him, and I must make this very clear: No one else, no other officer I have known, could have gained victory at Dong Ap Bia. The battalion was, for the most part, blessed with excellent junior officers, captains and lieutenants, and we did our jobs well, but we would not — could not — have achieved what we did without his leadership and his fierce, unyielding will to defeat the enemy. If we have attained any small measure of renown, it is due to him.

Newspaper and magazine accounts exaggerated greatly the anger directed at him by the surviving troops after the battle, including the absurd and thoroughly unsubstantiated claim that someone placed a $10,000 bounty on his head, but there is no doubt that many of them, in the immediate aftermath, did believe he had pushed us beyond our limits. But a truer measure of how he is viewed is that in 2012 the Hamburger Hill Chapter of the Rakkasans voted to change our name to the Weldon F Honeycutt/Hamburger Hill Chapter of the 187th Airborne Infantry Regiment. Make no mistake: Leadership counts for something.

Author's Note

Historians and military analysts will quickly recognize that there are major discrepancies between this account and numerous details in the official 3/187th after-action report for operation Apache Snow. I am fully aware of them all.

This book is not the place to go into this matter in depth. Many of the surviving officers of the battalion have known from its issuance that the report is flawed and incomplete. Indeed, Brigade required the original report to be rewritten in early June 1969. None of us, however, had any idea, until recently, just how flawed it is. While discussing an annotated contour map with an illustrator, I noticed that Samuel Zaffiri's book, *Hamburger Hill*, in a similar map, had the battalion HQ located too far to the southeast. Thinking it a minor point, I nevertheless looked into it, and soon was appalled at what I found. Incidentally, I place no blame on Zaffiri or his editors: They based their map on the after-action report.

Simply put, almost none of the reported locations and events can be trusted. This is not just a matter of opinion, or based on remembrances of events more than 40 years in the past. The report contradicts itself with regularity. I will cite one specific point only, to illustrate: In appendix 10, the following entry is made: "At 1915 hours, B Company reported spotting several NVA carrying a mortar at YC314993, or about 300 meters NW of the upper LZ." In the next paragraph, B Company's location is given as YC324976. Even without a map, one can see that the report is physically impossible. The two locations are more than 1300 meters apart, in mountain rainforest terrain. With a map, one notes that there are two intervening ridges.

The reasons for these serious inaccuracies are identified in this book and, more tellingly, in the report itself. One of the very first incidents, early in the morning of May 11, was the friendly fire strike by errant ARA on the battalion CP, wounding 35 men, most of whom were evacuated that day. Among those evacuated were the very people who were supposed to maintain the dispatch logs and casualty reports. Dan Bresnahan, a platoon leader from Alpha Company, gave very valuable insight into the matter when he and I began going over the report in detail in November 2012. After the battle, Dan was temporarily assigned to the depleted battalion S3, to help reconstruct

Although taken in 2006, and on the opposite side of the mountain, this photo perfectly illustrates the broad, heavily-traveled man-made trails that we found all over Dong Ap Bia. It was such a trail that led Bravo Company, with Lieutenant Denholm leading, up the ridge and to the clearing that became the focal point of the most vicious fighting throughout the 11 days.

the report. Almost none of the dispatch logs were to be found, if indeed they had been maintained at all.

The second reason for the inaccurate report is also contained here and in the report: Dan told me that, faced with the absence of reliable information, their only recourse was to call the scattered companies and ask them to provide their recollections of events, times and locations—this in June, almost a month after the battle. But reflect: Who was there to call? Three of the four company commanders, all but four of the original platoon leaders, three of four company first sergeants, and most of the platoon sergeants were dead or evacuated wounded. By June of 1969, there were very few individuals left in the battalion who could provide firsthand, reliable information. My company commander in June, Captain Butch Chappel, perfectly illustrates the problem: Captain Chappel took over command of Bravo Company at about 1300 hours, 15 May, after Captain Littnan was severely wounded and evacuated in the morning. By 1800 hours, after an aborted assault, Bravo Company was withdrawn from the ridge and returned to the battalion CP. So Chappel had exactly five hours of contact, during which time the company did not move its CP. What information could Chappel possibly have given regarding previous events?

This scenario was repeated for every line company. Bresnahan agrees that their efforts became complete guesswork. This is not to place blame on Dan or anyone else; it does illustrate how flawed the process was.

Historians will also note that some of the names in my manuscript do not match the after-action report. This was deliberate on my part; I changed names to protect their privacy. What matters in any case is the position and rank, not the individual.

In the event, I have had to go with a reasonable and reasoned account, based on my diary, my recollections (and those of others, as mentioned), terrain and common tactical practice. Later, perhaps, I and others will compile a more thorough and detailed analysis of the after-action report, but for the present this is all I can do.

1

The Mountains of Viet Nam

YD490198; 14 December 1968

The mountains were unlike any I had ever seen.

It's not that they were taller, or steeper, or more densely covered than any I'd experienced before then. The Alps and the Rockies are taller, and as steep. The Blue Ridge and Appalachians are as heavily forested. The Apennines are sometimes as rugged and peaked. But none looked like this. Those nearby were a subdued green; farther off, a grey-green. Farthest away, barely seen in the western sky, they were a smoke-grey. Over all of them lay a carpet of unfamiliar vegetation: Tall, slender trees, branchless until the spreading crowns of light green at their very tops; palms; fronds; vines; low thorn bushes; eight-foot-high saw grass; and here and there dark green bamboo. I would learn to walk these mountains over the next 200 days, but they would remain forever alien.

The major standing beside me took my arm, turned me around and pointed back to the northeast, at a tall, solitary peak, over 2,000 feet high: Firebase Helen. That was my destination. I had flown by Helen on my way here from Camp Evans, some 25 kilometers to the east. Actually, I had flown underneath it: The west slope of Hill 674, on top of which Helen had been placed, fell precipitously to a narrow pass, on the other side of which another hill, not as tall but just as steep, rose to form part of what was locally know as Rocket Ridge. Hueys, such as the one that had lifted me from the sprawling headquarters of Third Brigade, 101st Airborne Division, usually flew through the v-shaped pass, only a few meters above the ground.

"There's your new home," he said. "Chopper'll be by in about ten. Your CO's name is Barry Robison. Sorry the Colonel couldn't meet you; he's at Eagle." Major Raffaele was the operations officer of the 3rd of the 187th — the Rakkasans. Bravo Company, to which I'd just been assigned, was currently on Helen, and there I would go shortly, when another Huey would chutter down from the sky; there were no roads, anywhere, in the AO, so everything traveled by helicopter, or, as I was to find, on foot. I would be a passenger on a regular milk run, bringing mail, water, ammunition, food and other needfuls to the remote base. Oh, and one new first lieutenant.

Raffaele glanced around, decided he needed to be elsewhere, and nodded pleasantly. "Good luck," he said. He strode away from the slotted metal surface of the landing zone toward the low, heavily sandbagged bunkers that made up the battalion's field headquarters.

I looked back at Helen. The hill rose from the pass to a high, squared-off peak, then fell slowly, irregularly, in a long series of peaks and draws. These ended at another, lower hill to its south. That was hidden from view by some intervening ridges. But Helen stood out; it towered over everything nearby. Hill 674 rose up from the coastal plain, its foothills barely above sea level, so its 2,300 feet seemed to touch the sky.

There was nothing much else to look at. My eye was untrained. Only a few weeks later, I would look at a firebase and note deficiencies, irregularities, sagging concertina wire, indolent or missing troops, trash, unsafe conditions and a hundred other details, but today all I saw was brownish-orange dirt, dull green metallic slats, dirty beige sandbags and dust. I didn't know enough yet to realize that Rakkasan was only half-finished.

I sweated. The sun was hidden behind a sullen grey haze, but this was a rainforest and it was damp and hot. Just over a week ago, I had been shivering in the cold, misty pre-dawn winter air at Raleigh Airport, saying goodbye to my wife. Thirty-six hours later I was stepping off a TWA charter at Saigon Airport, under a harsh, heavy sun; it was morning, but already 105° and dense with moisture. Eight days later, I was a few hundred miles north, but it was still hot, and still moist. I decided then I would never feel cool again until I returned home to Washington, D.C., itself no arctic clime. Less than eight hours later, I would find out how wrong I was.

A few minutes later, two soldiers walked up to the pad, to stand, as I was, awaiting the Huey. Both wore the same jungle fatigues I did, but theirs were immeasurably scruffier: faded, sweat-stained, worn, smeared with dust and dirt and mud, or with the errant remains of pear syrup, thin pork gravy, strawberry jam and other fugitives from a C-ration can. Both wore helmets, both carried M16s and nothing else. They glanced my way briefly, saw the shiny green of my newly issued fatigues, the virgin dark green of my almost empty rucksack and looked away dismissively. Neither spoke, to me or to each other.

A few minutes later, I heard the heavy hammering of an approaching Huey; it appeared suddenly from behind one of the raised bunkers to the west; nose up, skids limned against the dusty green underbelly, doors open, the blades scrawling a thin, shimmering smear across the face of the distant hills. A moment later, I was clambering aboard, awkwardly. I would soon learn to jump up and twist about in mid-air, even with a hundred pounds on my back, but not that first time. The two enlisted men jumped on behind me. I scooted to the center of the craft's floor, to give them room, but they scornfully turned their backs, and seated themselves on the edge, with their legs dangling out over the skids and one hand each casually holding onto the center post.

The one nearer me stared morosely out over the rapidly receding ground, silent.

The other fidgeted and hummed and tapped his fingers rhythmically against the post. After a moment, the first turned to him, scowling.

"What the fuck's wrong with *you*," he yelled.

The second man broke out in a huge grin. "R&R, man. R&R."

His companion gave a snort of disgust and turned away.

The flight took only minutes. We approached from the west, to land on the lower of the two LZs; the upper one, at the very peak, as I was to find out, was for the artillery battery that made Helen their permanent home. One of the men jumped gracefully to the ground, bent over a bit, and ran slowly from the helicopter. The other, still grinning madly, waved a cheerful and derisive goodbye. I had to squeeze by him, dragging my pack with me. I imitated the other soldier and ran, bent slightly, to where a couple of men were standing. They paid no attention to me but scuttled to the still-hovering craft; boxes of C-rations, ammo and a bright red mailbag were tumbled out of the Huey's interior, to be hauled away by the waiting soldiers. Then, with a sudden clamor, the helicopter's tail lifted, and it began a curious crab-like scuttling across the LZ pad, to the edge of the mountain. Its departure was not so much flight as a fall; it tilted a bit to port, nose down, gathering speed. A moment later it reappeared, well below us, to our northwest, tilted to starboard now as it rounded the stem of the hill, on its way to Evans. The lone passenger waved again, a tiny figure in the open doorway. He was still grinning, I thought.

The silence, now that the Huey was behind the mountain, was noticeable. There were a few muttered words; a thudding sound came from behind a tall mound of long, flat boxes, in which the 105mm rounds for the firebase's artillery were shipped; as I was to find out, they also made good construction material. Above me, connected by a steep, rock-studded road, was the upper LZ, around which the 105s were placed. Faintly, I could hear voices and movement from there. Nearby, a low structure of sand-filled boxes, PCP (Perforated Construction Plates, the ubiquitous slotted metal panels that were used for landing pads, bunker walls, sidewalks and almost everything else) and sandbags was topped by a half-dozen or so long whip antennas. Even I could figure out that this was probably the CP — Command Post — and that my company commander, Robison, would be there.

No one had so much as looked my way. I walked over to the command post, around it, and found the entrance, a small opening with a flap of canvas nailed across it as a curtain. A narrow, clean cut, good-humored face, with grey government-issue eyeglasses and a mop of short, tangled pale blond hair, popped out from behind the curtain. "Thought Ah heard a choppuh," he said. "C'mon in."

I had to stoop to enter; inside, it was a dark, cramped space, much longer than wide. Up front, next to the entrance, were four radios, two PRC25 mobile units and two PRC10 field units. Planks ran down the length of the structure on either side; a pair of upturned ammo crates made a rough table. It was too dim to see much, but one of the men seated at the table was an absurdly young-looking, very blond man, pale of skin and hair, with a thin, triangular face and a pair of protuberant blue eyes, which gave him a perpetually startled look. There were three others seated around the table with him, including the young soldier who'd greeted me — I found out his name was Carter, and he was Robison's RTO — a short, wiry Hispanic, with a platoon sergeant's chevrons on his lapel and a big, muscular, bare-chested black man seated at the far end of the table. But the only one who spoke was the blond man. I noticed that he too wore a black bar on his collar (all combat fatigues used black insignia, instead of silver). That meant he was, like me, a first lieutenant.

"Who're you?" His voice was midway between a tenor and a baritone, with a slight hint of a Virginia drawl mixed with the flat accents of the Midwest.

"Lieutenant Boccia. I'm assigned to Bravo Company."

"Bosha." The blonde man grunted. "Yeah. I'm your CO." He nodded toward the sergeant. "That's Sergeant Garza, my first sergeant. And that's Al Jones, Second Platoon." He indicated the black man.

I had pronounced my name the way I always did — to rhyme with "gotcha" — but it didn't matter. No one in the army, or any military service, ever pronounced it that way, no matter how many times I said otherwise. Only a month or so into my army career, I stopped trying. Not because I despaired of ever getting them to pronounce it correctly, but for the very practical reason that, in the service, no surname is ever left entirely alone; almost all are truncated, one way or another, and the universal shortening of Bosha is Bo. I can live with that. The short name for Boccia, on the other hand, is Botch.

The CO turned back to the table. "Did you say two?" Then he glanced back at me before examining his cards. "Your platoon's not here. Al, did you say two?" he asked again.

Uncertain as to what to do, I sat down along the wall and watched. The game featured a lot of grunting and swearing, quick decisions and surly exclamations. The only one who had any real idea of how to play was Carter. The others were betting blindly. I watched the game for a quarter of an hour, with nothing else to do.

He looked up after a while. "Where'd you say you were from?"

"Washington, DC."

"Oh, yeah? Luis, you gonna bet or not?" He frowned at his cards. At Garza's bet, he threw them down in disgust, cursed, and looked at me again.

"We got nothing to do. You play poker?"

I thought now might not be the time to mention that I preferred bridge. "Yeah."

"Siddown."

They say that you can learn a lot about people by watching them play cards, but after a few moments I was hoping devoutly that that wasn't so. Robison, profane, loud and petulant, had a real weakness for inside straights and unlikely flushes. As the game progressed, I gave a heartfelt prayer that Robison's recklessness in cards was no indicator of his approach to life in general and tactics in particular.

1. The Mountains of Viet Nam

After an hour or so, I had had enough. I was no expert at poker, but I knew the basics and trying to play with three scattershots was irritating. Besides, Carter was on a roll, and my hands weren't that good. When he beat my two pairs with three sevens, I had the excuse to back out, pleading bankruptcy. I stepped outside, and took a walk around the lower firebase.

It was a hazy day, as days often are there, but even so the view from Helen was imposing. It lay along an extremely narrow ridge; nowhere did it measure as much as 40 meters across, and the main portion of it, on which I stood, was less than 25 meters from side to side. The slopes were precipitous. By walking off the PCP pad to the edge of the ridge, just feet away, I could look almost straight down the flank of the mountain. To the east, the ridge fell away in a series of dips and rises. One moderately high rise hid the eastern end of the ridge, almost three kilometers away; I was to learn that Firebase Long, a smaller companion to Helen, lay at its very tip. To the north and east was the coastal plain; on a clear day, I could easily see the China Sea from here, but not today. Almost directly north was Camp Evans. Hue was almost exactly east of us, but the Imperial City was veiled by both haze and distance. Directly below, at the foot of the precipitous flank, were some low, bare rounded hills—the foothills. They seemed inadequate and absurdly small, unsuited to the massive mountains they presaged, like size five slippers on a ponderous dowager.

But it was the west and south that drew my attention. Helen towered over the nearer hills and mountains. What I was looking at, below, was the valley of the Song Bo, a river that wound its way north and east through the hills, to exit through a gap east of us, and eventually join the Perfume River north of Hue. Rakkasan, indistinguishable at this distance, lay behind a couple of lower hills. But beyond that, beginning a few kilometers away, was a succession of hills, ridge after ridge, each succeeding profile higher than the previous one, marching on endlessly, until they were lost in a featureless grey. These were the real mountains of Vietnam, and beyond, Laos. At a later time, when I had my maps, I could stare down at the sheets and read them off, like the names of gods in a geographer's pantheon: Hill 950, Hill 1044, Dong Ngai, Dong So, Dong Tien Cong, Coc Muen, Coc A Bo, Co Trang, Phou Reck, Eagle's Nest, The Dragon's Tooth ... and, although I had no knowledge of it then, Dong Ap Bia, a powerful, round-shouldered mass, called, by the Pacoh tribe that had made it and its valleys their home for millennia, The Mountain of the Crouching Beast.

That night I almost froze to death.

I was shown a small hutch, not really even that: It was little more than a tunnel made of artillery cases laid end-to-end in parallel rows, covered by a few others laid athwart them. It measured perhaps eight feet long, two wide and perhaps 30 inches high. The floor was PCP, hard and unyielding. But the worst feature of it was that the opening faced southwest, into the cold, thin wind that began blowing soon after nightfall.

I couldn't believe that Vietnam, the land of the steaming sun, of the 105-degree sun, of the unrelenting, merciless sun, could be so cold. The wind leached away the warmth from the metal plates, whistled into the shelter and picked at me with wicked, gelid nails. I had nothing but my fatigue shirt on, and that, while it had seemed too heavy during the day, was pitifully inadequate now. I had no liner, and the thin poncho did nothing to keep in the heat. I shivered throughout the night, never getting warm, never feeling comfortable. I may have dozed for a moment or two, but if so that was all: a moment or two.

The night in Vietnam lasts a long time. It is too close to the equator for the seasonal variation to have much effect. Sundown had come at 1800; sunrise at barely 0600. Long before then, I was up, walking along the PCP to start my blood circulating again. First light performed its magic at about 0500, or a few minutes past it: That moment when, from one second to the next, grey, featureless lumps become men. Or bunkers, cases, water tanks, bulldozers, piles of sandbags ... I went in search of breakfast.

I didn't realize it then, but I was an orphan, a motherless child. I was a platoon leader without a platoon, and there is no more helpless individual on earth. There is also no more bored individual on earth. I had nothing to do.

Soon after dawn, a tall, string bean figure ambled across the PCP toward me. I recognized him as one of the men who had drifted in and out of the CP the previous afternoon. He had a long, thin face and short, wavy light brown hair; his eyes were hidden behind a pair of army-issue sunglasses. He held out his hand.

"'Bout time someone says hello," he said pleasantly. "I'm George Bennet. Third Platoon leader."

I shook his hand and nodded. "Hi, I'm Frank Boccia. And I have no idea what I am."

He laughed. "Not exactly the way you thought it would be, is it. Well, Barry's not a bad guy. And you'll be taking over First Platoon. They're out on a RIF right now," he pointed to the west, "along the Song Bo. They should be back in a few days. Sleep okay?"

"Damn near froze to death."

He laughed. "It surprises everybody. And last night was dry. Wait 'til you get a rainstorm. You'll see how cold it can really get. Want some coffee?"

Before joining the army, I never drank coffee, but I was now addicted to it, or at least to something hot in the morning. "Yeah. Love some."

He laughed. "Well, too bad, 'cause what we got ain't coffee. But c'mon."

He led me along the firebase, past the LZ, to yet a third, lower level, at its far eastern end. Here, the PCP deck ended; beige-yellow dirt, studded with grey rocks and boulders, floored this part of the firebase. This third level was long and narrow; two bunkers stood on each of the long sides, and a fifth, directly in front, faced east down the ridge. I had seen bunkers in training and at Bien Hoa, but this was the first time I would enter one on a firebase. From where I stood, I could see only a narrow, impossibly short opening amidst a neat rank of sandbags. These were stacked about 15 feet across, and perhaps two high; the opening was almost precisely in the middle. On top of this bunker, and on each of the other four, two soldiers, shirtless but helmeted, sat casually holding M16s. Their backs were to us, and they looked out over the surrounding area. On one of these bunkers, a good-sized portable radio blared out "This Is Dedicated to the One I Love" by The Mamas and the Papas.

As I approached the rear of the bunker, I saw that I'd been deceived as to its height. A narrow trench had been dug across the back, about three feet deep, so that the tiny opening I had seen was actually over five feet high, as was the wall of sandbags. The bunker was on a slope; the front of it, also sandbagged, as was the roof, was perhaps eight feet high. Stooping, we entered. Inside, the floor, rear wall, sides and roof were formed of PCP; only the front wall was timbered. A slit, heavily sandbagged, 18 inches high and about six feet across, was cut into that front wall. Glancing through it, I could see that it commanded the trail and ridgeline approaching from the east, along with the flank to either side.

Dried mud covered most of the PCP floor; along the right wall, a small, rough table, probably hand made, held a PRC25, a deck of playing cards and a bayonet in its scabbard. Along one part of the back wall, two timbers laid parallel, covered by a sheet of the PCP, formed a narrow bed, bench or table, depending on what you wanted to use it for. On one end of this bench sat a stocky, bespectacled trooper, bareheaded and shirtless. Beside him was a field stove — not the army issue field stove, but the one that we would make ourselves, almost every day: A small C-ration can, emptied with its top removed, the sides at its base perforated by a can opener, so that a series of triangular holes were punched all along its base, and a bright blue-green tablet of sterno, brittle and chalky, set inside. The perforated base allowed a steady stream of oxygen, the tablet burned a bright blue, and a can or cup placed on top would be heated. If it seems crude, it was, but, as I was to find out, this was as much comfort as we would get over the next few months.

This morning, a large canteen cup was placed on the stove, filled with water; it had already begun to boil, so the trooper opened two packets of C-ration instant coffee, poured them in, stirred, and then removed the cup from the fire.

"Good timing, Lieutenant," he said, reaching out for a dirty, used styrofoam cup. "Just made another batch."

"Great." Bennet took the styrofoam cup, handed it to me, poured in some of the coffee, and kept the rest in the canteen cup for himself. It was vile, gagging stuff, and burned my tongue, but it would be a part of my morning ritual for the next year.

We talked for a while — or, he did. The company, along with the rest of the brigade, had just moved into the AO (Area of Operations) around Hue only a little over a month ago; they had been operating in the area around Cu Chi until then. The hills and valleys to the west, George said, had been used as infiltration points by the NVA for their massive Tet offensive against Hue. Previous American units, including the First Cav, had tried since then to deny them access to Hue a second time.

Lt Col Sheets was the battalion commander, Bennet told me. Raffaele was the S3.

The problem was, he said, that everyone, from Sheets on down, was used to the flat terrain around Cu Chi, and simply hadn't gotten around to understanding the nature of the mountain terrain we operated in now.

"Down there," he said, swirling his canteen cup, "we'd move five, six, seven klicks a day with no problem. The S3 shop would look at a map, pick out a spot they wanted you at, and tell you to move. But up here ... they look at the map, tell you to move the same distance — on the map — and don't realize that you're climbing up and down some of the steepest jungle in the world. That's why your platoon isn't here, by the way: They sent them out a week ago, figured it would take them two days to go out and back. It's been six, now. Most you can do, usually, is one, maybe one and a half, klicks a day."

I considered that for a moment. "But it's been a month, you said. Haven't they learned anything yet?"

He laughed. "They aren't the ones doing the humping. It's the same old shit. They can watch us sweat all day and not get tired. Want to fix that? Send *their* sorry asses out on a RIF up and down Helen."

"I take it they don't go out on RIFs?"

Bennet laughed again, without humor. "Those sons of bitches never poke their heads out of the fucking TOC. I don't think any of them's even looked around and noticed we're in the mountains now."

He went on about it for a while, obviously aggrieved — I would find out later that he was exaggerating a little, but only a little — but I finally was able to steer him to the one topic I wanted to hear most: First Platoon.

"You're lucky," Bennet said, laying his empty canteen cup down. "You got a good — no; a damn good — platoon sergeant. Wright's his name: Lifer, with about 15 years. He's good. You got a bunch of cherries, but at least you got him."

I wanted to know more, but by then Bennet decided he needed to check his bunker line. Besides, he noted, the morning poker game would be starting soon.

The next day, we were lifted off Helen and deposited at Fire Base Rakkasan. The troops weren't thrilled: It meant hard work, because they were there to fill sandbags and build bunkers, string concertina wire and cut down trees around the perimeter to make the Hueys' approach easier. I wasn't thrilled, because my platoon still wasn't there: They'd been directed to Helen, and had already begun to climb its slopes, when the rest of the company was moved into Rakkasan.

Robison saw me standing, looking very alone, by the pad after our arrival. Frowning, he came up to me.

"Want you to hang around with Al Jones for a couple of days, until Wright brings your platoon in. Learn something."

Al Jones was big. He was a graduate of Alcorn State, and had played football there, at halfback. He looked it. He was six one, 220 pounds. Except for Sergeant Wright and one or two others, he was the biggest man I was to see in the line companies. It wasn't just size: He was chiseled, with a huge upper body. His strength was legendary, and his men in awe of it and him. Once, one of them told me, they'd been climbing a steep, difficult ridge. One of the men had passed out — a frequent occurrence, with the weight of the packs, the extreme heat and the pace they were expected to maintain — and he'd simply picked the man up and carried him on his back. Man and pack together weighed about 190 pounds, and he carried them both for a good 20 or 30 minutes, until the man revived enough to walk on his own. Jones kept the pack, carrying both his own and his trooper's the rest of the way.

He nodded when I showed up at his CP bunker a little while later. He was cordial enough, but, unlike Bennet, had little to say. He spent most of the day stumping around Second Platoon's assigned sector, talking to the men, checking the wire, the bunkers and the slit trenches behind them. I tagged along, most of the time, and he seemed not to mind, but he made little effort to tell me what was going on. At night, both platoons were required to put out an LP (listening post) 100 to 200 meters in front of the perimeter. They normally consisted of four men with a radio. He sent his out before dark, around 1700, usually to the same spot each night. It was easier that way, he said to me, on one of the few occasions when he explained himself. He would return from checking his bunker line around 2000, after dark; a portable radio, tuned to one of the Armed Forces Network stations, played Motown music, and he and his CP group would settle in for the evening. The only cogent thing he said to me during that time was one night when the CO raised hell with him about a missing starlight scope. Jones heard him out, nodded, spoke a brief word into the radio and tossed it aside. Looking up to meet my gaze, he shrugged.

"Robison's a pain in the ass," he said.

By the standards I was to learn over the next few months, Jones and Bennet were incredibly lax. In their defense, this was not only a new AO but, at least in the immediate area of Helen and Rakkasan, along the Song Bo valley, relatively calm and safe. Not much happened there. But what little I learned over that first week I had to quickly unlearn, because I was soon to be made aware that such ways were unacceptable.

My teacher arrived two days later, on the 18th of December. Carter pulled me aside as I walked by the CP.

"Bravo One's comin' in," he told me, quietly. "They'll come through the wire in Third Platoon's sector, probably in 'bout 20 minutes."

Third Platoon's bunkers were on the southeast side of Rakkasan. I stood by one of them, eager but trying to appear detached, as the first of them came plodding tiredly up the slope, a half-hour later.

They were a scruffy lot, compared to the others, but that was because they'd been humping in the field for over a week, while the other platoons had had access to clean fatigues and even a portable shower. These were the men I would get to know intimately over the next few months, but on that first day they were barely individuals: Short or tall, thin or heavy-boned (there is no such thing as a fat or overweight airborne trooper), black and white, blond, brown-haired or otherwise, they all seemed the same: Tired, quiet, with a certain air that distinguishes combat troops, at a glance, from all others. Forty years later I still can't define the difference, but I can recognize it instantly.

The sixth man in line climbed the slope and stepped through the inner ring of barbed wire. He wore a floppy jungle hat, which hid his hair and part of his face, but what I could see was a smooth brown cheek and a firm, large mouth. He was tall, over six feet two inches, and big: 240 pounds— huge for an airborne soldier, most of whom tended to look a lot more like me: 5'7" and 145. As he neared me his dark brown eyes settled on me and the black bar on my collar. Peeling off from the line, he walked over to where I stood.

"Are you One Six?" he asked, in a mellow, soft baritone.

"Yes, sergeant. I just got here." I looked up at him. Sweat stained his fatigue shirt almost black; a similar black line rimmed his jungle hat. He took that off now, running his hand over short, crinkly brown hair, sprinkled here and there with grey, that framed a proud, tranquil face, with large dark brown eyes, high cheekbones and a firm, rounded chin. Small lines around his eyes could be laugh lines, or they could simply be wrinkles earned from years staring into the sun.

"Welcome aboard, Lieutenant. I'm Sergeant Wright. Sam Wright." He offered a huge hand, dark brown on the back, but with an almost pink, light-hued palm.

He was sizing me up as much as I was him. "Where's your gear, Lieutenant?" He asked, after a moment.

"Back over in Second Platoon's command bunker."

"Well, I hear we're taking over their sector, so I reckon I'll meet you over there, sir."

I nodded; moving through the group of soldiers, who had dropped their packs and were seated on the ground behind the bunker line, waiting, I made my way over to Jones' bunker to retrieve my rucksack. As I walked away, I could feel more than 30 pairs of eyes fixed on my back. That was no wonder: For the next few months, for good or for ill, I would be the most important person in their lives.

Jones and his platoon were getting ready to move out on a patrol of their own; characteristically, Jones had said nothing to me about it. I thanked him for showing me around, but he was busy and preoccupied with inspecting his troops, and only gave me a brief nod in return.

Sergeant Wright stared at my rucksack as he entered the bunker, a few minutes later. It hung limp, obviously empty: The only things I had in it were a couple of books, some stationery, a compass and a couple of cans of C-rations.

"Where's your gear, Lieutenant?" he asked again.

I shrugged. "This is it."

"Did you talk to Sergeant Sandler when you were down at Evans, Lieutenant?"

I shook my head. "Who's Sergeant Sandler?"

"Bravo supply sergeant. At Evans."

"Oh. No. I didn't have much time at Evans. Clerk was there, name of Meyers. He said the sergeant was busy."

He compressed his lips, and for the first time I saw the Sergeant Wright Glare. Whirling, he said, "give me that radio" to the RTO, who was busy sweeping out the bunker floor. Picking up the black receiver — it looks exactly like a telephone receiver, with a earpiece and mouthpiece joined together by a handle — he called in to our company area, 25 or 30 kilometers away, at Camp Evans.

"Get me Sandler," he said to whoever answered the call. "No — now ... Sergeant? This is Sam Wright. My lieutenant came in about a week ago. You said you was too busy to deal with him. Did I hear that right?"

Whatever Sandler said in response apparently wasn't what Wright wanted to hear.

"Sergeant, I will tell you this once. You *ever* do that again, I'll be on the next bird to Evans to deal with you personally. Do you understand me?" He listened and nodded this time.

"Good. I want this: harness, two ammo bandoliers, ten magazines; canteen and cup, two-quart canteen, two jugs; poncho, poncho liner; jungle sweater, rain jacket, floppy hat; two pair socks; binoculars; map case; ten plastic bags."

He listened for a moment, and his lips tightened even more. "No. I want the stuff tonight. You can eat later, Sandler. You're fat enough already. Tonight. Don't make me get on no Huey an' come back there an' pay you no visit."

He listened for another moment or so. "Well, what do you think he's doing here? He's the new One Six. And you make sure that stuff's on its way tonight. Wait one."

He looked over at me. "What'd you do with your duffle bag and other gear?"

"I left it at the supply room; they said something about a storage area."

He snorted. "Might as well 'a dumped it in the ocean, Lieutenant." He turned back to the radio. "This is Wright. After you're done getting' that gear out to us, you get yourself over and personally get the Lieutenant's duffle bag n' other gear, you heah? ... No, don't you wait 'til tomorrow. Tonight. You savvy? ... Out."

He handed the mike back to the RTO, visibly upset. "Boys in the rear need their butts kicked, now 'n again," he went on, softly.

I looked up at him, no longer an orphan.

2

Firebase Helen

YD515219; 19–25 December 1968

I met only a portion of the CP group that day. A platoon CP consists of the platoon leader, platoon sergeant, their respective RTOs, an artillery forward observer and *his* RTO, and a medic. Spec4 Brown and PFC Hash, his RTO, although assigned to First Platoon, were over at the FDC of the 312th Artillery, undergoing some additional training, and Muldoon, our medic, was similarly engaged at the battalion aid station. That left only the two RTOs in the bunker with us that first night.

The senior RTO, who would carry my radio, was a thin youth from Wisconsin, named Conzoner. His round Italianate head was framed by wavy dark hair, perhaps an inch or so too long. His face was sharp and thin, with heavy-lidded dark eyes and high, round cheekbones. He had a casual, off-hand manner, breezy and somewhat detached, that bordered on impertinence. Part of that, I accepted, was that I was in his view, and that of every man in the platoon a cherry; a newcomer: An untested and unknown quantity. Hathaway, Sergeant Wright's RTO, was smaller, slighter in build, with a shock of cottony blond, almost white hair, a freckled Huck Finn face and an outrageously nasal Eastern Tennessee accent. He maintained a perpetually breezy, impudent air, a sly insouciance in the way he drawled out the serial numbers of the gear we checked that night—I was comparing the list Meyers, the supply clerk, had given me with what we actually had: Despite assurances, I had learned the hard way not to sign for so much as a tooth brush without checking.

That done, I was called into a meeting with Robison, along with George Bennet, to go over work assignments for the next two or three days. When he'd done laying them out, I blinked in astonishment. I totaled up the manpower requests for the following day and came up with 36. My entire platoon, full CP group included, consisted of 35 men. I pointed this out. He waved it off petulantly.

"Forget it. Goddamned numbers don't mean anything anyway. They'll change by tomorrow morning. By the same token, I want you to remember this: They're on my ass about finishing up the work here and I'll be on yours, so just get it done. Shit," he snorted, "Delta was here for a week and didn't get shit done, and now we gotta get it all finished in three days. The point is, we got 26 bunkers, and commo wire laid out to three of 'em, and they all gotta get wired. Got no claymores, trip flares or shape charges put out. Sump by the mess hall hasn't even been started yet, the aid station's got only two layers of sandbags, the TOC's only half-finished — shit, I could keep going all night. Now, I tell you one thing. I want my platoon leaders humping. None of this bullshit of sittin' around all day playing fucking cards and scratching your asses. And," he aimed his bulbous blue eyes at me, "I don't wanna see you sittin' around writing letters and fucking off, like you been doin' all week, you hear?"

I blinked in surprise. I started to open my mouth to protest that the reason I'd been sitting around was that I had nothing to do: My platoon had walked through the wire less than four hours ago, but then I snapped my mouth shut. Jones was right. Robison was a pain in the ass.

We settled down for the night. I had the first watch, from eight to midnight, and the last, from four to six, so I lit a cigarette, leaned back up against the wall, and concocted several foolproof mutinies. Actually, by the standards he was to set over the next few months, Robison's performance bordered on the genial, but I was unable to appreciate that the first time. Wright was in no hurry to get some sleep, although he had the middle watch. The rear entrance to the bunker was covered by a heavy canvas flap, now lowered, and the RTOs had strung ponchos across the front slit, so no light escaped, allowing me to smoke and Wright to light his Coleman lantern and pull out his second bible — a two-day-old copy of the *Stars and Stripes*. No London barrister or New York stockbroker read his *Times* with the same gravity, absorption and sensual pleasure as Sergeant Wright read the Army daily. In it was contained all that he needed to know.

The men went about their daily work, which in itself was sheer drudgery: Filling sandbags, hauling concertina wire about, stringing commo wire, felling trees, digging sumps, ditches and fills ... the list was endless. Mess and ammo-hauling details, battalion runner duty.... Dangerous work, the last: one of my men, whom I never even had a chance to meet, was suspected, accused, tried, judged and found guilty of being able to type, and was spirited away by the battalion TOC and never seen again.

To make things even worse, on the third day I lost an entire squad: Sergeant Stempin, my senior squad leader, and his squad were temporarily assigned to the TOC: They were to be the battalion CP's security force on a small operation to the west of Rakkasan. They were to be gone the entire week, leaving me with only 25 men. The nights got longer for the men. To make their joy complete, the mess hall was closed down until the sump and other related construction was completed. The men were back to eating C-rations, and that as much as anything aroused a sullen resentment. But there was nothing to be done: The mess was closed at the orders of the battalion surgeon, and not even the battalion CO could override them.

The first grumblings were heard, and I was too new to realize how normal all this was. But even Sergeant Wright was concerned. The first casualty of war is sleep; many of the men were getting less than an hour, because of the constant alerts, Mad Minutes, "condition yellows," when the bunkers went from one-in-three to two-in-three awake, and stand-to, when everyone donned gear and weapons, usually once at midnight and again at 0400. Bennet dropped by my bunker one afternoon, and voiced his dissatisfaction. The problem was becoming critical, he said, but he was pessimistic about our chances of getting Robison to do anything about it.

"Robbie's the only first lieutenant with a company in the brigade. He wants to stay that way. He sure as shit isn't going to stick his neck out and go against SOP, or risk getting his ass reamed by the Old Man. He sits up in that CP of his, waited on hand and foot by those suck-ass RTOs and Garza, and he doesn't know what the hell his troops are gong through. Think he loses any sleep at night? Matter of fact, do you think he even wakes up during the Mad Minutes? Bull. Only people you ever hear then are Garza and Carter. Robbie's sacked out."

I shrugged. "I guess so. I don't know. But you don't think it's worthwhile at least asking him to give the guys some slack?"

He gave his head a quick, emphatic shake. "Shit, no. You and me, we look out for our people. Only person the CO looks out for is First Lieutenant Barry Robison. He could care less if the whole damn company drops dead of overwork, as long as they don't blame him for it. And as long as he's following battalion SOP..." he waved his hand.

"Okay," I said, "could be. But I thought we could ask."

Bennet shrugged. "Okay. Ask him, then."

I hesitated. "I was ... well, I was thinking, since you're senior platoon leader, your opinion would ... I mean, we could both go."

"Nah." Again, he gave that quick shake. "Look, you want to try, you go ahead. It'll be a waste of time. The only thing that'll happen is he'll get an even bigger case of the ass and we'll have to put up with even more bullshit during those goddamned morning meetings of his."

He got up and left, leaving me frowning. Looking about the bunker, I saw Conzoner hunched over his radio, fiddling with it. Hathaway was out somewhere, and Sergeant Wright was supervising a work detail. On sudden impulse, I got up and walked to the company CP.

I found Robison seated at his desk, an empty C-ration can on top of a pile of paperwork. He looked up, scowling, as I approached.

"What's the problem, Boccia?" He, of course, pronounced it Bosha.

Giving a mental shrug—in the immortal words of Bill Baymont, one of my OCS roommates: What will they do? Send me to Viet Nam?—I outlined the problem as I saw it, and, hesitantly, mentioned my idea of a partial solution: scheduling the mad minutes at the same time as the stand-to, cutting down the interruptions. I expected an angry or scornful reaction. Instead, he nodded thoughtfully, dropping the pen he was holding back onto the desk. He leaned back in his canvas field chair and stared at me.

"I know the guys are getting worn down. I can see it. The problem is, we've spent way too much time on a firebase lately. Haven't been out on patrol as a company since November. Helen, Long, here ... I wish to Christ they'd send us out to the field. Goddamn S3 is on my case every day, about the work, about the security, the mad minutes— all that bullshit. By the same token, when Sheets is here, he's even worse. I keep telling them that if they want the work done in a hurry, they should bring in the 326th. Engineering should be done by goddamn engineers, not line troops. But..." he shrugged, looked down at his hands and then back at me. "We can only do the best we can. You've been doing okay: I see you out there, busting chops. That's the way it goes. I don't like it any more than you do, but that's our fucking job, right now.

"As for those mad minutes ... that idea comes down from Brigade S3. Some fucking genius there, never spent a day in the field and never gets less than eight hours, dreamed that one up, along with the goddamn condition yellow shit. I know it's killing us, and I don't like it and I've talked to Sheets about it, but, what the hell. Seems like there's a war on."

He stood up and stretched. The company CP on Rakkasan was the only one that allowed a man to stand erect. He shook his head. "Sorry, Bo. Hang in there, and tell the troops to do the same. I hear we're moving out after Christmas. I hope so. Until then..." he shrugged.

I returned to my bunker puzzling over how to reconcile the immature, brash, petulant Robison of the morning meetings and the calm, reasonable, even thoughtful man I'd just spoken to.

There was a new member of our CP present when I returned there. He was seated in a corner of the bunker, cards spread out before him, playing solitaire. He had thick, silky black hair, already spiced with premature strands of grey, over a long, bony face with high cheekbones and a smooth white complexion. He lifted a pair of sullen light grey eyes as I entered, but dropped them quickly back to his game. I stood for a moment, appraising him. As a thin-faced boy of 20, he was remarkably ugly; probably by 30, he'd be a handsome man. He bristled with an unsubtle air of belligerence and defiance. I had no trouble guessing who he was. Wright had already spoken to me of him.

"You're Muldoon?" I asked, after a moment.

He looked up. "Yeah." His voice was high and hoarse.

"Where are you from, Muldoon?" I kept my voice mild.

He gave a brief, almost imperceptible shrug. This was a game, his manner implied, and he knew it was a game, and he knew the rules. "Wilmington."

Even that one word betrayed his east-coast urban, ethnic background. I had no trouble deciding that he didn't mean the one in North Carolina.

"I'm Lieutenant Boccia. Your platoon leader."

Finally Muldoon looked up, reluctantly laid the cards down and stood up. I kept my face impassive but my tone mild. Wright had warned me that Muldoon was a hard case, but that, given time, he could be brought around. I took his word on it. But of all the uncertainties that I had about the coming year — and they were many — dealing with the troops was no longer one of them. Possibly the only personnel decision the army got right in Vietnam was that, unlike in World War II and Korea, they had stopped sending newly-commissioned second lieutenants to combat units. I'd had an entire year to learn how to handle the men, and in particular, the hardened, sometimes bitter, often contemptuous veterans returned from Vietnam.

Muldoon was no veteran, but he had the same attitude that most of them displayed back in the States, when they came into contact with officers and NCOs who had not yet served overseas. Muldoon was a fairly common subset of this type: A man who invariably measured himself against anyone he met, like a fighter observing an opponent across the ring, and with an instinctive resistance to authority.

Once he stood up, I waited an extra second or two before speaking. "Are you going back to the aid station tonight, or staying with us?"

"I gotta be here. They told me to check the platoon for foot problems and infections."

"Good. Glad you're with us." I glanced down at the cards at his feet. "You play pinochle?"

His eyes flickered. "Yeah. Sir."

"Good." I smiled. "Maybe you and I can challenge Martin and the CO sometime. I hear Martin plays a good game."

He nodded, thoughtfully. "Yeah. Maybe." The first round, his eyes said, had been a draw.

I went about my business, only slightly pleased with my guess. The chances had been about four in five that he would play pinochle.

It wasn't long after that, only about an hour, that I met the last of the CP group. Brown and Hash — their names inevitably led to a long-standing series of jokes, good, bad and horrible — joined us that evening, fresh from their training; they were with us just long enough for me to notice that Brown was very tall and thin and Hash short and thin. Beyond that, I could learn nothing more, because they were taken from us again, the next morning, to accompany a senior FO for field experience on the same operation Stempin's squad was on.

Three first impressions within an hour: Two were too brief to learn anything, and the third had been slightly negative. By the time the night was over, I would have two more, and these were decidedly negative.

I made a routine check of the bunker line at 0230, the morning of the 23rd. The fourth bunker I came to was missing the two hunched, poncho-shrouded shapes on its roof that I expected to see. Grimacing, I climbed to the top of the bunker and found one man stretched out, asleep. Condition yellow was in effect that night: There should have been two soldiers on that roof, both awake, both carrying weapons and wearing helmets. Instead, there was this one man; his helmet and rifle lay next to him. I shook my head. One of the bunkers I'd just checked had had only one man awake, but his comrade had been up on the roof with him, steel pot on his head, rifle laid across his lap, head bent down at a painful angle, asleep. That, I could understand and tolerate; I had ostentatiously turned my attention to something to the rear of the bunker, while the man hurriedly elbowed his comrade.

But I couldn't overlook this. I shook the man's shoulder. He stirred, made a faint sound, and then bolted upright. His face was a pale, indistinct white blotch in the darkness.

"What's your name, soldier?" I asked, in a low voice.

There was a moment's silence. "Kaminski. Who's there?"

"Lieutenant Boccia. Where's your rifle?"

"Over here." He felt along the roof beside him; I could hear the scrape of plastic against the sandbag as he lifted his weapon.

"Who's supposed to be on guard with you?"

There was another, longer silence, during which I could hear only the lonely squeaking hoot of a gecko lizard. "Morris," he said, finally. "Morris's got the guard with me."

Jesus. This is just great. Terrific. I've never even met these two yet and my first encounter with them is going to mean an Article 15. What a great way to start.

"Where is he?"

"I don't know." Kaminski's voice was husky. "Down in the bunker, I guess."

"Get him. Bring him up here."

I waited while Kaminski slid off the roof and disappeared into the bunker. A couple of minutes passed; I could hear an indistinct mutter, and one single, sharp expletive. I was getting impatient when two shapes emerged from the bunker entrance and climbed onto the roof. I recognized Kaminski; the other's face was totally indistinguishable beneath his bush hat.

"Where's your weapon?" I asked the newcomer.

"Right here." The man's voice was hard and sullen.

"And your helmet?"

"Don't got one."

"You were issued one, weren't you?"

There was a mulish silence.

"So where is it?"

"Lost it."

I was angry. SOP was that all men on guard would wear their helmets. I wouldn't always make an issue of it; a steel pot is a damned uncomfortable thing to wear, and as long as the men had theirs with them, on the bunker, I wouldn't say anything if they wore the more comfortable bush hat. But this was too much.

"Go below and borrow one from one of the others. Move it."

He raised his head to stare at me for a moment, then groped past me to the edge, jumped down and entered the bunker again. I could hear the subdued slap as he thrust the canvas cover against the interior wall. Then there followed a muffled curse or two, and a clanging sound, unnaturally loud and sharp in the stillness. Morris's dark shape emerged from the bunker and returned to the roof, a steel helmet on his head.

"When did you two come on guard?" I asked.

"Two. 0200." Kaminski answered.

"See me at 0600. And when I come by here again you both better be awake."

I finished checking the rest of the bunker line, feeling upset. I had a fleeting wish that someone else — Wright — had found them asleep. But then I shook my head. No matter who found them, I would have to deal with it. It was bad luck; now I would have no choice but to bring disciplinary action against them, without ever having even seen them before. I would have preferred that affairs had gone otherwise. I wasn't worried about my popularity within the platoon; I'd long since realized that an officer who fails to enforce discipline because of a concern over his popularity with the troops will soon have neither discipline nor popularity. But I was being paid to lead these men, not court-martial them. It was just plain bad luck. Another few days, perhaps no more than one or two, and the word would have made its way around the platoon that I did indeed check the bunkers, and I did insist on the guards being alert, with weapon and gear ready. The troops would have adjusted accordingly. That was the equivalent of preventive medicine. But now...

I found Sergeant Wright awake; he had a sort of instinct about these things. Time and again, over the next few months, I would see him rouse from the deepest slumber when something went wrong. Now, he propped himself up on one arm, clad in a jungle sweater and bootless. He clicked on his flashlight; a red plastic lens over the bulb allowed us to see without destroying our night vision.

I sat down next to him. "I found two men asleep," I said, without preliminary.

He grunted. "I was expectin' that. Who?"

"Kaminski and Morris. Kaminski was on the roof, with weapon and steel pot, but asleep. Morris was down below. I told them both I want to see them in the morning."

He grunted again, almost pleased. "Morris. I figured he'd be the one."

"They've been in trouble before?"

"Morris. Kaminski's been clean up to now. But that Morris is a bad actor. Been one since he got here."

"Great." I thought for a moment. "Have we had much trouble with the guys falling asleep, before this?"

"No, suh. But this here Morris's been spoilin' for a Fifteen."

"Shit." I felt bad for Kaminski; there was no doubt in my mind he'd simply fallen asleep from exhaustion. He was dressed, with his weapon and helmet, on the roof. But Morris ... he'd never had any intention of standing watch. But I could hardly punish the one and not the other. Nor could I ignore what had happened.

"I don't see any help for it, Sergeant. I'm going to have to get Robison to hand out Article 15s to both of them."

He nodded. "Yes, sir. You let these two slide, it'll be all over the firebase by breakfast. Half the platoon'll be asleep tomorrow night, jus' on principle. You got to land a boot up their backsides."

"I know. But I hate getting off to such a bad start."

He snorted. "Now, Lieutenant, that's just plain foolishness. Ain't you startin' off bad, it's them two."

"I know. But, considering how tired all these guys are ... well, I don't have a choice."

"Yes, sir. First Call's at 0400. Night." He switched off the flashlight.

"Good night, Sergeant." Seconds later, I could hear him snoring.

The operation ended on the morning of the 24th; the battalion CP, and with them Stempin's squad, returned to Rakkasan. Stempin's people were full of harrowing tales, not of combat — they'd had no contact at all — but of the extreme conditions they'd had to endure while accompanying the CP group. Most of their stories centered around the final two nights, and Sheets' choice of NDP.

"Barracuda picks this spot," moaned one of them, a bespectacled and diminutive trooper named Samuel, "on the side of this ... this rock slide. It was nothin' but boulders. Like trying to sleep on the steps of City Hall. Roll over and you'd bounce all the way down to the friggin' bottom of the hill."

The others nodded solemnly and assured us that it was so.

The administration of the platoon was simple. I had a little red notebook, about three inches across and five long, with three small rings and a few dozen sheets of ruled paper. It had been the first thing that Sergeant Wright had given me, the day I joined the platoon. It was already partly filled, in his small block lettering. Each sheet held two entries, and they were all laid out the same way. He had given it to me perhaps a half-hour after my gear had arrived that first night, but he'd already made an entry under my name:

Boccia, Frank J
O-2 O5352304
DOR Dec 12, 1968
DEROS Nov 14, 1969
Married Yes Child No
Mrs Alma Boccia
200 Country Club Dr
New Bern, North Carolina
wpn 842754

Directly underneath it, he had placed his name:

Wright, Samuel J
E-7 RA53143177
DOR Nov 1965
DEROS Nov 6 1969
Married Yes Child Yes
Mrs Ruth J Wright
1001 Hanover ST
Bluefield, West Virginia
wpn 529986

There was an entry for every man in the platoon, in that same neat block lettering. The notebook became my personnel file, my operations file and occasionally a scorecard for our bridge games. Not that there were any bridge games, at this point. I took a look at the list one day: 22 states were represented, with Ohio leading the way with three. Five hailed from eastern states, 14 from the Midwest, nine from the south, and one each from the southwest and west. That didn't count the FOs or Sergeant Wright and myself. Some, like Hyde, whose drawling, backwoods speech and appearance belied an intelligent, sophisticated mind, had gone to college; others had barely graduated from high school, or had GEDs instead. There were Catholics, Baptists, Presbyterians, Methodists, and of course, with all the upper Midwest boys, several Lutherans, and a few who listed no religion at all. Aside from Wright, there were four blacks and one Hispanic. It was as complete a cross-section of America as you could reasonably expect.

That day, the 24th, we were given the best Christmas present we could have, and were taken from Rakkasan to Firebase Helen.

Christmas arrived. I hadn't thought about it, although I did receive a more personal present: The first of the letters from home arrived on Christmas Eve. The brigade celebrated the Holy Day by calling in all patrols; all units were either at a firebase or back at Camp Evans. We were perched on Helen; it was a beautiful winter morning, as winter mornings go in Vietnam: Clear, warm, brightly lit. At about 1100, the heavy thumping of a Huey sounded from below the north face; a few moments later the pilot climbed to our level, hovered briefly over the LZ with that characteristic swaying, bobbing motion of the Huey, and then settled its skids on the PCP deck. Eight or nine large green canisters were offloaded, and behind them, to the marked delight of the troops, several cases of beer.

Our feast delivered, the pilot, Black Widow Four Four, gave us all a friendly wave, throttled up, skidded across the deck and, as usual, fell off the ridge, on his way back to Evans and his own Christmas dinner. A furious Sergeant Garza fought through the crowds of eager soldiers, to stand like a little Mexican bantam cock in front of the beer. Cursing freely, he warned everyone to back off.

"Dis beer's for fuckin' Chris'mas," he bellowed.

So we had Christmas dinner. The ham was limp and damp; the turkey dry, the stuffing crumbly; peas, green beans and sweet potatoes were all one jumbled, overcooked, sodden mass. There were no seasonings. The ice cream, by the time we got to it, was a lumpish liquid. Still, it was better than C-rations. Wasn't it?

Soon after the meal was served, Robison called for me. I entered the CP to find him and Garza seated at the rough table, drinking gin and cool-ade. Even in the dim light, I could see Robison's face was flushed and his eyes glassy.

"Siddown," he said. He shook his head. "Hell ... helluva party, isn't it?"

"Yes, sir," I said neutrally.

"Pay for this inna mornin', right, Top?"

Garza smiled and nodded.

"You be ready to go, uh — whadda they call you? Frank?"

"Yes, sir."

"You ready for tomorrow, Frank?"

"If my guys survive tonight: Yes, sir."

"Well, it's your goddamn job see they survive tonight, Lieutenant. You been roun' see if anybody's drunk on his ass yet?"

I had to clamp my jaws together. The temptation to say "No one but the commanding officer" was great. After a second or two, I said, "I will in a little while, sir. After I leave here."

"Yeah. You know where the hell you're going tomorrow?"

"Yes, sir."

He looked at me owlishly, his protruding blue eyes focusing. "Tell me. Show me on map."

I pulled out my notebook and flipped it to the right page. It took me a moment because I had already wrapped and sealed it in a heavy plastic bag. He stirred impatiently while I did this.

"Yes, sir. We're supposed to set up an NDP at 496243. That's Hill 254, sir."

He nodded. "Yeah. Okay. Show me on your map."

I looked at him. "I don't have my map with me, sir. It's in my pack."

"Well, Christ on a crutch," Robison yelled. "What kinda sorry shit's that? You s'posed to carry your fuckin' map with you at all times, Lieutenant. *All* the time! I don't s'pose you got your fuckin' compass with ya, either."

"No. I thought I could find my way around the fire base without it."

Robison slammed his fist down on the crate, nearly breaking through the wood. "Goddamn platoon leaders can't fin' their way 'roun' their own goddamn *bunkers*, Lieutenant! You're takin' thirty 'merican troops out in the fuckin' jungle first thing tomorrow mornin', an' you so goddamn unprepared you don't have your fuckin' *compass* on ya. There ain't a goddamn platoon leader in this company can navigate worth a shit — am I right, Top?" He shook his head angrily, not waiting for an answer. Garza simply smiled his thin-lipped, toothless smile.

"Shit. I could take a platoon out tomorrow, no map, no fuckin' compass, no radio ... bring 'em all back alive. Could you do that? Shit. Need thirty fuckin' body bags. Wish they'd send me some real platoon leaders. Somebody knows somethin', not *this* shit. I gotta wipe your goddamn noses for ya, all goddamn day. Go get your people ready, you, and next time have your shit together."

"Yes sir." I turned to go.

"Hey! Frank!"

"Yes, sir?" I turned back. Robison still sat in his chair, blinking unsteadily.

"Merry goddamn Christmas."

I stared at him in disbelief, my jaw hanging open. "Right," I said, recovering. "Happy fucking New Year."

I went back to my sector and checked the bunker line. Things seemed okay; Sergeant Wright had already been through, and although there was probably a bit too much noise and horseplay, each bunker was manned with a helmeted, armed sentry. But it was when I made it back to the command bunker that I found I had a problem.

The army had considered carefully, and had decided that two cans per man were sufficient. No one can get drunk on two cans of 3.2 beer. They hadn't counted on the ingenuity and persuasive abilities of Francis "Duke" Muldoon.

In every platoon, there will be a given number of men who don't drink, or who don't drink beer, like me — at least, not warm, foamy 3.2 beer — or who stop at one can; or who have their own supply of illicit whiskey or brandy or gin or whatever they could smuggle into a rucksack. Add all these people up and it comes to a sizeable number — about a dozen of us. Two times a dozen is 24, and while Muldoon might not have scarfed up all two dozen cans, he certainly got the lion's share.

I found our platoon medic hammered as flat as a human being can get. Fortunately, he was past the disruptive, belligerent phase — and such a drunk is no small thing, in a small restricted space with weapons available — so he was, by this point, relatively quiet; head lolling back against the sandbagged wall, eyes glazed, slurred words and loose, flaccid limbs. Sergeant Wright and I stood over him, considering. Wright's normally impassive face was a dark, stormy brown.

Helen's long, precipitous flanks beckoned. "I think we should just pitch him over the side," I growled.

Sergeant Wright shook his head, slowly, but he was glowering at Muldoon. "No, I'd like to..."

I thought about it for a few more seconds but then decided he was right. It might be against regulations. "Article 15?" I asked.

Wright looked up, still scowling. "No, sir. You leave Private Muldoon to me. I'll take care of 'im."

I shrugged. Wright had 15 years in the army; I had been commissioned just over a year. His experience in these matters was greater. I agreed, although I reserved, to myself, the right to come down hard on Muldoon if this happened again in the future.

A couple of hours later, I was no longer concerned with the future.

Firebase Helen was designed for an artillery battery, usually about fifty men, and an infantry company minus — two or three platoons, totaling perhaps 80 or so. With that in mind, the engineers had built two latrines, one on each main level of the firebase. These were wooden hutches about 15 feet long, with a screened door at one end. Inside was a wooden plank that ran the length of the hutch; in it were cut four holes. Spikes driven into the wall held rolls of toilet paper. Under the holes were cans; 55 gallon drums cut in two. One of the less pleasant duties of the medics — a literal shit detail — was to periodically drag the cans out from under the hutch — the lower back end of the hutch had a hinged, upward-opening door, for that purpose — and then fill the can with kerosene. The resulting odor, as kerosene, ordure and urine burned with a greasy, brownish smoke, became a staple part of our existence on a firebase.

Four latrines per level were usually sufficient. There was rarely a wait. That night, around 2200, I stumbled out of my bunker, arms pressed against my stomach, in considerable pain. It had started about an hour earlier: A queasy, unsettled feeling, moving swiftly to stabs of pain, a rising nausea, and then the full-throttle assault by unknown but voracious bacteria on my bowels. I walked with the shuffling, mincing steps of a man who has only seconds left, and stopped in horror.

The line to the latrines was endless; men, looking exactly how I felt, were strung out across the entire length of the upper LZ, bent over, arms pressed against raging abdomens, shaking in misery and pain. I took a few faltering steps toward the road leading down to the lower LZ: Perhaps there ... but as I did so, a half-dozen suffering troops were climbing *up* from the lower level; obviously it was the same thing below.

I got in line, praying that I could last. The conversation around me, among those who could talk, was grim.

"Had to be the turkey, man. The turkey."

"Nah. I didn't eat no turkey. It was the fuckin' ham ... oh, Christ! The ham...."

"That stuffing...."

One voice rose above the others. "It was everything, man: All of it. They poisoned the whole fucking dinner."

"I ever go to Evans, I see a fuckin' cook, I'll shoot 'im," one man whispered weakly.

"Shit. Only way any of us is goin' back to Evans is on a medevac."

"I mean it. I'll shoot the next cook I see."

It was a punishable offense to defecate or urinate on any part of the firebase other than the latrines: Usually the troops didn't have to be told; they policed themselves far better than their officers and NCOs could. Nobody wants to live with the smell of pee or crap. But that night, the discipline broke down. Most of the time, it wasn't a conscious decision; it was simply a case of a man reaching the end of his endurance. As I crouched there, waiting, I would see one man after another stagger away, toward the bunker line, to find a spot outside the barbed wire.

It was a dark night; the three-quarter moon and the stars were hidden by thin, high clouds. The sides of Helen are steep; almost sheer, particularly along the flanks. It was a dangerous business, moving past the wire and keeping your balance as you squatted. Several men found it to too difficult. The night was punctuated by the curses and despairing yells of men who toppled over and rolled down the steep, gravelly flanks. One man, in Third Platoon, happened to fall on a more than usually steep and open part of the hill, and was so weak that he rolled helplessly all the way to the tree line, which was over 200 feet down the flank, to be stopped there by a fallen tree trunk. He lay there all night; only the next morning did his squad mates, looking for him, spot his feebly waving arms far below. He was lucky; he'd broken a rib and bruised his chest but was otherwise okay.

I ended up making four trips to the latrine, but it didn't help. Dawn, clear and cool, found us still lined up, still crouched over, still groaning. The firebase was a shambles. The smell was indescribable. The trooper's words from the night before, about shooting the cooks, were no idle remark. The men of Bravo would remember this night for a long time.

Captain Robison, looking disgustingly fresh and rested — he'd suffered no ill effects at all — called me into the CP just past dawn. He nodded at me, with no sign that he remembered anything from the afternoon before. He briefly went over the day's planned route. "Okay. Password is Legit Abide. Keyword is Alvin Comet. Tomorrow, you continue following that ridge to where the river cuts through to the plain; turn southwest there and follow the river back up this way. You'll be out a week; re-supply in three days. Understood?"

I nodded weakly.

He looked at me closely. "What the hell's wrong with *you*?"

I shook my head. "Not much sleep," I whispered.

"Shit. Too much beer and turkey. Damn good thing I'm sending you out today: You need to get whipped into shape. Okay, move out."

I felt aggrieved. It was the alcohol, I guessed. Muldoon hadn't suffered either.

3

The First Patrol

The Ridges West of Helen; 26 December 1968 – 1 January 1969

It was a descent into Hell.

Well, it seemed that way. It was probably the most physically exhausting ordeal many of us were to go through. The west slope of Helen juts out into the pass like the inverted prow of a huge ship: High, knife-edged and steep, it slopes down at an impossible angle. The heavy rains and prevailing winds of uncounted generations have eroded its thin edge, exposing bedrock and boulders, large and small, through which a few wretched trees cling to a stunted existence. The descent is steep enough that there were times when we were forced to climb down by hand; in a few places, the drop was sheer.

Most of us were still wracked with the diarrhea of the previous night. Dehydrated, weakened, sleepless and still feeling discomfort if not pain, we stumbled and fell down an endless slope. In several places, our only recourse was to jump from one boulder to another, a drop of five, six, eight, even ten feet. It was on my first such leap that I made a dismaying discovery. My body had just enough strength to control one set of muscles. I had a choice: Take up the shock of nearly 230 pounds (my pack weighed over 80) with the muscles of my legs, or ... control my sphincter muscles. I couldn't do both. After the first time, when I chose the wrong muscle and almost pitched forward in a potentially fatal fall onto another set of rocks 15 feet below, I glumly realized that I had to, er, let go. I wasn't the only one so afflicted.

I had never been overweight, and was very athletic; moreover, I had recently gone through eight straight weeks of, first Jump School, and then Jungle School in Panama, and I thought I was fit, but I found out that there is fit and then there's combat fit. We achieved, all of us, after a few weeks of carrying anywhere from 60 to 100 pounds in 90°-plus heat up and down some of the steepest, most densely vegetated terrain on the planet, a level of physical fitness that could be matched only by world-class decathlon athletes. But not that first day; not for me, anyway.

By the time we reached the base of the slope, my legs were jelly and my back one continuous spasm. Moreover, if any NVA in the area happened to be both deaf and blind, they could still have noted our arrival from the smell alone. I felt worse when I realized that this was the first day of the patrol; under normal circumstances, from what I'd been told, it could be weeks before we could expect a shower or even a change of fatigues.

And then, late in the morning, we began to climb another slope, not as high but just as steep. If the descent had been hell, then this was reaching down into one of its lower circles. A few weeks later, the climb would not have bothered me at all; the ridge we were ascending rose to just over 250 meters, so by the standards we were to reach later, it wasn't that great a task. But after that descent, and in the condition we found ourselves in, still weak from the night's ordeal, it was brutal. Moreover, the sun decided to come out from the mid-morning haze and was beating on us with stunning force. I almost crawled the last few meters.

Once there, Conzoner handed me the receiver. I was supposed to report back to Robison when we made our noon objective. I was sucking the air for oxygen, in deep heaves, as I called in. An amused but sympathetic Carter answered. I gasped out our position; he chuckled in response.

"Kinda beats your butt, doesn't it?" he said in his Kentucky drawl. "Don't worry, One Six. It'll get better tomorrow."

My legs and arms were quivering, my back was knotting spasmodically, my lungs burned and my head was light and spinning, but I did note one plus: The diarrhea was gone. The bacteria, somewhere along that slope we'd just climbed, had looked around and decided, like wise rats on a foundering schooner, that the body they were feasting on wasn't long for this world. They got off, I guess.

I was too tired to eat, and I was hungry. I ended up opening a can of peaches and eating that, eagerly swallowing the juices. Sergeant Wright had been at this longer, but not by much — he'd come aboard in November, and the last patrol had been his first — and he was an older and much bigger man, so he wasn't too much better off than I was, although at least he could breathe normally.

I was dreading the afternoon's move — it was four times as far as we'd come — but I found out that we'd been through the worst. We had descended and then climbed an interminable distance, but on a straight line we'd come less than 800 meters. The 3,000 meters we tramped that afternoon were along the ridge top, with few dips and climbs. We had taken six hours to make our first point — at 1300. It took us only three hours to cover the remaining three kilometers.

Once at our NDP — night defensive position — I dropped my pack and watched as the squad leaders set up the perimeter. We would not be digging in, but each four-man position was carefully and thoroughly cleared of leaves, sticks, stones, roots and any vegetation over a few inches high. This was not done only for the comfort of the men; it was to eliminate noise during the night if a man shifted position. Then the area to the front was cut down with a machete, to the height of no more than six inches, creating a clear field of fire. While three of the team were engaged in that, the fourth was moving out 10 to 20 meters, there to set up an array of claymore mines, trip flares and cowbells— empty C-ration cans strung across a possible avenue of approach and filled with a handful of small pebbles, ball bearings, empty cartridge casings or anything else that would rattle satisfactorily when shaken. While this was being done, the squad leaders walked from position to position, sighting and ensuring that there were no gaps or blind spots in the perimeter.

A trash sump and a latrine were dug, the first inside and the other outside the perimeter, and finally, Brown, the FO, after double-checking with Sergeant Wright, radioed our exact position to the Artillery FDC. That was vital: As time passed, I would check our position, gradually weaning myself from dependence on Sergeant Wright, who was a masterful navigator. No matter how tired or distracted I was, that was one task that I put everything else aside for. The worst thing a platoon leader could do was to mistake his own position and have artillery fire called in on top of his men and himself. If he survived, he would face a general court-martial.

Sergeant Wright stood by my side while I watched this. After a moment, he turned to me and asked, in a soft voice, where I wanted to set up the M60s.

Two of the locations were easy: One facing the trail ahead of us and the second facing back along the trail we'd just traversed. I looked around for a likely spot for the third ... there was a relatively bare, shallow slope to the east, leading up to the ridge and into the heart of the NDP. I indicated the spot.

Sergeant Wright nodded his massive head, but slowly; I was to learn that this was his way of saying no. He spoke in a low voice, so no one would hear. He was the most professional soldier I ever came across in the army; far too professional to embarrass his officer: He knew that I would be vital to the welfare of the platoon. But he had to teach.

"Yes, sir," he said, nodding. "But ... that there slope looks bad, but look behind it: Only way anybody gets to that slope is to come over that ridge there, right behind it. Ain't no other way. And anyone comin' over that ridge'll be lit up against the sky. Easy targets. But look over here..." he nodded in the direction of a small, narrow, densely vegetated ravine to our left. "That little draw there? Goes down into the ravine below; got two approaches to it and we can't see neither one. Someone comes down the ravine, up that draw ... they'd be here before we know it. Best set the Sixty up there, sir. Have the gunner clear out a field of fire right in front. If they come, they'll come that way."

That began my post-graduate training. It wasn't the tactical training that I needed; I'd had plenty of that already and anyway tactics are, for the most part, common sense. What I was launched into that afternoon was a crash course in topography, taught by Professor Samuel Wright. I was a city boy born and raised, and for the next few months I was to have crammed into me the accumulated lore of generations of hill-raised hunters and trackers. I prided myself on my map-reading ability; in OCS and subsequent training I'd always ranked very high in that discipline. What I was to learn was that reading a map is of no use. A map is a human creation, one man's interpretation of the earth's surface. What I needed to read was not the map but the terrain. The terrain was real, the map fiction. Accurate or not, a map could never tell me what the slope of the hill, the turn of the ridge, the angle of the stream, could reveal.

It is a very scientific discipline, but it was not taught scientifically. It couldn't be: Sergeant Wright hadn't learned it that way. He *knew* it. Some of the lessons were easy, and easily passed on: I learned to read the treetops along an opposite ridge. The leaves of one tree are a slightly different color than those of another. A line of light green broken by a patch of darker green, no matter how straight and uniform the line appeared, no matter that the map said that it was a long, unbroken ridge, meant that taller, heavier trees formed that darker patch: In the middle of that ridge was a substantial cut, unseen and un-guessed at from the air. One day we found ourselves at the base of a ravine, steeply walled; it emptied out into a narrow valley; behind that was a jumbled mass of hillocks, dales and low ridges. To our left was a solid mass of a heavily forested hill; to our right the terrain fell and rose in a confused but visible array. Behind it, I could see the horizon. A small stream bubbled across our path, from right to left. We were supposed to rendezvous with the rest of the company, on a high ridge not far from where we stood. My instinct was to turn left, in the direction of that massive hill. But Wright nodded at the stream; it flowed from right to left. Water can't run uphill. The high ground was to our right, not, as the hill seemed to suggest, to our left.

An animal trail in the mountain rainforest, typical of the ones we followed throughout most of our patrols. Visibility is no more than three to five meters.

3. The First Patrol

The earth, he made me realize, has a strict, precise logic of its own; a logic that can't be explained in human terms because it isn't human, but it is a logic nonetheless. Learn that logic, think like a stream or a ridge or a hill, and you will never be lost.

I had other teachers besides Wright; Jones, from the hill country of east Tennessee; Nate Hyde, college man that he was, had nevertheless been raised in the woods of Louisiana, and, probably the best of them all, Phil Nelson, a member of the Occoquan tribe from Milford, Virginia. They all did their best to bring some sort of rural literacy to this neophyte city boy.

But that was a long, long time in coming.

The next day, I received another lesson — two of them, really. We were to continue following the ridge, and then descend along a spur to the valley of the Song Bo, south and west of our NDP. We set out early the next morning, traveling, as we almost always did, in single file. I was following the lessons of OCS, placing myself and my RTO between the first and second squads. Later that day, I began to follow the file as it descended a spur, in the general direction of the valley. Conzoner tapped me on the shoulder and handed me the mike. It was Sergeant Wright.

"One Six, this is One Five. Where are you headed, over?"

"Five, this is Six: Down the ridge to the Song Bo, over."

"No you're not," One Five replied, with finality.

And, of course, we weren't.

The point man had missed another, smaller, leaf-choked spur a hundred meters back. The one we were descending would have eventually taken us to the east and north, directly opposite where we wanted to go. Another terrain-reading exercise, but also something else: By walking behind the first squad, as training dictated, I was placing myself a hundred meters or more behind my point man. And a hundred meters in mountain terrain is an infinity. I was to experiment over the next few days, but I eventually ended up with a configuration that I was to follow for the rest of my tour: I would walk third in line, behind only the point and slack men. I had two tools vital to the platoon: The map and the radio, and neither would do us any good carried a hundred meters behind the point.

The next morning, the platoon quickly reversed its procedures from the previous evening. The equipment was picked up, the trash buried, the dead branches and leaves scattered across the sump and latrine to hide them as well as possible, packs and gear were donned, and we moved out. Our trek that day took us to another rarity — it was remarkable, how many events or terrain features I encountered on that first patrol that I would never come across again — a small, sweet, clear pool of spring-fed water, near the hill where we set up for the noon meal.

That evening, I accompanied Spec4 Skinner and his squad as they set up; I noticed details that I had missed the night before: The angle of the fan-shaped field of fire that was cut in front of each position varied with the slope and configuration of the ridge; care was taken that all paths between positions were cut well inside the straight line between them, so that at night, in the dark, there was no danger that a man would find himself even briefly outside the perimeter.

I followed Skinner and one of his people, a tall, heavy-eyed man from New Mexico named Hernandez, as they set out their trip flares at the base of the low ridge. Working quickly but meticulously, frowning in concentration, Skinner wrapped a length of thin, pliable, almost invisible wire around the base of an inch-thick branch, about ten inches up the stem of a leafy bush. He cut off a two-foot length and attached the free end to the base of the flare, a slender dull-grey cylinder about six inches long. A sapling about two feet away provided the anchor for a second length of wire, this roughly four or five inches long. Normally, Skinner explained as he worked rapidly, he would leave the longer wire attached to the base of the flare when he retrieved it in the morning, but tonight he was discarding the old wire and using a new one because the thin wire tended to kink and bend with use.

Up to this point, Hernandez had been standing behind us, rifle ready, watching the forest around us. Now, he laid his weapon down and knelt beside Skinner, holding the flare off the ground with the long wire taut. Carefully, Skinner eased the spring-loaded piston out of the body of the flare until he heard or felt the faint click that indicated that the flare was now armed. He threaded the shorter wire through the tiny eyebolt at the end of the piston and quickly took up the slack on the shorter wire. Then the two of them got up and carefully backed away. Skinner turned to me and nodded in satisfaction. The flare was hidden underneath a small branch of the sapling; even in daylight, and having seen him do it, I could barely make it and the attached wire out. At night, both would be invisible.

They then turned their attention to the claymore that Hernandez carried. Choosing a spot about ten feet upslope of the flare, Hernandez brushed aside the leaves and twigs to create a bare spot about five inches long. He thrust the four thin legs of the claymore into the ground there, wiggling it about to make sure it was fixed and fairly level. Then, carefully, he unscrewed the two small nuts on top of the mine's surface; looping a bare end of a wire around each post, he then replaced the nuts, finger-tightening them to make sure they were snug. He then picked up the wires and began unreeling them behind him as he climbed the slope to the position above; there, the two ends would be attached to a small, hand-held dynamo, looking vaguely like a stapler, that would, when squeezed, generate the low voltage needed to set off the C-4 explosive in the claymore.

I noticed two things about this operation, that might seem like trivial common sense, but were not. Inexperienced troops could and did neglect them. The first was that the claymore was angled so that it covered the area immediately behind the trip flare, but also so that its back-blast would dissipate among the small trees and bushes well off to the side of the position above. The other was even more fundamental, but was surprisingly often ignored: The flare was set with two criteria in mind. Obviously, it was set along what Skinner thought would be the most likely avenue of approach for an enemy soldier, but also it was set in plain view and in the direct line of sight and fire of the position above. Third Platoon, a few weeks later, with an inexperienced platoon leader and new squad leaders, set up a series of flares along the base of a small ravine that led directly up into the heart of the platoon position. As it happened, the enemy probed them that night and set off the flares; one or two of the dead-white phosphorus lights sparked in the night. The three positions set up to cover the ravine opened fire and poured hundreds of rounds of ammo down the ravine — and over the heads of the startled NVA, who crouched at the base of the hill, well out of sight of the crest.

That evening was marred by only one thing: After we'd set up, and Sergeant Wright and I had each checked the entire perimeter, we sat together going over the next day's planned route. Gradually, I became aware of a constant but sotto voce muttering, a baleful litany coming from behind me. It was Muldoon, speaking to no one in particular.

"Goddamn Army sends a man out here to fuckin' nowhere, makes him eat like a jerk, talk like a jerk, act like a jerk, tells him where to sleep and where to shit and where to fuckin' croak. Won't leave a fuckin' man alone."

I glanced at Wright. "You sure you're going to make soldier out of him?"

Wright smiled, benignly. "Sir, I said I would. You'll see."

I shrugged. Wright had 15 years in the army; I had been commissioned just over a year. Still, it seemed unlikely.

The fourth day of the patrol, on a broad, open bluff overlooking the Song Bo, we were resupplied, and along with the rations we got mail. While it and the rations were being distributed, I heard a loud burst of laughter from Stempin's squad. Moving over to see what was going on, I found a knot of soldiers surrounding a diminutive figure. It was Samuel. His mother, either a woman of enormous optimism, or someone who had no idea what conditions in Vietnam were like, had sent him a goody box — a carton filled with food and other desirables. This was a common thing, and they almost all ended up disastrously. Most foods simply aren't meant to withstand the travel, rough handling and extreme heat.

I moved closer to see what Samuel was holding. He was staring mournfully at a cardboard box, crushed and stained beyond recognition. Heat and mishandling had reduced its contents to a brownish, semi-liquid, scatological goo. He reached down with one tentative finger, dipped it into the mess, brought it to his mouth and tasted. Making a face, he sighed, shook his head and turned the whole thing over, dumping it into the garbage sump.

"Chocolate cake." he said sadly. "It was for my birthday." Not even Samuel could think of a more plaintive complaint than this.

The following day, we tracked west and south, along yet another ridge, reversing the Song Bo's course but well above it. It was hot, extremely hot, and dry; we hadn't had any rain since before Christmas. We moved all day along the barebacked ridge; what few trees dotted the ridge were low, scrubby little things, offering no cover and less shade. By the time we reached the end of the ridge, we had all long since run out of water; the spring water was long gone. Since we were following the Song Bo, no one had thought to send water out on the resupply. The Song Bo was there, all right; less than 50 meters to our west. But it was 100 meters down.

It was getting late. We didn't have time to descend that bluff, almost sheer in many places, collect water, and then climb back up and move into our NDP; it would be dark long before we got there. And we needed water. I stood by the bluff and glared at the river, far below. Sergeant Wright moved up beside me.

I glanced at him. "What a fucked-up way to make a living," I said bitterly.

Wright smiled. "Now, sir, don't get shook 'til I get shook."

I had to repress an urge to hit him. Wright would repeat that phrase perhaps 200 times over the next six months, and what was irritating about it was that he never said it when I was nervous or uncertain, but only when I was, like now, angry or frustrated. Off hand, I can't think of anything less calculated to calm me down. Still, Wright could get away with it. Punching a man who outweighs me by close to 100 pounds lacks appeal.

We ended up sending a party of six men down the flank of the ridge, burdened with straps threading dozens of canteens like fat green beads on a necklace. They didn't have to descend all the way to the river: One of them found a small, muddy spring about 75 meters down the hill. The water, when I got my canteen, was warm and slightly odorous. Dropping two iodine tablets in it, and shaking it for a minute or so, I tilted my head back and drank deeply. As I did, something wriggled down my throat along with the water. I never found out what it was and probably that's just as well. Frankly, I didn't care.

The following morning, we struck out again, along a series of low, tangled ridges and hills. The sun was hot, the air dry and dusty. It was hard going, and as we moved along I noticed that the men began to bunch up, especially behind me. I stepped off the trail, allowing Conzoner to move past me; I was snarling out a command to spread out to two particularly chummy troopers when a sudden burst of automatic rifle fire shattered the morning silence.

I spun around but stayed on my feet. We all did. My muscles tensed and I was trying to decide what to do — I hadn't yet developed the nano-second reflexive response to gunfire — but by that time my mind realized three things: The shots had been outgoing, not incoming; they were M16 and, most importantly, they weren't continuing. My hand reached out to take the mike from Conzoner, but pulled back. What was I doing calling the CO when I had no idea myself what had happened?

Hyde appeared around the bend. Helmet swinging casually in one hand, rifle carried nonchalantly in the other, he approached me with a sheepish grin on his black-stubbled, sweaty face.

"No problem, suh. It's all raht."

"What's all right?"

3. The First Patrol

"Nothin' happened. Ski was on point."

Oh. Of course.

Even in the short time I'd been with the platoon, I'd heard all about Ed Mareniewski: Big, hard-working, mild-mannered, friendly, accommodating, and a dangerous menace. He wasn't, but should have been, called Tank, from his habit of trying to go through trees instead of around them.

He was purportedly the only man in the history of the United States Army—or any other army—to have accidentally discharged a weapon while it was disassembled. I confess that I first treated this story with considerable skepticism, but as time went on and my acquaintance with him grew, I gradually adopted a more agnostic position. I wasn't going to make it an article of faith, but anything was possible. I did personally witness the time when, while boarding a Huey during a CA, Ski ran up to the craft, turned in mid-air and executed that backwards jump onto the floor of the waiting craft—with results all his own: Instead of arcing up and onto the floor, like everyone else, Ski simply kept on going, like a berserk bowling ball, and cannoned into a startled and profanely distressed door gunner, his M60, its mount and the webbing of the seat. Everything collapsed in a tangle of limbs, muzzles, straps, helmets, packs and boots. For a delicious moment, it seemed exactly like one of those cartoon fights, where the participants are hidden inside a whirlwind and only an occasional glimpse of an arm or foot is seen. When it was all over, the shaken door gunner glared at Mareniewski with wide-eyed but wary dislike. As far as he could tell, he had been the victim of an unprovoked, maniacal attack. Assurances that it had all been an accident left him unconvinced.

"What'd he do? Trip?"

Hyde's grin became wider. "No, suh. He didn't trip. He was point, and he came aroun' this bend in the trail up ahead, and he ran smack into this deah."

I blinked. I wasn't sure I heard right. "A deer?"

Hyde nodded. "A deah. Critter jumped raht out o' those bushes, raht at 'im. Ski jus' blew 'im away."

"You mean the klutz just shot up a goddamned deer? For God's sake."

"Yes, suh. Let off fouh, fahv rounds 'foh he knew what he was shootin' at. Didn't leave much of that deah."

"Jesus Christ. Okay, let's move on. And for God's sake put someone else up on point before he blows one of us away."

Hyde nodded, still grinning, and returned to the point. I considered calling the CO but decided not to. The chances were that they hadn't heard the shots—we were a good ways from Helen—and I saw no reason to call Robison to tell him that one of my men had just gone wild game hunting.

A moment or so later I came across the body of the ruminant—not a deer, but a species of small antelope, which had stood no more than 30 inches high. Its slender fawn-and-brown body had been ripped almost in two by the burst from Ski's rifle and its large, soft brown eyes, dulled and still in death, stared sadly out at the world.

Hyde had misinterpreted what I'd said to him, apparently. Mareniewski, visibly upset, stood by the side of the trail: *His* large, soft brown eyes were almost filled with tears; he studiously avoided looking at the small body of the animal he'd just killed. I could see why. It was an awful lot like shooting Bambi.

"Geez, sir," he said in a husky, uncertain baritone. "I'm sorry. I didn't mean to do it. It was an accident, Lieutenant. Honest. I don't hunt. I don't like hunting. I *like* animals, sir."

"Okay, Ski," I sighed. "I know. I'm sure you didn't mean to do it. Just be more careful. And ... uhh, you have unloaded your weapon, right?"

He nodded vigorously. "Oh, yes sir."

"Okay. Move out." The reference to unloading his weapon wasn't pointed only at him; it was SOP in the entire battalion that, unless in contact with the enemy, only the point and slack man on patrol would carry chambered weapons. It was a precaution, but with Ski around, I thought, it was also a necessity.

That afternoon, as if in recompense, we found Heaven. I realize that my definitions of Heaven and Hell may seem parochial, but they were all we had. The celestial sphere we came across that day was the Song Bo itself; we ultimately descended from the ridge and followed the river upstream, until we came to a bend. Here, the stream had dug out a channel for itself; on the inside of the bend was a broad, gravelly beach, bordered with a thin slice of pure white sand. On the outside was a low bank, and close to the bank the water was clear and about five feet deep: A pool, in other words.

We were well ahead of schedule. In fact, by this point, Robison was no longer relaying the NDP sites to me; I was supposed to pick my own. Sergeant Wright and I agreed that this was as likely spot as any. There was a small, low hill some 200 meters from the bank: That would be our actual NDP. In the meantime, it was still mid-afternoon, and the water beckoned.

And so I was able to clean up after all. God knows I needed it. We all did. Alternating between bathing and standing guard, everyone in the platoon cleaned up.

Everyone but one man, that is.

It is a settled fact of human nature that if everyone smells bad, no one notices or, if someone does notice, he doesn't care. But the corollary is that once you've cleaned up, you notice those who haven't—very much so. I have no idea why this young man was afraid to enter the water: It might have had something to do with snakes, or with modesty, or hydrophobia. I never found out because he was gone from the company within the month, a victim of an undiagnosed fever. I don't even recall his name. But I do remember the look on his face that afternoon. I've mentioned that Sergeant Wright was a big man—more than 6'2". This boy was small, and weighed perhaps half of Wright's 240 pounds, so the sergeant had little difficulty in picking him up by the collar (after repeated, patient attempts to talk him into a bath) and carrying him down to the bank and throwing him in. When he came up for air, his buddies, armed with soap and grim determination, scrubbed him clean.

3. The First Patrol

In a way, that day was unfortunate, in this respect: Coming so early in my tour, I expected that all or most patrols would be like this. I found out, sadly, that this wasn't the case. It may seem strange, but mountain streams are a rarity in a rain forest. It takes a lot of moisture to keep that triple canopy growth alive, and very little water is left over after the 200-foot monsters suck it up through their roots. During most of the year, except for the Monsoon, the hundreds of streambeds shown on our maps were dry, debris-choked ruts. Only twice more in that entire time were we to have a chance to clean up while in the field.

I was stretched out in the shade, propped up against my pack, cool, clean, rested, smoking a cigarette, profoundly, if only temporarily, content with my lot in life, when Sergeant Stempin walked up. His short brown hair was covered by a damp jungle hat; his fatigue pants were still soaked a dark green. He was barefoot and barebacked; the deep brown of his forearms contrasted sharply with the white of his upper arms and torso. I smiled quietly up at him, still full of mellowed brotherhood.

The author, Bravo One Six, on his first patrol in late December, 1968, along the Song Bo River (photograph by Dennis Helms).

"Talk to you a moment, Lieutenant?"

The smile disappeared. If he'd wanted to talk sports or books or anything like that he'd have merely sat down. This sounded too much like business. I gestured at a nearby fallen log.

He sat down facing me. His smooth, beardless oval face was serious, but then it usually was. Stempin was not burdened with a great sense of humor or a lighthearted approach to life. Before starting, he took a plastic cigarette case from his trouser pocket, extracted a filtered cigarette, along with a pack of matches, lit it, and returned cigarettes and matches to the case, carefully tucking it away in his pocket. Then he took a short drag, releasing the blue-grey smoke in a thin smooth stream. Stempin's every motion, no matter how trivial, was stamped with an intensity of concentration, an absorption in detail, that left the onlooker somewhat apprehensive. Something important had to be going on, you felt, and you were at a loss to understand what. It was difficult to make small talk with him, but he was conscientious and reliable.

"I've got a man with a real problem. Do you know Abbot?" His voice, like everything else about him, was measured and precisely defined.

"I've met him, talked to him. Not much, though." The name brought a vague recollection of a short, shapeless man, with an undistinguished face; doughy, wizened and round.

"We got mail." He made a small, intricate gesture with his left hand, while shaking his head, as if to apologize for reminding me of the obvious. "Abbot got another letter, from his ... uh, wife. I don't suppose you're familiar with what's happened, sir?"

I stared glumly out across the river, at the white sand glaring cleanly in the sun. This was beginning to sound more and more like work. "No," I answered, shortly.

"Abbot has a — well, let me start from the beginning. Abbot got married, right after he was drafted. Has one child, a son. Right after that, he and his wife started having problems. You know how it is."

"Great." I sighed again. "Okay, Sergeant. I take it you want me to talk to Abbot?"

"Well, yes sir, but I wanted to tell you the story be —"

"No," I interrupted him, in a spasm of irritation. "I'll get it firsthand from him. No need to hear it twice." I realized how abrupt I'd been: Stempin was just doing his job. And now I'd have to stop relaxing and do mine. I softened my tone. "I'll get the details from him anyway, Sergeant, and you know how things can just get a little twisted when they're second or third hand. But thanks for bringing this to my attention."

"Yes, sir." He stood up, hesitating. "Sir, I wouldn't have bothered you with this, only ... well, the whole thing's getting pretty rough. Not just on Abbot, but on the whole squad ... it's been going on for some time. I think it's a morale problem, sir."

"Okay, Sergeant. I'll talk to him." I glanced at my watch; it was still relatively early. "Why not send him up here now."

Yes, sir." Stempin had finished his cigarette. Carefully, he stubbed it out against the toe of his boot. Then he reached down, dug a small one-inch trench, laid the dead butt into it precisely, and with his boot smoothed the dirt back over it. I watched in fascination. *Everything* that he did had to be just so.

I heard footsteps approaching from behind me a few minutes later and gave a subdued sigh, but when I looked it was Sergeant Wright who stood there. He flashed a wide, relaxed smile.

"Now, how's that feel, Lieutenant?"

I grinned, stretched, and got up. "Top, between us we ought to be able to figure out how we can spend the rest of the year right here."

"Wish we could. Look, Lieutenant, I was just gettin' ready to send a fire team up to that hill, check out our NDP for tonight."

"It's only a couple of hundred meters, right?"

"Yes, sir. Right up this little ridge behind us. I was gonna send Skinner. He'll know what to look for."

"Okay. Oh, Top..." I stopped him as he turned to go. "One thing. Abbot. Are you aware of what's going on?"

His lips twitched and his eyes twinkled. "Oh, yeah. Has Stempin been talkin' to you?"

"Well, yes. I've told him I'll talk to Abbot. But he said something about this becoming a morale problem with the rest of the squad, so I —"

Wright laughed. "Well, Lieutenant, you could say that. In a way. You ever come home in the afternoon and found your wife watching them watchamacallits, them soap operas? On TV?"

I shrugged. "My mother does, sometimes. Why?"

He nodded. "Then you got an idea of what's goin' on with Abbot."

"Oh, great." Out of the corner of my eye I saw a small, wizened figure trudging up the bank towards us. "Speak of the devil.... You staying for this?"

"No, sir." His lip barely twitched with a hint of a smile. "That's my officer's job."

I couldn't quite repress an answering smile. "Thank you, Sergeant."

He nodded affably and clumped off.

Abbot, who had remained waiting out of earshot, looking across the stream, turned and stared at me. I made a beckoning gesture with my right hand and, as he approached, waved him to the log lying nearby. I sat on my pack, a few feet from him.

Abbot sat gingerly. He still hadn't said a word. He was short, of average build, with a round, pasty face. His torso was bare, hairless and oyster white. His mouth was soft and round under small, close-set eyes and an undistinguished lump of a nose; his ears lay small and flat against a rounded, mouse-haired skull. I waited for him to say something, but he sat there, staring at the ground between us; his face registering both anxiety and apathy, and a certain querulous brooding. After a moment, I realized that I could wait by this stream for the rest of the month before Abbot said anything.

"Did you want to see me, Abbot?" I asked pleasantly.

His eyes, dull and dun brown, like his hair, remained fixed on the ground. After a moment he raised them almost to the level of my chest before dropping them again. "Uh, no sir."

Terrific. "I understood from Sergeant Stempin that you've been having some problems?"

He shrugged. "Nothin' much."

Great. *Thank you, Sergeant Stempin, and remind me to shove my boot up your ass the next time I see you.*

"Well, if that's the case, then you can go."

Now his eyes did meet mine; there was a hint of panic behind them. He hadn't expected this. "It's my ol' lady," he said, reluctantly. His voice was low, with a curious bipolar accent; a mix of the rounded vowels of the South, and the flat rhythms of the Midwest. Similar to, but not quite like Robison's.

"Okay. Do you want to tell me about it?"

"Yeah. She — I don't know. Woman got no call doin' that to a man."

I sighed. "Where are you from, Abbot?"

"Laurel."

I raised an eyebrow. Laurel, Maryland was a far suburb of Washington, D.C., but that accent had never been heard anywhere within 500 miles of the Potomac. "Where's that?"

"Indiana."

I took a breath and released it slowly. "Look, Abbot, if you don't want to tell me anything, that's fine. I don't want to pry into your private life. On the other hand, your squad leader tells me you're having a problem of some sort, and he's asked me to help. I can't help you if I don't know what's going on. So let's get right to it. If you think you need help and I can help you, then tell me what you think I need to know. If not, then go on back to your squad. We both have things to do."

He sat there, rock still for a moment, and I thought he was about to get up and go, but then a tremor of emotion passed through him, and he nodded, stiffly. He began to talk. His voice, to that point, had been like the rest of him: Dull, stupid, featureless and uninteresting. It was still dull, but it took on a plangent, unpleasant whine. It was the voice of a man who was suddenly determined to relate all the wrongs in his life.

It took quite a while to get the whole story out of him, between the irrelevancies and non sequiturs; a good deal of it consisted in monotone imprecations against his wife. But I finally understood this much: Abbot had married his wife in Laurel, Indiana, and she'd given birth to a son. A few weeks later he'd been drafted, and was eventually sent to Fort Ord in California, leaving her and his son living with his parents. A few weeks after that, Betty Jean expressed a desire to move out to California to be with her husband; he'd told her not to come but she did anyway, leaving the baby with her in-laws. Then when he'd shipped out to Viet Nam, she'd stayed, living in a cheap motel just off the base. Once he understood that, he'd tried to stop the allotment to her, but the Army refused — as was the law. The full allotment continued to be sent to her in California; none of it, according to Abbot, made its way to his son.

It all came down to this: Abbot was angry that the money was being sent to her at Seaside, and wanted it stopped. I explained patiently, or as patiently as I am capable of being, which is admittedly not much, that he could not, by law, stop an allotment to his wife. This is how the conversation went, for much of the time:

"Abbot, you can't cut off the allotment. You can't, the Army can't, no one can. But you *can* decide where it is sent. Why did you have it sent to Fort Ord in the first place?"

He shrugged, and mumbled "'Cause that's where she was."

"Okay. But you can tell S1 that you want the check to be sent to Laurel. It'll still go to her, but she'll have to move back to Laurel to receive it."

"She ain't in Laurel. She's in California."

"But you *want* her to move back to Laurel, don't you?"

3. The First Patrol

"Jus' wanna stop the 'lotment."

Finally, he returned to his squad, leaving me irritated and skeptical that he had understood one word I'd said. Only months later would I realize how badly I'd handled this.

After a leisurely dinner, as the sun set and the twilight deepened, we climbed the wooded slope to our NDP site. It was on the northwest flank of the ridge on which we'd spent our first night; we were 500 meters from our first NDP. We set up on a small, lightly sloped saddle almost completely covered in triple canopy growth, except for a bare spot in the middle, where a couple of the large trees had fallen and created a gap in the canopy overhead. Setting up in a saddle was unusual, but neither hill was large enough or elevated enough to make a difference.

That night was the brightest I could remember. Months later, on the bare expanse of Firebase Blaze, which was not even a concept in an engineer's mind right now, we would see a moon as bright as the one that flooded the forest with a hard, silver white light. It gave the illusion of being as strong and illuminating as sunlight; only when I tried to read the print on my wife's letters did the moon's *travestimento* betray itself. If we couldn't read by it, however, we found we could easily write, and many of us took the unexpected opportunity to write home. I answered my wife's letters, and also wrote to my parents and my brother at college, shivering in the cold winter of Detroit.

One thing happened to break the quiet of the night; a tense half-hour during which we heard, and even saw, constant movement across the east sector of the perimeter, back and forth. We even called the artillery for a possible fire mission, but in the end nothing came of it. Long before they fired, Sergeant Wright, and even I, neophyte that I was, had recognized that, whatever was moving along the tree line over there, it wasn't the enemy; what would he be *doing* out there? As a matter of fact, subsequent events led me to believe that what we heard and saw that night was one of the stunted, ever-hungry tigers that made the rainforest their home. We were less than a kilometer, on a straight line, from where Ski had shot up the antelope. Because of what happened later, it isn't too much of a stretch to believe that the animal, having fed on the remains of Ski's kill, had taken to following us. After all, we represented, to him, a delightfully surprising lunch wagon, and so he tagged along in our wake, full of antelope meat and hope. We'd encounter Monsieur le Tigre some days later.

4

Mud Is the Universal Constant

The Song Bo Valley; YD423215; 2–9 January 1969

The next day held two firsts for me, within minutes of each other: My first departure from an unsecured PZ, which led directly to my first CA. I was to make more than 25 combat assaults over the next few months, earning the Air Medal, and the first one is rather blurred by time and the intensity of some of the later ones, but all CAs are alike in some respects. There is the constant hammering of the Huey's blades overhead, and the muted vibration of the steel deck. There is the air moving across exposed legs that dangle over the sides, and the look of the forest as it is never seen otherwise, lying thick and green across the sloped shoulders of the hills. Then there is that moment, as the ground suddenly looms closer, and the Huey begins to sway slightly; the last shreds of colored smoke are blown across your path, and the leg muscles tense for the shock of over 200 pounds jumping to the ground. And there is that sense of disorientation, of the sudden awareness of being someplace different, somewhere you've never been before. This first time, it was truly different: From the dense forest along the riverbed, we were taken to a high, open plateau, covered with ankle-high brush, tufts of coarse green-yellow grass and huge, moss-grey rough-skinned boulders, strewn all about.

We were the last platoon in, so I was the last man to jump off the lift ship. Second and Third Platoons were already in place, as was Robison. As soon as the last Huey had climbed away from the LZ and was on its way back to Evans, he called the platoon leaders to the center of the LZ. Standing by one of the boulders, he had his map spread across its surface.

"We're here," he said, pointing to the map. "425199. Earlier today, somewhere around 415205, in this valley here, Charlie Company lost a man — KIA — to a sniper. Probably nothing more than a trail watcher who got lucky, but Charlie Company and us are gong to sweep this valley and ridge. Charlie's on Hill 504, just to the west of us. They'll move down and sweep the valley. We're going to move north down this ridge, to 423315. We'll check the ridge and the slope on this side."

He folded his map and replaced it in the top pocket of his rucksack. Straightening up, he lit a cigarette. "Charlie's not supposed to send anyone north of 504, but tell your

4. *Mud Is the Universal Constant*   49

people to make sure what they're looking at or hearing." He shot me a glance. "They're uptight, so they may shoot first and ask questions later."

"How'd they lose that man?" Bennet asked.

"It was Dandridge. Mike Dandridge. You guys know him?"

Bennet nodded, whistling. "Yeah. Geez. He was in OCS with me, same time, but in 52nd Company. They graduated a month ahead of us."

Robison snorted scornfully. "Well, he must not a' learned jack shit while he was there, 'cause he has to be the dumbest son of a bitch I ever heard of." He waved a hand in the general direction of Hill 504. "His platoon was moving up a ridge, supposed to rendezvous with the rest of Charlie. According to his platoon sergeant, Dandridge ain't sure he's on the right ridge, so he stops the column, walks up by himself to a clearing about 50 meters ahead, takes out his fuckin' *map*, and stands there readin' the goddamned thing. Musta thought he was back in the fuckin' World, waitin' for a bus. Charlie Six said when they found him he still had both hands on the map, like he was readin' a newspaper."

We all shook our heads.

"One round." Robison continued. "That's all that gook needed. One round in the chest. Probably aimed right in the middle of the map. Good target." Robison's expression changed from contemptuous disgust to malicious amusement, as he glanced at Al Jones.

"You know how many days Dandridge had left in the platoon?"

Jones ignored him and started walking away.

"Five," Robison shot out. "Five fucking days." He pronounced the words slowly and painstakingly. "How many days you got left, Al?"

Jones turned and gave Robison an icy, mean-eyed stare. "I can take care of myself," he said.

"Yeah. So could Dandridge. I'm just telling you to be careful. All of you. Don't fuck up. It's bad for morale, you know what I mean? By the same token, all you Short-Timers getting yourselves wasted your last week in the field ... bothers the troops, see? Gives them the wrong message."

"Don't you worry about it, man." Jones was furious.

"Oh, I don't," Robison said, smiling. "Because we all know that it's only the dumb shits get themselves killed their last week. Dumb shits like Dandridge, dumb shits like platoon leaders who go on one-man RIFs."

Jones turned away and stalked off toward his platoon, still glacier-angry. Robison watched him go with a mean smile on his lips. We all knew that Jones was noted for reconning a new area by himself. The CO watched for another second or two and then turned to me.

"Okay, Bo. Order of march will be 1-2-3. You know where you're going?"

"Sure." I pointed to the northwest. "Right down that ridge."

"Okay. Get going. And watch yourself. A sniper makes a clean kill like that, he gets all jacked up and they all want another GI for their trophy room. Dandridge got his in his last five days; don't you get yours in your first five."

I nodded and walked away. George Bennet walked with me for a few steps, until we separated to go to our respective platoons.

"That was a great morale booster," I grinned. "A real shot in the arm."

Bennet said nothing, but shook his head; he seemed preoccupied. With a nod, he turned aside and made for this platoon.

I saw immediately, within ten steps, the obvious difference in the way we moved that afternoon. The point man especially was far more controlled, far more sparing in his movement. There was not a turn of his head, not a glance from his eyes that did not serve a purpose. It was Jefferson, the most experienced man in the platoon: His was the total economy of effort typical of a combat veteran.

Trees covered the slope leading down from the LZ; they were large-boled, gray and widely spaced. The mid-afternoon sun slanted through their branches and filled the glades with a soft golden light. We were moving northwest, and the light lay across our path in pale amber bars. There was a clarity, an almost liquid luminescence to it that washed away the shadows in the same moment it created them. Soft, subtle colors emerged from the dun grey forest floor, where they had slept, waiting for the sun's salute: A patch of moss, vivid emerald green; a pale yellow vine, streaked with apple-green and the softest hint of russet; the rich, speckled umber earth. A broken boulder glinted rose and amber amidst the stern, surrounding grey stone. Grey-green lichen carpeted the rock and tree trunks. Even the fallen leaves, dry and curled, revealed, under the warm light, a tinge of brown and olive, as if the sun could restore life even to the dead. A part of me wondered. I had never seen things so clearly before.

There were few sounds; nothing flew overhead and the forest animals were unusually silent. Jefferson moved slowly but steadily. As we neared the valley floor, the vegetation changed; gone were the open park-like glades of the upper slopes, with its vital patches of grass and moss. Now we moved through dense triple-canopy forest, choked with dead and living plants. The sun disappeared as the relentless green roof covered us and everything else below it. We replaced Jefferson on point. We were now forced to use our machetes and cut our way through the rampant clinging vines and branches, and Jefferson was a waste; any muscle-head could wield a machete.

We reached the valley floor, found a path leading north toward our destination and followed it. There was no sign of the enemy, no hint or feeling that he was around. The path showed no sign of use, although, from its size, it was man made, and not an animal trail. Jefferson took the point again. Another half-hour of slowly moving along the path brought us to a low slope; climbing it, we reached a wide, rolling, semi-bare hilltop where we would set up the NDP. The sun was just reaching the western horizon, and had already dipped behind the far mountains.

Once all three platoons had arrived, Robison called Jones, Bennet and me together. He indicated two locations, one to the southeast and the other to our west: Second and

Third Platoons were to move out immediately and set up ambushes at these spots. Jones accepted the news with an indifferent nod; he left for his platoon without saying a word. Bennet argued and protested for a while but then shrugged. Muttering to himself, he turned away. Robison scowled at his back and then looked at me.

"Get your people set up and put a four-man LP back down the trail we just came up."

Together with Sergeant Wright, I made a tour of the perimeter. It took a while, because the perimeter was both large and scattered. It was deep twilight; darkness was only minutes away. By the time we finished, a quarter of an hour later, it *was* dark, and I had to pick my way carefully over the rough grass and low brush to Robison's CP.

"I don't think I can put an LP out tonight," I said, as I walked up.

He finished spooning some steaming chicken noodle into his mouth before answering. "Why not?"

"Because the perimeter's too big, and I can't spare the men. Besides, we've got two full platoons out there on ambush anyway."

Robison scowled; at least, in the dark it looked like a scowl. "Five days in the field and you know it all, huh?"

"I don't know it all, but I can do arithmetic. The perimeter's 200 meters around with a lot of little gullies and draws; even at 20 meter intervals, that means ten positions. I have 30 line troops, and I gotta put three men at each position. That also works out to ten. I think that's what they mean by a balanced budget."

Robison suddenly laughed. "Okay. No LP. But if we get overrun tonight I'm gonna court-martial your ass."

The next day of the patrol was routine. Granted, nothing was routine to me at that stage; I was far too new to know what was ordinary and what was not. Even the swim, although a rarity, was not something that soldiers would swap stories over, years later. But what we came across the day after that, was, well, unusual.

It was two days later; First Platoon was, again, on point. We were following a ridge for most of the morning, but at a certain point we were supposed to move down the flanks of the ridge and reach the valley floor, to continue to sweep along the base of the ridge for the rest of the day. Navigation along the top of the ridge was, of course, easy, but I was a bit concerned about what would happen when we descended. "Valley" gives an image of a broad, open level space, like my beloved Shenandoah, but that sort of thing was the exception here; valleys in this area tended to be a confused jumble of knolls, draws and twisted slopes, all covered by a thick wall of triple canopy.

Clary was my point man, as we walked through the dense growth atop the ridge; I had checked the map only moments before, and told him to turn off the ridge and begin the descent. He merged from the shadows into bright sunlight, and stopped, suddenly. Moving past the slack man, I hurried to his side.

I had never seen anything like it. I still haven't, all these years later.

Stretched out below us, in a broad swathe 70 or 80 meters wide, and extending all the way down to the valley floor, was a tangle of fallen trees. Here and there a solitary oyster-grey skeleton, limbless and dead, stood among the piled-up corpses. I stared in wonder. Here was a scene of devastation out of the Apocalypse. The thought passed through my mind that this was a bone yard, and what I was looking at were the fossils of some huge, unknown creature. We stood for a moment, uncertain about what to do. The trees had not been cut down; I could see that clearly. They were uprooted, lying in thick piles on the ground, stripped of bark and leaves, gleaming a dead, dirty white in the day's light. They *did* resemble bones more than trees, I thought.

We began our descent, carefully. I assumed, initially, that all this was the result of an Arc Light — a B52 run — because I could conceive of nothing else that could destroy an entire mountainside, but as we picked out way along I saw that I was wrong. There were no craters of any size, anywhere, and a B52 strike leaves dozens of deep, wide craters. My next thought was that someone had poured thousands of rounds of artillery onto the slope, but I dismissed that idea, too: Artillery may shred trees bare, leaving them skeletal and blackened, but it doesn't uproot them whole. Defoliation wouldn't answer either. And, most puzzling of all, the trees weren't laid out in rows, as I had seen in photographs of the huge tree fall in Siberia, thought to be a result of an asteroid strike. These were all tangled together, their crowns and roots pointing every which way.

Movement became difficult. No, movement became impossible. There was no path through the fallen trees; we had to clamber from one to another, often finding ourselves 10 or 15 feet above the ground. The trees were dry and rotten; time after time, a limb would break off with a sharp crack, sending one of us flailing and grasping for support. Several times, none was to be had, and then the unlucky trooper would fall, to the ground or onto another limb or trunk. What worried me were the hundreds of short, thick limbs, some splintered, sticking straight up in the air, like hungry teeth. If a man fell on one of them, he risked impalement. After a few moments, I stopped. Looking ahead, I could see that we had another 200–300 meters to go.

I called the CO. Carter answered. "Roger, One Six."

"Give me Six. We've got a problem down here."

"Roger. He's up front. Wait one."

While I was waiting, another worry struck me; it is a measure of how bad the movement was that I hadn't thought of this other problem before now. We were spread out across an open slope, helpless and immobile. Facing us, on the other side of the valley, was another ridgeline. An NVA detachment, even a small one, armed with a couple of light machine guns and a mortar or two could wipe us out, and there would be nothing we could do about it; running away would be impossible.

"Okay, One Six, what's the hold up?" Robison's voice rasped over the speaker on Conzoner's radio.

"This is One Six. Have you reached this belt of dead trees, over?"

"Roger. Just walked up to take a look. What's the problem?"

4. Mud Is the Universal Constant

"Have you tried moving through it yet?"

"Negative. What the hell's the problem?"

"These trees are brittle as hell. They snap off in a heartbeat. Sooner or later someone's going to take a bad fall."

"You only got a coupla hundred meters to go, right?"

"Roger, but this is rough going."

"Well, keep on pushing. I don't feel like going back up and around. Out."

I started to protest but desisted. "Out" means end of conversation and, what the hell, he was the boss. Tossing the mike back up to Conzoner, who was perched, like an apprehensive large green parrot, on a large limb just above me, I motioned for Clary to continue. We hadn't gone 50 meters when the CO called.

"One Six, this is Six, I think you're right. We'll never make it down this slope. Turn around and head back up towards me, over."

"Roger." I grinned as I handed Conzoner the mike. The CO had just taken a good, hard fall.

It was two nights later that I discovered, to my painful humiliation, the true gap between a new lieutenant and a 15-year NCO. The good weather we'd been enjoying — if 100° heat can ever be enjoyable — gave way to a series of storms that at last settled into a dreary grey rainfall. We moved into an NDP late one evening; the rain had stopped, for the moment, but the night promised to be wet. The prospect of setting up on the already-soaked ground lacked appeal. Sergeant Wright showed the way. Choosing a pair of saplings about eight feet apart, he strung up his poncho between them, as a hammock. The six-feet-long, green draw cord of the poncho, when removed and cut in two, made an adequate string to hang the poncho from. It was strong enough to hold a man's weight and pliable enough to tie easily.

I watched Wright swiftly set it up in the growing dark. I noticed that he took the time to tie four knots in each string; he spaced them out some three or four inches apart. I did as he did, but when it came to the knots, I skipped them. It was late, starting to rain again, and I could see no reason for them. One thing I did pick up on was that he hung the poncho sideways; I saw at once, when he got on it, that this allowed him to button it up on the side, and not directly on top, making the whole thing perfectly waterproof.

I had the first watch, which was the best to have, really. When it was done, the rain was coming down in a steady downfall. Taking off my rain jacket and donning the dry jungle sweater I had in my rucksack, I blissfully jumped in my field hammock, buttoned it up and settled down to a good night's sleep. And that is when I discovered a curious property about water that I had never considered before.

My poncho, empty, had hung limply all throughout my watch. When I got in it, however, my weight pulled it down and also pulled the supporting strings taut; they now formed a perfectly straight line from tree to poncho. I discovered what the knots were for. The rainwater collected on the tree, ran down the length of the string, but, in Sergeant Wright's case, reached a knot and dripped to the ground below. In my case, with no knot, it happily ran all the way down the string, to the poncho and into it. It collected in a nice, cold pool, to an impressive depth of about three inches.

The next morning, stiff, cold and wet, I eyed my platoon sergeant with a jaundiced glare as he got out of his poncho—he'd had the middle watch, and so had returned to its comforts afterward—and stood before me, smiling, relaxed, refreshed, and dry.

"Mornin', Lieutenant," he greeted me cheerfully. "Sleep okay?"

The rains continued, and life became misery. Later, we would go through a pattern of heavy, intense afternoon thunderstorms; those were violent but, in the end, bearable because they were followed and preceded by strong sunlight. This rain was relentless, and the few times it stopped, the clouds stayed in place. We never dried out. Even Wright couldn't hold off the wet forever. But we continued to move across our AO, trudging up slopes made slick with a heavy, brownish mud, or, worse, descending those slopes later. My left hand, the one not holding my weapon, became a single bleeding sore from the cuts, abrasions and punctures the sodden vegetation inflicted on me as I clutched at it to keep from being washed down the hill.

Wearing a poncho or a rain jacket became a joke. Neither could keep anyone dry. The many straps and laces that crisscrossed our bodies became conduits for the rain; they directed cold water along our chests, down our backs, under our arms. The plants became so waterlogged that even when it stopped raining, we got soaked moving through the brush. The point man, in particular, was affected; visibility, in real terms, was often reduced to mere feet, if for no other reason than that his eyes were constantly filled with water, splashing directly into them, or trickling in a constant stream down his forehead. We changed the point constantly.

Everything was wet, and everything was coated in mud; grainy, rough-edged mud, or liquid, oily mud, or pasty, cloying mud; smelly, or slick, or abrasive ... mud became our element, like seawater to fish. Our weapons were impossible to clean, because there was absolutely nothing left to clean them with that wasn't itself full of mud. Food was tasteless, and best eaten in huge, rapid gulps. To linger over a can of peaches was simply to convert it into a watery, foul-tasting soup. Cigarettes became a distant dream—how could you light one? No one was optimistic enough to try writing a letter.

This went on for four days. Rations were low—nothing flew. Worse, the other companies were inserted into the AO, and what had been two line companies stumbling about became four, with the predictable results that movement became a series of countermanded orders; we were pulled first in one direction and then another; yesterday we were headed east; today north, and tomorrow south. Yesterday, today and tomorrow became morning, afternoon and evening: Contact, or suspected contact, by one platoon of Delta at the far southern end of the AO inevitably meant that everyone was diverted and made to slog through the misty hills and valleys, until, an hour or two later, a platoon from Charlie, far to the east, made contact and everyone was turned around and made to move that way.

How the men stood it is something I had difficulty understanding. We'd already moved, as a company, over three kilometers—a vast distance in that jungle, in those conditions—to arrive at a proposed NDP site. First Platoon was immediately sent out on a RIF to the northeast, over a kilometer away. Robison tempered the blow by assuring me that we were due for pick-up in the morning at a PZ no more than a few hundred meters from our target site. We were just reaching the indicated area when I received a call from Robison.

"Change of plans. The wind's changed again and the whole valley's socked in. Nothing's gonna fly. Barracuda wants Bravo to rendezvous at Yankee Lima Lima Foxtrot Alpha Golf. Got that? We're waitin' on you, so get the lead out."

I pulled out the map and tried to make sense of the rain-splotched paper ... and then my internal thermostat went off the charts. The rendezvous point was to the southwest — the precise opposite direction we'd been moving in. Robison ignored my curses by simply handing the mike back to Carter.

We got to the vicinity three hours later, at 1730. The clouds were low and dark, and twilight already gripped the valley. But it wasn't too dark for me to see this huge mass directly in front of us—the rendezvous point. I was stunned.

What is that?

We were on a low, bare hill; a shallow saddle led off to the south where Robison and the company waited for us, 300 meters away...

And about 200 meters up.

I pulled out the map and re-checked the coordinates of the rendezvous point. They were right. I checked Robison's last position. That too checked. Then I looked, in growing consternation, at the map. There it was, plainly shown: Our hill, the saddle between us and Robison, and the small hill the rest of the company was on ... all within the 20-meter contour line, as next door to flat as you could reasonably expect in this area. But what I saw in front of me, its top already lost in the late-evening mist, was a mountain a good 600 feet above the point where I stood. I shook my head, incredulous. I'd been checking azimuth headings constantly. Surely I couldn't have made such a colossal error in navigation?

I flipped my compass open and took a heading to the mountain. 173°. I looked at the map and estimated the heading there ... 170°, give or take a degree ... where the hell *were* we?

Robison chose that moment to call. "One Six, where the hell are you?"

I restrained any of a large number of visceral responses. "Six, this is One Six. We're about 300 meters north of you, and closing. But we've got a pretty tough climb in front of us."

"If you hadn't been fuckin' around out there, taking your time, you could 'a been there by now," he told me.

Sergeant Wright walked up beside me.

"We gonna rest here for a moment, Lieutenant? I thought we..." his voice trailed off as he looked at the slope in front of us. He carried his own map; he pulled it out, looked at it, blinked, looked at the slope again, and then carefully put them map back in its plastic bag. He was reaching for his compass when I stopped him.

"Just took a heading, Top. One Seven Three — on the nose."

He grunted, scowling.

"Top," I said, "there's no way we could be anywhere other than where we're supposed to be, is there?"

He shook his massive brown head. "No, sir." Then he shrugged. "Well, it ain't the first time I seen a map be wrong."

"Yeah. Great." I stared resentfully at the mountain. Climbing that, in the dark, at the end of an exhausting day that was only one of an exhausting week, would be an absolute trial.

The follies weren't over. After a night in which no one got any sleep, the clouds sill lay low and heavy over the hills, and we understood immediately that there would be nothing flying again today. Robison was crouched on his haunches, Vietnamese-style, over a flickering stove boiling water. I shook my head. He had to be the only man in the company with a heat tab. He grunted when he saw me.

"Gather up the others, Boccia. We need to be moving out."

He sounded in a foul mood, and after I collected Bennet and Jones, we all found out why. Incredibly, we were to backtrack almost the entire route from the previous day; our objective was a large, flat-topped hill three and a half kilometers from where we stood. But between us and that hill were two moderately high, steep ridges, which we would have to climb and then descend. And when we got there, our maps told us, the southwest side of the hill, which we would have to climb, was a 300-meter rise; from the dense reddish contour lines, almost as steep as Helen's flanks.

We all looked at each other.

"Mother *fucker*," Bennet said, quietly.

The entire battalion, except for Alpha Company, was being pulled into that one hill; it was open on top, treeless, and would make an adequate PZ, if — but this was a huge if — the weather cleared. What we would do if we got there and the weather continued bad was, frankly, beyond our comprehension. Perching an entire battalion of infantry on top of a vast open space miles from any known objective for no other seeming purpose than to stand dripping in the rain would not be something that later generations of infantry officers would study at the War College as an example of brilliant tactical maneuvering.

The rest of the day, until late in the afternoon, was simply one long, frustrating, exhausting series of two steps forward and one back, as we struggled up and down the mud-lathered ridges. After a while, we entered that dangerous zone, the one that kills: Our numbed minds had room for only a limited number of sensations, and they were focused on our feet and backs and shoulders. Move your foot forward ... shift weight, lift the other foot and move that forward ... at a certain point, we could have walked

4. Mud Is the Universal Constant

right through an entire regiment of NVA all lined up at parade rest and we wouldn't have noticed them.

It got late. The dark heavy clouds and the pervasive mist cut the waning sunlight to almost nothing. Well before sunset, we were moving in deep twilight. Our order of march that day was two-three-one, which meant that First Platoon was taking up the rear; easily the most exhausting and infuriating position to find yourself in while moving. Aside from the dreaded accordion effect — the alternate bunching-up and spreading-out of the last ones in a file, ensuring that half the time they would have to be running to keep up — there is the truly depressing feeling of never knowing what in hell was going on; starts and stops occurred all day, without us having a clue as to why. And, on a day like this, after a week of rain, by the time 100 fully loaded troops had climbed or descended a path before us, the trail was reduced to a thin muddy liquid surface over a slick, clay-like undercoat. It would often take us three or four tries to climb two or three feet.

We approached the hill from the west, more or less. Delta came in from the northeast, on a much easier approach; Charlie had to move the farthest that day, but had the easiest approach of all, from the north. For them, the slope from the ridges they'd been following all day to the hill itself was hardly noticeable. So, even though they'd had the longer trek, they were the first ones there, arriving only a few minutes before Delta. We were last, and that had some serious consequences for us.

Jones's lead element began climbing the steep, boulder-strewn south slope at 1630. As steep as it was, there was one positive; there was no trail here, worn into the hillside. Instead, the entire slope was covered by a tough, coarse grass growing amongst the massive boulders and rock face. Slick grass was tough, but a vast improvement over the grease-like mud we'd been trying to negotiate all day. Jones radioed back at 1710 that he'd reached the top. I uttered a prayer of thanks. The lead elements of First Platoon were by now about a quarter of the way up the slope, and it looked like we'd be on top ourselves by 1800.

But I hadn't counted on the mass confusion of three full companies entering the NDP area all at once. Movement became an inexplicable series of fitful starts interspersed with long, tiring waits. At 1745, Bennet announced his lead element had reached the top, but we were still not even half way. 1800, and sunset, came and went, leaving us in almost total darkness, but we were scattered all across the slope of the hill, at its steepest part; the men were literally clinging to tufts of grass to keep from sliding or falling back down the slope, often for five or ten minutes at a time.

I had made, already, at least a dozen calls to Robison, asking what was going on, but he'd had little to tell me. I knew he was on top of the hill himself, because his CP group had been between Second and Third Platoons, but beyond assuring me, repeatedly, that it wouldn't be long, he told me nothing.

It was 1830. By now, it was almost pitch dark. The rain, which had ended sometime in the early afternoon, returned as a steady, soaking drizzle, making our ascent even harder. The men were beyond exhaustion; resting in place with 60 to 80 pounds on their backs while clinging to the slope of a steep, wet, grass-covered slope is not rest.

How I had held onto my temper all throughout the day remains a mystery to this day. But somehow I had. Now, however, I was on the narrowest of ledges; one small fraction of an inch of control remained between me and a berserk eruption.

That fraction disappeared with the next transmission, I called the CP to see what was gong on—we hadn't moved in ten minutes—only to be told by Price, Robison's other RTO, that the CO was unavailable.

"Well, *make* him available. I need to talk to him now."

"Roger, One Six, but he's not here. He's checking Second Platoon right now."

"Then get yourself over there with the radio now, because I can't wait. Clear?"

Something in my tone must have told Price not to argue. About 20 or 30 seconds later, Robison's voice, peevish and harried, sounded in my ear.

"Okay, One Six, what's so goddamn important?"

"What's important is that you've got one of your platoons strung out on an open slope, in the dark, and we haven't moved in half-an-hour. What in the hell is gong on up there?"

"We got some problems up here, One Six. The S3 is changing some positions on the perimeter and he doesn't want you up here until he gets it straightened out."

Sergeant Wright told me later that he didn't need a radio to hear my next transmission.

"Well, fuck the S3! Do you understand your men are spread out all over the fucking map? Get them up there, for chrissakes. There's got to be room up there for one lousy platoon!"

Robison's voice was placating, almost pleading. "Okay, One Six. We're trying."

"Well try harder, damn it!"

I hurled the receiver away; it flew as far as it could, about three feet, before the coiled cable pulled it back, almost hitting an astonished Conzoner in the head. If Robison responded, I didn't hear him. I was still fuming and muttering to myself, unaware of the stares of the men who had been in earshot, which turned out to be about half the platoon. I didn't realize it then but I had just become their hero. I had said exactly what every one of them had been thinking for the past hour.

My tirade might have had some effect: The column began to move again a few minutes later, and this time there were no more delays before we reached the top. A silent Sergeant Garza led us across the south flank to the east, where we were to set up for the night. It was too dark, and too late, to do anything except break the men up into five man positions—there wasn't enough room along the perimeter for positions smaller than that—and the set up the CP group behind them. The word had already been passed down to maintain 40% alert—two on, three off, but Sergeant Wright and I arbitrarily changed that to one in five. There was no time to dig in, or to clear fields of fire. All we could do was put the men in place and trust in the fact that the NVA wasn't about to probe an entire battalion.

Then I went hunting for Robison. I still had blood in my eye. Fortunately for me, because otherwise I'm fairly sure I would have crossed the line between mere insubordination and outright assault, Robison again spoke in a placating, almost apologetic tone. He knew it had been a bad day, he understood that we had borne the brunt of it, and he agreed that the battalion staff had been incompetent and clueless. And here, have some hot chocolate.

5

The Poor Guys in Korea

YD477205; 7–9 January 1969

When we woke up the next morning, we found ourselves on a massive plateau, or more accurately, a connected series of shallow, rolling hills and valleys, none more than a few meters above or below another.

It had to be massive, because a better part of three full companies was there. Alpha had moved into Rakkasan three days earlier, but the rest of the battalion was all over that plateau. Robison called us in for a briefing at about 0630. Delta and we would leave here and join Alpha at Rakkasan; Charlie would move up to secure Helen and Long. Once there, Alpha would vacate and go on a RIF to the west, and Delta and we would take over the firebase security. We estimated our march to be about four hours. For once, we were pretty accurate. We moved out about 0730, and entered the barbed wire of Rakkasan at just before 1200.

But the Furies weren't done with us yet.

I suppose I should have suspected: 20 minutes after entering the wire, First Platoon was still sitting in the drizzling rain on the PCP of the helipad, waiting. Garza found me there and told me the CO wanted to see me.

Robison had placed his CP in an unfinished bunker, destined to be an auxiliary aid station, about 30 meters behind the north bunkers. I found him there, stripped to the waist, toweling himself dry, or as dry as someone can get from rubbing a piece of cloth only slightly drier than a waterfall over his body.

Clue number two was that he wouldn't meet my eye when I entered.

"Bo," he said, with real reluctance, "I ... they decided Alpha's not moving out after all. They want them to wait here until the weather breaks and then chopper them out to the west. We'll be hiking up the Helen tomorrow morning — the whole company — but ... the firebase is too crowded. You're the last platoon in, so they told me to send you out on an ambush. Uh ... to this ravine over here. 477205."

I took one look at the map and steeled myself to stay calm.

"If we're going to climb Helen tomorrow, wouldn't it make sense to at least send us out to the east, in the same general direction?"

5. The Poor Guys in Korea   61

He shrugged. "Yeah, it would, only this is where they want you to go. Hell, it's only a klick or so. Won't take you but an hour."

"When do we leave?"

"Uhh ... now."

Despite my best intentions, the fires began to build. "It is 1230. As you say, we'll be there by 1330. What the hell kind of ambush am I going to set up in the middle of the after—" I broke off. This was useless. It was obvious they weren't sending us out on a real, honest-to-god ambush. They were merely getting rid of an unwanted group of men. I took a deep breath.

"This shits, you know," I said to Robison.

He shrugged again. "War is hell."

I found Conzoner seated on the PCP, moodily playing with his PRC25. "Steve, tell the platoon we'll be moving out in 20 minutes, after they get their Cs. Form up over there, order of march 1-2-3."

I started to move off in search of Sergeant Wright when Conzoner spoke up.

"Uh ... Lieutenant. About those Cs...."

I came to a halt, almost sliding in the slick yellow mud just off the tarmac. "What about 'em?"

"Uhh, there hasn't been a resupply in four or five days. There aren't any C-rations."

"No rations? Who says?"

"That's what Garza just told me. It looks like they gave Alpha Company all the Cs because they thought they were moving out. I guess they got 'em all."

"Are you telling me they gave Alpha Company our C-rations?"

"I don't know about that, Lieu—"

I didn't hear the rest because I was already on my way back to Robison's CP. Twenty minutes later I left, having vented my spleen and pushed Robison to the point of court-martialing me.

An hour later, Jones, our point man, walked through the gap in the concertina wire, along the mud-slicked trail leading down the northwestern slope. Every second bunker had a solitary forlorn figure, huddled in a poncho, seated on its roof. The sentries watched us file by. None waved or jeered, as was the custom. It was cold and wet. To wave meant to move, and to move was to expose yet another portion of the body to the rain and wind. Better, much better, to sit motionless.

We had no choice; we had to move. At least that warmed us up, after a while. The men were subdued, resigned, more than a little scatological in their comments, but not particularly surly. At the last moment Robison had scrounged some Cs from the artillery battery, so we had enough food to see us through the morning, and at that point, that was as much as we could ask for. Things could be worse. Things could always be worse.

We made our NDP by 1400; we still had five hours of dim grey daylight ahead of us. That would have been laughable, had we been setting up an ambush, but we had no intention of staying in ambush posture throughout the night. Things would be bad enough, and anyway, no one, including the S3, seriously thought there'd be any enemy activity where we were. The steady drizzle had become a downpour soon after we left Rakkasan; it had stopped altogether now, but the dirty grey clouds and the wind promised more of the same. Visibility, once again, was terrible: We could barely make out the tops of the trees under which we stood.

There was no hilltop for us to set up on, nor was there any appreciable extent of flat terrain. Wright looked about and then performed a bit of his magic. We were on the slope of a long but low ridge, just one of a series of folds and draws that were just one large tumbled mass. One spot would have been as good as another, but he chose the east slope of a small spur that ran off the ridge. The wind and rain, he explained to me, as we started setting the men up in a rough oval at the base of the slope, were from the west; we would be behind the sharpest piece of terrain in the area, at least partially protected from the wind. The little draw at the base of the slope was split by a small rill, normally dry, that today was full of brown, swift-flowing water. We set up positions along the slope and the rill. As a tactical location, it was horrible, but no one cared that night. No NVA in his right mind would be out in this stuff anyway.

The platoon was on its last legs; days of constant movement, up and down steep, mud-covered ridges, perpetually wet, cold and sleepless … there was little left in them. Not even Wright could stay dry and warm, after all this. And we were out on a useless patrol in the middle of what was probably the safest AO in Eye Corps. Sergeant Wright and I weren't slackers, but it took us only a moment to make our decision: Minimum security, and a fire.

Three fires, we decided: One at each end of the rough oval and one in the middle.

It was a lovely dream, but I reluctantly punctured it. "How are we going to light a fire? I doubt there's a man here who has so much as one dry match. And a whole troop of boy scouts would work themselves to death trying to do the stick-lighting thing."

That's when Hyde, who'd been standing there silently, spoke up.

"Uh, Lieutenant? While we were on Rakkasan? Saw some C4 lyin' there … thought maybe we could use it. You know, for blowin' an LZ or…."

"Or lighting three fires," Wright finished for him.

"C4, huh?" Hyde had just misappropriated government property. Bad, Nathan. Bad. I grinned at the thought. Hyde had just ripped off the U.S. Tax Payer for about a hundred dollars. I think the entire platoon would have spoken as one: Fuck the U.S. Tax Payer.

C4 is lovely stuff. It is a plastic explosive, and it comes wrapped, like a vanilla candy bar, in a thick brown waxed paper with a waterproof lining. Each bar is about ten inches by two by one, and is composed of a grainy white substance that, when squeezed, becomes plastic and malleable. C4 is the least temperamental of all explosives: You can stomp on it, mash it, throw it, chew it, jump up and down on it. Nothing happens. It just sits there. You can even burn it. *Especially*, you can burn it.

It burns with a fierce, spitting blue flame. A warm, heat-emitting blue flame. Lovely stuff, C4. An expensive blue flame, too. Thirteen dollars a stick, they told us at SERTS. The good people at S4 would be having fits and falling in them if they'd known what we used their prized $312-a-case C4 for. But then, the S4 was invariably to be found back at Evans, in a nice warm hutch, and as he sat there, relaxing in his easy chair, sipping a Makers, listening to the tape deck and the sound of the heavy rain clattering against his roof, did he cast a thought out to the grunts who were sitting out there in the cold and wet? Did he wonder to himself, *gee, how do those guys keep themselves warm and dry on a night like this*? Did he? Oh, I'm sure he did.

Well, if he did, here's his answer: We burned C4. By the crate, when on a firebase. Not tonight, of course. Hyde had liberated six sticks, and they had to be husbanded. But it wasn't long before Hyde and Wright had three fires going. Wet as the wood was, these two men, raised in the woods, knew to take the larger branches and split them open; inside the wet bark and outer half-inch, the wood was dry and ignited instantly under the intense blue flame of the C4. Soon, the three fires became the foci of three groups of shivering, damp bodies. Oh, we had security out; two positions, of four men each, one at the top of the slope and another at the head of the draw, but we rotated them every hour, which meant that everyone had three hours by the fire for every one spent on duty.

We strung out ponchos as shelters, but that was only moderately effective. The ground was soaked after days of rain, and it was uncomfortable to lie on. Some men tried to buddy up: One poncho was used as a ground cloth and the other as a lean-to, but in the end, the water got us all. There was simply too much of it. Muldoon and I stretched both our ponchos across the fire, hoping to keep the rain off of it, but that still meant that we had to lie or sit on the muddy ground.

Even with the fires, this had to rank well up there among the most miserable days I've ever spent. The rain, as expected, picked up again, the wind gained in velocity and the temperature fell even lower. We had intended to put the fires out — not even under these circumstances could we allow them to burn throughout the night — but nature saved us the trouble; an exceptionally heavy deluge hit us around 1700, and literally washed the fires away.

Muldoon, Conzoner and I were stretched out under the lean-to; Wright, Hathaway and Brown were in another. I was wrapped in a sodden liner, shivering. The rain, no longer able to penetrate the waterlogged earth, began to run down the slope of the ridge in tiny waves, leaping and burbling down my back. To lie, as we all did, with our heads pointed upslope meant that this constant, night-long runoff of rainwater simply poured down our backs, bringing with it thousands of little grains of silt, tiny twigs, fragments of leaves, drowning spiders and — oh, yes: Leeches; leeches by the hundreds. As time went on, the silt built up along the inside our shirt backs; every shift of position, every shiver, pushed it further down our backs, until we were literally lying on a pile of grit.

"This is unreal," Conzoner said, at one point.

"Reckon there's a dry spot left on earth? Anywhere?" Muldoon muttered.

"Goddamnit!" Conzoner cried out. "Duke ... can a leech really crawl up a man's dick?"

"Anywhere it's warm," Muldoon answered.

"Oh. Well, that lets out my dick, then. Jesus! It's cold."

I could hear some murmuring behind me. Sergeant Wright was up, too, along with the others. Not even Wright could stay comfortable tonight. More comfortable than me, maybe, but not really comfortable.

"We're gonna have 35 cases of trench foot for sure," Muldoon said. "But that don't matter 'cause we'll all be dead of pneumonia before that."

"Or we'll drown."

"Did you say you checked the platoon this evening?" I asked Muldoon.

"Yeah. They're wet."

"Good man," I said. Wright was, of course, right: Muldoon was turning into a fine soldier, much as it pained him to realize it.

"I heard you went after the Old Man today," Muldoon said, after a moment.

"What?" I started to sit up but shuddered. No; best lie in place. "Where'd you hear that crap?"

"Me," Conzoner answered. "I was outside the CP when you lit into him about the Cs. Made my day, if you don't mind my saying so, Lieutenant."

"Mine, too," Muldoon said, full-throated approval in his voice. "And yesterday ... on that fucking hill. Goddamn, Lieutenant, I'll make an Irishman out of you yet."

The wind picked up even more, and now the temperature really started to fall. Hypothermia became a real possibility.

"This shits," Conzoner said, as the wind whipped across the slope; it had turned, as was coming from the north now, bringing stinging shards of rain with it.

"Yeah," I said, shivering. "It does. But as bad as this is, it could be worse. A lot of guys had it a lot worse. I read about Korea, and — that was bad. They had some serious cold, those guys."

"Yeah, you're right," Conzoner agreed. "My uncle — my father's brother — he was in Korea, and he told us about it once. It was damned cold there. Real cold. Guys froze to death. Weeks at a time, below zero ... trench foot, frostbite, amputations ... bad, bad shit."

"Yeah," Muldoon said.

"They had it bad," I nodded.

"Yeah, they had it bad. Poor bastards." Muldoon brooded for a moment. "Course, that don't make me no drier."

Around midnight, I made the rounds. Sleep was impossible, and I could hardly get any wetter or colder. Surprisingly, I found the prevailing mood among the men to border on hilarity. We had reached the point where only two reactions were possible:

Either we'd sink into a rasping, mutinous anger or we'd start to laugh. At the last position, Tim Logan was holding court, stretched out along the ground wrapped in a muddy liner. Logan, an Indianapolis boy with bright red hair and freckles, was big and very strong; he had immediately been tapped as his squad's Mike Sixty man.

"Lissen, man. Think about it. Years from now, we'll be sittin' in a bar somewhere, sippin' a brew, and laughing our asses off about all this. No—seriously."

"I will like shit. You laugh. You're a retarded fuck, anyway, Logan. You laugh at everything."

"Nah. We'll get a million grins from tonight. It's like my ol' pappy told me, the day I put the John Deere in reverse and backed over the outhouse. He was up*set*, mainly 'cause he was in it at the time. But when he finally crawled out from under, he just smiled and said, 'Son, you 'n me's gonna laugh like hell about this.' That was just before he beat the living shit outta me. An' you know what? Ol' Pap knew what he was talkin' about: To this day, he laughs like crazy when he thinks about beatin' me up."

"Shut the hell up, Logan. You were raised in the city and you know it. You ain't never *seen* a tractor or an outhouse."

"Never seen a—why, slop mah pigs! Talkin' to an ol' Indiana farm boy like that."

"Shit. You ain't never seen no live pig in your life."

"Never seen a pig? I dated your sister, didn't I?"

"Logan, just what was it you did back in the World?"

"Me? I was press secretary to President Lyndon Baines Johnson."

"He ain't fuckin' president no more, you moron."

"That's why I'm not the press secretary anymore." Logan replied.

"Ohhhh, man. I'd like to press a secretary right now. Right in her—"

"You poor, shriveled-up little mouse-dick, you. Just what in hell do you think you could do with a woman? Better you should keep your mind where it belongs, on pigs and outhouses."

I returned to the CP area and found Wright standing up, wrapped in his liner.

"How are the troops, Lieutenant?" he asked.

"Bearing up," I replied.

The next morning, I was shocked to find out I'd actually slept, at least for a half hour or so. It took an act of will to move. Even a slight twitch of the muscles brought some portion of the skin in contact with the clammy, gritty abrasive fabric of fatigue shirt or pants. I walked, stiff-legged and mincing, down to the rill, and then up the draw. The remains of the fire were a blackish smear against the dun brown mud. Nothing looks as cheerless and dead as a spent, washed-out fire.

Some of the men were already up. Others still lay on the ground, shivering, groaning at the feel of their wet clothes and the raw, sodden morning air. I stepped over Logan, who was still stretched out under his poncho liner, shiny with water.

"I feel like a duck," he announced to the world at large. There was a brief pause. Then: "Quack, quack," he said.

"Quack quack quack" sounded all around the perimeter, as squad leaders began to prod their men up. They also were urging them to clean — as well as they could — their mud-encrusted, silt-clogged weapons. I continued walking around the perimeter until I saw Muldoon, kneeling beside a trooper. It was Abbot, I saw, who sat on a small log, wrapped in his poncho, stiffly holding out his left hand.

"What's wrong?" I asked, approaching.

Muldoon looked up. "Bad stuff." He indicated the hand.

I grunted softly. The base of the thumb was swollen to almost twice normal size, and was an angry cherry red. Along the back of his hand, the skin was puffy and dead white — a sure sign of cellulitis.

"Hurt bad?" I asked Abbot.

"A bit."

"Can you carry your weapon?"

"Yeah. I can do that."

I looked at Muldoon. "Will he last until we get to Helen?"

Muldoon shrugged. "If we can get him back to Evans right after that. Man needs a lot more than I can give him."

"Abbot, do you think you can hold out until we get back to Helen? We should be able to get you out of there."

"Yeah, I can make it."

"Good man."

As we walked away, I asked Muldoon if there were any more cases like that.

"Some," he said, morosely. "But not as bad — yet. It's bullshit, Lieutenant B. I checked yesterday an' half these guys got skin missin' on their toes an' the top of their feet. We don't get them settled down and dry, you're not gonna have a platoon left."

I sighed. "I know. And nothing's flying."

As expected, we returned to Rakkasan just in time to join the rest of Bravo in a hike to Helen. Three klicks, (plus the additional klick and a half we'd had to negotiate in the morning) brought us to the base of Hill 674. Six hundred seventy four meters high, and almost all of it rose up from the valley floor; the contour line at its base read 80, on the map. Six hundred meters vertically, and only about 800 horizontally. Even on the best of days, this was an official ball breaker. In the rain, after what we'd been through ... and, oh, yes: As a fillip, each of us carried a round of 81mm mortar ammo, which the good people at Rakkasan had pressed on us, as a sort of going away present.

6

The Tiger Dines

Firebase Helen; 10 January 1969

It took us all day to climb Helen's flanks. As we entered the firebase from the west, Charlie Company's two platoons were filing out the east end, along the ridge that would take them to Firebase Long; from there, it was an easy descent to the plains, where they would probably spend the night. If the weather remained as it was, they would walk north to Highway 601, where they would be picked up in trucks and motored directly to Evans, which straddled the road. It was ludicrous: On the east side of Helen was the coastal plain, with roads, towns, cities, electric lights and running water; on the other side, separated by barely a thousand horizontal meters of mountain, was absolute wilderness.

The weather remained as it was. If anything, it got colder. I remembered what Bennet had said, after my first night on Helen almost a month ago: Cold as I'd been, he'd warned me that it would get worse when it rained. I hadn't believed him then. But he was right. The wind came sweeping across our bunkers uninterrupted, from the southwest, bringing with it hard, icy almost sleet-like shards of rain.

It was 1900. Four of us sat in the CP bunker, arms wrapped around ourselves, flexing stiff, puffy fingers. Even Wright was no longer comfortable: He'd tried laying out his jungle sweater, to dry it, but it was just too cold and wet. Hathaway and Brown sat huddled together in a corner, back to back, wrapped in the same poncho liner, hoping to warm each other. I simply lay on the rough bunk, shivering. My clothes were clammy, filled with grit and sand, and at least three leeches clung to my armpit; I was too cold to remove my shirt to get at them.

Conzoner entered; he'd been up at the CP, getting next day's password and keyword. "Hey, guess what? Guess what's up at the CP right now?"

"Six hundred pounds of bullshit," Hathaway said, peering out from over his liner. "What?"

Hathaway counted on his fingers: "Robison's about 170. Garza's 140, n' Schoch's 180."

Conzoner shook his head. "That's 500, dumb shit."

"Oh." Hathaway shrugged.

"Listen: Beaucoup kerosene. Beaucoup, in a five-gallon drum. I saw the son of a bitch sitting there, right behind the CP. Whattaya think, Lieutenant," he said eagerly, "think we could use some of that?"

I shuddered one more time, feeling the slimy touch of my shirt against my skin.

"Conzoner," I croaked, "I have no idea what you're talking about and I don't ever want to know. Clear?"

Conzoner tapped Hathaway on the head. "C'mon, man. Let's go." He looked at me. "Ell Tee, I promise you that you won't know a thing."

I didn't think it possible, but I must have fallen asleep. I didn't remember setting the watch schedule, and it's probable that none was set. I vaguely remembered Muldoon coming back from his rounds of the bunkers, and then, some time later, being awakened by Sergeant Wright's insistent voice.

"Sir. Wake up. Wake up, Lieutenant."

He was shaking my shoulder. I lay on the bunk, unable to open my eyes. I still felt exhausted, although, I noticed, I was no longer trembling with the cold. I made an effort to speak.

"Yeah, Top?" I said thickly, still barely able to articulate.

"Wake up, sir. The CO wants you on the radio."

I groaned. "Jesus Christ." I finally forced my eyes open. Wright's face, a slight smile playing across his heavy features, was just above mine. In the corner, casting enough light to see by, was a mess hall coffee can half full of burning kerosene. The brown shadows on Wright's face shifted and melted in the flickering light, so that each second he seemed to change identity, like a television program gone berserk. The thought finally trickled through my sleep-fogged brain that the kerosene lamp must also explain why I no longer felt cold.

"Okay, Top," I said, sitting up. "I'll take it." Then I sat paralyzed at a sudden thought. "Jesus, Top! I didn't check the bunker lines."

He smiled as he handed me the receiver. "It's okay, Lieutenant. I checked them an hour ago."

I grinned sheepishly. He nodded and went directly to his bunk, where he wrapped himself in his liner and was asleep before I was done with my conversation.

"One Six here," I yawned into the horn.

"Where the hell you been, One Six?" Robison's voice was sharp but low. "We got movement inside the perimeter."

That was an eye opener! Do you want to wake an old infantryman up? Don't bother with alarms, trumpets, buckets of water or anything like that. Just whisper "movement inside the perimeter" in his ear and then jump back.

I sat bolt upright, my fatigue not even a memory. With one hand I held the mike, and with the other I frantically tried to put on the boots I'd kicked off a few hours before. Meanwhile, I gestured urgently to Muldoon to wake up Conzoner and Wright.

6. The Tiger Dines 69

"Okay," I whispered into the receiver. "I copy. Is it in my sector, over?"

"Negative. It's over by the mess tent. Three Six heard it come through his sector about ten minutes ago."

"Right." But even as I said that, my sleep-fogged brain finally began functioning. What the hell kind of alert was this? Bennet saw it, reported it, and then Robison took the time to not only call me, but to wait while my platoon sergeant woke me…

"There's a tiger in the mess tent. I want you to go check it out."

That totally befuddled me. A "tiger" is what we called an ambush patrol. Was Robison telling me that one of our patrols was raiding our mess tent and I should go check on them? It seemed unlikely.

"Say again, over?"

"I say again: There's a tiger in the mess tent. Check it out."

"Uhhh … this is One Six. Did you say 'tiger,' over?"

"Yeah. You know. A tiger. A big goddamn orange pussycat."

I shook my head, trying to clear it. "Are you telling me that we have a live tiger in our mess tent right now?"

"That's affirmative, One Six."

I stared at the receiver for some time before responding. "And what do you want me to do about it?"

"I want you to check it out, over."

My brain refused to come up with anything to say.

"Let me know what you find, One Six. Out."

I stared at the receiver. Out. The goddamn weenie.

I looked up to see Wright taking off his shirt again and replacing his weapon in the rack over his head. Conzoner and Hathaway were industriously trying to disappear under their poncho liners. Muldoon, his ugly mug grinning gleefully at me from his little corner of the CP, shook his head in false sympathy.

"How would you go about checking out a live Bengal tiger, Top?" I asked him.

"Very carefully, Lieutenant," he replied. "Good night, sir."

I looked around the bunker. All four of them were asleep, or striving mightily to appear so. Outside, the wind howled and the rain splattered against the ponchos we'd strung across the bunker slits. Somewhere behind me, perhaps 50 meters away, a live, hungry and probably very frustrated tiger was prowling about, looking for something to eat. I was armed with an M16, an admirable weapon for shooting 125-pound North Vietnamese soldiers, but not exactly suited for big game hunting. Then too, if I did have to fire my weapon, I was in the middle of a firebase with armed troops in all directions. What if one of them took it into his pointy little head that I was an NVA infiltrator?

What was a tiger doing … and then it occurred to me suddenly that this must be our old friend from the ridge two weeks ago, when Mareniewski shot the antelope.

Officers are paid to make quick, firm decisions. I made mine. Replacing my rifle in its rack and kicking off my boots, I lay back on the bunk and rolled over.

"Bon appetit, kitty," I murmured.

There was a shortage of toast at breakfast the next morning. Kitty, frustrated in his attempts to get into the meat containers, had ripped open the bread stall and scarfed up the better part of ten loaves of bread. He also left, as a comment on what he thought of our hospitality, a fairly decent pile of scat, in a corner of the tent. The NCO in charge, a burly E6 with a mass of tight blond curls sticking out from under his white cap, giving him an unnerving resemblance to Harpo Marx, was profanely directing the cleanup when I entered the mess tent at 0530. These cooks, by the way, were not from the battalion mess hall. Even the battalion commander had better sense than to put the cooks who'd prepared our Christmas dinner on the same firebase with armed troopers from Bravo. I was one of the first to eat, that morning. The pancakes were cold, astonishing considering that they'd just been fixed, the syrup watery, the eggs powdered and soggy, and the bacon would have made an excellent gasket material, but standards change. I ate it without comment.

I did come across something of interest as I left the tent. A couple of paw prints were firmly embossed in the mud just outside the tent, and I raised both eyebrows when I saw them. The Vietnamese tiger is nothing like his 500-pound cousins in India; most of them are stunted after years of war, and are usually not too much larger than our own mountain lion. Even so, the size of the print impressed me. That was one big paw.

The sun was just now rising, looking red and watery under the distant clouds on the east horizon. I paused to look at it, knowing that within minutes, after it had risen some more, it would disappear behind the grey cloud cover again. I just wanted to be able to say I'd seen it. I ducked inside our bunker and squelched my way through the mud to my pack. Just then Hathaway turned to face me. I broke out laughing. His blond, almost white hair framed a face that was as black as a coal miner's. Conzoner, still in his bunk, looked up; his face was the same. I blinked. Mine would be the same as theirs. I wondered for a moment that the mess NCO hadn't commented on it, and then realized that probably more than half the firebase had availed themselves of the kerosene and we all had a coating of soot.

I was staring at my pack, trying to decide if I should simply pitch the whole mud-fouled thing over the side, when Muldoon stuck his head in the door.

"See you a minute, Lieutenant?"

"Sure." I willingly left the rucksack to its fate and followed him outside.

He stood by the entrance, looking both angry and apprehensive. "Lieutenant, we got a problem."

"Abbot? His hand?"

He shook his head. "Over here." He turned and walked to one of the bunkers, only a few meters away. It was one of Hyde's. Hyde himself was standing over a seated figure, a deep scowl on his face. I recognized the man on the crate as Kenzy, one of Hyde's team leaders. His right foot was bare, and stretched out before him, resting on a pack.

Muldoon stopped beside the man and shot a troubled look at me.

"What's the problem?" I started to ask, but the words stuck in my throat. "Oh, Jesus!" I thought.

Kenzy's foot was indescribable.

The right side of it, the outer side, was one raw wound, caked with dried blood and pus. The toes and the upper part of the foot were an angry red; the skin there was shiny and stretched, like a balloon about to explode. Shreds of dead grey skin, remnants of popped blisters, hung from his ankle and his heel. Blood still oozed wetly from the outside of the foot, which must have worn against the accumulated grit and water inside his boot. Above all else was the horrible smell of pus and dying flesh.

I whirled on Muldoon, furious. "How in the hell did this happen? I thought you were checking the platoon every night!"

Muldoon, astonishingly, hung his head. "I know. I'm sorry, Lieutenant. He just never said nothin', I asked him every night if he was okay...."

"Well, for Chrissakes," I started, but I broke it off. Anger wasn't going to do anyone any good, and in any case it was more my responsibility than Muldoon's.

I looked at Kenzy. He was short, burly, with a round, smooth face, high cheekbones and light grey eyes under sandy brown hair. Hyde and Wright both thought highly of him, and I had been impressed by his calm competence and willingness to work. He was in pain now, I could tell: His eyes were narrowed and his mouth pulled back tightly, but he hadn't said a word yet.

"What happened?" I asked him.

He shrugged. "Got a blister or two. Just got worse."

"Blister? That's a damn sight more than a couple of blisters you've got there. Why didn't you say anything?"

"Well, I got the blister the first day we went out, you know? I didn't say nothin' about it then 'cause I figured it was gonna go away — they usually do. You know how blisters are. I always get one my first day. Only this one got worse."

"Why didn't you say something then? I know Muldoon was checking with you guys every night."

He grimaced and shifted his foot slightly. "Yes, sir, I know. Ain't Doc's fault. By the time I realized it was getting' worse, weather socked in and I knew we weren't gonna fly out anyway. No point in botherin' him about it."

I took a deep breath, although I had to turn slightly away to do it. "But you should have told us, Kenzy. Damn it."

"I don't know, sir. If I told ya, what couldja do about it? We'd 'a still hadda walk, right?"

I opened my mouth and then closed it. He was right. Nothing was flying during that period. Still ... "If you'd told us, Kenzy, we could have helped you."

He looked at me levelly. "Sir, the only way you coulda helped me was to carry me and my pack. And the other guys were goin' through enough shit over the last week without havin' to do that."

"Damn it, Kenzy. How much farther could you have gone on that foot? We'd have ended up carrying you anyway." I turned to Muldoon. "What about it, Doc. What's it look like?"

Muldoon swallowed. "Lieutenant, I ain't never seen nothin' like this. Not even in pictures. This man needs a hospital and a doctor. Nothin' I can do now."

I shook my head. Hyde was standing off to the side, looking mortified. He felt as bad about this as Doc. And I felt worse than either of them.

"Look, Kenzy ... I know you were thinking about your buddies. I understand that. I can't imagine the guts it took to walk on this thing. You've been unbelievable. But..." I paused for emphasis. "Your buddies are going to have to go without you, at the very best for a long time — weeks, maybe months."

It was Kenzy's turn to swallow. "You mean I gotta go back to the rear? To the hospital? I thought ... I thought maybe Doc here could just patch me up. You know, give me a coupla pills, put some cream on it."

I stared at him. The funny thing was he was serious. "Kenzy, you will be god-damned lucky not to lose your foot. For sure, you're going to be off of it for at least two weeks, while they try to save it."

Hyde shook his head. "You know, Lieutenant, I've been walkin' behind Kenzy for two weeks, 'n I never even saw him limp." He looked wretched.

"Doc, I was told the resupply is going to fly later this afternoon. Can he wait until then? What do you think?'

Muldoon stared at me. For a brief fraction of a second, he looked scared, but then something flashed in his eye and he gave a firm, resolute nod. "I say call the medevac right now, Lieutenant."

"For an infected foot? Who's going to scream if we're wrong?"

"Medevac team. Maybe the battalion staff."

I looked at Kenzy's foot, the red and grey and yellow ruin of it, and then out over the bunker line at the dim grey green forest and hills, still shrouded in fog and mist. Kenzy had walked at least 20 kilometers with close to 100 pounds on his 150-pound frame, up and down some of the steepest mountains in the world, through some of the worst weather I'd ever seen. The pain he'd endured was unimaginable.

Compared to that, a dressing-down from the battalion staff wasn't even a pimple.

"Okay, Doc. You're covered. It's my decision. Call the medevac now. I don't care what you have to tell them. Get them here. And — Doc," I placed my hand on his shoulder. "I'm sorry I yelled just now. This is all my fault."

The medevac arrived within 20 minutes. Abbot and two others were sent back with Kenzy. They weren't emergencies in any way, but Kenzy certainly was and we thought we'd take advantage of the flight. I told Robison about what we'd done, and he shrugged it off. We got our share of grins out of the whole affair about a week later, with the simultaneous reception of two memos from the rear. One was a terse warning from Brigade over the indiscriminate and unjustified use of medevacs to ferry personnel who were merely sick and not critically wounded. The second was a scathing letter from the Division Surgeon at the 22nd, apoplectically critical of Bravo Company's officers for holding back, until it was almost too late, the worst case of infection he'd seen in all his years of service. Robison cursed routinely upon receiving the messages, and was inclined to be a bit snappish with me, until, at Garza's suggestion, he sent a copy of the surgeon's letter to Brigade and vice versa. We never heard back from either one.

7

Black Jack

YD553176; 12–22 January 1969

The weather continued cold and wet for two more days. Finally, on the 12th of January, the clouds vanished overnight, and the sun beat down on the sodden firebase with all the unrelenting force of the tropics. Magically, the ankle-deep mud that had been our torment over the past ten days was replaced by rough-surfaced, crumbly piles of dirt. A portable shower was flown in, along with fresh fatigues, and we enjoyed the unspeakable luxury of clean skin covered by clean clothes. Two more of my men were sent to the rear, for treatment of sores and abrasions and the accumulated effects of prolonged dampness. Word came back from the 22nd that Kenzy would be gone for at least three weeks. Had another two or three days elapsed, we were told, he might have lost his foot.

We never got started on finishing up the construction work. The 14th of January, we were lifted off of Helen and taken on a CA into the area south of the Song Bo, onto Hill 142, YD553176. For the first time, I would lead the assault; that meant I was on the first Huey into the LZ. Robison briefed us on the general tactical situation, and then gave us the plan. First Platoon, as first in, would secure the perimeter from ten o'clock to two o'clock; twelve o'clock would be the direction of flight of the lift ship. Bennet's Third Platoon would come in next, and secure from two to six; Al Jones would then complete the perimeter, from six to ten. The company CP would accompany Bennet's platoon.

It was my first time on the lead ship, and I got a new perspective on CAs. Our lead Huey circled lazily over the LZ, about a thousand feet up, as puffs of grey-white smoke dotted the ground beneath us. This was the artillery prep; a concentration of 105mm fire from one of the firebases nearby. After perhaps ten minutes, the artillery ceased firing, and the ARA ships, flanking us on either side, began making their runs, rocket launchers snarling and screaming audibly. I could follow the path of the rocket by its trailing white smoke; a tiny pinprick of intense yellow marked the explosion when it hit the ground.

Then the lift ship began to lose altitude. The LZ disappeared as the pilot turned his craft and headed directly for it. We flew lower and lower; the trees and bushes became individual plants, three-dimensional. The sound of the motor overhead became an obliterating roar. Suddenly my ears were assaulted by a solid, hammering sound, just behind me. It was the M60, opening up. I felt a moment's fear: Were we under fire? But no; this was routine. I was keyed up, tense and ready. It was like my first parachute jump, in a way, but far more intense.

The ground was there, all of a sudden, directly below my feet. I lurched forward and threw myself off the Huey's platform — too hard; I went tumbling and landed on my face. Scrambling up, not even noticing the 90 pounds on my back, I ran to the center of the LZ, where Conzoner, his receiver already in his hand, waited.

The other Hueys followed us in; the men, fatigues whipping in the hurricane wind of the blades, jumped out and ran to their pre-assigned positions on the perimeter. Sergeant Stempin, whose squad was the first in, pulled out a smoke grenade and armed it, throwing it into the center of the LZ. Intense cherry-red smoke boiled out, lifting quickly into the sky. This not only served to mark the LZ for the other lift ships, but also gave the pilots an idea of wind direction and velocity. I was preoccupied with the placement of the troops, and didn't notice that the wind had changed direction at some point.

The result, to use Robison's considered phrasing, was as complete a rat fuck as the U.S. Army had produced since Little Big Horn. With the Hueys now approaching from a different heading, Bennet, who had no way of knowing the original 12 o'clock direction, sent his troopers into the same positions as mine. While we were yelling at them and each other, Robison landed with Second Platoon; he and Jones stood there in consternation at what seemed to be a mob of soldiers milling about aimlessly. Robison added his voice to the din. While we were all happily engaged in producing as much sound as possible, two troopers, one from Two Six and the other one of mine, reacting to the apoplectic snarls of their respective platoon sergeants, ran full tilt into each other and went sprawling, packs, weapons and all.

With that, we all started laughing. If you're going to fuck up, do it right. We finally figured out what had happened and moved everyone to where they were supposed to be. There were no recriminations, mostly because, as even Robison realized, this was primarily his fault; never again would we use direction of flight as an indicator. He was, if anything, relieved it had not been worse.

Robison had another cause for relief. Barracuda — Lt Col Sheets — had left while we were on Helen, and a new commander had just taken over the battalion. He had in fact been hovering over our LZ, observing the insertion, but fortunately for all of us, immediately after First Platoon landed, Charlie Company, going into an area west of us, had erroneously reported a hot LZ, and he'd sped off to see what was going on there. He hadn't been there to see the afternoon follies, then.

It's a measure of how little impact the outgoing battalion commander had had on us that none of us, except for Robison, even knew he was gone, or that a new commander was already in place. I may have been the first line officer in the company, perhaps in the entire battalion, to meet Black Jack, as the new commander called himself, and that meeting took place about an hour after our insertion.

We began a sweep of the area along the east bank of the Song Bo. A year before, this had been a major staging area for the NVA, used by them to launch their Tet attacks on Hue. The NVA were gone, at least in any appreciable force, but their bunker complexes and caches remained. It was these that we were looking for, and, as well, we were assuring ourselves that the enemy had in fact left the area.

First Platoon was in the lead; we were moving along a low ridge, through dense forest, when we came suddenly upon a wide, long clearing covered only by sparse shrub and low, coarse grass and reeds. The ridge flattened here; the clearing stretched about 40 meters across and some 60 meters long. The forest surrounding it was the same dense tangle we'd been moving through.

Jones, my point man, had stopped at the tree line. This was SOP, and what I did next was strictly according to the book: Calling up my M60 machine gunner and an M79 grenade launcher for fire support, I deployed a fire team and the two weapons along the tree line. Then Jones and Bresina, the point and slack, began making their way slowly along the left side of the clearing. Ulrich and Hernandez, the next two men, moved as slowly along the right side; eventually, the four of them would meet at the far side of the clearing and give us the signal. Only then would the rest of the platoon move out into the open.

It was, as I said, strictly by the book; I didn't even bother to call Robison myself but had Conzoner tell Carter what we were doing. I was kneeling there, on the edge of the clearing, watching the four men advance slowly along the sides, when I heard the rustle of movement behind me. Before I could turn to see who it was, a green-clad shape thrust itself through the vegetation and into the clearing. Whoever it was stood there, well into the open, hands on hips, looking out across the clearing.

I opened my mouth to snarl a reprimand when the man turned his head and looked at me. I immediately saw the black rosette on the collar of his new, still-shiny green fatigue shirt. I was looking at our new battalion commander. He was short, wiry, with a hard face and ginger hair tinged with grey, and two of the bluest, coldest eyes I've ever seen in a man. His name, I saw, was embroidered over his breast pocket, in thick black lettering: Honeycutt.

He turned back to the four men making their way along the flanks for a moment, and then back to me. "Good morning. You're Bravo One Six, right?"

"Yes, sir."

"Good looking platoon you have here."

"Thanks, sir. Uh ... Colonel? We haven't secured the far tree line yet."

He smiled but said nothing. Turning away from me again, he concentrated on the four men. Bresina, I could see, was closing in on the far side of the clearing. I shrugged. Short of grabbing him and dragging him back by force, there was nothing I could do if he wanted to stand there, in plain view, with the heavy black insignia of lieutenant colonel contrasting starkly with the shiny green of his new, unwrinkled fatigues. I could only hope there was no sniper around. I would have a hell of a time explaining to Colonel Conmy or General Zais how I'd managed to lose a battalion commander in his first few minutes in the field.

Looking back on this, months later, I would reflect that almost everything we would come to know about this man was on display that morning: His arrogance, ego, courage, contempt for the ordinary, commitment to direct oversight and aggressive drive were all there, even if masked by a relatively benign smile. Had I known, of course, I would have treasured that moment: The friendly tone in which he said "Bravo One Six" that day would be the only time those words were said in anything but a snarl or a bellow.

The tree line was cleared and we began to move across the open space. When I looked back, a few seconds later, he was gone.

That entire week passed in what could only be called our golden time — with one horrendous exception. The weather was good; the sun shone daily, making the rains of the previous weeks seem like a dark dream, but the temperatures were moderate — for the tropics, I mean: A fairly constant 85° to 95°, which is downright temperate. There was no contact, although we constantly ran across long-abandoned bunkers complexes and trails. Perhaps more than anything, the new commander made a great difference. This was the same S3 staff that had had us chasing our tails all over the AO in that miserable stretch around New Year's, but this time the movement was rational, methodical and to a purpose.

The platoon blossomed. To a man, they all agreed that pounding the boonies, as they called it, was far preferable to life on a firebase — at least, when we weren't facing a constant deluge and harassed by seemingly imbecilic operations orders. No sandbags to fill, no police calls along the barbed wire, no ridiculous condition yellows and mad minutes, no irritating duties like latrine or trench digging. Movement was moderate, the battalion S3 finally having learned the difference between movement along an open plain and movement in dense mountain forests.

Hyde, Stempin and Skinner, the squad leaders, were all experienced, industrious and reliable men who knew their business and took care of their squads. Besides that, they allowed the men considerable latitude in how and when to do their jobs. Stempin was humorless and meticulous, but took a hands-off approach to delegating work; as long as it was done to his satisfaction, he said nothing. Hyde, easy-going and laconic, relied on patience, good humor and a certain let's-get-this-over-with attitude to cajole his squad into working hard. Skinner was the classic in-your-face leader. None of the three tolerated sloppiness or outright insubordination. I was the envy of Bennet and Jones: I was blessed with not only the finest platoon sergeant in the company — some said, the battalion — but the best trio of squad leaders too.

Al Jones had departed soon after our insertion, his DEROS date finally arriving, leaving Second Platoon without a leader. Until his replacement arrived, they became the palace guard, under the eye of Garza and Robison. That left George Bennet and me as the workhorses, and Robison worked us hard.

Still, with the weather continuing fair, and the battalion staff moderating their demands, life wasn't that bad, until the third day of the RIF, the 15th. I mentioned earlier that we had one horrendous exception to a generally easy series of moves, and this was it, and it made up for all the others.

We were along the Song Bo again, on the north and west bank, across the river from our earlier sweeps. First Platoon was on a detached mission, searching out a series of old (and thoroughly abandoned) bunkers. Robison called at mid-morning, telling me to return to the company as soon as possible. Sergeant Wright and I checked the map. We were on a low hill, not far from the river, covered with a familiar reed-and-grass mix. Northwest of us lay a broad, shallow valley, on the other side of which was a long but low ridge, leading directly to the rendezvous point. Wright and I congratulated each other; for once, we would have an easy time of it: We had to traverse 100 meters of valley, climb a low knoll, turn to our right and move an additional 200 meters—400 meters in all. Piece of cake.

Four hundred meters: A world-class sprinter can do it in a little over 40 seconds. It took us eight hours.

The first 75 meters took only a few minutes. But as we neared the slope we were going to climb, we were stopped by a solid mass of living stuff. We all looked at each other. None of us had ever seen anything like it. We never would again, although we saw some areas that came close.

Weeks before, we found ourselves moving through the true saw grass; it's a name given to many different grasses, but the real stuff is about six to ten feet high, two or three inches wide, and aptly named because of the serrated edges consisting of thousands of microscopic razor-sharp teeth. Moving through saw grass is certainly possible, and it doesn't slow you down much, but it *is* painful. Think of a hundred or so paper cuts.

We'd also had several encounters with bamboo thickets, where the ten and 12-foot high stalks grow so closely together that you have to force your way between them, or spend long minutes hacking at them one-by-one with a machete.

And, of course, the "wait-a-minute" vines and creepers were our constant companions; these snaked their way around and between the vegetation wherever we went; here too, a strong right arm and a machete were required.

But we had never seen all three together, and not only together but intertwined so closely that they formed a literally impenetrable wall. The nastiest Georgia briar patch is an open meadow compared to what lay before us. The bamboo provided vertical structural strength, contemptuously turning our machete blades. The intertwined vines and creepers buttressed the bamboo, holding it stiff and unyielding, like a raft lashed together. And the saw grass filled the few gaps, its edges lying in wait like a million knives, ready to draw blood.

7. Black Jack

Our progress was measured in feet per *hour*, or, as Samuel glumly noted, pints of blood per minute. Point men were changed every few minutes, after extending the trail a few inches. Point and slack men had to wear leather gloves, with rolled-down, buttoned-up sleeves, and preferably a scarf around their throats, to keep from being sliced to ribbons: This in 90° heat. Even so, we received cuts on parts of our bodies I would have thought impossible to get to.

We tried something different: Putting one of our bigger men up front—Logan, Ski, Snyder—and having him fall backward, with full pack, trying to push the mass down, becoming a living bridge for the next man to walk over his body and then do the same. It didn't work: The mass was too dense, too strongly held together. After struggling like this for about half an hour, I sent two teams out on a recon, to the right and the left of our position, to see if we could bypass this nightmare. They returned after more than hour; this incredible belt extended for a klick in one direction, and almost that in another. Again, Sergeant Wright and I checked our maps ... and reluctantly concluded that we'd lose more time going around, primarily because going in either direction would lead us to some fairly hefty, steep ridges which we'd first have to traverse, and then backtrack. Besides, we agreed, how far could this mess extend?

We both believed that this was an isolated patch, perhaps only meters in depth. Better, then, to punch our way through. As it turned out, we were wrong, but even in retrospect, our reasoning was good. What we ran into that day could hardly be called typical: Never again did we encounter this grisly mess, so we had reason to believe that it would extend back only a short distance.

It depends, of course, on one's definition of "short." In the event, we hacked and pushed our way through 75 meters of the bloodthirsty thing. When we finally pushed through the last few inches, we looked like men who'd just fought with a berserk meat grinder. At one time or another all of us had taken a turn at point. Every one of us was covered with scratches, cuts, punctures and scrapes: Not just our hands and wrists—that was normal—but our upper arms, faces, necks, shins, waists, bellies—we sustained an incredible amount of damage.

My mood, bad as it was, was not improved by the constant calls from Robison, sitting up on the hill only a few hundred meters away. No matter how often I tried to explain why it was taking us so long, he refused to believe that anything could impede an infantry platoon for so long a time. Transmissions between the CO and me were reduced to profanity-laced snarls. Finally, at around 1500, five full hours after we started, I told Conzoner to turn the radio off.

We finally staggered up the short slope to where he and the rest of the company waited at 1800, just before sunset. The others looked at us in awe: Even in the gathering twilight, they could see the dried blood staining our clothes and skins. We found out why we'd been brought back: There was an intelligence report that a battalion of NVA had been spotted, or more accurately, heard, by some of the thousands of sensors we'd placed along the approaches from the west. Alpha Company was being moved into place north of us, between the Song Bo and the ridges to the west; we were to move north and west to drive them between us.

It was too late to move that night, but early the next morning, just past first light, Bennet's platoon moved out from the hill, descended to the same valley we'd traversed the day before (but much further up, well past The Wall, as we came to call it) and began moving through the low, dense country bordering the river. North of us, the Song Bo made a large, semi-circular loop, so that it looked, on the map, like a backwards question mark. Two platoons of Alpha were at the top of the mark, stretched out in a line that cut off the escape north. The third platoon was sent to a ridge west of the river, and blocked the retreat in that direction. Our job was to seal off the south and southwest.

Almost immediately, Bennet encountered a bunker complex laid across a low ridge that blocked our way. Robison, reluctant to move into the complex — our approach would be confined to a single file, while the enemy, if present, would be arrayed across our front, allowing them to bring many weapons to bear on our few — decided to call in artillery, and for some 30 minutes we simply knelt in place while 155 and 8 inch shells pounded the ridge. It was my first experience with concentrated artillery fire and it was impressive; the volume of sound that two batteries can generate is sobering — and deafening.

After they lifted the fire, Bennet began to move again but within moments stopped; his point man reported possible movement again.

Robison got on the radio, talking to the S3. He dropped the mike after a moment, and told us to sit tight.

"S3 says they've got some assets coming in." In answer to our looks, he shrugged. "That's all I know."

A few minutes later, we heard the heavy thumping and droning of a helicopter, approaching from the east. We exchanged puzzled looks. The sound was unlike anything we expected; it was too heavy, too loud, to be a Huey or Cobra. Then, hovering over the ridge directly in front of us, we saw the source of the sound: It was a Chinook 27, looking like a misshapen grasshopper, with rotors at each end of its ungainly, chunky body. We stared at it and each other with uncomprehending frowns. What on earth was a Hook doing in a tactical situation? It was the equivalent of rolling out a deuce-and-a-half truck in a tank battle.

This one had a net dangling from its belly. Inside the net were eight or ten 55 gallon drums. The Chinook hung ponderously over the bunkers for a few long seconds, and then dropped the net, drums and all. It lifted slowly up, turned, and moved out of sight.

We blinked and stared. Not a single one of us, Robison and Garza included, had any idea of what was going on. Seconds after the Chinook cleared the area, a Cobra, from the sound, fired a pair of rockets into the ridge where the drums lay. The entire ridge erupted in a ball of intense yellow and roiling black.

"Jesus Christ!" Robison yelled, over the whooshing sound, "that was fuckin' *napalm!*"

In fact, it wasn't: It was JP4 aviation fuel, among the most volatile substances on earth. The bushes, reeds and vines around the bunkers crackled and spat flame for several minutes, burning with a fat orange flame and greasy back and grey smoke. It hadn't rained in a week, and we were concerned the entire forest could catch fire, but eventually the flames flickered and died down. Half an hour later, a still-stunned Bennet took his troops in the hot ashes; after a search of about 20 minutes, they reported finding nothing.

While they were looking, the CO shook his head in awe. "I wonder what lunatic thought up this idea?"

No one ever claimed credit for it, which is probably just as well. It *was* a lunatic notion.

The rest of the day, we followed the Nuoc Ke Trai, a small tributary of the Song Bo, encountering several more abandoned bunkers, but finding not a trace of NVA. Battalion S2 finally concluded, a few days later, that the large enemy force the sensors had picked up was us. Technology is wonderful.

So we had to revert to old-fashioned infantry work: Grunting our way through the hills and valleys along the Song Bo and its tributaries. On our last day, we finally made a significant find: A recently-used bunker complex, well to the south of where we'd previously looked, containing documents indicating that elements from the 64th NVA Regiment had been in the area a month or so earlier. They were back in Laos now, but G2 was pleased. We also found a cache of medical supplies and some rice. Glory enough for everyone.

The following day we were airlifted across the Song Bo to an LZ at the base of the ridge on which Helen and Long were located. We were below the eastern end of the ridge; Long was only a short hike up from there — nothing like the strenuous climb to get to Helen.

We weren't there for very long, but two notable things did occur there. The first was an OCS reunion of sorts: Joel Trautman and Jim Goff, OCS classmates of mine at Fort Benning, were with Charlie Company, who were leaving as we entered, and we got to say hello and exchange a lie or two; and waiting for us there was Al Jones' replacement, a short, bespectacled, dark-haired man named Chuck Denholm, who turned out to have been a classmate of Bennet's.

The second event came the next day: Jimmy Stewart, the actor, and his wife and son visited us there. Flanked by Colonel Conmy, the brigade commander, they circulated among the troops, shaking hands, asking questions and chatting effortlessly. Most celebrities, when they did come to Viet Nam, stayed in the rear areas, at the big bases like DaNang or Bien Hoa or Quang Tri. Thousands of GIs saw them, but they tended to be, naturally enough, the REMFs who worked in the rear; some combat troops were able to attend, but the majority was not. Few of the performers and other celebrities came out to a firebase, and particularly not a small, scruffy place like Long.

I am not given to hero worship, and even if I were actors would be pretty far down on the list of people I admire, but Jimmy Stewart was something of an exception. In a college course on film making, we'd studied several Alfred Hitchcock movies extensively, including *Vertigo*, which I saw at least eight times. Our professor regarded the movie as Hitchcock's finest, and one of the things he admired most about it was Stewart's performance. I did too, and it was a thrill for me to meet the man and shake his hand. I said nothing to him about the film, however. I'd always thought that those people who insist on saying "I saw you in..." were pretty tacky.

Stewart and his wife were gracious, sincere and thoroughly nice people, so completely the opposite of the artificial and self-absorbed movie stars of today (or then, for that matter). To take the trouble — and it is a lot of trouble — to come out to a remote firebase is something for which I will always remember him with affection and respect.

The Stewarts left after about an hour, and we weren't far behind them. That night, we were lifted off the firebase and deposited at Evans.

There were several personnel changes in addition to Denholm's arrival. Of the most consequence to me were four: Robison got his captain's bars; Hathaway, Wright's RTO, left the platoon to become, of all things, a Chaplain's Assistant. Of the 34 men in the platoon, Hathaway would have ranked perhaps 25th or 26th on my list of men suitable for the duties of Chaplain's Assistant, but, oh well ... Conzoner took his place, temporarily, until *he* left the platoon and became the first sergeant's RTO. Stempin, reliable and steady, was gone, ruthlessly pirated by Bennet. Wright and I screamed in outrage, but Robison stood firm. I had three good squad leaders, he pointed out, as well as the best platoon sergeant in the company, while Bennet had nothing; his E7 was gone to Bangkok for R&R and he was left with nothing but Spec4s as squad leaders. I pointed out bitterly that this was communism, and hell, that's what we were over here fighting, but Robison was unimpressed.

In fact, I didn't have three good squad leaders anymore. Skinner, potentially the best squad leader, was gone, returned to Bien Hoa for training. Wright, who almost never raised his voice and who *never* cursed, let out a loud, militant obscenity on hearing the news. Skinner was up for E5: Sending him to the rear for additional training practically ensured that he would be sent to another company, and perhaps even a different battalion, when he was done training and was promoted. Garza, and through him, the battalion sergeant major, swore on their wives' honor that he would be returned to us, but neither Wright nor I believed them. For one thing, Garza wasn't married.

RTO is a very important job; he is at the nerve center of the platoon. A good RTO can save his platoon leader grief and trouble; at the very least he can relieve him of the tiresome but necessary logistical and administrative duties. Calling in a resupply order is important but routine; far better that an RTO does it than a busy platoon leader.

He must also be able to get along with the lieutenant and the others in the CP group, treading the fine line between obsequiousness and insubordination. Jeeves would have made a good RTO.

Unfortunately, my platoon was in short supply of British valets, but there were several men who could have done well, which is why I thoroughly shocked myself, and Sergeant Wright, by proposing that Morris be made RTO.

Wright stared at me for a good five seconds when I mentioned it to him. "Now, sir," he said finally, "why would you want to do that?"

I cleared my throat. I had to be pretty convincing, inasmuch as I had to talk myself, as well as Wright, into believing that this was a good idea. I ticked off the reasons.

1. Morris has been a discipline problem wherever we placed him.
2. Only Stempin, of all our squad leaders, has been able to handle him, after a fashion, and Stempin is gone.
3. There isn't a hope in hell that he will listen to or work for Eden, our new shake-n-bake E5 who took Stempin's place, as inexperienced as the man is.
4. Even if Skinner comes back — and we had no faith in the sergeant major's assurances — Morris has already shown in the past a disinclination to work for him.
5. Placing Morris in Sergeant Hyde's squad will be tantamount to fomenting mutiny.

Even Sergeant Wright had to admit the justice of that remark. The fireworks that had gone off when Morris, a sullen, tight-lipped black man from Arkansas, received the first, drawling, high-pitched order given by the Louisiana born-and-bred Nathan Hyde, had been brief but spectacular. He and Hyde had been about to square off when Sergeant Wright arrived. Morris wasn't a small man, but Wright had picked him up and *thrown* him into the nearby bushes. Then he'd gone and sat on him. Literally

"So," I finished up, "either we transfer him out of the platoon, or we let him run wild, *or* we put him where we can keep an eye on him. You and I can handle him, I know."

Wright frowned. "Maybe," he reluctantly agreed.

"And another thing," I went on, "it might do him some good to be given some responsibility. RTO is an important job. A guy like Morris's been put down all his life. Maybe this is a way of putting some pride back in him."

Sergeant Wright pursed his lips in an expression with which I had become familiar over the past six weeks. That slow nod ... he disapproved, but had already stated his objections, couldn't think of another way of presenting his argument, and, because he was Army and disliked people who argued against orders, decided to leave it at that.

"Yes, sir," he said, as neutrally as he could. "We'll see."

"Right," I said, pretending, as I watched him walk away, that I wasn't conscious of the very real possibility that I had just made a horrendous mistake.

8

Firebase Barbara

YD329337; 23 January–15 February 1969

January and February were the worst period of my tour. All the mad chaos of pitched combat lay ahead, in April and May, but these two months were the worst.

The six or seven days spent slogging around the rain-drenched hills around the Song Bo, culminating in that horrendous night on the "ambush," had set what I thought would be the standard for sustained misery. But now came Firebase Barbara, an old First Cav base, long abandoned, out in the middle of nowhere. When the CO first gave the coordinates, YD329337, I thought he had to be wrong. They were miles outside our AO. We had to have new maps issued.

But, on January 23, we were flown in on Chinooks, those big ungainly green monsters capable of carrying a platoon at a time. Barbara was nothing more than a brownish grey scar in the green forest.

The firebase was on a long, low ridge that runs roughly WSW–ENE. It lies just beyond the southern confines of the So'n Phan Cong Hoang Quoc Gia, or national forest preserve, which itself is some 30 kilometers due south of the provincial capital of Quang Tri. We were there to secure the firebase for an ARVN battery, whose mission was to support a joint ARVN–U.S. operation far to our southwest, below Ba Long, a spur of the A Shau. The main effort was by the Marines, who were sweeping the Da Krong River, west of Quang Tri. The whole operation was called Dewey Canyon. Of all the places I was to go in Vietnam, this was by far the most desolate and remote.

All the bunkers were torn down, the barbed wire taken up, claymores and trip flares removed, gun emplacements leveled. On its western end, the ridge dropped dramatically into a southward-pointing spur, broad and flat, that made an almost perfect natural LZ. This was connected to the main portion of the base by a rough dirt road that still led up through the exposed rock of the upper ridge.

The land south, west and north of the ridge was low, a series of valleys and gently rolling hills, almost featureless under the unbroken forest canopy. To our east, there was a short but steep drop to a saddle, from which the ground began to rise gradually, toward a peak some distance away. This was the most vulnerable part of the firebase, and was assigned to First Platoon.

Firebase Barbara had last been used by the ARVNs, and it was, charitably, a mess, littered with old ammo cases, spent 105 and 155 casings, open garbage sumps, broken or abandoned tools, discarded timbers ... it was one big dump. In all that jumble of old and rusted equipment, empty cases and rusted artillery casings, we would not have had a prayer of finding a booby trap before it was too late. Fortunately, none was present.

I suppose that, had the events of those weeks not been so nearly and completely disastrous, there would have been an element of humor in them: Murphy's Law was in full force. I had a contentious encounter with our ARVN allies on that first day, when they'd located a 105 emplacement right over our CP bunker, and test fired the piece without warning. Then came a running argument with Bennet's temporary replacement (George had left on R&R but, in the event, never returned), a Lieutenant Thomas, over the equitable distribution of the workload among the platoons; an inattentive OP, manned by some of my best troopers, was shot at and almost hit and daily, I could see the discipline and unit pride Sgt Wright and I had tried to instill deteriorate under the pressure of constant rain, hunger and mind-dulling work. I was in a foul mood.

But I was a beaker of sunshine compared to Robison. I admit that having to put up with me was probably a large part of his personal hair shirt, but I was but one of many. For one thing, Black Jack, our new commander, had changed overnight from a quiet, almost affable man to something close to a raving lunatic. He found fault in almost everything and everybody, and he very quickly made it apparent that he was not a man to keep his opinions to himself. At that, except for one brief but appalling visit early on, we were left to ourselves— our location, so far outside the battalion AO, gave us that much, at least — but the new ground rules had been established. Robison was looking forward to one thing: His R&R in Hawaii, where he was to meet his wife. Between Black Jack, the weather and our daily dose of madness, Robbie began to despair of ever going.

As I say, I played a not inconsiderable role, but Lt Thomas far outdid me. George Bennet had been laid back and a bit loose now and then, but he knew what he was doing; Thomas appeared to be clueless and, worse, lazy. As I said, I had clashes with him constantly, but that was my problem. What he did on the fifth night was everyone's: He sent, or allowed to be sent, an LP with no designated leader, inadequate instructions and almost no ammunition — and then they got probed. The young PFC in charge— in charge only because he happened to be the one by the radio— was scared spitless while we, and Robison in particular, were incredulous and angered.

Robison was still in a rage the next day. He never got the chance to calm down: 18 hours after the LP incident came the Love Affair. This one finished Thomas but unfortunately three or four others got caught up in the mess with him. As it happened, I was at the company CP, fighting a losing battle with Robison over work assignments—

it was a dispirited, lackluster argument, done more for form's sake: He knew I didn't have the men available and I knew he had to get the work done — when a dull, low boom, not at all loud, sounded to our west. There was nothing else, so Robison and I exchanged looks, eyebrows raised. We waited for something to come over the radio, from the squad leader on that side of the perimeter, or anyone else. We were still sitting there when Sergeant Garza, his flat brown face a mean, grim mask, stuck his head inside the hutch.

"Trouble," he said, in his sharp Mexican voice.

"What now, Top?" Robison asked. He was worried, I could tell. He had just finished telling me his R&R date was less than two weeks away; he would be flying to Honolulu to meet his wife, and he was obviously thinking that so much had already happened that Black Jack might make him postpone it.

"Some sommbitch shot up a bunker," Garza said, bitterly.

"Oh, Christ." Robison and I exploded out of the hutch. Garza took us to the west side of the perimeter. Schoch, our senior medic, was already there. He was bent over a figure lying on the ground; a couple of bloody bandages, white and bright red against the dull brown soil, trailed off from the body.

Robison's eyes searched the area, anxiously. "How many are hit?"

Thomas, who'd gotten there ahead of us, replied. "Just this one. Savoy."

"How'd it happen?"

Thomas nodded toward a group of men standing a few yards away. Two large troopers stood alongside a third, each holding one of his arms. The third trooper was small and slight. Bruises and cuts showed stark against his white face; one eye was already showing signs of turning black.

"Towson," he said. "PFC Towson. Fired off an M79 round."

Robison swung around and glared at the man. Towson was swaying slightly on his feet: The men on either side of him were holding him up as much as they were restraining him. "Was it an accident?" he asked.

Thomas shook his head. "No, sir. I guess not."

The glare shifted to Thomas. "You guess not?"

Thomas shrugged. Robison scowled, cursed under his breath, staring at the ground for a moment. Then he walked over to Towson.

"What the hell's going on, soldier?"

Towson blinked up at Robison in surprise, or perhaps fear. He said nothing. Robison whirled and glared again at Thomas. I knew what he was going to say: Even from 15 or 20 feet away, I could see it too. Towson was thoroughly drunk.

"Where'd this man get hold of liquor?" Robison ground out the question between his teeth.

Thomas shook his head. "I don't know," he protested. "Damn if I know."

"Top!" Robison snapped out.

"Sir." Garza, his mean little Mexican smile looking meaner than ever, trotted up to him.

"I want this man's squad leader and every man in that bunker at my CP right away. I want you to detail two men from First Platoon to take care of Towson: Guard him, don't let him talk to anybody, and if he so much as takes one step in any direction tell them to blow him away. I want his M79 and his ammo pouch up there too. And —" he grabbed Garza's arm for emphasis: "I *especially* want that goddamn bottle. Understood?"

"Yes, sir." Garza nodded crisply and stalked off. I raised a surprised eyebrow. Robison right now was completely different from the huffing, puffing, semi-ineffective screamer I knew. He was concise, taut and dangerous. There were times, I had discovered, when I could play him like a piano, tinkering here and there and getting the sound I wanted. This was, decidedly, not one of those times.

As busy as we were, Robison still wanted me to sit in on the interrogations of the squad members. The first two wouldn't say anything, but the third, a scared youngster named Andersen, folded quickly. As well he might: Aside from his furious CO, the kid looked around and saw me, with a face never intended to radiate reassurance, and a hatchet-nosed Garza, apparently fully capable of human sacrifice. Curiously enough, the hardest time Robison had was getting Andersen to tell us where Towson had gotten the bottle in the first place. Finally, after some fierce browbeating by Robison and even more so Garza, it came out that a trooper named Rodgette had bought the whiskey, a crude, harsh Korean product named Colt 45, from the ARVN troops. But the real jaw-dropper came when, at the end of the interrogation, a by now thoroughly rattled Andersen recounted exactly how Savoy got shot by a drunken Towson.

"And, well ... they was both talkin' trash, real trash, by then. So Towson, he says, Savoy, you're part of this fuckin' platoon — and Savoy say, no I'm not. I'm jus' a nigger from Alabama, and Towson says, no, man, no. We all are in this together, and we all love each other, and Savoy says, fuck you, you don't love me. Ain't none of you loves me, you lyin' sack of white shit, and he starts to walk out the hutch, an' Towson, he says, I do too love you, we all do, you son of a bitch, and then he says, come back here and Savoy keeps walkin' and ... then Towson fires him up."

Robbie and I exchanged incredulous glances. I placed my hand over my eyes, rubbing the bridge of my nose with my palm. If the incident hadn't been so serious, so nearly fatal, and if the future hadn't held at least one if not more courts-martial in store, this would have been hilarious. *I do too love you ... bang.*

After the shaken youngster was dismissed, Robison looked at me, almost speechless.

"I don't believe this," I said, shaking my head.

Robison snorted in disgust. "I believe anything coming out of that platoon," he said through his teeth.

I left the CP angered and upset. Of course, I didn't care about Andersen or Towson or any of the others involved — they weren't in my platoon, after all — but their squad leader was Sgt Stempin, who'd been transferred to Bennet's platoon earlier that month.

Towson was going down—facing court-martial for attempted murder—but he was dragging others with him, and Stempin, as his squad leader, was one of them. Stempin wanted a career in the Army, and this wasn't going to help him at all.

I had other problems. Abbot had also returned on the Four Four flight, after a week in hospital, with the news that the finance office at Evans had screwed up and not only had not decreased his allotment but had actually *increased* it. This news was greeted with predictable profanity by the troops. Combat infantrymen come in all sizes, colors, religions, political persuasions, dietary habits, cultural backgrounds and educational levels, but we are as one in this: The cold hatred we feel for the REMF, who lives a life of sybaritic ease, surrounded by comforts unimagined, dining on steak and fine wine, pampered and petted by bevies of horny young women, sleeping on soft feather mattresses, working in bullet and shell-proof, air conditioned bunkers ... well, perhaps we overestimated their life style, but we despised them anyway. And when something like this happened—when one of our own was mistreated by the miserable bastards—the anger flared and righteous wrath filled our hearts.

But there is a fine line there, and it began to appear that First Platoon was in danger of crossing it. To be an elite unit, the us-against-the-world mentality is not only natural but healthy. We are the chosen ones and everyone else is unworthy, and particularly so the people in the rear. On the other hand, not only Abbot but also the rest of us were drifting into a decidedly unhealthy and self-indulgent recitation of the litany of wrongs. In a word, Abbot, and by extension the platoon, were feeling sorry for ourselves. And after only a day or two, that perception intensified and I began to worry about it. Abbot was moping along, head hanging, morose, sullen, completely embittered. He could speak of nothing but the wrongs he was suffering and the pain he was enduring. All of us felt sympathy, to a point, but sooner or later, we wearied of it. I was probably first to feel that way—after all, there were 34 men in the platoon, and they all had problems, and they all had work to do. Even his buddies, after the initial paroxysm of fury, began to lose a little patience. They continued to feel sorry for him, as did I, for that matter, but ... damn, Abbot; your wife's 12,000 miles away and the platoon's *here*.

Nevertheless, I did promise that, as soon as I could, I would talk to the people at Evans myself. More than that, I could not do.

Muldoon startled me, in a good way, by confessing to me one night that the best thing that had happened to him was a chewing out by Sergeant Wright. Top, apparently fed up with Muldoon's attitude, had pulled him aside and made it clear: Keep this up and he'd end up in Bien Hoa jail. The only possible loser in a fight featuring Francis Muldoon and the U.S. Army, and specifically in the person of Sgt Samuel Wright, was Muldoon.

"I thought about it that day, an' all that night. An' he was right. Saw it real clear. Every time I kicked you or Top, you guys didn't even bother kickin' back. So I decided I'd try. An', tell you the truth, it was easy. Once I stopped tryin' to pick a fight wit' youse, damn, life was easy. Or better, anyway. Don't get me wrong: I still hate this fuckin' Army. But youse — you and Top; you're all right. I can handle this."

"Well, I'm glad to hear it, Muldoon. Seriously. You're a good medic."

"Yeah." He smiled, looking off into the dark. "Just count the nights, ya know? One more night in Viet Nam...."

And that became our own personal litany, from that night on. Each night, at an NDP or firebase, as one or both of us settled down to sleep, he'd turn to me and say, "Well, Lieutenant, one more night in Viet Nam." And my response would be: "One more night, Francis."

Throughout that week, the CP continued with its other litany. We met the complaint about the cold and wet by observing that, as bad as we had it, we were still better off than the troops in Korea had been. We were facing 55 degree weather and rain. Those poor bastards, we reminded each other, had had to endure deadly sub-zero temperatures for weeks at a time. So any complaint now was met by the mantra: "Yeah, but think of those poor guys in Korea."

Until the night Brown, his long, lanky body bent into a pretzel shape as he tried to keep warm, was shivering and staring morosely at the sodden canvas curtain over the entrance, suddenly gave a sharp curse.

"Damn!" he yelled. He grabbed the back of his upper thigh and began rubbing vigorously. "Cramp," he muttered.

Muldoon, his own thin frame shaking with the chill, crawled over to him and helped him until the cramp went away. Then he flopped back down in the mud. A smear lay wetly on his cheek, and his breath showed grey in the dank, chill air.

"Fucking weather's gonna kill us," he muttered.

"You been checking the guys' feet? For trench foot?" I asked,

He nodded, snorting. "Yep. They got it, all right."

I smiled. Muldoon, at least, was still Muldoon. "We'll all have it, if this shit keeps up."

"But just think," Conzoner spoke up from the far corner, "just think how much worse this'd be if it was really cold out there. We'd have immersion or frostbite by now."

Brown groaned. "God, no, man. Don't even say that. It can't get any worse than it is."

"Yeah it can. Just think about those poor guys in Korea."

There followed a morose silence of some duration.

Then Muldoon stirred. "You know what?" he asked softly.

None of us said anything; no one had the energy to play the straight man.

Muldoon was undeterred. "*Fuck* those poor guys in Korea. You wanna know where those pricks are right now? They're at home, back in The World, boozin' and fuckin' like rabbits, and do you think that even *one* of those sorry sons of bitches is thinkin' about us poor guys in Nam?"

We sat quietly, examining the profound truth in his heresy.

"Good point," Conzoner agreed.

I *had* made a horrendous mistake.

Bad weather — a singularly inept description for what we were enduring — had closed in a few days after we arrived. At first, the rain, cool temperatures and constant wet were bad enough, but soon an enormous blanket of dense cloud and fog covered the entire area, from the coast to the A Shau, many kilometers away, and from Quang Tri in the north to well below Hue to the south. Nothing could fly. Well, that's not true. The guys in Black Widow tried repeatedly, but although they could fly above the cloud layer, they simply couldn't find us in that soup.

No Black Widow flights, no resupply. No resupply, no food. And now it had become a problem. The entire firebase was tense, on edge, almost mutinous. Relations between the ARVN artillery battery we were there to secure and our company were at the breaking point, but even within the company, tensions were dangerously high.

And in the midst of all this, just when the whole firebase was smoldering, Morris poured gasoline on the glowing tinder.

Our last resupply had been nine days earlier. We were all, by that time, out of food. Many of us were reduced to hoarding and eating one last cracker, gleaned from the depths of our sodden rucksacks. Morris had half a meal left; somehow he'd kept it through the nine days. No one begrudged him; some of us had rationed ourselves, some had not, but we'd all started with the same amount and no one could accuse another of having too much.

One of the last items he had was a can of pork slices. We had long since seen the last of the heat tablets, so everything had to be eaten cold. Pork slices, warm, were unpalatable, almost inedible. Cold ... it was like eating rancid grease. Morris opened the can, tasted it, and then tossed it aside.

"Can't eat that shit," he said, morosely. "Fuck this shit."

I, personally, agreed with him. I couldn't eat that shit either. I'd have to be a lot hungrier than I was to willingly bite into the gristle and fat that seemed to make up 90 percent of the meal. But there were men in the platoon who had run out of food entirely the day before, and who would be glad to eat anything. I pointed that out to Morris.

He didn't respond for a moment; his head was lowered, his shoulders set in an angry line. My jaw tightened; I felt a sharp anger. The constant question asked and answered within any group of men is a basic one: How much of myself do I give to the group, and how much do I retain for me alone? It's a balance that each man must determine for himself, but in truth, the fulcrum on which it rests is broad and inclusive; there is room for any number of answers, almost any degree of movement from one end to another. Human beings are remarkably adaptable in that sense.

But regardless of how broad that fulcrum or inclusive the answer, Morris placed himself outside of it, always.

"It's my food," he muttered, finally. "I saved it up. If I want to throw it away, I can throw the shit away. Ain't nobody's business but mine."

"Throwing it away is just wasting it," I pointed out. "If you're not going to use it, why not let someone else have it?"

He raised his eye to mine. "Because it's *mine*," he snarled.

I heard a growl from behind me: Muldoon was aroused. Duke's world of trust was small; he included few people in it, no more than a handful, but to those few he offered complete and limitless loyalty. The selfishness and disdain in Morris's words offended him.

Hurriedly, I broke in, before he could say anything. Tempers were bad enough already. Muldoon had never been raised to suffer in silence; his reaction to Morris's attitude would have been direct and visible. I grew up in an Irish neighborhood. They tend to be a pugnacious lot.

"That's not really yours, Morris, anymore than this water here"—I pointed to my canteen—"is mine. If I don't need it and someone else does, he gets it. It's the same with food. If you don't want it, let someone else have it."

Morris gave an irritated shrug. "Yeah, okay," he said after a pause. "So I won't throw it out. I'll eat the shit." He got up. Sullen anger lay across his face like a closed curtain. Picking up the can of pork, he took it with him outside, leaving behind an empty silence.

Muldoon finally broke it. "Now there's a sorry son of a bitch," he said angrily. "There's a guy..." he shook his head, for once unable to come up with the words.

I studiously avoided looking in Sergeant Wright's direction. Professional as he was, he wouldn't say anything, but his body had to be just radiating *I told you so*.

I stopped worrying about Morris; we were in danger.

Not from the enemy—although they were out there, somewhere—but from ourselves. Relations between the ARVN battery and our men continued in an ominous downward spiral: Food and cigarettes, so freely shared early on, now became a font of bitter anger, as the ARVNs sold back our gifts at exorbitant prices. We saw them as lazy, shiftless, ungrateful, sneaky and incompetent. They saw us as arrogant, clownish, domineering and feckless. Tensions quickly reached the point where Captain Trangh, the battery commander, and Robison realized they were at the point of detonation. All that was needed was a spark.

That came on the tenth day, when a dispute over the placement of a new ARVN latrine, judged to be too close to a Second Platoon bunker, suddenly turned into a shoving match, and then came the sound the officers had been dreading: rifle fire. The ARVN mascot, a white mid-sized mongrel, had wandered out in front of one of our bunkers, as he often did, but this time the men opened fire, blandly asserting that they mistook him for an NVA infiltrator—in broad daylight. The infuriated ARVNs grabbed their own weapons. We were seconds away from fratricide when Robison and Trangh stepped in. They averted the violence, but the bad blood remained, and we were all certain that it would manifest itself again, and soon.

And then, finally, the weather broke. Almost not enough, because a solid mantle of fog remained over Barbara, but one of the Black Widow pilots reported clear skies less than a klick away, beyond what we called Monkey Ridge, named after a troop of Howling Monkeys who had serenaded us at dawn and dusk throughout our stay. I led a reinforced squad out to collect the supplies and mail. We weren't worried about the enemy. Any NVA foolhardy enough to get between us and food was doomed. The load we had to carry back — including two weeks' worth of mail — was staggering but the men didn't mind, at all.

We celebrated by having our first square meal in a week. For most of us, it was also our first cigarette in two or three days. Tensions and bad feelings dissipated; the ARVNs bowed ingratiatingly, we grinned and waved back at them. It's surprising how much brotherhood and tolerance a full stomach and a Camel can bring about.

The next morning dawned pale rose and yellow; our first glimpse of the sun in 11 days. Robison let out a yell of relief: Today was the last day that he could leave in time for his R&R. Thomas was going back with him, having shown himself incapable of handling a platoon; Savoy and Towson were sent back also.

The chopper settled down on the LZ. Two new officers, both lieutenants junior to me, jumped out. Robison jumped on. He grinned, waved at me, and with a happy shout, told me, as the ship began to lift, that it was all my show.

His actual words were, as I recall: "It's your fucking nightmare now, Bo, and I hope it chokes you."

I blinked. I realized, suddenly, that I was the Bravo CO.

The CO's hutch offered a wealth of amenities I had more or less forgotten: A Coleman lantern, unlimited hot sauce and onions (courtesy of Sgt Garza), a field cot with air mattress and, hidden under a poncho, an honest-to-god pillow.

I got to know a couple of the CP tenants much better. Lieutenant Russ Crenshaw, our pipe-smoking artillery FO from California, wore heavy frame glasses and a pleasant expression. He was affable in his own way, and I liked him, but conversations with him tended to be short and, let us say, sparse. He wasn't at all unfriendly; he was just one of those rare individuals who keep quiet when he has nothing to say. About the only personal bit of information I got from him, other than his home state, was that he considered himself a Rockefeller Republican. Since my interest in politics at the time rivaled my fascination with Mattawoman hand pottery, we spent several nights in the CP in companionable silence.

Nicholas Schoch, our CO (no, not commanding officer, conscientious objector) and company medic, was more talkative by quite a bit, although that still didn't make him a prattler. He too was a California man, with a year or two at Berkeley under his belt, and it showed. His attitude toward me was a bit mixed; he knew I had a degree from Georgetown, and that seemed to impress him, but he also saw me as a hard ass, and that made him wary. Still, we got along, and he even became my bridge partner whenever we had the chance. I came to admire him, although I had little patience with his rare political screeds. One thing stood out: Regardless of his feelings about the war and the Army, he was determined that the men of Bravo would get the best medical care he had to offer. More than that could be asked of no one.

It also gave me a chance to get to know our new officers. The first one to come forward was short, of medium build; he held out a small, smooth hand, but his handshake, for all that, was firm and strong. His helmet, covered by a crisp new camouflage cover, was tilted low over his forehead; the lid almost touched one of the largest noses I'd ever seen. It was slightly slanted, and set between two small blue-grey eyes under thin light brown eyebrows. His mouth was large and mobile, and his face flat, broad and creased. It was an attractively ugly face, full of good humor and sense. His voice matched his handshake: low but firm, full of warmth and self-confidence. I liked him immediately.

"Jerry Wolosenko," he introduced himself.

"Frank Boccia. Good to have you with us."

The other young man hung back, a little off to one side. He was short, too—most of us were, in the Airborne, for one reason or another. I personally suspected that any new officer over 5'10" was segregated at Bien Hoa and assigned to Division or Brigade staff, so we could all have something to look up to. He was thickset, with light brown hair and thin, pale blue eyes. He seemed very young, smooth-cheeked, slightly pink faced. His voice, when he spoke, contrasted with Wolosenko's firm baritone: It was a thin reedy tenor. You almost expected it to crack suddenly, like a 12-year-old's. Wolosenko's eyes had rested on mine, in frank appraisal, when he greeted me. Dickson's (so his name tag read) slid off quickly and flitted nervously about.

I turned to Garza, who was standing close by. "Did Captain Robison leave word on their assignments, Top?" Although I had had no idea they were coming, Robison must have.

Garza smiled his gap-toothed, mean little smile. "Yes, sir. Lieutenant Walla... Wolo..."

"Wolosenko," Jerry said.

"Yah." Garza nodded. "You got First Platoon, Lieutenant."

A cold spasm went through me at those words. I don't know why I didn't expect it. I was an English major, but I could do simple arithmetic: Three platoons, four lieutenants. One—me—was the acting CO. So the other three...

But I didn't want to be acting CO and even less did I want to be the XO when Robison returned, a week from now. But that was the fate that stared me in the eye. Denholm was brand new himself; he wasn't going anywhere. Wolosenko and Dickson hadn't even been unwrapped yet. Incredibly, I, with fewer than 50 days with the company, was now senior lieutenant. And that meant that when Robbie got back, I would have to move to the XO spot. An executive officer in a line company spent most of his time in the rear, safe, comfortable, well fed and with access to wine, the thought of women, and song. No more straining up 60 degree slopes in 105° temperatures carrying 100 pounds. No more dusty, muddy or otherwise objectionable firebases with too much work and not enough sleep.

No more leading a platoon.

I hated it.

I hated what came next even more.

Two days later, the operation ended and we were pulled out, on February 16. We left Barbara with no regrets. Of all the miserable hellholes in Eye Corps, this place had been the worst. Until Brick.

First, we were taken back to our home — Helen — to spend two days there, running RIFs out into the valley below. It was all routine, even rote, except that the platoons were told to walk down and back up Helen's long, steep sides: The weather was still too uncertain to plan on airlifts, and besides, the Black Widow squadron was needed elsewhere. Something was up: We could tell. Major Raffaele, the S3, was all over the place, including Helen. He asked a lot of questions but told us nothing, which alone was an omen. On the 18th we were flown to Camp Evans.

9

Firebase Brick

Ten Very Bad Days; YC835995; 19–28 February 1969

Normally, a stay at Evans was something to celebrate: Hot showers, real food, and, above all, sleep. Blissful, uninterrupted, restorative sleep. Wars are fought by very young men for two reasons: They are foolhardy enough to charge machine gun fire and they are able to withstand the effects of sleep deprivation far better than their elders—and a 30-year-old is an elder. But even the kids reach the point of utter exhaustion, and bad things happen, in almost every way.

But a night or two of sleep ... the magic wand that restores health, rationality, equanimity. Not even modern medicine has a cure so effective.

However, by the afternoon of the 19th my mellow mood had evaporated like a dewdrop in the Sahara. It wasn't even a distant memory; by 1500 of that day, I was able to take stock and come to this realization: In the period of 24 hours, I had managed to piss off, alienate, infuriate and make sworn enemies of: A battalion commander; his XO; a Brigade finance officer and both his clerks; the Brigade S1 and one of *his* clerks; a JAG officer; my first sergeant and two of *my* clerks, and a host of others I must have gotten to along the way. The tally, by my own modest estimation, was impressive.

First came Black Jack.

The occasion of his call was the morning report, which I hadn't seen yet—paperwork in Vietnam wasn't quite up to stateside standards—but it would have made no difference if I had. Three troopers from Bravo Company had been admitted to the 22nd field hospital with high fevers. Black Jack, who put the Mayo Brothers and Johns Hopkins to shame, being able to diagnose malaria without ever seeing the patient, had already publicly roasted a senior captain over this same thing, so he had no trouble in working himself up into a fury with a junior lieutenant who was only playing at being a CO while his captain was off in Hawaii getting reacquainted with his wife. By the time he was done, my prospects with the Army were already settled: What was at issue was my future in the human race. He didn't think I had one.

I was accused and convicted of laziness, ignorance, failure of command, irresponsibility, dereliction of duty, cowardice in the face of the enemy (the mosquito, in this case), incompetence, lack of supervision, loss of control, failure to carry out lawful orders and general imbecility. Added to that were deficiencies of character, upbringing, intellect and moral fiber. My forefathers were questionable and my offspring doomed.

And that was only the first five minutes.

I made one attempt at reason. I pointed out that the incubation period for malaria was several days, and I had been in command for only three, at this point.

That was not a good answer. This time the tirade lasted closer to ten minutes. When it was finished, and Black Jack went off somewhere, presumably to torture kittens, I was left in a rage of my own. My adrenalin levels that day must have been off the charts. I was humiliated, angry and filled with a great sense of the injustice of it all. To make it all perfect, all three troopers came from Third Platoon. I was beside myself.

Of course, I reacted rationally and reasonably. I stomped about the morning room, yelling at the top of my lungs, demanding to see the morning report, asking why this had not been brought to my attention earlier, threatening everyone there with instant transfer to a line platoon ... I made myself a pain in the ass to everyone, and accomplished nothing of value.

A couple of hours later, we held the promised party for the troops: steaks, ice cream, the usual two cans of beer per man, loud music blaring over the PA system ... and then some damn fool, almost certainly not from Bravo, threw a grenade behind one of the buildings. No one was close to being hurt, but...

After the grenade, came another call.

"Sir! Black Jack's on the landline, at the office. He wants you ASAP."

This conversation was, if anything, worse than our previous one about malaria. It lasted a few minutes less, but made up for it with an intensity of vituperation that transcended the merely mortal. His diatribe led to the blunt observation that I was *this* close to a court-marital.

"Boccia," he ground out, in his ice-edged tenor, "the only fucking thing that's keeping me from relieving you on the spot is that fact that Robison's due back in a few days and you'll be his fucking problem."

When he finally finished talking he did so with an iron-cold "out" that cut through the transmission like a saber.

Except for my opening sentence, I had yet to say a word. Now, just to show that I had learned nothing from the afternoon's conversation, I ventured to point out that there was no certainty as to who had thrown the grenade, and it was unfair to automatically place the blame on Bravo.

The answer came, not from Black Jack, but from Major Hansen, the XO.

"You've got the word, Lieutenant. Black Jack wants those troops put to bed. Make it happen."

"But *anybody* could have thrown that grenade. The evidence indicates it was someone from another unit. Why would someone from Bravo screw up his own party?"

Hansen's voice was heavy with disgust. "Look, Lieutenant: Get them to bed. I'm tired and I want to get some sleep, and I won't be able to rest as long as you and Bravo are on the loose. It doesn't matter one sweet damn to me who threw the son of a bitch; I just want you to shut up and get your troops out of there and in their barracks. Now. Out."

But I am a resilient man, if not a very astute one. The following day, suitably angry, I tried to straighten out Abbot's allotment. First came a completely useless hour at the finance office; next an equally profitless half-hour with an even less helpful brigade S1. Still fuming from that, I managed to get a JAG captain out of his chair and bellowing within six minutes. I didn't time him; Jerry Wolosenko, who'd come along for the ride (Abbot was, after all, now his man) did, and, as we stomped out — well, I stomped; he walked — he turned to me and said, in his quiet Boston way, "Uhmm. That's your idea of how to get things done, is it?"

I glared at him. We got in the jeep, and he began driving, looking straight ahead at the road, but I could see one corner of his lip twitch. Other than that tiny movement, his face remained perfectly deadpan.

"I didn't want to interfere," he added, after a longish silence, "but you did sound like Attila the Hun negotiating with some village elders. And calling the JAG officer an asshole wasn't the best legal argument I've ever heard. I'm new here, and all, but I have the feeling you're not going to get a whole lot of cooperation from JAG, Finance or S1, in the future."

'We weren't getting anything from them before this, so what's the difference?"

Jerry drove slowly and carefully along the pitted, heavily rutted road. This was a back way to the battalion, not the main road, and it led us through an empty, flat, reed-covered area just behind the north berm and bunker wall.

"Don't get me wrong," Jerry continued, "I don't know you all that well, and I'm not trying to rattle your chain or anything, but, well ... I ask because I really want to know: I kind of got the idea that you were, oh ... looking for an excuse to raise hell back there."

"Where the hell did you get that?" I erupted angrily.

"Hard to believe that anyone could get that many people pissed off by accident."

"What the hell," I muttered. "You make me sound paranoid."

Wolosenko said nothing.

"Okay." I continued. "Maybe I lost my cool. But what the hell — you were there. You heard them, in all three places. They couldn't give one shit less about Abbot, or anyone else out in the field. You saw their attitudes."

"Well, they weren't very enthusiastic, I'll give you that. And I'll also admit that the troops like to see that — I mean, if they hear about today, and they will, well, it'll be even more points for you with the guys. They think a lot of you already, for taking on the REMFs for them."

I was slightly nettled. Jerry brought the jeep to a halt in front of the battalion quad. "That's not why I do these things, to make points with the troops," I protested.

"This shit upsets me. Here's a guy who gets asked—no, he gets *told*—to do the toughest job in the army, who goes through more physical privation and suffering in one week than most of these clowns will go through in a lifetime, and these sorry bastards sitting on their ass in the rear won't do a single thing for the guy. Look, I don't enjoy losing my temper, but—"

"Yes, you do," Wolosenko said, getting out of the vehicle.

"What?"

"Yes, you do enjoy losing your temper. I've never seen anyone have such a good time at it."

I glared at him again. "You're crazy."

"No, I'm not. Look, you're Italian, aren't you?"

I glared some more. "Yeah. And the first word from you about hot-blooded Italians and I *will* enjoy losing my temper."

He waved a hand, grinning. "That's what I mean. Italians have it down to a fine art. Yelling. Screaming. Posturing. Gesturing. It's all there. You really do enjoy it. It's like putting on an opera."

"Yeah. I enjoy wiping the dirt off the sidewalk with Polish lieutenants, too, so—"

"Polish?" It was Wolosenko's turn to glare. "Where in hell do you get the idea I'm Polish?"

"Well, aren't you? You sure as hell aren't Scottish."

"I'm Ukrainian. Wolosenko is a Ukrainian name."

"Oh, Russian."

"*Ukrainian*, asshole."

"Hmf. Makes no difference. What's a russki doing in the U.S. Army? Aren't you supposed to be on the other side?"

We stopped at the entrance to the Day Room, and suddenly we were both grinning. Jerema Wolosenko, I would find, could get me smiling in less time than anyone I knew.

And it was good that I calmed down, because otherwise, I wouldn't have had my Archimedes moment.

Chuck Denholm, if he only knew it, was the author of his own demise—well, demise may not be the right word. Serving as XO of a line company sucks, but it doesn't actually equate to death. It's nothing he said; he came in to check about some matter or other, we talked a few minutes and he left. Seeing him reminded me of when he joined us, back on Long, when Jimmy Stewart visited that tiny firebase, and I recalled that Chuck was introduced as George Bennet's classmate at OCS ... and then I sat bolt upright in my chair.

George Bennet had a DOR at least a month earlier than mine—closer to two months, actually. And Chuck, being his classmate, had to have the same DOR. I was stunned and chagrined—that it had taken me so long to figure this out.

Chuck Denholm's DOR preceded mine. Chuck, bless his Iowa heart, was senior to me. Chuck, not I, would be the next XO.

9. Firebase Brick

I sat back and smiled, ecstatically. Jerry Wolosenko didn't know it, but I was returning to First Platoon. But all that would have to wait until Robison returned, still several days hence.

Less than an hour later, I was sitting in the battalion conference room, joining the other company COs, including Captain Ogle, the newly appointed CO of the HHC Headquarters and Headquarters Company—for the battalion. Why he was there was, initially, a mystery. HHC personnel—the clerks, the cooks, the maintenance mechanics, the supply people—had nothing to do with field operations, and one glance at the maps displayed on easels throughout the room showed me that this *would* be a field operation. I raised an eyebrow as I peered at the map coordinates. For the second time in three weeks, we would be going completely outside our AO, this time to the south. If this kept up I'd end up with maps of all of Eye Corps.

When Black Jack showed up, about 15 minutes late, there was already an air of anticipation in the room. The senior captains had taken one look at the maps and had already guessed where we were going and why. That was confirmed by the battalion CO almost immediately after he joined us. We, along with the 2/501st, whose AO this was, were to go into the mountains southwest of Hue in search of the elusive and infamous Colonel Mot and his 5th NVA Regiment. It had been his unit that had infiltrated the route along Highway 547, that linked Hue to the lower end of the A Shau valley, just before Tet; it had been his troops who had entered Hue and, in the course of just a few days, had slaughtered over 6,000 civilians—government clerks, teachers, doctors, nurses, religious leaders, policemen and wealthy land owners. They had also, ironically, lured 3,000 Viet Cong military leaders and political cadre from the surrounding areas to the Citadel, northwest of the Perfume River, and there massacred them in long ditches under the walls. The political leadership of the North used the Viet Cong in the South, but never trusted them, and some people speculated that the failure of the Viet Cong to organize an uprising of the people in the south during Tet was the last straw. In any case, Colonel Mot's units were responsible for the deaths of close to 10,000 people in Hue alone.

So he had a price on his head, and we had been seeking him for months following Tet. Now, intelligence reported that his regiment was operating in the low hills and small valleys in the area almost directly south of Hue. There, the Song Ta Trach meandered through the hills until it formed a series of extraordinary loops, bending north and south, so acute that, at a few places, you could cut off two miles of river by walking less than a quarter of a mile. Sometime in the past, at one of those points, the water had forced its way through the shallow valley, and joined two of the loops; the land in between was known as Leech Island, and with good reason.

Leech Island was approximately five kilometers long and about one and a half wide. From its north point, the Song Ta Trach flowed almost due north to join the Song Hou Trach a few kilometers below Hue: They entered the city together and became the Perfume River. But there was nothing remotely perfume-like about Leech Island.

The land was low and completely open; only a few scraggly trees and low brush could be seen. Once again, mosquitoes would be a problem, and, of course, the leeches, along with scorpions, flies, rats and a species of centipede that was purportedly deadlier than a back widow. It promised to be another pestilential hellhole.

But the local vermin weren't my primary concern. What bothered me was made known within the first minute: The entire battalion CP group and its equipment was to be transferred to Leech Island for the duration of the operation, and Bravo Company was to be the security element. I closed my eyes in horror and disgust when I heard that. The prospect of spending two or three weeks in close proximity to Black Jack and his staff, while manning another damned firebase, with all the problems associated with that, was too much. Of course, a moment's reflection told me that this was inevitable. The other three companies would move out immediately on combat operations, and they weren't about to trust an entire company to a new lieutenant with two months in rank and less than seven weeks in the field.

It also explained the presence of Captain Ogle. When the colonel said that the entire HHC staff was going, he meant just that: Except for maintenance and a few administrative personnel, all of HHC was being moved out. Ogle collared me as soon as the meeting broke up. He and I would have to work together closely over the next few weeks. While I would be responsible for the security, to include the bunker line, barbed wire, claymores, patrols, LPs and so on — the routine — he would be responsible for everything else, and especially the logistics. We spent the next two hours going over that.

I had never met Ogle before. He was tall, with light brown hair, a broad, moon like face dominated by a short beaked nose and two large grey eyes. It lent him an owlish appearance, somewhat abetted by his voice and manner, a sort of mildly humorous cynicism coupled with a weary, worldly fatalism. Ogle's presence seemed to shout Staff! at you; I had difficulty visualizing him as an infantry commander. He seemed much more at home in the clatter of typewriters and the smell of ditto ink.

And he was thorough. I filled several pages of notes with information about the aircraft loads, contact points, contingency frequencies, liaison personnel, CP layout and all the myriad details needed to plan and execute such a mission. Or, at least, all the myriad details that I needed to know, which were about one-tenth the number he had to deal with. I was to get to know Ogle very well as time went on, and found him to be an amusing, even-tempered and competent man, but those days just before and during the Leech Island operation he was constantly nervous and under stress — as indeed he should be, given the responsibility that he'd been given.

As it turned out, the ten days on Brick were among the worst of my tour, and I would not have thought it possible that that could be said after Barbara. It all began badly, as load after load of Chinooks, Cranes and dozens of Hueys scoured the island with the heavy fanning of their blades, landing or taking off, raising huge clouds of dust and making ordinary conversation an impossibility. This continued throughout the day, and well into the first night. Flights were misdirected, equipment went lost or misplaced, Alpha Company was inserted into the north side of the firebase, when they should have set down to the south, and vital communications gear was rendered inoperable by a combination of dust, noise, confusion and plain operator error.

Regardless, the mission was launched; the three line companies trudged off into the surrounding hills, and we settled down to the unimaginable dreariness and back-breaking work of constructing and manning a firebase, one that was easily three times the size of the largest we'd yet occupied.

Captain Ogle was a nice enough fellow, despite his nasal, sardonic delivery and his apparent conviction that the North Vietnamese Army's sole purpose was to annihilate him personally. Still, I tried my best to avoid his presence. The way it worked was classical in its simplicity: The commanding general jumped on the Task Force Commander, who flayed Black Jack, who in turn spat verbal poison at Ogle, who sought me out and...

The only thing that was different was Ogle's unique verbal style; he almost never could pass on mere vituperation:

> The CG and Black Jack found four C-ration cans in the barbed wire around the Third Platoon area ... I assured them that this was merely the location of the new garbage dump, but honestly, they expressed their doubts.
>
> Third Platoon hasn't quite finished their bunker line. Is the problem cost overruns, or is the union on strike?
>
> We have an arithmetic problem, Lieutenant. I asked your first sergeant for six men and got four. Without launching an extensive investigation, I must conclude that your first sergeant can't count.
>
> That LP last night was a fiasco. One of your intrepid warriors was seen lighting up a cigarette at 0230. I understand that he's a Marlboro Man. Excellent.

It got so I winced every time I saw him. After a while, I would honestly have welcomed a good, old-fashioned ass chewing. Of course, if I needed that, there was always Black Jack.

That was how the operation began. It never got any better. The following days were to become a wretched purgatory. For the companies in the field—Alpha, Charlie and Delta, it was to be the most frustrating, nerve-shattering period of the war. Colonel Mot was a wily and experienced commander, a superior tactician who knew his terrain and who was skilled at dealing with larger forces.

Almost daily, one or more of the companies would make contact, always trail watchers and snipers, never more than two or three NVA at a time. Bunkers were found, scores of them, some in groups of two or three, some in large and well-built complexes, but they were always empty, always abandoned months or weeks or days or even hours before we got there. Tracks would lead the units along trails and down into ravines and shrouded valleys.

Then they'd hear the first shot, perhaps two or three. Sometimes an RPG would be launched; most times not. A scream or a soft grunt, the rustle of leaves and snapping of branches, the thud of a falling body, and then the moans. Too late would come the shouted commands, the patter of M16 fire, the artillery, the steady drone of the ARA.

After a couple of days, the pattern became all too evident. The trail watchers would lead a unit on, down into a dense valley, up along a tree-covered ridge, to the ambush point. Then the scattered shots, the fall of a body, the moaning...

The rumors came back, filtering through the official dry antiseptic reports. There were no dead, only wounded. The majority of casualties were from AK rounds to the groin area.

The troops seized on this with all the sick enjoyment of a teenager watching a horror movie:

> *They're shootin' them guys in the balls, man. I hear every guy's been hit in the balls.*
> *That's what I hear, man. You seen the list? Ain't nobody killed. Nobody. They ain't shootin' to kill, man. They're aiming low. Put a man down, take his family jewels.*
> *Jesus Christ, what kinda war is this? Shootin' a man in the balls? God damn it.*
> *Tell you one thing, Joe. I ain't walking point. No fuckin' way. I got R&R comin' up, an' what the fuck good's Bangkok gonna be to me if my balls are hangin' from some goddamn tree?*

Whether the troops were right is debatable. In reality, combat in heavily forested mountain terrain is almost never visual, and it would be very unusual for snipers to get clear, unrestricted sightings and the luxury of time to select a specific spot. These weren't trained snipers with a scope and sniper rifle; they were trail watchers with AK-47s. A cool assessment of the casualties could bring this explanation: An American GI on patrol moved with anything from 60 to more than 100 pounds of gear on his back. The vast majority of them walked leaning forward, to distribute that huge weight more evenly across their backs. This foreshortened the chest area, presenting a smaller surface, and, in addition, if enemy activity was rife, he would carry his rifle across his chest at the ready position, further decreasing the available area to hit on his chest. But a man's lower torso and upper legs must remain erect, lest he fall over. So the easiest, most available shot would be to the lower stomach and groin.

It's a good, scientific explanation, but I wouldn't have tried selling it to the troops.

Whatever the intent, the result on our operation was significant. Only one man was killed during those eight days, but dozens were wounded. A man shot through the head or heart falls instantly and usually silently to the ground. His comrades, with hardly a glance at his body, will step around him and continue. But a wounded man lies on the trail, moaning or crying, in pain. The men behind him stop, and begin firing. The medic rushes up to treat him. Two or more troopers are assigned to carry him back to the rear or the column. If his wounds are serious, the whole company's movement is stopped while a medevac is dispatched and the man extracted.

One bullet, properly placed, will bring 120 men to a halt. So maybe the troops were right after all.

Those of us on the firebase were spared all this, of course. We had only to put up with the demands of senior officers, from General Zais on down, who wanted everything done perfectly, and done yesterday. I came to understand Robison far better, during those eight days he was gone, than I ever had in all the weeks we were together. My respect for him went up. During all his loud, profanity-ridden tirades against us, back at Helen or Rakkasan, I had sat silently (or not) fuming, thinking SOS: same old stuff: *Shit runs downhill in the army, and Robbie's had his ass kicked and now he's taking it out on us.* What I discovered, during that week, was that in reality Robison had shielded us from more crap and unreasonable abuse than anyone not in his position could imagine. There may be, in this unhappy world we inhabit, a more demanding and thankless job than that of an infantry company commander, but I would shudder to think of it. Simply put, a company commander is responsible for *everything*.

And even at that, I had to remind myself that I was experiencing only half — the easy half — of Robison's job: I didn't have to face the enormous responsibility of taking an entire company out on a combat mission.

But at the time, those thoughts comforted me little. The badgering and harassment I received from the senior officers, walking around the firebase, spouting flames and self-importance, kept me in a tight-lipped and sullen rage all week.

I came to know the three platoon leaders well. Wolosenko and Dickson, of course, were new, and Denholm had spent almost his entire month with the company either at Firebase Long or on patrol, so I'd had no chance to work with him before. He was probably the best of the three: Quiet, competent, relaxed, but filled with a muted aggressiveness that somehow made its way into the spirit of the men in his platoon without the need for exhortation or dramatics. While on Long, he'd encountered some NVA in the valley just below the firebase. Reacting quickly, aggressively but not recklessly, he chased them all over the valley, and forced them back into the ridges west of Long. They eventually got away, but he harassed them constantly, never giving them the opportunity to set up an ambush or drop off a sniper. He'd done well, but more important than the results was the respect he got from his men, and especially the old hands. It can't be bought or traded for. Chuck also possessed a low-key sense of humor, and a steadiness of temperament that made his presence in the CP welcome.

If he wasn't the best, then Jerry Wolosenko was. With his big nose, receding fair hair, and short, blunt body, he was certainly nothing to look at. And then there was his background: ROTC, staff-oriented, somewhat academic in tone, comfortable with paperwork and rote … all this was a recipe for disaster. But Jerry took his duties, if little else, seriously. There was a tough inner core in him, a mixture of self-deprecating humor and an unassuming willingness to accept responsibility. Unlike many of us, there was little visible ego in Jerry, but for all that he was no pushover. Walking all over him was a remarkably hard thing to do. What he and Chuck had in common, above all, was a conscientious concern for and appreciation of their platoons; neither spared any pains in ensuring, as well as they could, that their men were safe, comfortable and as prepared as they could be in a world where safety and comfort were in short supply.

Dickson, the Third Platoon leader, was something else again. He exhibited a broad streak of round-faced, adolescent immaturity, an undisciplined unwillingness to put out the necessary effort. Dickson was almost never prepared. He was uncertain of his authority, ignorant of his responsibilities and uncaring about his appearance and demeanor. Denholm and Wolosenko were close to their men, and did everything they could for them, but they were officers first. Dickson substituted familiarity for concern, and never had a prayer of gaining respect. Days after First and Second Platoons had finished their bunkers, Third Platoon was still digging in: The ground was too hard. There weren't enough men. The shovels were too small. The NCOs wouldn't push the men. The sun was too hot or the rain was too cold.

Robison returned on the 25th of February. I felt like kissing him. Perhaps not. But I did shake his hand with something more than customary fervor. He arrived tanned, relaxed and full of stories about his week in Hawaii. He had changed, somehow, or perhaps I had.

After an exchange of casual pleasantries, I briefed him on the conditions on the firebase, the mission and in general how things were going. I left out the two incidents at Evans, with Black Jack: Either he'd hear about them from the CO himself or he wouldn't, so bringing them up would accomplish nothing. Neither did I pass on my thoughts on the new platoon leaders; he would see for himself and Third Grade had taught me to abhor tattle tales. All that done, it was time to get down to serious business.

"One thing," I said casually, after he'd just finished telling me, for the fourth time, that he had never realized what a good marriage he had until Honolulu, "I don't know if it's escaped your attention or not, but we have three platoons and four lieutenants."

He grunted, smiling. He was still in a good humor. Ogle was nowhere to be seen, and his mind was still in Honolulu. "Okay. We got ourselves an XO. You."

"Wrong. Not me. I'm not going back to the rear as XO. Give me liberty or give me First Platoon, but not that."

He shook his head. "You're senior platoon leader. That's it. End of story."

"Not quite." I'd been savoring this moment for a week. "It's true that I got here first, and have been with the company longest. Chuck Denholm got here only a month ago. But..." I loved the stress on that word ... but is such a beautiful, expressive word: "But, Denholm came here direct from Alaska, as you know." We all knew that story: Chuck had told us of the effect it had on him, to step on a plane in -30 degree weather and then step off into 100 degrees. "He never got home for leave before Nam. And the reason why, as you may or may not know, was he'd just returned to his unit in Alaska from emergency leave, just a week or so before that." I hurried on, because he was beginning to get impatient. "The point is ... because of all that, Chuck didn't get his promotion to first lieutenant at Bien Hoa, the way most of us did. He made O2 while he was still in Alaska. On October 30th. Six full weeks before me."

I leaned back and smiled beatifically. "He ranks me. I may be senior platoon leader, but he's the senior lieutenant. Ergo, he's XO."

Robison eyed me suspiciously. "Are you making this up?"

I raised an eyebrow. "It's on his orders. Check it out yourself. The man ranks me and that's that."

"Shit." Robison looked thoughtfully at the radio in the corner. "Okay," he said finally, shaking his head. "If that's so ... then you take Denholm's platoon, and —"

"No," I interrupted firmly. "First Platoon. My platoon."

Robison grimaced, shaking his head forcefully this time. "Wolosenko's got that platoon, and from what I hear he's doing a good job. Why shift everyone around? It'll be a rat fuck. I'd have to move Denholm to XO, Wolosenko to Second, you to first...."

"Robbie," I leaned forward, my voice pleading. "Look, it's not as if I'm asking for the moon here. All I want is to go back to my platoon. That's all. There are probably a thousand lieutenants in Vietnam right now asking to leave their platoons and go to the rear. I'm asking to leave the rear and go to my platoon. What the hell!"

Robison thought about it for a moment. "Okay. You're a pain in the ass, but ... okay."

I stood up, overjoyed. "Thanks. Has anyone ever told you that you're a prince? No? Well, not surprising, really. But this once you are." I looked him in the eye. "Thanks, Rob. I mean it."

And I did, too.

The men, I was grateful to see, were genuinely pleased. They liked Jerry, but they were happy to have me back. As Muldoon said, that first evening, Lieutenant Wolosenko was a great guy but the CP just didn't seem the same without somebody yelling all the time.

The operation ended a few days later. There was some brave talk about a "fairly high body count" but that's all it was, talk. In fact, we were licking our wounds. Colonel Mot had led us a merry chase and administered a stinging lesson. The CG had erupted, sometime during the last couple of days, with predictable results: Not a single commander was fit for human consumption for a week, and the acid indigestion trickled down to our level quickly. Robison and I had a good, old-fashioned, hands-on-hips, eyeball-to-eyeball confrontation over some ridiculous matter on the afternoon of the 28th. Robbie would later refer to it as the Gunfight on the Streets of Laredo, because it had started over the radio and had ended with the two of us approaching each other along the dirt trail between our CPs, staring at each other in the approved narrow-eyed, tight-lipped John Wayne manner. Only a month later, neither of us could remember what the disagreement had been over.

10

Firebase Rakkasan: Abbot's Tale

YD490198; 2 March 1969

One hundred and fifty Chinook 47 and twenty-five Chinook 54 sorties later, we were all deposited safely back at Evans. The dismantling and evacuation of Brick had been, in Robison's delicate wording, a complete rat fuck. The weather had remained dry the whole time, with the result that the bare clay surface of the island had turned into lightly compacted sand and dirt particles. The resultant dust clouds, under the lash of hundreds of whirling blades, some of which, like the ones on the CH54 Crane, were 80 feet in length, gave a fair imitation of a sirocco scouring the Sahara. We spent most of the time slumped by the PZ, heads tucked low on our chests, towels wrapped around our faces. There are moments when combat just isn't any fun at all.

Back at Evans, we took hot showers, donned clean fatigues and made a mandatory appearance at a battalion officer's party, organized by Black Jack. In addition to the beer and steaks, we were treated to the presence of a half dozen nurses from the 22nd, the brigade field hospital, as well as the august presence of three or four colonels, from the brigade and division staffs. The party had all the verve and charm of a hanging. It had been planned in advance, possibly as a celebration of the anticipated success of the operation against Colonel Mot. If so, there was nothing to celebrate. He had cleaned our clocks with embarrassing ease.

The colonels all hung about in a single, suspicious knot, scowling at us on occasion, but more often talking in grave undertones to each other. Occasionally, Black Jack would pause to listen or add a comment. The nurses, none of them under 40 and lower in rank than captain, stood in a separate corner in an even more suspicious and closed group. If their presence had been intended to add a dash of feminine sparkle and laughter to the event, someone had miscalculated dreadfully. They were all clad in fatigues, with short, mannish haircuts and grim, mannish faces. I don't suppose there's any DOD regulation against it, but I have never seen an army nurse smile. These didn't. Besides, it was awfully hard for me to find any sex appeal in a group of women whose main function in life, as far as I had been able to determine from personal experience, was to skewer me with every sharp object at their disposal.

The Bravo Company lieutenants left the party early, careful not to wake the others. We gathered instead at the company HQ building. Robison joined us soon after that, and we spent the rest of the night relaxing and getting better acquainted. Denholm was there, of course. He let me know, later, without rancor, that he would have preferred staying in the field, but he accepted his move to XO with a certain grace. He had known all along that he was the ranking lieutenant. Besides, he confided to me later, he'd heard that the battalion had already decided that there would be no more XOs and an additional platoon, a fourth, would be staffed for each company, with the lieutenants currently serving as XOs to become the platoon leaders. He sat quietly tonight, his dark, heavy eyebrows slightly lowered under the equally dark, heavy glasses he wore. Seen like that, in repose, he looked dour and grim, remarkably like a young Leonid Brezhnev. In fact, Denny was full of puckish good humor, and bore the details of his job, the paperwork and the bullshit, with surprising equanimity. The heartland of America is full of men like Denholm; competent, solid, comfortably faithful to their own moral values but recognizing that others could differ, and imbued with a certain sense of rightness, and not righteousness. It was hard not to like Denholm.

It was impossible not to like Wolosenko. Jerry, in his own sly way, was as flamboyant and eccentric as Check Denholm was Middle America straight. It was all in his own way, of course. Jerry had graduated from CCNY with a degree in political science, an indiscretion for which I never tired of needling him. He in turn never tired of reminding us that his was a venerable Ukrainian name, and he was never to forget it himself. He went out on patrols with a small blue and yellow flag, the banner of the defunct Ukrainian Republic, attached to the back of his rucksack. Despite the heat, he wore a long white scarf wrapped around his neck, removing it only when the tactical situation dictated. He also complained bitterly, and threatened to write to the Secretary of Defense, Laird, about the lack of Ukrainian food in our C-rations. All other ethnic groups, he pointed out, were over-represented—chili, spaghetti, over-cooked vegetables, omelets, pork slices, it was all rank discrimination against his heritage.

As the time passed, and the drinks added up, the CO started to become more and more belligerent. He began on his favorite theme, that the lieutenants coming out of OCS and ROTC these days were capable, on their better days, of crossing the street on their own, if that street was in a small Midwestern town with no traffic, and even then only at a corner with a traffic light. That we could take a platoon of infantry, fly out to the boonies, engage the enemy and return in anything other than a body bag was an impossibility. Water would flow up a mountainside, he said, and people would walk on the moon, before any of us could survive one day in the field. What would happen if we ever ran into anything more than a pair of woodcutters, without him to guide us, was something he didn't want to think about. You might think, reading this, that Barry Robison was a West Point man. He wasn't. He'd graduated OCS, but, of course, an entire year before us, and that made all the difference.

It was familiar stuff; Chuck and I had heard it before. In a way, we took pleasure in it, as Jerry and Dickson sat there, open-mouthed, listening to Robbie assure them that any patrol they took out would quickly turn into a rat fuck *and* a Chinese abortion, before they'd made it 500 meters. It's like sitting through a favorite movie with someone who's never seen it before; you can anticipate the good moments, and watch the others as they react when they come.

After a while, however, it turned personal. His target was Wolosenko. Jerry had mentioned, during the course of the conversation, that eventually he'd like very much to join the battalion or brigade S2 or S3 staffs—intelligence or operations. I'd known Jerry only a short time, but it doesn't take long to size a man up in the army, and I knew that he wasn't motivated by either cowardice or, as some men are, by an unwillingness to lead. In fact, Jerry made an outstanding platoon leader, as he was to show over the next few weeks, but he reasoned, correctly, that his talents and background suited him to one of those staff jobs more than to a line company. He was just being objective about his abilities.

Robison chose to make an issue of it; his remarks, although seemingly made in the same spirit as the rest of the evening's banter, turned ugly. Jerry kept his calm, shrugging it off, and pointing out, when pressed, that a good staff officer was preferable to a bad platoon leader. Robison kept mulishly plugging away.

"Look a' Bo," he said, waving drunkenly in my general direction. "Now, *he* had a chance to go to the ... uh, rear, an' he turn' it down. Now, whaddaya think abou' *dat*?"

Jerry sighed patiently. "I think that's great. He likes being out there. That's okay. But I'm not Bo. I *like* staff work. I'll do anything they ask me to do, but I think I'd do better in a staff job."

"Shit. Shit on a goddamn stick. Only one kin' job worth havin'—right, Bo? In the whole yew-nited state' army ... goddamn right. 'm I right, Bo?"

"Always," I said.

"So, tell me." Robison's eyes crossed and uncrossed as he tried to focus. "Wha—I mean, why you wanna leave platoon ... you scared?"

Jerry smiled. Thinly, but he smiled. "No, never."

"What, never?" I murmured.

"Well, hardly ever," he allowed, grinning.

Robison squinted at us suspiciously. He could tell we were sharing a joke, but he didn't know what it was. He decided to change his focus.

"Sheeee-it. Never. Huh. But lissen. Lissen ... Why you wanna stay inna field, Bo? Huh? Why?"

I shrugged. "I love mud. Couldn't do it, as a kid, 'cause mom used to beat me senseless. Now I get to play in mud all day long, and I'm a happy man."

"See?" Robison settled back with a pleased smile. "See wha' I mean? Fucker likes *mud*. Makes all diff'rence."

Chuck broke in at that point, with a very filthy joke about a boy and a girl playing in the mud on a farm, and the evening passed.

Fortunately, we remained on Evans for another two days. Hangovers were the rule the next day, and while my moderation the night before spared me that, just being around the pale-faced, bleary-eyed mincing corpses that morning was bad enough. I shuddered to think what it would have been like had we gone on a combat assault at 0700. I tried to imagine the effect the noise and motion of an assault helicopter would have on aching head and queasy stomach, but I gave up. Some possibilities were too horrible to contemplate.

Instead, we spent the next two days teaching classes. I gave a class on navigation and map reading. A month before, I would have been embarrassed to give it, but after the tutelage of Sergeant Wright, I was confident and expansive. I could never know what he knew, simply because it was a part of his upbringing, but I managed well enough. We taught courses on radio procedures, starlight scope, machine guns, first aid, grenade launchers, claymore mines and trip flares ... we reviewed them all. The troops were properly appreciative. They hadn't had a chance for so much uninterrupted sleep since they'd gotten to Nam.

There were changes. Matters with Morris had come to a head while I was acting CO. Wright had lost patience with him. He was shipped, with warning label, to Third Platoon. Proof that Henry Ford was right, history is bunk, was provided by my selection of the new RTO. I had learned nothing from the Morris fiasco. Kaminski had been the other man I'd found asleep along with Morris, back in my first week with the platoon. I was remarkably fortunate with the men I commanded. Other than Muldoon, and him only for a short while, there were no real discipline problems—except for the two men I chose as RTOs. The reasoning with Kaminski was the same as with Morris: He was a handful for his squad leaders. Skinner (who, naturally, never was returned to us, as we'd known all along) had been his squad leader and had been able to handle him, but the young and inexperienced Sergeant Eden, the recent NCO academy product, didn't have a prayer. Hence, with the idea that if at first you don't succeed ... this may be viewed as unwavering optimism or persistent stupidity. Take your pick.

The rumor was that we were headed for a long operation, but before that we were sent to Rakkasan for a few days. Same old stuff, of course: A soldier's work is never done. Some genius at Brigade S3 decided to relocate the bunkers on the west side, perhaps on a whim. Moving a finished bunker is not quite the same thing as simply digging a new foxhole. Sandbags have to be removed, land wires unstrung, PCP pulled out of the ground, timbers pried loose, a massive hole filled in and another one dug ... all because some captain or major from Evans decided to improve the view.

The rumors kept flying about. Robison himself was convinced, by something the S3 had said, that we would soon be on our way to the far west, almost to the A Shau. That was pretty sobering news: We'd tamed the AO along the Song Bo; the enemy rarely moved about in anything larger than squad size, and most of the time they were present only as a pair of trail watchers or an odd sniper or two, or perhaps a wood cutting party. But that region to the west, where the really high, steep mountains stood, with their deep, tree-covered valleys and ravines, was not only unknown territory but adjacent to the A Shau, and the A Shau valley was the NVA's home ball park.

The weather had finally cleared for good; the heavy, relentless rains of the monsoon and later were, for the moment, a memory. In their place came a heavy, relentless sun, often glazed over by high thin clouds that served only to spread out the light and increase the humidity. In this respect, it was just like summer back in Washington; the same brassy pearl sky and the heavy heat, the same clinging moisture that became, after moments, unending sweat, the same hazy horizon. Here, it was just more intense, and there was no air-conditioned Teehan's to duck into when it all became unbearable.

The good news was that the rains were gone, and that meant a general improvement in the platoon's health. The bad news was that the increased heat could lead to heat fatigue, men passing out, and even deadly heat stroke. And the cuts and abrasions would not stop; any time the skin was broken in the tropical forest, there is the potential for infection, with rampant cellulitis being the most common effect.

Leeches, not mosquitoes, were our biggest fear. A leech in itself was a disgusting little creature; time and time again, we would stop momentarily on a mountain slope, under the dense canopy. Almost immediately, as if by magic, dozens of the tiny threads would emerge from the damp soil, each about a quarter to a half-inch long, and barely two millimeters wide. They would raise their front portion into the air, waving about, and inch closer to the boot: They sensed the heat, and were drawn to it. To avoid them then, of course, was easy; one simply moved his foot. But at night...

They were dangerous. Not because of the blood they took from us, although that tiny little thread became, once it had feasted, a fat, gorged sack about an inch or longer and a good quarter-inch wide, or bigger, if it was a river leech. They were there by the dozens, in the morning: Under a man's armpits, on his neck, between his thighs, along his forearm, all along his calves and in the small of his back. Removing them was a painstaking task. What worked best was either a lit cigarette, or the powerful insect repellent we carried. In either case, a man's buddy would have to do it, since many of the things were in places where he himself couldn't reach.

Their real danger lay in this: Pulling one out left its head in the body, where inevitably it would fester and lead to infection. This could happen accidentally, without a man's noticing that he'd just scraped a leech off his forearm, for example. Even worse was the instinctive appeal to the leech of human body cavities: The warmer, darker, damper a spot was, the better the leech likes it and the more it would strive to get there. What some newcomers thought of as a crude joke was in fact absolutely correct: Leeches sought out places like the anus or the foreskin of the penis, along with the armpits and the scrotal sack, because they were the warmest and darkest parts of the body. The ones who settled under the arm or the scrotum eventually either fell off, gorged, or were seen and picked off. The others ... men did end up in the hospital with painful infections when the leech, full of blood, dropped off but could no longer exit the body; it died there, then, and days later the infection set in.

Muldoon and I were going over all this in the CP bunker, trying to work out a plan to keep this at a minimum. Rubber bands were popular: upon bedding down for the night, troops would pull their sleeves down, button them and then wrap the rubber bands tightly around their sleeves and their ankles, sealing off the arms and legs. Liberal use of insect repellent about the neck and upper chest might keep them off. And, of course, Doc would have to perform or at least oversee a mandatory morning inspection. The troops resisted this a bit at first, but after a couple of incidents and rumors coming back of men ending up in Japan with severe anal infection, they took to it willingly enough, to the point where many of them would strip naked and have their buddies carefully look at their backs and buttocks.

We were still at it, trying to reach a balance between maintaining the platoon's health and bringing operations to a halt by frequent inspections and treatment, when Sergeant Eden entered the CP. He went to Sergeant Wright, so I ignored him, but after a moment or so the gist of their conversation made its way into my consciousness.

"...he just won't do nothin'" Eden was saying.

Wright shook his head, majestically and angrily. "Eden, why do you keep comin' back to me with this stuff? You're his squad leader. Ain't my job, ain't the Lieutenant's job, to run your squad. I'm sick n' tired of hearin' 'bout Abbot. It's Abbot this n' Abbot that. Got me 35 men in this platoon, n' the only one I got time for is Abbot, 'cause *you* can't deal with 'im. You get your butt back there and do your job, n' get 'im to do his."

Eden shrugged, whining. "What can I do? Shoot 'im? He won't move. Sits there, that's all he does, moanin' about his ol' lady. None of the other guys can get 'im to get up either."

Wright seldom raised his voice but this was one time he did. "Other guys? Eden, there's only one guy in a squad's got the job o' getting' a man up. That's *you*. You want your squad to do your job for you now? Along with me n' the Lieutenant?"

Wright and I exchanged glances. He shook his head again. "This acre's just about worn out, Lieutenant."

Eden raised his hands in despair. "He won't go, Top. The rest of the LP's ready, but he won't go. Whaddaya want me to do?" He looked down at the floor, as angry, in his own way, as Wright was. When he looked up, his face had changed. He had made a decision.

"It's ... there's somethin' else. I mean — this stuff's been goin' on a long time. You ain't never seen it, 'cause we all agreed ... we thought the right thing...." Slowly, he took something from his cargo pocket on his trousers; it was a plain white envelope, soiled and slightly torn. He glanced at Wright and then at me, hesitated, and then walked over and handed me the envelope.

It was white, a common cheap drug store variety. The address on the front was in crude, spidery block letters, in thin and faded pale blue ink. There was no return address. The envelope was heavier than it should have been; when I opened the flap, I found, in addition to a ruled piece of yellow paper, five stiff-backed Polaroid photographs. I looked at the first one.

"Oh, God," I whispered, my lips moving in an involuntary invocation. The photos—I shuffled quickly through them all—were of a young woman, presumably Abbot's estranged wife. She was nude, as were the men—there were three different ones—featured in the photos with her. They were ... I gagged in disbelief.

I'm hardly the prudish type. A lifetime spent going back and forth among several capitals of Europe, and a normal college career, had exposed me to every shade of erotica, from Rueben's art to comic books. I reacted to it mostly with indifference; the standard commercial pornography had almost nothing to do with love, sex and even lust as I had experienced them, and so found me neither drawn nor repelled. But this...

There was, truthfully, nothing erotic about the pictures. The girl was skinny, with ugly, sagging small breasts, scrawny limbs, and a face devoid of intelligence, beauty or mystery. Her poses were clumsy and awkward, unnatural in their stiffness. Her skin was pasty and dull at best, and in the glare of the flashcube, was rendered corpse-like by the hard shadows and glistening flash points. The men—one tall and bony, with a wisp of beard; another paunchy and oily, a third short and compact—had leering, drunken grins. They were merely disgusting. But the woman ... her grin was terrifying. It was a skull-grin, a graveyard grin, a grin of hate and bestial pleasure—pleasure derived, not from the sex, but from the pain she meant to inflict.

Numbly, I opened the letter and read it. It too was printed in block letters, in pencil

Dear Ed, it began: I hope you like these pictures. You know Bob. That's his cock Im sucking. His cocks biger then yours. I love his cock.

The next few paragraphs were more of the same, a detestable, unnerving litany. I stopped reading after a while, stunned. There was one photograph of her in full face, smiling directly into the camera. I had seen such a smile, years ago ... I searched my memory and then remembered: A woman in our Glover Park neighborhood, a thin, primly-dressed lady with grayish brown hair pulled back in a tight bun, sequined glasses and a smile on her face, always ... she and her smile would peer out from behind the curtains of her house on 37th Street, avidly, eagerly watching her stepson, a boy of six or seven, at play. Waiting, hoping ... until he did something wrong, some minor transgression—stepped momentarily into the street, or dropped a toy in the yard and left it, or perhaps raised his voice too high—and then she would run out of her house, quickly, before he had a chance to undo his wrong, and, always with that tight, gloating, horrible smile, she would spank him, viciously, slowly, calmly, inexorably. Her face was incandescent with pleasure. I grew up in fear and loathing of that woman.

This was the same smile. Already nauseated, I read the last paragraph.

Dont com home. You got a needle dick anyways an you aint no use to a wumin. You aint no use to me. Bob an me hope you die so I get the inshorance. You aint no fuckin good to nobuddy. Die, motherfucker.—Betty

I stood there, staring at the soiled paper, for several seconds. Sergeant Wright was now standing behind my shoulder, reading it. I glanced back at him. He was looking at Eden, only now the thunderous disapproval of moments before was gone, replaced by something very like thanks.

"Sir?" Eden finally broke the silence.

"How long has this..."

"Weeks, Lieutenant. Months. Me'n the guys ... months."

"And you didn't tell me or Top."

"No, sir. No ... I ... we didn't...." He made a helpless gesture, as he'd done so many times before, only now I understood it. "What could we do? A man has to...." He shook his head. He had no words for this. Neither, I realized, did I.

"Months of this shit?" I pointed to the envelope.

"Yeah. Well — today's the first time with the photos, I mean. She never ... this is the first time with the photos," he repeated.

I let out a soft sigh. "Jesus."

Eden merely waited, quietly.

I took a deep breath. No wonder Wright was now silent. Top, a deeply religious man, married to the same woman for some 20 years, couldn't deal with this. Neither, really, could I, only I had to. Nothing in my experience could have prepared me for this. Marriages, where I came from, were ... nothing like this. I was almost 26 years old and had never seen my parents argue; I spent untold hours in the homes of my friends, dozens of them, and had never seen *their* parents argue. I had never seen hate like this, homemade hate, hate that was as intimate and personal as lovemaking.... My wife's often-repeated phrase came back to me just then.... *Ugly as homemade sin....* I'd always seen that as one of her funny southern expressions, before this.

"I suppose I need to...." I shook my head, angry with myself. *You're the platoon leader, asshole. Act like one.*

"Take me to Abbot. Top, you coming?"

For the first time ever, I saw indecision on Sergeant Wright's face. Before he could answer, I said "Never mind. You've got a lot to do."

Wright hid his gratitude by turning swiftly away.

Eden nodded. "Yes, sir. He's still over by the squad."

The ten minutes with Abbot were among the worst of my life.

I dismissed Eden; a glance at his face and mine sent the others scrambling to their bunkers, leaving Abbot and me alone. Faced by him, seated on a stack of sandbags, head down, shoulders slumped, hands clasping and unclasping, I suddenly realized I had not the slightest idea what to say.

"Abbot...." That was all I could get out.

He shook his head, eyes still fixed on the dirty beige soil of the firebase. Finally, he said, in a low monotone, "Ain't nothin' I can do."

I nodded, and then cursed myself for a fool. Twice. He couldn't see me, and if he could I wasn't supposed to be agreeing with him about that. I was supposed to be helping him. "I know you feel that way right now, Abbot, but you can't let this eat at you forever. At the very least ... you could see the chaplain."

He gave a quick, angry shake of his head. "Ain't gonna show them pics to no fuckin' chaplain."

"He's seen worse, Abbot." Actually I didn't believe that. Nothing could be worse.

Abbot sighed; his left hand was squeezing his right fist; the knuckles showed white and red in the setting sun.

"Or you could request compassionate leave; I'll back you, and so will the CO."

"What for?"

"To go home and straighten this out."

"Ain't nothin' I can do." He repeated this quietly, but obstinately. And then he looked at me for the first time. His eyes struck me a mortal, pitiless blow; they were filled with hurt, and shame, and a deep, despairing anger that seared me like jagged lightning. I had never seen pain like this before.

I lowered my eyes and turned away, unable to face Abbot. Head down, I swallowed reflexively. I felt sick. I forced the words out; they lay thick and squalid in my throat.

"I'm sorry, Abbot. I'm...."

"It's okay." Abbot's voice was remote but calm. I looked out across the bunker line, down the orange clay slope. I fixed on a small, bent sapling, one of the few left standing. I concentrated on it. It all seemed so easy, so natural, before reading the letter. I had known all my life this truth: Only if you can describe your pain do you really feel it. That is what I believed. And so only Michelangelo can feel the depth of a mother's grief; only Beethoven can rage at fate, and Shakespeare alone among us can despair over the body of his dead beloved.

It was a perfect syllogism, straight out of Logic 101. Stones and lumps of earth are inarticulate. They can feel no pain. Abbot is inarticulate. Therefore, Abbot can feel no pain.

I stared at the tree for a moment longer, and the thin trunk became the tall, spare frame of the Reverend William Pauley, SJ, who had taught that logic course. I remembered him well: Short, slender black eyebrows over deep set black eyes, a gaunt, hollow-cheeked face, a surprisingly round, soft mouth. And his voice: thin, cutting, cool as an ice pick, detached as a distant star: *Boccia, the fact that the premise — either the major or minor — is false does* not *obviate the syllogism. That remains valid, correct and perfect. Remember: A correct application of the logic will always lead us to a* valid *conclusion, although it may or may not be true.*

I realized, with a dull pain of my own, that for once in my life I had absolutely nothing to say.

"There ain't nothin' I can do," he repeated, not as a question now.

"No." I started to say something about filing for divorce, but then thought better of it. Divorce? For *this*?

"I want...." Abbot shook his head.

Justice, I realized. That's what Abbot was asking me for. He wants justice. Was there a court anywhere that could dispense justice to Abbot's wife? Lacerations of the human spirit: They cry out for justice. We invented a heaven and hell, precisely because, as Abbot said, there ain't nothin' we can do. Of what crime would she be convicted? Only that of being human, and the universe itself had already passed sentence: The verdict was death, and it came to us all, good or bad, kind or cruel, gentle or harsh.

"I'm sorry, Abbot."

"Yeah."

I hesitated. "Tell Sergeant Eden I want to see him. And — Abbot: I don't want you going on the LP tonight."

Abbot nodded. There was no hint of triumph or even relief on his face. "Yes, sir." He stood up and walked slowly to Eden's bunker.

11

March Madness

The 3/187th AO; 3–21 March 1969

The next day was Monday, March 3rd. We would not see Rakkasan, or any other firebase, for the next 22 days, not until the 25th. For three weeks, we would be on patrol. But we returned well rested, in excellent condition, and content. It was by far the longest patrol we had, but the weather was consistently good, with only an occasional shower, the movement, for the most part, was easy and contact with the enemy was minimal. And by this time we knew our AO well; the low hills and smaller mountains around Rakkasan held few mysteries for us.

There was one moment of slapstick comedy just before we boarded the helicopters. While we were waiting, I made my routine inspection of the platoon. Half way through, I stopped dead, thunderstruck, and turned in astonishment to Sergeant Wright.

"What's this!" I asked, pointing.

"This" was one of our new troopers, transferred from the 4th Division. He stood there in line, with his pack, ammo, canteens and rifle ... and two machine gun ammo belts across his chest, like a Mexican bandito in a cheap western.

Wright just stared, without making a sound. Then the two of us advanced on the trooper with grim faces.

I believe the man found the next few moments to be very illuminative, as I explained to him, in my usual calm, polite, even-tempered way, that First Platoon did not do this kind of thing.

Why not? Well, for one, we were operating in a rain forest, where the ground was almost always damp and moldy. If shot at, I explained patiently, your first reaction will be of course to hit the dirt. And when you do that, the bright, shiny 7.62 cartridges on that belt will get ground into the mud and would then, eventually, get fed into an M60, and M60s, sadly, do not perform well when dirt, small stones, twigs and other such material enter the chamber.

"You fuck up one of my mike sixties," I said, "and I will send you on a one-man patrol in the A Shau."

In addition, the crossed belts, with that beautifully glittering brass twinkling in the sun, make an excellent crosshairs target for an enemy rifleman.

Finally, John Wayne starred in Hollywood movies, and did not actually serve in the U.S. Army.

When we finished with him, Sergeant Wright, his face still thunderous with disapproval, went looking for Eden, the man's squad leader.

I don't recall his name; he was with us four days, and then left on the first resupply flight — not because of this, I must add. He was called home on some kind of emergency leave and never returned.

We left Rakkasan and were flown into the same area, across the Song Bo, that we'd patrolled earlier in late February. Alpha Company was inserted with us, but in an LZ a bit to the northwest, closer to the river. From then on, the two companies were to sweep upriver, parallel to each other: Alpha close by the Song Bo, Bravo some 1,200 meters to their southeast. Alpha was sweeping an area we'd been through before, with little result, but they were to encounter constant contact over the three weeks. We never saw him; beyond a sniper round or two one night, that caused no damage, we would have been hard pressed to offer any evidence that he was even in the area.

Alpha, moving along the riverside, was encountering the same vegetation we had earlier, on the opposite bank of the Song Bo: The mix of bamboo and creepers, with occasional saw grass, although no one except Bravo One ever ran into The Wall. I nodded my head in sympathy and understanding when I overheard the snarling conversations between frustrated, bleeding platoon leaders and equally frustrated, disbelieving CO. We, by contrast, found ourselves moving through gently rolling and moderately forested hills, with only a very few steep slopes or tangles of vines and saw grass to impede us. Some of the trails we found were unbelievable. Jerry, moving his Second Platoon on point the second day, radioed back in awe. He informed us he had just come across the Los Angeles Freeway. When we reached Hill 154, on which he was located, we saw what he meant. The trail was at least three feet wide, smooth, cleared of stumps and large stones, and, in a part of the world where straight lines appeared to have been outlawed or never conceived, stretched direct and unwavering as a ruler.

It's not that nothing went wrong over those 22 days; we had our share of problems, as I'll recount, but over all that patrol has to rank as the easiest, most carefree time I spent in Viet Nam. Day followed day with almost unnerving ease. Our chief concern was how to invent tastier, more appetizing meals. Beyond that ... move a kilometer or two, stop, send out squad or occasionally platoon-sized patrols, then set up, rest, eat, rest some more, sleep, get up, move a klick or so...

I shouldn't give the impression that we were slacking off: We weren't. When we sent out recon patrols, they *searched*. It's just that we never came up with much. Poor Alpha, less than a mile away, was constantly being harassed by trail watchers, snipers, or occasional squad-sized ambushes, while we simply could find nothing at all.

Until the sixth or seventh day. Each platoon had, on this mission, a Chieu Hoi.

These were NVA or VC defectors who now worked for the U.S. Army as guides and advisors. They were supposed to know the terrain and AO, and, of course, the enemy's SOP. In fact, we rarely found them of much use, partly because of the language difficulty—they spoke very little English and we spoke no Vietnamese—but mostly because we didn't trust them. The day would never dawn that would see me place even a small part of the responsibility for the lives and safety of my men in the hands of an NVA turncoat.

Nevertheless, our scout, a stumpy, moon-faced fellow by the name of Trangh, did make himself very useful that day.

The occasion was a recon patrol First Platoon conducted. The previous day, Alpha Company had made significant contact, and eventually found a recently abandoned bunker complex, perhaps only a day or so empty. They found large quantities of rice, several weapons and 200 or 300 pounds of documents and maps. Bravo was diverted from its planned route and sent into an adjacent valley, one that was broad, flat and densely forested. Almost immediately, Jerry found a small complex of about seven or eight bunkers. Fifteen or twenty minutes later, he radioed Robison with the news that he uncovered 60 or 70 pounds of documents. First Platoon at the time was a short distance behind but to the east of Second Platoon. Within ten minutes of Jerry's second call, Jones, our point man, raised his hand. We had found our own bunkers. Calling Robison and relaying the news, I set up two squads as security and took the third—Hyde's—into the complex with me.

It was a typical NVA bunker complex. Each bunker was built into the ground, low and deep. Less than 18 inches showed above ground. The roof was made of heavy logs covered with a foot or so of dirt, over which fallen branches, reeds, leaves and live plants were set. Seen from the rear, a bunker was almost undetectable. The entrance was narrow and shallow; a big man, like Mareniewski, had difficulty entering. Once inside, you would see little except for four dirt walls and a dirt floor, with the heavy timber beams overhead. The smooth floor also contained a grenade sump, with the floor angled to roll the grenade toward the sump; a small niche with a tunnel leading downward into the hillside, or more steeply downward if it was on flat terrain, and now and then a drainage ditch. It seemed, at first glance, to be primitive and crude. In fact, these were well constructed and supremely functional. A bunker like this, with its flat roof, would sustain direct hits from anything but heavy naval artillery or perhaps a 175. Anything smaller would merely raise some dust. Even a 500 pound bomb landing a short distance away would do relatively little damage. (To the bunker. The people inside might not fare so well, in that case: The concussion would kill them. But many of them had tunnels leading down into bombproof shelters, designed to withstand even the heaviest of ordnance.)

And these were the flat-roof type. Further west, in the high mountains, we would encounter the A-frame construction, so sturdy and so well designed that even heavy ordnance wouldn't damage them. A 1,000 pound bomb was needed to crack those nutshells, and it took a direct hit at that.

The bunkers were only marginally vulnerable to small arms fire, because of their narrow slit opening, and the dirt construction rendered it impervious to LAWs or even the 90mm Recoilless Rifle — until we learned to use flechette rounds against them, and those just killed the people inside; they did nothing to the bunker itself. They were never placed just anywhere; they were carefully spotted and angled, so that each bunker would support, and be supported by, two others. Terrain and cover were used to the fullest. Most complexes, even very large ones, were invisible from the air and almost so from the ground. Most of the time we found them by the one thing the NVA couldn't hide — the trail leading to them.

But search though we might, there was nothing there. Vandenburg, one of Hyde's men, did find an old weapon, rusted and with a broken stock, leaning up against a wall. It was at least World War II–era, if not older; probably an old French Army carbine, from the looks of it. Even as a souvenir, it was valueless. The rest of the bunkers were empty and showed signs of being long abandoned.

Trangh, however, did save us a bit of time, when he dissuaded an enthusiastic Tim Logan from digging down into a noticeably softer patch of earth behind one of the bunkers. Logan's fertile imagination conjured up visions of a document cache full of secrets, but the scout, through emphatic gestures and one or two words of broken English, informed him, to the delighted derision of the rest of the platoon, that he was in fact digging up an old latrine. Logan, who showed no mercy when it came to ragging on the others, could expect none in return, and the next few minutes were filled with catcalls and witticisms, culminating in Sgt Hyde's assurance that Logan's effort had just changed the name of the battalion to the Turd of the One Eighty-Seventh.

This patrol marked the first time we made extensive use of LRRP rations—the new substitute for C-rations. The acronym stands for Long Range Reconnaissance Patrol; they were a freeze-dried meal with the entrée wrapped in a stiff plastic bag, into which you could pour hot water and let the meal steep for a few minutes. The rations were far lighter than the C-rations, and, actually, most were far tastier. A five-day ration would weigh only a couple of pounds, an obvious advantage on a long patrol.

Nevertheless, they had one enormous drawback: In order to eat the damned things, you needed boiling, or at least hot, water and plenty of it. Even with the hot water added, there were pitfalls. One of the tastier meals was chili with beans. But the beans, no matter how long you let the meal steep in the heated water, would never soften. One of the commonplace sounds at mealtimes was the agonized yelp of a trooper biting down on a shriveled, pebble-like kidney bean. Water, as I've said, was at a premium, and even when we had it we often didn't have time to heat it, and a LRRP meal eaten cold was no better than pork slices. In the end, we went back to the heavier but more practical C-rats.

Neither my diary nor my letters home reveal anything important happening, and I suppose nothing did. Very few things stick out. There is the image of Jerry Wolosenko, stumping along the trail, his blue and yellow Ukrainian flag fluttering hanging limply from his rucksack. I remember one hilarious evening with him, on one of the rare occasions when our two platoons were together at an NDP: He sat cross-legged on the ground, fussing with field stoves, canteen cups, C-ration cans, LRRP bags, onions, hot sauce and other assorted material, concocting some dish or other, muttering constantly in an exquisitely horrible French accent. He'd fashioned something that looked vaguely like a chef's cap, and called himself Chef Escargot. Sadly, the food, when done, afforded us nothing like the pleasure of its preparation. Candidly, it was awful.

The following day, having had to endure my comments as a food critic, Jerry returned the favor. Due to a misunderstanding about the coordinates of a streambed, the CO and I had a difference of opinion over where I should be at that particular moment. It ended with Robison's waspish query whether I'd lost my bearings. Wolosenko called in a moment later, apologetic. He'd just called in a resupply, he said, but had he known I'd lost my bearings, he would have ordered another set for me from Evans.

Perhaps two weeks into the patrol, we received our monthly book drop. Every four or five weeks, the good ladies at the USO would prepare several boxes of used paperbacks, for our reading pleasure. I don't want to make light if this: Their efforts were extremely welcome. I gave a glad cry of delight that particular day at finding an almost new copy of Jane Austen's *Emma* — of which more anon — but there were other worthwhile titles: *Michel, Michel; Diary of a Country Priest; To Kill a Mockingbird; Life with Father*. There were more, besides. But I did have to wonder at one particular offering.

The books were sent to us directly by the USO but they were usually gathered, back in the States, by various civic-minded groups. Many of the ones that came to us that day had been collected and sent on by the Women's Worship and Bible Study Committee of the Clarksville, Tennessee Free Will Baptist Church. I was flipping through them all — I unashamedly pulled rank when it came to getting first choice. Damn it, a commission ought to be good for *something* — when I ran across one that seemed a bit out of place. It was called *The Ways of a Man with a Maid*, and a glance at the cover had me wondering. It just didn't seem to.... Opening it up at random, I read about half a paragraph, and choked. My eyebrows reached the highest point of the war so far.

Jerry Wolosenko was seated nearby, also going through some of the paperbacks, looking for books with a lot of pictures. Turning to him, I held the book out.

"Did you see this?" I asked.

He took the proffered volume, glanced at the cover, frowned and shook his head "What is this, a Harlequin Romance? Frank...."

"Uhhm. No. Read a line or two."

He did so, and then *his* eyebrows met well up on his forehead.

"Holy shit," he said. "What in hell...."

"Foul. Really disgusting stuff."

"Filthy: Absolutely filthy. Perverted."

"It's as perverted as anything I've ever seen."

"Yeah." He closed it back up and returned it to me. "I get it next when you're done."

Doc Muldoon was not exactly a sterling character, even compared to Morris or Kaminski, but I eventually learned to enjoy his company. He opened up a new world for me, truthfully. I had led, admittedly, a sheltered and privileged existence, until I entered the Army. We were by no means rich — my father's income was always decidedly middle-class—but I had been given advantages that few others enjoyed, including the very rich. Among other things, my schools had been select: Parochial School, located in the heart of Georgetown, DC; a Jesuit prep school for boys, sited within a view of the Capitol Building, from which 163 of my 164 classmates graduated to college; and then Georgetown University. I believe it is safe to say that I'd never met anyone quite like Muldoon before.

It's not that I was unused to Irish Americans. One cannot go through Holy Trinity, Gonzaga and Georgetown—Jesuit institutions all—without accumulating a list of friends that reads like a County Mayo census roll. My closest friends in childhood were named Sheahan, McCarthy, Finnegan and Rafferty. But every one of these was a college graduate, some with advanced degrees. Inevitably, I had far more in common with them than I had with an Italian-American stevedore from New Jersey.

Muldoon, from the blue collar neighborhoods of Wilmington, Delaware, would have felt right at home with the stevedore, and completely alien to my friends. He did most of the talking. He told me of his upbringing in a tough, blue-collar, ethnic, factory-union urban neighborhood, and of his alcoholic father, his mother, his hard-fisted, hard-drinking brothers; he admitted that he worried about slipping into alcoholism himself.

"Hell, it's beer what does it, Lieutenant. Beer and a shot. But, it's the beer. You just sit there an' *drink* it, y'know?"

He talked, often, of his fiancée, but without a hint of sentimentality or even, as far as I could understand, love. "Dumb bitch just won't shut her mouth. Can't leave a man alone, know what I mean? Man, Lieutenant, I hope your ol' lady don't have a mouth like hers. You'll hafta shoot 'er."

Routine became ritual. Each night, after I'd checked the perimeter, talked with the men and made my radio checks, and he'd returned from his sick call, and his treatment of the blisters, cuts, boils or sores, we would unroll our liners, stretch them out, remove our boots (unless I had first watch), and then, before lying back, he would turn to me.

"Well, Lieutenant: Another night in Viet Nam."

"Another night, Francis."

After the first week, Robison changed tactics. The Scouts were unanimous in telling is that the preferred tactic of the trail watchers active in the area was to follow a platoon or company, usually 500 to 1,000 meters to the rear. If they were in larger units, they would do so until they determined where the American units were going, then slip by them and set up an ambush ahead. But the smaller trail watcher groups, which rarely exceeded four or five and often were only two, would remain behind the Americans, just keeping tabs on them.

Robison decided to make First Platoon the drag, or anchor platoon. The rest of the company moved along the general route we'd been following, roughly north and east, while I took First Platoon on a RIF due east, to a small hill there. But then I looped back behind them and maintained a gap of about 1,200 meters between us and the last squad in the larger group. Perhaps this way, he said optimistically, we would run right up the backs of the NVA trailing the main element. I didn't argue the point. I much preferred to be on my own anyway. Henceforth, we were the phantom platoon, heard but never seen, as Jerry said of us. We never caught any NVA, but on the bright side it kept Robison out of my hair and vice versa. Perhaps that's all he intended all along.

There was plenty of time for letter writing. I had never been what one would call a conscientious correspondent, reasoning that writing is hard work and should be approached with due caution. Besides, there was always the telephone. But the Army had not gotten around to installing telephone booths in the Vietnamese mountains, so I was forced to fall back on pen and paper.

I was appalled, although genuinely gratified, by the sheer number of people who wrote me. My wife and parents were to be expected, of course, and my brother and Jim Sheahan, my best friend through grade school, high school and college, would no doubt send a line or two—so much had I anticipated. But I was embarrassed by the letters that came from my in-laws, friends of the family, parents of college or high school classmates, neighbors, even an odd teacher or two. I quailed at the thought of responding to them all, although I did the best I could.

Unlike many, to be truthful, I rarely spent much time on thinking of the people at home. It distracted me. I was as close to my father as any son could be, but it took an act of will to recall his face, even when reading his letters. Perhaps there was just too much of a gap between the person I had been in Washington, D.C., and the man I had to be here. I could never convey this to the ones back home. In fact, I had trouble conveying anything at all. Rereading my letters is painful and humiliating: They are the dull, pedestrian quackings of an illiterate mind.

I said that little of importance happened on this patrol, but that isn't true. It was during this time that First Platoon became, indisputably, a seasoned fighting unit. It seems, at first glance, to be an exaggeration. Other than a few errant shots at Barbara, we had had no contact at all. Bravo as a whole had seen almost none. In the months from December to the end of March, until late April, in fact, we would not suffer a single casualty to enemy action. All we did in March was walk up hills and down hills and along ridgelines and across saddles and down into valleys and ravines. Walk. Move. Hump. Set up. Eat. Sleep. Wake.

Alpha Company, to our northeast, was in daily contact. We saw and heard nothing.

But somewhere in that time, along those kilometers walked and pounds carried, during the hours spent staring into darkness, listening to the whispered hiss of the radio and the pattering of the forest night, we became a seasoned platoon. We changed from 34 individuals led by a young and uncertain lieutenant into a disciplined force. When I joined the company, in December, I had — usually — known what to do; I often had no idea how to go about doing it, or, more precisely, how to get the 34 or 35 men to do what I thought had to be done.

Now, it was almost magic. There seemed to exist a sort of ESP that ran through the unit. I could actually *feel* where everybody was, who was too far from or too close to the man in front of him; who was facing out, rifle ready, in alternate directions, when we stopped, and who was not; who sat alert and armed, in the pre-dawn watch, and who instead sat, head down, draped in his poncho, struggling to keep leaden eyelids open.

Fatigue, anger, fear, boredom, disgruntlement, satisfaction — I could read them all, at an instant, in the postures of the men, or in the tone of voice.

We had gained an intangible: Confidence in ourselves and each other. This is the basic stuff of a combat platoon. Weapons, ammunition, uniforms, food and water — all of these may be in short supply, or even nonexistent; you may still survive. But trust in the man next to you, absolute trust, regardless of rank or position — it has to be universal — is a necessity of war. Lacking that, a small unit like a platoon lacks everything.

By late March, we were all known to each other, judging and judged in turn. A few — a very few; no more than two or three — had been found deficient. That didn't matter; we knew who they were. We could compensate. Never mind that we had not yet faced fire, serious contact. You cannot spend three months in those mountains, moving through the rainforest, in enemy territory, without becoming well aware of each other's strengths and weaknesses. There had been times, by the dozen, when we'd had to do something inherently dangerous. How many men had walked point, along the forest trails, knowing the enemy was somewhere about, when the next turn of the path might bring a man face-to-face with the black muzzle of an AK-47? How many of us had taken a deep breath and crawled into a darkened bunker? Or a tunnel, or cave, or overgrown ravine, with tight stomachs and prickly spine? How many cliffs had we rappelled, with full packs, dangling 30 or 40 feet over sharp rocks? (Well, to be honest, one. That's how many cliffs we rappelled. It was nothing I would care to repeat.) Movement in enemy territory is dangerous. Routine infantry movement, if carried out in the States during peacetime, would reduce the average civilian male to nervous exhaustion within hours.

Did I need to see Kenzy shot at to know that he would do his job under fire? Kenzy, the man who'd carried 80 pounds on his back for days, on a foot that would have rendered many men sobbing hulks within hours? Hyde's demeanor and subsequent actions, on that day he'd tripped the flare on Barbara, told me more about him in seconds than his wife would learn in years. We had seen each other react; we had seen the decision-making, the resolve, the responsibility, the fear, the courage — we'd seen it all. How realistic was all this? Let me put it this way: In the terrible month of May, when we saw more concentrated violence than almost any other unit in Viet Nam, I was to be wrong about two individuals—and they performed far better than I expected. Not a single man in whom I had confidence, at the end of that March patrol, would fail me or the others.

Most of the memories of that patrol come to me in disconnected fragments, but together, they give a flavor of the whole. The look of sick horror on Mareniewski's face as he stared at a peanut butter-covered cracker he'd bitten in half—with half a leech on top of it. The stoic patience on Andrew Hannah's dark, sweaty face as Doc Muldoon lanced an enormous boil, the size of a golf ball, on his black thumb. An overheard conversation, mumbled, diffident, half-embarrassed, between St. Onge and Olson, as they talked about their hometowns in upstate Michigan with yearning. The gritty feel of sweat and grime chafing my shoulders as we climbed one more hill; the sweetish smell of tomato sauce bubbling in the can of spaghetti being heated over a blackened field stove. The deep, pungent feel of the forest just before dawn, when the shadows magically turn from black to dark grey. The acrid, hot taste of cigarette smoke being drawn into my lungs during a break, or the crackle of laughter and endless lascivious comments when Alpha Company reported finding three crates full of bras—all 34C—in an abandoned bunker, or the quick, explosive surge of fury when Kaminski, violating platoon and Company SOP, walked with loaded and chambered rifle, tripped and let off an accidental shot that passed between me and Jones, the slack man. And there are a couple of incidents that can't be summarized in one sentence.

PFC Clark was a small, intense boy, with black eyes and heavy, curly black hair. He was stocky, well muscled, but no more than 64 inches tall. He surprised me one afternoon by confiding that he had hopes of a baseball career. The Chicago White Sox, he told me, with anxious, uncertain pride, had offered him a try out. Center field, he answered my question. He played center field.

"I don't hit for much power," he admitted, "but I sting the ball, you know? Hit it to all fields. I think I got a shot, you know? I mean, I can catch anything hit to the outfield—I got legs, you know?"

I smiled and nodded politely. But, who knows? I was a Washington Senators fan, and who of that strange breed, of the Fifties and Sixties, can forget Albie Pearson or Del Unser, neither of whom was much, if anything, over 5' 4".

And then there was the afternoon, very late in March, when I caused untold anguish to Timothy Logan. We had a long, interminable, hot wait on an LZ, waiting for a pickup that never came. With nothing to do but sit, I pulled out my current book, which happened to be *Emma*, and gave myself up to the pleasures of the cool green English countryside. It is one of my favorite novels, and as I came to the passage when Mrs. Elton picked strawberries in the hot sun, I suppose a smile came over my face. Rereading a great novel, after all, is like meeting an old friend. I forgot where I was and gave myself utterly to Jane Austen.

"Watcha got there, Ell Tee? Must be good."

I looked up to find a broad red face beaming down at me.

"It's a book," I muttered. I dislike being interrupted while reading.

I should have known that this would have no effect on Logan. "You're kinda laughin' to yourself, readin', Must be good. What's it called?"

I lifted my head to stare at him, meanwhile lifting my left eyebrow in the most pointed way possible. It did no good. No one I've ever met could possibly stare Logan down. I sighed.

"Okay. It's called *Emma*."

"Em A?"

"Emma."

"Yeah? Good book?"

"Very good."

"What's it about?"

"Oh, people. You know. Men and women."

Logan nodded sagely. "Yeah. Sex book, huh."

I smiled. "Yeah. Sort of."

He nodded his large red head. "Surprised at you, Lieutenant. Wouldna figured you for one of those guys reads cock books." Then he noticed my smile. "C'mon, Lieutenant B — you're shittin' me. What's it really about?"

"Okay. You want to know? It's about this rich, popular young woman, only 21 years old, who spends her time trying to run everyone else's life, and in particular for her younger girl friends, who she's trying to arrange marriages for, only she screws it all up and causes more harm than good, which is what her friend, who's old enough to be her older brother keeps telling her but she won't pay any attention to him because she's too full of herself until she really messes up and thinks she's arranging a marriage for this girl with one guy but finds out instead the girl thinks she's giving her the go ahead to make up to her older friend, and she realizes she loves the guy herself and things just work out in the end."

I had to rush to get the last sentence or so out, because I'd run out of breath.

Logan stood absolutely still, as if stunned. His little blue eyes darted anxiously to mine, then down to the book in my hand, and then back to me. He was waiting for me to laugh, telling him I was joking again. When I did nothing of the sort, but began reading, he made a small, uneasy sound.

"Uhhhh ... Lieutenant ... you mean ... it's a love story? Like my mother reads?"

I looked up and smiled. "Not at all. It's what's called a comedy of manners."

"Oh." I could see the alarm creep into his eyes, as he regretfully but resolutely tried and convicted me of Wimphood. I could read his thought process. *This can't be.... The guys won't believe this. Jesus ... the Ell Tee....* Finally, shaking his head, he wandered off, not without one last pleading look over his shoulder.

I resumed reading, smiling, not at Jane Austen's prose this time, but in satisfaction for at last rendering Logan speechless.

12

Dickson's Shining Moment

Song Bo Valley; 22 March 1969

We didn't get picked up that day—it was the 22nd—so we continued our trek across the valleys and low hills west of the river. The next day I received an early call from Robison. We'd been operating on our own for so long that it was a shock to hear the CO order me to rendezvous with the company at an NDP. We would be probably be extracted the following day. The coordinates he gave me were for a place almost 3,000 meters to our west, and across some tough terrain, so I wasted no time in getting the platoon up and moving. We had a long way to go. In the meantime, Dickson's Third Platoon was conducting a sweep just south of us, and would join us later.

We made good time at first, for the first hour or so, but then we ran into the first really bad terrain we'd encountered on the patrol, as I'd feared. It was a tangled web of shallow ravines, draws, twisted ridges and indistinct hills, much of it covered with the saw grass-creeper vine combination. It was nothing like The Wall, but it was bad enough.

It was early afternoon, about 1400; we were within a klick of Robison's NDP site when Jerry Wolosenko called the CO, who was moving with Dickson's platoon. He reported finding a perfect, natural LZ, on a good-sized hill, near where Alpha had found some bunkers much earlier. Jerry read off a string of letters which I decoded, and then checked the map. I cursed viciously. He was almost 4,000 meters to the east, behind us. We'd just come 2,000 tough meters in the wrong direction. I prayed that Robison would nix the idea.

Robison's voice reflected doubt; he had the same concern I had. "I don't know, Two Six. That's a long way to move. You say the LZ there is good?"

"Affirmative. It's perfect. Flat, level, not a tree in sight."

"Yeah. What about an NDP site?"

"This is Two Six. Listen, it's perfect. All of it. Plenty of water nearby, big wide LZ, and story book fields of fire." Jerry's voice reminded me of a real estate agent selling a vacation home in Arizona. Gushing enthusiasm tinged with desperation.

"Story book fields of fire, huh?" Robison sounded skeptical.

12. Dickson's Shining Moment

"Perfect. Just perfect. You'll love it. Couldn't ask for anything better. And then there's the water — nice clean pool."

"Okay. I'll take your word for it, but it better be good. Break. One Six, this is Six. Did you copy, over?"

I made no effort to hide my displeasure. Jerry was a great guy, and all that, but there are limits.

"Roger, Six. I copied. Break. Break. Two Six, this is One Six. The main advantage of this NDP site of yours wouldn't happen to be that you're standing on it, as opposed to being five klicks from the one we were all headed for, would it?"

I wasn't sure Jerry could decipher my tangled syntax, but apparently I'd been clear enough.

"Negative, One Six. Negative." Jerry was all injured innocence. "Seriously, Frank. This is really something. You'll see when you get here."

We did an abrupt and profane about face and began retracing our steps. The book says you should never go back over a recently used trail, and in general the book was right, but we really had no choice. If we were to make the Mad Russian Monk's storybook fields of fire anytime before tomorrow morning, we'd have to use the trail we'd just hacked through the saw grass and creepers. Besides, I was pissed. The platoon was pissed. Any NVA who messed with us that afternoon would do so at their own peril. We were in a decidedly foul humor.

Approximately 600 meters along, we rendezvoused with Dickson and the company CP. Robison stationed himself behind my last squad, and Dickson swung in behind the CP group, and we continued to file along the trail we'd blazed earlier.

We descended a small knoll into a saddle, and there ran into another one of those bamboo and saw grass thickets, and within seconds we were measuring progress, in Samuel's happy phrase, by the pint. My milk of human kindness had pretty well curdled much earlier in the day, so there was nothing left of it by that time. Jerry called three or four times, wondering where we were and further extolling the wonders of his LZ and NDP; by the time he was done, the place had taken on the combined magic of Manhattan's 42nd Street and a Barbados lagoon beach. Robison called approximately 47 times, wanting to know (a) when I was going to get a move on — "hell, this trail's clear; what's taking you so long?" And so it was — after the 35 men of First Platoon had hacked their way through it — and (b) had we heard movement to our left, right, rear and above, as reported by Dickson's platoon. Also, (c): Would I get the lead out of my butt because he, Robison, didn't want to be moving through the dark while surrounded by platoons of NVA. Dickson called three times, just so I could hear his voice.

I was cursing Jerry, Robison, Dickson, the Army, the NVA, Ho Chi Minh, Nixon, Johnson and the Little Sisters of the Poor when Eden shut me up very effectively.

"Hey, Lieutenant! Movement to our right — across the ridge."

We all ducked and froze. We'd finally cleared the bamboo, and were in a partial clearing, the first such we'd moved into in quite a long time. The ridge fell sharply to a thickly covered ravine, and then rose just as sharply to another ridge, double-canopied, about 100 meters away. Between the small trees, we could see the sway and rustle of leaves among the brush. There was no question something was moving over there, and it seemed to be too high off the ground to be an animal. Throat suddenly dry (*I'll be damned*, I remember thinking, *Dickson was right after all!*) I called Robison and, in whispers, telling him of our sighting.

"Roger," he whispered back, so quietly I had trouble hearing him over the hiss of static, "Can you fire on them from your position?"

"Affirm."

"Roger. Three Six, you see anything, over?"

"Negative. We're behind you."

"Okay. Three Six, move your element up to where I am, fast. One Six, deploy and wait on my command. I'm calling for air."

"Roger." I replied, but the sudden howl of static told me I hadn't gotten through. Someone else was talking. Dickson, that moron, was ignoring protocol: The man in direct contact with the enemy always has priority on the radio. In this case, it didn't matter, but the man's stupidity was going to get someone killed one of these days.

I handed the mike back to Kaminski and moved cautiously forward. I gave whispered commands to Hyde: Logan and Westman, stepping as quietly and carefully as two big men can, brought the M60 up to a large fallen tree; they laid the barrel of the weapon across the log and stretched out behind it. Carlton moved in beside them, with his M79. I was crouched alongside Westman, who was carefully and silently unpacking a belt of gleaming 7.62 ammo. Within seconds, I would report to Robison that we were ready and we'd open fire on those still-moving branches across the ravine. I took the receiver back from Kaminski.

"Six, this is Three Six." I almost jumped. Dickson's voice, coming over the radio, sounded loud and unexpected in my ear. His voice, as usual, was excited.

"Roger."

"I got movement! I got movement! Off to my left — uhh, south." His voice cracked with the tension.

"Roger." Even Robison sounded excited. South? The movement we were seeing was to our north. Were we surrounded?

"Roger that. I can see somethin'. 'Bout one hundred meters to our left, across this valley...."

One hundred meters across a valley? To his left? I gave a snort of disgust. "Hold up, Lo," I said.

"Jesus Christ!" Even as I was saying that, Logan was shaking his head. His eyes had picked out the unmistakable outline of helmets and rucksacks, moving through the brush.

"Six, this is One Six."

"Roger. You ready, One Six?"

"I'm ready to put a boot up Three Six's ass. Shit. Double shit. That's Three Six over on the other ridge. I can see him."

"Three Six? Hell, no! He's right behind me!"

"Negative. Come up here and see for yourself. Break. Three Six, did you copy? That's us you're looking at. I say again, that is First Platoon you're seeing. Do not fire, over."

"Negative! Negative! That's NVA! I can see 'em! I can see 'em!"

Fuck this, I thought. I was furious. I jumped up on the log, putting me in clear view. A moment later, Robison hurried up. He stood beside me and looked across the ravine. By now, some of the Three Six people were showing themselves, and stood gazing across the ravine at us. One or two waved.

Robison's face was an ominous red. He took his mike from Conzoner. "Three Six, this is Six. Stand down. Do you copy?"

"Three Six. Negative, Six. We got contact. I can see 'em."

"STAND THE FUCK DOWN!"

"Uhh, roger."

"How the hell did you get on that ridge, Three Six?"

There was a long moment's silence. Then: "Uh, this is Three Six. We're on the right ridge. One Six must be lost, over."

Robison and I exchanged looks. I would have opened fire on Dickson but he had too many good men near him.

"This is Six. One Six is where he's supposed to be. Get your ass back down to the trail; I'll have an element from One Six back there to guide you back up to us. Do you copy, over." The last four words were spaced out, and shot through Robison's clenched teeth like bullets.

Eventually, we moved on. It also— naturally; what else were we lacking?— began to rain. By now, there was no doubt that we would not make Wolosenko's position before dark. Movement was stop-and-go, because the terrain suddenly turned vicious on us, and Robison called every two or three minutes, wanting to know where and when. Jerry called again, sounding amused. He'd overheard the recent fiasco, and was inclined to make light of it. After about half an hour of this, I could stand no more.

"Kaminski."

"Yeah, Lieutenant?"

"Turn that fucking thing off."

"Sir?"

"The radio." I pointed to it. "Turn it off, *now*."

He looked at me doubtfully but did as he was told.

Two hours later, long after sunset but before the heavy grey rain clouds had turned completely dark, we stumbled up a slight incline onto a broad, reed-covered hill. I looked around me in consternation. There was not one shred of cover on the whole damned hill. There was not one single incline or rise that would have slowed an arthritic grandmother. There was nothing on that hill but acres of rain-slicked reeds, about two or three feet high. To our south, west and east were high ridges, looming black and ominous in the near night.

"Hiya doin', Frank. Finally made it, I see," Jerry Wolosenko, looking dry, calm and rested, stood in front of his prepared hutch, smiling and holding a canteen cup full of hot chocolate, from the smell. Jerry gave me a smile of pure affectionate brotherhood.

"You son of a bitch!" I spat out.

His eyes popped in surprise. "Wha...?"

"You moron!" My voice rose. "*This* is what I just humped five klicks through a goddamn bamboo patch for? *This* is the goddamned story book field of fire you've been yapping about?" I waved an outraged arm. "*This* is the fucking Shangri-La you've been promising us?" My voice by now had reached full throttle, up around D over middle C and as loud as I can get. Strident. That's a good word.

"What's the matter?" Jerry looked about, all wounded innocence. "What's wrong with this place?"

"What's wrong with it? What's *right* with it? This is the most miserable —"

"What *is* this shit?" Robison, eyes popping, mouth set in a furious downturned U, came striding up to us. His eyes kept shifting back and forth between us. He didn't know whom to scream at first.

"What the hell is wrong with your radio?" He finally asked.

"I turned it off," I replied coldly. "It wasn't working. All I got over it was meaningless gibberish."

"Yeah." He glared at me. He knew damn well I'd turned it off and why. He swung around to face Wolosenko. "Are you shitting me? *This* is your idea of a perfect NDP?"

"What the hell's wrong with it?" Jerry was exasperated now. "Look." He swept the now-dark horizon with his hand. "Not an inch of cover in sight. NVA can't bring a jackrabbit through here without us seeing him. What's wrong with that?"

"What the hell are *we* supposed to do for cover, you goddamned rat-fuck Russian?" I think it was the sight of Jerry standing there with the steam from his hot chocolate still curling over the rim of the cup that infuriated both of us. Robison was about to expand on his remarks when Dickson wandered by.

"You!" Robison yelped in rage. "You goddamned idiot son of a bitch, how the *hell* can you lose contact with the CP group? You nearly got some people killed out there today!"

Dickson stopped, a look of combined petulance, tepid arrogance and trepidation on his face. "It wasn't my fault! Bo here took the wrong turn! I —"

The next several minutes could charitably be described as emotional. There was a singular lack of brotherhood and good feeling among the officers of Bravo Company that night. I went on to my own CP a little later, having calmed down, or so I thought. I did notice that Sergeant Wright placed himself between me and Third Platoon's position, and kept a wary eye on me all night.

12. Dickson's Shining Moment

The following morning, wet, stiff, chilled and sore — in every sense of the word — we moved out, at first light, crossing a broad flat plain to our north. Treeless and reed-covered, it was simply an extension of that low hill we'd spent the night on. We moved easily through the reeds for an hour, and then, in one of the truly Herculean efforts of my tour, we climbed the flank of Hill 105, which juts straight up from the plain along the banks of the Song Bo. Straight up. One hundred and five meters is a mere bagatelle, when compared to the two and three thousand-meter summits to our west, but that is still over 300 feet, and straight up means just that. It took us three hours to make the climb, with 90 or so pounds on our backs.

When we did reach the top, we were afforded one of the rarities of life in the mountain forests: A panoramic view. The Song Bo meandered its way across the valley, in classic ox-bow turns, to our west, north and east. Sighting along the general path of the valley, to our northeast, we could make out the steep mass on which stood Firebase Strike, perhaps five or six klicks away. Looking southeast, we could plainly see our NDP of the previous night, and had a splendid view of Nui Khe Thai, another massive and steep hill. Between the Hill 105 and the Khe Thai was the Ngoc Ke Trai, the small stream along which we had spent the night — it skirted the broad hill and Jerry's Story Book Fields of Fire — and which flowed west and north into the Song Bo. To our south were the low, rolling forested hills we'd spent the previous weeks in, including Hill 154, whose broad trails and bunkers were hidden under the smoky green carpet of trees.

It was just past noon, and the sun, softened by the high haze, lay lightly on the land like a thin sheet of yellow gossamer. I smiled in appreciation, my chest still heaving from the climb. It was one of those rare scenes of beauty and mystery — the far vistas and the solitary, proud-standing hills beckoning like sirens across a green sea. I lingered for a minute or so, while the platoon moved through. Moments like this were so few.

Plans changed as I stood there. Instead of descending the north slope, as we'd intended, we were ordered back along the way we'd come, back toward Hill 154. Alpha Company, again, had run into contact, including, this time, .51 caliber machine guns. That raised the level of interest considerably. Trail watchers and scouts do not carry Fifty Ones with them.

We hurried toward Alpha as fast as we could, which was not all that fast, at that. Robison told me to resume my anchor position, a klick behind the company. Weeks later, we would admit to each other that this was not the brightest tactic we'd ever tried. Splitting a company as we'd done earlier made sense, when we thought we were facing small units. But the .51 is not a small-unit weapon. What we did bordered on folly. A likely scenario was this: The NVA would insert a small force between me and the company. Choosing a suitable spot, they would hit my lead element hard, with small arms fire and RPGs, pinning us down. Robison would turn the company and hurry back down the trail, to reach us. And run right into a full ambush, of company size or larger, hidden along the trail. There was nothing far-fetched about that: These were precisely the tactics that both the VC and the NVA had practiced all through the war. And while our air power and artillery would eventually drive them off, we stood a very good chance of losing a lot of men, to include, I realized, a certain handsome, dark-haired lieutenant from the tree-lined cobblestone streets of Georgetown. Nope, it wasn't a bright move.

Nothing happened however, except for late than night, after we'd settled into an NDP. Four 122mm rockets landed in our vicinity, ironically coming from Nui Khe Thai, the hill I'd admired earlier. None of them came close enough to do any damage, although we did suffer a casualty when Mareniewski cut himself on the jagged edge of a C-ration can he was opening when the first rocket hit. I suppose that qualifies as contact.

All good things end, and this patrol did the following day. Robison radioed me at dawn to tell me to rejoin the company because we were at long last going to be extracted. Late that morning, we set up on a ridge overlooking a tributary of the Song Bo; the proposed PZ was on the flank of the ridge. I sent Hyde on a recon to locate it, and he returned less than an hour later with news that he'd found a huge, football field-sized clearing less than 500 meters away. We settled down in contentment. We were in place, and the rest of the company had a hike to get to us. Perfect.

Around 1400, Robison called. The extraction mow was scheduled for 0700 the next morning. We were to hold in place; he, along with Second and Third Platoons, would set up an NDP on the same ridge but a few hundred meters away. I acknowledged, and we spent the rest of the day resting in the shade of the forest ridge.

At 0630 the next morning, as we were winding our way along the easy trail to the PZ Hyde had located the day before, Robison got a call from the S3 that sent him up a tree: extraction was delayed. His curses could be heard for miles. Move to the PZ, he said, and wait in place. Out.

I shrugged. This neither surprised nor bothered me. We were only 100 meters or so from the PZ by then. Putting out security, we flopped down and prepared to wait.

I'd started a new book, *Michel, Michel*, and it was a long one, about 500 pages. I was only on page 50, but I tackled it anyway, expecting to get only part way through it. At 1430, I started a second book, *Terrible Swift Sword*. One thing about the ladies from the Clarksville Free Will Baptist Church: Their reading tastes were certainly eclectic.

Word finally came, at 1600: Prepare for extraction. We saddled up and made our leisurely way down to the PZ, only minutes away. When we got there, I looked at it appreciatively. It was everything Hyde had said: Big, featureless, grass-covered, with not a fallen log or boulder to mar its dark green surface. It was perfect. Except for one thing.

It was the wrong one.

By the time we got that straightened out — Jerry was sitting on the right PZ, an almost identical meadow some 200 meters north of us — it was almost 1800. It didn't matter that much, because it was still an easy move for us, and from Jerry's point of view it was a godsend. He'd had to listen to a substantial number of witticisms from me about his Story Book Fields of Fire, and he had reason to hope that this would shut me up. It didn't, actually.

13

Father Haney's Lament

Camp Evans; 25 March 1969

Twenty-two days in the field, and at last, a stand-down. We were flown to Firebase Rakkasan, were picked up within the hour and taken to Evans, where we found hot (*hot!!!!*) showers, clean clothes and empty bunks waiting for us. The first touch of that hot water on my shoulders, and the feel of it running down my back, offered me a glimpse into the orgiastic rites of Pan: Sheer, unconstrained, voluptuous luxury.

A shave followed, and then a reflective cigarette, before I walked back to the company HQ. My rucksack, filthy, stained, still stinking from the field, lay by the CO's office door. I debated whether to unpack it and clean it out — I wasn't positive but I suspected an open can of peanut butter was lodged in one of the side pockets, buried under my compass, spare bootstraps and a strobe light — but then I decided against it. I was clean, for once, and it was too dirty.

I joined the others in the CO's office; someone had placed a tub of ice and Pepsi by his desk. Jerry reached down and offered me one as I sat beside him. I wasn't particularly fond of Pepsi, or any other soda, for that matter, but I drank that one with deep satisfaction. I couldn't remember the last time I'd tasted a cold drink.

Our conversation, while we waited, was desultory and constrained. Jerry and I loved ribbing each other, but we avoided doing so when Dickson was present, because of the very real danger that he would take one side against the other, which was intolerable. We had tried, but had never been able to disabuse Dickson of the notion that he was one of us. After his performance of the last week, when he'd taken the wrong ridge and almost precipitated a fratricide, even casual conversation with him was more than I was willing to do. Besides, there was little to do at this point but speculate.

Robison entered as he always did, profanely, loudly and emphatically. He sat at his chair behind his desk, leaned over, rummaged in the bucket and screamed in outrage.

"Shit! There isn't a goddamned drink in this shittin' thing. You bastards drank every goddamned one of them!"

Jerry frowned. "Hell, there're plenty of drinks left, Robbie," he protested. He pulled out a Pepsi and offered it to him.

Robison glared. "I said a fucking *drink*, not that shit. TOP!" he bellowed.

Garza stuck his head around the corner. "Sir?"

"Top! Where's my goddamned beer?"

Garza's Aztec face was unmoved. "No beer, Cap'n. Colonel's orders."

Robbie's eyes popped, not hard to do since they always protruded anyway. "Fuck the colonel! Top, you get me some beer or by God you'll be back with a platoon tomorrow — on a fuckin' thirty-day RIF!"

"Yes, sir." Garza nodded and withdrew.

Robison shifted his attention to the three of us. "Well, that was a rat-fuck operation if I've ever seen one," he snorted.

"Terrible command-and-control," I agreed. "Worst I've ever seen." Despite his yelling, I judged that Robbie was actually in a good mood — as who wouldn't be, after a hot shower and clean clothes for the first time in months? I thought he could take a bit of kidding. Of course, if I was wrong, I was in for a tirade but life is risk.

"Shit," Robison snorted again. "What am I supposed to command? A regular Chinese fire drill: One of my goddamned platoon leaders gets his ass lost and doesn't even know it, and damn near gets his sorry ass shot up by his own side, and another takes all fuckin' day to move 500 meters, and the third sets up an NDP on some wheat field with story book fields of fire and high ground all around us. The only fuckin' command I shoulda given that night was for you all to form an inward circle and commence firing."

Jerry smiled thinly. He was going to get awfully sick and tired about the "story book fields of fire" before his tour was over. He'd already taken a lot of grief over it, mainly, to be honest, from his good friend One Six.

"It was a rat-fuck," Robison continued. "I never saw such piss-poor navigation in my — yeah? What do *you* want?"

We turned out heads. Leanahan, the Commo/supply NCO, was standing in the door. He'd taken over the supply job as well as his own when Sandler left, unlamented. "Good evening, Cap'n," he said pleasantly.

Leanahan was our local phenomenon. Every army unit larger than a company has one. Sergeant Bilko was fiction, but he could have been modeled on any one of 1,000 NCOs. He is the fixer, the Man in the Know, the dealer, the Ace, the dude with the pull, the Provider, the one individual who rises above rank and position and organization and has things his way.

Is your unit stationed in northeast Alaska, with daytime temperatures in the minus thirties, and inadequate sleeping bags? Leanahan has somehow finagled the first and only experimental arctic sleeping gear, rated for minus 100-degree temperatures. Is your unit on a desert patrol, with nothing to drink but warm water, and only mouthfuls of that? Leanahan has a locker full of cold Budweiser. Has your unit been stationed on a deserted island 1,000 miles from the nearest land? Squeals and feminine giggles can be heard coming from Leanahan's hutch.

13. Father Haney's Lament

In our company, Leanahan was the Commo NCO; there might exist, in all the armed forces, a softer job, but it's hard to imagine it. And few offered what his job did: Being in the rear, with the company spending 350 days a year in the field, with no permanent XO and only the supply clerks and the company clerk for company, he had pretty much an open checkbook. It was a mystery, but at any given moment any type of rotary-winged craft could land on the battalion pad — sleek, deadly Cobras, unmarked Hueys, ungainly Chinooks, LOHs, Sikorskis, even a civilian craft. Leanahan's short, dumpy form would then be observed running along the wind-swept ground, mysterious satchel in one hand and his non-regulation Australian bush hat pinned to his head by the other. A swirl of dust, and the craft would lift off, bound for — where? No one — no one, including Top — knew. Hours, or days, later, he would return, round face smiling, carrying his satchel, now a trifle thicker and heavier, and radiating bland self-satisfaction.

Leanahan was tolerated because he had long since discovered the secret of survival for one in his line of work: Keep the CO and the first sergeant happy. There was, for sure, not a single legal case of beer anywhere in the battalion area, this side of the Brigade NCO club, but Top would have some beer for Robison in a few minutes.

Despite that, or perhaps because of it, Robison didn't much care for Leanahan — none of us did — and his greeting was less than cordial. "I'm fine, Leanahan. What do you need?"

Leanahan's round baby face creased in a smile that never reached his bright little pig eyes. "Nothing, Captain, not a thing. Heard you all had a good time, this trip."

Robison started to glare at him, remembered the beer, and thought better of it. "Right. Real good. We're busy, Sergeant. Check with me tomorrow morning about those new PRC 25s, will you?"

Leanahan beamed and nodded. "Sure thing, Cap'n." I was reminded, incongruously, that Leanahan had once confided to me that he was an original member of the first Hell's Angels club in Oklahoma. "Uh, one more thing, Cap'n. I got some great flicks the other day. Some real Tijuana Oscar-winners. I was gonna show 'em in that hutch over by Delta's area — the empty one, by the berm."

"You mean the one right across the from Recon Platoon's hutch?" Robison asked.

"Yup. These are good, clean skin flicks like mother used to make, Cap'n. Y'all gonna come?"

Dickson snickered. "We will if we see 'em," he said. He looked around to make sure we got the joke. "They real hot pussies, Wally?"

Leanahan nodded. "The best, Lieutenant. The best. The hottest and the best. Starts at 2000. Uh — Cap'n: In order to defray some expenses, I'm chargin' a dollar a head, but you and the lieutenants get in free, 'course. See you there?"

Robison nodded. "Maybe. We'll see."

Leanahan grinned and disappeared. While Robison fumbled at his desk, looking for something, Jerry leaned over to me and whispered.

"You going?"

I grimaced scornfully. "You serious?"

Jerry grinned. "No."

"What?" Dickson crowed. "You two little goodie-two-shoes too holy for that? Scared of seein' a real man-sized dick?"

Jerry laughed. "The only thing those flicks have that's man-sized are the women. They drag the back streets of Tijuana for the fattest, drunkest, ugliest whores in Mexico and shove a glass of tequila and a five-dollar bill in their hand. The man is a condemned criminal; he's given a choice: This or the firing squad. The sensible ones take the bullet. There's your cast. Plus they use hand-cranked cameras from the Twenties and candlelight. No thanks."

Whatever Dickson was going to say in rebuttal was lost, sadly, by the entrance of Garza, carrying a case of warm beer. Dumping the soda cans out, he tossed as many beers as the bucket would hold into the rapidly melting ice.

"Der' you go, Cap'n" he said.

But Robison had time for only one beer before we were called to an impromptu briefing by Black Jack; a call that left Robbie—and us also—apprehensive about the possibility of a change of plans for the next few days. He was so upset he swept the cards from his desk onto the floor with a loud curse. As it turned out, that wasn't the reason for the meeting, and we filed back in to the office 90 minutes later.

We talked briefly, and with feelings of real empathy, about the horror that Captain Harkins had just gone through at the meeting; two of his troopers had been sent to the 22nd with high fevers, and that's all Dr. Kildare needed to tear Alpha Six a new one. Add to that the report that a third Alpha trooper had been admitted with a badly infected toenail, and Black Jack spread himself pretty wide and high.

Still, Harkins and the rest of us made it out of there in one piece. Robbie insisted that we hold a foot inspection first thing next morning. And from now on, he added, if any of our men ever demonstrated a temperature over 99°, we were to take him out behind a tree and shoot him. Better that than another case of "malaria."

That started it. His face took on that patient, long-suffering look, and I groaned. He had embarked on his favorite theme.

"Now, when we get to the Rak, I want my platoon leaders to hump their asses this time, instead of sitting around playing cards all day." He paused while Jerry, with perfect timing, dropped the cards he'd just picked up from the floor onto the CO's desk. Robison ignored him.

"Last time," he went on, "you guys remember: we got our asses reamed for just about every mickey-mouse piece of crap you can think of. Discarded soda cans in the barbed wire. Butts on the bunker floor. Men on duty without their shirts and helmets. Food in the bunkers—every little chicken-shit thing that he could find. By the same token, I want you to make sure your bunker's as clean as you can get it, this time. I mean, last time, it was a fuckin' disgrace, the way you left it. And you, Bo: you left your claymore wires disconnected and trailin' all over the—"

13. Father Haney's Lament

"That wasn't First Platoon," I said firmly. "You know —"

"That's what I mean!" Robison interrupted my interruption. "That's it. Right there. So what if it wasn't your shit? Think about the company, for a change! You got 30 guys to worry about. By the same token, I got 130. Shit! If you guys had to deal with half the shit I do, you'd...."

Jerry snuck me a look, winking. Robbie was off and running. We settled ourselves back for a good, long wait, wearing suitably blank expressions, but this time he was cut short, before he'd really gotten going, by the entrance of Sergeant Garza, whose hard brown Mexican face showed five parts genuine concern and one part awe.

"Der you are, sir! Where you been?"

Robison stopped in mid-sentence, swung his feet of the desk and straightened in his chair, alarmed by Garza's expression and tone of voice.

"We've been over at the briefing, Top. What's up?"

Garza slipped into the office and closed the door behind him. "All kinda shit, Cap'n. You remember Leanahan an' 'is movie?"

"Yeah. So?"

Garza licked his lips. He really *was* worried. "Well, de chapl'n, 'e's walkin' round, li'l while 'go, n' 'e sees dese lights comin' dis buildin' — de one Black Jack tol' 'im 'e could use for 'is chapel."

Garza at least had a fighting chance of keeping his face impassive. Robison didn't have a prayer. His eyes popped and his jaw hung. "You mean to tell me that that dumb son of a bitch picked the *chapel* to show his goddamned skin flicks?"

Garza nodded solemnly. "Yes, sir. 'N de chapl'in walks in an' see dis movie — 'e was mad, sir. Piss'. Beaucoup piss'. So 'e call Brigade. De colonel."

Robison's mouth worked open and closed, rapidly. "Colonel *Conmy's* already heard about it, for chrissakes?"

"Yes, sir. I trie' talk to 'im, but 'e didn' lissen." Garza paused. "It was Major 'aney, sir."

Robison, who'd been working his way up to a supreme bellow, blinked, stunned. "Haney?" he whispered. "Again? Chaplain Haney?"

"Yes, sir." Garza looked unhappy. He hesitated, and then shrugged. Much as it pained him, he decided that Robison needed to know the worst. "'E was beaucoup, beaucoup mad; not jus' 'bout de movie, but, see, Leanahan, 'e put some new cherry at de door, didn' know the chapl'in. So de stupid sommbitch try to collec' a dolla' from 'im — de chapl'in."

Robison sat down, heavily. His eyes still protruded, and his mouth was open, but he made no sound. Wolosenko and I struggled manfully to keep our faces properly deadpan and sympathetic. I could feel Jerry shaking with the effort. We watched appreciatively as the full beauty of the situation began to register on Robison's face. Of all the chaplains in the brigade, the last one Robison could have wanted to deal with in this case was Haney. First, there had been the incident on Helen, when Garza had called the troops to Mass with a profanity-laced tirade from the top of the ridge. Then, there was the Abbot case, and then after that ... Bravo—and Robison—had a long, sad, unfortunate history with Father Haney. Robison's respect for the cloth was already suspect, after the Helen fiasco, and now, to find the men of Bravo leering at a dirty movie in the building designated as the chapel ... well, Haney was really a tolerant guy, but enough, he'd decided, was enough. And now Conmy was involved...

Garza was still shaking his head. There was more.

"Sommbitch walk' in at a bad time," he went on. "De men at de door, dey tell me: Momen' 'aney walk in, dere dese two big balls, red as a spank' baby's ass, jus' 'angin' dere on de screen" Garza held his hands out to either side. "Sommbitch musta been five, six feet across. Each."

That was the end for Jerry and me. He started making urgent, harsh sounds, shoulders shaking, head bent to the floor. I was pressing my elbows into my sides, trying desperately to keep it in but it was no use. A moment later the two of us whooped out loud, bent over and gasping. I dropped to my knees and laid my head against the desk; Jerry was pressing one hand against his jaw and the other to his stomach. The look on Robison's face was that of a man who'd just stepped on a rake and had the handle slam him between the eyes. As our laughter mounted, his eyes narrowed and he sent an angry, resentful glare our way.

"What the fuck are you two laughing at?" he yelled. "And you too, Dickson. You're all in this, too. And so's that fuckin' XO of mine—where *is* that son of a bitch? Where the hell was he—WILL YOU TWO FOR CHRISSAKES SHUT UP!"

I buried my head in my elbow, trying to stop, but after a second my shoulders started shaking again and I was laughing harder than before. The image of those two large red testicles splayed across the screen ... I was helpless.

Robison started to yell some more but he closed his mouth with a snap and switched his glare back to Garza. "Top, get me that son of a bitch," he said between his teeth. "Bring him to me right now. I'm gonna tear him a new asshole. I'm gonna slice his balls off and feed 'em to him. I'm gonna rip his heart out and flush it down the toilet!"

Garza nodded glumly. "You mean Lean'n, Cap'n?"

Robison exploded. "You're goddamned right I mean Leanahan! Who the fuck do you think I want—the Pope?"

Garza opened his mouth to reply but Jerry beat him to it. "Under the circumstances," he said, straining to keep his voice from cracking, "I feel mention of His Holiness is in poor taste at this time."

"Shut up, Wolosenko!" Robison glared at Garza, who still stood there. "Well?"

"'E not 'ere," he said reluctantly."

"I know he's not here! That's why I want you to haul his ass down here!"

"I mean, Cap'n, 'e not 'ere at Evans. 'E gone."

Robison opened his mouth in a soundless scream of outrage. "Gone!" His voice cracked when he finally was able to speak. "Gone? Where —" Robison shut off abruptly. Pausing to take a deep breath, he let it out slowly. "Where is he?" he asked, quietly.

"'E lef' right afta de chapl'in walk in de movie ... 'e 'ad bizzness at Eagle."

Robison swallowed. "It's 2200, Top. How'd he get from Evans to Eagle at this time of night?"

"Way I 'ear it, sir, sommbitch, 'e 'itched a ride wid a medvac on its way to de Twen' Secon.'"

Robison, who'd stood up, sat back down again, heavily. He closed his eyes, briefly and then opened them again. Speaking in a low, tight voice, he said, "I'm gonna shoot that bastard if it's the last thing I do. I swear to God I'm gonna shoot 'im. No. I'll put his ass in the field and the let the NVA shoot 'im." He smiled at the thought. "I'll make him walk point in the A Shau. I'll make him crawl through every tunnel and bunker in 'Nam. I'll make him disarm booby traps with his *teeth*."

Garza shook his head sorrowfully. He hated to interrupt the CO's fun, but ... "One mor' t'ing, Cap'n. De colonel, 'e want to see you. Firs' 't'ing, tomorr' mornin'."

Robison's jaw twitched. "Who? Conmy?"

Garza nodded.

"Why?"

Garza made a gesture with his right hand, but said nothing.

Once again, I was in imminent danger of bursting out. I suppose I should have been more sympathetic, but the day he'd had First Platoon chasing the CP all over the AO was still fresh in my mind. And besides, while I was sure that tomorrow's meeting with the brigade commander would be decidedly uncomfortable, I doubted that Robbie was in any serious danger. There are hundreds of reasons for relieving a company commander in combat, but this probably wasn't one of them. Still, there was little doubt Conmy would announce his displeasure.

Jerry must have had the same thoughts as I, only he carried them one step further. At least I was willing to just sit and grin. Jerry decided to rattle the CO's chain even more.

"That's going to be some interview tomorrow morning," he said softly.

Robison glared but said nothing.

"Yes, sir. I can just see it. The Old Man here is going to march up to the colonel's office, the colonel is going to demand an explanation, and do you know what our CO is going to say?"

"No," I said, "what's he going to say?"

"He's going to look the colonel right in the eye, and he's going to say: 'Colonel Conmy, sir. I cannot tell a lie. It was my mistake in judgment that led to this, and I accept full responsibility. If I'd only listened to my platoon leaders—particularly Lieutenant Wolosenko, the handsome, intelligent one—none of this would have happened. It is my fault and mine alone that Bravo has screwed the pooch.' There won't be a dry eye in the house."

Robison scowled in irritation. "Fuck you guys. And get out of here."

We left him glaring at the desktop. Squeezing by Sergeant Garza, who was eyeing us reproachfully, we walked through the morning room and into the supply room in the rear, where Jerry commandeered Leanahan's padded reclining chair. I sat in one of the smaller but still comfortable padded chairs by Leanahan's desk. It really was remarkable what the man could scrounge. Dickson did us the enormous favor of leaving.

We laughed some more, but we also agreed that Robison's career wasn't in real jeopardy. Had Colonel Conmy really been pissed, Robbie would be on the carpet this minute.

"You think Leanahan's gone—for good?" I asked.

Jerry shrugged. "Maybe—but probably not. That guy has nine lives. I mean, he could be down at G1, right now, getting orders cut for the 82nd, but he's got it good here. And you know Robbie better than I do. He'll calm down."

"Yeah. Maybe." I grinned. "It's been a good evening, hasn't it?"

Jerry smiled his sad, sweet smile. "Sure has."

14

Dennis Helms, Bravo One Six Romeo

Firebase Rakkasan; 25–29 March 1969

There were more changes. For one thing, I lost Hyde, by far my best squad leader, to R&R. (*Australia, Lieutenant B! Australia! Reckon I might not come back.*) Wright and I decided that Eden simply wasn't capable of running a squad. Nevertheless, we moved him into the first squad, to serve as squad leader until Hyde's return. We made that clear to Eden, and he was inclined to pout, but Wright put it best: "You already lost your squad. You screw this up, an' I'll take your stripes."

Evans and Nelson, both Spec4, took over the other squads. This was a bit tricky, since waiting for us at Evans had been three new shake-and-bake E5s—Drozd, Burnetta and Dickerson—but we never even considered making one of them squad leader. Having an E5 with stripes on his sleeve report to an E4 was a bit awkward, but it was all we could do.

We lost some people to DEROS or transfer—Denholm had a grim smile as he handed me the 1049s—but we gained a couple, in addition to our E5s. A sandy haired, wrinkle-faced youngster from western Georgia, named Wright, and a taller, heavy-faced man named Besack. Sergeant Wright wrote PFC Wright's name down in our notebook without comment.

One other loss: Kaminski went to Second Platoon, at his own request. Jerry agreed. Although Kaminski could be a handful—he was a bit immature and unrealistic—he could be a good soldier if he tried.

Rumors floated through the company that morning. Denholm was ecstatic about the first one: All XOs would be returned to the field as platoon leaders.

The other rumor was less positive, from a personal point of view. Jerry was slated to go to S3. Actually, his name wasn't mentioned, but the word was that Raffaele had told the S1 that Bravo would need a new lieutenant, because one of theirs would be joining his staff. Well, that was a no-brainer. It wasn't Denholm; he'd have heard about it and anyway, he was begging to get away from the field, not stay in the rear. Me? Certainly not. Aside from the fact that I didn't want to leave the field and my platoon, there was the little matter of Black Jack. Horned demons would be holding snowball fights in Hell before Honeycutt accepted me on his staff, where he might have to see me every day. Dickson? I grinned. I would be named Army Chief of Staff before Dickson was placed in S3. I would be very sorry to see Jerry go. Not only was he a friend, but about 90 percent of the fun would go with him.

Rakkasan welcomed us back. There was work to be done. After one day, Logan proposed that the Army strike a new medal, a sandbag with crossed shovels, to be awarded to the trooper who distinguished himself in the art of filling.

With Kaminski gone, I needed a new RTO. St. Onge was now the senior RTO, but I hesitated. He was working with Wright, who was satisfied with him, and I had my eye on a tall young North Carolinian named Helms. He was a slow talking, quiet man, well liked in his squad, and he was big, or at least tall, about six feet. That's important in choosing an RTO. The PRC25 weighs about 25 pounds in itself, and the spare batteries add another four or eight — that, on top of his own gear. The only break an RTO got was that he was normally exempt from having to carry extra ammo, ropes, starlight scopes or any of the other odds and ends that added 10 to 15 pounds to a trooper's pack.

Helms was sturdy enough to carry it, and he seemed willing enough, when I asked him. "Third time's the charm" is one of those folk sayings that I have always found particularly imbecilic, but in this case that was exactly the case. His personality fit right into the CP and enhanced it greatly. His quiet, dignified determination perfectly offset Muldoon's sharp-edged candor and my tendency to the dramatic. Wright took to him immediately; he later told me that he wished he'd taken Helms first, back when he had the chance. St. Onge welcomed the change, too. He'd suffered under Kaminski's domineering self-promotion, particularly when it came to watch schedules and work details. Helms was far more equitable in temperament.

Dennis was my RTO for only a few days more than two months, but when I think back on the platoon, when I called to mind a particular day or incident, it was always Dennis' arm that was extended with the receiver held out, and it was his face that frowned in concentration over his tuning dial. I

Dennis Helms, my RTO, taking a break (courtesy Dennis Helms).

would have to remind myself that the event I was recalling had happened in February, or early March — it couldn't be Helms I saw.

Rakkasan wore on us quickly. Logan was right; the sandbag had replaced the rifle as our most common instrument of war. A couple of amenities had been added since our last visit: The mess had not only been reopened but had been extended. They even had an officer's mess tent now, alongside the other. The portable showers were now permanent, and several of the interior buildings, including the company CPs, now had electricity from a generator. But at the end of the day, these improvements, although appreciated, did little to improve conditions beyond the barely tolerable. The mess tent was nice, and it felt great to put my hand around a real mug of coffee, and feel its warmth on a cold wet morning, but the eggs were still powdered and the milk had never gone through an udder, and shit on a shingle is still just that.

The shower suffered from one major drawback — lack of water. It had to be hauled in from Evans, in huge containers slung under a Chinook 27, and they couldn't keep up with the requirements of well over 150 men. Besides, there is another basic problem with the showers we had. They were gravity fed, basically large tanks on a frame under which the men stood, pulled a handle, and dumped water in a thin drizzle over themselves. And therein lay the problem. On one of those unbearable hot days, when the sun was punishing us with 105° heat, and we would have committed battery to feel cool water over our faces and torsos, the sun brought the water in the overhead tanks to a near boil; it could actually be scalding hot. On the other hand, if the southwest winds brought the cold rain and temperatures in the fifties, when a hot shower was my one wish in life, then the water would be a chilly 60 or 65 degrees.

But it was neither the mess hall nor the showers that made Rakkasan our bane. The work was never ending: Fill sandbags, lay them in place around the bunkers, cut down vegetation in front of the barbed wire, lay more barbed wire, clean out bunkers, string out telephone lines, fill sandbags, fill in old latrines, dig new latrines, string out concertina wire, put out claymores and trip flares, take up old claymores and flares, fill sandbags, send out LPs, police the perimeter, clean the TOC and the mess tent and aid station, fill sandbags, clean the showers, go on RIFs around the perimeter, fill sandbags...

By the time a week had passed, the troops were ready for a 50-day operation. So were we. The one magnificent thing about the field is that as long as you are on a routine mission, no one knows or cares where you are, and above all, no one comes paying a visit.

It often seemed that every officer in Viet Nam above the rank of lieutenant colonel descended on Rakkasan to inspect it. Sometimes two or even three Hueys, distinctive because of their polish and doors and seats, so different from our work-worn stripped-down slicks, would flutter into the LZ and out would pop a general and two or three colonels, fatigues fresh and pressed, boots polished a soft ebony, insignia and name tags glinting bright and conspicuous in the sun. And there we stood, grubby and dusty and scruffy, in that same sun, looking for all the world as if we were in a different army. And, in fact, we were.

It quickly became apparent to us that, with one or two exceptions, the inspections were of the most trivial and superficial kind. Rarely were we asked about real deficiencies in equipment, weapons, supplies, tactics or morale. Seldom were our answers even listened to. There was one exception: A tough, razor-faced senior colonel, with infantry insignia and an attitude, stood me in the sun for a full half an hour, asking probing, pointed questions on First Platoon's proficiency with our weapons, reliability of our ammunition, communications problems with our radios, my training program, and a concise description of our tactical movement. He refused to accept generalizations or evasions, demanding full and relevant answers, and wanted to know what really was taking place, and not what I thought he wanted to hear. By the time he was through with me, I was almost limp.

But that colonel was an exception. Had there been more like him ... but there weren't. Most of the visitors walked around, hands behind their backs, bodies leaning slightly forward in the classic pose of the Field Commander Reviewing the Troops. Those who were in a good humor or otherwise kindly disposed would stop by a group of working troopers and ask an affable and meaningless question or two. Those who weren't so disposed would stalk the base, eyes searching for something, anything, to raise hell with Black Jack about. It is a measure of the inanity of these men that these discrepancies had nothing to do with firebase security, weapons proficiency, fields of fire, placement of mines and shape charges, bunker layout or anything else that might contribute to the death of an enemy or the safety of a GI. Instead, a general's outrage would be triggered by a coke can in front of a bunker, or a shirt, doffed by a sweating trooper filling sandbags, draped carelessly over a radio antenna, or maybe the most capital crime of all, an unshaven face. These senior officers might not know how to drive the enemy from the A Shau, but, by God, they knew how to deal with *that*.

General would turn, frowning, to Colonel, who would speak in glacial tones to Lieutenant Colonel, who would call over the captain, who would immediately scurry off looking for the platoon leader responsible, whose first act would be to demand an explanation from his platoon sergeant, who would grab the nearest trooper unlucky enough to be around and curse him expertly while he removed the offending item. Had things ended there, it might not have been so bad, but they rarely did. Like sharks who've tasted blood, they went on a mindless feeding frenzy for the next half hour or so, ranting and raving while the rest of the firebase was subjected to a minute and probing search for discarded cigarette butts or other acts of high treason.

Eventually, general and colonels would mount their shiny air busses, amidst a swirl of dust and wind (which, on one memorable occasion, blew half the contents of the trash dump across the bunker line) and return to their air conditioned quarters at Division or Corps or MACV, there to write scathing reports and plan their next descent into the lower regions. Left in their wake would be a battalion commander whose temper had been ratcheted up to hot-eyed incandescence. It would take him a week to calm down, and since these inspections occurred almost on a daily basis, the resulting state of Black Jack's disposition can be imagined. Or perhaps not, if you've never seen him in action.

I tried to be fair about the whole thing, telling myself that these senior officers had a job to do, as did I, and that we were all God's children, but there were times when I wanted to echo the words of Phil Nelson, spoken softly and barely audibly to a retreating general's back: "Good God Almighty, General: Ain't you got nothin' better to do than look for coke cans, for chrissakes?"

The week passed. Sunny, in the main, which was good, as we'd long since become accustomed to the heat, while nothing could ever inure us to the damp and cold of the monsoon. Rumors were swirling, as was the dust from a dozen Chinooks, bringing in equipment, food, water, ammunition and, oh, sandbags, in case we ran out. There was a new firebase being built, out in the valleys west of our AO. The name was Blaze, and it was supposed to be huge. Why it was placed there, and when we'd see it, formed the core of most of the rumors.

One afternoon, Jerry sent word that he wanted to see me in his CP bunker. The last time I'd gone to his bunker at his request he'd cajoled me into helping him blow down some trees on the west slope, and what happened next took ten years off my life. After mulling over the idea of sending back word that I'd died and was unavailable, I decided that I had to face the music sooner or later.

I knew something was up because as soon as I entered his RTO got up and left. After a quick greeting, I sat down on a bunk along the rear wall, facing him. He got right to it. "I wanted you to be the first to know. I got word from Raffaele this morning."

I nodded. "S3?"

"Yeah." He smiled and shrugged. "Been waiting for it. Didn't know it was going to happen just yet."

"So," I said, with a straight face, "why you wanna leave the field? You scared?"

Jerry laughed. "Hardly ever."

I smiled, but then said, seriously, "I hate to see you go, Jer. I know it's what you want, and I'm glad for you, but..." I stopped there. The words "I'm going to miss you" were not supposed to be part of an airborne officer's lexicon.

"Well, I'm torn, to be honest." His eyes involuntarily went to a small table to his left. I looked there. A framed color photo of a lovely young woman — his wife — stood prominently on the small wooden surface.

"I guess Donnie will feel better about it," I said casually.

He nodded. There was no need to belabor the point. His wife was intelligent, and knew very well the difference in life expectancies between an infantry platoon leader and a staff lieutenant.

I rested my eyes on the picture; an easy thing to do, because she was truly lovely.

In this photo, her long blond hair was woven in braids and crowned her head with a gold far more subtle and appealing than mere metal. Her blue eyes were wide and wide-spaced, and her other features delicate and perfectly proportioned. I could never look at her photo — I'd seen it two or three times before — without a momentary and visceral sense of wonder that so beautiful a woman could link herself to an ugly man like Jerry, but of course that was stupid, shallow nonsense. Jerry Wolosenko was one of the kindest, smartest and funniest men I knew, and no woman of sense would fail to look past the big nose and the off-center Slavic face and see what lay behind it. A bimbo might not, but then that's why bimbos deserved what bimbos got.

I looked at the photo more closely. I had never quite gotten past her face before. Now I noticed something evocative about her costume, what could be seen of it, from a little below the neckline up. I nodded ... National Geographic.

"She's beautiful, Jerry. Is that a Ukrainian costume she's wearing?"

He nodded. "We were married in a Russian Orthodox service. That's her wedding dress."

"You take that pretty seriously, don't you?"

"Yeah. We're both active in the Ukrainian community in the area. My parents are, and so are hers. It's funny. I'm second-generation American. My parents have been over here for years. But ... I don't know. That flag I carry means something. I don't know why, really. Except that maybe it's got to do with the fact that the fucking Soviets wiped us from the map. The country is still in my blood." He shrugged, "It's ... do you feel the same way about Italy?"

It was my turn to shrug. Only Jerry, of them all, knew that I'd been born in Italy, and he had learned that more or less by accident. It was nothing that I was in the least ashamed of, but it was a lot more than I was willing to share with others. I could talk non-stop until people begged for mercy, but I rarely let on anything really private.

"I don't — no. I love Italy; I love its people, the food, the language, the art, the music, the architecture, the cities, the countryside, everything about it; but I wouldn't cross the street to save the nation of Italy. America is my country."

He made a vague gesture, with a quick, half-embarrassed smile. We were perilously close to crossing that thin line that none could define but all recognized. We were as close as any group of men could be, far closer than we'd been with our classmates and friends back home. We lived together, worked together, sweated and feared and triumphed or lost together. We would die for each other without a moment's hesitation. That was no hyperbole or romantic myth. Men did it every day. I would trust Jerry, as he trusted me, in a way that no civilian can even hope to comprehend.

And yet we lived in terror of revealing to each other even a minor part of our innermost thoughts and emotions. Jerry, as did I, maintained a bantering, cynical, detached surface. That was our armor, and we never shed it. We looked at each other closely, searchingly and without pity or sentimentality. We looked for specific, vital things in each other: courage, coolness, awareness and, above all, competence. Beyond that, there was no need to look and every need not to. I didn't want to look deeply into Jerry's soul, or allow him to see into mine, for one fundamental, imperative and all-sufficient reason. We had this habit of dying, you see.

I couldn't think of anything more to say. "When do you leave?"

"Don't know for sure. Couple of days. Soon as my replacement arrives. But I'm pretty sure I've been on my last patrol."

"Well." I stood up and made to leave. "I'll be glad to see you go, you rat-fuck Russian, you and your storybook."

"My very first act at S3," Jerry assured me, "will be to give Colonel Mot the coordinates of your NDP."

The following day was the 29th, and brought more rumors. It also brought two more bizarre incidents. The first, early in the afternoon, was over before most of us even knew what happened; we ignored the routine sound of an approaching Huey, focused instead on the job at hand, improving the bunker line. And then came yells, several of them, of alarm; our heads jerked around, just in time to see a shape, dangling from the chopper on the end of a long rope, go slamming into, first the concertina wire, and then a bunker. It was a pathfinder, we found out, whose insertion into a potential LZ had been interrupted by suspected gunfire; he'd clung to the rope while the pilot thought he'd dropped off. The terrified man hung precariously to the rope for the 20-minute flight back to Rakkasan, and only after he was dragged into the bunker did the chopper crew realize what had happened. Miraculously, the man survived with a few broken bones.

That over, we bent back to our tasks. Several hours later, we were still at it. We'd finished with the wire and the claymores and were working on our favorites, the sandbags, when I was told to report to the mess tent, to join Robison and all the other officers. I entered and groaned. Black Jack stood there, along with Raffaele and a couple of other staff officers. Good news is seldom to be had at a gathering such as this.

It wasn't as bad as I feared, merely a stern but (by his standards) muted lecture from Black Jack about firebase security procedures. He hadn't liked what he'd seen over the past week, and took the occasion to issue a friendly (again, by his standards) reminder. While we were standing in the tent, the lights dimmed perceptibly and the heavy canvas flaps began whipping and flexing to an increasingly vigorous wind. The monsoon was far behind us, and now we were entering the period of afternoon thunderstorms, often of a violent nature. This was merely one of them. The temperature dropped, dull, low booms sounded from the west and south, and lightning began to flash and crackle. I listened to Black Jack with half a mind while the other half tried to remember if I'd left my poncho liner out to dry in the sun earlier. The meeting dragged on while the storm raged on, and then broke up in an aimless, irresolute mixing and milling about of officers, most of us unwilling to brave the lashing rain and the winds outside. We were all still in the tent, then, when a brilliant white bar of lightning slashed across the treetops.

BOOOOOM! BOWHUMP!

The first two were distinct. After that, and following within a split second, it was a continuous rolling booming, like a dozen bass drums gone berserk. It was impossible to distinguish the thunder from the explosions. We all stood stock-still for a moment, our minds trying to understand what in hell we were hearing. Everything had gone off at once, within one or two seconds; now there was silence, except for the continued heavy drumming of the rain and the whistle of the wind. A shout, and then two. That galvanized us. We bolted outside, scattering toward the perimeter, to our respective sectors. Troops were standing, some in rain gear, others, emerged from bunkers or tents, bareheaded and streaming with rain, still pelting down with undiminished fury. The thunder resumed, but farther off.

"What the hell happened?" I yelled at Sergeant Burnetta, who was standing, open-mouthed, not too far away.

He whirled and saw me. "Damn if I know, sir. Everything went off at once."

"Everything? What are you talking about?"

There we all stood, a group of officers and NCOs, staring wildly around us, absolutely baffled. There was no more incoming—if it *had* been incoming. It hadn't really sounded like it. It hadn't really sounded like anything we knew.

Sergeant Piccorelli, the artillery liaison NCO, walked by a knot of us. He smiled in grim amusement. "Claymores and shape charges— anything that was wired up. They all went off when that lightning hit."

"The lightning set off the claymores?" Major Raffaele said in amazement. He looked around him. "Anyone hurt?"

"Not on this side, Major," Piccorelli answered. "Don't know about the other side there." He nodded toward the other end of the base. "But we were damned lucky we didn't have a work party or a patrol coming back in just then."

"Jesus H," Robison said. We looked around. There was no visual damage. There shouldn't have been, of course: The claymores and shape charges were set up to explode out, toward the forest. But we'd been lucky, as Piccorelli had said, that no one was outside the wire at the time. Only later did I recall that a couple of hours earlier, we'd been standing out there, working with those claymores. If that storm had come through at 1530 instead of 1730...

Ted Billings, whom I hadn't seen since our first night in Camp Evans, months before, stood on a bunker and looked around, hands on his hips. "Jesus," he said, to no one in particular, "there are more damned ways to get killed out here."

15

The Banana Tree

Firebase Rakkasan; 30 March–10 April 1969

March 30th brought the end of the month, and Marsh Eward, Jerry's replacement. Moreover, Denholm moved in from Evans, ready to take over Fourth Platoon. I had to give up some people — we all did, of course — and so Clary, Hannah, Jacobs and Wilson, along with two of my new E5s, Burnetta and Drozd, joined the new platoon. I liked Denholm, and moreover understood that a company was only as good as its weakest platoon, and so I resisted the temptation to send him troublemakers and screw-ups. Besides, when I got right down to it, I didn't really have any. Even Abbot appeared to have put his domestic troubles behind him, or at least off to the side. Others were not so scrupulous: Morris, Kaminski and Towson, for example, were added to his roster, along with some other tough cases from Third Platoon.

"Think of it as an expansion draft," I told Denholm. "The Washington Senators did just that, ten years ago, when that asshole Clark Griffith scuttled off to the Great White North of Minnesota." I paused. "On the other hand, the expansion team sucked rock slime, now that I think about it."

Denholm didn't care: He was desperate, and would take anything, including REMFs, even cooks, as long as he could field a platoon. He was determined to pull them together and make something out of nothing given the chance.

Early one morning, Robison called us to his CP for a briefing. I entered the dark and (relatively) cool structure to find everyone present. The CO looked up from the grey notebook he always carried and waved me to a seat, an upturned crate by the rear wall. He was visibly irritated about something, but that was hardly news. Robison had been in a constant foul mood all week, as had we, for that matter. Brass hats have that effect.

The CO flipped through a couple of pages of his notebook and then favored us all with a brooding scowl. A thin beam of fiery sunlight slipped through a crack in the PCP wall and slashed across his face, highlighting his thin, tight lips and banishing the rest to deep shadow. It gave his face a disjointed look, like a torn photograph carelessly pasted back together.

"I don't know how many goddamned times I have to tell you that Black Jack wants all troops shaved every day," he began. "That's *all* and *every*. Yesterday we sent a squad up to the TOC on a work detail and Black Jack came back from Evans and found two of 'em with beards and one hadn't had a haircut in a couple of months." He fixed a glare at Eward. "That was your platoon, Two Six."

Marsh nodded silently. He didn't bother to point out he'd taken over the platoon that morning.

Robison held his glare for a second or two and then looked back down at his notebook in disgust. "Bunker line's still not finished and I'm catching some real heat over that. I see guys farting around all the goddamned day when they should be working. I want you guys to start doing your jobs instead of sitting around all day writing letters and bullshitting. Get out there and start making your guys hump, or by Christ I'll find some lieutenants that will." Once again he stopped to glare, this time at us all.

"I'd like it if I saw one of you lazy bastards checking the barbed wire and the claymores once in a while. No hurry: Once a month would do. And the perimeter. I went out there this morning and found two goddamned soda cans and a paper plate right in front of Bunker Thirteen. Who's got Thirteen?"

Dickson cleared his throat. "That's mine."

"Well, don't sound so fucking proud of it. Your area looks like pigs live there. And you, Bo," he turned his slightly protuberant eyes in my direction. "Two of your guys were sitting on top of a bunker with about 20 empty sandbags laying there, playing cards. Where the fuck were *you*? I don't want any goddamned card playing during working hours, you got that?"

I nodded, although two remarks wanted to push their way through my lips. The first was to ask him if the men or the sandbags were caught playing cards—he hadn't made that clear. The second was a question: Does that mean your afternoon poker game is called off? But I kept my mouth shut. There is a time to needle Robison and a time not to.

Robison ducked his head back down in a characteristic gesture, while he read the next entry in his notebook. Each entry, I knew, was preceded by a circled number, with all important words or numbers underlined with a heavy stroke. I felt a brief twinge of mixed amusement and sadness that I knew far more about my CO's habits than I did of my wife's.

"Okay." He flipped the notebook shut, and then reopened it. "That's all I should have to say about that. Let's go on. 1300 today, I want a 30-man detail—that's ten from each of you—to report to Sergeant Whitley at the battalion TOC. We need two men from each platoon for KP at the mess tent—0900." He flipped to the next page. "Mad Minute tonight at 0200." He paused and shook his head at the general groan "All right, it won't kill you. Might even wake some of your people up, for once. Oh, yeah—Top here needs two bodies from each of you at … what, 1300, Top?"

Garza shook his head. "No, sir. In one hour. 0830."

15. The Banana Tree

"Okay. You guys copied that. Now, listen up. General Ewell—he's the Corps Deputy CG—will be here at 1400 hours for an inspection. I want one bunk—"

The rest of what he had to say was drowned out by our united cries of outrage. I threw my notebook to the floor in utter disgust.

"Jesus Christ, Rob," I said, "will you listen to yourself? Two minutes ago you're chewing ass because we can't get the work done on time and now you're telling us to clean ourselves up and look pretty for some half-ass inspection by some fucking son of a bitch of a REMF general whose main function in life is to peek under sandbags looking for cigarette butts. How in the hell are we supposed to get any work down around here when every day we spend half our time with our thumbs up our ass waiting around for some asshole inspection that doesn't mean shit to anyone except that moron of a general whose brain isn't big enough to handle anything more important than that?" My voice had gotten higher and higher, and louder as I warmed to my subject, but I had to stop; I was out of breath.

He glared at me but before he could say anything, I picked up my notebook and waved it in front of his nose. "And as if that wasn't bad enough, every other word from you is ten bodies here and two bodies there and—Jesus Christ! How are we supposed to get any work done at all? You've got all my people doing something else. Look at this! So far today, I got 16 men going to you or battalion. I've got six bunker positions to cover, one man at each. I got a permanent orderly at the officers' mess tent, I got a man at the TOC on detail, two men TDY at Evans, three men on sick call and my medic is attached to the battalion aid station for the duration. If you add that up, that's 30 men gone. You know what that leaves me with? My two RTOs, Top and me. That's it. Would you mind telling me how I'm supposed to get any work done around here when I don't have any people to do it?"

My breath was now coming in snorts. I glared at him and he glared back. And then Robison fooled me. Instead of throwing his notebook at me—as he had several times in the past—he unexpectedly leaned back and nodded sympathetically.

"Okay," he chuckled quietly, "I see your point. And I've got the remedy." He leaned back some more, his field chair creaking as it teetered on its rear legs. The bar of sunlight had passed on, leaving his face in complete shadow. I narrowed my eyes as I tried to read his expression. Had I finally gone too far? But, no: I'd been far worse on several occasions. I lost my temper with Robison about twice a week, and it was now almost an established routine.

He smiled in genuine pleasure. "0700 tomorrow morning, I want you to take a squad and RIF to the west." He looked at his notebook. "You'll go to the vicinity of 482185, perform your mission and return tomorrow evening. Whole thing shouldn't take you more than six, seven hours."

I frowned and took out my map. It took me only a couple of seconds to locate the coordinates. I looked up from the map, puzzled. What the hell was supposed to be there?

The spot he'd designated was 1,200 meters from the base, a little north of west from it. There was, as far as I knew, nothing of interest out there. And the whole thing made no sense: We ran sweeps all the time, of course, but that's what they were — sweeps. A platoon would search an arc some 2,000 meters or more from the base; they'd normally be out for several days. This was ... I shook my head. It made no sense at all to send 10 or 12 men — one squad plus at least part of my CP group — on what amounted to little more than an afternoon hike, especially at a time when we were up to our ears in work.

I was determined, nevertheless, not to ask questions. I suspected something was going on, and I didn't want to be the straight man for one of Robison's punch lines. He, however, was more than ready to tell me everything.

"This location," he went on, with a smile of joy on his face, "was personally selected by the battalion CO after careful reconnaissance. He's been looking for this place for two weeks, he told me. So, tomorrow morning, Bo, you'll take your people and move down to that ravine there, and pick up three banana trees and bring them back."

I blinked and sat there, stunned. My ears are good, so I knew that I'd heard correctly. I could hear Dickson laughing and Chuck was grinning and sniggering softly. Even Eward smiled. No wonder Robbie hadn't flown off the handle when I'd just popped off. I promised myself, not for the first time, to refrain from ticking him off again.

"You want me to go a klick and a half and pick up some banana trees?" I asked, carefully.

Robison nodded his head. "Three of 'em," he said happily.

"You can't be — why?"

"Black Jack wants three banana trees, in good condition, by tomorrow evening or it's someone's ass."

"You *can't* be serious."

"Serious as a heart attack. Now," he said briskly, straightening up in his chair, "the keyword today is Black Night and the password is Broken Shaft. Got that?"

"Yeah, I got the shaft all right," I said wryly. The hell of it was he had me, period. I had zero room to maneuver here. After all, what was he asking of me? To take a squad of infantry to a certain location. I was an infantry platoon leader, wasn't I? What part of leading men on a RIF through jungle terrain and returning couldn't I handle? No one's asking me to fill sandbags or string wire, or stand still for a candy-ass inspection.... You're a grunt. Just do grunt work.

There was nothing I could say. To beg off, after the scene I'd just pulled, would make me the laughing stock of the company. Even Dickson would feel entitled to snicker. But to actually go ... I suddenly realized, in horror, that I would have to tell Sergeant Wright. I couldn't just grab an entire squad and disappear for the day. How could I face him? And the worst part would be that he would instantly know *why*. He knew me as well as anyone ever had, and he knew my temper and my tendency to shout from the lip. Wright would know immediately that the CO was shoving this up my butt in payment for indiscretions, past and present.

But *why*? Not why me — that was clear. But why go at all? I had not, at that time, seen *Mr. Roberts*, so the parallel didn't occur to me, and anyway, even if I had, that still didn't answer the fundamental question. Why banana trees?

Robison was exchanging a word or two with Garza when I recovered my voice.

"Okay. I'm on my way. But just why does Black Jack want banana trees? Is he going to camouflage himself as a fruit?"

Robison broke off his conversation. Why not? He was enjoying this. "He wants them, two of them, for decoration in front of his TOC. He's gonna pot 'em. The third's a spare. And he wants them in good condition, whole. Not cut down, but pulled up, roots and all." He finally broke out laughing. He never could keep a straight face.

I was furious, but there was nothing I could do except nod and accept it all. Robison, his good humor restored, went on with the rest of the briefing. There was still no word on when we would be sent back out, but things were happening and none of us doubted it would be soon.

I left the CP in search of my platoon, which was no small trick, since they'd been devoured piecemeal by Rakkasan's voracious appetite for warm bodies. I dreaded telling Sergeant Wright and the men about tomorrow's mission, but I stepped up and took the manly way out. I collared Helms and told *him* to inform Wright and Hyde's squad. Then I more or less moped about the bunker line for the rest of the morning, contributing my fair share of misery and contention to the general welfare. I left Samuel and Snyder, both good, hard working, conscientious troops, muttering in baleful near-mutiny after finding them on their respective bunkers, on guard but without helmets and their weapons lying on the roof next to them. Normally, I'd have said nothing, this being daytime; if nettled, I'd have simply mentioned the SOP. Today, I snarled and carried on like a Black Jack wanna-be.

Jerry's departure from the company was decidedly low key, in part because he wasn't going anywhere; he took Ted Billings's place on the staff and simply moved his stuff a few hundred feet to the TOC area. I hated to see him go, but at the same time I was happy for him, or more accurately, for his wife.

Marsh Eward was a New Englander, an OCS graduate, and a slow-talking, taciturn man. He was sandy-haired and husky, a couple of inches taller and 30 pounds heavier than I. My first impression was that he was humorless, serious and slow, in body and mind. I felt a twinge of trepidation. I already had Dickson to deal with; I didn't need another dud to have to pick up the slack for. Of course, first impressions were sometimes wrong. But he looked as if he'd be perfectly at home selling women's shoes in a discount store.

Denholm's release from the exile of XOship almost made up for the Mad Russian Monk's departure. Eward was untried, and I had no confidence at all in Dickson, so it was comforting to me, and I'm sure to Robison, to have a known quantity in Chuck. The occasion had not yet arisen, but it would, sooner or later, that I would have to trust my life and platoon to the good judgment and competence of one of the other platoon leaders. I hoped that when the time came, Denny would be the one.

Each day over the following two weeks, one of the platoons would fly out of Rakkasan on a CA into the surrounding area, patrol for the day, and then be returned to base. Occasionally, we would walk off the firebase and run sweeps around the perimeter, in arcs 2,000 or 3,000 meters out. By now the situation had become clear. Our AO, which extended roughly from the first ridgeline overlooking the coastal plain (on which were placed Helen and Long) south to the valleys of the Song Bo and the Song Trac, and westward to the hills overlooking the Song Bo valley, was as empty of significant NVA presence as could be expected. We made the comment, among ourselves, over and over, that we felt safer on patrol in familiar territory—Hills 154, 178, 105—than we would have sitting in a bunker in DaNang or Quang Tri. But west of us, in the high steep mountains east of the A Shau, lay unknown, unpatrolled areas. We all had a feeling that we would become better acquainted with those areas—a deep, forbidding green on our maps—very shortly.

The banana trees were planted by the colonel's hutch on Rakkasan; a few days later someone else was sent out to retrieve a pair of palm trees, the small, low-lying ones prevalent along the river valley. These took their place alongside the banana trees. It was then that someone—I think Denholm—acquainted me with the movie *Mr. Roberts*. We debated whether this was a case of life imitating art, or if insanity was endemic in commanding officers. The plants, by the way, met a sad end, a few weeks later. Our whole valley, surrounding Rakkasan, was sprayed with defoliants and...

April 4, we heard news of a grimmer sort. Robison called us to his CP to announce that Firebase Jack, on the same general coastal ridgeline as Helen but north and west of the Song Bo's entrance into the plain, had been probed and then hit by sappers overnight. Alpha Company, again, bore the brunt of the enemy actions. Two were killed and several wounded. We all looked at each other. Jack was less than 15 kilometers west of Camp Evans—on a clear day, you could stand on its bunker line and see our base camp. Furthermore, it was on the northern edge of our AO, the one we thought safe. Reports were mixed, but the consensus was that Alpha had been hit by a platoon reinforced by a sapper detachment. That was way too many NVA wandering around our AO for comfort.

There was no specific intelligence that the other firebases would be probed or attacked, but we all went on alert. Robison opened his notebook and began ticking off items.

"All the claymores and shape charges have been replaced from the other day, right?"

"Yeah," I said. "That concertina wire's been replaced too, along the west side."

"Okay. What about the telephone lines to the bunkers?"

There was a mulish silence, broken only by Dickson clearing his throat. This was a sore subject, for Chuck and me. We'd spent an entire day, while Dickson was out on a CA, straightening out the mess in his sector; some wires were hooked to nothing, while others were crossed, linking one bunker to its neighbor but not the CP, and others simply baffled even the RTOs; there was no telling where they led. To make things

15. The Banana Tree

worse, Black Jack decided to take a personal interest in the project, freely making suggestions and other, more pointed remarks while we worked. It all should have been finished days before, but once again, Third Platoon was a week or more behind the rest of us. We finally got it straightened out, only to have Dickson return from his day in the park and accuse us of screwing up his bunker line. Denholm and I had a serious falling out: We each demanded the right to shoot Dickson first.

"Okay," Robison said, finally. "I guess the less said about that, the better. What about the ammo? Everything up to par?"

"Yeah," Denholm answered. "We replaced all our old M16 and M60 ammo with new stuff, and we visually checked all our M79 rounds."

"Me too," I added.

"And me," Eward said.

Robison waited a moment, looking at Dickson, who remained silent. "Well?" he asked after a long moment.

"Uh ... no. Uh, not yet."

"Jesus H," Robison said in disgust. For a moment we thought he was going to go off the handle but he ended up just shaking his head. "Okay. Grenades? Weapons? Cleaned and checked? Starlight Scope—I know, but goddamnit, we're supposed to carry the goddamn things. Strobes? Radios."

We all looked up. The last had a slight tone to it. "Check your goddamned radios. Now. Tonight. Tomorrow morning. Check 'em in your fucking sleep. I don't want another session with Black Jack like the last one, when I had to explain to that son of a bitch why my platoon leaders' radios never work. Understood?" He was looking right at me while he spoke. A few days before, I'd gone on a CA to a shallow, open valley, with no hill around higher than 100 meters, and Black Jack, flying overhead, had been unable to establish contact with me. He had not been happy, and had shared his feelings with Robison.

I shrugged. "You know it's bullshit. I could hear him. *He* couldn't hear *me*. Rakkasan could hear me, Eagle could hear me, Helen could hear me, Bastogne could hear me, and so could Strike. Bayonne, New Jersey could hear me. Tell him to check his own fucking radio."

Robison started to flare up but stopped and grinned. "You tell 'im. I'd pay to see that."

He continued on down the list for a few minutes and then flipped pages.

"Okay. Tonight, it's condition orange. 50% alert from dusk to 2200, 75% alert from 2200 to 0500." He ignored the groans and curses. "Mad minute at 2230 and 0430. Stand to at 0500. And I want 100% stand to."

This time he was looking straight at Dickson. The last time we'd had a pre-dawn stand to, Dickson had decided to skip it and remained sacked out. Unfortunately, that was the morning that Raffaele happened to wander through the bunkers on a lark, and found Three Six curled up in the corner of his CP.

Robison waited patiently while we all vented our collective spleen over the condition orange announcement. Basically, it meant no sleep.

"You really think they're going to hit Rakkasan?" Denholm asked, after we'd complained long enough.

"Who knows? It's a fact that they've hit a lot of firebases in the division AO lately. By the same token, Jack's the first one of ours they hit. Who knows? But Black Jack wants us to be on our toes, and it won't hurt your guys to stay awake one night. Tell 'em there's a war on."

Nothing happened that night, or the next. It didn't end the silly season—condition orange continued for several nights—and it ensured that the platoon leaders fought each other over the right to go on overnight RIFs. Even the daily CAs were popular. At least we were out from the base and blessedly free of colonels, inspections and a harassed and harassing Robison.

Chuck Denholm took his brand new platoon of cast-offs, rejects, rookies, wailing REMFs and some good men into the area just west of Helen, on the southern slopes of the ridge along which I'd made my first patrol, back in December. It wasn't, on a straight line, all that far from Firebase Jack, although a couple of steep ridges intervened. Coming across some fresh tracks, he followed them to a large cache of weapons and 122mm ammo. This caused some consternation in the S2 shop at Evans. The only explanation for the 122mm ammo was that they were going to use it to rocket Camp Evans, or possibly even Hue, something they hadn't done in a year. Along with the attack on Jack, this was evidence that they were determined to infiltrate back into our AO.

Apparently Chuck's discovery, and the subsequent destruction of the ammo, irritated the NVA, because when he lifted out that evening, from a saw grass-covered valley at the southwestern foot of Helen, they peppered his PZ with small arms fire and some RPGs. Denholm kept things under control, however, which was remarkable considering how new his platoon was and how inexperienced some of its troopers were. The extraction went off without any casualties or a serious hitch. ARA and Cobras from Evans arrived with their deadly snarls within minutes, and covered his last ship—with him in it, of course—and plastered the valley and its surrounding ridges.

The following day Dickson was inserted back into the same area, to see if the NVA were still around or if they could find signs of casualties. He found nothing, but the incident, however minor, did worry the S2 and S3. Damn it, didn't the NVA know we'd chased them out of this area?

By now the rumors were swirling so thick about the base that a Huey trying to land got waved off, or so Jerry said, one day at the TOC. Most of them centered on one name: Every war has a place or a name that transcends its time and enters the lexicon as something more than a geographic appellation. Valley Forge, Gettysburg, the Somme, Iwo Jima. Ours was the A Shau.

It is a broad, long valley, slashing across the central west of Viet Nam, in spots only a few kilometers from the Laotian border. It is not only broad, it is flat, and bare.

15. The Banana Tree

At its northern apex, among the hills there, lies Khe San. Far to its south, the abandoned village of A Luoi, alongside which lay the Special Forces camp by the same name, and its airfield, sat athwart Highway 547. This was the last American presence in the valley, before being wiped out in 1967. Highway 548, a mix of PCP, dirt and rotted tarmac, splits the valley, running roughly along the path of the Khe Tre river, to intersect 547 at the village. Highway 547, in colonial times the principal link between the precious hardwoods of the western mountains and the lumber mills and ports on the coast, cuts through these mountains in a winding, curving, dipping path, to eventually exit through the gap between Firebase Long and Firebase Strike, far to the east, and thence curve back up north to Hue.

It was along these two roads that the NVA mounted their attacks on Hue during Tet. Although 547 was more or less closed to them, since Long and Strike, and our other firebases, stood sentinel duty now, 548 continued to be the enemy's road through the valley and into the massive mountains on its east and west flanks. This was the infamous "Yellow Brick Road," down which trucks and even tanks flowed into the south from North Viet Nam prior to the Tet. The Ho Chi Minh trail was not one road, but dozens, perhaps hundreds, and this was one of them, and a major one at that.

Just west of the valley were the staging areas, R&R camps, supply centers and permanent bases of the NVA. All during training, even at OCS, right on up to SERTS, the enemy had routinely been referred to as Victor Charley, the VC, or the Viet Cong: black pajamas, funny looking conical hats, primitive guerrilla tactics, armed with ancient bolt action carbines and punji stakes, cut-up automobile tires on their feet and a few grains of rice in their bellies. Too bad it wasn't true.

The Viet Cong, by 1969, were just about totally used up, militarily. Even at their peak, they had never been particularly formidable opponents. Popular myth and Hollywood (which may be synonymous) insist on glamorizing guerrilla warfare and vastly overrating their effectiveness. In fact, guerrilla units generally suffer the fate of all amateurs who tangle with professionals: They get hammered.

But we were facing the fourth-largest standing army in the world, not a bunch of guerrillas. The NVA in Eye Corps had more tanks, vehicles, artillery and heavy weapons that we did. Their defensive networks were superb, and almost impervious to artillery and air attack; their logistical network was excellent. In one area and one only were they completely outmatched, and that was in air power. Even discounting the fact that they had effectively lost control of the air space over North Viet Nam by 1968, they simply never had it over South Viet Nam, ever. They would never have dared to send a helicopter anywhere in the south, and their few sorties by fixed-wing aircraft ended in humiliation. Air power, while valuable, was severely limited in the steep, forested terrain of western Viet Nam. You can't hit what you can't see, and the NVA were excellent at camouflaging their roads, base camps and other facilities.

With sanctuary across the border in Laos, with trackless triple canopy forest covering the steepest, most hidden draws, ravines, hills and paths, the A Shau was ideal for the NVA. And make no mistake, they considered the A Shau as their own. The last time we'd disputed their claim to it, in 1968, the First Cav lost 96 helicopters, almost all of them Hueys, but including Cobras and Chinooks. They'd been chewed up by .51 caliber machine guns, RPGs, shoulder-held missiles, rockets, 40mm anti-aircraft fire and small arms fire. The Marines had gone into the northern end of the valley several times; the last had been in February, when Bravo had sat on Barbara. That had been called Operation Dewey Canyon, and it had had the same result as earlier efforts. We went in, kicked a couple of chairs over, but left with the house intact.

16

The Rao Trang

YD462014; 11–24 April 1969

April 11 brought us First Sergeant Tim Murtiff, a block-faced, small-eyed, buzz-cut bear of a man, almost a caricature of the career NCO; red-faced, profane, gravel-voiced and tough. He took over as Bravo Company First Sergeant; Garza, an E7, reverted to platoon sergeant for Denholm. It was an all-around improvement in the company, since essentially we gained an outstanding platoon sergeant. Garza, whose ambition shone as bright as his glittering black eyes, took it well, as he had to; he was still too far away from his E8 to do anything more than smile grimly and begin whipping Fourth Platoon into shape. Denholm was lucky. Despite his personality, which left some of us uneasy, Garza was a tough, professional and very competent soldier, and a skilled leader. I had the best in Sergeant Wright, but if I couldn't have him I wouldn't have minded having Garza.

We had more changes forced on us. Hyde finally returned from Australia, after a short stint in the hospital, a conjunction of events that gave his men endless material for speculation, insinuations, suspicions and accusation, almost all of them ribald in nature. At the same time, Wright decided, reluctantly, that Nelson, an outstanding soldier, simply didn't have the experience to run a squad; he needed more seasoning. We'd lost several men to Fourth Platoon, and one of the replacements we received was a transfer in from the 173rd, a recruiting poster-type E5 named Novak: tall, firm-jawed, big-shouldered, with blue eyes under short blond hair. He was taciturn and cocky at the same time, an unusual but not necessarily disturbing combination. Coincidentally, Evans, quiet, somewhat colorless, unassuming but competent, got his stripe. We now at last had three experienced E5s: Hyde, who of course took back First Squad, Novak, who took over Second, and Evans, who retained the Third. Nelson and Clifton became team leaders under Novak, Snyder and Grump Ulrich, who liked working for the lead-by-example Evans, became his team leaders. This left Sergeant Eden and Sergeant Dickerson as odd men out; the only thing we could do was make them team leaders in First Squad, under Hyde, a move that left Eden pouting and resentful. That also meant that some very good men, like Kenzy, Gann and Jones, remained as riflemen, which seemed a waste; any of the three would have performed better than Eden and Dickerson, we thought.

The CP became a very pleasant place; Helms was all I had expected and hoped he would be, as RTO, and even more. Even though he was junior to St. Onge, he immediately assumed a quiet but effective leadership role within the CP; even Muldoon listened to him and followed his lead. He had a knack, rare and priceless, for making decisions and presenting them to the others so that they saw them as not only good ideas but inevitable, without in the least appearing overbearing or overconfident. Similarly, he could back off a potential confrontation without appearing weak or intimidated. He struck the perfect balance with me: Attentive without being slavish, firm (in the face of my frequent tantrums and explosions) without insubordination, and agreeable without at all becoming cloying or sycophantic. Once I got past his shy and diffident exterior, I discovered a core of steel under that quiet demeanor.

On April 13, we received confirmation, or at least a very strong hint, that the rumors were true. Robison, along with his four platoon leaders, were loaded on Black Jack's seldom-used Command Helicopter, a Huey stuffed with communications gear, and taken for an aerial reconnaissance of our next patrol area; not the A Shau itself, but the high, steep mountains that formed the valley's eastern border, some 20 or 30 kilometers southwest of Rakkasan. The flight started cheerfully enough, but our expressions sobered quickly when we arrived and began flying at 100 or 200 feet above the forest. We exchanged carefully expressionless glances as we flew over or by peak after upthrust peak, fold after dark green fold, ravine after v-shaped ravine. Firebase Helen, 680 meters high, was the tallest feature we'd seen to date. Its mountain was dwarfed by the mighty peaks here. 800, 900, 1000, 1300, 1500, 1800 meters — 6,000 feet — and more they rose. But it wasn't their height. The forest carpeting the steep slopes and sharp valleys was nothing like

John Snyder returning from a squad recon patrol in the Song Bo valley (courtesy John Snyder).

the thinned-out, partially defoliated meadow-studded terrain around Rakkasan. Here it was an unbroken dark green shield, absolutely featureless, completely impenetrable. Mile after mile, they stretched to the horizon. We whistled in awe as we flew between two peaks, no more than 200 meters apart; their tops towered at least 200 meters above our heads, while their flanks plunged to dark, almost hidden ravines 500 or 600 meters below us. I had spent quite a bit of time in the European Alps, and have never seen anything quite like this.

Robison, uncharacteristically thoughtful, finally broke the silence. "God knows what's down there," he said soberly.

We all nodded in understanding. And none of us relished the idea of climbing these monsters; Helen was close to an all-day ascent; some of these beasts might take two full days to reach their summit. And much of it had to be virgin forest, and trackless, except for some meandering animal trails, which never led anywhere we wanted to go. Animals have little use for a straight line, after all. Finally, water would be a problem, and a huge one. There was little chance that we'd find streams or rivulets under those monstrous trees; their huge greedy root systems sucked it out of the ground as quickly as it fell. Only in the monsoons, months behind us, would the ravines and draws hold running water. When we turned and left for Rakkasan, we remained quiet, with none of the banter we usually exchanged. I felt a vague depression. I wasn't looking forward to this operation; it looked entirely too much like work. The operation was scheduled for the 16th, three days hence.

I was in my CP bunker, writing a letter, when Jerry stuck his head in the entrance. "Goofing off, as usual," he sniffed. "C'mon, Major Raffaele wants you."

"Hmm. The question is, do I want him? Tell 'im I'm busy." I frowned at the letter, one to my brother, that I'd been trying to write for three days now. But Wolosenko stood there, and the weight of his stare finally got me to down pen, stand up, stretch and utter two or three elegant curses.

"I follow the Mad Russian Monk. Avanti."

Jerry didn't want me to follow him, however. A step or two from my bunker, he took off for the mess tent. I was a big boy, he reasoned, *and* an infantry platoon leader, and could almost certainly find the TOC by myself. But Major Raffaele wasn't as convinced, apparently: He met me half way, his face stern and grim. The major was normally a very mild-mannered man.

"You took your time," he growled. "Come on."

He about-faced and led the way to the commo center, adjacent to the TOC. I opened my mouth to ask what was going on but shut it. I probably didn't want to know. While we walked the 30 or 40 meters, my mind went back over the past two weeks. How had I pissed Black Jack off this time?

We stooped to enter the low-set commo center; Raffaele took me to a PRC30, a powerful commo link for the battalion. One of the battalion RTOs was seated in front of the unit; he looked up as we entered.

"You got it?" Raffaele asked. At the RTO's nod, he took the receiver from the man's hand and thrust it into mine. "Here," he said brusquely

I put the receiver to my ear. "This is Bravo One Six," I mumbled, most of my mind still searching my memory for transgressions, real or imagined.

A thin, tinny voice, almost lost in static, began saying something. I finally caught the words "wait one," and did so. Then another voice, much louder and clearer, came on.

"Is this Lieutenant Franco Boccia, of B Company, of the Third of the One Hundred Eighty Seventh?" the voice asked.

I smiled. It had been so long since I'd been referred to, over the radio at any rate, as anything other than Bravo One Six that I almost said no. Besides, only my mother ever called me Franco.

"This is he," I answered.

"From New Bern, North Carolina?"

I almost said no a second time. My home was Washington, D.C., and had been from the age of four. New Bern was my wife's hometown, and where she was living while I was overseas. We hadn't been married long enough to establish our own place before I left for jump school at Fort Benning.

"Yeah, that's right."

"Okay, I have a telegram which was just received at 1137 hours, 13 April, addressed to First Lieutenant Franco J Boccia, B Company, Third of the One Hundred Eighty Seventh. Break. Message follows. Break. Red Cross personnel in New Bern, North Carolina wish to relay the information that Mrs. Alma L Boccia, of New Bern, gave birth to a male child at 0720 Hours, April 12th, local time, at Physician's General Hospital, New Bern, North Carolina. No information available on child's weight, height, health or that of its mother. Therefore Red Cross authorizes Lieutenant Boccia to place a call to New Bern, North Carolina in order to ascertain health of mother and child. End of message. Break. That means, Lieutenant, that you should return to Camp Evans, to the Red Cross facilities there, where you will be authorized to place a transoceanic call on a priority basis. We'll be expecting you." The voice went silent; I could hear only the rush of static.

"Congratulations." It was Raffaele, his voice and expression relapsed to their customary benignity.

I opened my mouth to say "thank you" but found I couldn't speak. I was numbed by emotion, unexpected, and curiously daunting. Geoffrey Lidano Boccia. My son. I realized I couldn't speak for the lump in my throat; it simply wouldn't go away.

Raffaele grinned. "Come on, Lieutenant. You look like someone's smacked you on the head with a two-by-four. Christ, it couldn't be that big a surprise, now. You *did* know she was expecting, didn't you?"

I finally managed a weak smile. "She did mention it," I said in barely above a whisper.

"Okay. Come on, we've got to get you down to Evans."

"Huh?" I looked at him blankly.

He shook his head in disgust. "Evans, Boccia. Camp Evans. I know you've heard of it. Let's *go*." He practically had to take me by the arm and drag me. On our way to the pad, we stopped by the CO's hutch. Black Jack, his blue eyes just a degree or two less frosty than usual, shook my hand and muttered something that might have been congratulations. Then he admonished me to return ASAP. "You got work to do," he reminded me.

His LOH was on the pad, warming up. Raffaele pointed it out to me, slapped me on the back, and returned to the TOC. As I walked toward it, Jerry popped out of a hutch and advanced on me, hand outstretched and his face split by a huge grin.

"Congratulations, Frank. How do you feel?"

I shook my head. "I don't know. I'm not sure I feel anything."

His grin grew wider and warmer. "Do you know, boy or girl?"

"Uhh, boy. It's—he's a boy."

"I'm glad for you. That's terrific. How's Alma?"

"I don't know. That's why I'm on my way up to Evans. They wouldn't say." Now that the original shock was wearing off, I began to worry. *Why* wouldn't they say?

"Oh, I'm sure she's fine. My best to her, and to your son, Frank. I mean that."

"Thanks, Jerry. Thanks ... I—"

He nodded at the LOH, by now fully revved up. "Hop aboard, man. See you."

The LOH lifted off a few seconds later and 25 minutes after that I found myself in a large, bare building in the middle of Camp Evans. At the end of the room were six curtained booths, each with an overseas telephone. Benches and chairs lined the other walls. I took a seat in one and waited. Four hours later, a voice, tiny and remote, unrecognizable, finally came through the receiver. Only after several seconds did I realize that I was speaking to my father-in-law.

"Hello? Hello?" Are you there?"

"Yeah, I'm here. Who is this?"

"Frank?"

"Yeah?"

"Is this Frank Boccia? Lieutenant Boccia?"

"Hello! Yes, it is."

"Frank! Gene here. How are you?"

"Gene? How's Alma? How's Geoff? What's—"

"...trying to get a hold of you all day. Alma's fine. She's fine. She's asleep right now."

"How's the baby? Was there any trouble? The way they were talking here, I thought maybe there was a problem."

"No, no. No problem at all. The kid's fine. Ugly as homemade sin, but fine. Got hair, feet, hands and a mouth. Reckon that's all he'll need for right now."

"How much did he weigh?"

"I don't know. Fifteen, twenty pounds ... no, six or seven, I think. Haven't heard exactly. Blue eyes, but I guess they all have those. Lots of dark hair, like yours. Butt-ugly, though. Got wrinkles on top of wrinkles, and looks like someone spray-painted him with red ink. Alma's fine, though. How are you? You doin' okay?"

"I'm great. Look, tell Alma I love her, will you?"

"Sure. She loves you too, only not a whole lot right now. Having a baby takes a lot out of a girl. She may forgive you by the time you get home."

"Right. Okay. But, she's okay? No problems?"

"Good Lord, son. She's fine; don't worry. I—"

A nasal voice broke in to inform us our time was up. I yelled some belated greetings to Alma's mother and aunt, and the rest of the clan, but the connection was broken before I'd said much more than a word or two.

I took a flight back to Rakkasan that evening, late. The sun had already set when we reached the firebase. I jumped off the chopper in near darkness, almost without feeling. The reality of having a son was still far distant. After the first rush of emotion, I could only know that I was a father. It would be eight more months, when I at last held him up to the ceiling and looked into his eyes, before I truly felt it. The others—Robison, Denholm, Eward, even Dickson, crowded around and shook my hand and laughed and made remarks, but my face was back to its usual deadpan. Black Jack was right. I had work to do.

The next morning, we were briefed on our mission. Hill 990, one of those anonymous green giants we'd flown over two days before, was to be our insertion point. It was located about five klicks to the northwest of Firebase Blaze, still under construction, and only six or seven klicks east of the A Shau. The enemy was known to have supply depots and bunker complexes in the area. Our job was to find them.

We looked over the maps and shook our heads. Even without the recon we'd flown, the nature of the terrain jumped off the page at us. Thin red contour lines were massed together, so closely that they almost seemed a continuous smear across the deep green. Movement would be by ridgeline, period. Trying to strike out across a valley, something we'd done routinely in our AO, would lead to unacceptable delay, at best, or disaster. A platoon caught down at the base of one of those v-shaped draws, surrounded by peaks and ridges hundreds of meters overhead, would find itself isolated and almost helpless. Air strikes would be extremely difficult and hazardous; even artillery support would be limited. There were deep folds there that nothing could reach.

We evolved a plan, or at least a general approach, which we were to refine once we actually walked those ridges. Once done tinkering with it, we sat back, well pleased with ourselves. It solved most of our problems.

It all looked good on paper, and in the event, it *was* good. Looking back on it, that was a considerable achievement, for us to sit down in a CP bunker and in one afternoon come up with a workable tactical plan to use in terrain so formidably different from any we'd experienced to that point.

April 16 dawned cool and clear. While we assembled on the PZ, waiting the arrival of Black Widow Four Four and his squadron, we were apprised of a change: Instead of Hill 990, we would be inserted into another LZ, Hill 770, a bit to the south and east of 990. This made no difference, really: Since the entire area was unfamiliar to us, one ridge was just as good or bad as the other.

As usual, First Platoon was the first one in. I found it hard to remember the last time we weren't the lead platoon on a company CA. Even though it was only about 20 kilometers from Rakkasan to the area around Hill 770, the weather changed dramatically. Heavy white mist and low-lying clouds covered the shoulders and flanks of the mountains. We slowly circled the peaks while artillery and then ARA pummeled the chosen LZ, hidden below the clouds. It had been blasted out of the forest the previous day by a pathfinder team of engineers, who'd been inserted by jungle penetrator while the Huey hovered overhead. An infantry platoon leader's life expectancy was three weeks, but I wouldn't have traded jobs with one of those guys for anything.

The sun was still too low in the sky to burn off the mist, so it clung to the hills tenaciously; we could see nothing, not even the intense yellow flashes of 155mm HE rounds pounding the ground. Finally, the guns and ARA fell silent, and Black Widow Four Four, in whose craft I was riding, began a slow, cautious descent through the grey mist and cloud. The air felt clammy and cool. Our stomachs tightened into the familiar ball of anticipation. We broke through the clouds and found ourselves directly above the hill; its slopes looked black and smoky in the dim grey light. The LZ was a dull orange and grey patch ahead of us, across a saddle nestled between two sharp twin peaks. Wisps of smoke still curled from some shattered trees standing blackened and bare around the edges of the LZ. As we neared the saddle, I could make out the dozens of shallow craters, only a few inches across, that marked the impact of the 155mm rounds. I smiled slightly as the crew chief's M60 began thudding a few inches from my ear, recalling the first time I'd heard it, and how startled I'd been. Now it was comforting and expected, a passage in a familiar ritual.

As in all combat assaults, the ground rose up swiftly at the last moment. Suddenly the roar of the engine and the swaying motion became noticeable again — I'd blocked them out as unimportant during the flight — and so too the fact that I was on a terribly vulnerable platform several feet above the ground. I began to lean forward in anticipation as the ground seemed almost to lunge at me, and then Black Widow Four Four tilted his nose up slightly and it was time to go.

M16 held across my chest, equipment flapping and jostling, I thrust myself forward and hit the ground in a crouching run, without pausing, to a spot along the eastern edge of the LZ. A quick check of my compass confirmed my position; north was to my left; my platoon was to cover eleven to one, which meant I would have to move across the LZ.

Behind and around me were Helms and St. Onge, with their radios; Hyde, with Logan and Westman and their M60 and ammo, were across the LZ, having exited from the opposite side. I pointed to the north and all of them began to move to our sector. Logan's gun, by prearrangement, was to be placed exactly at 12 o'clock, or due north.

Hyde now stood on the LZ, arms raised like some ancient necromancer, directing in the other lift ships. I crouched on the ground, ignoring the buffeting wind from the Hueys, and called in the LZ time and status to Black Jack, hovering, unseen in the clouds overhead, in his command helicopter.

"Black Jack, this is Bravo One Six. LZ is green; LZ time is 0726, over."

Black Jack, his voice warbling and fading, acknowledged.

I moved up beside Hyde. The second ship had landed while I was on the horn with Black Jack; now the third touched down and six figures jumped out, hunched over against the weight of their packs and the prop blasts, running to their assigned positions, automatically registering where Logan's gun was as a reference. The fourth, and fifth, and finally the sixth, with Sergeant Wright, Brown and Muldoon, all touched down in rapid succession. Only one small incident marred a perfect insertion: Bresina, on the fourth ship, had been unable to jump in time. The pilots were barely touching down, hovering for only seconds on raised skids before taking off again. I was fortuitously looking straight at Bresina as his chopper approached; I saw him tense with the others, and lean forward, and then check — probably a strap or a buckle caught on an eyebolt on the floor of the craft — and then present me with a surprised, woebegone look as the ship roared up and away, with him still in it.

But I had no time for that now; the rest of the company was on its way. Eward's people came in next and secured the western part of the perimeter, from seven to ten. Dickson's platoon followed, with Robison's CP group; he covered the east, from two to four. Finally, Denholm arrived, to plug the gap at the rear, or south. Hard on his last ship's arrival was Black Jack, who jumped off his command ship and strutted around the perimeter, without helmet or weapon.

The perimeter was now too crowded; it was time to expand it. At a nod from Robison, I raised my hand and flicked my fingers forward. I grinned with a fierce pride as the men responded instantly, right by the book (our book): Two men from each of the four-man positions jumped up, ran forward some 20 meters and threw themselves down, covering the advance of the other two, who had of course been covering them. It was all done in seconds, without a single voiced command. They ended up some 40 to 50 meters away, lying or crouching in place, weapons ready, alert and exuding confidence. Sergeant Wright and I exchanged pleased, fleeting smiles. There was no hesitation, no fumbling and no uncertainty. This was a far cry from the Mack Sennet comedy of a few months before. I turned around at that point, to watch the other platoons maneuver, and found Black Jack standing silently behind me, with something that, in anyone else, I might have taken as approval. I had told myself over and over that I didn't care what the flinty old bastard thought, but of course that was moonshine; I did care, and I wanted him to know that Bravo One was a tough, aggressive and professional unit. I could hide my professional pride behind wisecracks and sardonic mockery, but it was there. It didn't matter what he thought of me personally, as long as he understood that First Platoon, Bravo, was the best in the battalion.

The proposed NDP was only about 1,000 meters to our east, and we made it by noon that day. The ridge was razor-thin and so heavily forested that we could see nothing of the slopes below. We set up immediately, with Sergeant Hyde and his squad running a quick sweep about 100 meters to either side. Chuck Denholm moved through us and started poking into the hollows and spurs to the east, while Eward did the same behind us, to the west between us and the LZ. Third Platoon remained back on the LZ with Robison.

It was Denholm, then, who almost immediately found a small bunker complex nestled into the north flank of the ridge, about 300 meters ahead of and a couple of hundred below the NDP site. His voice was laconic but pleased as he called Robison to report that the bunkers, showing signs of very recent occupancy, had been searched and found to contain ammunition, food and a large medical supply cache, including boxes of gauze, several crates of plasma bottles, some morphine and hundreds of hypodermic needles and several cases of antibiotics.

"No bras?" Robison asked, after Denholm had finished reading off his list.

"Nope. No bras. They must not have any nurses around here."

"Shit. I was hoping for nurses. I got a headache. Okay. What's in those documents, anything good?" (It was years after the war before I finally found out what those titillating 34C bras were for: Not nurses but coffee filters. The high humidity and frequent rains would turn regular paper filters into limp paste after only a few days, but the bras worked just fine.)

Denholm's last act was to destroy the entire cache with thermite grenades. Normally, we'd have lifted the medical supplies out, for distribution to the South Vietnamese civilian hospitals and clinics, but the terrain said no. The cache was hidden in a small but deep hollow; it would have been impossible to bring a Huey in to lift the stuff out, and the idea of humping those hundreds of pounds of material back up the steep ridge was not even considered.

The find made us even more enthusiastic in our search; we knew there was something here. Dickson found a second depot on the third day, also hidden in the fold of a deep and precipitous hollow. This one was mainly food — rice, dried fruit, some canned stuff — and some weapons and ammo. These bunkers, and their contents, were also burned. On the following day we got word that Delta Company, several kilometers to our west, just east of the A Shau itself, had uncovered a huge transportation depot, including over 50 five-ton trucks, as well as large quantities of diesel fuel, spare parts and tools. They'd been found in a valley just north of Highway 548. That find, and a similar one made by the 2/501st, who came across two or three tons of ammunition, served notice that we were indeed in the heart of the enemy's territory. We had very little trouble, this time around, keeping the men alert at night.

After Dickson's find, however, we came across nothing of interest. As we looked over our maps, we decided to change direction. The ridge we were following appeared to lead into a dead end; a small but deep valley surrounded on three sides by very high steep mountains. It made little sense to us that the enemy would place anything substantial in that valley — what for? How would they get it back out for their use? Instead, we followed a spur that led south, and then a saddle took us to another ridge, this one also running east-west, a couple of kilometers south of Hill 770.

Eward had proved already to be a good soldier and a solid platoon leader. The more we saw of him, the more confidence Denholm and I had in him. On first acquaintance, I'd judged him to be stolid and humorless, even somewhat stupid. My first impressions are invariably correct, unless they're wrong. It was true that Eward was slow of speech, often maintaining a stubborn silence, especially during our moments of banter and chops busting, and it was also true that he often was literal-minded, but he was far from stupid. And as to stolidity — he was, in his own way, even more aggressive than Denholm and me. In his case it took the form of implacability, a sort of unnerving thoroughness and attention to detail. He was like a glacier; slow, seemingly inert, but inexorable and unstoppable.

The ridge we'd followed was skirted by the Rao Trang, which flowed out of the valley and toward its junction with the Song Bo, near Blaze, several kilometers to the east. We reached a steep bluff overlooking the stream; below us was a valley a bit broader than the others we'd seen, no doubt because of the waterbed, but just as densely forested, save for a small belt of saw grass and reeds, easily seen from where we were, that lined one bank of the Rao Trang. Our NDP was on that ridge, near its western end. Our plan was to descend the south flank down to the valley, turn east along the stream and follow it to a small low hill, tomorrow night's NDP. Beyond that was a clearing on the north bank of the Rao Trang; on the following day, we'd move to that clearing, only a half a klick from the hill, and be picked up for extraction.

Almost 24 hours later, I was standing on the same ridge. Well, no, I wasn't standing: I was walking, as quickly as possible, away from Robison, who *was* standing, hands on hip, looking down at the valley with an expression that would have curdled a mother's milk at 1000 meters. For once, I wasn't the cause of the glare. The reason I was walking away was humanitarian; I didn't want to see a grown infantry captain cry.

Okay, I wasn't the best subordinate, and we argued more often than Matthau and Lemon, but I honestly felt sorry for him. Just a few hours before, Robbie had stood on this ridge, map in hand and valley spread out below him, in a state of grace that very few commanders in the history of warfare had ever had the good fortune to experience: He knew, with virtual certainty, where both his unit and the enemy were, where they were going and what would inevitably happen within the next quarter of an hour or so: The destruction or capture of a sizeable enemy force.

16. The Rao Trang

It had started that morning. Two Six had moved south off this ridge, to the Rao Trang; he was to then sweep east along its banks. Three Six had also moved down to the Rao Trang, but not before following our ridge to the east, and only then descending the slopes. He would follow the river west and link up with Eward at a prominent bluff that jutted out from the southern banks of the Rao Trang, forcing the river into a u-shaped detour; it was this bluff that would be the rendezvous point.

Almost immediately upon reaching the valley floor, Eward was caught in an ambush, a sizeable one. Reacting instantly and correctly, he pinned the NVA down while sending a squad in a loop to the southwest, flanking the enemy and forcing him to retreat along the banks of the river. That was how Robison, almost a kilometer away, knew exactly where everyone was.

All that had to happen to trap the enemy force was for Dickson to take his Three Six element and establish a blocking position on the river where it rounded the bluff, the sides of which were too steep and bare for them to climb, not with a platoon of infantry right behind them. Prevented from following the Rao Trang on its eastern course, they would have had to cross the river where it was at its widest and shallowest, leaving them vulnerable to Two Six's fire and ARA, which was already on its way.

Robbie was beaming happily, already hearing Black Jack's commendation ... then it all fell apart on him in an appalling five minutes.

The plan, although hastily improvised, was perfect, brought about by Two Six's skill and bulldog tenacity. But it depended on Dickson performing one simple, basic act: Follow the river west to the bluff and horseshoe bend.

He was nowhere to be found.

I won't go into the tedious two hours that followed, as everyone from Black Jack (who became involved early on, having had to call in the ARA) to Robison to the Arty commander back on Berchtesgaden to the Bilk Two Two pilot, who had a brace of deadly F105s circling in a holding pattern like hungry sharks, cursed Lieutenant Dickson and all his progeny: He was called more names by more people than almost any individual in history; even Denholm and I added our invective.

Finally, when it became evident that the NVA had slipped around the bluff, climbed its east slope, which was heavily forested and much shallower, and then disappeared into the ravines and hills to the south, everyone went home who could, and all that was left for us was to make sure that Two Six and Three Six linked up; it was nearing sunset and Robbie didn't want them separated and unsure of the other's location after dark.

I suppose I misspoke a little when I said Dickson wasn't to be found. He didn't disappear; we had radio contact with him the whole time. It's just that where he was reporting himself to be and the reality on the ground bore no possible correlation. Somehow or other, he conceived the notion that he had *passed* Two Six and was now to Eward's west, while also insisting that he'd seen no bluff or bend. It had been a long day; Robison was beyond frustration, and the sun was nearing the horizon. Eward, even more angry than Robison, broke in to say, curtly, that he was going to pop smoke, and Dickson should close on him.

None of this, however, was the reason I was trying to move away from Captain Robison. It's what came next that did it.

Eward popped two red smoke grenades and got on the radio. "Do you see the smoke?" he asked Dickson.

"Yep. I see it. It's to my east, like I said. I'm behind you."

"Well, move toward it. We'll be on the lookout for you, But you're sure you see the smoke?"

"Yeah, yeah; I see it."

"What color is it?"

And now came the words that would forever enshrine Dickson in the pantheon of Army greats. "I can't tell; the sun's in my eyes."

There was a moment of stunned silence up on the ridge. By now the RTOs had switched on the speakers and we could all hear the radio transmissions. Robison and I looked at each other. "The sun's in my eyes" ... this from a man who had just spent an entire hour insisting that he was facing *east*—at sunset. It was truly one of the great moments in life, when you realize, with a thrill, that you are in the presence of perfection. Nothing, no one, ever, anywhere, at any time or place in human history, had ever raised the Art of the Stupid to such heights.

You can see why I wanted to leave the poor bastard alone.

The next morning, we trekked along a ridge on the south bank of the river, west to a small bare hilltop, from which we were extracted. Instead of returning to Rakkasan, as planned, we were taken directly back to Camp Evans, and another stand down.

Late that night, Denholm, Eward and I sat in the supply room, talking until late in the night, or early the next morning. We went over the past week, the actions we'd taken and the tactics we'd used and critiqued them. Even after only two weeks, Eward was now one of us, fully accepted, admired and, more importantly, trusted. If Denholm was a terrier — he kind of looked like a scottie, with his heavy black bushy eyebrows — then Eward was a bulldog, big-jawed and implacable. Me? I don't know. Something elegant and swift, I think.

Dickson wasn't there, uninvited. We didn't really talk much about his series of fiascos but the feeling was there, the same thought in all our minds. There are times when you can afford a mistake in navigation and times not, and chief among the times not is when you are moving as fast as you can to the aid of a fellow platoon leader. Eward had *depended* on Dickson's getting to the right spot on time, and Dickson hadn't delivered. Motives, excuses, explanations and reasons were all irrelevant. Dickson was our weak link. Until now, it hadn't mattered. But now, the A Shau loomed. It mattered.

17

Zeus Frowns

Firebase Blaze; YD538022; 25 April 1969; 0630–1630

The morning of the 25th found us waiting on the PZ under an already hot sun, awaiting pickup, speculating about the operation ahead of us. The A Shau had its reputation, but beyond that we knew nothing about what we'd be getting into. That it would involve more contact than we'd had over the past few months seemed possible or even probable. It occurred to me, with a little shock of surprise, that our company had not suffered one casualty from enemy fire in the entire time we'd been up north. I mentioned this to Wright and he grimaced.

"It don't pay to talk about that, Lieutenant."

After a wait of half an hour, Robison informed me that there had been a change of plans: I was now to lead the company into Firebase Blaze, hold in place and await further direction. Beyond that, he said, he knew nothing. Minutes later, a big Chinook settled slowly on the dusty LZ and we filed aboard.

Blaze was still nothing more than a smear of dirt in the valley floor. Dozens of caterpillar tractors were crawling all over the place, pushing tons of dirt around and raising clouds of dust that sometimes obscured the sun which had finally broken through the early morning mists. We were deposited on a grassy knoll, right above a small stream. From where I stood, I could see nothing of any bunkers or prepared positions. I assumed we had some type of security somewhere around here. In the meantime, I told Sergeant Wright to form the men in squads, drop packs, and relax.

As usual, we had hours to wait. It was infernally hot, and only two things made the wait bearable; the first was an encounter with a supercilious lieutenant from the brigade staff, who had no information but told us to stay in place, to bake in the sun. That irritated me, but on the other hand it validated my belief in my moral superiority over REMF staff officers in pressed fatigues. The second was a presence of a small pool in that stream. I allowed the men to go swimming, a squad at a time, which went a long way toward preventing heat stroke — there was no shade at all here.

So we all got a chance to get in the water and cool off, which was just as well, since the temperatures rapidly climbed to well over 100 degrees. When Robison and the rest of the company hopped out of their Chinooks, they found us leaning against our packs, relatively cool and rested.

Robison was registering querulous envy — they'd been waiting on a hot LZ for the past hour — debating with himself whether to give the other platoons permission to emulate our example, when another jeep came skidding and bouncing down the dirt trail. This time, however, it was a Lt. Col. Kraciewski, and not the S3 lieutenant, who jumped from the vehicle.

"Where's the CO?" He demanded.

Robison walked over to him and saluted. "Afternoon, sir."

Kraciewski glared at him. "What the hell are you doing here? You're supposed to be at the other LZ!"

Robison blinked. "We just got here about ten minutes ago. The hooks dropped us off right here."

"Well, where's your advance man? He should have been over there three hours ago."

Robison looked at me. "What about it, Frank?"

I returned the colonel's stare. "We've been here for over four hours sir. A Brigade S3 lieutenant named Rentzle told me this morning, right after I got here, to wait right here until further notice."

"Rentzle?" He looked as if he'd had to repeat a bad word. "What the hell does he know?" He turned back to Robison, his manner brisk. "Get your people over to PZ Laura." He pointed downstream, where, half seen in the whirling dust, several Hueys sat on a PZ. He started to get back in his jeep, hesitated, then turned back.

"On second thought, you'd better come with me, Robison. You're going to need a briefing and there isn't much time. Hop in."

Robison reached down and picked up his pack and weapon, threw them into the back seat of the jeep, and looked over at me. "Get 'em over there, Frank." He climbed in beside his gear, and the jeep jerked and bucked into gear and up the hill.

I looked around for Sergeant Murtiff and caught his eye. "Get everybody moving, Top. We're headed downstream to the PZ. Order of march will be 1-2-3-4." I sighed, moved to my pack, and began to put my gear on while Sergeant Wright called out the squads' order of march to the squad leaders. Within a minute, Hyde, his spare frame draped with harnesses, moved out at the head of his squad, leading the company toward the PZ.

Naturally, 30 minutes later, when we assembled on the PZ, we found out that there would be another wait. I looked at my watch; it was already almost 1400. We dropped packs and sat in the hot sun, waiting. First Sergeant Murtiff looked at me and winked.

"Army don't never change, Lieutenant."

I agreed. "Let that be a source of comfort to you in your old age, Top."

17. Zeus Frowns

He laughed and walked over to where Sergeant Wright and Sergeant Micheaux sat in the dust.

It was almost half an hour later, at about 1430, when the jeep drove up again and dropped Robison off before speeding back the way it had come. Robison tossed his pack and weapon down at a spot a few yards from the company and called for the officers and senior NCOs.

He waited until we had clustered around him, then hunkered down on his heels, spreading a map of the A Shau in front of him. "Anybody hear about what's going on in the A Shau right now?" He asked.

Sergeant Murtiff nodded. "I heard somebody's run into some shit."

Robison pointed to the map. "2/17th Cav ran into something here, at about 345052." We looked at the spot; it was on the east side of the A Shau, near the valley floor. "They got into it yesterday; since then one company has lost over 40 men."

Whistles and raised eyebrows greeted this news. Forty casualties in one day for one company? That was about twice the number our entire battalion had suffered throughout the previous four months.

"It's a good-sized enemy force," Robison continued. "Might be battalion or bigger. They're using RPG and big-caliber automatic weapons fire. We're going to be inserted at 347051." He pointed to a small hill that stuck up from the valley floor at the base of the mountain slope. "We'll move in and support the 2/17th units. Charlie and Delta companies will go in at another location and try to pinch the NVA between us." He looked up and stared at us. "It looks like the gooks might be sticking around and giving us a fight, this time."

"What have they got down there, a big supply depot, or what?" Eward asked.

"Something like that. They're stirred up, though. We'll have two gunships from Evans—call signs are Crazy Otto One Seven and One Eight. Do your RTOs have the net frequencies for Battalion and Brigade?"

We all muttered assent.

"Okay." He looked at his watch. "At 1500 hours, we'll take off. Bo will go in first. Dickson next, then Eward. Denholm, you're the company reserve; you go in last. I'll be with Eward's people. The LZ will be secured by people from the 2/17th, but we'll have to be careful; they've lost three slicks since yesterday. Bo, you take ten o'clock to two on the ground; Marsh, you go two to six, and Dickson six to ten. Denny, when you get in you move your people out of the perimeter right away; I'll show you which direction when you get on the ground. ACL will be six, so plan accordingly. Bo, I want you to take both your radios in with you, since you're gonna be on the first bird. Set one to Battalion freq, the other on Brigade. I wanna have a working radio as soon as I hit the ground. Okay?"

"Right," I nodded. "What freq are those guys from 2/17th on?"

"Same as Brigade. They're OPCON to us, or we are to them, or some such bullshit. Don't count on a liaison man on the ground when you get there; they might have one there or they might not." He picked up his map and started to fold it. "Any questions?"

"What about C-rations, Captain?" Sergeant Wright asked.

"Forget 'em. We'll catch a re-supply when we're on the ground."

"What about these goddamn gas masks; can't we leave 'em behind?" Eward asked.

"Negative. Division says carry 'em, so we carry 'em."

"They're a pain in the ass."

"Then you're wearing yours wrong. Anything else? No? Okay. Get going and get your people ready. We move out in 30 minutes."

We were assembled, in good order, on the PZ a few minutes later. It was about 1540. I sat on my pack, smoking a cigarette and chatting idly with Muldoon and Sergeant Wright. Sergeant Murtiff ran up to us.

"Get your people over to that dumpster, Wright! You got five minutes to load up with C's!"

I threw my cigarette down viciously. "We're all packed now; no way we can be loaded up and be ready in five minutes!"

"Black Jack wants us loaded up. CO wants to see you." He ran off, bellowing for Garza to get his men over to the large green container sitting on the far side of the LZ, where two or three men were tossing cartons of C-rations on the ground and splitting them open. Each carton held a dozen meals, and the ground was littered with well over 100 of the individual boxes the rations came packed in.

Robison was standing over near the dumpster, so I picked up my gear and moved it to where he was. The place was a madhouse, a large broken anthill with dozens of green ants scurrying about. I could see our troops stuffing the boxes into their packs, their careful, neat packing gone for naught. A few were trying to pick through the boxes, looking for their favorite meals, but Sergeant Murtiff and the other NCOs cursed and bellowed; there wasn't enough time for that. I asked Helms to fill my pack for me while I spoke with Robison.

The CO wasted no time. He looked me in the eye, his face grimmer and older than I'd ever seen it. "There's been a change, Frank. 2/17th has taken over 40 more casualties in the last hour. Black Jack doesn't think we're going to do any good going into that same LZ. We're going in on top of the mountain, at"—he glanced at a note—"363064. Got that? Okay. They daisy-chained it some time ago; made an LZ up there near the peak. It's on a place called Hill 1485.... Shoulder of the Dong Ngai: see it on your map? Right, Frank.—this LZ is unsecured. You understand?"

I nodded, the butterflies beginning to twitch and jiggle in my stomach. "Same procedure on the ground?"

"Yeah. Ten to two, like I said. The way this is supposed to work, we're gonna go in up there, on top of the hill, and work our way down towards where the Cav is catching all the shit. Delta is gonna come in right behind us." He took off his steel pot and wiped his blond hair. "Okay?"

"Right." I walked back to where Sergeant Wright, Helms and Muldoon stood. My pack, which this morning had been neatly closed and balanced, lay on the ground, a lumpy amorphous mass with the edges of green C-ration cans peeping out of the inside compartment and side pockets, where Helms had stuffed them. I hefted it and grunted. It weighed 10 or 12 pounds more than it had a few minutes before.

"Helms, if you've given me pork or beef slices, I'll have your ass."

He grinned and shook his head. "Nah, I took good care of you, sir."

"Listen up, Top," I said to Wright. "We're going in on a different LZ. This one's unsecured. I'm going to change the loads. Helms and St. Onge will come with me, and so will Hyde. But I want Logan with me, too, with his M60."

"Yes, sir. That's five. Who else? Muldoon?"

I hesitated. "Who has the M79 in your squad, Hyde — is it Carlton?"

Hyde glanced up from tossing rations into his open pack. "Yes, sir," he drawled, "Short Round's mah man."

I bit my lip, frowning. Carlton was new, and young; not one I'd normally pick to be with me on the first ship in. But, I reflected, I wanted Logan — and Hyde — with me, and Carlton was in Hyde's squad.

"Okay," I agreed. "Carlton's on the first bird. Top, I want you on the last one, as usual. Muldoon goes with you. But I want Brown on the second ship in, with the rest of Hyde's squad, just in case."

Wright nodded his massive head. "Okay, sir. You sure you don't want Muldoon with you?"

"Yeah, I'm sure. If we run into shit I'll want firepower, not bandages."

"Yes, sir." He moved over to where the other squad leaders stood, making sure that everyone understood which helicopter they were to get on.

I looked down at the pile of gear at my feet. I was debating what to put on first. I decided that the gas mask was the one item I would least likely be needing, so that went on first, the long strap over my left shoulder and the mask itself, in a large green canvas cover, resting against my right thigh. Next came two bandoliers of ammo, one thin green strap over each shoulder. Because the straps were so thin and the ammo heavy, the bandoliers tended to cut into your flesh after a while, and I normally donned them last, so that they rested against the thick, wide padded surface of the pack straps. But I wanted nothing on those pack straps, in case I had to pull the quick-release tab and dump the pack in a hurry. The two canteens, each holding two quarts, came next, and then a thick green strap, borrowed from a radio harness, from which dangled a plastic gallon jug of water. Next were the binoculars, and finally I grunted and swung the pack, now weighing about 55 pounds, over my back and onto my shoulders, squirming until I adjusted its weight evenly. I squatted down, like a woman in a tight skirt picking up a handkerchief, grabbed my helmet and M16, placed the helmet on my head, thrust the stock of the rifle against the ground in front of me and leaned slightly forward, resting against it. It occurred to me, as I stood there, swaying slightly, searching for the most comfortable stance, that a medieval knight might have gone through a similar routine to don his battle dress, probably with the same exasperation. I now weighed, instead of my normal 150 pounds, about 250, or just about what a knight in full armor had weighed.

Instead of a prancing charger, however, I would mount a whirling, swaying, dancing, roaring, olive drab helicopter. When the first lift ship arrived, six of us ran forward. One hand holding my weapon, the other my helmet, I ran toward the helicopter and, as I got within a couple of feet of it, pivoted my body so that I faced away from it and in the same motion jumped backwards, landing with a soft grunt on the floor of the compartment. I then wrapped my right arm around the center doorpost, and hung on.

Helms and Logan sat to my right; on the other side of the craft were Hyde, Carlton and St. Onge, their backs to ours. Above and behind me, the handles of his M60 firmly in his hands, sat the starboard door gunner.

The tail of the slick lifted slightly, pushing the nose down; the skid lifted an inch or two off the ground. The muted rumble of the motor suddenly became a throbbing roar, and we started to scutter crab-like across the face of the low, gently sloping hill the PZ was located on, building up speed as we went until, reaching the small stream we'd swum in an hour or two earlier, we tilted to port and soared up. The horizon disappeared from my view; all I could see was blue sky, with an occasional cloud. Then we settled back on an even keel, and the mountains reappeared; dark green close by, a smoky grey along the horizon. We built up altitude quickly, until we reached about 5,000 feet, heading straight down the valley, to the west. Normally we would have circled the LZ until all the lift ships were airborne, so that we could fly in tight formation, but today we headed straight out. There were so many helicopters taking off or landing (ours was not the only operation to be channeled through Blaze) that the air space would have become dangerously crowded if they'd had the pilots circle.

It was less than 15 minutes later that the steep, high, forested slopes below us fell away to the floor of the A Shau. We were over the abandoned airstrip of A Luoi. A muddy, meandering stream, the Rao Lao, strung its tired way through the middle of the valley.

The valley itself was flat and treeless, but immediately to either side of it, as it lay northwest-southeast along the Laotian border, were the steep, thickly forested mountains which the NVA had for years been using as supply and headquarters areas. To the west, visible but indistinguishable, was Laos. To the east, peaks jutting green or grey against the sky, were the mountains we'd just flown over; beyond their eastern slopes lay the valley where Blaze was located.

I noticed, after a few minutes, that we'd begun to circle; behind us, silhouetted against the southern sky, looking, at that distance, like fat ungainly tadpoles swimming in a light grey sea, were the other lift ships. I looked at my watch: 1605. We should have been approaching the LZ. Then I saw, to the northeast, in the direction of Hill 1485, a thick, dirty grey blanket of clouds. Red flashes suddenly lit the interior of the cloud mass, turning the outer edges a deep mauve. I could see the rain and hail as it fell in raging sheets onto the valley floor below.

It was the first time I had ever seen a mountain thunderstorm from the air, and it was an awesome sight. We circled around an area just south of the storm, out over the valley. Well to the southeast, miles away, we could see stringy patches of blue sky, but everywhere else there were clouds: Grey and silver-grey above us, deep grey and purple directly ahead of us. The lightning flashed and glowed, usually showing only as a red or purple smear within the clouds; occasionally it shone orange or yellow. Only once or twice, when it slashed across the outer edges of the clouds, did it become that brilliant, mind-stopping, jagged bar that turns the whole world white. The thunder was constant; deep, booming waves of sound that washed over the puny roar of the helicopter engine as the surf washes over and obliterates a child's pool scooped out of the beach sand. I gave a slight smile. I could see why the Greeks, rationalists though they were, could still believe that only an irascible god could wreak this havoc across the skies. Zeus was angry.

The temperature began to drop; scant minutes before, on the ground at Blaze, we'd sweated and cursed the heat. Now we shivered and hunched our backs against the cold wind that clawed at our exposed bodies. I looked around the compartment. Helms sat on my right, his left arm wrapped around the center post. His boyish face looked almost child-like; his eyes were closed and a curious half-smile was on his lips; he was thinking of his home, and his young wife. Logan, holding his M60 across his body with his left arm, held onto a brace on the bulkhead by the open door. At one particularly loud burst of thunder, he turned to me and raised an eyebrow, in mock alarm. I nodded back, grinning. Glancing back over my right shoulder, I could see Hyde and Carlton; they both sat staring out at the furious sky. Catching Hyde's pinched, worried look— he hated thunderstorms—I smiled again, and winked. He gave a slow, sheepish grin back.

I turned back to the view in front of me, where the clouds still boiled and scuttled across the mountains. I was still grinning. But I knew. It wasn't fear, or the usual butterflies I had during a CA. I knew.

This would be a hot LZ.

The knowledge came to me unnoticed, without volition, the way a man lost in a strange city will suddenly, on turning a corner, recognize the road ahead of him. There was no fear or even apprehension; it was knowledge, that was all. I even lost my awe at the thunderstorm raging across the sky. For all its violence and might, this was after all merely a prelude.

Soon after that the pilot made one last turn over the valley floor and began to fly northeast. I watched, fascinated, as the peaks approached. I looked at my watch; it was 1624. We began to descend, or rather, the mountain slopes rose to meet us; the hill we were headed for stood at 4500 feet.

18

The Crater

YC363064; 25 April 1969; 1630–1730

1625: Out of the jumble of peaks standing green against the still sullen sky, one, tall and steep, shows directly ahead.

1626: Closer. I can see individual trees. Our air speed begins to drop off.

1627: Closer. Where is the LZ?

1628: There! A crater, or perhaps two, across the back of a saddle running between two hilltops near the peak of Hill 1485.

1629: SEEEEWHOOOSHHH! Gunships and Cobras, flying parallel to us, loose lightning of their own, as rocket after rocket slams into the ridge. Overhead and to my left, the barrel of the door gunner's M60 dips and swivels as he brings it to bear on the LZ just ahead. Then it thunders in a staccato roar.

1630: The LZ looms suddenly ahead. The trees which just seconds before, seen from overhead, had seemed like child's toys scattered across an abandoned playroom floor, were now real trees again, reaching high over our heads.

Pack! Pack! Pack! A hollow, snapping sound, from the trees. I hear it for the first time; the sound an AK-47 makes when it is fired directly at you. It is unmistakable; a metallic crack! that reverberates along all your nerve endings. The bird sways and shudders, hovering over the ground; the pilot strains to keep it away from the close-hanging branches of the nearby trees, which reached out long gaunt arms to clutch the whirling blades. More snapping sounds, coming from directly in front of me as I face out.

We are under fire.

Suddenly a sort of laughter bubbles uncontrollably from some unimagined place within me. For the briefest of moments, I feel a fierce joy at being young and alive and staring down the ancient tribal enemy.

At last the pilot touches down. I see Helms jump out, then Logan. I tense my muscles and push, but nothing happens. I push again, and curse; the strap on my gas mask has snagged across an eyebolt on the aircraft's floor. I struggle and squirm; already two or three eternally lasting seconds have passed. The door gunner reaches down and shoves me just as I finally free the mask, and I tumble out of the helicopter, off balance. In those few seconds, the pilot has begun to drift backwards, off the summit of the saddle; I fall on the slopes below the crater in which Helms and Logan have landed. The weight of the pack drags me down; I roll down the bare slope before fetching up against a fallen log. I can't see anyone else, from where I am lying, but I can hear the continuing spatter and crackling of AK-47 fire, and then, briefly, a heavy burst from an M60, whether from the ship or from Logan's gun I cannot tell.

I start to push myself up to my hands and knees, to make a dash for the crater above me, but once again the mask snags, this time on a protruding stump of a limb. Panting, snarling, I finally free the mask and run toward the crater some ten yards away. I land on the bottom; just above me, leaning against the east slope of the crater, I see Helms, eyes big, mouth tightened in a straight line as he holds the radio microphone out to me. At the top of the saddle, just inside the crater, helmet off, red hair limned against the grey-green trees, Logan jerks and shakes as his M60 sprays the wood line a few meters away.

The Huey is still swaying and bucking behind me; I wonder why the pilot doesn't pull straight up. There comes a slam, a scream of ripping metal and then a sound like a huge sheet of aluminum foil being ripped and crumpled. The slender tail of the chopper whips across the LZ; the Huey, like a wounded bird, gives one last useless shudder and crumples to the ground, blades gone spinning into the forest behind us. It lies partly on its left side, with the nose and body on the saddle above us and the tail, shattered and twisted, sticking out over the crater.

I take the mike from Helms, pause to take a deep breath, and then realize that I am perfectly calm. I feel neither fear nor uncertainty; I know what to do. My hand presses the tab.

"Black Jack, this is Bravo One Six, over."

"This is Black Jack."

"This LZ is Red; I say again, the LZ is Red. LZ time is 1630."

"Roger, One Six. I copy. You have a red LZ."

"Affirmative. The bird is down, over."

"Roger. Are you returning fire?"

"Affirmative. I'm going to pop smoke, over."

"Roger."

I pull a smoke canister off my harness, remove the pin and toss it into the trees. Ocher clouds billow out and stream away in the wind. I become conscious of something: the thudding chatter of the M60 is absent. I feel a twist of alarm as I look to my left, but Logan isn't hit. He is swearing, almost weeping, as he tries to clear his jammed and useless gun. Helms, between me and Logan, rises up and fires a burst from his M16.

"We're taking incoming from a hill just east of us. Request ARA, over."

"Roger, One Six. I see your smoke."

"Roger."

Logan, spurning his gun, pulls the pin from a grenade and throws it at the hill. I watch in a mixture of apprehension and irritation as the grenade flies about 20 feet before striking a tree and bouncing right back at us. It rolls up against a log several feet from the lip of the crater and explodes, as we duck.

"Where the hell'd you ever learn to throw?" I yell at him, but he doesn't hear me. I press the tab on the radio, and as I do a flat, wet smacking sound comes from behind me; then another. RPG. That sound is also unique.

"This is One Six. We're taking RPG fire now. Where's that ARA, over?"

"It's on the way, One Six. Any casualties?"

I look around. A figure in flight dress lies outside the crater below me. I can see no one else. "At least one. I want a run southeast-northwest. Azimuth from smoke is one zero zero; distance 75 meters, over."

"Roger, I copy direction 100, distance 75. They're coming."

I look back at the crewman; he is moving his head, from side to side, but he still lies out in the open. I crouch and run to him, grab his feet and pull him into the crater. He gives a ragged scream as I drag him. He lies on the crater bottom, breathing in short, harsh gasps.

"You okay?" I ask him.

He nods, his face white. "Arm ... broken." I start to leave him but he reaches out with his good arm, wincing. Major D ... hit."

I nod and run back to Helms. Before taking the mike from him I fire a burst of M16 fire into the woods. I can hear the gunships firing, but the slam of exploding rockets is too far off. Too far!

"Black Jack, this is One Six. Drop 50. I say again, drop 50."

"Roger. Drop 50."

I can hear Logan shouting at me, but I can't make out the words. I have already pulled the quick-release tab at my shoulder and dumped my pack. Now I shrug off the rest of the gear. I hand the mike back to Helms. There's so damn much noise! I pull a fresh magazine from one of the bandoliers, eject the empty one, insert the new, and lock a round into the chamber. I pick up the bandolier and turn to go but Helms grabs me.

"Somebody's been blown to hell back there!" He yells in my ear.

I nod. "You didn't see who it was, did you?"

"No, sir. RPG got him. You watch yourself, Lieutenant."

"Right." I scuttle to the top of the crater where Logan, his face purple with rage, is still trying to clear his M60. I tap him on the shoulder, hand him my rifle and the bandolier, and then run, crouching, across the few yards to where the helicopter lies.

As soon as I round the nose of the beast, I see two figures on the ground; one big and burly, the other small and slight. The small one still has his flight helmet on, but the bigger man, with a major's rosette on his collar, has taken his off, revealing ginger hair and a large, flat red face, creased with pain. The name tag on his flight suit reads

18. The Crater

Dougherty. His lips are pulled back in a grimace; he lies on his side, right hand holding a .38, left hand braced against the ground. When he sees me, he drops the revolver and holds his hand over his chest.

I kneel beside him. "You okay?" I yell.

"No. I'm hit in the back," He says through a tight, straining throat muscles. He half-falls, half-lowers himself forward; in the middle of his broad back I see a tiny red-black hole. I turn to the other man; he lifts his head, and from under the green flight helmet blood trickles down his forehead.

"Leg!" He yells. "I'm hit bad in the leg!"

"Right. Wait." I look around. No one else in sight. I can hear Logan firing my M16, but nothing else. I run back around the helicopter, past Logan, and jump into the crater again alongside Helms. His M16 lies propped up against the side of the crater, smoking; he's fumbling with a grenade, which is hung up on the buckle of his pouch. Freeing it, he pulls the pin quickly, stands up and throws in one motion, and then ducks down beside me again. His aim is better than Logan's: the grenade explodes somewhere on the hilltop above us. Even while the grenade is still in the air, he pulls the mike off his shoulder strap and hands it to me.

"Black Jack, Black Jack, this is One Six. Request a medevac, ASAP. I say again, I request a medevac, over."

There was a pause; while I waited, I could hear the ARA firing again, closer than last time, but still not close enough.

"Roger, One Six, we'll have one to you as soon as we can. How many casualties, over?"

I hesitate. You're not supposed to radio this in clear but, shit on a stick, the NVA are right on top of me and can probably count them better than I can. "Three. Two hit by small arms and one with a broken arm, over."

"Roger. Keep me informed."

I grunt an affirmation, then run back up to the major and his crewman. The major is lying on his stomach, still holding the almost useless .38. "Where's my pilot?" he asks. "You seen him?"

I shake my head, looking back over my shoulder at the wood line from which we'd been ambushed. I see nothing.

"Big ugly fellow, name of Watson," the man persisted.

I turn back to him. "Negative. You've got a man down in that crater, on the other side of the bird, but he's your starboard door gunner."

"See if you can —" He stops, suddenly. We both realize two things: First, Logan and Helms have stopped firing, and, second, we are still shouting to be heard. All this time there had been a noise in the background, unnoticed because of the firefight, but now we can hear it plainly; a rough, harsh, multi-toned whine, like a dissonant nine chord played on grating wind instruments.

Dougherty stares at me. "The engine...."

The engine. The engine is still running; the blades are gone but, high up on the housing, I can see the naked shaft turning.

The major grabs my arm, winces, shakes it. "Got to turn it off!" He shouts. "Overheat! Fire!"

I nod. "Okay."

He rolls over on his back, gasps with pain, tries to sit up, then eases back down, his face trembling with the effort. "Switch–center console ... next to yellow handle ... grey switch, on-off ... got that?"

"Right. Center console, yellow handle, grey switch."

"Be careful."

If I was careful, I wouldn't be here.

I crawl into the dying bird and perch on the tilted pilot's seat. The instrument panel lies in front of me. Through the cockpit windows, cracked and starred by bullet holes, I can see a ridgeline leading off the knoll from which they've hit us. The front hatches are open and I feel naked and vulnerable, exposed to the world. I hear the same vicious sound I first heard minutes before, of an AK-47 being fired at me, but from farther away this time; they must be shooting at me from the ridge. No time to be daydreaming. I look at my watch: 1634.

Where's the switch? The yellow handle jumps out at me; there, in the console between the two front seats. And just to the left of it is a grey switch. I reach for it. As I do so, I hear the distinctly heavy sound of three or four rounds slamming into the co-pilot's seat beside me. They etch an interesting rhythm in my brain: thup! thup thup! thup! With my right hand I toggle the switch.

Nothing happens.

Well, shit. I snap it again, in the opposite direction. Still nothing. I see a similar grey switch next to it and try that, then another, and another. My helmet keeps slipping down over my eyes as I bend over. I curse, pull the helmet off, and fling it through the open hatch to the ground below. The slight breeze blowing through the open cockpit feels cool to my sweat-soaked hair. I grimly snap all the switches on the console. Nothing.

As I scramble out of the aircraft, I think to myself, in a detached sort of way, that the NVA must be pretty poor shots. The major shakes his head as I scamper across the saddle and kneel down by his side.

"See that cowling?" He raises a hand and points to the green nose of the Huey, a few feet away. "Lift the cowling up ... underneath is a blue handle ... pull handle down." He makes a quick jerking motion with his hand. "Straight down."

"Right." I rise and do as he says. Still the engine whines and grates on. I turn back to the flyer. "We'll just have to leave it. Medevac's on its way."

"Okay." Sweat and black dirt now cake his cheek and forehead. "Where's my pilot?"

"Don't know." Come to think of it, where are the rest of my people? I think back to those RPG explosions and grimace. How many had I heard? I race back to Helms, realizing, as I run, that the shooting has stopped now. Out of the corner of my eye I see Logan trying once again to clear his machine gun.

"Black Jack's been trying to get hold of you," Helms says, as I run up.

"Okay. Black Jack, this is One Six, over."

"Roger, One Six. Medevac's on its way. What's going on?"

"I've been trying to cut the motor off, over."

There was a short silence. "Roger. You got all your people together?"

"Negative. I'm getting ready to do that now. How long before the medevac gets here?"

"Three, four minutes. Are you still taking incoming?"

"Negative. Not now."

"Roger. Out."

I tap Helms on the shoulder, point to Logan, then to the saddle on the other side of the helicopter. He nods, gathers my discarded gear — his is still on his back, of course — and darts off. I slide down the steep crater slope to the center, directly under the shattered tail, where the door gunner, Fleagane, is half-sitting, his face a monochrome mask of fear and pain. The engine noise here is much worse. I tap him on the leg, lean over, and shout in his ear.

"Medevac coming. Can you move?"

He nods weakly, and struggles to an erect sitting posture. Bracing himself against the crater floor with his good arm, he jerks himself up, and begins to crawl and stumble painfully, up the crater's west wall, alongside the exposed underbelly of the helicopter.

I go around the other way, conscious, suddenly, of having neither helmet nor weapon. I scurry across the nose of the Huey. With the cowling open, the nose of the craft looks like the gaping beak of a nestling, a starved eaglet. The other two crewmen are on their feet; Logan has his arm around the major's waist, supporting him. The crew chief leans against the face of the helicopter. Blood streaks the grey-green dress.

"Here he comes," Helms says, gesturing to the sky to our south.

Looking fat and stubby and terribly vulnerable, the medevac helicopter is approaching, nose-on, about 2,500 meters away. To its east, I see another shape; sleeker, deadlier: a Cobra, rocket launchers snarling, on a run to protect the rescue ship.

I am suddenly conscious of something else; there are still four men unaccounted for, and I have only seconds before the medevac gets here. I get my rifle from Logan and move up the saddle, to the west. Reaching the base of the west hill, I turn and face the crater again; to my upper left stands the knot of wounded men. Directly ahead lies the Huey, on the crater lip. To my lower right is the bare southern slope of the saddle. To my immediate right is thick heavy vegetation. Two bushes, about four feet high, stand directly in front of me, a gap of two feet between them. With my thumb I slide the safety catch off, then immediately snap it back on.

There are none but my own people around here; I'm standing in the open. If the NVA were going to shoot me, they'd have done so by now. I move between the bushes, rifle at the ready port position. A log lies in the middle of the path; I raise my foot to step over it.

A log? I look again.

A leg.

It is cut off — no, not cut: it is as if some titan had wrenched it off; the ends are ragged and trailing ribbons of skin and tissue — at just below the knee. The trouser leg has been blown off, revealing skin that has already turned a mortal grey. A dirty, scuffed jungle boot remains fixed to the foot. A part of my mind that somehow seems detached from all this says, as if in answer to a quiz, that the leg comes from one of my people, since a pilot's boot would not be dirty or scuffed.

I complete my step over the leg, and glance at the bush to my right. It is speckled with crimson berries, and for a disorienting moment I am reminded of Christmas and holly bushes. But then I know what they are; small pieces of flesh, scattered across the leaves, white stained red, like the bread my great-aunt would dip in the rough new wine and give us children, on Sundays during those summers we returned to Italy on home leave.

In the middle of the bush, face-high as I crouch, is a hand, blown off at the wrist. The fingers are half-curled, empty, and grey. Again that unbidden part of my mind answers an unasked question: the hand and the leg are a dead grey because the force of the RPG explosion has literally blown the blood right out of them; not just the venous and arterial blood, but the capillary and lymphatic fluid as well.

I take another step. On the same bush is another leg. There is rather more of this than of the first; it has been blown off above the knee. At my feet is a red stain on the brown hillside, about a foot square. One more step; to my left, a few feet away, I see a flight helmet, lying by the lip of the crater. The inside of it has blood and other matter smeared over the plastic and leather.

I take one more step; by now the medevac is only meters away. I realize with a start that Helms is moving behind me now. A branch sways on my right: whirling, swiveling at the waist, I bring my rifle up in a reflex action, my right thumb hard against the safety, my finger leaping unbidden for the trigger. I recognize Hyde, white-faced and grim. I let out a slow sigh of relief.

"Who's with you?" I ask.

"Short Round," he answers. Ducking his head, he shoulders his way through the bush he'd been sitting behind and joins us. Behind him, barely visible in the foliage, crouches Carlton. It occurs to me that I hadn't noticed any M79 fire during all this.

I look at my watch. 1637. I glance back at the leg, involuntarily. "Where's St. Onge?" I ask. I know where, but I have to ask anyway.

Hyde shakes his head. He's seen the leg too.

Then, with a thumping of the blades, the medevac arrives. The only flat open spot was the middle of the saddle, across which the Huey lies crumpled. The medevac can't land, so the pilot hovers over the crater, only the front of his skid touching the side of the hill. Hyde and Logan help the wounded men into the medevac, while Helms and I search the surrounding wood line with quick-moving, nervous eyes. Now is the moment when I expect the NVA to hit us again, while we are helpless. But the three men scramble or are pushed on board quickly and the pilot, unable to take off straight ahead, backs away from the slope, his tail bobbing and swaying; then, when he's only a few meters away, he roars straight up, the sound of his motor almost doubling in volume as he pours on the power, in a maneuver that at any other time would have been called wasteful. Tilting to starboard, he soars away, leaving in his wake heaving branches, waving their arms mournfully like disappointed acolytes.

I motion for Logan to take his M60 and set up on top of the saddle, just behind the nose of the helicopter. I tell Hyde to move back to the concealing thick brush to our right, where Carlton still crouches, unmoving. Helms and I kneel down by the west lip of the crater, just below the fuselage.

There is no sound, nothing at all, except for the faint hissing of Helms' radio. I examine the area, really for the first time. The saddle we landed on runs roughly east-west, between two low, rather flat-topped knolls. The west hill is fairly clear of vegetation, with just enough trees on it to make landing an impossibility. The east hill, from which the NVA had been shooting at us, is thickly covered with underbrush and trees. The two hills are about 100 meters apart. The saddle itself is completely bare of trees, having been swept clean by bombs designed to do nothing more than to clear a small area of trees so that a helicopter can land. The clearing, partly natural, partly a result of the daisy chain, extends about 30 or 40 meters down the southern slope between the two hills. This slope is steep, and continues all the way down the mountain until it eventually reaches the valley floor almost four kilometers away. The northern slope of the saddle descends only a few meters, at a shallow angle, until it runs into a rough, gorse and weed-covered tableland that humps and tumbles its way northwest for some distance. To the east is another hilltop, higher than the two we are sitting between — Hill 1485 proper. It is steep and thickly wooded, and falls away to the valley floor in a long, narrow ridge that follows an almost straight line to the southeast. The ridge, also heavily wooded, lies about 100 meters to our east. Another ridge, this one jutting off in a northwesterly direction from the near-by east hill, stands about 200 meters to our northeast. Finally, between us and that ridge lies a third, much shorter and lower, that slopes to the northwest until it merges into the tableland to our north. Behind me, to the west, I cannot tell what lies because of the intervening hill.

It becomes apparent that we are in a bad position. The only existing landing zone is right here, at the saddle, and is partly blocked. It is also surrounded by higher ground, ranging from 25 to 200 meters away. I have only four men with me; it will be impossible to secure both the east and west hilltops. Even had we been able to do so, of course, the enemy could still have delivered accurate, heavy fire from any one of four different ridges lying in three different directions. And if I occupy only one of the hilltops — it wouldn't matter which one — all the NVA will have to do is stroll on up to the unoccupied hill and shoot downhill at helicopters that are forced to hover, back off, and then turn before soaring off — at a range of less than 50 meters, at most.

It strikes me that I ought to be a helluva lot more worried than I am.

A firefight breaks out to our south, at the base of the mountain. I have no way of telling if it is the 3/187th or the 2/17th. After a few moments of staring tensely at the forested hilltop to our east, Helms hands me the microphone.

"Iron Raven," he says.

"Iron Raven, this is Bravo One Six, over."

The Colonel's gravely, grandfatherly voice comes quavering over the speaker — the vibrations from the command helicopter he's in scramble his voice into a rough vibrato. "This is Iron Raven. How are you doing down there?"

"This is One Six. We're okay, over." Boccia, you liar.

"Roger. Can I have a casualty report, over?"

"This is One Six. Roger. Three wounded, already medevaced. One confirmed KIA, over."

"Okay, son. Is the KIA yours or a crew member, over?"

I hesitate. Am I really sure that leg back there belongs to St. Onge? I bite my lip. The hell with it. Surely, they were both dead. "It's hard to say — there are pieces scattered all over the LZ. I think he's my man, though."

"This is Iron Raven: Do you have any idea where the missing crewman is, over?"

"Iron Raven, this is One Six. The other crewmember is almost certainly dead. I've found his flight helmet, and it's got blood inside of it, but we haven't found his body yet. There are so many pieces scattered around that they may belong to two different bodies. They've been hit by RPG fire."

The Old Man's voice comes down, low and soothing. "Okay, One Six. Keep me informed. You're doing a fine job. Good luck."

I look at my men. Logan, on my far left, is crouched behind his M60, his broad ugly face a profile in impassive red granite. Helms kneels beside me, his face boyish and still. I hear him swallow, and his shoulders are tensed, but I know he's under control. I can't see Carlton's face, off to my right, but Hyde's narrow visage reflects a sheen of sweat as he constantly moves his head back and forth, eyes searching the wood line along that east hill.

"Lieutenant!"

I look up. Logan's voice. "Yeah?"

He points to the east hill. "Thought I saw something move. Right over there by that big tree right in the middle." His voice is calm but urgent.

I look but see nothing. "Hyde: You see anything?"

"Nossuh. Not a thing."

"Dennis?"

Helms shakes his head. "No, sir."

"I saw something," Logan insists.

"Okay. Carlton, pump about five or six rounds into those trees." I kneel down and watch the hilltop, waiting for him to fire. After five or six seconds of silence, I stare over in his direction. He's shown no sign that he heard me at all. "Carlton!" I say, more loudly. "Carlton! Move it, man!"

Hyde looks at me and shakes his head. He places his rifle down, gently but firmly disengages Short Round's fingers from his weapon and takes it from him. Breaking it open, he takes a short, stubby M79 found from Carlton's belt, drops it into the open chamber, snaps the launcher closed, places it on his shoulder at a 45 degree angle, and pulls the trigger. The weapon gives out a hollow thump! and we watch the grenade lazily spiral up and into the treetops. A second thump, and a third ... eight in all. Explosions, not loud but sharp, shred the branches ... tree limbs and leaves cascade to the ground.

Hyde, after firing the eighth grenade, leaves the smoking weapon open and hands it back to a bemused Carlton. Once again, there is a deep silence, broken only by the radio static and the far-off popping of the distant firefight.

Helms makes a distressed sound and grabs my arm. I turn and follow his pointing finger with my gaze. Lying a few meters to our left, underneath a bush, are the lower two-thirds of a man's body. Everything from the sternum up is missing; most of the rest of the torso is an empty red cavity. From the waist down the body is intact, enough so that I recognize the lower part of a flight suit.

I start to take a step in that direction, but settle back quickly. What can I do but stare at it? We've found the missing pilot. Helms, unbidden, hands me the mike.

"Black Jack, this is One Six, over."

A pause, then: "This is Black Jack."

I look at my watch. Incredible — it's 1642. Only 12 minutes have passed. "This is One Six. Confirm two KIA. I say again, confirm two KIA."

"Roger. Two KIA. Have you identified them yet?"

"Affirmative: One Five's RTO, and the other is a crewman off the bird, over."

"Roger. Which one, do you know?"

"Roger. I think it's the pilot, over."

A brief pause. "Roger."

I take another breath. "This is One Six. I don't want to appear pushy or anything, but do we have anyone coming in, over?"

"They're on the way, One Six. Do you have the LZ secured?"

I stare at the mike. What is he, a comedian? "Negative. Negative. I've got too much area to cover."

"Roger. The slicks are enroute."

I look at my watch. 1645. We wait.

1650. Waiting.

1655. Nothing. Still waiting.

1659. No sound. The firefight to our south has ended.

1702. Waiting.

1705. Waiting. Where are those slicks?

1710. Waiting. Where are the NVA?

1715. There! At last! A drone, faint at first, but rapidly growing in volume, swells to our southeast.

I feel my breath leave my body slowly, involuntarily. In a few moments, I think, almost giddy with relief, we'll be safe.

19

Death Dance of the Ghost Riders

YC363065; 25–26 April 1969; 1730–0800

It was 1724 when, high and stubby, dark green against a darkening eastern sky, a slick began its descent. I felt a partial relaxation of the rigid control I'd kept for the last 45 minutes or so. The Huey came in, as all Hueys do, thumping and swaying, buffeting us with dirt and leaves and wind, filling our ears with the comforting roar of 10,000 pounds of thrust. Six green, hunch-backed figures jumped out and started up the hill. The three closest flattened themselves to the ground as the slick pulled out over their heads, turned, and roared off. I recognized Dickson as one of them and groaned inwardly. Why not Eward or Denholm? I waved Dickson and his people to the other side of the crater, to get out of the way of the next slick, which was hard on the tail of the first.

Within two minutes, four more birds had landed, 24 more men jumping out. The area around the LZ was getting crowded; six newcomers, in addition to my four, were strung out along the west hillside, but all the others were bunched on the eastern side of the LZ. No one had started up the slope to the east hilltop yet, however. I waved twice at Dickson, trying to get his attention, but he didn't see me. I had just turned to Helms to tell him to try raising Dickson on the radio, when shots started whining through the treetops.

Heads snapped all around as everyone automatically tried to pinpoint the source. Hyde was pointing to the ridgeline southeast of us, some 200 meters away. At that distance, RPG's weren't accurate, but small arms fire was...

Small arms fire was enough. I don't think the next Huey was hit all that badly, but the pilot, realizing he was under fire, tried to maneuver, swung his tail too sharply, and crumpled it against a tree. The slick dropped just outside the crater, on the east side; blades and pieces of tail went flying through the LZ. I had taken an instinctive step forward, but I turned immediately and grabbed the radio handle from Helms. As I pressed the button to call Black Jack, the next bird, close behind the preceding one, lurched and caught a branch with one of its blades. A sudden wobbling racket, like an unbalanced washing machine, filled the air. I watched in sick disbelief as this one too started to shudder and pitch; it then dropped 15 meters or so to the ground at the base of the clearing, 30 meters down the hill.

For a moment I could do nothing except stand and stare. The extent of the disaster was immediately evident: this LZ was a death trap for the Ghost Rider squadron. I felt like whimpering: when was this going to end?

"Black Jack, this is One Six." The words, familiar and repetitive, had become part of a rite, like the half-forgotten Latin responses from my childhood. Like them, they seemed meant to bring a comforting refuge in a hostile universe. The words themselves were meaningless but the act of speaking them...

Agnus Dei...

"This is Black Jack."

Qui tollis peccata mundi...

"This is One Six. We've just had two birds go down. The LZ is blocked. I say again, the LZ is blocked. Hold off sending any more, over."

"Roger." The next lift ship, a hundred meters away, swung sharply to its left and pulled away.

I realized suddenly that all hell had broken out below me.

I dropped the horn in Helms's hand and raced down the hill toward the downed slicks. Along the way I felt dismay and a sort of futile anger at events: None of the men I saw were from my platoon. I reached Dickson, who was lying propped up against a log, staring stupidly at the mike he held in his left hand: about two feet of cord dangled from one end. Behind him sat his RTO: three feet of cord trailed off the radio.

Dickson saw me and gave sort of gasping giggle. "Didja see that? Man, didja see that? Goddamn blade off that chopper came right through here and cut the cord on my radio! Man, and I'm holdin' the goddamn mike in my hand! Man —"

I cut him off savagely, pointing downhill to where the last helicopter lay crumpled uselessly. By some miracle, none of the birds that day caught fire. "There're some injured men down there. You got anybody checking them out?"

His gaze moved from the cut cord to me. "No. I —"

"Well, get somebody down there, goddamnit."

Some troopers — I recognized Stenger, the Third Platoon medic, among them — were already helping dazed and injured men out of the closer of the two slicks. To my left, a small knot of men lay huddled at the base of the east hill, just above the crater. I ran over to them. That sinking feeling in my stomach was getting worse; there wasn't anyone here I could trust. I grabbed one by the shoulder, started to say something, and then spotted Nolan, who'd been transferred to the Second Platoon some weeks back. Thank God! I thought. I beckoned him over and he ran up the slope, his face wearing a big grin of recognition.

"Take these guys," I indicated the five or six lying at our feet, "and set up some security on this hill here. Got that?"

He nodded, his thin, good-looking face showing nothing but easy confidence. I left him and spotted Hyde helping extract an injured crewman from the helicopter. I ran over and pulled his arm.

"Nate, get some people — a squad, at least — and set up on that west hill."

"Right."

"Hurry it up." I turned away, then reached back and grabbed him as he started moving off. "Another thing: take a Mike Sixty up there. Got it?"

"Roger." He left me, running around the fuselage. The injured and wounded were starting to pile up, clustered around the crater. I spotted two more medics, Tunney, from Fourth Platoon, and Powell from the Second, and I felt a small measure of relief; one medic could not have handled all the casualties.

For the next few minutes, I tried unsuccessfully to get an exact count of the injured and wounded. This proved difficult; I found I had elements from all four platoons, some with their leaders and some without, and of course the crewmen from the helicopters. Stenger was able to tell me, though, that he had three men, so far, who definitely had to go: one with a broken back and two with badly broken legs.

"Can we move that guy with the broken back?" I asked.

He shook his head. "Not a question of 'can.' We have to move 'em; they can't stay here. But we'll have to bring in a jungle penetrator and pull 'em straight up from where they're lying, 'cause I don't want to have to move 'em up here and then have to move 'em again to load 'em on the medevac."

I grimaced. Everything seemed to be conspiring to make the near future as dangerous as possible; we would have to ask the medevac to hover for several minutes for each extraction, moving from one spot of another. It also meant that the pilot would have to hover at or near tree-top level, making himself and his craft vastly more vulnerable to enemy fire.

"Are you sure," I asked him, "that it wouldn't be better for them if we gather them all up, keep them over night, and then blow an LZ in the morning?"

"No sir, absolutely not. Two of those guys are in shock already. I can't guarantee they'd last the night."

I pointed out the difficulties that the medevac would face, but he remained adamant that at least those three be evacuated. In addition to the broken back, another man had both legs broken, one a compound fracture.

The injured — all the casualties on the last two Hueys had resulted from the crash and not small arms fire — had by now made their white-faced, teeth-gritting way up the slope. My heart leaped as I saw that the ones in the last helicopter had been from my platoon. Gann came struggling up the hill, supported by Kenzy. Behind them were Eden and Dickerson, carrying their gear. That particular slick, I realized, had been the second in line behind mine, earlier in the afternoon. It carried the rest of Hyde's squad.

But I had no time to greet them just then. I glanced behind me and saw that Nolan had not yet succeeded in getting his group up the east hill. I spotted Dickson down by the other slick and yelled for him to come up. He ran puffing up the hill towards me.

"Get those guys moving," I said, pointing to Nolan's group. "We've got to get the high ground secured now, before those medevacs come in."

He nodded and ran off in their direction. I moved around the crater, below the tail of the first chopper, and to the base of the west hill, where the majority of the injured were gathered. Hyde and seven or eight men were scattered across the slope, heads down, unmoving. I saw Micheaux, Dickson's platoon sergeant, among them.

"Why the hell aren't you moving up this goddamn hill?" I shouted.

Carlton, lying at my feet, looked up, his face white and his eyes huge. "There's a sniper up there! He's been shooting at us!"

I erupted in rage. "Well, shoot back, you stupid son of a bitch!"

Hyde, Micheaux, and one or two others were now kneeling, but no one had moved yet; they were all looking anxiously up the hill.

"Get up! Get up on your feet, damn you!" I felt the fury rise in me. "Get up, damn you! Move! Follow me!" I yelled and started up the hill, looking straight ahead. I sensed Helms behind me, with his radio. As I moved up the hill, my eyes searched the hilltop for any signs of a sniper. At any other time, I know, I might have been moving tensely, body braced, waiting for the sniper's bullet to hit, but by now I was so full of anger and frustration, so sick of crouching and ducking and wondering where the next blow was coming from, that I didn't care and, even if my conscious mind wasn't spelling the situation out, step by step, my training and my instinct both gave my mind one message: Get to the high ground or die.

I reached the hill's summit, turned, and saw, without surprise, 10 or 11 men behind me. I set Sergeant Micheaux to placing them around the hilltop in a rough perimeter.

Then I called Black Jack. "This is One Six, over."

"This is Black Jack." His voice was icy with rage. "Where have you been?"

"I've been trying to get organized, over."

"Let me tell you something, One Six. You keep your ass planted right by that goddamn radio from now on. I've been trying to raise you for 15 minutes now, trying to find out what the hell's going on. Now, what's happened, over?"

I sighed. Before I thumbed the mike. "This is One Six. We've been trying to get the wounded collected and treated. I've got the west hill secured, and by now the east hill should be too. The medevacs will have to use a jungle penetrator, over."

"Roger. There'll be a bird over there in a few minutes with some dynamite and C-4. Blow an LZ tonight or tomorrow morning. Where was that fire coming from, that got the second bird, over?"

"Seemed like it was coming from a ridge to the southeast, about 200 meters out, over."

"Roger. And if you'd been on the goddamn radio over this last half hour, we might have been able to do something about it."

I bit my lip. I had been about to retort angrily that I had been on the radio when the choppers had been shot down, but I decided to shut up. At this point in my young life, I reflected, I needed all the friends I could get.

The injured were toiling painfully up the slope. Brown, my FO, was among them; he walked gingerly, wincing; his body and clothing were soaked by JP-4 aviation fuel, which chafed his skin raw. I could see Vandenburg lying at the base of the saddle, both legs encased in heavy splints. His specially designed sniper rifle lay broken in two by his side. He was the one Stenger had referred to.

Kenzy and Eden struggled by me, both limping. I put a hand on Kenzy's shoulder as he passed me. "How're you feeling?" I asked.

He shrugged. "Okay." His eyes searched the hilltop. "Things been movin' since we got down here," he said, keeping his voice casual. "Ain't had a chance to look around. I seen everyone 'cept St. Onge."

I didn't say anything.

He looked at me. "St. Onge didn't make it, did he?"

"No."

He glanced at Eden, then lowered his head. They moved on.

Helms tapped me on the shoulder. "Medevac's on its way," he said.

I nodded and glanced at my watch, then did a double take.

1745! I couldn't believe it; a full half-hour had passed since the two Hueys had gone down. I tried to swallow and found I couldn't; the insides of my mouth and throat were sere and grainy from lack of moisture. I fumbled through my equipment and found a canteen, unscrewed the top, tilted the container up and drank deeply. The canteen had been in the sun all day and the water temperature was well over 100 degrees, but it was liquid and I didn't care. I needed it badly. Then I went to check the perimeter.

I stepped past someone lying not far from Dougherty's aircraft, one of the crewmen. He clutched my loose trouser leg; his face awash with sweat, eyes staring but almost unfocused. I recognized fear, and something else ... Captain Watson's body, or what was left of it, lay only a couple of meters away. I turned back to the man: The name tag on his flight suit read Molinar.

"What can I do?" he asked.

I almost left him; I had too much to do, but instinctively I knew that leaving him there in his condition would be wrong. I wasn't being altruistic; I didn't want to deal with potential hysteria. A few meters away lay a pile of gear belonging to the injured troopers; I told a trooper from Three Six to give one of the weapons to Molinar and take him to the perimeter.

"We're going to need you to guard a position on the perimeter, okay? The guys will show you what to do. Can you do that?"

Molinar sat up, took the rifle in his hands and nodded. "Yeah. Yeah, I can."

I looked about. A knot of pilots and crew sat together, high up in the saddle. One wore captain's bars, and the nametag on his flight suit read Gouch. "Are you the ranking pilot?"

He nodded. "Yeah. Captain Gouch. That's Searcy and Genna; they piloted that last one to go down. And...."

I cut him off. "I have to get the perimeter secured first. Then I'll tell you guys what to do. Just stay where you are."

A few minutes later, I watched — it was all I could do — while the medevac arrived and hovered for what seemed hours over our shattered LZ. The medics, with the assistance of two or three others, worked like men possessed to strap the wounded into the baskets lowered from the helicopter overhead. They had to work slowly, painstakingly, gently, with the broken back case, and the longer they were at it the more pressure I felt building up inside. I wanted to scream, to yell at them to get on with it. Any second now, I knew, one or two NVA, hidden in the gathering darkness, would slip through the surrounding vegetation and at point-blank range fire an RPG at the stationary, helpless medevac. I hardly moved the whole time; I stood and waited for the inevitable. My eyes and ears were ready, anticipating the harsh yellow-red flash, the dull metallic slam, the mortal crumpling and snapping as a destroyed chopper fell 15 or 20 meters to the ground, and the savage yellow flare of exploding JP-4 fuel...

When, finally, the pilot backed the over-loaded medevac away from the slope, turned, and flew off safely, I remained on the side of the hill, still in disbelief. Surely they would, even now, as the retreating medevac disappeared into the murk, blast it mockingly from the sky ... surely we were not, even now, with all this...

"Hey, Lieutenant!"

I started slightly. Micheaux, Dickson's platoon sergeant, was looking at me strangely and I became conscious that Helms' hand was on my shoulder, shaking me.

"Yeah. What do you need, Sergeant?"

"One of my guys was talkin' with them door gunners an' got 'n idea, 'bout strippin' them guns off 'em birds and puttin' 'em 'round the perimeter tonight."

I looked at him for a second, my mind picturing six — no seven, including Logan's — machine guns set around a small perimeter. I looked around me; it was fast getting dark. They would have to hurry to get the job done. "Good idea, Micheaux. Tell them to get right on it. By the way, are those other men still on that east hill?"

"Yes, sir."

"Have somebody gather them up and bring them over here. We won't be able to secure both hilltops tonight, and I don't want to leave them over there by themselves."

"Yes, sir." He trotted off. As he did so, I realized that I had explained myself to him, something that I would never have felt the need to do with my own platoon. I couldn't think why. Perhaps it was because I felt my own people understood me, after five months together. I stood and watched five or six troopers, accompanied by a limping crew chief, disconnected the M60s from their mounting brackets on the helicopters and carried them uphill, along with all the ammo they could scrounge up.

Meanwhile, the medics were combing through the interiors for anything useful, such as emergency first aid kits and containers of water. Sometime previously — I had

19. Death Dance of the Ghost Riders

Looking south from the crater, the wreckage of Gouch's and Genna's ships. Although Genna's craft spilled volatile JP4 fuel all over the area, no fire resulted (photograph by Pat Lynch).

not even noticed its arrival — a slick had flown over the hilltop, hovered briefly, and dropped three cases of TNT, a strobe light, and some other supplies. Hyde and a couple of others were presently engaged in breaking open the boxes and taking the TNT around the perimeter, distributing it among the men so that there would be no large concentration of the explosive to go off in case we were hit.

Eventually, all the activity ended, and I walked around the steadily quieting perimeter, taking stock. What I discovered wasn't too encouraging. First, I had elements of all four platoons on the ground with me. We had several wounded or injured still with us, including several crewmembers from the helicopters. The lightly injured were placed into the perimeter, but the more gravely hurt had been kept back in a group, with the medics. One or two of them had begun to groan and fret, and I asked the medics to keep them quiet, to dose them with sedatives if necessary; we would have to be as quiet as possible that night.

There were nine men from my platoon — all of Hyde's squad except for Westman, whose place on the second slick had been taken by Brown, and Vandenburg, who'd been evacuated. While having a complete squad from my own platoon was a big plus, it was tempered by the fact that all of the squad members who'd come in on Genna's craft — the one that had dropped from tree-top level — were bruised and shaken. Gann's ankle and Eden's knee were so puffed up they could barely hobble. Kenzy was one massive bruise; characteristically, he refused the medic's offer of Darvon, because he didn't want to get sleepy during the night, but he ached all over. Brown suffered from a wrenched shoulder, and in addition was chafed raw by his fuel-soaked clothes; he was on the verge of hysteria from the pain.

Second Platoon had seven men on the ground, including Sergeant Randolph and his RTO, Delorean, whose knee was so badly smashed Stenger had given him sedatives almost immediately. There was Nolan, and I knew Stenger; the others from Second Platoon I knew only by sight.

Dickson had 19 men with him, only one of whom was injured. Fourth Platoon had landed two men: Tunney, their medic, and a trooper named McAllister. There were eight crewmen, four of them hurt, one very badly.

So that was that. I had a total of 37 troopers and eight crewmen with me. The three medics were inside the perimeter, along with three of the crewmen, Brown, DeLorean, Gann and Parsons, Dickson's man. Dickson, his RTO, and Helms were also back there, along with me. Sergeants Randolph and Micheaux went on the perimeter, which thus had 32 men, including five crewmembers armed with M16s taken from the evacuated troops. Well, not quite, I reflected. I'd forgotten those M60s we'd stripped from the slicks.

Eight positions, considering the size of the hilltop, would be stretching it thin. I grew more and more worried as I walked around the perimeter. They could come at us from any direction. To the east and southeast there were the saddle and the slope that, although bare, were littered with downed helicopters, which were excellent cover for attacking infantry. To the south, the slope was steeper but heavily forested, allowing a quiet enemy the opportunity to get quite close to the perimeter. The west was convoluted and also thickly vegetated, to within a few meters of our positions. The north, though, was my chief worry. That small ridge jutting off to the northwest from the east hilltop was separated from us by a shallow ravine, even and bare. I decided to place three of the machine guns here.

But the more I stood on that north slope, the less I liked the idea. The ridge, thickly covered by double-canopy vegetation, was but a menacing 50 meters away — point blank range for rifle fire and RPG. Our slope, on the other hand, was bare, with the exception of one huge old tree standing a couple of meters off the crest of the hill. I paced back and forth; it was already dark, although the western sky still retained a purple glow. I knew I had to make a decision soon. I didn't care a bit for the situation on the north slope, and I was nagged, too, by an uncomfortable feeling about the southern and western sides of the perimeter. I looked at my watch: 1945; the luminescent dial was barely visible. I moved back up the slope to the top of the hill, turned, and looked back at the black mass that was the ridge ... okay, I thought. Do something, dummy.

"Sergeant Micheaux," I called out quietly.

"Yes, sir." He materialized out of the darkness behind me; I could hardly see his brown face underneath the helmet.

"Put one four-man position here," I pointed to the ground at my feet, "and another over there. I want M60s at both positions."

"Yes, sir." I couldn't see his face, but I could hear the doubt in his voice. The two positions I'd indicated were on top of the hill, about 20 meters apart. I was abandoning, then, the northern slope, the "military crest" of the hill, the importance of which had been drummed into us practically from the first day of Basic Training. I moved quickly to a point just above the saddle and indicated I wanted a third position there. I placed a fourth on the southeastern slope, just above the spot where St. Onge's body lay scattered—it wasn't until that moment that I remembered, with a start, that I hadn't had time to do anything about either of the two bodies, and they still lay where they'd fallen.

I placed the next three positions along the southern and western slopes, but downhill, right up against the wood line. I felt that this would be safer than leaving five or ten meters of clear ground between the heavy growth and the positions. The last position went into the northwest corner, about 30 meters from the first. Machine guns were placed at all positions, except the middle one on the southern slope. We had been able to salvage five M60s from the helicopters—one had been too badly smashed to be useful—and we had a gun from Dickson's platoon and, of course, Logan's gun, to give us a total of seven.

After giving the NCOs time to set the perimeter up—there was no digging in; there was no time—I made the rounds, checking each position and gauging the morale and determination of the men. Many were dispirited and nervous, but there were others, fortunately several, who were calm and grimly determined. There would be no panic, and, I reflected wryly, no trouble keeping anyone awake tonight.

I came to the key northern position; I had told Sergeant Randolph to place Hyde's squad on the north slope, since I trusted them most, and here I found Kenzy, Logan, Carlton and Eden. Hyde, with Dickerson, was in the adjoining position, along with McAllister and one other man from Second Platoon. I squatted down beside Kenzy. Sergeant Eden was lying on his stomach, right leg held out at an awkward angle; even in the darkness I could see that his knee was twice normal size.

"Hiya, Lieutenant," Kenzy greeted me.

"How're you guys doing?"

"Okay." He paused, his eyes searching the dark ridge to the northeast. "Van sure messed his leg up, didn't he?"

"I don't know; I never got a chance to take a close look. Stenger told me it was bad."

"Yeah, it was. I seen it." There was another pause. "We been busier 'n shit since we got here," he continued diffidently. "Ain't had time to even talk to Hyde or Short Round." He continued to stare out at the darkness. Carlton sat huddled by a tree a few feet away; Logan was stretched out behind a fallen tree, his M60 perched against the log, facing the valley.

Eden turned his head; I could see only a vague grey blob below his helmet. "How many gooks we got out there, Lieutenant?"

I shrugged. "Don't know."

Kenzy cleared his throat. "We're in kinda deep, ain't we?"

"Yeah. You could say that."

"Well, shit. Guess we'd better dig ourselves out, then."

I grinned. "Yeah. Guess we'd better."

"Logan's good at diggin', ain't that right?"

"Fuck you guys," Logan muttered. He was tired of being reminded of the NVA latrine. Then he looked up at me. "We're gonna make it, right, Lieutenant?"

I nodded. "We'll make it."

"They don't know who they're messin' with," he growled.

By the time I finished checking the perimeter, it was almost 2100. Some of that time I'd spent on the radio, talking to Black Jack or Iron Raven. There wasn't a whole lot they could do for me, beyond giving me verbal encouragement. It reminded me of when I was a boy of 12, at summer camp, going into the boxing ring to face an opponent a year older, four inches taller, and about 20 pounds heavier than me, and hearing my camp counselor optimistically urging me to punch the guy's lights out...

Well, I take that back. There was one thing Iron Raven mentioned that improved morale considerably: Spooky would fly for us tonight. Spooky was a specially equipped C147, a fat, lazy four-propper with a large cargo opening in its flank. In that opening rested two miniguns. A minigun looks like an old-fashioned Gatling gun, but each of the six barrels is an M60, so that each minigun is firing the equivalent of six machine guns. The volume of fire each minigun could put out is unbelievable; a bullet could hit every square foot of a football field within one minute. No one in his right mind would be wandering around an area where Spooky was flying.

A call came at 2145 that Spooky was on his way. Helms had prepared a shelter for us—a poncho stretched out among four trees, at a height of about 30 inches—and it was here that his radio was. I took out the strobe light, which is a stubby container about five inches long and three wide, made of heavy plastic, with a clear plastic lens on one end. Within the lens there is a strobe, or high-intensity light bulb, which, on activation, begins pulsing rapidly, giving out an extremely bright, piercing light. The light is aimed upwards, and is easily visible from the sky. The pilot spots the light, begins a narrow circling orbit around it, and then his gunner begins to lay down a carpet of M60 ammo all around the focal point.

For the first half-hour or so, I sat by the radio, with the light held over my head. I noticed that the others in the CP had begun edging away from me, and I grinned. I suppose the spot I was sitting on wasn't the safest in Viet Nam ... after a while, though, my arm got tired and my brain started working again, and I crawled over to a dead tree, took a couple of boot straps—I always carried six or seven extra pairs of the long, tough leather straps—and lashed the light to a branch of the tree.

I joined Helms, who sat with his head on his knees, legs pulled up against his chest and cradled in his arms. I thought for a moment that he was asleep, but I saw his eyelids flicker in the dim starlight. His pack, with the radio, lay on the ground between us; I could hear the faint hiss of the squelch and an occasional whisper of static. It was ridiculous, I thought, how much older than my troops I felt; only three or four years separated us, but it seemed to be so much more than that. Helms, now; he sat beside me, this boy from North Carolina ... 20 years old, and married to his high school sweetheart, an assistant manager at the local supermarket ... a life of hard work during the week, and church or family picnics on Sunday, an occasional outing with friends, a life of placid gentleness and comfort, a life without dark shadows or ominous strain; Helms, of all the men in the platoon, even more than Westman, was the very essence of small-town decency and innocence, I thought. Slowly, the image I had of him faded; the churchyard and shopping center, the young wife with the bright smile, the dark, intense middle-aged man who was his manager, the schoolyard where he'd played, the small-town cop who'd known him since he was a boy ... all this gave way to the reality of dark hilltop and darker forest.

The night passed slowly. For entertainment, we could sit and watch the green tracers from Spooky; they covered the entire sky around us, lightning without thunder, a shimmering aurora that no natural sky had ever seen. And all you can hear while Spooky flies is the drone of his engines, and a faint, comical burp! as the miniguns fire.

The hours went by. Iron Raven made several brief calls during the night, as much to keep my spirits up as for anything else, I guessed. Except for one of them: It was to inform me that we'd landed almost in the middle of the headquarters of the 6th NVA Regiment, many of whose troops were engaged with the 2/17th and the 3/187th at the base of the mountain. I took the news with a quirky satisfaction. If you're going to land in the shit, it might as well be a big pile of it.

I finished both canteens that night; going an entire afternoon without water had almost dehydrated me, although I hadn't felt it at the time. My body welcomed the warm, stale water as if it were premium beer, cold and delicious. My body would have welcomed some sleep, too; I could feel my brain fogging over with fatigue, especially around 0300, but there was no way I could sleep. I was tense and expectant. I expected the NVA to attack any time, but especially after 0400; this was their usual pattern. Twice that night I crawled around the perimeter, making sure that there were at least two men awake at each position. The quarter moon rose late that morning, well after 0400, but when it did rise, it transformed the forest around us. Poets speak of "soft moonbeams," but moonlight is hard and brittle. The jungle, never colorful even in full sunlight, loses the soft green and brown patina of day and becomes etched in black and silver-grey; a thing of shapes and shapelessness, a montage of things that might be and things that aren't. Your eyes betray you at night, especially under moonlight. They see things that aren't there, and, worse, fail to see things that are.

I found myself listening. An earlier wind, which had covered the night sounds with the heavy rustling of unnumbered leaves, had died down now, and I could hear the soft call of early-rising birds, the liquid hooting of the gecko, the whistle and peeps of tiny life-forms. Behind me I could hear a muffled clank as a man struck his helmet with a careless rifle butt. Faintly, from my right, I heard a whispered sentence — perhaps two men exchanging the guard. The world had become, suddenly, a very small place. All I could see was shadow, black or silver. All I could hear was whispers. All I could smell was my own rank sweat and the leftover taint of gunpowder, scorched tree sap and burnt metal. All I could feel was the damp black earth and the chill of early morning. Now, indeed, all traces of The World were gone. I looked at Helms again; he was now curled up by his radio, eyes closed. Helms the assistant store manager and small-town bridegroom was gone, perhaps forever.

It was now 0500. Spooky, his tour of duty as our guardian angel over, had flown home, leaving us to face the dawn. The sun had not yet risen, nor would it for another hour, but in the east the trees had lost their silver moonshine and were already taking on the grey mantle of early dawn. The geckos and the night birds were quiet, while the day birds were now awake and shrill, pricking the night silence with tiny needles of sound. Suddenly, as always in the tropics, the dark shadows fled and revealed the hunched-over, grey-green bodies of men, asleep or awake, motionless, weapons held in cold, stiff hands, bodies and gear daubed with morning dew ... the night slid quickly into day.

0550. Behind the inevitable early morning clouds, the sun reared over the hills. The light, still grey, became stronger and clearer each minute. Men were shaking each other awake, quietly. There was no conversation, no sound. A shake of the shoulder, a nod, and everyone was turning to look at the forest. Now everything was quiet; the birds and monkeys were still. Nothing moved, nothing sounded. I felt a tightening of my stomach muscles.

They were coming.

The unnatural silence deepened, and lengthened. A rasp of static sounded loud and cataclysmic; Helms hastily picked up the mike and muttered an answer. Micheaux, crouched low, walked around the perimeter, from position to position; the slight rustle of his boots against the weeds carried easily over the intervening distance. From the

19. Death Dance of the Ghost Riders

corner of my eye, I saw Dickson rise up and stretch cautiously. I licked my dry lips. 0556.

I realized that I'd forgotten to turn the strobe light off after Spooky had flown home, over an hour before. I crept over to the tree, turned the light off, and unstrapped it. Hyde, hearing the sound, turned and looked at me, expressionlessly. I moved back to my pack and stuffed the bright red container into a side pocket of my pack. I heard faint clicks as the men carefully checked their rifle chambers.

I was puzzled. They were coming, I was sure, but when? I felt a moment's impatience.

0600. Dickson stood a few meters away, staring down at the helicopters, lying forlorn and discarded on the slopes below him. Brown, eyes puffed and groggy, was quietly splashing water over his face. Eden, head bent in concentration, was loading M16 ammo into an empty magazine...

Blam! Blam!

Dickson hit the ground hard, on his belly; Eden whirled and dove behind the log next to Logan. I flattened out and in the same motion grabbed my steel pot and slapped it on my head. Two RPGs had landed on the north slope, followed immediately by a stuttering hail of AK-47 fire. About damn time, I thought crazily.

For a moment there was no response from our perimeter. Then, hesitantly, an M16 here and there spat and snapped. There was a mounting volume of sound coming from the ridge, as more and more AK-47 and light machine gun fire poured in. Suddenly, shockingly, gloriously, at least four of the M60s opened up with their deep-throated, insistent booming and, like a runaway orchestra overwhelming the soloists, drowned out all the other sounds. Sergeant Randolph, seeing where the fire was coming from, quickly moved two more M60s from the south side of the perimeter to the north, adding their voices to the song.

Each machine gunner has slightly different rhythm, and the combined voices of five or six M60s were awesome. I smiled, at the sudden thought of what must have been going through the mind of the NVA officer who was directing the attack ... his eyes opening wide in shock at the sound of five M60s answering back. I smiled again a few seconds later when I realized that my decision of the night before to move the men back off the north slope was paying dividends; all the NVA fire, and particularly the deadly RPG rounds, went slamming into the empty northern slope. We were not to take one single casualty that morning.

Once I stopped smiling, however, I decided I'd better get on the radio. I reported the attack and requested artillery. Brinkman dragged his radio over and lay on the ground beside me, attempting to call on his artillery net. Brown, now awake but still groggy, crawled painfully over and tried to help out. Between the two of them, I thought, they might be able to get some 105s or 155s in. Black Jack had gotten on the line immediately on hearing about the attack, but there wasn't a whole lot to tell him just then except that we were returning fire and had taken no casualties. He mentioned that ARA was on its way, but that it would be a while before they got to us. In the meantime, he said, bring in the 155s from Berchtesgaden.

We never got that far. Less than three minutes after it started, everything was over. The NVA, possibly a platoon-sized force, certainly at least a couple of squads, left abruptly, unwilling to face the firepower of the massed machine guns, to say nothing of the ARA or other artillery we were sure to be calling in.

After the stupendous racket of the firefight, the ensuing silence was almost eerie. I looked at my watch: 0604. Less than five minutes had passed. Word came quickly from around the perimeter that no one had been hit. Gradually, the noise level around me began to rise; I heard excited voices and some laughter as the men reacted to beating off an enemy attack with no losses. After the shambles of the day before, it was a heady feeling.

Hyde came back just then to tell me that he could still see movement along the ridge from which the attack had come, as the NVA retreated. I told Brown and Brinkman to continue their efforts to call in artillery. While they were doing that, I spoke with Black Jack, giving him the results of the morning's contact. He was noncommittal about that, but quickly became emphatic about the need to blow the LZ as soon as possible. I heartily agreed with him. The sooner we finished the LZ, the sooner we'd get more troops in.

"Do you have enough troops to send out a recon, over?" He asked.

I hesitated, considering. "I don't think so. I don't have enough men here to back them up if they run into something."

"Roger. Do you have that other hill secured?"

"Negative. I don't have anywhere near the manpower needed to cover both hills and the saddle in between them. I don't want to split my force up, either."

"You might have put an LP out there; might have saved you some grief."

"Roger. But everything we've gotten since coming in yesterday has been from the ridges around us, and not that hilltop. I don't see how an LP on the east hill will do anything as far as covering the ridges is concerned."

"Roger." Black Jack's voice was cold and cutting. "Your job is to secure that LZ, and so far you've done a mighty piss-poor job of it. I don't care how you get it done, but I want that LZ secure when those next birds come in."

I bit my lip, infuriated by the unfairness of the criticism. I had to admit, though, that from his point of view I had failed in my primary mission, which was indeed to defend an LZ until the other troops could be landed. Three crumpled helicopters were ample testimony to the failure of that mission. On the other hand, I thought, looking around me with tightened lips, I might want to have a word or two with the turkey who'd picked this spot as an LZ in the first place.

I dropped the phone in disgust and joined Brinkman and Brown, who were still trying to call in artillery fire. I looked at my watch: 0615. The NVA had by now almost certainly left the immediate area, unless they were stupid enough to have left behind an observation team. Brown shook his head at my query of how long he would be. I told him to let me know as soon as he was ready, and then went off in search of Sergeant Hyde, my resident explosives expert.

Hyde, as aware as I was of the importance of the LZ, had already started preparations. He had one case of C-4, he explained, which he was saving for an emergency. The dynamite sticks he was wrapping in white det-cord, in bunches of three, around the trunks of selected small trees and saplings. Fortunately, there were no really large trees on the hilltop; that one huge old veteran on the north slope, some four and a half feet in diameter at the base, was well out of the way. Most of the trees on the level surface of the hilltop were five or six inches thick; only a few were more than ten inches in diameter.

I had never before worked with dynamite, and I wondered why so many sticks were needed for each tree. Once, I'd accompanied Jerry Wolosenko down to the base of a slope at Rakkasan, where we'd blown some good-sized trees down, clearing an approach path for the helicopters. He'd used C-4, and two or at most three sticks of that had sufficed. Hyde told me, as he carefully fitted a thin, fragile metal fuse to the end of the det cord, that C-4 was considerably more powerful than dynamite. Three sticks would certainly do the job right, he explained, backing his way carefully from the tree he'd just finished wiring, playing out the explosive white cord behind him until he reached the next tree. "Two sticks might do it, or they might not," he drawled. "If they don't, then you done nuthin' 'cept waste some dynamite. Better be one over than one short, you know what I mean?"

"Okay," I said. "You know what you're doing. Just make it as quick as you can without blowing yourself up."

Hyde's dark face flickered into a grin. "Amen."

On my way back through the CP I checked with Brown, who was standing barechested, sweat already shining over his thin ribs and shoulders, an angry red from the chaffing and fuel. He held the radio mike up to his ear. Some day, I thought, looking at him, if they ever sculpt a statue of a soldier in Viet Nam, it ought to be with a goddamn radio stuck in his ear. It was now 0640, and he still had not been able to coordinate with DivArty.

I paused, irritated. I wanted to check the perimeter. On the other hand, I needed to find out what was taking so long. Granted, I had no need for the artillery just then, but if I ever did need it — and I had a feeling I would before all this was over — I sure as hell didn't want it taking so long. I dithered for a few seconds, trying to make up my mind, but I finally decided that the perimeter was more important. I told Helms to stay back at the CP. I could be at his side within seconds, if I were needed, and, besides, walking around a perimeter with an RTO following you, in plain view in an area known to contain the enemy is just not the smartest thing in the world to do.

I made my rounds quickly. The south, east and west sides were quiet and undisturbed. When I reached the north side, however, I noted with interest the shallow depressions along the slope of the hill, where the RPGs had exploded. I counted at least five, and every single one was along the military crest of the hill. If we had set up there, as normally we would have ... Logan pointed out fresh scars in the bark of the trunk of the big tree, where RPGs had exploded in the thick branches just above the ground. At least two RPGs, he told me, had hit there, shredding the ground directly underneath with deadly shrapnel. One of the positions had originally been placed directly below that tree.

I was on my way back to the CP when Hyde's Louisiana drawl yelled out, "Fiah in the hole" Others took up the cry, "Fire in the hole!" and we all knelt or squatted behind a tree, ducking our heads. The boom! of exploding dynamite was followed by a tearing, crackling sound as a 30-foot tall sapling toppled slowly to the ground. I looked at Hyde, who allowed a slight, pleased grin to flicker across his face.

"Jus' raht, Lieutenant," he nodded, in satisfaction.

He proceeded quickly to blow several more; each one came down smoothly, and it seemed that he would be soon finished. The air was full of the stink of burnt sap, sawdust, and trinitrol. I decided to leave him alone and see to the perimeter again. I called Black Jack, told him how the work was progressing, and guessed that we would be ready within an hour. He told me that Delta Company was sitting on an LZ, waiting.

I felt better. It was now 0715; by 0900 we would have all of Delta inserted, and we'd be able to go on the offensive. We would no longer be sitting ducks, waiting for the NVA's next blow. It was shortly thereafter that Brown limped up to me and reported that Arty was ready. I glanced at my watch, and then at him, in consternation.

"What time did you first call this strike in?" I asked.

He shook his head. "0605, sir. It wasn't five minutes after they hit us, I swear!"

I stared at him. Of course, it wasn't his fault. "And one hour and 12 minutes later, they're ready to fire?"

"Yes, sir." He shook his head again. "Captain Dufresne held it up. He kept telling us our coordinates were way off."

"Didn't you tell him we're sitting on the same damn hill he prepped yesterday, for God's sake? On the same damn spot?"

"Yes, sir. I told him that a hundred times! He kept telling me I was crazy. He said we'd moved off the hill by about five hundred meters. I kept trying to tell him where we were, but he kept tellin' me I was crazy."

I felt my anger rise. Dufresne was a supercilious bastard, I know, but even he should have been able to understand plain English. Furious, I called Black Jack, but he was unavailable.

Minutes after that, Hyde came up to me, shaking his head. Two of the trees he'd just blown down had landed across some previously fallen timber; he would need two or three men, with hatchets, to chop them up. He admitted this would slow him up considerably.

19. Death Dance of the Ghost Riders

"Okay. No help for it. Go to it."

"Yes, sir. Uh ... sir? You reckon you could maybe ask for a couple chain saws? Go a lot faster that way."

"Okay, Nate. I'll see what I can do. But get going. The sooner we get Delta inserted, the better."

He nodded and trotted off, calling out to Eden to bring over a couple of men from the squad. I dutifully called in the request. Black Jack still had not returned, and I ran into some unexpected difficulty. The S3 — not Major Raffaelle, who had DEROSed, but a new one — got on the radio, wanting to know why we needed a chain saw. I wasted time explaining it to him, fuming the whole time, only to have him say, at the end of it all, that there were no supply slicks available anyway. By this time my patience, never in great supply, had eroded to the vanishing point. I was getting ready to ask him why the hell he'd wasted my time wanting to know why I'd needed them when he'd known all along he wasn't going to send them, when I was interrupted by Brinkman, who told me that Dufresne had just finished yelling at him. Arty, it seemed, was still standing by, awaiting our go-ahead to fire. Captain Dufresne, Brinkman informed me nervously, was getting impatient.

"Is he now?" I said, with forced calm. "Is he really? Tell Captain Dufresne to do something for me. Tell him to insert every single 105 and 155 muzzle on Berchtesgaden up his rear and pull the lanyard. Tell him that the next time I'm in contact and it takes me more than an hour to get artillery, I'm going to come looking for him and pull the fucking lanyard myself. Would you tell him that for me, soldier?"

Brinkman blinked, uncertainly. "Uh ... I ... uh."

"Right."

20

Welcome to the 6th NVA Regimental HQ

YD365065; 26 April 1969; 0800–1900

Hyde was back to me within half an hour, requesting more men, to help in clearing the LZ. The trees, he explained, were coming down well enough but he'd been trying to have them fall in parallel lines and instead they were falling at odd angles, across each other, piling up in spots. He admitted that he wasn't as expert with the dynamite as he'd thought. Using the dull hatchets and machetes we had with us, he would need several men to cut up the piled-up trunks and drag them off to the side. Things were going a lot slower than expected.

"Never mind," I said. "You're doing fine, Nate. You're doing a helluva lot better than anyone else here could do, so keep it up. We'll just have to wait until you're done, that's all."

"Right." He nodded and went back to his work.

A little later Powell, one of the medics, came up to me with a worried expression. "Lieutenant, we got a problem. We gotta do somethin' about them bodies."

I stared at him, a bit taken aback. I'd actually forgotten about them. "I guess you're right." I turned to Stenger. "What can we do about them?"

He shrugged. "I don't know. Let's take a look."

We followed Powell down the hill to where the bodies lay. The pilot's body was covered by a poncho. Powell uncovered it; the chest cavity was no longer bright red and liver purple. It had turned black and dull brown, with several large white spots. My stomach lurched as the spots seemed to pulse and sway before my eyes. It lurched even more when I realized that what I was seeing were actually masses of crawling maggots. Powell dropped the poncho and led me to another. The medics had gathered the various parts of St. Onge and piled them together, where they lay, like some mad-man's assembly line and spare parts bin; two legs, a hand, and, worst of all, his head, untouched, but cut off at the neck cleanly, as if by a guillotine.

I knelt beside it. The smell here was worse than by Watson's body, but the flies and maggots were fewer. "When did you find this?" I murmured, indicating his head.

"Little while ago," Powell answered. "It was down there." He pointed to a spot at the base of the slope, near Genna's helicopter. "One of the guys stripping that slick found it."

I gazed at it. His features were still clear. The skin was grey, the muscles around the eyes and mouth were slack, but it was recognizably St. Onge's face. His eyes were open, and still blue and mild, as they had been in life. I felt a quick stab of pain. It was grief and guilt: Guilt, because I had mildly disliked St. Onge. Grief, because he was one of mine and I had loved him. He was the first of my men to die, and I felt the burden like a weight across my back.

St. Onge, while he lived, had often had a slightly puzzled expression in his eyes, as if trying earnestly to capture something beyond his understanding. That was to be his now for eternity; there would be now no chance he would ever understand.

I started to take a deep breath, and gagged reflexively. Powell covered the pile again.

"I see what you mean," I said quietly. "They're a bit ripe."

"Too much longer," Stenger interjected, "and we'll have to bury them if we can't get them into bags. Sun's too damn hot."

"I'll see what I can do."

Black Jack was back on the radio soon after this. I debated whether to bring up the matter of the morning's fiasco with artillery, but decided against it. Later perhaps, but there were other things to do now. I requested the chain saws and the body bags, and also some water; with the large number of wounded we'd had, water had been used at a higher than normal rate.

"Negative on the chain saws," he replied. "By the time I can spare a slick for you, you should have the LZ finished. How's it coming?"

"We've got the trees down, but we're going to have to clear them off the middle of the hill, over."

"Roger. How much longer?"

I glanced back over my shoulder at Hyde. He was busy showing Kenzy where to cut one of the fallen trees, so I decided not to interrupt him. "I'll say 30 minutes. Maybe longer." I glanced at my watch and did a double take. It was already 1030.

"Roger. Hurry it up. When Delta gets there, they'll have some body bags and some water with them. How's the security on that damned LZ?"

"Lousy as ever. Until we get some more people in here there's no way we can cover all this ground around us. When you bring Delta in I'd say we ought to have at least a couple of ARA or gunships around, over."

"I'll see to that. The rest of the battalion is running into some heavy stuff down below you. Bravo's up to their armpits in it. They may need those gunships worse than you. Out."

"Rest of the company going to make it up here, Lieutenant?" Helms asked, a bit too casually. His face was as placid as ever, but he'd been through a lot these two days. I felt a surge of affection and gratitude. I knew the strain this youngster had been under;

I'd felt his fear and hesitation, and yet not once had he shirked or hidden. Always, whenever I turned around, he'd been there.

"No." I relayed what Black Jack had told me. "Delta'll be here sooner or later," I assured him, "and then maybe we can relax a bit. What's that you're eating?"

He smiled shyly. "Beans and franks. I'm hungry."

I stared at the can. Hungry? I realized that I hadn't eaten since dinner, two days earlier. I noticed that his little stove was flickering. "Mind if I borrow that?" I asked.

He nodded, his mouth full. I went to my pack, took a heat tablet from one of the side compartments, and dropped it into his stove. Then I rummaged inside the pack. The first can I pulled out contained pork slices. So did the second.

"Helms," I said, through my teeth, "I'm going to wear you out."

He looked up from his meal and saw the two cans in my hand. "Keep trying, sir. I know I put something good in there for you."

"You'd better hope so," I said, pointedly. I finally found a can of spaghetti and meatballs, opened it, and put it on the stove. While it was warming, I opened a can of cheese (colored cellulose) and spread some over the crackers. As I swallowed the stuff, I wondered briefly if I could ever get hungry enough to eat those damned pork slices. I doubted it.

Things going as they were, I had no right to expect that I could finish my meal uninterrupted, and I didn't. About halfway through I got a call from Black Jack, wanting to know how much longer we'd be, and immediately after that Hyde warned us all off the hilltop, as he had one last tree to blow. By the time he was through with that, the food was cold. It didn't really matter; I'd been too hungry to enjoy it anyway.

After the dust settled, Hyde was able to report the LZ finished. It was just past 1100 when I radioed Black Jack and gave him the news. He replied that Delta would be enroute immediately.

I told the NCOs to check the perimeter and make sure everyone stayed alert while the birds landed. I wanted no repeat of yesterday's carnage. Then, I settled back to wait.

The first of the slicks became visible as a black dot on the southern horizon about 20 minutes later, at 1125. It grew rapidly into the dragonfly shape of a Huey; strung out behind it were several more, each smaller and blacker against the sky. The first bird approached the LZ. Hyde, standing in the midst of the fallen timber, pulled the pin on a smoke grenade and brilliant purple smoke gushed and eddied into the air, finally streaming away in a northeasterly direction. The pilot swung his Huey around in a wide arc, bringing himself into the wind. I held my breath. This maneuver brought him over the ridge from which we'd been hit that morning. But he touched down safely, shredding the smoke into frantic violet puffs. Six green-clad, hunch-backed figures jumped out and ran towards the perimeter. I glanced at my watch. LZ time was exactly 1130.

The second slick followed the leader's path, but I noticed as it neared us that it was acting erratically. I pulled my lips back in a grimace as I watched; it hovered, shuddering, over the LZ. It was still about ten feet up when it dropped, not swaying and jerking, the way they usually do, but straight down, like a rock. There appeared to be no damage, but when the pilot and crew scrambled out along with the infantry, I knew something was wrong. I ran up to the pilot, a thin, dark-haired warrant officer, who was in the act of throwing his flight helmet at the helicopter in disgust.

"What happened?" I yelled, over the sputtering and whining engine was making.

He shook his hear, cursed briefly but imaginatively, and spat. "Took a round through the hydraulic reservoir." He gestured disgustedly at the housing surrounding the main propeller shaft. "We're grounded." He resumed his cursing.

Oh, this was beautiful. I could hear the other slicks circling, awaiting instructions. He had landed right in the middle of the LZ, blocking it. I grimaced again and trudged over to Helms, who handed me the mike.

"Black Jack, this is One Six, over." He was going to love this.

"This is Black Jack. What's the problem?"

"One Six. This last bird here is sitting on the LZ stuck. He took a round through a reservoir, over."

"This is Black Jack. Where did that round come from?" His voice was deceptively mild.

"I don't know. I couldn't hear it. Wait one, while I check with the pilot." The WO had moved back from the helicopter and was standing nearby, hands stuck in his rear pockets, head shaking, muttering. I asked him if he knew where the fire had come from.

"Damn if I know," he shrugged. "I heard it hit while I was cuttin' down over that hill there —" he pointed to the east.

"Which side did it hit?" I asked.

He squinted up at the housing. "Starboard side. There. Almost head on, about six inches from the lip. See it?" He pointed.

I squinted, but I couldn't see anything. That's why I was infantry and he was a pilot, of course. Twenty-forty vision just doesn't make it.

I returned to Black Jack. "This is One Six. The round appears to have come from a ridge to the northeast or east, probably about 300 meters out, over."

"Roger. Is he blocking the whole LZ?"

"Affirmative."

"Okay. If your LZ's blocked, pick another spot and blow a new one."

"Roger." I said, without enthusiasm.

Delta Company had landed 12 men, of whom one was Lieutenant Mattioli, the Second Platoon leader. I knew him only to say hello, but he had a good reputation in the battalion. We got the preliminary greetings out of the way, and then I briefed him. I called in Sergeant Hyde, and Mattioli got one of his NCOs, who was supposedly an expert on blowing LZs, having served briefly with the Engineers. We discussed the problem. The only other place we could blow an LZ was on the east hill, which, though heavily wooded, could still be used, provided we had enough dynamite. The only other possibility was to leave the vicinity entirely. Mattioli agreed that, considering the size of our force, to say nothing of its splintered command structure, this would not be a wise move.

While we were holding our conference, the crew were holding one of their own; one of them was working on the housing of Major Dougherty's craft.

I had some trouble raising Black Jack; apparently, things were happening at the base of the mountain. I could hear small arms fire from down there. I waited for a few minutes, radio mike stuck in my ear. I watched idly while Crew Chief O B Carlson ran up the hill from the Dougherty's chopper — the one I'd been on — jumped onto the fuselage of the newest addition to our junk pile, and began fiddling with something on its housing. In that moment Sergeant O B Carlson became a legend, replacing the hydraulic reservoir and securing it with a C-clamp and duct tape.

By the time Black Jack got back to me, they had finished whatever it was they were doing and had gathered in a group; one of them, WO Parson, whose craft it was, was arguing and gesticulating. I was explaining our choice of LZ site to Black Jack when WO Luis Molinar came up to me.

"Wait one," I spoke into the mike, and turned to the pilot.

He grinned. "Thanks for the hospitality. We'll be buzzin' off now."

"What?"

"Look, we took a reservoir off of Dougherty's bird and put it on Parson's. We think it'll work; we want to try, anyway. Tell your head honcho we'll be off the LZ in a couple of minutes." With a friendly nod, he turned and strutted back to his helicopter. I noticed that the two door gunners were still standing with the other crewmembers, but Parson was in the pilot's seat. The blades started to swish slowly, and the noise level rose.

I returned to the radio. "Uh, this is One Six. Good news; we won't have to blow that LZ after all. The pilot says he's fixed that problem he was having and he's lifting off right now."

"Dammit!" Black Jack's voice exploded in my ear. "You tell him to get the hell out of that bird! Do you roger? Get him the hell out of that thing and shut her down!"

"Roger." Right. Parson was revving the motor up, already well past the warm-up point. The blades were whirling fast enough to pick up dust and leaves and blow them around the LZ. I moved up the hill a bit and waved my arm, but his attention was on the instruments in front of him. Even with the noise of the engine, I could hear Black Jack yelling into the radio. I thumbed my mike. "Can't get to him; he's lifting off right now, over."

"You tell that son of a bitch I'll court-martial him and everyone else down there if he doesn't shut that thing down! And that goes for you too, One Six!"

I sighed. "He's not on the radio net and he's not paying attention to us on the ground. I think he's pretty well made up his mind to go, over."

"Goddamit, I said stop him! Get moving and stop him."

I glanced up the hill and spotted one of the other pilots, standing off to the side, watching intently. It was Captain Gouch. I ran up to him.

"Hey! Black Jack says to shut her down!"

He shifted his small brown eyes from the chopper to me. "Who's Black Jack?" he asked mildly.

"Our Battalion CO."

"Oh. Well, go ahead and tell him, then." He waved his hand at the helicopter, which had already begun to tremble and sway as the pilot lifted it an inch or so off the ground.

The grounded crews working on WO Parson's aircraft, replacing its punctured hydraulic reservoir with one taken off Major Dougherty's ship. This action cleared the second LZ, on the west hill, for Alpha Company's insertion later that day, April 26 (photograph by Pat Lynch).

I grinned. "I don't think he's paying any attention to me."

He nodded agreement. "I don't think so, either."

The engine noise suddenly increased to a roar, the tail tilted up, and the Huey, bucking and swaying its familiar dance, edged up into the air. I held my breath; I was aware that the captain next to me had become tense and motionless, while the Huey hung briefly a foot or so over the LZ. Helms handed me the radio, from the receiver of which poured a steady stream of abuse and orders. Black Jack was upset.

He was going to be even more upset if that damned thing crashed, I thought, and I forced a brief but heartfelt prayer as Parson held his craft steady over the LZ. After what felt like hours, he rose suddenly, banked and roared off inches over our heads, headed straight down the southern slope. We continued to watch until we saw him swoop sharply and gain altitude. The captain let out his breath in an explosive snort.

"By God, we made it. I really didn't know whether that would work or not."

I stared at him. "You mean you guys weren't sure?"

"Hell no. We'd never done anything like that before. Guess now we know. Nothing against you, and all, but we damn sure didn't want to spend another night on this goddamn hill."

I swallowed. "Do you have any idea what would have happened to you, not to mention me, if that son of a bitch had crashed?"

"Not really."

I stared at him some more. "You must be out of your minds! All you had to do was wait another couple of hours, and we'd have another LZ ready. There wasn't any need to take that kind of chance."

"Well, it worked out, so don't get your tit in a wringer."

I stared at him some more. "Well, all things considered, I'd sure like it to be you instead of me who explains this to Black Jack."

He grinned. "Now there's a guy who's really nuts."

"Yeah. He's a colonel *and* a pilot. He definitely belongs in some sort of home. Speaking of which..." I thumbed the mike. "Black Jack, this is One Six. The pilot went ahead and lifted, over."

"This is Black Jack. I'm going to find out who that little maniac is and tear him a new asshole. And if you don't start carrying out my orders, Boccia, I'm gonna kick your ass out of this battalion."

"Roger. I relayed the message." I smiled crookedly. Of course, I hadn't relayed it too hard. Hell in a bucket, I'd wanted the guy off my LZ. And what was more, Black Jack knew it.

"Alpha's on their way in. Keep that damn LZ secure. Out."

I handed the mike back to Helms and shrugged. The pilot, who'd been listening to the conversation as it came over the speaker, grinned and shook his head in wonder. "Flight school's the best damn thing ever happened to me. We never have to put up with that shit."

I shrugged. "You get used to it. Up to a certain point, his bark is a lot worse than his bite."

"Here they come!" Helms yelled at me, from where he was standing on the south slope. I looked back over my shoulder; the first of Alpha's sortie was chop-chopping its way into the LZ. Sergeant Hyde waved a hand at me, nodded, pulled out a can of smoke and popped it. It hissed out, yellow and thick in the middle of the LZ, billowing almost straight up. The wind had died down. The slicks, then, would probably make their approach from the southeast, the easiest approach available to them. WO Searcy guided the Ghost Rider craft in. I quickly made the rounds of the positions on that side of the perimeter, reminding the men to keep their eyes open for any possible movement on the hilltops and ridges over which the Hueys would come.

The first of Alpha's birds touched down at almost 1245; it was jerking and swaying — the pilot, with excellent reason, was nervous, and was allowing only the first three

WO Searcy, Genna's seatmate, guiding in a Ghost Rider bringing in the first of the Alpha Company troops, at 1300 hours, April 26. Genna was badly wounded, and Searcy killed, during the NVA attack that night (photograph by Pat Lynch).

or four inches of runner to make contact with the ground. Out came the scuttling figures, dancing their ritualistic fandango under the blurred blades. The men had barely touched the ground when the pilot lifted off, banking immediately up and to port. The next slick touched down, and then, swiftly, the next ... it was all going so smoothly.

Captain Harkins was on the third slick in. He looked around as he ran off the LZ, spotted me, veered, and came up to me. Harkins was short, blade-thin and wiry. With his close-cropped sandy hair, prominent, angular cheekbones, and tight ropy muscles bunched around his thin lips, he looked mean and professional. Anyone seeing him for the first time assumed that he was either West Point or, perhaps, a prior-service OCS graduate. In fact, he had gone through ROTC, a fact that Black Jack, who despised ROTC graduates, never tired of reminding him of. Nevertheless, Harkins had acquired the reputation of being hard-bitten and tough, especially on his platoon leaders. He demanded quite a lot, and none of his lieutenants cared to meet those cold grey eyes and confess failure.

He greeted me in a friendly enough fashion, however. "How're you doing, Lieutenant? Heard you were getting lonesome down here."

"A bit, yes sir."

"Right." He looked around. Where's the shooting been coming from?"

I waved a hand at the perimeter. "All over. Yesterday, they hit us from that hill over there to our east. Later they were firing from that ridge to the southeast — over there. This morning they hit us from that other ridge, the one to the northeast — the nearer one. Oh. You can't see it from here, but it's just over that saddle there. And later this morning, that slick with Delta people on it got hit by a round from the east. So take your pick."

He frowned. "Jesus Christ. I was wondering why the hell you couldn't secure this LZ. Now I see. You got anybody over there?" He pointed to the east hill.

"Negative. We just didn't have the people to extend our perimeter out that far. And I didn't want to split up, and put half my people on one hill and half on the other. I didn't have enough to cover the hills and the saddle in between"

He nodded. "I see that." He ran his eyes over the saddle, to the timber-covered east hill. "But tonight we'll be able to man the whole thing. Bresnahan!" He called out to his Third Platoon leader, a man I knew. Dan's tall, string bean figure was almost jack-knifed under the weight of his pack as he bounced along the slope. We exchanged grins as he joined us.

"Dan," Harkins said, without preliminary, "I want you to take your platoon and secure that hill over there. Move 'em right out, but be careful. That's where they ambushed the CA yesterday, and they might have left some booby-traps behind. You got that PRC-25 working any better, now?"

"It's working okay now. Uh, one of my guys sprained his ankle coming off that last bird."

Harkins made a face. "Jesus, what a bunch of retards you got. Tell the little SOB to join the rest of the mob over there." He jerked his thumb in the direction of the group of wounded and injured sprawled out along the south slope. "Sprained ankle, for chrissake," Harkins muttered. "Top! Top! How many slicks in so far?"

Joubert, his first sergeant, who was standing on top of the hill, at the center of the LZ, was moving the Alpha Company troops out into the perimeter as they disembarked. He yelled back his answer, but we couldn't hear it over the roar of the helicopters.

"C'mon," Harkins said to me, "let's move up closer to the saddle."

We ran up the slope to where the saddle merged with the west hill. From there we could hear Joubert; he cupped his hands over his mouth and shouted the information that eight slicks had landed so far. The ninth was settling in as he spoke, so he turned his attention back to the LZ and gestured at the troopers getting off, waving them toward the west and south slopes. The Hueys were landing southeast northwest, giving their pilots the best angle for taking off. I noticed that these pilots were hovering longer, in contrast to the first two or three, who had barely touched down before lifting off.

Harkins turned his back to the LZ, keeping the dust and leaves out of his face. "How many positions did you man last night?" He asked.

"Eight. We had two right here, facing that ridge behind me, and another right over there —" I pointed to my left. "Two along the south slope, and one at the southwest corner. One over there — you can't see it — on the west slope, and the last one on the north side. We did have seven M60s, though."

He nodded. "Okay. You got enough ammo for 'em?"

"Yeah. We raided the dead slicks for everything they had."

"Good. Okay, move your people down to the sou — Christ!"

We both hit the ground as the BLAM! of an exploding RPG rocked us. I'd been gazing right at the tenth helicopter as it landed some 60 feet away. I had seen the door gunner, looking bored and uncomfortable, glance out at something to his right rear, probably Dougherty's chopper lying by the crater. The troops had already jumped out, and the Huey had started to sway and shudder, in that second before lift-off, when a harsh white light glared blindingly across the fuselage, just over the door. I saw the gunner's face dissolve under his green flight helmet. I threw myself down; the whole side of the chopper was enveloped in a yellow rush of flame as the extremely volatile JP-4 fuel ignited. The blades continued to whirl, fanning the flames into monstrous red and yellow billows. I could hear the hiss and crackle of burning flesh, and a high-pitched, ragged screaming from inside the flaming fuselage. I stared at the shriveled, blackened body of the door gunner, just visible behind the flickering, shifting flames; the nauseating odor of roasting flesh suddenly became obvious. Sgt. Joubert and Searcy, who had been knocked to the ground, picked themselves up and raced to the burning hulk, where the co-pilot sat slumped against the starboard door. Harkins and I had risen, in an instinctive move to reach the screaming man, but we saw that others had already gotten there, from the port side. Searcy pulled the co-pilot out — the back of his flight suit was torn and bloody from shrapnel — and laid him on his side a few meters away. Two troopers, thinking quickly, had raced to the pile of gear taken from the downed helicopters and brought back two fire extinguishers. They began to spray the foaming liquid across the body of the Huey, but it was far too late to save anything.

We stood, transfixed, and watched it burn. Then, explosively, Harkins whirled and glared at the ridge behind me. "Where the fuck did that come from?" He growled.

"Had to be from over there," I answered. "Same place they hit us from this morning."

He searched the ridgeline grimly, his eyes darting back and forth across the vegetation. "Son of a bitch," he said through his teeth, "there's not a goddamn thing we can do about this until we get out there and shove 'em off that ridge. Innocenti! C'm'ere." His RTO ran over, ducking low and dragging his pack with the radio along the ground behind him.

All that was left of the Ghost Rider craft that was destroyed by an RPG while on the LZ at Dong Ngai on April 26 (photograph by Pat Lynch).

"Black Jack, this Alpha Six, over."

I left him reporting to Black Jack and moved around the still-burning hulk to the other side. The crewman who'd been screaming was stretched out on the ground, with Stenger and Powell both working on him. He was the portside crew chief, who'd been peppered by shrapnel but also covered by burning fuel as it exploded above and behind him. They had smothered the flames by wrapping ponchos around him, but he'd suffered a serious burn across the back of his neck, between the helmet and the protective flight suit. The pilot, looking dazed and sick, sat on the ground nearby, untouched; he'd taken a lung full of acrid fumes when he'd attempted to rescue his wounded co-pilot.

As I stood watching, a couple of Alpha Company medics brought the co-pilot around from the starboard side. One of them held an IV bottle high over his head, the tube snaking down to the wounded man's arm. The co-pilot's eyes were opened. He groaned, but not with that soft, life-ending sigh of dying.

He would live. There was no hope, of course, for the starboard door gunner. Pray God, I thought, that he had died instantly, and hadn't been alive while those fiery yellow sheets, which still danced across the fuselage, had seared his body into a shriveled black lump.

I looked out over the saddle. Dan Bresnahan had begun moving his people over the saddle towards the east hill, but they had dropped to the ground and were lying there, weapons pointed at the ridge. Dan got up, walked, crouching, over to his point man, tapped him on the helmet, and pointed to the hilltop. The troopers scrambled to their feet, weapons still leveled, and ran up the short slope. Dan set up a machine gun on the saddle and, as his troops hurried across the exposed ground, the gunner began a stuttering tattoo, spraying the ridge and valley. It took his platoon less than two minutes to cross the bare saddle, however, and he quickly silenced his gun and shifted it to the hilltop.

Captain Harkins immediately called a meeting of the various—and I do mean various—leaders. There were elements from four platoons from Bravo Company, a squad and CP group from Delta, and two platoons and the CP from Alpha. He had assembled around him two platoon leaders from Bravo, one from Delta and two from his own company. Harkins, who was known as a by-the-book commander, shook his head in disbelief.

"I guess you gentlemen realize that this thing is beginning to look like a Chinese fire drill," he said, in a hard, mid-western baritone. "I can't ever remember seeing a mess like this on an operation. That just means we'll have to work harder, so we don't have any screw-ups. Dan, how many people have you got here?"

Bresnahan, knees bent and body folded in an oriental squat, sat next to his CO. He answered quickly. "Thirty-one. That includes the man I told you sprained his ankle."

"Yeah. Frank?"

Frank McGreevy, his other platoon leader, a short, intense-looking guy with a vague resemblance to George Goble, hesitated. "I got two squads and my CP group.

That's twenty-two. Then I got that FO from Gordy's platoon, and a Kit Carson. Twenty-four."

"Okay. I'm glad you got Gordy's FO, because Scranton didn't make it in. Okay. Boccia, watcha got?"

"I've got ten from my platoon, seven from the Second, two from the Fourth. Of those, three are pretty badly injured and can't be used on the perimeter; a few others are just shook up a bit, and bruised. Nineteen bodies on the ground."

"Okay. You — what's your name? Dickson?"

Dickson blinked and nodded. "Yes, sir —" He stopped and cleared his throat; his light tenor voice had cracked and emitted a falsetto squeak, eliciting grins all around, except from Harkins, who merely stared, waiting.

"I've got ... eighteen, I guess. That is— uh, yeah. Eighteen."

"Nineteen," I interjected.

"Uh, yeah. Nineteen. But one of them's hurt."

"Uhm." Harkins continued to stare at him for a moment, then glanced at Mattioli.

"What about you?"

"Twelve," Mattioli replied, "but four of them are from Captain Sanders' CP and five are from my CP. I've only got three line troops with me."

"Right. Boccia, how many medics do you have?"

"Two."

"Okay, Dickson?"

"One."

"Mattioli? You got a medic?"

"Two. Mine, and the Senior Medic."

"Good. I've got mine, and Dan, I saw yours on the ground. How about you, Frank?"

"No, sir. Mine was on my last load; he didn't make it in."

"Right. What about NCOs?" Harkins plodded on for the next 20 minutes, systematically putting together a picture of our assets: NCOs, machine guns, special weapons, starlight scopes, radios, rations, water, ammunition — everything that goes into making up an infantry unit. I admired his thoroughness; many commanders, presented with this mixed shambles, would have thrown up their hands and simply scattered us around the perimeter. Some purists would have just thrown up.

Some of the grounded flight crews had hopped aboard the slicks as they deposited Alpha Company. I couldn't blame them: the ground is no place for a pilot and crew. Many remained behind, however, as had our wounded. Black Jack had decided to not even try extracting them by Medevac until we'd had a chance to patrol the area and secure the nearby ridges. None of them was in any particular danger, medically speaking, so why take a chance on another helicopter being blasted from the sky?

"All right," Harkins finished. "That's the picture, then. Let me remind you that we're still in a bad position here. The latest intelligence estimates are that we've got a battalion or more of NVA troops in the immediate area, for whatever that's worth. No matter how many of the little fuckers there are in this area, they've got the high ground around us, and there's nothing we can do about it unless we move out and push 'em off these ridges. So tomorrow morning, Dan, I want you to take your platoon on a RIF to the northeast. There." He pointed behind him at the ridge leading off the east hilltop. "Follow that ridge down to the tableland to our north. That ridge is where they've been hitting you from, right, Boccia?"

I nodded. "Mainly. They've had snipers all over but that's where the heavy incoming comes from. All the RPGs—"

"Yeah. I know. Dan, I want you out first thing tomorrow morning. Maybe we can catch 'em napping. Or maybe not."

"They hit us at exactly 0600 this morning." I offered.

"Yeah. So?" He gave me a look, which plainly said that interruptions were not welcome. "Bilk Two Three was on a recon flight a while ago and spotted two, maybe three, bunkers in a ravine just north of that ridge. That might be where they've been coming from. Dan, you'll have ARA and artillery ready for you. What Iron Raven and Black Jack think we've got here is a headquarters area, maybe regiment, maybe division. Most of the line troops— we think — are down there beatin' on the 2/17th, but there are plenty to go around, so watch yourself, capishe?"

Bresnahan nodded.

"Another thing. Until we can get off this damn hill and onto some higher ground, we're not going to even try to bring any more choppers in, except for emergency medevacs. The rest of the battalion is gonna start working its way up the mountain to us, on foot. Might be as long as three or four days before they get here, though, and until they do we're gonna be pretty much on our own. Keep that in mind."

Harkins then quickly segmented the perimeter by platoon. Using the north azimuth as 12 o'clock, he assigned Frank McGreevy five positions, from the saddle to the northeast corner of the east hill; in addition to his own 24 men, Frank placed the pilots Genna and Searcey in his line. Dan Bresnahan covered the east hill around to the south slope below the crater with seven positions; like McGreevy he too was assigned a couple of crewmen. Dan's last position was at six o'clock. I placed my four positions from there to the junction of the south slope and the west hill; like Dan I was instructed to push my positions all the way to or in the tree line; Harkins was emphatic that he wanted no empty space between us and the dense vegetation. Dickson was told to cover the west with four positions, to ten o'clock. Finally, Al Mattioli filled in between him and McGreevy with the final two positions. Twenty-two four-man positions, plus six able-bodied crewmen.

"Now, for the rest of the time we're here, Harkins went on, "Four man positions, 50 percent alert all night. Claymores and trip wires in front of every position. I want each position checked by you or your platoon sergeant at least once every hour. I want absolute noise and light control as soon as the sun sets. No idle bullshit chatter on the radio, no runnin' around tradin' war stories, no goddamn cigarettes puffin' in the dark. Keep your people quiet and alert. Password for the day is Gentle Coin. Get the word out. Any questions?"

"Yes, sir." Dan Bresnahan spoke up. "How about a couple of LPs on that ridge over there?" He pointed at the low ridge to the northeast.

"No." Harkins shook his head decisively. "Not the way this terrain lies. We don't know what's on the other side of that ridge, but we do know that's where all the stuff's been coming from. You put a four man LP out there, Dan, are you sure you could get 'em back? Until we get off this damn hill, we've just got to sit tight and hunch low. That's why I want you out first thing in the morning. The sooner we start punching back at these bastards, the better off we'll be."

The briefing broke up and we went back to our various platoons. The next hour was spent in getting the men positioned, responsibilities delegated, and machine guns set up. While I was doing this, Stenger came up and asked to speak to me.

"What's up, Doc?" It wasn't until I saw Stenger blink that I realized what I'd said. Just one of the many times I've managed to sound like an imbecile with no apparent effort.

He ignored it, though. "I just checked with Robertson — he's Alpha Company's Senior Medic. Those body bags they promised: we didn't get 'em."

I raised my eyebrows. I could see the reason for his concern. "Damn, Doc. Did he say why not?"

Stenger made no effort to hide his anger. "He says they were on the last of Alpha's slicks. When the LZ got blocked nobody thought to have the bags just dropped down to us. Lieutenant, we've got to get those bodies out of here. They're starting to blow up. Another few hours in the sun and God knows what they'll look like. I asked Robertson to call in and have another bird fly out and drop some bags, and he tells me his CO says no go, that they won't fly anything out here unless it's an emergency. Lieutenant, we've got ourselves an emergency."

I admit I was as moved by the vehemence of Stenger's manner as by the cogency of his remarks. Mild-mannered, retiring men like Stenger simply don't make a fuss over nothing. And besides, the idea of leaving the bodies to rot out there, like carrion, was distasteful.

Leaving aside the obvious health problems, there was also the question of how it would affect the morale of the troops. With the tropical sun beating down on them and Hell's own galaxy of flies swarming over them, those bodies were not something you could long ignore. None of the troops would say so, I'm sure, but the unspoken thought in everyone's mind would be ... will they leave me out here to rot like that if I die?

This passed through my head as I walked up to Captain Harkins' CP after leaving Stenger. Surely, I said to myself, Harkins feels the same way. I found him leaning against a tree, with a radio mike in each ear. I waited while he talked, for about seven or eight minutes, and then spoke quickly when I saw he'd finished.

"Captain. One of my medics just asked my about those body bags. Can we get some—"

Harkins shook his head, and turned his back to me while he handed one of the mikes to his RTO.

"Negative." His voice sounded hard and flat, from over his shoulder. "No good. My medic asked me the same thing. I've already checked. Nothing's coming out here until we get this area secured. That's final."

"Look, Captain, we're going to have a serious problem soon. We've got to do something."

He took a cup of coffee proffered by one of his RTOs and turned back to face me. The late-afternoon sun glinted redly off the canteen cup as he sipped slowly. "I know it's bad. Robertson told me. Hell, I can see for myself. But we won't get anything in here until at least tomorrow morning. If then. We've got to secure this area before we risk any more slicks." His level grey eyes flitted quickly around the perimeter. "If it's that bad, though, why not have the medics move the bodies outside the perimeter until we get the bags in?"

I shook my head, tiredly. "Those aren't bodies, Captain, they're goddamn omelets. We'll need a shovel to get 'em off the ground even now."

Harkins swirled his cup gently, and frowned at it. "As I said, Lieutenant, that's final. End of discussion."

"Captain, will you call Bla—"

"Shut up." He looked directly at me, and his eyes were chilly indeed. "I'm not in the habit of explaining myself to my platoon leaders, Boccia, and I don't really need to say anything more to you than I've already said. But since you're from another company, and since you don't seem to know just when to shut up, I'll tell you this: I've called Black Jack three times with a request for those bags. The second time I was told not to bring the matter up again. I won't tell you what I was told the third time. Is that all right with you, Lieutenant?"

I swallowed and felt my ears burn. Talk about stepping in it.

"Yes, sir. Sorry, sir."

Harkins drained the last of his coffee. "Get your ass back to the perimeter and start doing your job, Boccia. I'll do mine."

I went.

21

The Body Bags

YD365055; 26–27 April 1969; 1900–0600

Dusk came early that afternoon; the sky overhead was clear and the sun would not set until 1830, but it was hidden behind distant storm clouds to our west. Darkness began to close in quickly. After checking the perimeter twice — more to gauge the men's morale than for any other reason — I settled down to a cold meal; by that time it was already too dark to risk using a heat tablet to warm anything up. I was hungry, but still not hungry enough to eat cold beef slices or ham and eggs or turkey loaf, which was all I had left — despite what Helms had promised. I opened a can of peaches and started spooning the sweet syrup into my mouth. I was vaguely aware that Harkins' RTO was giving a time check; it came over Helms' speaker: 1900.

The NVA must have very accurate watches. Seconds later the first RPG slammed into the north slope.

I dropped the can and rolled down the hillside to my rifle, spattering sticky peach syrup over my legs. Helms snatched up his radio and stretched out alongside me. We had both instinctively faced north, in the direction of the shooting, but after a couple of seconds I reminded myself that my responsibility was the south side of the perimeter. I swiveled around, accidentally kicking Helms in the process. RPGs were going off, one after another, along the north slope, I could hear someone crying out for a medic in a harsh, ragged scream, and then everything was drowned by the furious cascade of sound as at least eight machine guns opened up. I saw, off to my immediate left, an M60's characteristic red sparkle, and cursed. I got to my hands and knees and scrabbled and twisted down the slope to where the idiot was firing. I was thinking along the way that Logan had cleared his gun and wanted to show everyone that it would too work, but when I got about halfway there, I saw Logan's unmistakable bulk rise up from behind the gun and run to it. Seconds later the firing stopped.

From that particular gun, at least. The rest of the perimeter, especially along the north slope and the saddle, was still putting out a heavy volume of fire. I flopped back down to the ground and grabbed the mike that Helms held out. Bresnahan and McGreevy were talking back and forth, trying to pinpoint the RPGs. Harkins would be on the other net, calling ARA or artillery. I sat there and listened; I had nothing to say, and, for the moment, nothing else to do.

By the time ARA got there, about ten minutes later, the NVA had ceased firing and left. Two machine guns from Bresnahan's sector kept up a sporadic, random fire, trying to keep the enemy off that damned ridge, but everyone else had settled back to lie still and stare into the darkness. The hellish thing about firefights at night is that you can't see. Of course, you don't normally see much during broad daylight, either, but it's worse at night.

It hadn't gotten completely dark, yet. There remained enough light for me to see, as black patches against deep gray, the medics and others as they pulled wounded off the perimeter and brought them back to the CP. An exhausted Stenger returned, about one hour later, with the word that we had lost three killed and six wounded. Two of the dead and two of the wounded, he informed me, had been in an M60 position, directly underneath the big tree on the north slope. The enemy had slammed round after round into the branches and trunk about ten feet above the ground, shredding the area directly underneath with a rain of shrapnel.

The other KIA was WO Searcy, the copilot of the last craft to go down, the one with my people on it. Wounded by the same RPG was his seatmate, WO Chris Genna, whom I'd talked to only hours before. They'd been behind a large fallen log, but here again the NVA used that against us. Almost all the casualties we were to take on Hill 1485 were the result of RPG fire.

And so, despite everything, Stenger got his body bags. Two of the wounded were hurt too badly to last through the night. Around 2100, a dark shape hung roaring and throbbing over our LZ; the medevac pilot, guided only by a strobe light, settled his craft blindly, his fragile blades swishing inches from the unseen branches around him. We sent as many of the wounded back as we could, including one of the crewmen from the slick shot down earlier, but we still had to retain several. By now, every time a helicopter approached the LZ, we expected to hear a crackling, grinding crash and see it plummet to the ground. I don't suppose it's possible, but we all said later that we'd held our breaths the whole five or six minutes he was there. The wounded had to be hoisted up, one by one, while the pilot grimly held his position over the clearing. During this time, of course, the entire perimeter was putting out a huge volume of fire, and two gunships raked the ridgelines, but with as much high ground as there was around us, and as exposed as that medevac was, it was still a highly risky operation. When the pilot finally pulled up and flew off, the breath exploded from my lungs as if out of a burst paper bag.

Stenger brought a couple of body bags by, about ten minutes later. He threw them on the ground, beside his pack. "Tomorrow morning, " he said, to no one in particular.

"It's too late for tonight," I agreed, although he may not have even been listening. I peered closely at him. Even in the dark, I could see a dark stain on his left arm and shoulder. I thought it was sweat, at first, but then I realized that it was blood. "Are you all right?" I asked, leaning forward for a better look.

He glanced at the shoulder. "Yeah. That's from one of those guys we put on the medevac. He started to bleed while I was holding him on the penetrator. I guess he dripped on me." He fell silent for a moment. "I'd change shirts but I don't have another one."

"Here." Helms held something out to him. "That's a jungle sweater. Wear that."

Stenger nodded. His pale torso gleamed momentarily in the starlight as he shrugged off his stained shirt and donned the rough olive green cardigan.

We settled down to await the night. Exhaustion enveloped me like a bed of quicksand, immobilizing me. I had not slept at all the previous night; my nerves had been under constant strain since the afternoon of the 25th. My body wanted to surrender to the pull of the damp, cool ground, and sink into a deep and engulfing sleep. I could feel some of my larger muscles twitch and jerk with fatigue. But my mind grimly refused to dim. Even though the need for sleep was like a pain, even though my brain felt blurred and heavy, I could not close my eyes.

I suspect that not many of us could. Finally, after an hour, I got up and crawled around the perimeter, as much to relieve the growing tension between my taut nerves and flagging body as to actually check the positions. Everyone was awake, as I'd thought. Of course it was still early—about 2230—but I doubted that I'd find anyone sleeping on guard at any time during this particular night.

I had just returned to my CP when Helms shook me silently and handed me the mike. I lay back against the ground with the black earphone in my ear and listened as Captain Harkins informed me that movement had been spotted along the west side of the perimeter. I just nodded and yawned into the mike, a strange lassitude overcoming me. It's not that I disbelieved him; I just couldn't get too excited about the news. A month, or even a few nights, earlier, and hearing news of that sort would have brought me bolt upright, to go scrambling about the perimeter alerting the troops and preparing for a firefight. Now I just lay there and nodded. Movement? So what's the big deal? I suppose it was rather like a young man being offered a chaste kiss by his girlfriend the night after he'd squandered a couple of hundred dollars on his first trip to a bordello. It seems like such a letdown...

Oh, I got up all right, and crawled around, making my rounds, but I felt anything but virginal and wide-eyed. We stayed on alert for about 20 minutes or so, and then gradually relaxed. Sergeant Randolph made the rounds to tell the troops they could go back to two on, two off.

An hour later, at 0015, we had another alert.

At 0300, we had another.

0430, and I crawled around again.

By 0500, when we went off the last alert, my brain had quit working. I fell at last into a confused and uncertain slumber, which was ended by the wake-up call at 0530.

Dawn had already tinged the eastern sky a half-hour earlier; the sun would be rising soon. I made the rounds one more time, although this time it was harder to convince everybody to get up off the ground. Not many of them were sleeping, but a good number of the men were simply lying on the ground, eyes opened, but barely able to move. I knew exactly how they felt.

Getting back to the little hutch Helms had manufactured the previous night, I crawled into it and picked up the radio mike. I could hear Helms snoring softly, his back to the radio. I called the CP and mumbled into the radio: "Bravo One Six. Perimeter on alert. Out."

Then I just lay there, my cheek pressed against the cold angular surface of the PRC 25. The metal felt cool and comfortable. My body, twisted around with my legs stretched out and my chest up against the pack, felt warm and relaxed. I closed my eyes, just to rub the grit and sand from them...

"Wake the hell up!"

I opened my eyes, blinking. Harkins' face, red and granite-like in the morning sun, glared at me, a few inches away. I nodded agreeably, rolled off the radio, stretched and looked at my watch. Of course, I'd just closed my eyes for a second ... 0730! "Jesus Christ," I muttered, as I sat straight up.

Harkins withered me with a look. "Check your goddamn perimeter, if you can get your ass out of the sack."

I started to tell him that I'd checked it at 0530, but then thought better of it. There wasn't a whole lot for me to say.

Dan Bresnahan had begun to move his people out an hour earlier, but he'd been held up as a result of some confusion between Harkins and DivArty. Incredibly, Dufresne continued to insist that we were some 500 or more meters from the original LZ. It took the combined efforts of Harkins and Black Jack to finally get things straight. Even so, Dufresne was often heard to say, over the next few weeks, that only his alertness had prevented an inexperienced company commander from calling 155s in on his own position. Fortunately for Dufresne, Harkins was not among those who heard him say so.

Dan eventually moved on, and about half an hour later, while I was dispiritedly attacking another cold can of C-rations, his point squad found a complex of bunkers, about 300 meters from the east hill, just beyond the farther ridge. They were deserted, Bresnahan radioed us, but they did show signs of recent occupancy.

Minutes later, while we sat in the morning sun, cleaning our weapons, rifle fire broke out to our north, followed by a curiously hollow, dull explosion, unlike anything I'd ever heard before. I was standing right beside Helms' radio, so I merely knelt down and picked up the mike. Nothing came over the speaker for a few minutes, while the fire petered out. After a few seconds of silence, Bresnahan's voice sounded in my ear.

"Alpha Six, this is One Six."

"Roger, One Six. Go."

"We just took some fire from three trail watchers. Nobody hit on our side. We returned fire. Confirm two NVA killed over."

A thin cheer sounded from around the perimeter, as those few who were close enough to a PRC 25 to hear the news relayed it to others standing nearby. Harkins' response cut through the noise with a rasp of static.

"Good 'nuff. What was that explosion we heard?"

"Gook was set up behind a bunker with his RPG armed and aimed, if you know what I mean. My slack man spotted him and fired off a few rounds, and I guess one of 'em hit that damn RPG square in the nose. Blew the launcher, Charlie and his buddy and about five square yards of jungle all to hell."

Laughter and loud cheers greeted this news. I felt pretty good myself. That bastard with the RPG had been making life hell for us. The bodies of five of his victims still lay inside our perimeter. We savored the irony of his having been blown up by his own deadly weapon.

"Good man," Harkins chuckled. "Keep on moving. You need ARA or anything like that?"

"Negative. There was just those three trail watchers, and the third one split quite a while ago. We'll take our time and be careful, over."

"Roger. You do that. In any case, I don't want you to go more than 500 meters from the hill. You copy?"

"I got it. Looks like they've hit the road, though."

"No more than 500 meters, period. Out."

Norman Stenger walked up a few minutes later, holding two body bags slung over his shoulder.

"Me and Powell are going to get those two bodies down there, Lieutenant."

"Right. Helms and I will give you a hand."

Stenger stared at me. "Maybe you ought to detail somebody else, sir. It's going to be pretty nasty work."

I looked back at him. I could feel a muscle twitch along my jaw. "St. Onge was my man, Stenger."

"Yes sir." He hesitated, than continued. "I'm not kidding about it being nasty, Lieutenant." He dropped his eyes to my equipment, then raised them back up to meet mine. "You'll need your mask."

Well I'll be damned, I thought. I'll get some use out of this miserable thing after all. I pulled the floppy black thing out of its container, flung the latter aside, and walked down the hill to where Stenger and Powell were already gathered. Behind me, I could see Helms putting his mask on, with no noticeable enthusiasm. Helms had by now gotten used to being volunteered.

I knew it would be bad, but I wasn't prepared for what it was like. Even with the gas mask on the stench was so bad I could barely bring myself to breathe. I swallowed three of four times, rapidly. Somewhere, floating back to me from some long forgotten lecture, the thought came that a man who vomited in a gas mask stood an excellent chance of smothering himself. I fought back the nausea and bent to the task. Helms was helping Powell with the body of the pilot, while I helped Stenger with St. Onge's remains. In addition to his mask, Stenger wore a large, thick pair of gauntlets; he was trying to pick up the pieces. A couple of them — the head, and one leg came easily enough, and he placed them into the gaping bag. But the other leg slithered through his fingers as he tried to lift it, and my stomach gave a desperate wrenching lurch as I saw that much of it had liquefied. I had to turn away, fighting back the urge to run off and vomit. I shut my eyes, bent over and stopped breathing for a moment.

When I turned back, Stenger was gone, but he reappeared quickly. He had gone to get an entrenching tool, which he was opening as he came down the hill. I held the bag open for him while he shoveled PFC Thomas St. Onge, RA 1123452, into it. When he finished, there remained a brown-black stain, the color of old, spent wine; it crawled with maggots and small black beetles. He scraped dirt over the stain and covered it up, then handed the shovel to Powell, who needed it too. I zipped closed the long gray bag.

We each grabbed an end and started for the top of the hill. The bag was disturbingly light, as if it were some child in there, instead of a full-grown man. But there was little enough left of St. Onge.

We added our bag to the three that were already stretched out alongside the burned chopper. As bad as that was, Stenger informed me, as we stripped the masks from our sweat-soaked faces, we had been fortunate compared to Robertson and Calloway, the senior medic from Delta. They had had to scrape the scorched body of the door gunner from the bulkhead of the helicopter.

Scrape was the word, Stenger said. Parts of the man's flight helmet had melted and stuck to the frame, with his head still in it.

The rest of the day was spent in improving our defensive posture. Around 1400, Helms made brief contact with our company CP but was chased off the net before I had a chance to talk with Robison. Gordie Atcheson, Harkins' Third Platoon leader, was the point element of the battalion as it tried to move up the long steep southern side of Hill 1485 and link up with us. They were running into constant sniper attacks, delaying their progress. Rather than risk any men, Black Jack was ordering ARA, artillery and gunship attacks against any sniper position. That's why Helms was unable to get through to Bravo for very long; the operational requirements for the battalion net were too great.

There wouldn't have been a whole lot to say, anyway. Bravo and Charlie Companies had been left behind, to continue to search out the enemy units at the base of the mountain, while Atcheson's platoon, the bulk of Delta Company, and the Battalion CP tried to link up with us.

I spent most of the afternoon watching my men dig in and improve the four-man foxholes along our sector of the perimeter. I also listened to the radio, getting a running commentary, almost step by step, of Atcheson's progress. Somewhere around 1400 Harkins came up behind me while I stood there.

"Come over here for a minute, Boccia. I want to talk to you."

I turned and followed him to a spot a little removed from our respective CP areas. I hesitated and then looked him in the eye. "Sorry about this morning, Captain."

He scowled, making a waving motion with his hand. "Forget it. Just don't let me catch you doing that again. That's not what I wanted to talk about." He shifted his gaze to a spot over my left shoulder, toward the west side of the hill. "This man Dickson. How long has he been in the battalion?"

"Dickson?" I said, surprised by the question. "I don't know ... three months, I guess. About that, anyway."

Harkins brought his hard gray gaze back to me. "Has he seen much action before this?"

I raised my eyebrows, feeling the skin along my forehead rub against the leather bank of my helmet liner. "Hell, Captain; nobody in Bravo has seen a whole lot of action, except for Marsh Eward last week."

"What is it about this guy? Is he a little bit yellow?"

I blinked. Then I looked away, silent and, to tell the truth, stunned. None of us had any great regard for heroism, at least in the sense that civilians would use the word. A professional soldier is far more impressed by competence than he is by bravery. Bravery, after all, is given, a basic necessity; it was, or should have been, part of a man's physical equipment. A soldier needs two arms, two legs, two eyes, and bravery. Heroism ... the only time soldiers use the word "hero" is in derision, as a synonym for dummy, or as a term of contempt for a showboat or one who thinks too highly of his importance in the overall scheme of things. The objective of professionals is to win wars, not medals.

But if heroism is not a word used seriously, cowardice is not a word used lightly. A man like Harkins could no more accept a coward as a platoon leader than he could countenance a blind man or a paraplegic leading troops into battle. Harkins could cheerfully and unceasingly label his platoon leaders as incompetent fools; incompetence, after all, can be cured. But yellow...

I swallowed and tried to choose my words carefully. "I've never seen any evidence that he is, sir."

"Do you know how many alerts we had last night? Or did you sleep through them all?" His face remained deadpan. Harkins probably did have a sense of humor, somewhere, but why waste it on lieutenants?

"Yes, sir. I know. I was awake all night. We had four alerts."

"Yeah. Four goddamn alerts. And every damn one of them on the west side of the perimeter. Dickson's people. Four alerts coming from the one side of this miserable goddamn hill we haven't been hit from yet." Harkins paused to light a cigarette. "He had his men so damn spooked," he continued, blowing a thin gray stream of smoke out from the side of his mouth, "that they were calling an alert every damn time a leaf moved. Dickson spent the whole damn night going around his perimeter, from one position to another, getting his people so stirred up one damn sneeze would have spooked them off the hill. I hear he was going around telling his men we didn't have enough ammo and we couldn't get any supplies in and we were surrounded and we're gonna get overrun and all kinds of bullshit like that.

"Now, I don't mind going 'round and keeping his people alert; rather have him doing that than catching Zs under a goddamn poncho. But all this bullshit about how we're all gonna die in 12 minutes is too damn much. I don't mind keeping your people tightened up, but God damn." He emphasized the last two words. He paused. "I hear he wasn't exactly front and center the day before yesterday when you got shot down."

I blew out my cheeks with a puff. "I don't know, really. Look, it's no secret that the rest of us think he's a loser. And he wasn't any ball of fire Friday. Okay. But he wasn't hiding any place, either. I don't really know what to say, Captain."

Harkins snorted. "Well, you're a lot of fucking help. I talked to him this morning and he was still scared spitless. If you can spare the sack time tonight, I want you to check his people along with yours. Get 'em calmed down. I can't relieve Dickson — that'll be up to Robison — but I sure as hell don't want him in control of a platoon if we get hit again tonight. Capishe?"

"Yes, sir."

The rest of the day and the following night were mercifully uneventful. I checked both the south and west sides of the perimeter that night, but by then every one had apparently calmed down. We held a mad minute at 0300, which effectively cut everybody's sleep, but who knows? It might have disturbed the slumber of some NVA, too. The night passed much more swiftly than the previous two, partly, I suppose, because I was finally able to get about three hours of sleep.

The next morning the officers assembled at Harkins' CP, sipping coffee and talking in low undertones, while Harkins spoke on the radio with Iron Raven. Bresnahan, McGreevy and I were discussing a problem we'd encountered the previous night, concerning the coordination between my easternmost and Dan's westernmost positions, when Dickson ran up the hill to where we stood.

"Hey!" he puffed, his round baby face taut with excitement. "We got probed last night! They came right up to our positions, man!" His thin, reedy tenor, scratchy at the best of times, sounded shrill in my ear.

The three of us looked at each other with raised eyebrows.

"I didn't hear anything last night," McGreevy said mildly. "Where were they?"

"I didn't hear nothin' last night either, but this morning my guys found some signs right out in front of one of our positions. Tracks and shit."

"Really? Are you saying they crapped on one of your positions?" Bresnahan asked.

"All kinds of signs there, damn it," Dickson persisted. "All over the place."

I sighed and caught Harkins's eye as he swiveled around with raised eyebrows himself. He was still listening to the radio but he'd overheard some of what Dickson had said. He nodded at me and then in the direction of the west side of the hill. I took that to mean that I was to go and check the situation out.

"Okay, Dick," I sighed, "let's go take a look."

Dickson's third position was located in the southwest corner of the perimeter, where a 15-foot long thicket thrust out from the forest. Alongside this thicket was a patch of earth about six feet square that had been cleared of ground cover; nearby were some packs and other gear, and few discarded C-ration cans. A slim path had been cut into the thick growth directly in front of the position, and this went for a short distance into the forest. A pair of thin grey-green wires led out from a detonator lying by a man's helmet.

Two scared-looking troopers were manning the position. They greeted us nervously and pointed down the path. "It's right there, sir," one of them spoke up. "We left it just like we found it."

I raised an eyebrow at Dickson and motioned for him to follow me. I traced the wires down the path until I reached what I expected to find: a curved steel case, with the wires attached to the two small posts sticking out from the top. The convex side of the mine faced our perimeter. I sighed when I saw it. I knew what Dickson was going to say.

"You see it?" He whispered. "Man, I thought I could hear somethin' last night! Goddamn good thing my guys didn't hear 'em or they woulda blown themselves away, for sure."

"I see it. Good thing they didn't hear what last night?"

I couldn't see Dickson's face — he stood behind me — but I could just about hear his eyes pop.

"NVA! Little tuckers came up and turned our claymores around on us last night!"

"Dickson," I asked in a hushed voice, "why are we whispering? Never mind. How many claymores got turned around, did you check?"

"Uh, yeah. Yeah, I did. This is the only one they got to, so I guess we musta scared 'em off 'fore they could get to the others. You can see where they were standing — right there!" He thrust an arm past my shoulder and pointed his finger at a mark scuffed into the black earth, about four or five inches from the claymore.

I looked where he was pointing, and then gave a slow look at the immediate area. "Dickson," I asked quietly, have you ever seen an NVA wearing GI jungle boots?"

There was a silence, then: "What's that got to...."

I raised a hand, cutting him off. "Look at that foot print, and then look at the soles of your boots and tell me if the patterns aren't the same."

Some of the tense eagerness went out of his voice, to be replaced by a faintly expressed mulishness. "Well, they might be ... but all the same, somebody turned that thing around."

"You are so right. Tell me, what time did your guys put their claymores out last night? Was it after dark?"

"Uh ... I dunno. Six or seven. Why? What's that got to do with it?"

"Come on. Let's go back and check." I waited while Dickson turned; I couldn't really blame Dickson, I thought, as I followed his rear end down the path. The fact was that some otherwise fairly intelligent soldiers had convinced themselves that the NVA had nothing better to do than to crawl around American perimeters at night turning claymore mines around and leaving them pointed in the wrong direction. It did no good to point out the utter imbecility of such an action.

Let's consider it for a moment. A highly trained NVA soldier, a sapper, for instance, crawls along the ground in thick jungle growth, to within spitting distance of a U.S. position. It is night, the unit in question has undergone three attacks and suffered several casualties, and is correspondingly nervous and jumpy. Having crawled over broken branches, leafy vines, thorny bushes and swaying, crackling reeds, any one of which could give him away, our industrious friend then sits down alongside a claymore mine. Does he proceed then to cut the wires leading to it, so that in case the American troops—who are only some 15 to 30 feet away—hear him and try to detonate the mine, he doesn't get blown to Socialist Heaven? No. Does he take advantage of the fact that he has somehow gotten close enough to the GIs to smell their socks by casually tossing a grenade or satchel charge into their position? No. No, he carefully loosens the mine, which has four thin posts stuck into the ground, picks it up, and turns the thing around, so that it faces back toward the U.S. perimeter. Does he then toss a grenade and scurry away, chuckling orientally over the surprise the GIs are about to receive if they survive the grenade and try to blow the mine? No. Does he run off a few feet, duck behind a tree, and yell out "Fuck Nixon!" to the sleepy GIs, thus awakening them from a pleasant slumber and inducing them to blow the claymore? No. What does this highly trained soldier do? He replaces the claymore gently and then crawls away, softly, softly, leaving it to be found the next morning.

It seems absurd even to consider this possible; the NVA would have to be insane or moronic to do anything similar. But there remains an exceptionally vehement group of soldiers who swear a thousand oaths that the NVA did this all the time. Reasoning with them does no good; they simply smile and shrug. This group takes its place alongside others such as believers in creationism, astrology and extra-terrestrial UFOs in demonstrating a celestial contempt for facts and logic.

Dickson's two men confirmed that they'd laid the claymore out after dark, at about 1930. As far as I was concerned, that was it. They were tired, scared and inexperienced. I had no doubt in my mind what had happened. I started back up towards Harkins' CP. I could hear Dickson coming up behind me, trying to catch up.

"Just a minute, Bo," he yelped, "You can't—"

"Shut up!" I turned on him, irritated and disgusted. I'd had it up to the eyebrows with Lieutenant Dickson. "I don't have time for this. That man of yours stuck the damn thing in the ground backwards. SHUT UP!"

I compressed my lips, and then took a deep breath. Dickson's small blue eyes were fixed on mine and his mouth was open but I have a lot of lungpower when I need it. "Okay, that happens. We all make mistakes when we're tired. But your guys are so high-strung right now they're ready to blow sky-high. And you're so damn jumpy yourself you can't even think straight. Last night we had four goddamned alerts, and every one of them was because one of your men got jumpy and thought he heard something. I'm not through yet so shut up. You ever hear of the little boy crying wolf? Well, another night like last night and Charlie could bring his whole damn army up this hill and nobody'd believe you. So settle yourself down and keep your people calm. And if you don't like what I'm saying, then understand this: Better me than Harkins. You fuck up again and he'll shove a stick of C4 up your ass and blow it."

I turned away. I could feel Dickson's stare in the small of my back. It didn't bother me. With Eward or Denholm or Jerry — assuming one of them could have ever screwed up like Dickson, which is a hell of an assumption — I would have felt bad about what I'd just said, since it bore more than a trace of condescension and contempt. But with Dickson I didn't care; I didn't want him as a buddy, or a fellow platoon leader, or anything else. If his feelings or sensibilities were hurt that was just too damned bad.

Harkins turned an eyebrow in my direction when I reached his CP, but I shook my head.

"Forget it," I said, waving a hand toward Dickson's positions. "Gremlins. Elves. Brownies. Things that go bump in the night and turn claymores around." I plopped down on a fallen tree trunk and pulled out a cigarette.

Harkins grunted and returned to his map.

22

Rescued by the Gnome

YD 365065; 28 April 1969

Late that afternoon we received word that Atcheson's platoon — Alpha Three Six — was on the final slope leading to our location, and would be entering the perimeter within 30 or 40 minutes. The rest of the battalion was still strung out a couple of kilometers behind him. Since his lead element was expected to reach us by 1700 or so, Harkins and Black Jack decided that there would be enough time to get the last of the column in before darkness fell.

I knew Gordon Atcheson by reputation. He was considered to be absolutely fearless and almost insanely aggressive. In less than six months, operating in an area where contact had been — until now — sparse, he had already earned a Silver Star and a recommendation for the DSC.

I made the rounds of the perimeter, warning the troops to look for his approach from the southwest. No one said anything, but the almost inaudible sighs and imperceptible relaxation of tense shoulder muscles indicated that the troops had been fully aware of the seriousness of our position.

At 1722 precisely, (yes: I did check my watch) a tall stringy black soldier, branches and leafy twigs covering his helmet, pack and M16, ambled through the perimeter, entering at a point just south of that position where the claymore had been "turned around." Two or three men followed him; all were puffing slightly and their uniforms were dark with sweat. Gordie had pushed hard over the last 200 or 300 meters. He himself was the fourth man in, short, stocky, fair-haired, with a broad, flat, bulldog face glistening with sweat under his branch-festooned steel pot. He clumped his way up the hill, looked about, saw Harkins standing at his CP, dropped his pack and gear and swaggered over to join us.

He greeted Harkins first, then nodded to McGreevy, Bresnahan and me. From a distance he gave the impression of being stolid and phlegmatic. Seen up close, tiny lines around his mouth and eyes betrayed a lively sense of humor. Above all, though, one sensed the tremendous self-confidence and determination in him.

"Rough trip, Gordie?" Harkins asked. Atcheson was a lieutenant, of course, but

Harkins no doubt consoled himself with the thought that Atcheson would be a captain, and therefore eligible for membership in the human race, within three or four months. He was undoubtedly one of the very few platoon leaders for whom Harkins felt a genuine respect.

Atcheson shook his head; beads of sweat flew off. Even that gesture reminded me of a bulldog. "No, not that bad. Slow, mainly. Some half-ass sniping going on, but nothing serious. They'd just fire off a couple of rounds and split. Never let us get too close."

"How far back does the rest of the column go, do you know?"

"No. I never bothered about that shit. Keeping up with us was their job. I had enough to do to get up here on time."

Bresnahan snorted. "We notice you took your sweet time getting up here. Hell, it's too late now; we chased the NVA off a long time ago. But we can still use you. We need someone to run a police call around the perimeter."

"Where do you want my people?" Atcheson asked Harkins.

"I don't know yet. Let's wait until the rest of the battalion gets up here. For right now, take 'em over to that other hill over there," Harkins pointed at the east hill, "and keep 'em out of the way."

"Right." Atcheson looked at me. "You're Boccia, aren't you?"

"Yeah. You're Atcheson, right?"

He grinned. Smiling, his face became totally different; the laugh lines around his eyes and mouth became more prominent, his cheeks filled out, and he suddenly seemed to have become one of those florid, bonhomous men whom one sees in a bar getting drunk and doing remarkably silly things. But his voice remained the same; flat, hard and confident, with nothing of the clown in it. "Heard you on the radio the other day. You sure were making a fuss."

I shrugged slightly. "Just sharing my thoughts."

"Yeah." He waved a hand at his platoon sergeant, who was standing nearby, talking with Sgt. Joubert. "Get 'em over to that hill there, Sarge. I'll be right there."

Harkins grabbed his arm for emphasis. "Soon as you're set, I want you to cover that ridge over there—" he pointed to the northeast—"and lock it down. Black Jack wants to bring in his staff and I don't want him blown out of the sky, Capishe?"

Atkinson nodded. "Roger." With that he turned and walked away. There wasn't much casual chitchat with Alpha, I saw.

Thirty or forty minutes later, after the last of the column entered the perimeter, Black Jack and his Battalion staff landed without incident and immediately began setting up an impromptu TOC by the crater.

Black Jack, while that was going on, walked up and greeted Captain Harkins. Together, they began inspecting the perimeter and the surrounding terrain. He paused briefly as he passed through my sector, and gave me a cold, level stare.

"Boccia," he'd said, in a voice like two bricks being rubbed together, "just what in hell do you think your radio's for?"

22. Rescued by the Gnome

Fine, thank you sir; and how are you? "Yes sir," I said.

I braced myself but apparently he'd just thrown that out in passing. He grunted and moved on. Helms, standing beside me, smiled sadly and shook his head.

"He don't have any idea, does he," he said in his soft drawl, "what we were going through all that time."

I smiled back, ruefully. "I'm sure he does, Dennis. What the hell. If he ever said anything nice to me I wouldn't know how to act. Come on, let's go harass the troops."

Before I did so, though, I received a pleasant surprise. A couple of the battalion staff officers were busy setting up an impromptu briefing area, using discarded ammo or TNT crates, and I saw that one of them was Jerry Wolosenko.

"Jerry!" I said, "what the hell are you doing up here?"

Wolosenko looked up; his face split into one of his emphatic smiles. He dropped what he was doing and ran up to me. "Frank! Goddamn!" He placed a hand on each of my shoulders and squeezed. "Man, I'm glad to see you, buddy. You had us worried there, for a while."

I grinned back, feeling warm. The sincere friendship in Jerry's voice was a badly needed tonic. "Nothing to it, Jer," I said. "But what the hell are you doing up here? I thought you'd be back at Evans, or at least Blaze."

Jerry shook his head. "Nope. The Staff *will* accompany the Battalion CO."

"Let's get to work, over there. We've got a lot to do."

I looked up at the approach of another officer, one I hadn't seen before; he wore a major's insignia, and I assumed he was the new S3. Jerry returned to his work. "Got things to do, but I'll get with you later, Frank," he said, and turned away.

I received the distinct impression that new S3 was nothing like the easy-going Major Raffaelle. Still, I had things to do, so I left Jerry to his tasks and returned to my CP.

I didn't get a chance to do much, however, because we were called in to the Battalion CP, which had been set up on the saddle, just above the crater. The briefing was quick and to the point. There was a short report on the events that had occurred at the base of Hill 1485, a run down of some intelligence estimates, and an outline of what they would be doing tomorrow. I say "they" because I found out that I, with all of Bravo's people except for the injured, would trek back down the mountain to rejoin Robison and the rest of the Company. All things considered, I found that to be very welcome news.

"I want you to leave no later than 0700," Black Jack emphasized. "Take everybody with you who can move. Do you still have some wounded here?"

"Yes, sir. Three of them probably won't be able to make it; they've got leg injuries."

"All right, leave them here. I brought two men from Bravo with us; they'll guide you back down the mountain. I want you to link up with Robison by 1400 tomorrow."

I didn't say anything, and he was looking right at me so I didn't even raise an eyebrow, but I wanted to. Seven hours to cover a distance it had taken them almost two full days to traverse ... okay, granted: this would be downhill instead of up, and we'd hopefully not be facing sniper fire every step of the way, but even so...

"...there's a regiment or so out there somewhere," Black Jack was continuing. "I want good, tight security tonight. Keep your people alert. That's all, but I want Captain Harkins and Captain Sanders to stay behind. The rest of you are dismissed."

We were making our way out of the CP area, filing by Black Jack, who was in conversation with one of his staff, a new S2 whom I'd never met, when the colonel looked up and saw Atcheson, who was directly in front of me. I had to pause while Black Jack grabbed Gordie's arm and spoke to him.

"First thing tomorrow, I want you out of here; I was just going to get with your CO about that. Those gooks are out there somewhere; I want you to find 'em."

Atcheson nodded. "We'll get 'em."

"Right." Black Jack's ice blue gaze shifted to me. "You too, Boccia. On your way down the hill, keep your eyes open; the NVA's all over the place. You might run into 'em on your way down."

Dickson, right behind me, chuckled. "I sure hope not," he said.

In a split second the ice in the CO's stare turned to blue fire. "You hope not?" he exploded. "You goddamn well hope not, do you? Why you miserable gutless little sonuvabitch! You sniveling little bastard, you hope you don't find the enemy, do you? And just what is that you're supposed to be doing out here? Running from him? You're supposed to be a goddamn officer in the U.S. Army Infantry, goddamit! You're supposed to *want* to find the enemy, you miserable little bastard! How else are you going to beat him? Get the fuck out of my sight before I puke."

Dickson left, looking stunned. It had not been, I reflected, one of Dickson's better days. He had been chewed out by me, by Harkins, and now by Black Jack, all in the span of a few hours. Oh, well, there was no one I could think of who was more deserving.

About an hour later I received word to report to the Battalion CP. I went fully expecting to have my head handed to me on a platter. Black Jack, I was sure, was about to make up for lost time.

Instead, I found Captain Harkins, with Dan Bresnahan beside him, and Lieutenant Walden, a Platoon Leader from Delta, waiting. The sun would set in an hour; it would be dark soon. Around us, we could hear the sounds of the men digging in, improving old positions or digging new ones. I'd been supervising that effort when the summons came. None of us knew what was going on. Harkins knew only that Black Jack was conferring with Iron Raven and the Brigade S3 on the scramble-net radio, and that Captain Sanders was with him. We spent a few minutes speculating idly on what Gordie and the others would find the next morning when they moved out. We were all fairly sure that the regimental headquarters was close by.

In the hour or so that had passed between the time the Battalion had arrived, three or four slicks had made supply drops; included had been some tents, field tables and

22. Rescued by the Gnome

chairs, and other paraphernalia suitable for setting up a battalion CP; this in fact had been erected already. A figure emerged from the tent and walked towards us.

"Is everybody here?"

We all looked at the newcomer. I recognized him as the major who'd told Jerry to get back to work earlier. Beyond noticing that he was small, and had new bright yellow rosettes on his collar, I hadn't paid much attention to him. Now, in the fading daylight, I looked him over more carefully.

He *was* small. Of course, a lot of airborne officers are. At 5'7" I'm not exactly power forward material myself. Most short officers and NCOs tend, consciously or not, to compensate one way or another for their lack of height. They reminded me, in a subliminal way, of certain animals. Black Jack, with his puffed-out chest, strutting walk, quick movement of his head and the gleaming, beady expression in his eyes, was practically a description of a gamecock. Gordie Atcheson's resemblance to a bulldog wasn't confined to his face; he had wide shoulders and a thick short neck, and his head seemed to thrust forward, the way a bulldog's will. Lieutenant Walden, with a sharp, jutting face overhung by thick black eyebrows, and the trick of cocking his head to one side while eyeing you speculatively, reminded me so much of a cairn terrier I almost expected him to bark.

So the fact that this character was short was no great mark against him. The problem was that as I watched him approach the only word that kept flashing through my mind was gnome. He reminded me of nothing else but that. His face was small, with ordinary features, slightly concave, and already deeply seamed. His eyes were blue; not a bright, piercing, attention-grabbing cobalt, but a washed-out pale blue, like a summer sky seen through a haze. His body was stubby, and he stumped awkwardly up the slope, as if he were not used to moving in rough terrain. He gave us no greeting at all when he reached us, but nodded with his lips compressed tightly.

Looking Harkins in the eye, he announced, "I'm a better soldier than you."

Startled, Harkins looked down at him without speaking.

"Do you know why?"

Harkins, his eyes fractionally wider than usual, shook his head. "No. Why?"

The other smiled grimly, and leaned forward in what we would come to know as a characteristic gesture. "Because," he informed Harkins solemnly, "I'm *camouflaged*."

All of us, not just Harkins, involuntarily looked at his helmet. Stuck to the helmet cover were three or four bedraggled leaves, long since shriveled dry in the heat. There was a silence of some duration. Dan Bresnahan flicked a quick look in my direction but I looked down at the ground, shaking my head slightly. You're not supposed to laugh at your superior officers.

"I wanted the ground commanders of all three companies here. Is that what I've got?" His voice was a nasal tenor, with a curiously mixed quality; part querulous inquiry, part self-satisfied assertion.

Captain Harkins nodded. "That's what you've got. I'm Harkins, Alpha Company."

"Walden, Delta."

"Boccia, Bravo One."

He gave a quick shake of his head, an indeterminate gesture; one we were all to become familiar with. It was halfway between a nod and a negation, and could serve for both or neither. He seemed to tremble with suppressed energy; it showed in that nod, in the way he stood, in the quick, jerking motions of his hands. And yet, it gave nothing like the impression of competence and reserve that Black Jack's tension did. Black Jack reminded me of a battery, charged, powerful and ready to go or stop at will. This man reminded me of a boiling kettle, ready to explode.

"My name is Howard. Major Howard. I am the S3 for the battalion. I am responsible for the security of this firebase here and I am here to give you your instructions. I want your undivided attention."

Howard had a curious rocking motion, back and forth, but in slow motion. He began each sentence or speech back on his heels, but gradually his body would lean forward until his head was thrust out, almost like a battering ram.

We all involuntarily looked at each other. What firebase? We were standing on what was nothing but a semi-bare hilltop with not even the thought of a bunker.

"I don't care about what's happened here up to now. That's past. What's important is that you now have the Battalion CP here. Whatever you have done and however you have done it, from now on you will conduct yourselves in a thoroughly professional manner; remember that you will have the opportunity to be performing your jobs before the finest troops in the battalion. You will have to come up to their standards."

There was a moment of incredulous silence. I was looking at Howard, but out of the corner of my eye I could see Harkins, his sharp hard face impassive as usual, standing stock-still.

"We'll keep that in mind," Harkins said dryly.

I wish I could say it got better. It didn't. It got much worse. Howard, in the next half hour, mixed up our names, ranks, positions, unit designations and unit strength. He also mispronounced my name as no one had ever managed to do before. How does one get "Broker" out of Boccia? The highlight came when, attempting to indicate North, he poked Bresnahan in the eye following the wild swings of his compass needle.

But that was mere comedy. It turned serious: He dressed down Harkins, a senior and respected company commander, in front of three lieutenants, including one of his own. He grabbed troopers from both Alpha and Bravo and gave them orders with their respective commanders—Harkins and I—standing there. He assigned Alpha Company to a perimeter sector already occupied by Delta, and vice-versa. He insisted on relocating every foxhole or prepared position, often to within only a meter from the original; it was by now almost dark and that meant we'd not have a prayer of finishing the digging by nightfall. He—but why go on? By then, we were all—including Captain Sanders, who joined us late—openly incredulous: How had this man attained his rank? Rank, hell; how did he manage to feed himself?

I don't know how long the farce would have gone on, but as we reached Delta's sector, a headquarters trooper came up and told Howard he was wanted by Black Jack.

"I'll be back in a while," Howard said, jerking his head. "I'll expect to find the perimeter completed." He stumped off down the hill.

It took Sanders and Harkins about three seconds to decide that they would use the original perimeter line—the one whose foxholes were more than half done. The sergeant major joined us while they were settling this. Harkins turned to him, and asked where Major Howard had come from.

The sergeant major's face remained as impassive as Harkins', except for one corner of his mouth, which twitched imperceptibly. "Bien Hoa, Captain. I believe he was on the MACV staff there."

"I see," Harkins said quietly. "Has he ever had a field command, Sergeant Major?"

"Not that I know of. Not here, anyway."

"Uhm. Yes." Harkins said nothing else, but I spoke up.

"Interesting fellow, Major Howard. Glad to have him with us. By the way, Sergeant Major: you might see about getting him a new compass. The one he has doesn't seem to be working very well."

Harkins slowly turned his head and looked at me, deadpan. Under normal circumstances he'd have bitten my head off. He said nothing. The sergeant major was concentrating with fascinated interest on the tree line at the bottom of the hill.

A few minutes later, I was standing behind one of Dickson's positions, talking to him and watching as his men finished digging in. The sun had long since set and the trees around us had changed color, to the smoky gray of late twilight. The sky was almost the same shade; clouds had settled in during the afternoon, and now lay heavy and somber overhead. The night felt almost cool, or as cool as it can feel without rain. The forest sounds were reassuring; subdued but persistent. Dickson was trying to sell me the idea of putting a four-man LP out in front of his sector, but I wasn't buying. While we talked it over, Helms came up to me.

"Black Jack wants you and Lieutenant Dickson at the CP ASAP, sir."

"Right. Thanks." I glanced at Dickson. "Ready to go?"

"Yeah. Wait a minute: let me go get my stuff." He moved over to where his gear lay piled up and picked up his helmet and weapon. "Okay, let's go," he said.

We made our way across the hill and down the saddle. I thought about stopping off at my CP to pick up my gear, but decided against it. What the hell, I thought, it's only a few meters from the battalion CP to mine.

We found Black Jack, with a group of officers, standing by the tent. He glanced up from a map he was studying at our approach.

"Where the hell's your steel pot and weapon?" he growled.

Giving myself an enthusiastic, if mental, kick in the pants, I made a face and said, "Back at my CP, sir."

"Jesus. Okay, look now. I'm going to put three squad-sized LPs out tonight. One of 'em's going to be down the trail we came up this afternoon. That's your sector, right, Boccia?"

"Well, actually, it's in Dickson's sector, sir."

"Okay. Dickson, I want you to make damn su-"

POW! POW!

We all instinctively ducked our heads; someone was firing an AK-47 at us. We straightened up and faced east almost immediately, however. The shots had come from beyond the east hill, whose slope we were on. There was a brief instant of silence, and then Bresnahan's people — it was his sector that the shots had come from — opened up. Harkins and Bresnahan both sprang up the hill to get to the perimeter. As they raced away, Howard turned to me.

"You sure could use that helmet and weapon now, couldn't you, Broker?"

"Hell, sir; I didn't think I needed them anymore. Now that battalion HQ is here to protect me."

As soon as I opened my mouth, I realized that I had gone too far. I don't know why I say these things. The devil makes me do it. Howard swelled up, and was about to say something, but Black Jack said something to him, and he subsided and marched off. I wasn't sure whether Black Jack had heard me or not, but I don't suppose it made any difference. Black Jack was not one to get too upset by smart-ass comments. Everything else, yes.

A couple of minutes later, Harkins came back to report that a sniper had probed the perimeter with a couple of AK rounds.

"Stupid son of a bitch of a squad leader over there opened up with everything he had," Harkins said, in his clipped, angry baritone. "As many damn times as you tell those idiots not to fire blind and give their position away, they'll still start shootin' like crazies the moment they hear incoming."

Black Jack looked annoyed. "Did they see how many there were?"

"They didn't see jack-shit. They were just blazin' away."

The colonel grunted. "You got somebody there now who can control 'em?"

Harkins nodded. "Bresnahan's back with 'em. He'll keep 'em quiet."

"Jesus Christ," Black Jack muttered. He turned away, started to walk off, and saw me. "Don't forget about that LP out there. It'll be an Alpha Company unit in front of you; make sure your people know about it. I want you to be sure that the Alpha Company squad leader coordinates with the squad leader he'll be moving through. No damn slip-ups. Understood?" He looked at me, and then Dickson.

We nodded.

"Okay. You know the password for tonight. Make sure your people know it. Boccia, I want to see you tomorrow morning before you leave."

"Yes, sir."

He grunted again and moved on.

It was totally dark by the time I got back to my perimeter. The LP Black Jack had mentioned assembled behind our positions a few minutes later; eight men, with a machine gun and, of course, a radio. The squad leader was a thin, hatchet-faced E-5. Dickson and I took him from position to position along that side of the perimeter, warning each man that there would be a squad somewhere in front of them. The sergeant told me that his orders were to follow the trail down for about 50 meters, and set up alongside, in darkness. He had come up that trail earlier that day, with Atcheson, but he admitted he didn't remember exactly how the trail lay; he couldn't say for sure that he would end up in front of one position rather than another, once they reached their assigned spot.

So we made double sure everyone knew about it; a few minutes later, the squad, barely visible as charcoal gray shadows in the moonless darkness, slipped through the lines and made their way down the trail. I stood and listened for a minute or so, following their progress by the sounds of footfalls and creaking branches and swishing leaves. They were making far too much noise: they didn't move out of earshot until they were halfway to their destination.

The night passed uneventfully. The NVA apparently had decided that our force was now too large to tangle with. The worst thing that happened to me all night was that I fell asleep with the radio mike in my hand, and my arm twisted underneath Helms's pack. When I woke up, an hour or so later, my arm was numb, except for a million tiny needles someone was sticking into my wrist and hand. Even with that, I managed to get almost five hours sleep that night, which was a Godsend. I was tired.

23

Black Jack's Seminar

YD 365065; 29 April 1969

The next morning, at dawn, we got up and immediately began preparations for moving down the mountain. Brown and DyLong would remain behind; they would be flown out later. The rest of the troops began packing their gear and cleaning their weapons.

I found Jerry Wolosenko just outside the battalion CP tent, shaving. One half of his face was covered by a thin film of soap lather, while the other displayed two thin cuts, gleaming red and fresh on his chin.

"The Mad Russian Monk strikes again," I said. "Why not use a machete, or a hatchet? It'll be neater."

Jerry eyed me as he carefully drew the razor along his neck. "You could use one yourself. A machete, I mean. You're not shaving today?"

"I'm not Staff. Staff has to shave every day. Grunts don't have to meet the same high standards you guys do. Don't let me interrupt what you're doing, now; I know it's important. Tell me, when do I get to watch you polish your boots?"

"Immediately after you kiss my ass. I see you've been talking to Howard."

"Not really. Listening to him, maybe."

"Major Howard is here, and the war is practically over. You and I won't be needed anymore. Hey—hand me my towel, will you?"

I threw the towel over his head. "You're welcome, oh Mighty Assistant S3. That is your job now, isn't it? Assistant S3? A sort of Howard junior?"

Jerry finished wiping his face. There were now four fresh cuts on it, all bleeding. "Fuck you," he said elegantly.

"What's in store for me when I get down to Robison and friends? Anything interesting?"

"Nmmhmnn." Jerry was now brushing his teeth. He gave them a quick scuff and a rinse from his canteen, and spat onto the ground. "Don't know. I'm just the errand boy around here. Colonel Mot probably would know more about what we're doing than I do." He wiped his mouth with the towel, which he then began folding carefully. "So you're headed down the mountain this morning?"

"Yeah, in a while; soon as I talk to Black Jack. I don't suppose you know what he wants to see me about, do you?"

Jerry shook his head. "Nope. Except that he probably won't be pinning any medals on you. I think he's got a case of the ass."

"What for this time?"

"I don't know for sure; I just know he was pitching three fits the other day, when you got shot down. I can't figure why and neither can anybody else; Sergeant Major said you did a helluva job, and I think everybody else who heard what was going on thought so too."

I shook my head. "Jesus. That bastard never lets up."

"Don't let it get you down, man. Look, he's like this with everybody, so don't worry about it. You did a good job. You know it; the battalion knows it. Screw him."

I shrugged and gave a wry grin. "But I bet you Staff guys could have handled it standing on your heads."

"And we frequently do. Damn right. We are the cream of the crop." Jerry plopped his steel pot over his eyes. "And now I must leave you; I've got important business at the S3 shop."

"Yeah. Time I went into the lion's den anyway. Look, we'll be moving out right away, so in case I don't see you..." I put my hand on his shoulder as he walked by and gave it a quick squeeze. "Take care, Jer."

"Take care yourself, asshole."

I watched him stump off, his new fatigues and helmet cover an unaccustomed shiny green. I heard a noise behind me and turned to find Black Jack, his face streaked with shaving cream, standing by the opening to his tent.

"Good morning, sir." I saluted

"Come on inside," he nodded.

I followed him into the CP tent. He seated himself at a field chair, behind a desk with a PRC 10 propped up on it. Maps, on collapsible boards, were ranged on one side of the tent, while on the side opposite them a long field table held four radios. A narrow folding cot, with a rubber air mattress, stood immediately behind the chair he sat in. Shaving utensils littered the top of the desk, while steam curled slowly up from a white ceramic mug, with the black-gold-red Screaming Eagle logo on it.

He indicated another canvas chair, to the left of the desk. While I sat, he took a slow sip from the mug, replaced it on the desk, and eyed me quietly. His frosty blue eyes were neither aggressive nor hostile; they were uncharacteristically speculative.

"Boccia, I wonder if you could explain to me just what the hell you were doing the other day?"

The tone was milder than the words; I felt a moment's surprise, while at the same moment thinking, here it was at last: the royal reaming I'd been expecting since he'd arrived on the hill.

"Sir, I know you were disturbed by the fact that I wasn't on the radio as much as

I should have been. But." I took a deep breath. "But, there was a whole lot going on that you — weren't aware of at the time, sir."

"I know. That's why I'm asking you to tell me what was happening."

"Yes, sir. Things were happening fast, and I didn't have a lot of men there, and certain things had to get done in a hurry, and that took me away from the radio."

"What kind of things?" The colonel's voice was still mild.

"Well, for one, I had to deal with the wounded, and find out about the chopper. There was a wounded guy ... the engine kept on running and I had turn that off ... Logan's gun quit; I had to check on all that ... all this happened in the space of a couple minutes."

"Yeah. I know. Things happen fast in combat. They don't call time outs. And you're right; those things had to get done. But not by you. The number one job you had was to stay in touch with me. That was your only job. Staying on that radio and talking to me was the only chance you had of making certain you and everybody else down there stayed alive. You got damn lucky, this time. They didn't try to overrun you. But let me ask you this: while you were up there fucking around with the engine, and you were 50 meters or so from your radio, what would have happened if they'd hit you then? What the hell could you have done about it?"

I opened my mouth to say something, then closed it quickly. In point of fact, there wouldn't have been a damn thing in the world I could have done.

Black Jack drained his cup, set the mug on the desk, and resumed staring at me. "Why didn't you secure the east hill, after Dickson and his people landed?"

I tightened my lips; I could feel the blood rushing to my neck and jaws. "Sir, I did secure that hill. But when it got dark, I didn't have enough men to cover both hills, without splitting the force. I didn't have any leadership on the ground I was familiar with and could trust. We had a large number of wounded and injured and it would have been difficult to move them. I needed to stay on the west hill because it was half-cleared, while the east hill was covered with trees, and I knew I would be needing an LZ." Unbidden, my voice had risen and my jaws tightened. "I don't think anybody could have covered this LZ with the number of troops I had, sir."

Black Jack's fist crashed down on the desk. "You are so goddamn right!" He spat out. "Nobody could have covered that LZ. And so four goddamn lift ships get blown out of the sky because you weren't on the radio telling me what was going on! I don't need a goddamn lieutenant to tell me that this LZ couldn't be secured; not by you, not by me, not by anyone else. And that is exactly my point, you stupid son of a bitch: You couldn't cover it. So you should have been on that radio, talking to me, every single goddamn minute you were on the ground. I could have covered it for you. I had more fucking firepower at my fingertips than Napoleon had in his whole goddamn army, and instead of sticking to that radio and using that firepower, you were running all over the mountainside playing hide-and-seek with me."

He lowered his voice, although his eyes still blazed that strangely fiery icicle-blue.

"Right after you hit the ground, you called in the ARA, then you were off the radio for a few minutes. Where the hell were you?"

I blinked, thinking back. "I guess that's when I went over to the door gunner and pulled him into the crater. Then ... I suppose I went over to where the other two crewmembers were, and checked them out. Then I came back to the radio."

"Yeah. Tell me something. Was the door gunner lying out in the open? Was he getting shot at?"

I hesitated, puzzled by the question. "Yes, sir. I wouldn't have gone to get him if he weren't."

"And the two crewmen, they were getting shot at too?"

I shrugged. "I don't know. I guess so. At that point, yes sir, they were."

"Beautiful. You dumb son of a bitch. What would have happened if you took a bullet right then? What would have happened to your people?"

"I...."

He shook his head. "And this business of turning off the engine; why didn't you get one of the crew to do it?"

"Because ... well—" I made a motion with my right hand—"because they ... they were all wounded. Sir."

"You were the fucking *ground commander*, do you understand that?"

"Yes, sir," I said reluctantly, "but ... damn, I didn't have time to get someone else to do that."

He snorted in disgust. "Christ. You didn't have time. Listen, Boccia: Your responsibility was to everyone on the ground, and everyone in the air who was going to be using that goddamn LZ you were supposed to be securing. Not just to one door gunner. Not just to a downed pilot. To *everyone*. So what if that major was wounded? Prop the son of a bitch up against the slick and leave him. You've got things to do. If he gets killed, it's no loss. He's just a chopper pilot with no chopper to fly. *You* are the ground commander."

By now my face was furnace red; I could feel my anger building. What the hell did this maniac want from me? "Yes, sir." The pressure inside me forced the next words out. "I think I did the best I could, sir. Damnit it, five of the ten men on that bird went down within a few seconds. One of my guys was blown to shit, for chrissakes."

His small blue eyes spat fire and ice. "What the fuck's that got to do with anything? You think you're someone special, you're not supposed to lose anybody? Listen, you little son of a bitch, I'm going to tell you the truth, and I hope you listen to it.." He paused to glare at me for another few seconds.

"You make me sick, Boccia. You and all those other fucking assholes like you. You little son of a bitch. Why'd you get a commission? I'll tell you why. It was because you were too smart and too educated and too fucking privileged to be anything else. That's all. That's the only fucking reason you got a commission.

"That's all you saw, wasn't it? The gold bar, the fucking dress blues, all that shit.

And fuckers like you eat it up. Until the time comes when you find out that some pretty bad things can happen because of what you say or do, and then, all of a sudden, it's not fun anymore.

"Well, that's what it's about, Lieutenant. I don't give a shit if you like it. Now you see what it all means—it means sitting back behind a bunker and telling some 18-year-old with his whole life ahead of him to go and get his fucking brains blown to hell."

"Well, that's the price you pay for your commission, Boccia. It's your job. If we don't need someone to do that, we don't need officers. And especially not big-headed sons of bitches like you, who think they're smarter than God."

He stared at me, until I finally had to respond. "Yes, sir."

"From now on, you stick that fucking radio in your ear and leave it there. You understand?"

"Yes, sir."

His own jaw was twitching with anger. He held the stare for a long time, until finally he looked away. When he spoke next, his voice was softer.

"That major and that dead pilot were both good friends of mine. And that man of yours that got killed, he was as much my man as he was yours. So were all the other men killed up here. Do you understand what I'm telling you?"

I nodded, slightly. "Yes, sir."

He stood up and turned away from me. "Get the hell out of here."

"Yes, sir." My neck was furnace red, and my lips slashed a thin, ugly scar across my face. I stood and turned to go.

He waited until I reached the opening of the tent. "One more thing."

"Yes, sir."

Black Jack walked around the desk to the maps lining the wall and began inspecting them carefully.

"Those pilots recommended you for the Silver Star. I just got the paperwork on it this morning. I endorsed the recommendation."

I stared; I had nothing to say. He continued to scrutinize the maps, without looking at me, and after a moment, I turned again and walked out.

We left the hilltop soon after my meeting with Black Jack. I had Hyde's squad on point. I realized, with a wry grin, that I was doing to Hyde what Robison had done to me—there was nothing I could do about it, though; Hyde was the only squad leader I really trusted. Two men from Denney's platoon, Martini and Brinson, had accompanied the Battalion staff on their way up the mountain, and were returning with us, to serve as guides. Of course, in light of what they had found on their way up, guides were superfluous, but they'd no way of knowing that before leaving.

The first couple of hundred meters were routine enough, although we were, understandably, tense, but after a few minutes we came to a large, well-kept trail. Leaving the perimeter we'd followed a narrow rut that was nothing more than the result of a hundred or so men having passed through the underbrush the previous day. This, however, was obviously an old, well-established thoroughfare; it rivaled the "Los Angeles Freeway" that Jerry Wolosenko had found back on Hill 154 — seemingly years in the past, although it had been, in fact, less than two months. Paradoxically, we slowed down a bit upon reaching the larger path. We used trails often, of course — we'd never get anywhere if we didn't — but common prudence dictated that we not hurry down a large, well-traveled trail in the heart of enemy territory, and particularly not one that had been used the day before by our own troops.

After another 100 or 200 meters, the slope steepened abruptly. Someone — probably the NVA, although it may even have been the old Viet Minh — had cut large, even steps into the hill, and buttressed them with big logs. At first the steps were only a welcome curiosity; they made travel easier, and it was the first time we'd seen anything like them. But as kilometer followed kilometer, and the steps ran on and on, down the slope, one after another, untold thousands of them, a feeling of awe and disquietude began to grow in me.

I contemplated the enormous effort that had gone into their construction; a stairwell over two kilometers long, cut into the side of a mountain remote from the nearest town or habitation. It was a warning, a voice that first whispered and then gradually began to shout: this was the very heart of the enemy's territory. This belonged to him; it was his, and we trespassed. That he would be willing to expend the time and labor to place that mighty staircase there was indication enough that he would not soon leave.

I could feel the hair along the back of my neck stir and stand straight out at times, as we turned another bend in the trail, thinking that perhaps here they would end, only to see them stretching out again before us, down, down that seemingly endless slope.

After six hours, Brinson indicated that we were nearing the point where they'd left the Company on the previous day. We came to a small, level glade. The floor was bare and sandy. Tall trees towered over us like gray columns. The branches on those trees sprang out from the smooth-boled trunks 30 or more feet overhead; they met over the clearing to form a roof, dense, green-gray, and indistinct, as might a cathedral roof seem, above a veiling mist of incense. Daylight was dimmed and shadowy; the leaves were motionless and silent in the mid-day heat. The dense tangle of liana, bamboo, reeds and young saplings outside the circle of huge trees formed a vaguely-seen wall. The clearing extended only a short way along the trail; it was about 20 or so feet wide and perhaps 50 long. Martini, who'd been walking with Kenzy on point, stopped and waited for me to reach him. We all stopped momentarily. The place was hushed and expectant.

Martini pointed to a lone, dead branch, extending out from one of the trees; it hung overhead like a bare gray skeletal arm. I saw what looked to be part of the sleeve of a fatigue shirt dangling from the end. A foot or so away, on the same limb, a shredded green rag fluttered quietly in the weak breeze. All around us, I noticed now, a number of pinkish-red icicles hung from the lower branches, pointing like misshapen index fingers. For a moment, I thought them to be shards of flesh, so mortal did their color seem. But the smell told me that they were elongated blobs of sap and sawdust; wood pulped and melted and then scattered by the heat and force of an explosion.

"See that, Lieutenant?" Martini broke the silence.

I nodded. "Yeah."

"Engineers from the 2/17th were dropped in to cut an LZ a bit further down the hill. Slick got shot down; everybody was waxed 'cept one guy. He made tracks up the slope, running like a spooked deer, we figure. This is as far as he got." Martini gestured toward a spot a few feet away. "Gook musta been standin' there, listenin' to 'im run up them steps. Just waitin' for 'im. Soon's the poor bastard got into the clearing here, he hit 'im with an RPG. Musta got 'im right in the chest; all we found yesterday was a foot and part of the other leg." Martini shook his head. "Son of a bitch ran a long way just to get his ass blown away."

I tore my eyes from the rags. "Find many booby traps on the trail?"

"Beaucoup. But the gooks are markin' 'em. Makes it pretty easy. Usually take a branch on a bush 'bout five meters in front and behind the trap and bend it back. Once you know what to look for, they're easy to spot."

"Good. Why don't you get back up with my point man, then, and give him a hand. Show him what to look for."

"Right." Martini nodded, not quite as enthusiastic as he'd been a moment earlier.

I watched him walk off. I wanted to move on; I had no wish to stay long in this grim, leafless bower. This place, with its chambered gray gloom, was unsettling, almost terrifying, but I couldn't, for a moment, understand why. It wasn't until we'd begun to move on again, and were descending another of the series of endless stairs, that I realized why this particular place affected me so. It was, I thought, looking down the slope, a scene out a primal nightmare; something that lurked in the mind's deep shadows, from childhood on. The endless, gloom-shrouded staircase, leading like a dark tunnel on and on; the horror behind you, the wheezing, straining lungs, the hard muscles turned flabby and weak from unending effort, wide eyes frantically searching and staring, the feeling that no matter how fast and how far you run, that something behind you is reaching for you, gaining on you, playing pitilessly with you. Something unknown and slavering and evil and, above all, single-mindedly fixed on you. I wondered how the end had come; had he seen, in that last instant of life, the final terror? Had he glimpsed the enemy with the launcher in that micro-second? Or had he simply run on until his nightmare had been ended in that awakening blackness?

I found myself sweating. The picture was so real, so sharp; I felt I could give the dead man a name and a face. Yet, I knew nothing about him; not his name, or his height, or even the color of his skin — nothing. Nothing except that he and I shared — we all did — a common destiny; we would all make that final journey up a dark staircase, either desperately or quietly, either willingly, or not.

Helms, who, as always, was close by my side as we started to move, glanced up at the dead tree limb, and then down the trail. "That poor guy," I heard him say, softly, with pity. Helms understood, too.

It was still early afternoon when Gann, the point man, stopped, held his rifle over his head and waved. We were on a broad, low ridge; the heavy forest ended abruptly there where he stood. Moving up beside him, I saw that the ridge ended in a narrow, shallow valley, and on its other side, almost due west, was a broad hill. Behind that hill, clearly visible now, were the flat plains of the A Shau itself. On that hill, also clearly visible, were a couple of GIs, returning Gann's wave. Even at this distance, I recognized Grump Ulrich and Bresina. We were home.

The move across the open valley and up the hill took only minutes. Robison was waiting for me when I reached the top — of course, we'd been in radio contact the whole morning. He nodded as I walked up to him, reached out with his hand and shook mine. I almost toppled over from surprise. Robison, except in private moments, never let on that he cared for or even approved of his platoon leaders.

"Glad you made it, Bo. Good work." Good Lord; he even sounded sincere.

"Thanks, Captain. I'm glad to be back home."

"Yeah, I'll bet. Hey, we need to get together — say, 1500: At my CP. We got work to do."

I nodded and looked around; First Platoon's sector was off to my right, facing back up the mountain we'd just descended. Helms and I picked our way through the heavy tufts of grass and reeds to the thin tree line where they'd placed the foxholes. Cries of "Hiya, Lieutenant!" and "Dennis! Hey man, how ya doin'?" greeted us as we walked up.

Sergeant Wright turned and saw me; a small smile flitted across his face. Walking up to me, he suddenly stood at attention and saluted, catching me completely off guard; I had my M16 in my right hand and my rucksack in my left and had to just drop the weapon to return the salute. *A handshake and a salute: Absence does make the heart grow fonder.* But in reality I was flushed with pride. There was little doubt in my mind what that salute represented: I had finally earned Sam Wright's complete trust.

"Good to have you back, Lieutenant," he said.

"Top, you've got no idea how good it is to be back."

We had little time to talk, however, since I had to join Robison in a few minutes. I dropped my pack at the CP, exchanged greetings with several of the platoon as they walked by or made a point of coming up to us, and then walked back toward the center of the hill and Robison's CP. I paused as I passed one group, of about seven or eight men: Logan stood there, along with Eden; seated on the ground, talking animatedly, was Phil Nelson.

"...So me 'n Cliff low-crawl along the side of this bunker, see, and there's another bunker just ahead, spittin' machine gun fire, and we set up and I put a round right through that damn bunker, blew them all to fuckin' hell. Man, you shoulda seen it. Then, me 'n Cliff get up an' run over to this little rise, an' there's another spider hole, so Cliff takes his fuckin' grenade and throws it right in the fuckin' hole, just beautiful, and...."

Nelson talked on, and Logan turned and saw me. Raising his eyes up to the trees above, he nodded in Nelson's direction and winked.

I grinned. Logan had regaled us the previous evening with imitations of the rest of our platoon and what they'd be saying when we joined them. He'd gotten Nelson spot-on.

The greeting I got from Eward and Denholm was subdued but plainly showed they were glad to see me back. There was some kidding back and forth about exactly who had missed what, but we were all just glad to see each other. Robison was on the radio, but he finished talking and came over and joined us. As he did, I glanced around and noticed that Dickson wasn't there. I shook my head. Couldn't he ever be on time?

Robison had a small grin on his face, so unusual that I had an impulse to whip out my notebook and mark the calendar. He stood there looking at us silently for a moment.

"The three Mousketeers," he finally said.

"Does that make you Mickey Mouse?" Denholm shot back immediately.

Robison laughed, and now I *did* pull out my notebook.

There was something strangely upbeat about the CO, but whatever it was would remain unknown for a while, because he sat down with us, took off his jungle hat, and ran a hand over his short, sweat slicked blond hair. "So," he said finally, looking at me, "that was a hairy time up on the hill. What happened?"

As he said that, Dickson finally wandered up. Without greetings, given or received, he sat quietly to one side, looking both downcast and preoccupied. None of the others even looked his way.

I recounted the events that had taken place on Hill 1485, and tried to explain as well as I could the impossibility of securing the LZ. When I finished, Robison shook his head.

"I don't understand that bastard," he said, referring to Black Jack. "All that time you were on that LZ, that first hour or two, we were sitting around here listening to you over the radio, and we were all saying, damn, what a helluva job you're doing, and than Black Jack comes by a little later, tellin' us to move out to the north, like I said, and I mention to him how proud I was of the job you were doing, and he blows sky high. 'That little son of a bitch! I'll court-martial him! He's getting everybody killed up there!'" Robison shrugged. "I don't know what the bastard wants."

"He's a goddamn maniac," Denney said. "He's a goddamn glory-hound who doesn't know shit about what's really going on on the ground. Who cares what he says? Fuck 'im."

"One thing about him, though," Eward said thoughtfully, "he always goes in a straight line. Point A to point B. He's in a beaucoup hurry to get where he's going, and he'll bring you along with him, whether you want to go or not. He's a bastard all right, but he's a straight bastard."

"He can be Bruce King of the Fairies for all I care," Robison shrugged. "Fuck 'im. He'll be gone in another month, anyway. Then we'll have to worry about the next asshole." He suddenly smiled. "Or no we won't. You'll have to worry about him. I won't have to."

We all looked up in surprise. "What's this?" Denholm asked.

Robison grinned widely now. "The time has come, my man. I got the word yesterday evening. I've had this goddamn Company since October, and they finally figured that's punishment enough for one man. By next week, I'll be in Bien Hoa, soakin' in a sauna and drinkin' cold, cold beer. I'll be tellin' myself I ought to feel sorry for you assholes, but I won't."

That explains the good mood, I thought.

"Well, spit on mah doormat," Eward drawled. "First damn time you get shot at and you go running to Saigon to join the REMFs. Helluva thing."

"Shit. You're as ready to face life without me as you'll ever be. Hell, we all gotta grow up sometime. It's about damn time you get a chance to stand in front of Black Jack and have to tell him you can't carry out your mission because your platoon leaders can't chew gum and walk."

"Well, son of a bitch," I said, "I'll be sorry to see you go." I realized with some surprise that I meant it. Even with all the yelling and screaming that went on between us, we'd had a close relationship over the last two or three months, and now the Company was now a good, efficient team. I *was* sorry to see him go.

"You won't have anybody to get pissed at," he agreed, as if he'd read my thoughts. "You try some of that shit with the next CO and you're liable to end up in Leavenworth."

Denney asked the next logical question. "Who's gonna be the next CO?"

Robison smiled broadly. "Don't know and don't care. I hope he's a real son of a bitch. I'll enjoy that. Some meat-eatin', ass-kickin', head-stompin' son of a bitch of a senior captain who hates lieutenants, and especially wop lieutenants with a big mouth. Yep, I'd love that."

There was more of the same for a few minutes, but nothing of substance. He'd really called us together only to announce his departure. We eventually exhausted our store of Short-Timer comments and the meeting broke up. In all that time, I realized as I walked away, Dickson had not said a single word. A couple of times, during my account of the action up on the LZ, I'd looked his way when I mentioned something he and I had done together, but not even then did he say a word or even look up. I shrugged. The care and feeding of Lieutenant Dickson wasn't high up on my to-do list.

When I returned to the platoon CP, I found Sergeant Wright making the rounds of our positions, checking the men, making sure they'd cleaned their weapons, and looking over the fields of fire. Muldoon was setting up a poncho hutch in the middle of the CP — shades of Hill 114, I thought. Just like old times. Helms had already set up with Sergeant Wright — we were missing two members of our CP group; St. Onge, of course, and Brown, who'd been left behind, along with DyLong, on Hill 1485, to be evacuated by helicopter.

"Just like home, Duke," I said, making rare use of Muldoon's nickname.

"Yeah." Muldoon, in his own way, was glad to see me, I knew, but, once past the initial bust of approval and relief, he'd reverted to his eastern-urban, ethnic-tough, chip-on-the-shoulder, hard-mouthed abrasive sardonicism that he carried around with him as an Englishman carries an umbrella. He finished making a minor adjustment to it, then stood back and eyed it critically.

"Looks okay," I ventured.

He shrugged. "It'll keep the rain off. You know, damn television news is wrecking people's minds."

I didn't say anything. I was used to Muldoon's seeming non-sequiturs by now.

"Take my old lady, now," he continued. "She was writin' to me a couple weeks back. Now, I been tellin' her for months what the hell we're doin' out here — bout you an' me sharin' a hutch, and movin' every goddamn day, and all that shit. But you know what she thinks, now? I mean, all she's got to go on, 'cept my letters, is what she sees on TV, right? She thinks we stay in some kind of barracks or rooms, back in the rear, and that we get bussed out to the field every day and then, when we're finished, get brought back, and spend the nights in those goddamned barracks. Now can you top that?"

"It'd be a nice way to fight a war," I agreed.

"I keep tellin' her that ain't right, but what the hell. You know what broads are like. Ain't no tellin' them nothin' they don't wanna listen to."

"She probably thinks that would be safer. Hell, mothers are always going to think that way."

Muldoon shook his head, at the impracticality of mothers. "'Mom,' I says, 'that ain't the way things are done around here,' but she still don't pay no attention. You reckon everybody's as screwed up as that, Lieutenant?"

"I don't think that many people have any idea at all of what's happening, I'll say that. After all, most of the reporters and damn near all the cameras are in the rear, where the barracks are, so that's what she sees. You won't find any of them out here with us."

"Yeah. Wouldn't want those fuckers out here, anyway. What good's a goddamn camera gonna do? Gooks come out of the trees like monkeys, and some stupid sonuvabitch's holdin' his camera, yellin' 'Hold still, now, so I can get this picture!'" Muldoon snorted. "Shit on it. This war's got less'n seven months to go as far as I'm concerned."

"Amen."

Muldoon worked quietly on his gear, for a moment, while I sat and began taking my M16 apart. After a while, without looking up, he muttered, "You know, I didn't care a lot for Evans, 'cause he was always pretty stuck on himself, but he was okay when it come to runnin' a squad. He was right out front, where he was supposed to be. But that goddamn Ranger — you know, the new guy — he's somethin' else."

I glanced up from my rifle. "What new guy?" I couldn't think of anyone in the company, except for Robison, who was Ranger qualified.

Muldoon waved a hand, his raspy tenor certainly an uncharacteristic hard edge. "That new E-5 — Novak. Yeah, that's his name. Third Squad. He's Ranger. Least, he's got a ranger patch on his pocket."

"Novak?" I barely knew him, since he'd joined the company only a couple of weeks ago. I hadn't known, or noticed, that he was Ranger qualified. "What about him?"

Muldoon's voice was thick with disgust. "Yellow. Yellow as a chinaman's ass. The sonuvabitch has been goin' around with that damn patch on his shirt, actin' like Sergeant York and Christ knows who else, and makin' damn sure we knew how tough he was, and how we was all cherries and he's seen it all. Then we run into the shit, and he runs like a rabbit." Muldoon snorted explosively. "Yellow sonuvabitch."

I placed my half-cleaned rifle down, carefully. "Just what do you mean, Muldoon? What the hell did he do?"

Muldoon finished rolling up a length of bandage and carefully stored it away in his kit bag before answering. "You heard about when we run into them bunkers, right?" He said at last.

"Yeah," I nodded.

"Okay. Captain Rob sends us up to take 'em out. Sent that damn bazooka along with us."

"The 90mm, you mean." I said, automatically.

Muldoon waved a hand. "I'm just a medic, and I don't know about all that shit, so okay. Looks like a goddamned bazooka to me. Anyway, that first afternoon — no; it was the second. The day after youse got shot down — we hadda cross this ridge and down into a ravine. Gooks had these two bunkers set up, and we couldn't get through. Whole Company was stopped. Second Platoon went on around the side of the hill, hopin' to come at 'em from the rear — I guess that's what they wanted to do — but there was some more bunkers on the other side, with the 69 or whatever."

"Ninety," I smiled.

"Whatever. Wright sends Evans and his squad off, and they get pinned down, too. Then he tells this goddamn Ranger Rick to move up and support 'em. I'm sittin' right behind Wright when he tells him, so I know what I heard. So, a coupla seconds later, Top's on the horn, talkin' with Captain Rob, and he don't see what's happenin'."

"When he gets off the horn, there's Third Squad still layin' there right in front of 'im. They ain't gone nowhere. He yells a bit, and Snyder and 'Ski get up and move up, but they get pinned down again. Now Wright gets back on the radio, and he can't see what happens next, but I sure as shit did. The whole damn squad had picked up and moved after Snyder, but, when he got down, they did too. They was just layin' there again. Couldn't go nowhere. I'm lookin' around, thinkin' there might be some way I could maybe throw a grenade or somethin' and get 'em out of there, and, son of a bitch—" he spaced the words out—"there's Ranger Rick hidin' behind this fuckin' tree. I mean, he was hidin'. He wasn't even lookin' out to see what was happenin' to his own people.

"Well, I start to give him a ration of shit, cause his guys are out there gettin' shot at an' he's layin' behind this damn tree, looking scared as cherry in a whorehouse. I told him I was gonna rip that fuckin' ranger patch off his shirt and cram it up his ass if he didn't move his ass to where it was suppos' to be. Just then, though, Wright calls me an' tells me Evans was hit, an' I had to run on up there and take a look at 'im. But when I moved by Wright, I told him that miserable sonuvabitch was peein' himself yellow behind that tree. By the time I got back, it was all over. Those two guys with the bazooka—ninety, or whatever—they'd cleaned out those goddamn bunkers, and everything was back to normal. I don't know what happened between Ranger Rick and Wright, but I know for sure every man in his squad knows he was hidin'."

Muldoon took out a cigarette and lit it, his face expressive with disgust. Muldoon was neither a born soldier nor gung-ho; he was possibly the least military man I knew, if by military one supposes an adherence to and respect for orders and authority. I imagine, too, that one could spend a fairly longish afternoon listing his faults; but high up on his list of virtues was loyalty. Muldoon did not give one sweet damn about heroism or cowardice, as such. Leadership to him was a foreign concept, for in Muldoon's world, each individual was expected to go his own way, at his own bidding. Muldoon had no use for abstract concepts. Had Novak refused to move out at all, and kept his squad behind a ridge somewhere safe from harm, Muldoon wouldn't have turned a hair. Why should he? But for Novak to order his people out into danger, and then sit back behind a tree—no. Muldoon could never stomach that. I've said that Muldoon was not a born soldier, but of course that's wrong. He would not trouble himself to walk across the street for the sake of an idea, or any abstraction up to and including Country, Honor, God, or Motherhood; but he would throw himself into the pits of hell for his friends. Muldoon, much as it might distress him to realize it, was a soldier.

His disgust and anger were real enough, and I thought well enough of him to believe that he would not knowingly exaggerate something of this sort, but I had to find out more about what had actually taken place. If I took Muldoon's account to be accurate, then I'd lost two squad leaders at almost the same moment. There was no way that Novak could continue as squad leader if what I'd just heard was true. Telling Muldoon I'd be back shortly, I went off in search of Wright, who, Helms informed me, had just left for the perimeter. I found him, coincidentally, in the Third Squad's sector.

I gave a swift, involuntary glance at Novak, who sat on a large flat boulder, several meters away. He was writing a letter, and hadn't looked up. Taking Wright by the arm,

I moved him even further away; we stood beside two densely leaved saplings, away from the squad members. I asked him bluntly what had happened.

He shrugged his big shoulders. "I can't say for sure. All I can tell you is, he wasn't where he was supposed to be. I don't know where he was. Muldoon told me later that he was behind a tree somewhere, but I sure didn't see it. On the other hand, he wasn't where I needed him to be."

I drew my lips back in a grimace. "What about since then. How's he been?"

"Lieutenant, I'm not gonna say he was yellow. I don't know. I will say, he's never been where I can see him, and I spent a lotta time up front. To tell you the truth, what with Evans bein' hit, and Hyde up there with you, I ain't had time to worry about one man. I don't know what he's been doin', but I do know he wasn't much use to me."

"Has anybody come up and said anything about it? Or have you overheard any talk?"

He shrugged again. "A couple of 'em did say something. Snyder. Jorgenson. Nelson, too."

I let out a breath. "Terrific. Okay; answer this. You know the problem we've got, now. In your opinion, can we keep him on as a squad leader?"

Wright made a face. "Lieutenant, that's gonna be your decision. It ain't up to me."

I shook my head impatiently. "Look, you were down here and I wasn't. You've been close to what's been happening and I haven't been. So I'm asking you: what do you think?"

"Lieutenant, I ain't gonna say what I think, 'cause it ain't my job to think. It's my job to do what my officer tells me."

"Right. And your officer is telling you to give him your opinion."

Wright shook his head. "Sir, you're going to have to make that decision. It's not up to me. I gave you the facts, that's all I can do."

I grinned. Wright was one of the finest NCOs in the Army, but he could spot a mule team 50 pounds apiece and never budge. I've been accused, in later years, of being fairly stubborn, and maybe I am, but I assure you I'm not even in the same league as Sam Wright. I finally laughed. "Okay, Top: I don't know why I bother. I should know better by now. Why don't you go ahead with what you were doing and your officer will inform you of his decision later?"

Wright nodded in dignified fashion and left, without a trace of satisfaction on his broad unruffled face. Does a mountain smile after withstanding a summer breeze? I watched him move off and wished once again I'd had him with me on top of Hill 1485. Life, I reflected, would have been much easier.

I don't know what I would have done, or rather, how I would have gone about making the decision, but it was taken out of my hands less than an hour later. Before I'd had a chance to talk to anyone else, Murtiff came by and informed me that Sgt Novak was to be sent back to Evans the following morning.

I was surprised. Almost shocked, actually. "Why?" I finally asked him. "He just got here."

Murtiff shook his round, bristly head. "Division G1 fucked up. Or maybe MACV. Anyway, Novak shouldn't have been transferred to us. His DEROS is next week. Five days, I think."

I blinked. With that, everything became clear. And I no longer had to make a decision.

"Thanks, Top," I said. "We'll get him on the bird."

Sergeant Wright and I talked over the bad situation we were faced with. Hyde was our best squad leader, but even he was due to DEROS in less than a month. Evans had been steady and reliable, and he was gone; from Schoch's account, on his way to Japan for weeks of hospitalization and recuperation. And now Novak, an RA sergeant, was gone also. At one time, I reflected, we'd had an embarrassment of good, qualified squad leader-ready men in the platoon. Now ... I looked at Top.

"I don't like it, Top, but it looks to me like we're back down to Eden and Dickerson. Like it or not, they're the only E5s we got. You see anything different?"

He shook his head, frowning. "Snyder," he said softly, but not assertively; he could see the problem as easily as I did.

"John's a good man, and maybe in a month or so, but ... the problem is there's nowhere to hide them. It's not like before, when we could put them in as team leaders under a good E6. We're fresh out of E6s."

He sighed. "I know. Same with Kenzy or Gann or Nelson. They're all Spec4s." He brooded. "We've talked to them before, you know. Talkin' ain't done a bit o' good. It ain't gonna make 'em NCOs."

"Who else is there?"

He shook his head. "No one."

"Then that's it, then."

He nodded. "Yes, sir. Want to do it now?"

I shrugged. "Yeah. No use putting it off."

And so, despite our misgivings, our two shake-and-bakes, already tried and found wanting, were returned to their positions as squad leaders. I gazed at their young faces as we informed them of our decision, a few moments later: Part excitement and gratification, part resentment and humility (Sergeant Wright was unsparing in his account of all their previous errors of commission and omission) and part apprehension. I shook my head in silence — Sergeant Wright did almost all the talking — and thought, *God help you two young kids. You're leaders now, ready or not.*

I had to smile at myself as I thought that. Kids. Yeah. And I was an ancient 25 years old. Kids indeed.

24

Firebase Airborne

YD365055; 1–6 May 1969

The company riffed the base of Dong Ngai, running into a couple of trail watchers and killing one of them, but otherwise not getting much done. The enemy had either moved back up the slopes of Dong Ngai or made his way across the A Shau to the Laotian border, only a few kilometers to the west. Late that afternoon, Robison told us we were going to take over security for the new firebase, set on the spot I'd been shot down only six days before.

We were the second platoon into the LZ that had been bulldozed out of Hill 1485. I could hardly recognize the place. In the 36 or so hours since I'd left, they had flown in an Engineer platoon, with bulldozers and graders, and had begun construction of a new fire base — Fire Base Airborne — along the top of the hill. CH54 cranes had lifted out the downed helicopters. The saddle and crater where our lift ship had gone down and St. Onge and the pilot had died were gone; completely filled in and leveled. Bunkers had been dug into the bare slopes, and already sandbags had begun to pile up around a small TOC located approximately where the saddle had been.

We were assigned a sector along the northeast side of the perimeter, which was still nothing but freshly scraped dirt and an occasional tree stump. If we'd had any doubts at all as to why we'd been brought back up here (not that we did) they would have been dispelled immediately by the sight of stacks upon stacks of shiny new sandbags, flat and empty. No monument to Viet Nam veterans, I reflected, looking at that pile, would be complete or official without a statue of a man holding an entrenching tool in one hand and an empty sandbag in the other.

The work commenced immediately, and went on for the rest of that day, and all of the next. Lots of fun, filling sandbags. This was more or less like being on Rakkasan, except that the immediate area was not quite as well-tamed. We were actually bored most of the time. Granted, there were a few exciting moments. Dan Bresnahan, who seemed to be possessed of some sort of magnet which attracted NVA to him — or perhaps it was the other way around — made contact twice, killing two NVA and wounding two more, while losing only one man slightly wounded. We lost another slick, this time due to mechanical failure. It went down in a flurry of shredded blades and crunching metal. There were some injuries, but nothing serious. The biggest worry whenever a Huey goes down is the possibility of igniting the extremely volatile fuel. So far, by some sort of improbable miracle, only one of the downed helicopters had burned.

That second day also brought about another sort of disaster; a visit by the Division Commander, General Zais. One might expect that, considering that the fire base had been under construction for only three days, and that we were in the middle of a strenuous operation marked by frequent contact, that the general and his staff attendants might have overlooked items like discarded C-4 crates or empty fuel cans lying about, but one would have, in this case, been wrong. As much hell was raised over these items as had ever been raised over a soft drink can at Rakkasan. We shrugged it off. The Army, among its other virtues, teaches one tolerance.

I happened to wander by the TOC while Zais was still there. Colonel Conmy, standing by his side, saw me and called me over. "You're Boccia, aren't you?" he asked as I approached.

"Yes, sir," I saluted.

His lean wrinkled face creased with a slight smile. "I'll never forget that night you spent on this hill. I lost a lot of sleep, worrying about you, son. I was glad to see you made it through. That was a grand job you did."

"Thank you, sir. To tell you the truth, I didn't get a whole lot of sleep that night, either."

He laughed, clapped me on the shoulder, and moved on. I like colonels. It's those damn lieutenant-colonels you've got to watch out for.

Twenty minutes or so later, I rejoined the platoon; we were digging in some more, and dirt and dust filled the air. Muldoon, seated behind me, grabbed my arm excitedly; I turned in time to see a small snake, bright emerald green with brown stripes, slither into the protection of a fallen tree trunk. I raised an eyebrow. It was the first snake I'd seen in six or seven months of living in the jungle.

"Reckon it's poisonous?" Muldoon asked.

"I don't know. Why don't you stick your finger in there and find out?"

Muldoon scowled, then brightened. "Hey, yeah. Might get me sent home."

"More likely, the snake'd die of alcohol poisoning."

"You ever worry much about getting bit by a poisonous snake, Lieutenant?"

I craned my neck and scowled at him. "You've got to be shitting me, Muldoon. How many GIs have been killed in Nam, do you know?"

He thought for a moment. "Forty thousand, more or less."

"Right. How many of them died from enemy fire, and how many died from snake bite?"

He reflected on this. "Good odds," he nodded, emphatically.

First and Second Platoons were given north and east sectors to defend; Third and Fourth were placed to the south. The Battalion Recon Platoon held the narrow western

24. Firebase Airborne

end. Work proceeded; instead of bunkers we were preparing large fox holes, roomy enough for three or four men. The sun was hot, and baking; there was no hazy cloud cover today to soften its fierce rays. Water was at a premium, and I was worried that the men might suffer heat stroke. We made sure they took their salt tablets, and rested them frequently, and so the afternoon passed without incident. By 1700, the majority of the holes had been finished; most had been dug to a depth of four and a half or five feet. The men were heartily sick of digging, by then, and Sergeant Wright and I saw no need to push them any farther; these were temporary positions, anyway, to be replaced by more permanent bunkers within the next few days.

By 1830 they'd all been finished to our satisfaction, the men had eaten, and Wright and I had already inspected the weapons. Twilight, like a thieving footpad, had filched the colors from the forest and sky; and the men were gray shapes clustered about the black foxholes. The forest animals were beginning to quiet down; the diurnal animals reached a peak of activity just before sunset, and the nocturnal birds and lizards had not yet begun. Conversation among the men was muted and low-pitched, as they reacted in unconscious accord with the animals. The evening was warm and close, the air damp and heavy with the smells of forest mold, burnt fiber and cordite. It was a typical fire base smell, only heavier and more pungent tonight.

The work went on for four relentless days; sandbag after sandbag, foxhole after slit trench after sump after latrine. The men were bored and harassed, Robison was next door to catatonic; he had only a day or so left before DEROS, and this was becoming a replay of his last days before R&R But we were promised, over and over, that on May 6, we would be pulled out of there. The evening of the 5th, then, we were reasonably content.

I sat on the ground with my legs stretched out and my back resting against my pack. I was content to smoke quietly, and think. Muldoon was unaccountably silent and withdrawn tonight; he sat by himself, several meters away, with his chin on his chest, arms folded across his knees, and his eyes focused on the ground at his feet. Helms and Wright, the new RTO, sat side by side, with the radios set in front of them, but they spoke seldom. Of Sergeant Wright there was no sign; he'd probably gone to pass the time with his fellow senior NCOs. Brown, of course, was back in the rear, recovering from the injuries he'd suffered in the crash of his helicopter. There was no one to talk to, and I'd already made the rounds of the platoon, checking on their weapons and shelters. I thought about my son, now just over two weeks old. I tried to imagine what he looked like — I'd not as yet received any pictures from home — but gave it up after a while. I'd received one letter from my wife, obviously, from the scrawled handwriting and brevity, written within a day or two of Geoff's birth, which mentioned that the boy had lots of dark hair and looked like me. I gave up trying to imagine what he looked like after I had one startling, unnerving vision of a tiny red-faced squirmy thing with a nose the size of a small desktop. Later it occurred to me that perhaps she meant that he looked like me as an infant. I suppose that's more likely.

At 2200 I made another round of the positions, merely to have something to do. The men were relaxed and quiet; the men on duty were on guard, and among the others there was little conversation, so I had nothing much to say, except at the next to the last hole I checked, where I found Hernandez smoking a cigarette. It was, of course, completely dark, and the glowing red tip could be seen for a kilometer or more. Some of the other men had been smoking too, but they had taken the elementary precaution of getting into their foxholes, crouched low, and thus hiding their cigarettes from view. I made Hernandez put the thing out, and then spoke to him, harshly but briefly. Then I went and rousted Dickerson, his squad leader, and spoke to him harshly and at great length. I left him shaking my head in irritation and puzzlement; the irritation was for Dickerson, who seemed to taking up exactly where he'd left off — that is, doing nothing — and the puzzlement was over Hernandez's behavior. Until recently, Hernandez had been an excellent soldier, reliable and hard-working. Now, in the span of three weeks, he'd been found sleeping on guard and smoking at night. I was concentrating on my thoughts so much that I didn't see the dark shape in front of me until it was too late; I bumped into him even as I saw him. It was Eward.

"Been walking long?" he asked.

"Sorry." I looked around; for a moment I had a disoriented feeling, thinking that I had wandered off course and was in Eward's sector, but then I recognized my CP only a few meters away.

"Just coming for you anyway," Eward said. "Robbie wants us."

"Okay. Be right there." I stepped over the CP — Sergeant Wright was back, I saw and told Helms where I was going. Then I followed Eward across the dusty bulldozed hilltop to Robison's CP. There was plenty of light to see by; the cloud cover was high and scattered, and although the moon hadn't risen yet I could see Eward's shape clearly as he walked about 15 meters ahead.

Robison's CP was a large but shallow hole covered by sand-filled ammo crates, draped with weighted-down canvas to keep the light from the Coleman lantern from escaping through the chinks and cracks. The radios were outside; the place wasn't big enough to hold them. Robison, with Murtiff hunched down beside him, gave a brief nod as we entered; the flickering yellow light from the lantern danced and jumped across the pale stretched skin of his cheekbones. I tapped Chuck Denholm's shoulder in greeting and ignored Dickson, who crouched in the corner, by himself as usual.

The CO wasted no time in preliminaries, which alone was enough to tell us something was up. "S2 just put the word out," he began as soon as Eward and I had knelt on our haunches, "that a couple of NVA sapper units have moved into this area. Also, Berchtesgaden was probed last night, and took some incoming earlier today. The word is they may hit us before we get built up. So: 100% alert until 2400, 50% from then until 0400, stand-to at 0400. Got it?" He ignored the groans. "Checked your perimeters lately?" He glanced first at me.

"Just came from there," I replied, virtuously.

"Uhm. You?" He looked at Denholm and Eward, who nodded in turn, and then finally at Dickson, who stirred, coughed, and finally said, "Yeah — uh, earlier."

Robison said nothing; by now he was beyond reacting to Dickson. "Okay. That's that. This is my last night in the field, so I would appreciate it if you dumb fucks could keep me alive."

"They'll have to climb over my dead body; we'll fight like tigers to save you," Denholm assured him.

"Besides, you could always go hide in Black Jack's bunker," I pointed out.

"Fuck you guys. Marsh — you've got the tiger tonight, right?"

Eward nodded. "Yeah. I just checked with 'em, a while ago. No problems."

"Twenty men? Who's out there with 'em?"

"Mendez."

"Let 'em know what's happening."

"Roger."

The four of us left together, but immediately separated on our way to our several platoons. All except Dickson, who stood by the canvas flap covering the entrance to the CP.

"Hey! Uh..."

We all turned and gazed at him.

"I — uh — wasn't ... I had somethin' to do earlier; didn't get to the briefin'. Uh ... where's the ammo resupply point?"

Three long, hushed sighs sounded together. We were getting awfully tired of Lieutenant Dickson.

"Just off the LZ, on the side opposite the TOC," Denholm finally muttered.

"Yeah. Right. Thanks."

I broke the news to Sergeant Wright; then he and I made the rounds again, telling the men the glad news. Actually, there was very little reaction; two weeks before, the news — 50 percent alert meant a total of two hours of sleep — would have been greeted with groans, curses and some really inspired bitching by our acknowledged experts, like Samuel. But that was back when we'd had no contact for months. The men's comments were low-key and resigned. The sight of a body bag is a great stimulant. Of course, Samuel bitched anyway, out of sheer reflex, and the sound of his low-voiced muttering filled my ear as I made my way back to my CP.

"Man, I'm never gonna get enough sleep, you know? Last night Mareniewski snored like a fat dog, and the night before that I was out on that LP and I couldn't get any sleep out there, and before that I got the middle watch two fuckin' nights in a row, and I don't know how I'm gonna keep my eyes open, what the fuck does Robison think we're fuckin' machines and now I'm outta peaches and...."

He was still going strong when I came back by the position on my way back to the CP, several minutes later.

It was some time later — past 2300 — when I heard a soft boot step behind me; I craned my neck — I was seated, as before, with my back against my rucksack — and recognized Eward.

"What's up?" I asked.

He squatted down beside me. "Just wanted to let you know I'm going to move my tiger; S3 isn't satisfied with where they are."

I stared at him in amazement. "Are you shitting me?"

He shook his head. "Nope. I'm going to have to bring them around the whole perimeter; he wants them out on that peak to our northeast. I think that's 1485 proper."

"Jesus Christ. At night? Does Black Jack — did he okay this?"

"Don't think so; he's been tied up with Iron Raven most of the night. No, this looks like it's all Howard's idea."

"Some day, someone's going to open up his skull and find something completely unknown to medical science. What's Robbie say about this?"

Eward shrugged. "It's his last day, man. What do you expect? Only thing he cares about is making it through tonight so he can climb aboard that slick tomorrow."

"Howard is an asshole. You may quote me on that." I got to my feet; I would have to make the rounds again, this time to inform the men that Eward's people would be moving across their front in a short while. Eward and I were still standing there, commiserating, when I became aware of a stir behind me. We glanced at each other; something was up. Eward made a motion as if to head for his CP but then reversed his direction and followed me; he would find out what was happening faster this way.

Helms knelt on the ground by his radio, listening to it. PFC Wright was loading his rifle, and Sergeant Wright and Muldoon were listening to the other radio. Helms put the receiver down as I walked up.

"Berchtesgaden got hit just a while ago," he said. "Some 122s. They're expecting a ground probe. Here we go again, right?"

"Maybe." Eward and I glanced at each other. "What do you think?" I asked.

"Could be. If I was the NVA, I'd hit us tonight, before we get our bunkers up." He knelt down beside Helms. "Let me borrow that for a moment, okay?"

I nodded, and stood by while he called his ambush party.

"Tiger Two Six, Tiger Two Six, this is Two Six ... Roger, Tiger Two. You guys on the up-and-up out there? Eyes peeled and noses sniffin'? ... Roger; keep it up. One of the other firebases near here just got hit, so you all can go to sleep now.... Negative, I don't know.... Roger. Out." He handed the mike back to Helms and stood up. "That oughta keep 'em lively tonight. And now, when I tell 'em they're gonna have to move...."

"They'll love you for it."

"Yeah. I — what was that?" His head, and mine, jerked round to the north; a spooky hollow thump had sounded from out there. We'd heard the noise indistinctly, so for perhaps a second or two neither of us recognized it, but then, as a bright red and yellow flash erupted on the shallow slope before us, followed by the heavy crump! of exploding HE, we had no difficulty.

"What are they, sixties?" I asked Eward.

"No. They're bigger; four-deuce, sounds like."

We crouched beside the foxhole, but made no mover to get in, yet; the first round had landed a good 200 meters away. Another thoop! echoed across the shallow valley to our north. There was large hill mass, black and solid against the gray sky, about 800 meters or so to the northwest; it was from there that the hollow sound seemed to come. That was the sound of the mortar round being blown out of the tube by a small explosive charge; there followed a short, eerie silence, broken only by the faintest of reverberations — the same sound echoing, with diminished force, off the hillsides behind us — and then, finally, the loud crump of the exploding shell, preceded by the red, yellow and white flash. There was no whistling sound — mortar rounds are usually silent in flight — so you really had no way of telling where a round would land before the fact, but usually you could judge fairly well by the amount of time elapsed between the explosion of the first round and firing of the second; if little or no time has passed, then it is unlikely that any adjustments were made, and the second round ought to land near the first. But if several seconds pass, then the mortar team is almost certainly adjusting the aim, and the second round could land anywhere. In this case, Marsh and I weren't particularly worried; only a second or two had elapsed by the time the NVA had fired the second round. We were expecting it to hit on the slope in front of us, and it did; a bit closer but still completely out of range. Sergeant Wright crouched alongside the foxhole; he raised his head, placed his hands to his mouth and yelled around perimeter: "Get in your holes and keep your eyes open! Don't duck you heads 'til you have to. Keep a lookout for a ground attack!"

A moment later, we heard the third round leave the tube; several seconds had passed, which meant that the gunner had adjusted the strike. Wright glanced at me, then shrugged slightly and jumped into the CP hole; Muldoon and PFC Wright were already there. The CP shelter was actually two foxholes, spaced only a couple of feet apart; the nearer one, by which Eward and I knelt, was occupied only by Helms, who had reached out and dragged his radio in with him. Marsh and I looked at each other; we should have jumped in by now, but instead we held off. Eward was obviously debating on whether to try making it back to his own CP, 100 meters off. He was still making up his mind when the third round hit; much closer to the perimeter, but almost 50 meters to our right — toward Eward's CP.

"Guess not," he muttered. We jumped in as the fourth round left the tube.

He grabbed the mike from Helms, called his own CP, and told his platoon sergeant where he was. Then he called his ambush again; they were on a small spur just west of us, and so far the rounds had landed well to their east and north, but he wanted to make sure they were alert; these mortar rounds might be nothing more than harassment, but they might also signal a ground probe or even an attack. Satisfied that everything was well with Tiger Two — or as well as things can be, when 20 men are sitting out in the forest 500 or 600 meters from their fire base, with no cover during a mortar bombardment — he gave the mike back to Helms, crossed his arms, and leaned back against the crumbly dirt wall of the foxhole.

This was a deep one; standing fully erect, I could just see over the edge. Helms and Eward, both taller, had to crouch a bit, but nevertheless, it was more than deep enough. Only a direct hit — a one in a million chance — would cause any casualties. We listened as the next two or three rounds landed, a bit closer but still far out. Then a new sound, from behind us, interjected itself into the patter. A moment later first one, then a second green flare burst into bright, unearthly light overhead — some 600 or 700 feet up, and roughly 500 meters to our front. As they fluttered slowly to earth, and their light dimmed, a second pair appeared over them; from then on, as long as the attack lasted, our 4.2 mortar team kept a steady flow of flares.

Eward grunted in annoyance and picked up the mike again — he was no longer politely asking my permission, but under the circumstances I wouldn't blame him, because I'd be annoyed too — and called Robison.

"This is Two Six," he said, when Robison came on the horn. "Who's placing those flares?"

"This is Six. The Sierra Three. Why?"

"This is Two Six. Because my Tiger's out there, just west of where they're puttin' 'em up, that's why."

There was a pause, and Robison's voice came back over the loudspeaker. "If your boys are where they're supposed to be, then they should be all right. They're not taking any incoming, are they?"

"Negative. But those flares are gonna give 'em away."

"There's nothing we can do about those flares; NVA may be probing us any time now, and I sure as shit wanna see what's happening. Tell your people to hunker down and stay quiet. What the hell, they're supposed to be in ambush posture anyway. Doesn't matter what the light conditions are. You got your sector squared away? Everybody looking out?"

"What there is of it, yeah. I only got two positions besides my CP. We got any arty coming' in any time soon?"

"Soon as we get a target. Keep your people alert. Out."

Eward handed Helms the mike with a shrug. "Bullshit," he said to me, philosophically.

The NVA gunner had, by this time, walked his rounds up the hill and closer to the perimeter. Now he began to fire for effect, but the results were disappointing — to him, I mean. We were pleased. The rounds, fired at a rate of about one every six seconds, landed in a widely spread pattern across our front; a few burst quite close to us, but the majority were falling into a slight dip almost directly north of us. I made a mental calculation and came up with the figure of one quarter of an inch; by so much would the gunner have to adjust his tube in order to bring those rounds directly on top of us.

As if by cue, the gunner made that adjustment, or they began using mortar shells with a fresher propellant. One landed on the perimeter, some 50 meters to our right, directly on one of Eward's positions. There was the usual red-white-yellow glare, but also, as if in a surrealist's canvas, the figure of a man, black and twisted against the glare of the explosion, rose and fell to the ground. Eward gave an involuntary grunt, as of pain; before he could move, a second round landed almost on top of the first. As we watched, a man scrambled out of one of the foxholes—he was eerily green and flickering in the light of the flares—ran to where we'd seen the first man fall, and dragged him back into the hole. Eward, almost motionless up to that point, whirled explosively and grabbed the mike again. I was beginning to think about charging him rent for it.

"Two Five, this is Two Six, over."

The response was immediate. "Two Five, over."

"This is Two Six. Who was that that got hit? How is he?"

"This is Two Five. That was Adams. He got blown out of our foxhole by one of them rounds. Got some shrapnel from the next one. His head's ringin' an' he ain't gonna sit down any time soon but he'll be okay."

"All right. I'll be over there as soon as I can."

Marsh looked at me and shook his head. "Lucky."

The next few minutes got interesting.

Now, almost all the rounds were landing in or near the perimeter. And they were coming fast; sure of his trajectories now, the NVA commander added a second tube to his arsenal. What had been a relaxed, casual attitude — we had seen it as entertainment on a dull evening — became earnest and, after a while, as round after round slammed into the hill around us, one of controlled terror.

There is nothing worse than a mortar attack, once it zeroes in on your position. Artillery is more devastating and destructive, but with most artillery you rarely hear the piece fired; you only pick up the flight of the shell as it nears you, and if you can hear it, it's normally going to miss.

But with a mortar you can hear the moment of launch, and then nothing until the yellow flash and the sound of the exploding shell. Those 10 seconds become moments of fear: Where will it land? Over there, by the little knoll? Or here, on this spot, in this foxhole? The sound of it finally going off is only a momentary respite, because the hollow *thoop* of the next round had just sounded, and the fear mounts again ... and again.

Helms sat crouched deep in the hole, his arms over his head, pressing the helmet down. Marsh and I half-crouched, reluctant to blind ourselves by joining Helms. Besides, there wouldn't have been enough room. Instead, we looked out over the slope as the reddish-yellow flashes followed one another, like angry fireflies on a hellish summer night. Several times, we caught ourselves looking at one another. Pride, of station and manhood, kept us from showing our fear, because we were Airborne Infantry officers, but there was no doubt about its presence; you could almost smell it. There was no shame in that; no man I've ever known can go through a serious mortar barrage and not feel the terror of it. It's the randomness, the absolute statistical insanity of it, that turns your insides to water. In almost any other situation, there is something you can do. But here, all that is left to you is to crouch, listening to the mortar shoot, and then pray it lands somewhere else.

It ended about a half hour after it started, which is an eternity. Only the last five or ten minutes were bad, but that was enough. Our own artillery never got into the fight; I found out, later, that the same arrogant fool Dufresne, who had refused to fire the mission on the morning of the 26th, had held up the return fire again — and, incredibly, for the same reason.

In the meantime, though, all we could do was cautiously move from our holes and assess the damage. Fortunately, it was light, both to material and, more importantly, to the men. Eward's man, Adams, was his only casualty, and his was not a serious wound; painful and inconvenient, because he would spend the next several days on his stomach, but that was all.

I lost no one, nor did Denholm. Third Platoon, I heard, had taken one lightly wounded, a trooper who'd been caught running from one over-crowded foxhole to another; he had taken shrapnel in his lower legs, and that wasn't considered serious either. Dickson himself had taken a very small piece of shrapnel in his upper arm, but it was minor, and no cause for evacuation. One man in the battalion TOC had suffered a concussion from a near miss. That was all. Considering what might have happened, this was not a bad butcher's bill.

The main concern we had was to get the troops settled down for the night; we were all worried they'd be too much on edge, too trigger happy, and that's almost as bad as being too complacent. So the platoon leaders and NCOs got little sleep for the rest of the night, moving from position to position.

25

Sergeant Samuel Wright RA

Camp Evans; 7–9 May 1969

For once, they were true to their word; we were lifted out soon after dawn of the next morning, and returned to Camp Evans. Most of us dispersed immediately to our platoon quarters, for showers and rest, but the CO never left the PZ.

There wasn't much ceremony to Robison's departure. His replacement hadn't arrived yet, and anyway he had to leave now to make it down to Saigon and Bien Hoa. There was no emotion, no long goodbyes: A quick handshake, a nod, "See ya around," and he was gone. This was the Army way; the same thing would happen to me later, and to all of us; there are things to do, and the moment a man left the unit, he was history, and could contribute nothing to the present. In that respect, the dead and the living were exactly the same: Once you leave us, you are no longer in the present or future.

Robbie wasn't the only one who left. It may seem incredible, but none of us had noticed that Dickson wasn't around. Not all that incredible, of course: We move and live by platoon, and days could pass without seeing one another. But there had been a brief meeting, early that morning, before the flight, and it suddenly struck all three of us that Dickson hadn't been there. Robison was gone, but First Sergeant Murtiff was around. Denholm's straightforward question was answered with an impassive stare.

"Lieutenant Dickson was medevaced to the 22nd last night," Murtiff finally said. He turned and walked away.

We stared at each other, stunned. The first thought that flitted through my mind was "*By God, he was yellow after all,*" but it didn't ring true. Days later, I understood what had happened. We'd driven him away — Chuck, Marsh and I. Not even as insensitive and stupid a man as Dickson could endure the continued open, scathing contempt of his peers. Few men can. Dickson had seized the opportunity given him by a minor wound to leave this hell we'd subjected him to. I should have felt bad. The Jesuits had drummed moral theology into me for eight long years, and I was aware that I should not treat a human being so. I should have felt bad, but I didn't. For the sake of his men, and for all of us, I was very glad he was gone, whatever the cause.

Sergeant Wright came to collect me around 1100 that morning, the 7th of May. He escorted me to a small, screened hutch, just outside the battalion yard, that sat along the road leading to the perimeter bunkers. This was, de facto, the battalion Senior NCO club; sergeants below the rank of E-7 were not even allowed inside. There was little enough to attract outsiders anyway; a large metal tub, two feet high and about four across, was placed on the middle of the floor. It was filled with large chunks of ice and dozens of cans of beer. I had to smile when I saw it; I recalled Robison's outraged cries when we returned to Evans on stand-down only to find the battalion area dry. Well, no matter, I thought: He's at Bien Hoa by now and there's beer enough down there.

The only other accoutrements in the hutch were two wooden benches along the two long sides and a bare wooden table on the wall opposite the entrance. Two men sat on the table, their feet dangling over the floor. They were men made in the classic mode of the first sergeant: Broad red faces, barrel bodies, cold eyes, small thin-lipped mouths. I recognized one of them as Delta's first sergeant, Moran. I didn't know the other. Seated on the bench to my left was the Battalion sergeant major; spare, of medium height, with short ginger-grey hair over a face that was all flat planes and sharp angles. It looked as if it had been designed with a ruler. Two others sat on the right-hand bench; one was a well-known platoon sergeant from Delta, named Simpson, a huge black man with a massive bullet head, heavy jowls and small, mean eyes, and a chest and arms that would have crushed an ox. I wouldn't have believed that Sergeant Wright could ever have been made to look small, but this man did that easily. I almost missed the other E-7 seated next to him, a man I didn't know from one of the battalion staffs.

The NCOs interrupted their conversations to gaze at us as we entered. Sergeant Wright nodded familiarly to them but then focused on the sergeant major. With simple dignity, he placed his hand on my shoulder and said, "This is my lieutenant."

The others nodded back. The sergeant major got up from the bench, reached into the tub, brought out two beers and handed one to each of us, saying, to the room at large, "This is Bravo One Six. Here you go, Lieutenant."

I accepted the beer with a casual nod, but I was conscious that this was, in its own way, a ceremony as steeped in the traditions of the Army as the medal awards ritual, only far rarer and more meaningful. Of course, Meehan was being polite, but that's beside the point. Sergeant Wright would never have dreamed of bringing me here, to this place, to meet his peers—the senior NCOs of the battalion—on a merely social call. The gulf between junior officers and senior NCOs is wide and almost unbridgeable, and it's kept that way by the NCOs. Wright's pride of place and station was immense; he would never have brought me here simply because he liked me or thought I was a good storyteller.

Meehan opened a beer for himself, looked at me as he took the first swig, and then said, quietly, without much emphasis, "Good job up on Airborne, Lieutenant." The others just nodded in agreement, except for Wright, who looked gratified. I realized that this Miller I'd been handed was the equivalent of the DSC.

The NCOs resumed their interrupted conversation. Anyone listening in could be forgiven for concluding that these men were unaware of a world outside the Army. In a way, that is precisely so: Career NCOs, far more than career officers, are bathed by the dust of countless Army posts and stations. Their talk was about Fort Benning, Fort Campbell, Fort Bragg, Fort Ord, Fort Meyers, Fort Carson — at one moment or another almost every major Army post was mentioned — and the commanders and, more especially, the NCOs they had known there. The Army was large, but the community of senior NCOs was relatively small, and the clan of infantry NCOs smaller still. Perhaps no one man could know them all, but place five or six such men together, and it would be a good bet that among them they'd know every senior Eleven Bravo in the service. Commanders and peers were spoken of, praised, damned or merely mentioned. It struck me, listening to them, that the military NCO — Army or Navy — was among the last of the professions that actually defined and shaped the men who practiced it. It used to be so for almost everyone; it was no longer true for most. To know that a man is an attorney, or accountant, or bricklayer, or bus driver, is to know little more than what he does between the hours of 8 to 5. But to see the heavy chevrons on a man's sleeve is to know what he eats, where he sleeps, how he dresses and talks and even, to a large extent, how he thinks.

This sense of community, this sure knowledge of what one could expect from one's fellows, was a source of strength to the career man, but it also explained, at least partially, his traditional hostility — thinly veiled, or not — to young officers. A lieutenant like me would wear the uniform and lead men for two or three years. We were outsiders, not part of the community; we didn't speak the same language or taste the same food or wake up to the same sounds. Because we had different concerns and different views and even different goals, we were threats, weak links, potential trouble: How can you trust a man, *really* trust him, when he'd been a civilian two years earlier and would be a civilian a year later?

The talk meandered away from the past to the present: It touched here and there on the battalion staff, the companies, the brigade or division. Black Jack was ready to bust a couple of staff officers (please, I thought, let one of them be Howard); Delta was dissatisfied with his supply sergeant; Alpha *had* busted one of his shake-and bake squad leaders (this last was reported with morose but evident satisfaction); Charlie needed help with his navigation but wouldn't listen to his Top. No names were used; none was necessary. Who cared what the man's *name* was? Alpha Six, Bravo Six — that was what mattered. The Six. This identification of a man and his function seemed both strange and familiar; after a moment I realized where I had seen it before: Shakespeare. *My brother, France, must answer me ... I am dying, Egypt, dying....*

First Sergeant Moran's words took me out of my reverie.

"What's this shit I hear about them movin' the mobile units from the 22nd out to Blaze?"

That got my attention. The 22nd was the Division field hospital, headquartered at Camp Eagle. I had never heard before of moving a mobile surgical facility to a firebase, no matter how large it might be. The sergeant major glanced at Moran coldly.

"Where'd you hear that?"

"Charlie Stephens, down at 42nd maintenance. Me 'n him was havin' a beer last night but he said he had to go; had to get up early this mornin' on account of they was gonna get three Cranes ready so's they can fly them boxes out to Blaze, first thing." Moran's small, porcine eyes stared back at the sergeant major. "Why? Is that supposed to be some sort o' top secret bullshit?"

"No. Maybe not. But the troops hear about it, they'll start worrying. No need to go around talking about it."

Moran shrugged. "They'll see the fuckin' things for themselves when we get out there." He finished up his beer, crushed the can in one irritated motion and threw the crumpled thing into a trashcan across the room. "This goddamn Apache Snow sounds like a real bear-fuck to me. We're gonna get our balls clawed."

Simpson laughed, a deep, booming sound. "Top, you're getting' too old for this shit."

Moran jumped down off the table, reached in the tub for another beer, pulled out a small church key and punched the top open. "Fuck it," he growled in answer. "They'se some shit out there and we're fixin' to step in it, knee-deep. Movin' that hospital out there ... shit."

The sergeant major grinned sourly. "You can always go to the chaplain and request compassionate leave, Moran."

Sergeant Wright and I took our leave soon after that; there was much to prepare for. We crossed the road to the line of platoon barracks and entered First Platoon's. The plain, narrow cots inside were piled high with gear: rucksacks, C-rations, disassembled rifles, magazines empty and full, new and old fatigue trousers, blouses, sweaters, socks, field jackets, stationery, insect repellent, mail, unwrapped or open boxes from home, cans of Pepsi or coke, cards, portable radios and, sprawled out on two or three of the cots, troopers trying to catch up on two or three months of lost sleep. Someone had a radio going, and it was blaring out John Fogerty's *Bad Moon Rising*, our unofficial theme song.

Most of the troops were outside, shirtless in the sun. Westman and Logan sat together, as usual: Logan scowling and brooding over his disassembled machine gun, which he was inspecting carefully, and Westman patiently and meticulously cleaning and lightly oiling the long bandoliers of ammo, making sure that each individual 7.62 cartridge was free of dirt and corrosion. He looked up as we approached, his wide blue eyes beaming at us cheerfully.

"Morning, Lieutenant. Morning, Sergeant."

I smiled. I always did, on hearing his lilting Scandinavian accents. He always sounded like someone out of "I Remember Mama." "Good morning to you, Westy," I replied. "I see you're trying to keep Logan out of trouble."

25. Sergeant Samuel Wright RA

The Inseparables: Tim Logan (left) and Myles Westman, M60 gunner and assistant gunner, and an unidentified man in the background (photograph by Chris St. Onge).

Westman laughed, "You saw what happened when I wasn't there to take care of him. His gun didn't shoot and he almost got killed. I got to be with him all the time, Lieutenant, or he gets in real trouble."

Logan snorted. "Yeah. I wish you'd been with me on the hill, all right. I coulda used your head for a firing pin, you goddamned needle-skulled Swede."

Westman laughed again, in delight. "For sure, Timothy. For sure. But in meantime I clean your ammo for you, so it don't happen no more, right?"

"Go milk a reindeer," Logan growled. Then, after a pause, he grunted. "Right."

Westman smiled.

Camp Evans: 8 May: 1000

The new CO walked into the morning room at 1000 the next day. Tall, spare, with coal-black hair and an incisive but quiet manner, he was almost the polar opposite of Robison. For much of the morning, he was closeted with Master Sergeant Murtiff, the company first sergeant. Later that day, he met with us, the platoon leaders. First impressions are not, invariably, right or wrong, but I walked away from the first meeting with the notion that this was a cool, professional and very competent officer. I also noted that he maintained, in that first meeting, an almost visible barrier between himself and his platoon leaders. This never changed. Within hours of meeting Robison, I knew almost everything superficial about him: Where he'd gone to school, how he'd gotten his commission, his wife's name, the name of the street on which they lived, his favorite pro football team … from Littnan, I never even learned what part of the country he was from. Later that day, Chuck Denholm and I compared impressions. We ended up agreeing that, overall, we'd just had a significant upgrade in leadership. We were both fond of Robison, and wished him well, but Littnan had an air of maturity and purpose that Barry lacked.

Captain Littnan sent word that he wanted all officers and senior NCOs in the morning room by 2000. A briefing was scheduled for the company commanders at 1900 on the upcoming operation, Apache Snow, and he wanted to pass the information on to us. We assembled there after dinner, getting there early, only to find Littnan waiting for us: The briefing had been set back to 0700 the following morning. Since we were all there, he took the opportunity to introduce himself to those of us whom he hadn't met yet, so we were all still there when the call came.

Most commanders would have used the landline—the telephone—for the call. Black Jack used the radio—for maximum effect and exposure. The gist of the call became clear in short order. A Bravo Company Morning Report submitted to Headquarters a week before had listed three men on limited duty due to illness or injury. A report from the battalion aid station showed that the battalion surgeon had placed only one man from Bravo on limited duty. Black Jack requested an explanation.

He made his request in his usual fashion: At length, loudly and publicly. As the minutes stretched out, and the stream of abuse continued, we stared at our toes, or the floor, or anywhere except at Littnan; we were embarrassed and angered by what we heard. I know that I would have left the room if I could have figured out a way to do it without being disruptive. Through it all, Littnan sat quietly, while the totally unwarranted stream of abuse—the incident had taken place a week before—continued on for several more redundant minutes. When it was over, the silence in the room was broken only by the faint hiss of static from the PRC40 radio. None of us cared to look up; we were afraid to meet the CO's eye. Murtiff, in particular, was mortified: As first sergeant, the Morning Report was his responsibility. I would not have believed, before that moment, that anything on earth could mortify First Sergeant Murtiff.

The silence stretched out for another uncomfortable moment, and then Littnan spoke.

"First Sergeant, did you prepare the morning report he was talking about?"

Our eyes fixed on Littnan in what amounted to astonishment. His voice was cool and even. He gave no indication that anything unusual had happened at all.

"No, sir. But I'll check on it right away, sir." Murtiff, profane, growling, red-faced Murtiff, was almost babbling.

"Good." Littnan flicked a noncommittal glance at Murtiff and Braxton, the company clerk. "Let me know what you find out tonight, please."

That was that. No explosion. No yelling, no curses and threats, no screaming or pounding of fists—all things we'd gotten somewhat used to over the past few months—but there wasn't a man there who assumed that it would be perfectly okay with Littnan if Murtiff and Tanaka didn't get back to him until the next morning. Murtiff's chronically red face was now a vivid scarlet, whether from rage or shame. Mine was the same color, but in my case, it was definitely shame. I couldn't help but contrast Littnan's cool, professional reaction with my own. I remembered, with paralyzing clarity, how I had reacted under similar circumstances a few weeks earlier. It struck me then that I had an awful lot to learn about being a commanding officer.

We eventually did get our briefing on the afternoon of the next day. Apache Snow was big. Five battalions, four U.S. and one ARVN, would assemble at Blaze and then deploy into the western slopes overlooking the A Shau; we would be only a couple of kilometers from the Laotian border and the known NVA base camps and re-supply centers. The Task Force would be commanded by Colonel Conmy, our Brigade Commander; our principal mission was to search out and destroy the enemy supply depots and caches on this side of the border.

Our company was given the role of battalion reserve; we would be the last ones flown out, late in the day, and then take over as security for the battalion CP. We were to be, in effect, the palace guard, an easy assignment, except that we would be subjected to both Black Jack and Howard. There's always something.

We were given the assignment mostly because of the stiff hammering we'd taken at Airborne and the slopes below it, but also in part because this would be Littnan's first week with the company. But if that registered with Littnan at all, one way or another, he gave no sign of it. His briefing was so terse, concise and pointed that it was over before we were quite aware of it. There was none of the usual—the pep talk, the admonitions, the speculation—just the facts, cold, clear and unembellished. When he finished, Littnan nodded in our direction and retired to his office, leaving us in the morning room. Chuck, Eward and I remained behind as the senior NCOs filed out. Sergeant Leanahan, the commo sergeant, lingered behind for a moment but our looks plainly indicated that his presence wasn't required. As he left, Chuck took off his glasses and began carefully polishing them.

"What do we know about the area?" he asked, his dark eyes intent on the lenses.

Eward shrugged. "It's right on the border, ain't it? That's all we need to know. That—" he paused for a moment and smiled without mirth—"That, and that friggin' staircase on Dong Ngai. You both saw that, didn't you?"

I lit a cigarette and inhaled sharply; the smoke was hot and harsh on my throat.

"They're all over the area. We know that. Hell, it couldn't be any worse than Airborne. And, besides, we've got the easy job this time."

Denholm snorted. "Yeah. Two weeks of fun in the sun, with Black Jack as entertainment director." He shook his head. "One day of Howard would be enough...."

I nodded. "Maybe. A week of him, and—yeah. I was going to say that it beats getting shot at, but I don't know. Maybe we'll end up volunteering for a patrol—Laos, Cambodia, Russia, North Korea—anywhere."

Denholm grinned. "You know what would be great? Wait until the staff's asleep one night, and pick up and move out. Just leave 'em there. Let 'em wake up the next morning and find themselves on the damned hill with no perimeter." He laughed and waggled his dark, full eyebrows, looking vaguely like a young Groucho. "Howard would have a heart attack."

"Easier to just shoot him," Eward said, getting up and stretching. "Well, I got things to do, guys."

"Oh, really? You workaholic, you." I got up myself. "If nothing else," I continued, "this week ought to be interesting."

"All our weeks are interesting," Eward noted, as he left. Chuck and I exchanged glances while we gathered our gear and notebooks. Interesting, indeed.

Camp Evans: 9 May: 0730

The morning of the 9th, Captain Littnan held an early inspection. It would be fair to say that we observed him as carefully as he inspected us. I had been favorably impressed by his manner and character to this point, but this would be the first indication of what he would be like as a field commander. The ultimate judgment, of course, would be made when we came into contact with the enemy; then all earlier impressions, favorable or otherwise, would be as nothing. But for now, we watched him inspect the troops. What was he looking for? Would he know what was important and what was not?

I had no qualms about First Platoon. No unit run by Sergeant Wright would ever be deficient. He and I had inspected them ourselves earlier in the morning. Their boots were scuffed and muddy, some, who had not had a chance to draw new fatigues, were dressed in shabby and wrinkled, often stained or worn blouses or pants; their packs and other gear were no longer a shiny olive green but now were the hues of the mountain soil: dun and a deep, dirty buff. Not all of them had shaven as closely as they might. So much was so: Had this been stateside, Sergeant Wright and I would have been relieved on the spot. But I knew, and I waited to see if the new CO knew, what was important: The weapons were clean—indeed, spotless—and each man had all his magazines and ammunition, at least the requisite number of grenades, smoke canisters and other gear. Every man in the platoon had received a fresh, close haircut, not because it made him look more military but because long hair in a damp jungle environment where one might bathe once a month was inherently unhealthy. Their fatigues may have been scruffy but they were serviceable; none was torn, and the boots, no matter how dirty, were still in good shape; no one would wear through his soles or lose a heel. They all had adequate water (the food would be picked up at Blaze), and all had their salt tablets, iodine pills, malaria pills, heat tablets, complete first-aid pouches, insect repellent, plastic bags—all the items a man would need to stay reasonably comfortable and healthy in the mountain forests. So much was so: Sergeant Wright and I were determined that no combat unit would take to the field better prepared than ours. Captain Littnan finished looking over the company at 1030. I was pleased. We had both passed the inspection.

The hour 1400 was designated as Bravo's PZ time; this left us with about three hours to take care of last-minutes necessities, such as one last letter home. I had finished mine, sealed it in an envelope and handed it to Tanaka, the company clerk, and then settled down to wait. Fourteen hundred came and went; as most Army deadlines are wont to do, this one slipped away into the realm of lost time. The new time was 1600 or so. This left me the opportunity to write one more letter, one to my parents, whom I'd been neglecting shamefully. That done, I wandered around the company area, talking briefly with scattered knots of my troops, moving on, fidgeting, snooping, checking, growling, scowling, muttering. I wasn't nervous or apprehensive, but merely impatient. I hated waiting.

In the event, we boarded the ungainly Chinooks at 1545. Three of them arrived, one after the other, in an intense swirl of dust and wind, to pick us up and ferry us the 30 or 40 kilometers to Blaze. Alpha Company, who'd been waiting on the hot tarmac with us, were left behind to await the next flight, whenever that would be; Harkins, Alpha's CO, received the news with profane disgust. He stood in glum rage, buffeted by the powerful winds, as we lifted off. No one liked waiting.

26

Palace Guard

Firebase Blaze; YD538022; 9 May 1969

Blaze had changed substantially since we last had seen it; two weeks ago it had been nothing more than a tawny orange smear surrounded by dun green jungle. Now, it was recognizably a firebase; bunkers dotted the perimeter; bulldozers, levelers, back hoes and graders were growling all about, excavating more bunker sites, leveling off yet another landing site or building a berm along the river. Tanks and APCs from the 2/17th were lined up, squat and ugly, along the road. Interior roads had been leveled, surfaced and covered with sticky black liquid asphalt. Jeeps, deuce-and-half trucks, tankers and heavy construction equipment dotted the base in all directions. There were five principal landing zones, and these were a hornets' nest of Hueys, LOHs, 'hooks, cranes and even the occasional Marine Sikorski. Above all — and this hadn't changed — there was dust. Dust by the tons, by the cubic mile; a planetary envelope of dust. Dust that billowed and wafted and drifted and swirled and settled. Dust that penetrated and clogged air filters, cowlings, vents, exhausts, toolboxes, rifles, canteens, noses, eyes, ears and lungs. Dust that made us yearn for the monsoon rains: Even the filthy, sticky diarrheic mud of February was preferable to this.

The battalion was placed on the low hills that bordered the Rao Nai. Bravo, in fact, was set very close to the same spot where First Platoon had waited for the rest of the company, two weeks before. I knew that from the coordinates, but otherwise the place was unrecognizable. The swimming hole where we'd cooled ourselves while waiting was gone, silted over by the tons of dirt and gravel that had been scraped off the surrounding hills. Northwest of us, across the firebase, reared a massive ridge, now black and featureless against the setting sun: Hill 770 formed its western end. At the base of that hill, less than two kilometers distant, was the place where Eward had trapped the NVA platoon three or four weeks ago.

The moon was nearly full that night, and there were no clouds. The valley shimmered a ghostly, unaccustomed silver. The day's dust had finally settled; no helicopters flew, and the heavy equipment had stopped for the night. The high, sharp peaks to our west were shrouded in a faint, dusky gloom. They reared over us, dark and stern, like glowering justices on a courtroom bench. The night was quiet, open, oddly comforting in its cool clarity. It held no menace; at least, none that we could see.

Just before midnight, Littnan called: One of us was to take his platoon on a night reconnaissance along the Rao Nai. We were so used to hunkering down, motionless, at night that the novelty of it appealed to us: We all wanted to go. After a moment or two of squabbling amongst the platoon leaders, Littnan impatiently selected Denholm and told him to move out. Chuck did so, almost immediately, and he chortled and gamboled his way along the bare, flat valley floor. He enjoyed himself immensely. He had fine visibility, he was within shouting distance of 2,000 friendly troops, and, above all, he was able, for the first time in our tour of duty, to move in something other than a platoon file. Chuck was giggling with glee at the opportunity to actually maneuver his squads on line; he hadn't done anything like that since OCS.

We were too keyed up, and the moon too bright and alluring, for us to sleep. We sat around the radios, listening to Denholm's light-hearted chatter, and talked quietly. Some pulled stationery and Bic pens out of their packs and wrote an unexpected letter home. We weren't worried about losing sleep. After a couple of days' stand down, during which almost all of us had managed to get eight or even ten hours of uninterrupted sleep for the first time in weeks, we were fresh and rested, and besides, the following day we weren't scheduled to depart Blaze until very late in the afternoon, leaving us all day to rest up.

Sergeant Wright, as he frequently did, sat apart from us, either asleep or perhaps thinking of his family; perhaps going over some verses from the Old Testament, as he once told me he did on such occasions. Brown and PFC Wright lay by their packs, whispering. Helms, Muldoon and I sat up, gazing out over the valley. In the bright moonlight, the ugly orange dirt of Blaze was a vivid light grey. The talk was casual and unforced, including long companionable silences that might last five or ten minutes, punctuated by a low-voiced sentence from one or the other of us. We talked about the other platoons, or Camp Evans, or the changes we'd found at Blaze, the casualty rate among engineers, the way the C-rats had suddenly become tasteless, how mail that brought bad news always seemed to arrive right away, while the good news took forever…

That got Muldoon talking about his girlfriend, a sharp-tongued, strong-willed young woman from his hometown of Wilmington, Delaware. He admitted with mixed dismay and befuddlement that he would probably marry her when he returned from the war. But, he added morosely, in that flat, raspy tenor of his, he had no idea why.

"That broad," he went on, staring off across the valley, "could talk a starving dog off a meat wagon. I never seen her shut up for five minutes. Got nothing to say, but that don't stop her. And her mom…" he raised his dark Irish eyes to heaven: "her ol' lady is even worse. Two of 'em get together and it's goddamn non-stop. You know what, Lieutenant? If I could figure out some kinda gadget, I could hook up to their jaws? Run a generator? I could light up half of fucking Wilmington."

I smiled, and Helms did too, but Dennis often was uncomfortable when Muldoon started talking about his woman. Helms had married his high school girlfriend, and he loved her with a gentle, comfortable domesticity that was light years removed from Muldoon's sardonic, embattled, half-defiant, half-contemptuous attitude towards his intended mate. Helms never spoke of his wife except in the context of his life at home: a church picnic, Saturday shopping, a high school dance, a relative's funeral or a cousin's wedding; For Dennis, the realities of family, home, marriage, community, workplace and church were inseparable; his love for his wife, his home and his country were all one. But at the center of all of that was a slight, brown-haired girl who held all the rest together.

Dennis Helms was a gentle and decent man, and it was impossible to observe his serene smile and calm acceptance of events without believing that he was also a very fortunate and happy man. I wondered, at times, whether Muldoon—fiercely, proudly detached from everything, including family and friends, haunted by a demon that would not let him rest, alcoholic, often brutally indifferent to others—ever envied Helms. Probably not, I decided. Muldoon saw his environment as something to be fought against and conquered, while Helms drew sustenance and strength from the very things—family, community, friends—that Muldoon battled. I'm not sure the two understood each other. But they were both good men. Not just a good medic and a good RTO, but good men. Muldoon was possessed of that rarest combination of human virtues: utter honesty in his self-knowledge and full acceptance of responsibility for whatever came his way; he thought little of this world but he offered the people he cared for complete commitment, while Helms was a man to whom giving and embracing others was as natural as breathing.

Firebase Blaze; 10 May: 0630

Eventually, we slept. Any thoughts we might have had about a late sack time were dispelled quickly the next morning, at 0630. I had never seen or heard anything like it. No one had. Five battalions—2,100 men—were being lifted out of Blaze that day, and more than 100 Hueys were hovering and bobbing all over the valley. We arose and stared in wonder: One after another, rank upon rank, squadron after squadron, they spread out across the valley like a swarm of giant green dragonflies; their blades glinted and winked in the dawn light. I felt chills down my spine; the spectacle was awesome, frightening, inspiring and sobering. We watched silently as tiny green figures scampered under the whirling blades and into the gaping bellies.

The first battalion lifted off was the 1/502nd, followed by the 1/506th. The ARVNs departed soon after, and all of the 3/187th except for us—Bravo. The last battalion out was the 2/506th, but the firebase didn't quiet down then: In addition to the combat troops, hundreds of other men and tons of supplies were to be moved: support troops, engineers, artillery, supply, medical personnel and equipment, intelligence teams—all had to funnel through Blaze. Chinooks and even one or two powerful Cranes mingled with the Hueys, doing the heavy lifting. The noise was continuous and overpowering. Most of the support units had been dispersed among various firebases overnight, but they all converged on that one place deep in the mountains: YD 538022.

It was awesome, it was inspiring, but after a while cold logic reminded me that those Hueys were, after all, fragile things not much stronger than the gossamer-winged insects they resembled. I of all people knew that.

For most of the day, we had nothing to do. The officers gradually gathered around the company CP, listening to the radio on the battalion and task force nets, but nothing was being reported. There was little conversation for most of the day. Denholm, still yawning after a night without sleep, got into a brief, lackluster argument with Eward over some obscure point of radio technique; I listened without interest for a few minutes and then sniffed and informed them that neither of them had a clue what he was talking about, whereupon they united in reminding me that Black Jack had already made it abundantly clear what he thought about *my* radio technique, so it was best that I just sit, listen and learn.

Absolutely nothing of importance came over either net. We heard that Alpha was sent on a RIF west, toward the Quan Aim Hoa, the river that forms the Laos-Viet Nam border, and Delta to the high ground to the southeast. The only excitement came when a Delta platoon leader reported that one of his men had been bitten by a large spider. Our concern, we agreed, ought to be for the spider.

LZ2; YC314992; 10 May: 1730

Finally, our turn came, at 1630. The 18 Hueys that would take us to join the battalion came thrumming and whup-whupping down the valley; we were strung out along the river so the pickup was almost simultaneous. The flight lasted only ten minutes; it was not quite 1645 when we jumped from the lift ship onto the flattened light yellow grass of the LZ. Charlie Company was securing the LZ, and Alpha and Delta were by now sweeping either side of the ridge, so there was no drama to this CA. A combat assault in which you are the very last man of 2,100 troops to land ought not to rank very high on one's list of accomplishments, and I dismissed it from my mind until a month or so later, when I realized that this had been my 25th combat assault. Nothing like the 24th, of course.

Our orders had been to be the Palace Guard—the security element for the battalion CP—but that changed as we were landing. During the afternoon, while we had been waiting back at Blaze, Brigade S2 had called Black Jack and informed him of the existence of Area 82, a suspected NVA logistics center, thought to be located on a mountain less than two kilometers southeast of the LZ. It was called Dong Ap Bia, and the base was thought to be centered on or near one of its peaks, Hill 937. Looking at the map, Black Jack decided that, if nothing else, the peak would make a good battalion CP site. Accordingly, he ordered Captain Lee Sanders to take Delta Company and probe the area, and then establish a perimeter for the battalion CP.

Delta's First Platoon moved out, but before they had gone 100 meters, two NVA were spotted moving across their line of advance, toward the northeast. Sanders was ordered to pursue. Black Jack decided to send Bravo, still airborne, on Delta's planned mission to check out Hill 937. Grabbing Littnan as he arrived, Black Jack told him to move his company out immediately, to the southeast, and get as close to the mountain's peak as he could before dark.

Captain Littnan gave us our order of march: Eward, then me, the CP with Third Platoon, now run by Garza, and finally Chuck. Dong Ap Bia stood some 1,800 meters to our southeast; it was screened from our view by some intervening hills and ridges: Not quite two kilometers, as the crow flew (it occurred to me to wonder if there were any crows in Viet Nam), but as the grunt walked, it would end up closer to four or five.

An afternoon thunderstorm, at this time of year a daily occurrence, had blown in from the west, over the high steep mountains of eastern Laos, and had pummeled the LZ with heavy, driving rains and high winds. The rain had moved on, across the A Shau and into the mountains there, but the clouds remained and the dampened earth was somber and grey; the reeds and brush were still flattened and burdened with the weight of the storm. We pushed through the low scrub and stiff grass; our trousers and the lower ends of our fatigue shirts were soaked a dark green within seconds of moving out.

Eward reached a steep bluff, somewhat bare and sandy, spotted with chunks of rotting limestone, that descended to a treeless saddle some 30 or 40 feet below. The saddle was broad and wide, more like a valley, really; it stretched about 150 meters across. At its southeastern edge a belt of thickly leaved, low trees marked where the ground began to rise again to a small, low, heavily forested hill. The saddle, though treeless, afforded Eward a good deal of cover, its surface marred by dozens of folds, rills, humps and depressions. Vegetation was predominantly tough scrub brush and stringy gorse, with here and there a small, forlorn sapling or bush. Because the hill opposite was so far away, Eward did not follow the usual procedure of sending a fire team across the open space to secure the tree line before moving his platoon into the open space. One hundred fifty meters was too far to adequately support a small team if anything happened.

Bravo Two snaked their way across the saddle, dipping in and out and around the terrain features. I was watching them; when I turned my eyes back to my immediate front, my point man had disappeared. Edwards, my slack man, reached the lip of the bluff. Holding his M16 extended out in his left hand, as a counterweight, he turned his body to the right, balanced lightly on his right hand and then scrabbled and slid down the steep face of the bluff, loosing a small shower of gravel and dirt. I waited until he'd almost reached bottom, and then I followed him in the same manner. By the time I was half way down, Helms had begun his descent. Going down a steep, loose slope like that, carrying anything from 60 to 100 pounds on my back, was high up, perhaps at the top, of my list of least favorite activities. It always seemed to me to be a mere matter of time before someone broke a leg or a neck.

The daylight was beginning to dim; it was a quiet twilight grey now. The air about us seemed to become a shadow thing; the waning sun, which would have at least spotted the bare saddle with a hint of color, was sulking behind the heavy dark gray clouds. We picked our way silently across the rough surface. Sergeant Wright, all the way at the back of the file, had started a count soon after we'd left the perimeter. It now reached me: I heard Helms call out "twenty-nine." I glanced back over my shoulder; perhaps a third of the platoon had reached the base of the bluff. I turned my head back to the front and had already opened my mouth to say "thirty" ...

BLAM! ... BLAM! ... BLAM! BLAM!

I dove for the ground, one hand holding my rifle, the other pressing my helmet down on my head. *RPGs*, I thought. *Fucking RPGs.*

The initial explosions were followed by a light spatter of AK-47 fire and then, after a second or two, the steady thumping of a DP machine gun. The fire was coming from the low hill to our front; Eward's point man had to have been within meters of its base. For a moment, there was no response from Bravo Two, and then isolated M16 shots rang out. My mind noted how quickly I'd become adept at, not only distinguishing the sounds of the various weapons, but the far more compelling difference between incoming and outgoing. It only takes once.

I twisted about and saw Helms low-crawling toward me. I scrabbled and slid over the few feet separating us; by the time I reached him he'd pulled the mike off his harness and was extending it out to me. There was nothing on the net yet; Eward wasn't saying anything, and no one else should be speaking at all. From behind me, I heard the crackle of M16 fire, and a moment later the heavier pounding of an M60. Denholm, or perhaps Littnan, was directing return fire from the top of the bluff. I got up, cautiously. Most of the enemy fire was being directed at Eward's people, primarily his lead squad, which was probably caught in the open in front of the tree line. A few rounds were now being directed at the bluff behind me: First Platoon was, for the moment, being ignored. There was a rather lengthy fold, almost deep enough to be called a ravine, a few meters to my front right. I yelled to Sergeant Eden, who led the point squad, to get them into that ravine. He nodded and began calling out, motioning his men forward and pointing. I heard boots behind me: Muldoon, his aid bag flopping, came running up and knelt beside me. I noticed he was still wearing his floppy jungle hat, and not his helmet. I opened my mouth to say something but thought better of it. Muldoon wasn't placed on this earth to conform.

"Any of our guys hit?" he asked.

I shook my head. Just then, Eward was talking to Littnan. There was a crackle of static, then a burst, harsh and loud; after that, Littnan's voice came through.

"...casualties, over?"

"Two Six. Affirmative. I got two people down, at least." Eward's voice was always high-pitched, but it was even and calm.

"Roger. I'll send the medics up. Are you still taking casualties? Can you hold your position?"

"No problem for the moment. Start sending ammo up, if you can. Over."

"Roger. Have you been able to spot where the fire's coming from?"

Two flat booms sounded just then: more RPGs. Eward paused while they exploded. "Yeah, they're on that hill in front of me, near the top...." There came a sudden, sharp burst of static of long duration, and then his voice became intelligible again. "...Mike sixty up to where I can return fire. Have we got some air support on the way?"

"Roger, Two Six. Bilk Two Three is upstairs right now. I've got some ammo on the way to you. Out."

The initial heavy volume of enemy fire had diminished somewhat; it was now sporadic and less concentrated. Occasional heavy bursts served to remind us that they hadn't gone away, and that in itself was cause for wonder. They had to be able to see that they were facing an entire battalion. I felt a tiny prickling at the base of my scalp.

Muldoon left my side a moment later, called forward by Stenger, Eward's medic. Sergeant Wright, carrying only his rifle, a canteen and a bandolier of ammo, came puffing up. He'd had to run all the way from the rear of the platoon column, still on the slope of the bluff. We brought them down into the saddle, and formed them into a rough U, with the open end facing the bluff. Fourth Platoon was still on that hill, returning fire, and I heard Littnan acknowledge that a platoon from Charlie Company had moved up alongside them. There was a small depression a few meters behind the ravine where Eden's squad was set up; it looked a likely spot for my CP group. A smooth-surfaced boulder about three feet high formed a perfect chair back for me; I sat on the ground in front of it; Helms crouched beside me, with his radio sitting on the ground between us. Moments later, Muldoon returned, having bandaged up one lightly wounded man — Whitfield, he thought.

"Three more," he added, in response to our looks. "One's bad, maybe two, but I didn't see them. Nobody dead, far as I know."

If all this sounds a bit relaxed, it was. There was, at the moment, nothing for us to do. I lit a cigarette, sat back and, as the twilight deepened, watched the war.

Eward, at the first enemy burst, had been in a bad position, very ticklish indeed. The enemy had, in effect, "crossed his T"— they'd had their unit on line across, facing his column that was moving toward them. The net effect, although it was momentary, was that they could fire all their weapons at his column but he could return fire with only three or four weapons, until he had time to bring the rest of the platoon up and spread them out across the base of the hill. So even though he probably outnumbered the enemy, he was effectively out-gunned for some time. It was a classic case of using terrain and tactical position to bring a numerically greater force to a halt; the entire battalion was bottlenecked, with Eward's platoon the unwilling cork. Had this been 1864 instead of 1969, Eward would have been in bad shape indeed. If it had been 1864, I wouldn't be sitting at my (relative) ease, smoking a Camel and making combat a spectator sport; I would have been maneuvering my platoon to flank the enemy.

But it *was* 1969. High above our head, Bilk Two Three, the Air Force spotter plane, a frail, clumsy, slow, straight-winged craft, circled lazily in the air above the hill. Dense smoke, dull red in the twilight, gushed from a small patch of brush a few feet from the hill itself. Eward had thrown a smoke canister. The lazy buzzing changed pitch; Bilk Two Three flew over our heads. We heard the thin hissing as a marking rocket was fired into the hilltop. There came a low, dull slam and white smoke boiled out of the heavy foliage about halfway up the hill. Bilk Two Three's engine noise changed again as he veered away and ambled slowly back to the north, behind us.

No more than a few seconds later, the world came to a sudden end for a number of North Vietnamese soldiers. The F105s came in from the southwest, making the safest possible approach, at right angles to the line between Eward and the enemy. Someone — Littnan, Black Jack, or perhaps the spotter — had decided not to use HE bombs, since Eward's front squad was no more than 50 meters from the suspected enemy positions. Instead, the first sleek, mottled-green shark-shape that flashed across the valley, almost unseen in the gloom, spat out 20mm cannon, red and fiery, streaking through the evening air into the hill. Tiny yellow flashes signaled their arrival. The next jet emitted a distinct click; a napalm bomb, dead black, tumbled out of the sky in an ungainly wobble, to hurtle into the trees. We heard a low-pitched "whump!!!" and a greasy orange, red and black ball of flame roiled and writhed across the hill.

Evening began to cast a grey hood over our heads. The greens and browns of the forest began to meld into a faintly speckled grey. From far off, we could hear the booming of artillery. Someone was in contact; perhaps, from the direction, the 2/506th. Around us, however, there was a deep silence, broken only now and then by the dying crackle and oily sputter of the napalm. The heavy afternoon downpour had left the forest too wet to burn. After a while, I could hear a low uncertain noise: men talking to each other in whispers, moving about cautiously, one eye on the uneven ground and another on the darkening hills around them. There were things to do. It was too dark, or would be soon, to check the hill out now; that would have to wait until tomorrow morning. Instead, we set up an uncertain, ragged NDP where we were. Charlie Company, with the battalion CP, was on the bluff behind us; Alpha was to our west and Delta to our north, so we were in no real peril, but it felt *strange*, unnatural even, to be setting up on an open piece of ground surrounded by higher hills. I don't know if that feeling is instinctive. Possibly not; our ancestors probably avoided the high ground, like as not; but for an infantryman placing himself in a basin surrounded by higher ground is unnerving.

Five of Eward's men had been hit, but two were lightly wounded with superficial scratches from a RPG fragments and were still with the platoon. Two had been hit by AK-47 fire, one in the leg and the other through the upper chest. They both would be fine. The fifth was carried through our position by three men holding a poncho; his head was turned away from me, but I could hear the intense grunts of pain as the others moved as quickly as they could across the rough terrain, jogging him up and down. His right leg was gone from the knee down; someone had laid his right boot, with shards of pale red flesh coating the top, on the poncho, alongside his left leg. The boot flopped and jiggled crazily as the stretcher-bearers hurried by. I stared at it with cold eyes. *RPGs,* I thought bitterly. *Fucking RPGs.*

YC317992; 10 May: 2000

The night passed slowly. We hadn't had a chance to set up properly; we weren't dug in, our positions were haphazard and unplanned and no claymores, trip flares or other defensive measures had been placed. We hadn't had the time. C-rations were eaten cold that night, and few of us got any sleep. Sergeant Wright and I got none at all, because we spent a good portion of the night checking the perimeter or talking to our LP, which had been placed as far up the slope of the hill before us as we could, which wasn't, after all, very far. After dark, four men with a radio and a high degree of apprehension had moved up a trail leading up toward the hilltop; they had gotten perhaps 50 meters before moving off the trail into a dense stand of bamboo before setting up.

The platoon, other than the LP, was quiet and not overtly nervous or jumpy, but there was an unmistakable tension or expectancy in the air; it ran through us like a low-voltage current. Surprisingly, Muldoon and Helms showed it the most. Helms was normally placid and imperturbable, and Muldoon always presented a defiantly insouciant face to all circumstances. Tonight, however, Dennis was tight-lipped and downcast, uncharacteristically fidgeting with the radio microphone throughout the night. Muldoon sat alongside of me, huddled in his rain jacket, knees drawn up tight to his chest and cradled in his arms. For a long time we just sat there; I was listening to the radio, silent except for an occasional hiss; he stared off into some place only he could see. I could hear his shallow breathing. The night was cool and damp. The sun had never reappeared after the afternoon's heavy rain, so nothing had dried out and the moisture clung to everything: grass, leaves, our gear and us. I felt the tiny beads of dew forming inside the collar of my jacket. Overhead, the stars began to gleam and glitter in the black velvet sky; the clouds had at last moved back to the west.

"Bad-ass area, ain't it?" Muldoon broke his silence.

"Seems to be," I agreed.

There was another silence for a few minutes. I heard Helms accidentally break squelch on the radio, and his instant cluck of dismay. Gradually, the silence began to fill up with sounds; the cheeps and squawks and hoots and caws and soft-voiced twittering: The sound of a mountain forest; familiar, reassuring, friendly and safe.

"This look rough to you, Lieutenant?"

"Maybe," I said. One of the things I loved about both Muldoon and Helms was that nothing I said to them at such moments ever made its way to the others in the platoon.

"What's gonna happen tomorrow? You know?"

I grunted. I didn't want to think about tomorrow. Sufficient unto the day.... Then I remembered: We hadn't recited the litany.

"Well, Francis; another night in Viet Nam," I murmured.

Muldoon didn't respond. He was unusually serious. "This area ... it just *feels* different, you know? I mean, back across there," he waved in the general direction of the valley to our east, "on that goddamned hill there; that was— well, that was different. I mean, we were fighting, but...." He jerked his shoulders forward in irritation. "This just seems different," he repeated. "I just got this feeling someone's fixing to bringing a bag o' shit on our heads."

I glanced at him out of the corner of my eye. In the darkness, he was a huddled shape and nothing more, save where the faint starlight glinted off the parchment-like skin of his cheekbones. He seemed to want me to answer him. He seemed to need — not reassurance: What could I say? Tell him the war would end tonight? Tell him he was immortal?—but acknowledgement. He needed to hear from me that I— that we all— shared his fear. Muldoon was one of the bravest men I've ever met, a man of fierce and uncompromising independence and remarkable pugnacity, and yet even such a man as he needed to know that he was not alone.

The old refrain is that there are no atheists in foxholes. That's nonsense. They are there by the millions. There is little in combat that will lead one to look upon the Creator with favor. What can't be found there, instead, is the individualist, the selfish, the self-consumed, the self-centered, the aloof loner. Such a man cannot long survive. The terror of combat cannot be explained by the fear of death. There are worse things. The world can suddenly become a very cold place, like a northern steppe on a winter night: fear and doubt, like the glacial fingers of the north wind, begin to brush, lightly at first, along a man's spine; touching him fleetingly here, clutching painfully there. Soon or late, he realizes he is in the grip of a killing cold. He needs warmth, a fire, to survive: His discipline, his training, his duty, honor and country, his family and ultimately the very oak of his manhood are thrown into the blaze, but they are not enough to save him. At the end, he needs the warmth of his comrades. Otherwise, all he will have with which to face the cold dark will be his own spent soul.

Muldoon sat, waiting.

I stared at the dark forest; it was a charcoal grey against the coal black of the sky. I clapped him lightly on the shoulder. "We'll be okay. I don't like what we've seen so far, either, but what the hell. We'll just have to bring a bag of shit over *his* head."

"Huh." Muldoon paused. "One bag o' shit plus one bag o' shit equals *two* bags o' shit, right?"

"You got it."

"Let's just call it even. We won't start nothin' if they don't."

I grinned. "Where's the fun in that?"

He sighed. "You know what's funny, Lieutenant? I usta sit on my back porch at the house. All I can see from there is this goddamn dirty alley, an' this goddamn dirty smoke from the plant just up the hill. I'm sippin' a brew or two, an' my girl's standin' there, jawin' about my drinkin' ... Christ, she *never* shut up about that. I remember sittin' there thinkin', man, ain't nothin' I hate more than this. Starin' at that fuckin' alley, and listenin' to her mouth. I just had to get outta there." He laughed softly. "But you know what? If I was back there ... I'd sit there, and look at that fuckin' alley with all the fuckin' garbage, and the smell, and listen to her all goddamn *day*, and I'd have a fuckin' smile on my face."

I grinned. "And you'd drink your beer, wouldn't you."

"Lieutenant," Muldoon said reverently, "I'd drink the fuckin' brewery *dry*."

"Good night, Francis."

"Good night, sir."

27

The Broken Strap

YC319993; 11 May 1969; 0630–1200

The earth's rotation being what it is, morning had to come around sooner or later; it did so a little after 0600, with a smoky, dim sunrise. Overhead was clear, but evidently the storm clouds still lingered over the coastal plain to our east. Littnan called me over to his CP. Shaved and looking fresh, he nodded as I joined him. The radios were already crackling and hissing with traffic, and Price and Conzoner were busy monitoring them.

"I want you to take the point today, Frank," he said, with no preliminary. "Go up that hill there, and see what you can find, and then after that there's a ridge that seems to head in the direction we want. If all goes right, we should be on top of Dong Ap Bia by 1400."

I pulled out my map and opened it to the proper fold. Dong Ap Bia was at the very bottom of the sheet, only a centimeter or two above the end of the white border. I looked at the ridges and valleys on the map, and then at the terrain around me. The hill to our front obscured most of it, however. I studied the map for another moment or so.

"Okay," I said finally, pointing a finger, "I guess we'll turn south once we reach the top; follow the ridge for about, oh, say 400 meters until we reach this peak,"—I pointed to a hilltop at 320988—"turn slightly southeast and follow that; we'll approach the top of Ap Bia from the northwest and end up just south of Hill 937."

Littnan nodded agreement. "Black Jack's up in his LOH already, reconning the area. He says there are several large trails leading up to the top, coming from the west. If you find one, use it, but be careful. The word is they use booby traps in this area."

"Roger. When do you want me to move?"

He glanced at his watch. "It's 0645. Have your men eaten yet?"

"They're doing that now. We can be ready to go in ten minutes."

"Okay." Another look at his watch: "0700, then. Frank—take it real easy moving up that hill. Charlie's had all night to put in a surprise or two for you."

"Yeah. I know. Okay—ten minutes."

It was more like 45 minutes. We were ready; the battalion staff wasn't. Someone had the idea that perhaps we should wait until a pair of Cobras shredded the hill again, just in case the NVA had returned there during the night. I was agreeable. I would have been amenable to the idea of having a squadron of B52s carpet-bomb every inch of my planned route, that day and all the rest of my days in country. Ordnance, I reflected, was not only cheap but manufacturing it stimulated the economy.

So we sat, packs on our backs, already in file, and watched as the Cobras made their deadly, snarling runs. The sun was just showing itself over the rim of the ridge to our east when they finished. Littnan, who had left his CP a moment before to stand next to me, gave me a brief nod. It was by now well past 0730.

Terry Gann was the point man, and Phil Nelson, carrying his 90mm strapped across his back, was the slack. Gann moved into the belt of trees at the base of the hill and disappeared from view; a few seconds later Nelson followed him. I was about ten meters behind him; I stepped through the clinging vines and onto a broad, smooth, man-made trail. Nelson wasn't visible; the trail bent sharply to the right as it ascended. After I made the turn, I could see Gann, some 15 meters ahead of me. He was pacing slowly up the path, his head turning in careful, measured increments from side to side, with a determined economy of movement. I could hear the slight rustle and creak as his pack jogged slowly up and down on its harness. Nelson, consciously or not, was orchestrating his movements with Gann's: as Terry moved his head to the right, he would look to the left. I kept my eyes on Gann and Nelson. I was too far back, and the growth too thick, for me to spot anything they missed.

The vegetation on the slope was the usual mixture of small trees, bushes and vines. Halfway to the summit, however, we entered a dense thicket of bamboo, through which the trail, narrowed a bit, led. Gann had taken perhaps four or five steps when he halted abruptly; he gave no signal and remained standing, so I did too. Automatically, my hand reached back to take the mike from Helms, but I waved it off as I saw Gann beckon me with his arm. He didn't look back at me, but kept his eyes to his front. Stepping by Nelson, who'd sunk to one knee with his rifle at the ready position, I moved to Gann's side.

The path we were following penetrated the thicket for perhaps eight or ten meters. Presumably, it went all the way through, but at that point the bamboo lay across the path in swathes, forming a slanting roof about four or five feet high. Some of the stalks were broken off, others partially uprooted, and others still had simply been pushed down. A few were singed or charred. This was unquestionably the result of last night's F105 strike. I gave a quick glance around me. Off the path, the bamboo stood in dense patches, entwined with creepers, wines and thorn bushes. We learned the hard way how difficult it was to move through bamboo. Of course, I could always return to the bottom of the hill and skirt its base to one side or another, but considering that this was where the enemy fire had come from last night, I didn't believe Black Jack would approve. Nelson made a face: He'd just come to the same conclusion. I shrugged. There was nothing else for us to do but get on our hands and knees and crawl underneath the stuff. How far it extended, I couldn't guess, but I hoped it wouldn't be for more than a few meters. I sent word back for two riflemen to stand there and cover the rest of the platoon as we crawled through. I also called Littnan to tell him why we had slowed, and then gave Gann the nod to go ahead.

Gann blew out his cheeks, made a face of his own, dropped to his knees and then began crawling slowly along the path, rifle still held in one hand. Nelson, his 90mm strapped vertically on his pack, allowed him to get a several meters ahead of him before he too started on his hands and knees. I squatted in the dirt and watched him; the path turned sharply right after a few meters, and after he made that turn I followed.

I was a few inches shorter than Gann, and had no 90mm sticking up over my head, so I was able to duck-walk; faster but a bit more taxing and painful. After that first bend, the path turned almost immediately back to the left, and it was here that I almost bumped into Nelson, who'd halted. I dropped out of my squat to my knees with a soft grunt of relief; even after only a few meters, duck walking with almost 100 pounds on my back had turned my knees and thighs to jelly. I looked up the trail to see what was holding us up but at the moment the only thing I could see was Nelson's rear end topped by the barrel of his ninety, peering at me like an alien Cyclops. Then Nelson sat back on his knees, resting his rear end on his heels, and I could see past him.

The bamboo, thicker and more tangled than ever, had here been knocked down almost parallel to the ground; it formed a tunnel about 18 inches high. Gann had already flopped onto his belly and was now squirming along the ground; the top of his rucksack cleared the bamboo by only a couple of inches. His rifle was laid uselessly across the crook of his elbows; I remembered too late that I should have reminded him to put his safety on. Gann was both experienced and intelligent, and had probably already done so, but it was my job to remember things like that in time. I tapped Nelson on the shoulder and reminded him; he nodded and did so. He began to follow Gann, stopped, backed up into me, and then went through a series of impossible contortions in that small space, to remove his backpack. There was no way he was getting the Ninety through that tunnel. Clifton, his loader and ammo bearer, was behind Helms and Brown in file; he'd grab Phil's pack and drag it behind him, if needed. Taking a deep breath, Nelson got on his belly and began crawling; I watched as his boots, scuffling and scrabbling in the dirt, disappeared.

I drew a breath of my own, muttered a curse, and got on my stomach. Moving like this was a reminder of OCS; the pain was just as sharp, but at least here it served as an antidote to the fear, of which there was sufficient. We were, for the moment, helpless; we were crawling head first into a low and narrow tunnel, able to see only a few feet ahead of us, and if by chance we *did* see something there'd be little we could do about it. As usual, I relied on my ears, but there was little to hear: the noise of our own bodies scraping across the ground, the distant groan and whump of artillery, the heavy drone of helicopters somewhere to our south and an occasional chirp or hoot from a forest bird. Sweat began to pour from my head and face. My neck muscles hurt from the strain of holding my head back; I dropped my head to a more comfortable angle. What was I going to look at anyway, except for the rutted soles of Nelson's boots?

It wasn't my ears; it was my nose that warned me of what lay ahead. I suddenly smelled a strong, foul sweetish odor. By now, I knew it well. I brought my head up just in time to avoid bumping into Nelson; he was on one knee, staring, rifle held slackly in one hand. Just past my head, the bamboo tunnel ended.

"Jesus, Lieutenant," he called back over his shoulder.

"Let me through," I replied. He twisted to one side and I squeezed past him. The bamboo just past him, where Gann was crouched, was here again a lean-to, with the stalks four or five feet above the ground. After that harrowing tunnel, this seemed almost cathedral-like. The early morning sun glistened on the dew still clinging to the sides of the stalks. There was a heavy drone in the air, but it wasn't the distant Hueys. Flies: hundreds of them; faithful attendants to the dead.

Nelson pointed unnecessarily to the ground. Four NVA lay there, huddled in patches and rags, hued with the colors of death: grayish yellow, fly-black, gristly maggot-white and old, spent brown. There was a rustling, creaking sound behind me: Helms had moved up next to me. Automatically, he held out the mike. I pushed my helmet back on my head, placed the receiver to my ear, thumbed the switch and spoke.

"Bravo Six, this is One Six.... We're in a patch of bamboo on top of the hill right in front of you. We've got four NVA bodies here. From the looks of them, they got hit by that air strike last night."

"Roger. Any weapons or documents?"

"We're checking now. None in sight."

Sergeant Hyde brought some more men up and placed them farther up the trail as security. While he was doing that, I called Sergeant Wright to make sure he knew what was happening. Wright always monitored his radio, but you never knew. Then Nelson, Muldoon and I began to search the bodies.

The man I was kneeling beside had had his chest blown apart by a 20mm round; it gaped open, brown and purple and oyster shell white. I tried not to breathe through my nose, but that didn't help much; the stench was in the air and I couldn't avoid it. His head was twisted to one side, away from me. The hair along the back of his neck was short and cut in an even line. The khaki was new, still fresh and relatively unsoiled; so were his sandals. I picked up a grey, half-clenched hand; there were no scratches or cuts and the fingernails were clipped. The left side of his shirt had been obliterated by the cannon round, but the right side, with its pocket, was intact. I unbuttoned the pocket and found a sheaf of papers, all handwritten, in a small plastic bag. There were six of them, with what seemed to be dates in one upper corner and a signature at the bottom. The handwriting and the signature, to my untrained eye, seemed to be the same: These were letters he'd written and had been planning to mail.

There was also some money, in blue and red bank notes from the People's Democratic Republic; about 100 Dong. I turned my head, took a breath, turned back and carefully flipped him over, but his pants pockets had nothing in them. I let his body fall back; his head flopped to one side again. I glanced around. The others had finished their search and were holding up the contents of the dead men's pockets: some more letters, some documents, a comb, a couple of packs of cigarettes, a plain metal lighter, two ball point pens, a small roll of string and a very small penknife.

I called Littnan again. "No weapons, but here's what we got: Fresh haircuts, clean clothes, money — these guys just got here from Laos or the North." Of course, that, and a quarter, would buy you nothing at all. In this area, the NVA was *always* just getting back from Laos or the North. I took a quick second glance at the letters I held. "Six different letters, six different dates; looks like they were all addressed to the same person. Figure they've been in the area a minimum of a week, then."

"Roger. Could be. Anything else?" Littnan didn't sound too impressed by my deductions.

"Affirmative. Quite a bit more: Some documents and other stuff."

"Okay. Pass it all on back here; that'll save time. S2 wants it ASAP. Anything else?"

"Yeah. I'm moving on; these guys are a bit too ripe for my taste."

"Roger. Go ahead. Is there a way around that spot?"

"Negative. Only if you circle the base of the hill and come up from the west."

"Roger. Out."

I gave the signal to Gann to start moving. Helms had taken a large plastic bag and was collecting the material. I handed him the letters and glanced back down at the dead man. Despite my hurry to get away from the charnel smell and my cramped, uncomfortable crouch, I paused and stared at him for a moment. I felt a pang of pity. Not at his death; death, after all, belongs to us all. He had been trying to kill us, and we had killed him first. In another hour, that could be my body lying on the ground in an angular and flaccid heap. It was the thought of the letters; letters that would now never reach home. For some reason, that bothered me. The evil of war lies not in the acts of killing or dying, but in the thousands of casual knife-thrusts into the human spirit: The mother who, torn between abject grief and raging disbelief, stares, with rigid back and trembling chin, at the two somber strangers standing at her door; the ashen-faced father who cannot bring himself, even weeks later, to look at the bedraggled, neglected basketball net, where he and his son had played a thousand hilarious, incompetent but fierce games of one-on-one; the wife, in tearless bemusement, who prepares *his* favorite meal, and sets places for four when there are only three — but what else can she do?— and the child who stares at a picture on a mantle, a picture of a stranger who has never held her or talked to her or even seen her.

And all of these — the parent, the wife, the child — were now at home, waiting, waiting for the letter, a letter much like the ones I held in my hand just now; the one tangible proof that their son or husband or father was still a part of their world. Someone, I thought, as I placed the letters in Helms' bag, someone is waiting for these and will never see them — worse, will never even know they've been written. That was the greater evil than killing him.

I got up and gave the body one last glance. *I'm sorry. I wish that I didn't have to do this. But — truthfully — I would rather it is your mother or your wife who grieves, and not mine.*

A few meters up the path, the bamboo at last was lifted from the path, and we could walk upright. We all stretched cramped, sore muscles. A few meters beyond that, the bamboo disappeared entirely, replaced by the usual small trees and vines, as it continued its ascent of the hill. Twenty minutes later we reached the top of the ridge, a broad, flat hilltop; the path changed direction sharply, to the south. Soon after that, Gann halted. The trail, which up to now had been well-defined but relatively narrow, broadened out into what amounted to a road in these parts, some four or five feet across. But Gann wasn't stopping because of that; he, and now Nelson, were looking down at the path. I moved up beside them and saw what they were looking at: a broad, foot-long streak of dried blood. I called up Sergeant Hyde; he and Nelson, our two best trackers, knelt beside it and examined it and the surrounding area. I waited while they had a good, long look. Finally, Hyde turned to me.

"Old. Last night, I'd say. There's another one up there, and some foot prints."

"Okay. That blood's from one man? Or more?"

He shrugged. "Hard to say. Plenty of prints, though."

Nelson nodded. "Three or four, I guess. But the blood's from one man. These two patches are in a line, and ain't but one set of prints leadin' from one to the other."

I nodded. I decided to keep Gann on point, because I wanted him to concentrate on the *now*, while Nelson tried to decipher what had happened earlier. I also asked Hyde to move up to a position right behind Helms. It didn't occur to me until later that this was Nathan's last week in the field — he was going home, or at least to Bien Hoa, in a few days.

The thick, dense vegetation flanking the path disappeared after a couple of hundred meters; now we were moving through huge grey trunks, towering over our heads. These were the ironwood and mahogany trees, the largest I'd ever seen. The sun was now overhead, but the forest floor, shaded by the massive crowns, was hushed and gloomy; only here and there could you see a slender shaft of sunlight. I felt uneasy and insecure; this place was too open, too exposed. Visibility to either side and to the front was now as much as 50 or even 100 meters, which, in the mountain forests of Viet Nam, is the equivalent of an Illinois prairie. I didn't like it.

We found traces of blood all along the way; at one spot, Nelson and Hyde agreed, someone had stopped, perhaps to rest, perhaps — there was a large pool of blood — to die. Now Nelson agreed that there had been more than one man wounded; there was too much blood, and he and Hyde found several different trails of it. We kept finding footprints, a torn piece of gauze, a bloodstained scrap of khaki, a discarded sandal and even, at one spot, a few grains of uncooked rice. Nelson turned his broad warrior face toward me, shaking his head.

"Like following a fuckin' street sign," he muttered.

"Like, 'this way, dummy!'" I agreed.

"Yeah. They was in a hurry an' all, but ... God *damn*!"

I looked at my watch, surprised to see that it was already 1130. We'd come about 400 meters; the hilltop I'd pointed out to Littnan was just ahead of us. We went on for another 50 meters or so, taking our time — the more debris and tracks we found on that trail, the more cautious I became — before Littnan called to tell me to set up at the next suitable spot. Moments later we set up on the hilltop; Hyde, Dickerson and Eden spread their squads out in a security perimeter, and I set the CP group right on the trail itself.

Littnan joined me a few minutes later; Eward and Denholm were moving their troops into place behind us. "We'll take a quick break here, Frank," he said, dropping his pack with a satisfied grunt. "No more than 30 minutes. Black Jack's getting impatient. He wants us up there by 1500."

I looked at my watch. It was 1225. Half-hour for lunch ... two hours to cover the 800 meters ... "Okay, but ... have you been checking the trail out as you came up?"

He removed his helmet. Dark hair glistened with sweat. "Uhhm. You think we're heading into trouble?"

I shrugged. "Sergeant Hyde and Nelson are experienced men, and they don't like what they're seeing. Neither do I. Plenty of signs, plenty of blood. Tracks, all headed down this path."

Littnan nodded and glanced up at the sky. What could be seen of it was now a dark, ominous grey. "Rain's on the way." He looked at his watch. "It's about half a klick to this ridge here, right?" He pointed to a flat hilltop at 323984. His face furrowed in thought. "Send a recon — squad-size — down the trail, to check that out."

I looked at my watch in turn. "If I do, we'll be here for more than 30 minutes."

He shrugged in turn. "I know. I'll hold off Black Jack. Let's move."

Hyde was my best squad leader, but I didn't want to use him. For one thing, he had only days left before leaving; for another, I needed him and Nelson for point when we started back up, and they needed rest. I decided on Dickerson; young and inexperienced as he was, he had some good, savvy men in his squad and that would count for a lot. I walked over to his sector to give him the good news. He was obviously unhappy about it — the rain was on its way, and they had just started chowing down — but he had his men up and ready within a couple of minutes. I showed him on the map where I wanted him to go, gave him some general instructions, and then sent him on his way.

The storm came some 20 minutes later. This wasn't the monsoon; those rains came in February, and lasted for days at a time. This was a daily storm that swept in from the west, and it was a deluge. The worst rain I've ever endured was in Panama; that was not so much rain as an inverted lake. This was close. There was no avoiding this at all. All we could do was sit or stand quietly while the cold water flooded down our backs and chests; it streamed off our helmets in a continuous waterfall. Wind cut through the trees in thin, cold gusts, whipping the water into our faces. Water began to track slowly down every fold and crevice in our bodies, reaching places I would have sworn would be impossible. Those of us who had donned rain jackets soon found ourselves as wet as the others, with the added discomfort of sweat. Those who hadn't finished eating gave up and threw what was left away: The rain diluted whatever you were holding into a tasteless soup within seconds.

It lasted only about 20 minutes, but that was long enough to make the trail we were following a shallow pond, with a thin layer of water over an inch or more of sour, dun-colored mud. It ended as abruptly as it had started. One moment, it was falling with a continuous drumming roar, and the next there was nothing more than the patter of droplets falling on the leaves. That never stopped; for the rest of the afternoon, the huge crowns overhead would drip down onto the smaller plants below.

Packs, weapons, clothing — everything was not only soaked but spattered with the mud. Bodies were either chilled by the rain or overheated by the rain jackets. No one was comfortable. The only antidote to this was to move, but we couldn't do that until Dickerson returned. A few minutes later, Bresina, his point man, appeared on the trail, looking bedraggled and relieved. From me down to the newest rifleman, the disquieting aura of menace coming from the trees and ridges around us was palpable.

Dickerson had made it all the way down to the ridge we were interested in, some 500 meters to our south. Fifty meters before that ridge, he said, the trail doglegged to the southwest, and then branched; the right hand leg veered sharply to the southwest, and appeared to continue along a series of low hillocks and dales, partly wooded. The left branch turned back to a southeast heading and began almost immediately to ascend the ridge. He hadn't gone beyond that point, but he was sure it went on in a fairly straight line up to the peak of the mountain.

They had encountered the same signs Gann, Nelson and Hyde had earlier, except that the heavy rain had washed away the blood trails. It was becoming a bit too much.

I reported this back to Littnan but he let it go without comment. In any case, it made no real difference; we had to move out regardless. His thoughts were the same: "Move out, Frank. With all deliberate speed."

"Roger. All deliberate speed." I couldn't tell whether Littnan, who rarely joked, was being serious.

"Let's go," I said to the squad leaders, who by now had gathered around me. "Eden, you take point." I had changed my mind about putting Nelson and Gann up front again. Hell, with the red carpet the NVA had rolled out for us, Mr. Magoo could follow the trail. "Nate, you're next. Dick, you take up the rear. Good job, by the way."

I reached down, shrugged on my own gear, hunching my shoulders in an effort to distribute the 90 or so pounds as comfortably as possible across my shoulders. As I did so, I heard Helms emit a soft, hissing sound of disgust. Turning, I saw him kneeling by his pack, frowning at a ragged-edged strap in his hand; the rest of it dangled from

27. The Broken Strap

the lower end of his rucksack. It was one of the two holding his radio in place; his PRC25 sagged drunkenly to one side.

"Got something to fix it with?" I asked.

"Yes, sir," he mumbled, jerking open his rucksack. "Take a minute or two."

"Okay." The rest of the platoon was now strung out behind us, waiting patiently. I made a face. Littnan was moving up the trail toward us, as impassive as ever.

"Problem?" he asked.

I indicated the strap. "He's fixing it now. Should just take a minute or two."

Littnan grunted. "Okay. Go ahead. But I can't wait. I'm going to put Denholm on point." He turned away. His voice was cool and even, but I felt a hot blush on the back of my neck. When the CO asks if you're ready and you say yes, you'd better *be* ready. This was a Dickson-class screw-up.

28

The Ordeal of Bravo Four Six

YC325981; 11 May 1969; 1330–1730

Chuck Denholm walked by me as his platoon filed past. He gave me a slow wink and shook his head, smirking. I dreaded our next talk; if I'd made the mental comparison to Dickson, so would he, and the grief I'd take over the strap would be endless. He and his men began sloshing down the still-streaming trail. I waited as the rest of Fourth Platoon moved through, and then Littnan's CP group; when Peters, Russ Crenshaw's RTO, passed me, I signaled for Hernandez and Ulrich to fall in ahead of me, and we began to follow.

The deluge had washed away the blood and almost all the tracks, leaving only here or there a dimple or some discarded gear. The trail itself, though, continued broad and smooth. The sun occasionally broke through the still-heavy cloud cover, but the huge ironwood and mahogany trees filtered out even direct sunlight, leaving the forest floor a gloomy grey-green. The ground cover was thin and sparse; visibility often reached 100, even 200 meters, through the imposing grey, dun and brown boles. The forest was nebulous, smoke-green, crepuscular; rainwater still dripped in whispery patter all around us. And it was hot again.

Chuck initially moved out quickly. The trail, on leaving the low hilltop, dipped down into a broad, relatively flat and open saddle, which became a series of moderate rises and dips. We covered about 200 or 300 meters this way, in about 20 minutes. It was just past 1400: It appeared we'd make Black Jack's 1500 deadline with ease. Then I saw Ulrich come to a halt in front of me.

I had nothing to do but stand, wait and speculate. Chuck Denholm was now controlling the company's movement. Why was he stopped? The radio was no help; Chuck wasn't using it. Time passed. If Black Jack had been hoping for faster progress with Chuck in the lead, he was to be disappointed. Denholm was no more eager to rush into an ambush than I'd been. True, nothing was visible; the blood and footprints we'd been following were gone, scrubbed away by the downpour; we had seen no bunkers, no hutches, no spider holes— nothing tangible. But I could tell, simply by the way the men held their weapons and looked around, constantly pivoting their heads from side to side, walking with short, slow, controlled steps, that everyone felt the presence of the enemy. He was here, somewhere close.

Movement ahead, and then another long stop; the process repeated itself three or four times. By now, it was 1500; we'd moved perhaps another 200 meters in an hour. The path had now begun to climb a long, gentle slope. Word began to filter back, passed in whispered phrases from man to man: Fourth Platoon had found several footprints—*in* the mud. Someone had walked that within the last hour or so. The tension, already high, increased.

I began to feel tired: The pack dragged at me, the stop-and-go pace took far more energy than steady walking, and the afternoon heat, even with the sun behind the clouds, was sapping my energy. I noticed the silence; the forest was seldom very noisy at mid-day, but this was a much deeper silence than usual; it had a hollow vastness to it, like a cathedral in that moment just before the Angelus.

Suddenly there was a stir up ahead; I saw Littnan reach back for his mike. I was too far away to hear what he said, but he was speaking emphatically and forcefully. I turned to Helms with my hand out, but before he could hand me the mike, a burst of shots ripped the air. I whirled back around, crouching, uncertain whether to hit the ground or not. We all held that pose, between standing and squatting, while more shots rang out. These were unquestionably M16, and outgoing. Helms reached my side, the proffered mike in his hand. His pale, choirboy face was set and impassive, but his eyes asked a question: *What's going on?* The same look was in Ulrich's eyes, and Hernandez's. And in mine, probably.

The radio fell silent; I had missed the brief broadcast. Whatever Denholm was doing, he wasn't talking about it. My mind, with nothing useful to occupy it, dwelt on the initial burst; it had taken me off-guard, and my mind hadn't quite grasped the sound. Everything since then, I knew, had been M16, but were the first three or four rounds AK-47? I couldn't swear to it. I realized suddenly that I was staring at Littnan, less than 30 meters away. He was standing in the infantry officer's classic pose, with a mike in each ear. If I wanted to know what was going on, I thought, why not just ask him. He's the CO. He probably knows. True, I might end up with a blistering for leaving my platoon and my radio, but what the hell. Life is risk.

Littnan gave me a brief, cool glance as I walked up; he was speaking, alternately, into each mike. I waited patiently. There were no more shots, but overhead I could hear the high-pitched buzz of a LOH: Black Jack — or someone — was up there, reconning the area in front of us. This couldn't have been of much use: The massive trees were well-spaced, but their crowns had spread voraciously, to cover every square inch of available area, 100 feet and more above ground. From the air, I knew, this ridge and the surrounding hills would be nothing more than a vast sea of dark green.

The CO finished with the radio, handed the mikes back to Conzoner and Price, looked at me, then back at my platoon, and then back to me, with a slightly raised eyebrow. "You lost, Frank?" he asked pointedly.

"Yes, sir. Totally. I'd just like to know what's going on."

He shrugged. "I don't know. I'm beginning to wonder myself. Fourth Platoon's point man was coming up on that trail junction your squad leader told you about, and two NVA popped up from the upper trail and fired off a round or two. Then they took off right on up the ridge."

"We didn't hit anything?"

"No. Those gooks didn't stay around long enough to hit or be hit." His cool grey eyes flickered at me askance. "They *are* beginning to make it pretty obvious, aren't they?"

"More road signs." I made a face. "Question number one: Are they leading us into or away from something?"

"Good question, that. Black Jack wants us to move." His lips flickered with the ghost of a smile. "With all deliberate speed."

"Excelsior," I muttered. "Damn...."

"I told Denholm to make sure he knows what he's getting into before he makes a move."

"Who's he got on point?"

"McCarrell."

I nodded. I knew McCarrell from the days on Hill 1485; he'd been one of the Fourth Platoon troopers up there with me. I remembered him as a tall, rangy, dark-haired boy with an easy smile and a willingness to work hard. I hoped he'd make it, but walking point in the A Shau isn't the safest thing in the world to do.

I passed on what I knew to the platoon when I returned; nothing irks troops as much as being kept in the dark while things happened. Not unreasonably, they felt that if they were going to get killed in the next few minutes, they'd at least like to know who and what. The line began to move a moment or so later, but we'd gone less than 50 meters before we straggled to another halt. I felt a flicker of annoyance. What the hell was happening? Then I relaxed and mentally shrugged. At least I didn't have to worry about walking into a death trap. Chuck Denholm knew more than I did at this moment, but I would bet he was sweating a lot more than I was.

No word came down on why we'd stopped, and before much time had passed, we began moving again. I looked up and down the line. Usually, men on patrol carried their M16s balanced in one hand, leaving the other free to fend off branches, vines or thorn stalks. Today, every man I saw was carrying his rifle at the port arms position — up across the chest — with his finger and thumb on the trigger and safety. I wouldn't have been surprised to find out that quite a few of them, in defiance of standing orders, had already chambered a round. Even a neophyte, even a reporter, even a Secretary of Defense, should have been able to tell the difference between our normal patrol movement and how we were acting just now.

1545: Our section of the column reached the trail junction. To the right, one trail meandered across a shallow valley, skirting, on the east side, thick, tangled vegetation,

28. The Ordeal of Bravo Four Six

until it lost itself in a series of shallow ridges, folds and hillocks to our southwest. Behind all that, indistinct in the gloomy, wet air, were the mountains of Laos. But the company had turned left at this point, to the southeast. Here, the trail began what was at first a gradual climb along a broad, rounded ridge. I looked at the map again: We were at 322984. This ridge eventually steepened and narrowed into a true razorback, until it reached the top of Hill 937 — Dong Ap Bia.

Standing in the middle of the junction, in the very crook of the Y, like a great grey sentinel, stood a huge mahogany tree. As I passed it, I happened to look up. A foot or so over my head a heavy cylindrical object, a contrasting light green in color, stuck out of the heart of the tree. My heart skipped a beat when I saw it for what it was: an unexploded RPG. The first four or five inches had penetrated the hard, living wood. I turned to bring it to Helms' attention, but he'd already seen it; he was standing still, wide-eyed, staring at it. It hadn't been there long; the paint and surface were too clean and new. It certainly got our attention.

I was perhaps 20 meters past the junction when heavy fire broke out ahead of us. I reached back for the mike and Helms placed it in my hand. I listened a minute and was reassured. Handing it back to Helms, I told him to pass it on: Denholm's platoon was reconning by fire — spraying the trail and surrounding vegetation with a burst of M16 and M60 fire, to prematurely trigger any potential ambush. Sometimes, it worked. Even when it didn't, you felt better doing it. There was no question about giving our position away: Every instinct we had told us the enemy was watching us and knew exactly where we were.

More time passed: It was now 1600, a full hour past Black Jack's deadline, and we were still several hundred meters from the summit. To our right, the ridge flank now began to get both steeper and more thickly vegetated. To our left a few of the massive hardwoods still dominated a gentler slope. But with each meter the ridge became narrower and steeper; gradually the right flank became more and more hidden by increasingly dense growth. Even on the other side, as the last of the ironwoods was left behind, the terrain became dominated by the standard triple canopy growth: the tall, narrow hardwoods and conifers, the mid-level saplings and tall bushes and, at ground level, the impenetrable thickets, vines, creepers and thorny brush. After another hundred meters, we found ourselves on a true razorback; the path had narrowed to less than a meter, and the slopes on either side were precipitous and so densely tangled as to be for all practical purposes a solid wall.

YC323984

It was here, at about 1620, that we were halted once again. Fourth Platoon was reconning by fire, but no word came about anything else. We began to move forward in a brief series of starts and stops. Helms picked up his mike, held it to his ear and then replaced it. Moving up a few feet, he muttered in my ear: "Four Six just told the Old Man they've spotted a clearing up ahead. He's checking it out now. He says he's about 50 meters from the top."

I nodded. It was now 1630. Sergeant Wright, minus pack and most of his gear, shouldered his way up the trail to my side; one of the few times he'd ever left his post at the rear of the platoon column. He nodded at the unseen hilltop above us.

"How much longer will it be, Lieutenant?"

"Fourth Platoon's about 50 meters below the summit, I hear. Maybe another 15, 20 minutes."

He nodded his massive brown head. "Boys in the back of the bus are gettin' antsy. Wonderin' whether we'll make it up there before dark."

"Me too." I noticed that my throat and mouth were dry but my palms and neck sweaty. It's called fear.

Wright wasn't looking at me; his eyes were on the hill, which from here was a still vaguely sensed mass behind the dull green branches overhead. He seemed to have read my thoughts.

"Something," he said quietly, "just ain't right."

Helms tapped me on the shoulder and handed me the mike. "Black Jack's on the company net, raising hell with the Old Man about taking so long."

I placed the receiver to my ear. Out of the corner of my eye I saw Wright leave, on his way back down the trail.

" what's up there?" Littnan's voice boomed into my ear, too loudly. I motioned for Helms to turn the volume down.

"Four Six. Can't say. We're in this clearing. The trail kind of jogs to the left a bit, and then back to the right. Goes up east-southeast, looks like. There's another small knoll to our left, and a saddle in between."

"Roger. Can you see the top of the hill from where you are?"

"Negative. Not quite. It's behind these two knolls. But I don't think it's more than 100 meters from here. The trail seems to lead right up to it."

"This is Six. Okay. Good. Be careful in that clearing. See anything at all?"

"Negative. We're checking it out now. It's pretty level where I'm standing. I can see some heavy brush right in the middle of that little saddle; I just might shoot it up."

"Roger. Be careful. Out."

I handed the mike back to Helms and glanced at my watch. 1634.

Firing broke out again. For a second or two I stood there, unconcerned; this was Denholm's expected recon fire: the barking of an M16. But then that was cut off, overwhelmed by other sounds: Hollow booms—claymores: Two dull, flat slams— RPG. AK-47 ... like a stabbing icicle, the sounds registered. And then a vicious, mind-freezing, deep thumping, a pounding, crushing sound I'd never heard before but recognized instantly: A .51 caliber machine gun.

We hit the dirt, fast. Only a lunatic stands up when he hears *that* sound. A .51 caliber round will go right through a six-inch tree trunk without being inconvenienced in the least.

Then the screaming started: Yells for help, or a medic, and inarticulate screams of fear and agony.

We were a full 200 meters from Chuck Denholm's point squad, but even without the radio, I could hear the cries: "Medic! Chrissakes—MEDIC! MEDIC!"

All the carefully built-up discipline and organization of a military unit seemed to dissolve into a set of individual Brownian motion. Men ran here and there, or hugged the ground, eyes wide and staring. I realized then how great the tension we'd felt actually was. Schoch, the senior medic, stood in the trail above me, beckoning for Muldoon and Stenger to join him. I tried to get up and found I couldn't. I lay paralyzed by fear. For an immeasurable time, my mind had no place for anything but the steady, terrifying pistoning of the heavy machine gun, and the screams. The wet, muddy ground was a powerful magnet, and I was nothing more than a loose fog of metallic dust. For a moment, I was four years old, huddled under the flimsy sheets, wishing the dark away.

Two things made me get to my feet. The first was the sure knowledge that my platoon was strung out behind me, as afraid and motionless as I, and I was their leader; I *had* to get up. The second came a second later: Littnan, kneeling in the middle of the path some ten meters from me, one hand holding his mike, the other beckoning to me.

Once upright, I felt better. The fear was still there, but manageable. There is a little part of the human brain—I'd first noticed it on Hill 1485—which is recent and has had little to do with our ancestral savannahs, and antelope thigh bones, and shaggy, humped shapes huddled around a chance fire. This little corner is capable of a cynical amusement as it contemplates the tangle of blood and muscle fiber and glands to which it finds itself conjoined. It was snickering at the rest of me now, asking, with cool contempt, why I was so afraid *now*, when my own personal danger was remote, and not back on Hill 1485, when I had faced almost sure death. But it knew the answer: Fear is not a rational process.

I reached Littnan and knelt beside him. The volume of fire was greater than anything I'd heard to that point, and, chillingly, it was all NVA: I heard no return fire. Littnan was still calling into the mike, yelling to make himself heard. After a few seconds, he let the receiver fall from his hand. Turning to me, he placed his lips near my ear and yelled.

"I need two squads from you. Two squads! One to help bring the wounded down: The other to reinforce Denholm. You got that?"

I nodded. I started to turn away but leaned forward and shouted to him. "What's Chuck say he's got up there? Does he know?"

Littnan gave a quick jerk of his head, a gesture I'd not seen him make before. He looked up the hill, not at me. "I don't know. He's not answering."

The purposeless near panic of the first moment had now been channeled into swift, effective action. First Sergeant Murtiff, his tiny boar's eyes hot with wrath, was yelling at some men from Hyde's squad, telling them to strip the ponchos and poncho liners from all available rucksacks, for use as stretchers. Sergeant Dickerson, his round young face split by a rigid and determined mouth, ran by me; bandoliers and ammo pouches thumping against his body as he moved up the trail, followed by his squad. Sergeant Wright began organizing Eden's and the rest of Hyde's squad to secure the trail between us and the clearing. Murtiff set Third Platoon around the perimeter, gradually extending it upwards to link up with Wright. Finally, Eward set up security back down the trail, extending it as far down as he could and still retain a cohesive line. Intuitively, he knew that there would be a need for medevacs in the next few minutes, and the only possible location for inserting a chopper was the lower southwestern flank of the ridge, just this side of the trail junction, where the slope was relatively shallow and there were few trees.

Littnan himself was on the radio, talking to both Black Jack and Bilk Two Three, who was now back on station overhead. Price, on the company net, stood by his side, continuing his efforts to contact Four Six. At the moment, I had little to do: My platoon was dismembered; I had sent part of Hyde's squad, having finished scavenging for ponchos and liners, on their way up the trail to the clearing. Dickerson's squad was running ammo up to the rear elements of Fourth Platoon, and Eden's squad was by now melded into Third Platoon, with Garza, platoon leader now that Dickson was gone, pushing them up the ridge to close up with Fourth Platoon. Muldoon was gone as well; he, Tunney, Stenger and Schoch were needed up at the point of contact. Even Brown had been commandeered by Russ Crenshaw to help call in artillery. There really was nothing for me to do but kneel along the trail, with Helms beside me, monitoring the company net and listening to the sounds from above.

By now, Fourth Platoon had begun returning fire; I could hear the spatter of M16 fire, and at least two M60s. But those sounds were overwhelmed by the monstrous hammering of the heavy machine gun and the impressive volume of AK-47 fire, punctuated by a continuing bass obbligato of RPG and claymore explosions—a symphony of death. I didn't know it then, although I should have guessed it, but for the second time in two days the NVA had crossed our T—pinning us down on a narrow ridge while they fired down on us from a wide arc.

It wasn't long before the first casualties began arriving. The first two or three were ambulatory, running down the path with that curiously desperate air, like men being pursued by a dread beast, that the lightly wounded often have. I recognized a youngster named Meecham; his left arm was a montage of blood-brown and faded green: Shrapnel, from an RPG or claymore. Another appeared to have taken an AK round through his hand; he was holding it awkwardly in front of him, in his other hand, face twisted in pain. The third limped down, rapidly, despite a large splash of dark red on his upper thigh. All of them were helmetless and weaponless, a hallmark of defeat.

Then the first impromptu stretcher came down; four of Dickerson's men, one holding each corner, struggled down the path. The body on the poncho seemed absurdly small; blood, almost black in the dim afternoon light, covered his chest. The man's eyes were closed and his head swung purposeless to the swaying of the poncho. Morphine, possibly, or simply passed out from the pain.

It went on that way for several minutes, while the rifles and machine guns continued their steady hammering. Then the first body was brought back. It too was stretched out on a poncho, but only the legs identified the red-black mass as a soldier. Oh, and the head. Curiously, Rosenstreich's head and face were intact; his eyes too were closed, but everything between his groin and his neck was an obscenity, not even recognizable as meat. It reminded me of Watson, the pilot, on Hill 1485.

Another body was brought back; this one I didn't recognize. I found out later it was McCarrell. But I did see Larson, Denholm's RTO. His body was intact, complete, with no sign of war's heavy hand. His eyes were open, and for a moment, I stood there puzzled, wondering what was wrong; everything seemed normal. Any moment now he'd blink and sit up … and then I realized he had three eyes, not two. The third was faintly red-black, exactly between the other two, and just above the slope of his nose.

They continued to come, some on their own, some supported by one or two other soldiers, and some swaying and bumping in the ponchos, leaving trails of blood behind. They were all brought down to the lower slope, where the open spaces were. But then Eward, de facto in charge of the PZ, made a disquieting discovery: It was too difficult to bring in a Huey; the land there sloped just enough to make it impossible for a medevac to hover or land anywhere close to the ridge; the radius of the blades dictated that they would have to remain at least 40 or 50 meters from the ridge and trail, and Eward simply didn't have enough people to secure the ridge and the open slope alongside of it. There was too much high ground nearby, and too much open area.

It was at that moment that the legend of Crazy Rairdon was born. Rairdon was an LOH pilot, flying one of those bubble-faced insect-like observation helicopters, whose landing profile was perhaps half of a Huey's. They sat only two, *including* the pilot, and could lift only a few hundred pounds. They were also fragile and vulnerable; they could be shot down by rifle fire, and a machine gun would make short work of the craft and its inhabitants. An RPG would be redundant. But nothing else could insert itself into that small space along the trail, and the seriously wounded had to be evacuated immediately.

I don't know how many trips Rairdon made that day. Probably not many: Most of the wounded were evacuated via the trail back to the battalion CP. But the handful of men who had to go out or die were strapped into the tiny LOH; one ambulatory wounded in the spare seat, one crammed into the tiny space behind the seats, and one, on a solid stretcher, strapped to the platform on either side of the cabin. It was a precarious accommodation, but they didn't need to fly far: The battalion LZ, over which a half-dozen medevacs hovered, was less than a minute's flight from the ridge. Rairdon shuttled the badly wounded back to the LZ throughout the rest of the evening.

If it had ended there, Rairdon would have been admired but otherwise forgotten.

It didn't. As events were to prove, the problem with LZs along those ridges—ours, and the ones flanking us to the north and south, along which Charlie and Delta Companies would strive over the next ten days—was never really resolved. Rairdon went on to complete dozens of these missions of mercy, as well as an uncounted number of emergency ammo runs and other flights, often directly under fire from the surrounding ridges, often hit, and never once backed out. How do you think he earned the name Crazy?

While Rairdon was defying gravity, the terrain and the NVA, to say nothing of common sense, the rest of Fourth Platoon was disengaging and, slowly, pulling back. The wounded had by now—it was 1730—been evacuated from the clearing and ridge, at least down to the impromptu LZ at its base. Everyone in Fourth Platoon had returned—except for Chuck. I looked for him with mounting alarm, going from one dazed group of troopers to the next, asking if they knew where he was. I suddenly realized that an hour had passed since the ambush, and in that time I hadn't heard Chuck's voice at all, or anything about him. I was beginning to resign myself to his death when I heard a commotion from higher up the ridge. Artillery had by then begun firing into the hill above us; 105s, 155s and, I thought, some 175. But even through that constant booming, I heard the sounds of running feet, and some voices.

Chuck suddenly burst into view, half running, half staggering down the path. His dark glasses were gone; a bloody arm hung limply by his side. His breath came in deep, ragged gasps. I reached out a hand, both to support him and to bring him to a stop: I wanted to talk to him, to find out what had happened, but he went right through me, eyes fixed on the path below. I started to turn and follow, but Littnan saw me and emphatically shook his head. I watched Chuck continue to stagger away from us.

Littnan called us together a few minutes later. Rairdon continued his shuttles; he was at that moment, as it was getting dark, on the last of his flights. The artillery crumped overhead, and not far away we could hear the screech of F105s, possibly flying one last sortie for the 2/506th. We were a somber group. Eward and I were the only commissioned platoon leaders left. Sergeant Garza, relieved of first sergeant duties when Murtiff, who outranked him, joined Bravo, was de facto platoon leader of Third Platoon, since we'd finally seen the last of Dickson. And Chuck was on his way to a hospital ship in the Sea of Japan, although I didn't know that at the time. His platoon sergeant, Micheaux, was present. Before anything else was said, Littnan informed us brusquely that, until another officer was sent out to join us, he was combining Third and Fourth platoons under Sergeant Garza. I don't think it hit me until that moment just how serious the casualties from Fourth Platoon had been.

We were briefed on what happened, although no one who was actually in the clearing at the time of the ambush had survived; all were either dead or badly wounded and on their way to hospitals as we spoke. But a story was pieced together. It made grim hearing.

For some reason, just before they entered the clearing Chuck had called down about, he had replaced his point man with Rosenstreich, an unusual step, since Rosy was a squad leader. McCarrell was the slack man, with Mills behind him. Denholm, as was his practice, was the fourth man in file, with Larson, his RTO, close behind him. Garza, who had pressed forward all the way into the clearing when he and Third Platoon had reinforced the Fourth, described the terrain at that point:

The ridge, already steep and narrow, simultaneously increased its incline and became even narrower; its flanks became even more precipitous. It was like this for only about ten meters, or less, Garza said, before suddenly leveling off and broadening into a clearing, somewhat deeper than it was wide, but in comparison to the razor ridge they'd traversed, it seemed to be as wide as a football field. In fact, it was about 20 meters across and perhaps 30 or 40 deep. There were a couple of trees in the middle, but for the most part it was covered by small short bushes and scrub brush and creepers. At its far end, the vegetation became much thicker. A saddle connected two small knolls that dominated the clearing; the trail zigzagged through the clearing until it began to climb again, along the face of the right-hand knoll, the southern one. Well behind the knolls he could see what appeared to be the crest of Dong Ap Bia itself, perhaps 50 to 100 meters behind them. There were bunkers at the base of the knolls, across their slopes and on the mountain slope behind them. The floor of the clearing was dotted with fighting positions, one-man spider holes and perhaps one bunker.

This is what Chuck moved into. He was disturbed by what he saw — even an inexperienced soldier, which Denholm was not, could hardly fail to understand that the clearing was a perfect ambush location. Nevertheless, it was his job to move through it. Rosenstreich followed the trail for at least ten meters into the clearing; at this point, it jogged sharply to the left and then back to the right. The point man stopped there, looked back over his shoulder and indicated he was going to recon by fire: He did so, spraying the arc formed by the two knolls and the shoulder. Rosenstreich used up one full magazine; when he'd finished, there was nothing but silence. The time was 1634.

Sergeant Rosenstreich moved through the zigzag; from there the trail ran in an almost straight line to the base of the right-hand knoll. He took one or two more steps; McCarrell was a few meters behind him, scanning the underbrush at the base of the knolls. Spec4 Mills, the third man in file, had stopped at the zigzag, fingers playing nervously with the safety.

The NVA chose this moment to open fire. At least four claymores were sprung in that instant; McCarrell and Rosenstreich fell instantly. AK-47 rounds cut through the clearing, from a number of bunkers, spider holes and fighting positions. Denholm himself was blown off his feet; his rifle landed a few meters to his right. Weaponless, he found himself face-to-face with an NVA soldier hidden in a spider hole just to the right of the path. Their faces were inches apart. The man's attention was focused, not on Denholm, but on a GI a little further up the trail and on the left side of the clearing. With nothing else available, Chuck grabbed his bayonet from its scabbard on his hip and stabbed the man through the throat. Retrieving his rifle, he squirmed back onto the trail, trying to reach Larson and the radio, but gave up after one glance: Larson was down, across the trail, with his radio wedged under his body. Denholm couldn't reach him or the radio without crossing the exposed trail. Mills went down as he watched, with three rounds through his upper chest.

Then came the RPGs, with their evil flat sound; the second or third of them hit halfway up a small tree beside him, raining shrapnel down on his back and upper thighs. He lay there, bleeding now from wounds to his chest and shoulder, and his lower back and thighs. He had no radio, and, at the moment, no platoon to lead; he was the only one left alive of the lead element.

The fire from behind him began to increase, at last, although it was still no match for the intense fire coming from the knolls and saddle. Fourth Platoon's third squad, with elements from Sergeant Dickerson's squad, began to inch their way into the heart of the clearing, laying down suppressive fire while others began to retrieve the dead and wounded.

Two figures ran by Denholm, crouched down; they jumped over Larson's body and ran forward, toward something he couldn't see; moments later, they were back, each pulling one of McCarrell's arms, dragging his body back with them. Miraculously, neither was hit. Another pair grabbed Larson's arms and began pulling him behind them. Someone from First Platoon — Chuck never found out who — hoisted what was left of Rosenstreich onto his back and ran down the trail, until he placed what was left of him on a poncho. Denholm saw a young, pale-faced soldier reach out, pick something up, and then retreat with it. Only after the trooper had moved by him did the item register in Denholm's mind. It was Rosenstreich's left arm, dull green army issue watch still strapped to its wrist.

Mills was still lying in a heap a few meters to his left. Three light machine gun rounds had perforated his chest. In a movie, he would have flown back down the hill, arms outspread, to fall several meters back. In reality, he had slumped over onto his side, slowly, like a ship hulling over and sinking, to end up in a crouched, cramped position, head down, touching the ground, rifle still held across his chest. Tunney, Fourth Platoon medic, ran up the path. He knelt by Mills, turned him slowly and gently over on his back, and then turned his head to yell down the hill for someone to help him drag Mills away. As he turned his attention back to Mills, a round, probably from an AK-47, took Tunney in the chest. He instinctively lifted himself to a standing position, arms outspread for balance, and then toppled slowly backwards, to end up a few feet away.

From somewhere Sergeant Garza appeared; his broad, flat squint-eyed face as immovable as ever. "Let's get you outta here, Lieutenant. You hurt bad."

Denholm shook his head. "Fuck off, Luis," he said, or tried to. His mouth wasn't working, and all that came out was a gurgle.

"C'mon, Lieutenant, les' go." Garza, who weighed no more than 130 pounds, reached down and pulled Denholm's blood-spattered body off the ground. Looping one arm around his own neck, Garza began pulling the young lieutenant across the clearing. He'd taken perhaps three or four steps before PFC Leyden arrived, puffing, to take Denholm's other arm. Together they began to run down the trail to the lip of the clearing; even here, where it was so steep they could almost have jumped, they didn't slow down but continued to run as fast as Denholm's 160 pounds and dragging feet allowed. Only after they reached the bottom of that incline did they stop; sheltered now by the ridge itself, they could lower Denholm to the ground. Garza yelled for a medic.

Denholm was on one knee, still seeping blood from dozens of wounds, from pinpricks to gaping holes the size of a golf ball. His glasses were all fogged and smeared; he couldn't see. Taking them off, he looked at Garza, still kneeling by his side. "My rifle..."

"It's okay, Lieutenant." Garza nodded at Leyden. "He got it."

"Let me have it. I gotta go back! My guys are back there —"

"No, Lieutenant," Garza shook his head forcefully. "No one back der! Got 'em all."

"The hell you say." Denholm looked around, fiercely. "Where's Larson? Where's Mills? Where —"

"Lieutenant! They're all —" Leyden broke in, but a glare from Garza shut him up.

Denholm looked around; men were hurrying by, in both directions, but none of them were Fourth Platoon. And then the realization set in. "Oh, Jesus Christ," he whispered.

"Let's go, Lieutenant," Garza said, woodenly.

Chuck Denholm shook off the sergeant's proffered hand. He got to his feet, sick with the knowledge that his platoon was no longer on the clearing above him, but down at the base of the hill, at a PZ, waiting to be sent back to the rear, in body bags or with the heavy cardboard tags listing their wounds, condition and disposition — the triage. His helmet was gone, as was his rifle. So were his glasses; he couldn't see from them anyway. Almost blindly, he began to run down the trail, heedless of the steep slope, the tree roots, small boulders and vines that littered its surface. (*Note:* This account of the first few minutes was made to me, orally, by Chuck Denholm during the first commemorative ceremony at Fort Campbell in May of 1999. That was the first time I had seen him since the battle.)

When he reached us, some 200 meters below the clearing, he was gasping and sobbing, as much from grief as from the exertion. He ran right through us, but Doc Schoch happened to be on the trail when he arrived, and he immediately took him by the arm, slowing him down. Denholm struggled to free himself, but Schoch was a good-sized man, and in any case the wounds and the run down the hill had weakened Denholm to the point where he was almost passing out. Schoch led him down the trail at a slower pace, to the PZ, where he made him lie down; a moment later, morphine began to work quickly through Chuck's body, dulling the pain and his senses. A moment after that, he was unconscious. It would be 30 years before I saw him again.

29

The Clearing

YC324983; 11–12 May 1969; 1730–0930

The rest of us were faced with some decisions. Actually, only one of us was: Captain Littnan. The small arms fire had at last petered out; the .51 was silent, and only an occasional bark of an M16 could be heard. But the hill was hardly quiet; the artillery began to arrive in earnest. Bilk Two Three still flew overhead, judiciously moved to the west, out of the path of the 105 and 155 shells that rained down on Hill 937. Black Jack and Littnan agreed that, for the moment, air would be too hard to coordinate, particularly because there was no one left in the clearing to mark the targets with a smoke grenade. From the air, the crest and slopes of Dong Ap Bia still presented a featureless dark green carpet of trees to an aviator's eye. Garza, who had been up to the clearing, quickly dissuaded Littnan from any idea he might have entertained about pushing the company back up the ridge to the contact point.

"De clearing, it's zeroed in, Cap'n. We can't stay der. An' de ridge, 'tween 'ere n' der, like a razor. No room; mebbe a meter, mebbe less." He indicated the area around us. "Dis is as far up as we can go, Cap'n."

Littnan nodded. He probably had already come to that conclusion anyway. "Okay, then. Arty's going to fire for another hour or so, to keep them pinned down." He frowned down at his map; it was already dark enough that he had to shine a small flashlight on it, with a poncho draped over his hands. "We don't have enough people to secure here and the PZ, and anyway the PZ's no good to us. So we'll set up here, down to this spot here, about 100 meters or so above the PZ. Bo, you take your platoon and set up on the west end, down here. Four-man positions, 75% alert. Keep a clear path between your CP and mine. Top," he nodded at Garza, "you take Third Platoon and what's left of Fourth up here, around us; set up the same way. Eward"—Marsh had left his platoon down by the still-active PZ to join us—"after we evacuate the last casualty, pull your platoon off the PZ and set up between First and Third platoons. Send me one squad right now, and bring the rest up when you're done."

"And gentlemen," he added, "I want you to dig in. Don't know what we're facing but I want no chances."

It was Eward who spoke up, but we were all three of us thinking the same thing. "Captain, I want to dig in as much as you do, but this ridge is one big tree root, where it ain't boulders. And we've got only half-hour, maybe less, of daylight."

Littnan nodded patiently. "I understand. But your guys are going to want to dig as deep as they can, half hour or roots or whatever. If," he added grimly, "they need some motivation, send 'em down to the PZ and have 'em look at what's lying there." The wounded, of course, had taken priority in the evacuation; the dead still lay in their body bags.

Littnan paused, frowned momentarily, and then looked up. "By the way, Frank ... those documents you took off those guys today? They were from the 29th NVA." He glanced around at all of us. "The Pride of Ho Chi Minh."

Eward blew out his cheeks. "I reckon that's supposed to mean something? Nothing good, I guess."

I shrugged. "Probably not." I grinned at Littnan. "Who are we the pride of?"

He just shook his head and waved us away

We started to go back to our platoons, but the CO held out a hand to stop me. "Frank," he said, moving up beside me, "I'm afraid I had to borrow one of your squads. We're low on ammo and the LOH can't bring enough. I sent your man Dickerson back to the battalion, to bring back as much as they can carry. I should have told you, but I was busy."

I stepped back away from him in astonishment. My initial reaction was surprise; the anger didn't come until much later. But truthfully, my first thought was how dangerous the mission was. There was absolutely no security between us and the battalion, almost two kilometers behind us—along a path that had been traveled over just that day. We were within a few minutes' walk from the Laotian border; there would be NVA all over the area. And Dickerson was the youngest and least experienced of my squad leaders.

Some of that showed on my face, even in the gloom, because Littnan nodded. "I know it's going to be a hairy walk for them, and it's taking a chance, but we need that ammo. Not tomorrow morning, but tonight. I gave him one of Four Six's radios, and Black Jack knows he's coming. He's got ARA up and a pair of Cobras."

I nodded back. But my mind was focusing on the men in that squad ... Bresina, Olson, Ulrich...

I went in search of Sergeant Wright and found him, down along the trail, overseeing the set up of the perimeter positions. I asked him if he'd known about Dickerson. He shook his head.

"I just found out myself, Lieutenant, when I went lookin' for 'im. Matter of fact, I was just about to ask *you*."

"Uhm." The anger started to rise up then; Littnan had pulled a squad out of a platoon in contact with the enemy without notifying either the platoon leader or the platoon sergeant. But, after a moment, I settled down. It had been chaos during the time between Chuck's ambush and the last of the casualty evacuations. And it was late and getting dark; Littnan probably hadn't had the time to look for me.

Some of that must have gone through Wright's mind also, because he shook his head and looked back over his shoulder, in the direction of the battalion. "Guess it had to be done, Lieutenant," he said quietly. "I'll leave three positions open for Dickerson's squad — up here, tie them in with Third Platoon. I reckon we can have the CP group and a couple o' men from Eden's squad cover 'em 'til Dickerson gets back."

That's how it was. But that hour and a half before Dickerson radioed in to tell us that he as approaching the position was one of the worst I'd had to that point. Eight men traveling down an open trail in the dark in an area teeming with the enemy was the stuff nightmares are made of. Ulrich, Dickerson's point, finally walked through Snyder's position at 2100, two hours after nightfall. Each man was carrying 40 to 50 pounds of ammo, water and medical supplies and one carried a radio to replace Larson's. I let out a deep sigh. I could breathe again.

At about 2200, the word came down to us: Eward, with three volunteers, was going to infiltrate the clearing to retrieve the equipment left behind, including Larson's radio and an M60. How it was decided that Marsh would go was something I never found out; Littnan hadn't mentioned the mission while we were all together. In the event, it took Eward, a meticulous and very careful man, five hours.

The night was miserable. The weather became the enemy's friend; the clouds lay heavy and damp over us, blotting up the light and making it impossible to fly Spooky. Rain pattered down, off and on, all through the dark hours. Later, the wind picked up, blowing through the damp leaves with a restless whispering that sounded, incongruously, like surf breaking against a distant beach. I shuddered, perhaps at the cold rain that trickled down my back.

I was hungry, tired, cold, wet, but, more, I was afraid. It was completely unlike the first night I'd spent on Hill 1485. There, the sudden, intense violence and the knife-edge I had teetered on had left me alert, watchful and resolute. Now, the impersonal and dire unseen weighed on me and left me vague and purposeless. Like a mob of unwanted callers, beating insistently, cold-eyed and grinning, on my door, the sights and sounds of that last hour hammered away at my mind, demanding entry, breaking through the thin barrier of my will and strength into my consciousness: The stolid hammering of the .51 caliber; the metallic *slam!* of the RPGs; the hollow blow of an exploding claymore; the screams and cries; the black blood framing McCarrell's torn head; Bresina walking blank-faced down the trail, holding Rosenstreich's dismembered arm; Tunney gasping, blue-lipped and grey-faced, with a hole in his chest; Chuck Denholm — warm, calm, cheerful Denney — running down the trail, bloody, gasping, crying, almost disintegrated by grief and pain and fear. And, leering slyly, most persistent, most devastating, most heavy-handed of them all: The thought of the first few seconds, that first burst of claymore and gunfire, in which the first three men in Chuck's column died almost instantly. The first three, the wind hissed evilly. The first three, the leaves sniggered cruelly. The first three, the rain laughed harshly. The first three; and I always walked third in line. Always. The thought of Helms' broken strap, for which Littnan had switched First and Fourth Platoons, clawed at me with a clammy tomb-touch for the rest of that night, and 1,000 nights thereafter.

The rain had stopped by the following morning. Dawn was still a grim gray affair; we shivered at the touch of our clammy fatigues. Eward and the others had returned somewhere around 0300, but I hadn't heard anything more than that they'd successfully retrieved the gear. I tried briefly to imagine what it had been like up there, crawling about in the dark, and then dismissed the thought. This hill already had me spooked.

I made the rounds of the platoon, checking on the positions. I'd done so the previous night, but by then it had been too dark to really see anything. The men hadn't gotten very far; they'd had little time and the roots along the ridge were formidable. It was just as well that they hadn't dug deep, because I found it necessary to move two positions; their location didn't really offer decent fields of fire. That's what can happen when you set up in the dark.

The last position I came to was the one furthest west, on the lowest portion of the trail. Snyder, Jackson, Mareniewski and Edwards manned it. By chance, the soil here was relatively free of both roots and boulders; besides, Ski and Snyder were big men, and they'd been able to dig out a decent position, a broad V pointed down the trail, wide enough to comfortably fit all four, and already about three feet deep. An hour's work would finish it. The men nodded to me as I approached; they were busy with the details of morning life: heating water for the coffee or hot chocolate, munching on pound cake soaked with juice from the canned peaches or pineapple, dry-brushing their teeth, or wiping the night's accumulation of dew and damp from their weapons.

Mareniewski, trying to eat his breakfast and clean his rifle at the same time, looked up with a vague grin. "Hey, Lieutenant Bo. Howzitgoin?"

"I'm cold and wet, Ski. Don't ask." I squatted down on my heels beside them. "How'd it go last night?"

The others looked away with noncommittal shrugs, but Ski spoke up cheerfully. "Not bad, Lieutenant, 'cept for that guy waking us up."

"Waking you up? You weren't supposed to be asleep. Three on, one off, remember?" I said that automatically, but my mind was already on the upcoming meeting with Littnan and Eward, so I didn't expect Ski to answer.

"Well, that's what I mean, sir. It was Jackson's turn to sleep, and I woke him up when that dude walked up to us."

My mind was still far away, and I almost left it at that. "What dude? You mean Sergeant Wright? He checked the line last night again?"

If I'd been paying attention, I'd have noticed that the others were by now glaring at Mareniewski, so obviously saying "SHUT UP!!!" that a blind man could have seen it.

"Ah, nah. Not Top: It was this guy came up the trail."

Now he had my attention. "Up the trail? You mean, from down there?" I pointed down the ridge.

"Yeah. 'Bout 0300, right guys?"

I looked at Snyder, who was staring uncomfortably at his machine gun. "Someone tried to enter the perimeter last night? Why wasn't I called?"

"Well, he didn't exactly try to enter, sir," Snyder muttered. Edwards and Jackson nodded in concert.

"Then what *did* he do?"

Ski spoke up. He alone of the four still was heedless of my consternation and rising anger. "Well, I look up, around 0300, like I said, and I see this shadow right in front of me, so I wake up Jack, and point. And just then, the guy spouts off — he was maybe five, six feet from me — and says something, only I can't understand him."

I took a deep breath. "You couldn't understand him?"

"Nah. I think it was gook. Sounded like it. So I said, 'Hey! Who're you?' and he says something back, and then Snyder starts to say something, and the dude just turned around and walked away."

I was glaring now at Snyder. "Walked away?"

The others, including even Jackson, were a bright crimson by then. Snyder wouldn't meet my eye, and Edwards looked as if he was praying for a tornado to materialize, pick him up and carry him far, far away. Only Ski retained a smiling face.

"It all happened kinda fast, Lieutenant," Snyder muttered.

"He walked away?" I repeated.

"Yeah," Ski answered. "Later, me 'n the guys talked about it, an' we figured it musta been a gook got lost, took the wrong trail." He laughed. "Sucker musta shit his pants when he heard my voice."

Snyder, Jackson and Edwards by now were practically writhing with embarrassment. I was filled with so many conflicting emotions and impulses, from rage to stunned disbelief, from a monumental eruption to a court martial, that I was, literally, speechless. My mouth wouldn't work. And before I could break the logjam of competing reactions, I realized that I was late for Littnan's meeting. I had to go.

Contenting myself, then, with one last silent glare at Snyder, I walked away, talking to myself. I couldn't even guess what Sergeant Wright would say.

I met with Eward and Randolph a few minutes later; Captain Littnan was there, of course, along with Murtiff and Garza. Eward's report was concise and pointed.

"Couldn't see much. The bunkers and spider holes are up against the rim of the clearing, along those two knolls. The trail leads up to the middle, then kind of breaks off to the right, right past this one bunker complex; that's where McCarrell got it. The wires on their claymores are old and brittle; they've been here a good while."

There was an imperceptible jerking of heads and shoulders at that. We were all officers and NCOs in the Airborne Infantry, and not easily impressed, but Eward's

29. The Clearing

casual reference to crawling up and touching the wires leading to an enemy's claymore mine had to rank well up there on the list of historical understatements.

"Plenty of movement; we could hear 'em moving the whole time we were up there."

"I could see them," Randolph's deep baritone interrupted.

"Right. There's more than a platoon up there; they got at least one .51. We heard them arming it."

Littnan raised an eyebrow. "Did they spot you?"

"No; I think they'd have let fly if they had. No, they were just careless."

"The gear hadn't been touched?"

"Not that I could tell." Eward paused. "Maybe the artillery kept 'em in their bunkers."

Littnan grunted noncommittally. His lean dark face was creased in thought. After a moment, he turned to Garza. "Draw me a picture of the area." He nodded at Eward and Randolph. "You two can add or change it. I want it as detailed as possible."

Garza took out his bayonet and drew some lines swiftly in the loose damp dirt. "Here's de trail, comin' up de hill," he said. Right here's de steep part; real narrow dere. An' here's de clearing, wid de bunkers back up here."

Eward and Randolph made a few suggestions; after a couple of minutes the impromptu map was complete. Littnan sat on his haunches, eyes narrowed, studying it. "What's over here?" he asked, pointing to the areas on either side of the steep approach to the clearing.

"'Trip'-canopy stuff," Garza replied. "Real crap."

Littnan frowned. He thought for a moment more. "You got up here, right?" he asked Eward, pointing to the far side of the clearing.

"Yeah."

"And you"— he nodded at Randolph —"were over on this side. You both say there were plenty of claymores, is that right?"

"Beaucoup," Eward said.

"What about here?" Littnan asked, indicating the point where the trail narrowed and steepened, leading up into the level clearing. "See anything there?"

Both Randolph and Eward shook their heads.

"What about you, yesterday, Sergeant?" he asked Garza. "See any claymores here? Did any of the troops report them?"

"Nah, sir. Nada."

Littnan sat back, his face impassive. "Hmm," he said.

Hmm indeed. Now that he'd pointed it out, the thing was obvious. All reports indicated a ring of bunkers and claymores dispersed across the far side of the clearing. But that narrow neck just before the clearing would have been the logical, tactically most effective spot to place mines. And the NVA were at least as good as we were, tactically. The conclusion was so obvious that none of us needed to say anything. A bunker and a few claymores, placed at that point, would have kept us out of that clearing for days. The NVA knew that, and had had plenty of time to place them there. They hadn't. Therefore, they didn't want to keep us out of that clearing. And that conclusion led immediately to a few more, none of which was particularly reassuring.

There were a few more minutes of questions and answers; then Littnan looked at his watch. "0630," he said. "That's late." He looked at me. "Frank, I want you to take your people up there."

I nodded without surprise. I'd not expected anything different.

"I want you to recon the clearing. Tell me as much as you can about the bunkers and the automatic weapons they've got up there. If you meet with light resistance, fine; push on through. But if they start to pound you, I want you to pull back. Understood? I don't want to lose any more than I have to up there."

I nodded enthusiastically. "Understood. You can rely on me to run at the first opportunity."

Littnan ignored me. "Marsh, I want you to be support; keep your people as tight as you can, without clustering, and be ready to move up if Bo can push through that bunker line. Top, you and Sergeant Garza organize Three Six and what's left of Four Six into a perimeter defense; I particularly want the PZ secured." He looked at his watch again. "Bilk Two Three is on station now; I'll bring in some 105s if things start to warm up. Questions?"

"Have we got artillery coming in before I go up?" I asked.

"No. Not right now. For one thing, I don't particularly want them hunkered down; I want to see what they've got. Just remember; this is a recon. Don't take chances, and don't get yourself cut off in that clearing. The 105s have got plenty of ordnance if we need it."

"Right," I said, sincerely.

Marsh Eward pulled me aside as we got ready to go. "Be careful up there, Bo," he said quietly. "There's some deep shit there. Real deep."

I nodded. "Yeah. Just ask Denney."

YC325981; 12 May: 0645

Ten minutes later, First Platoon was assembled on the trail, weapons ready, ammunition distributed, ready to go. We left our packs behind; there was no need to encumber ourselves any more than was necessary. Each man had a canteen, and nothing else. Pockets bulged with grenades; bandoliers of ammo, loaded into the flat, black M16 magazines, each holding ten rounds of 5.56 ammunition, were hung around our necks or across our shoulders. Logan and Westman fussed and fiddled with their M60; Logan was crooning to it, reminding it that it had failed him in his hour of greatest need. "Don't do it again," he was saying. "I need you, baby; don't fuck up on me now."

Westman, wearing a tolerant half-smile, looked on. Westman was never quite sure when Logan was serious, but, then, he didn't care. Logan, he understood, just needed looking after.

Clifton and Nelson sat to one side, the long black barrel of their 90mm recoilless rifle sticking up in the air between them, like a ponderous medieval lance. A dozen rounds of ammo, blunt-tipped and heavy, were strapped to their backs. Muldoon and Helms sat nearby, backs against a large tree trunk, talking in low voices; their faces were calm and expressionless. I looked around at the platoon. These were good men. The only nervous gesture I saw was Samuel, blinking and tapping his extended index finger against the stock of his grenade launcher, and, hell, he always did that.

There was one change; Littnan was told to bring in some mortar fire. Why was another question, since there was nothing a mortar could do in this situation that a 105 or 155 couldn't do better. The dull crrrump-whump of the 81mms began shortly.

I did some thinking while waiting, and I had an idea of how I wanted to carry out the probe. Obviously the NVA were sighted on the trail as it came into and across the clearing. I pulled Snyder, Eden's point man, aside as we prepared to move out.

"Once you get up to that steep razor-back just before the clearing," I said to him, "I want you to move off the trail; stay off it entirely. Move at least five meters from it, to the left, even if it means pushing through the thick stuff. When you reach the clearing, especially, make damn sure you're not on that trail. That's their killing zone; that's where they're going to hurt us, so stay the hell off of it. When you do get to the clearing, stay out of it until the rest of us get up there with you. Got that?"

Snyder nodded down at me from his six-three height.

"Take it slow; there's no rush. And, Snyder: once you're in position up there, make sure to keep in eye contact with me or Eden. We're going to keep voice communication to a minimum. Okay?" I slapped his arm. "Good luck. Be careful."

Snyder adjusted his helmet lower on his forehead, turned, and started up the trail. As we filed through the perimeter, Marsh Eward, standing off to the side, gave me a leering wink and the thumbs-up sign. I shook my head, flipped him the middle-finger salute, adjusted the straps of the bandoliers on my shoulders, and followed Jorgenson, the slack man.

We moved cautiously, for two reasons beyond the obvious one. For this once, I had decided to forget about SOP; we all carried chambered rounds, with safeties off, ready to fire. Also, Russ Crenshaw was walking the 81mm fire up the slope ahead of us, and I didn't want to chance moving too fast and having a short round land amongst us.

As always, I tried to concentrate on watching Snyder and Jorgenson. We were now within 30 meters of that point where the ridge steepened and narrowed to a razor edge, just below the clearing. Snyder's progress was now literally one step at a time; branches were moved gingerly, quietly, to one side, carefully guided back. His eyes were performing a restless dance, peering ahead, searching for that metallic glint, the odd shadow, the quivering leaf, that would betray the presence of the enemy. Then he would give a quick glance down, as his foot descended, to avoid the dead branch, the vine, the loose pebbles, which might betray him in turn; down, back to the front, from side to side, a flicker overhead.... Snyder's eyes were busy. Jorgenson was not looking at the same things; his attention was concentrated on the ground immediately in front of Snyder: trip wires, unusually-shaped branches, vines that just didn't quite look right ... booby traps were of course set so that they couldn't be spotted by the point man, but an alert slack man sometimes was able to pick them out in time. Sometimes.

I was listening. The mortar fire was still falling on the hill, a couple of hundred meters above us, and the drone and buzz of ARA and Cobras whined overhead, but I listened anyway, for that faint click of an ammo belt slapping the side of a machine gun, or the soft unnatural thud of a rifle barrel accidentally striking a tree trunk, or the rustle of underbrush as an RPG gunner shifted his position ... no conductor, alert to pick out the faintest dissonance in his orchestra, ever listened with the intensity and concentration with which I sorted through the dozens of noises my ears were hearing.

We were now within a few meters of the clearing. The jetsam of yesterday's engagement littered the trail and underbrush to our right; empty IV bottles, bandages, ammo pouches, magazines, a pack, two or three canteens, a torn poncho liner, the heavy paper wrappings from the first-aid kits. Spent M16 cartridges glinted dull yellow; just a few, at first, and then, as we neared the lip of the clearing, they lay in brassy patches on the forest floor, marking the places where the men of Four Six had lain or knelt the previous day.

Snyder stopped. We had finally reached that point that Denholm had called back about; the ridge became very steep, leading up to the clearing some five meters above at about a 60 degree angle. It also narrowed dramatically, so that the trail took up almost the entire ridgeback. I inched my way up close to Snyder and was able to see for myself now what we were faced with.

The flanks of the ridge here were steep and thickly covered with vines, creepers and brush. A few yards to either side, however, they leveled off a bit, so that the slopes leading to the clearing on our left and right were much shallower than the incline facing us. Two ravines, steep-walled, narrow, and thoroughly overgrown, flanked the ridge; I immediately dismissed any thoughts I might have had about using them as routes to the clearing. A bunker or two at the head of each ravine, sheltered and invisible from the trail, and those narrow folds would become death-traps for anyone trying to make his way up. The clearing itself was directly in front of and above us; from where I stood, at the base of the incline, I couldn't see the front portion of it, but I was able to see, about 50 meters ahead of us, the tops of the two knolls, one on either side of the clearing, and the trees which covered the saddle linking them. According to Garza, the trail would, once it entered the clearing, bend back to the right, climb the slope of the saddle, and then ascend the knoll on the right, clearly on its way to the top of Dong Ap Bia. The .51 caliber gun, I thought, would probably be located in a bunker on that knoll — at least that's where I would have placed it — so that it could enfilade the trail and most of the clearing. It would no doubt be supported by several bunkers on the other hill, the saddle, and the upper slopes of Dong Ap Bia.

Well, I thought, this is peachy. We can't outflank them, and can't go up the middle, so what does that leave us? I felt an intense tightening of my stomach muscles. It is one thing to be thrust suddenly into a firefight, as I had been back on Hill 1485. It is quite another to sit at the edge of a killing zone and soberly consider the best way of entering it. The badger, set upon suddenly by the wolf, will fight back ferociously and instinctively. But that same badger, trotting down a trail, will pause, sniff disdainfully, and turn and retreat, growling, if he sees the wolf in time. I shook my head. Apparently, we just weren't as smart as badgers.

There was a small hump, not large enough to be called a knoll, on the slope at the very edge of the clearing, about 10 or 12 meters to our left; I signaled to Snyder to move in that direction, and he did so. I didn't need to tell him to make for that small rise; it would be the obvious thing to do, and he did it. I motioned for Jorgenson to move to the right; he crouched low and duck-walked across the trail, finally taking up a position about ten meters from me. Clifton and Nelson came next; they inched their way along the slope to a point about halfway between me and Snyder. By now the 81mm fire had ceased; my breathing, and the thud as I swallowed, sounded loud and disastrous in the silence. Samuel, his pale oval face set and impassive, moved by me, to the right. I gave my head a tiny shake, in wonder; the NVA still had not seen or heard us. Or perhaps they had, my body warned me. Perhaps they had, and were only waiting for more of us to fill their gun sights. Eden, who'd been crouching just behind me, now took Edwards and Mareniewski to the right, stringing them out in a loose line around the base of the slope. I glanced behind me. Helms, as ever, crouched within a few feet of me, his right hand holding his M16 and his left already clutching the mike. Muldoon, his white, bony face unusually grim and immobile, hugged the ground a meter or so behind him; I saw his tongue flick across his lips, his mouth tighten.

I heard a quick, faint hiss; Clifton made a flat, palms-down-pushing motion with his hand. Snyder had spotted the NVA. I inched my way up the slope, although I was still two or three meters below the clearing. I could no longer see Snyder, who was by now stretched out alongside that small rise, but Clifton relayed, by hand signal, the message that two NVA were occupying a bunker about ten meters to Snyder's left front. I glanced back to my right. Eden, who was closest to me, had seen Clifton's signals and was silently passing them on to the rest of the squad. My mind was crowded with a hundred thoughts, but I noted how much more confident and assertive Eden seemed; two weeks ago he'd have done nothing until I or Wright told him to.

The silence now became a force, squeezing the breath from our bodies. There was something hidden here, like a scorpion poised in featureless shadow. Twenty or thirty seconds had passed since Snyder had reached his position; Edwards, the man farthest to the right, had still not quite settled down. And then the enemy saw us.

Two, perhaps three, claymore mines were blown immediately ahead of us; the fragments whined overhead, into the trees behind us. Then the familiar crackle of AK-47s spat out of the woods, and, with paralyzing intensity, the solid bass hammering of the .51 caliber. The NVA fire started out as disjointed pattering, like the first tentative drops of rain; then, suddenly, as will a summer storm, the sound became a solid deluge. I gave a quick glance around: no casualties. I felt a flicker of elation; there was no question that the enemy had sighted their weapons on that clearing. As long as we stayed out of it, we should be able to escape the worst.

There was an answering spatter of M16 fire from my right. Eden was directing his squad's fire, firing back at the right-hand knoll. I reached back with my arm, knowing that Helms would place the mike in my hand. When I felt the smooth plastic handle touch my palm, I brought it to my ear and spoke.

"Six, this is One Six."

Littnan's response was prompt; he'd have been seated by his radio, waiting for me to call. "Roger, One Six. Go."

"We're taking incoming. Negative casualties. That .51 is definitely on that right-hand hill; I can hear it with no problem."

"Roger. Spotted any bunkers?"

"Affirmative. We're dealing with them now."

I flipped over on my back, my legs pointed down the trail; inching up by shoving my heels against the ground, I cautiously made it up to the lip of the clearing. By turning my head to my right, I could now see Snyder, about 15 meters away. He was firing his M16 in short bursts and then, every few seconds, casually throwing a grenade toward the bunkers to his front. He was in a good position, with a fallen tree, two or three feet thick, lying across his front, and the small crop of ground shielding his left. Clifton and Nelson now jumped up. They had spotted the bunker Snyder was firing at. Running forward a few feet, they dropped to their knees. Nelson held the 90mm; Clifton, in one practiced motion, rammed the canister round into the breech and tapped Nelson smartly on the helmet. An instant later the gun boomed with a flat, heavy sound. Dust kicked up all around them. There was a yell of manic glee from Nelson; his swarthy face was split by a white-toothed grin as he turned to say something to Clifton, who was already placing another round into the breech.

This time, as they fired, I risked a quick glance over the edge of the clearing. Heavy brush and small trees carpeted the saddle. A bent, burnt pack frame, with blood and shreds of flesh clinging to the upper arm, lay on the ground only a few feet from me; Rosenstreich's, I thought. McCarrell's had been brought back, and no one else had been blown apart like that. The 90mm boomed a third time, and a dull whummp! to my left marked another of Snyder's grenades.

Ducking my head back below the lip, and lying on my back, I pressed the thumb button to call Littnan. Just then two hard, flat bangs—RPGs—sounded to my right. They were going after Snyder, I thought. I looked over there, but could see no damage; Snyder was still busy firing away. I was looking directly at the 90mm team when, to my horror, an RPG hit directly in front of them. The black barrel of the gun went high in the air, emerging out of a cloud of dirt, leaves and explosives. I saw a helmet go flying; then Clifton and Nelson appeared, their bodies rolling down slope.

"Jesus!" I heard Eden mutter. I was still watching Nelson's limbs flopping loosely against the slope when two more explosions sounded, immediately above and behind me. They were firing into the trees over our heads. The vicious, heavy droning sound of .51 caliber slugs split the air a foot or two over my head; then another RPG landed above. I looked back to my left; Eden was yelling at one of his men, motioning him down. Another RPG hit; I could hear the rattle and snap of shrapnel, branches and wood splinters as they tore through the underbrush.

"Oh, Christ, Lieutenant!"

It was Helms, shaking; he pointed a finger down slope. I gave an involuntary cry; Muldoon was down, lying in a bloody heap at the base of a tree. His face was whiter than ever; his eyes were closed. Behind him, Hyde was on his feet, running toward him. It didn't occur to me until later that this marked the first time I'd ever heard Helms swear.

"Six, this is One Six. We're taking heavy RPG fire now, over."

"Roger, One Six. Are you taking casualties?"

"Affirmative. I need a medic; Doc's hit." A burst of heavy automatic weapons fire sent Eden, who had started to get to his feet, diving back to the earth. I slid back down the slope and turned back onto my stomach, so that now I was facing the bunkers. I saw Samuel bend his head down, load a grenade into his launcher, and with a quick motion bring it up to his shoulder and squeeze the trigger, sending the small grenade looping lazily into the brush at the base of the knoll.

"Sam!" I yelled out. "Can you see where that RPG fire's coming from?"

We ducked as two more RPGs exploded behind us. "No! That gun's in the saddle, I think!" he yelled back.

I looked back over my shoulder. Muldoon, his left arm and upper thigh bloody, was staggering to his feet; he stumbled and half-fell. Hyde and one or two others reached out to steady him. I gave a quick, preoccupied sigh of relief.

By now the RPGs were coming in a steady stream, shredding the trees behind us. Fortunately most of the branches had already been stripped off the trunks, so that many of the rounds passed right through them to land harmlessly in the ravine.

"One Six!"

I started. I'd forgotten that I still had the mike pressed to my ear. "Roger."

"Disengage and pull back. Do you roger?"

"Affirm." I gave a quick glance around me. "We're on our way." I flipped the mike back to Helms and spoke to Eden. "Pull back, Sergeant. Let's get out of here."

He nodded and began moving along the base of the clearing, gathering his troops. Helms handed me the mike again. It was Littnan.

"Pop smoke, One Six," he said. "I've got Bilk Two Three overhead."

"Roger." I turned over on my back again, slid quickly up the slope, reached down and took a white smoke bomb, untwisted the thin aluminum handle by which it was clipped to a ring on my harness, brought it up to my face, pulled the pin, and threw the green cylinder over my head, as far as I could. I squirmed back down slope. Eden's right flank was ready; I motioned for him to proceed. I glanced the other way, and froze, in dismay and a sudden, sickening realization.

Snyder, who was now all alone on the left flank, would have to remain there while the rest of the platoon pulled back. The sudden understanding hit me hard. Black Jack's words came back to me: I'd been given a commission so I could order men to die. In this case, I didn't even have to give an order; Snyder was where he was, and all I had to do was lie there, mutely, and leave him there. Eden looked past me, saw Snyder, and then looked at me. He opened his mouth, and then his eyes widened. We stared at each other for a long second. He turned away and with savage yells urged his men down the hill, past him. The last of them — Mareniewski — scuttled and stumbled down the trail. I motioned for Helms to go with them. Then Eden and I crept back up to the clearing's edge.

Snyder almost died. He should have died. Enemy fire was now concentrated on him; RPGs, machine gun fire, AK-47, and, as we watched, grenades. An RPG slammed into the ground a few yards in front of him, scattering shrapnel and rock fragments across the trunk behind which he lay. Two grenades, thrown from the knoll to our left, landed against the trunk, bounced back into the clearing, and exploded in a shower of dirt and leaves. Then, fat and lazy, floating in the air like a waffled pass in a touch football game, a third grenade came out of the tree line; Eden and I could only cry out as it hit Snyder's helmet, bounced straight up in the air, and landed beside him, inches from his chest. Snyder gave it one indifferent glance and resumed firing his M16. The grenade, a dud, lay there. Snyder gave one last burst of M16 fire, pulled out one last grenade — how had he even been able to walk, carrying all those things, I wondered — threw it, and, in a flurry of long arms and legs, scrambled and slid and crawled and rolled down the slope past us. Eden and I fired blindly, spraying the knolls and saddle, hoping to keep the NVA in their bunkers for a few extra seconds. Then we ran down the slope. Hyde and two or three of his men knelt along the trail, covering us.

Even before we made it back to the perimeter, the first of the F105s came screaming out of the west with its load of 500 pound bombs. The ordnance landed with a satisfying crump-*whump* high up on the slopes.

Company CP; YC324983

Littnan was waiting for me at the perimeter. He gave me a nod, and said, "We'll let Bilk Two Three beat up on 'em for a while. Did you spot any bunkers?"

"Yeah. That one that Marsh was talking about last night, the one right in the middle — that's empty. But there are two off to the left; my 90mm crew fired three or four rounds into them before they got hit. But I'd say they've got bunkers all over the place; there was a helluva lot of fire coming from the right and left, and that .51 was definitely on that right hand knoll. RPGs all over the place."

"Yeah." He was frowning. "What happened to your 90mm?"

I shook my head. "Had to leave it there; RPG hit right in front of it, blew it up, along with the crew. It was a direct hit, so I didn't see the point in risking anyone just to retrieve a piece of wrecked equipment."

"Umph. You're sure it was destroyed?"

I shrugged. "Not a hundred per cent, no. But I saw that barrel go straight up in the air; that RPG must have hit directly underneath it."

He grimaced. "Okay. We'll see what we can do about picking it up later. What else can you tell me about the defenses?"

I went over what we'd seen; there wasn't much more to mention. We had confirmed our belief that the clearing had been set up as a killing zone, but that was hardly a surprising discovery. The bunkers would have to be cleared one-by-one, which was not exactly news, either. I pointed out the one new wrinkle we'd come across: the RPG fire they were directing into the trees above our heads.

"It might be," I offered as explanation, "that they didn't realize that their fields of fire didn't extend past the clearing. I would guess that when they saw that we weren't getting hurt, they decided they'd try that."

Littnan shook his head in disagreement. "Not very likely. They know darn well that the slope below the clearing is adequate cover. No, I'll bet that the reason they didn't bother with that tactic yesterday is that they already had so many targets in the killing zone they didn't need to use it."

"Good point."

"Okay. Good job. We'll be bringing in Bilk Two Three for the rest of the morning; then I'll send Two Six up. I want you to start digging in; we may be here a while, and I don't want to go through another night like last one. Leave your people where they are, but make sure those holes are good and deep. "Oh — one other thing: 326th Engineers will be sending in a team later today, probably this morning. They're going to cut an LZ for us just below the NDP. They'll have to bring them in on jungle penetrator; I'll want you to send a squad down to cover them while they're being inserted."

"Yeah." We separated, each to his own CP.

My stomach was still tight from the tension of the previous hour. Only now, after leaving Littnan, did it hit me that Muldoon was gone. I wondered if I'd ever see that ugly face or hear that raspy, angular tenor again. I hoped so. I was going to miss the son of a bitch.

I got a surprise when I reached the CP. Nelson and Clifton were standing by a half-dug foxhole, bareheaded, grinning, obviously unhurt. The last time I'd seen them they'd been rolling and flopping down the hill; I'd been sure, then, that they'd been seriously wounded. Neither one had a scratch. Nelson spotted me and let out a crow of triumph.

"Hey! Lieutenant! We got that sucker, didn't we?"

Clifton nodded enthusiastic agreement. His face was split by a gap-toothed grin. "Two of 'em," he said. "We saw 'em come flyin' outta that bunker. That Ninety is a mean machine, by God."

Nelson chuckled. "Count coup, Cliff. When we goin' back up, Lieutenant?"

I made a sour grimace and shook my head. "What the hell will you two do when we do go back up? You left that mean machine of yours behind, you know."

Nelson stopped grinning. "No shit? You mean that? I thought one of the other guys mighta picked it up. You mean it's still up there?"

"Not only is it still there, but even if we get it back, I doubt you'd be able to use it much. That RPG landed right underneath it."

Clifton grunted. "Is that what that was? I didn't know for sure."

"First thing I knew, I was makin' like Superman—flyin'." Nelson grinned. "I musta gone 50 feet."

"More like 10 or 15," I said. "You guys are lucky to be alive."

Nelson blinked in surprise. "Nah. No sweat." Then he grinned again. "But did you see them fuckers come flyin' outta there? I mean...."

They went on about it, still flushed with the enthusiasm of the kill. That they had had a miraculous escape; that they should have been, by all the laws of probability, dead or severely wounded, did not occur to them, much less bother them. They were young, after all, and warriors.

Doc Schoch was coming up the trail; he walked slowly, bent forward, shoulders sagging with fatigue. I called out to him; he looked my way, and his eyes were neither young nor a warrior's.

"How's Muldoon?" I asked.

Schoch stretched, shrugged his shoulders, stretched again, trying to loosen up tight muscles. "Okay," he said. "He's back at the Battalion CP. He'll be lifted out in a while."

"You mean he's not gone yet? What's the holdup?"

Schoch made a dismissive gesture. "He's not in bad shape. He got hit by a lot of shrapnel, but most of it went barely past the skin. He had one or two pieces that got into him pretty good, but overall he hasn't lost much blood. And we've decided to hold off extractions until those Engineers blow us an LZ."

"They're coming soon, then?"

Schoch shrugged again. "Yeah." His eyes were glazed with fatigue; he couldn't have had much sleep lately.

"You look tired, Doc," I said, in concern.

"I'm okay. O'Keefe's coming up to give me a hand."

"Good. He's a good man."

"Yeah. He is." Schoch smiled briefly. "By the way, Muldoon says to tell you he'll see you back in The World."

I grinned. "As long as he can guarantee it."

There wasn't much for me to do; Sergeant Wright had already gotten the men started on their foxholes. I made a tour of the platoon sector. The men were digging in with a determined will. When I got to the last position, where Snyder, Jackson, Mareniewski and Edwards were digging in, I considered making a reference or two to last night's follies, but then decided against it. The story, by one means or another, had spread throughout the platoon, and the guys were already getting enough grief over it. Besides, Snyder had more than paid his dues.

I looked at my watch: 1130. I considered lunch; I hadn't eaten since noon of the previous day, but found out that I really wasn't hungry. I returned to the CP. Helms and Brown sat by their radios, talking quietly. PFC Wright had dumped his a few yards away; he was stretched out beside it, asleep. Sergeant Wright was nowhere to be seen. I shrugged, went to my pack, dug out my latest book — *Three Great Tales*, by Conrad — settled down with my back against a tree, lit a Camel, and started reading.

The F105s pounded the hill for the next two hours, flying sortie after sortie against the bunker complexes. After a while, it became routine, an unnoticed background noise that we heard but became aware of only when it ceased, like an air conditioner or refrigerator at home. First came the screeching, full-throated roar as the jet approached, a sound that was more insistent, more compelling, than the rumble of a commercial jetliner. Just as the craft drew even with us — the pilots were making their approaches from the west, following a ridge that paralleled ours about one kilometer distant — the pilot would release his ordnance with an audible click; then the pitch would drop suddenly to a low rumble as the Doppler effect marked the passing of the jet. Then came the faint, ghostly whistle as the bomb fell and the huge CRRRRUMP! when it exploded. Finally, soft and feathery, came the patter all around us as bits of trees and earth fell back to the battered ground. Then the next screech…

I'd already read the first and last stories, *Nigger of the Narcissus* and *Heart of Darkness* — it would hardly have been possible to attain a four-year degree in English Literature and not have read these two — but this was my first meeting with *Typhoon*. Within pages, Conrad had me hooked, as Conrad always does, and I read eagerly, paying no attention to what was going on around me. Only once, as Captain MacWhirr asked Mr. Jukes why he found it necessary to think upon Chinamen, did I happen to look up as one of the sharkish mottled-green F105s made its run. I heard the click of the release mechanism and followed the path of the 500-pounder as it tumbled, black and clumsy, to the ground. This particular one landed well short, down on a ridge instead of up along the hilltop; it hit where I could see it, about a kilometer away. A huge spout of dirty grey smoke and brown earth sprang up; inside was a harsh red glow, like lightning seen through dense clouds. Balanced perfectly on top of that cloud, upright and solitary, stood a tree, its trunk whole, its crown still intact; it hung outlined against the southern sky, motionless. I frowned; it reminded me of Muldoon's description of Tunney, with his arms outspread, teetering on the edge. Then it slowly fell, the crown still uppermost, until it hit the ridge, where it finally toppled and lay, shattered roots sticking up into the air like a hundred splintered bones. I raised an eyebrow, glanced around; no one else had seen it. I shrugged, half-annoyed and returned to the page. *Jukes took the plunge, like a man driven to it...*

30

The Book of Myles Westman

YC324983; 12 May 1969; 1300

Marsh Eward assembled his people at 1300. They were laden with extra ammo, M16 and M60. They stood, listening with appreciative grins, as Eward gave them a final briefing.

"...And one last thing," he added. "You know those assholes from One Six? They was already up there once today, and you know how they are: They left their Ninety behind. Last night it was Four Six couldn't keep up with their stuff. Seems like all we're doing up here is cleaning up after the other platoons. Well, can't be helped. So, if you guys are finished lunch, and are in the mood for a little police call...."

Eward gave his point man a casual nod. He waited until two more men had filed by, then he stepped onto the trail, giving us a wave. As soon as his last man had moved up the trail, we moved into place behind him. Our job was the relatively simple one of securing the trail between the Company CP and the contact point; it was important, but boring. I spent most of my time kneeling alongside the trail, with my radio mike in my ear.

There was nothing for us to see, and there wasn't much more to hear, either. Eward would of course not bother with the radio until he made contact, and so I could only guess, by the amount of time that had elapsed, when he actually made it to the clearing. I looked at my watch six or seven times, wondering when he'd get there. Finally, my watch showed 1330 hours; he had to be there by now, but I heard nothing from up front, nothing over the radio. For a second or two I wondered if my radio was working at all, and actually thought of calling Littnan's CP for a radio check, but I stifled that impulse hastily. Littnan would have my head if I got on the net while Eward was on the verge of contact.

There was more background noise — 105s or 155s from Berchtesgaden, and perhaps some 81mm from the battalion CP, all going into the eastern slope of Dong Ap Bia — but even so the first burst of gunfire which ripped across the ridge a few moments later seemed to have shredded a deep silence. There were four or five weapons firing, in short bursts of automatic fire — it was nothing like the hail of fire Four Six had encountered the day before. At that, at least two of the weapons were M16s; I recognized their metallic bark easily. There were, for the moment, no RPGs and no heavy weapons. The radio was still silent. I kept expecting Littnan to call Eward; I would certainly have done so by now. But Littnan was more patient than I. Gradually the volume of gunfire increased; now I could hear the thumping of a light machine gun — one of theirs. Finally, several minutes after the first burst, I heard the sound I'd come to expect: the flat slam of an RPG. Then another. And, quickly, a third.

"Six, this is Two Six."

"This is Six. What have you got?"

"Not much," Eward drawled. His voice was pitched high, as it always was on the radio, but it was calm and even. "Got some stuff coming in from my left flank — north — and a bit from straight in front of me. Nothing from the right flank. Small-arms and RPGs. No heavy stuff, yet."

"Roger, Two Six. Casualties?"

"Negative. We've got 'em bottled up pretty good. Got two gooks lying a few feet from me; look like pincushions. Must be those two One Six shot up this morning. One of my people just took out a bunker a minute ago; got at least one more there."

"Right. Where are those bunkers? Can you see them?"

"Negative. Not all of 'em. From where I am I can see three bunkers; the one that Four Six walked into yesterday, the one One Six shot up this morning, and the one my guy took out. I know there are plenty more, but I can't see 'em."

"Roger. Where are you now?"

"I'm on the left side of the clearing, over by the head of that ravine that runs off just to the north of the ridge. I got my people strung out along the rim of this clearing. They can't seem to get at us here, but I don't know if I can go much further; there's no cover between us and those two knolls."

"Roger. Anything else?"

"Yeah. I — hey! wait one!"

His last word or two was drowned out by a surge of noise as the automatic weapons fire intensified. The insistent thumping of an M60 was prominent amidst it all. Then it slacked off, and Eward got back on the radio.

"They got some fightin' positions — I don't think they're bunkers — up in the middle of that saddle; they just let fly. We got 'em shut up again, but I don't see how I can do much more, unless I take some heavy casualties."

"Roger. Wait one." There was a pause, during which the firing continued, but less radically. Probably neither side was hitting anything, and so neither saw any reason to expend further ammunition. After a moment Littnan resumed talking. "Break it off, Two Six. You got that Ninety of One Six's?"

I winced. "Yeah, we got it," Eward replied. "Tell those other guys I'm gettin' tired of pickin' up after them."

"Roger. Out." There was another pause. "One Six, this is Six."

I thumbed the mike. "Roger."

"Wait until Two Six is down past you; I want you to cover in case they try to follow him down."

"Roger."

Eward's people filed past us, grinning; they'd not suffered a scratch. Eward was carrying the Ninety himself. He stopped when he saw me, held it out, and arched an eyebrow.

"Excuse me, ma'am," he asked politely, "did you drop this?"

I took it from him with no comment. My wisest course was a dignified silence.

The digging was proceeding slowly, as was to be expected. The ridge here was narrow, the trees large; there were few places free of their massive roots. The sun had broken free of the clouds to the west. It dappled the tree trunks and bushes with a flickering, shifting light, and brought a steamy warmth. The men dug steadily, their bare backs slick with sweat. Low voices muttered and murmured. Occasionally there came a bark of laughter, or a sharp curse, as shovel met unyielding root or rock. The chink! of blade against earth and the soughing and whumping of thrown dirt were the only other sounds. It was, oddly, a scene of peace. I turned away momentarily from my platoon sector to stand at the edge of the slope, facing west. Barely seen were the mountains of Laos, draped in mystery — I had never seen them, and a part of me acknowledged that I never would. For some reason that saddened me.

"Well, fuck it, man. You gonna dig this goddamn hole or not?"

I jerked my head around. The angry shout shattered the smooth patter and murmur as a jagged rock does a pond surface. I never liked to hear that anger in my platoon. It almost invariably meant that Sergeant Wright or I had failed somewhere. I was surprised, almost shocked, to see that the man who'd shouted was Logan. He stood a few yards away, bare-chested and sweaty, glaring down at a diminutive figure. It struck me that I had never seen Logan angry before. The smaller man was Carlton; his round, little-boy face was a study in pouting stubbornness.

"I been digging," Short Round said, with a sort of hesitant willfulness.

"You have like shit! You haven't done a damn thing! Look at that damn hole! You haven't dug a fuckin' inch since I left!"

Carlton stared down at the ground. He couldn't bring himself to answer Logan — the man was twice his size, for one thing, and Carlton didn't have it in him to stand his ground for long. He was shy, and uncertain, and in all his life he had never challenged anyone, and certainly not anyone like this bristling, granite-faced ape who towered over him. I was surprised at Logan's anger; he was usually imperturbable, and I'd never thought of him as a bully.

He snorted in disgust. "Look, man; it's about time you started pulling your weight around here. We're damn tired of carryin' you."

"Why don't you just back off, Logan?" Grump Ulrich had been working on an adjacent foxhole; his entrenching tool was stuck in the pile of dirt alongside it. He advanced on Logan, hands on hips, sweat and dirt caked across his chest and neck. He wasn't as big as Logan—few of us were—but he'd spent a good deal of his life challenging people.

Logan whirled to face him, enraged. "Why don't you get back to your hole, chump? This ain't got nothin' to do with you."

"Who the fuck made you squad leader? You gotta fuck with somebody, fuck with me. Don't mean shit fuckin' with somebody half your size."

"Half my size or not, he isn't doing a damn thing. I'm not fuckin' with him, I'm trying to get him to do some goddamn work for a change. The little shit ain't worth a damn. He won't dig, he won't stand guard, he won't clean up, he won't take point; he froze up and damn near got us killed up on Airborne—"

"We all know the reason you damn near got killed up there was 'cause your fuckin' Sixty jammed; didn't have shit to do with Short Round," Ulrich sneered. "Why don't you fuckin' worry about gettin' your shit straight, 'stead of fuckin' with him?"

Logan's small eyes narrowed to dangerous slits. "Look, asshole," he growled ominously. He took a step forward.

This had gone far enough. But before I could make a move in their direction, a tall, thick-shouldered figure stepped out from behind a tree, carrying an open entrenching tool in his hand. Westman. Of course.

"Come on, Raymond," he said, holding out a hand. "Let me help you with that." Westman's lilting, upper-Minnesota accent cut through the anger like a heated knife. He was the only man in the platoon who called Carlton by his Christian name. Taking the entrenching tool from Carlton's hand, he began pushing it deep into the ground, his powerful farmer's shoulders bulging with the effort. He glanced up at the still-scowling Logan and smiled, briefly, before lowering his head again.

Logan and Ulrich stood there utterly baffled. The anger disappeared like light fog before a strong wind; a moment later Logan shrugged, shook his head, and picked up his own tool. Stepping up beside Westman, he began breaking up the tough, root-strewn surface. After a moment, he smiled. Ulrich stood uncertainly for another few seconds, and then turned and returned to his own digging. Carlton sat down and began kneading his tired upper arms.

I looked up and saw Sergeant Wright; he'd been attracted by the earlier shouts, as I had been. Our eyes found each other's, and we both gave a tiny, unbelieving shake of our heads.

Littnan called a meeting—Eward, Sergeant Garza, Sergeant Murtiff and I; the brain trust—so we could compare impressions and observations. We did so. We talked for half an hour and came to the conclusion that we didn't know what was going on. Littnan listened to each of us, then sat in silence. After a few moments, he looked at Eward.

"How many NVA are up there, Marsh?"

Eward shrugged. "I don't know. I figure at least ten bunkers. That's more than one platoon. Company, maybe."

Littnan transferred his gaze to me.

"I don't know either," I said. "A company sounds about right."

"They got a .51," Murtiff observed. "That's TOE for a company, not platoon."

The CO nodded thoughtfully. "The next question is, are they sitting on this one trail, or are they all over the mountain."

"Are we going to move to another ridge?" Eward asked.

"No. We'll stay here; keep your men digging. Charlie and Delta will move into the ridges north and south of us, I think." Littnan looked at each of us in turn. "Black Jack wants this hill."

"Fine," I said. "Tell him to walk up and take it, anytime."

Littnan ignored me. "So we'll find out then what we've got up there. There's one other thing; there's not much left of Fourth Platoon. I'm going to combine them with Third Platoon. I talked to Black Jack about this; he's got some new lieutenants down at Evans, but I don't think that this is the time to bring in a new man. He agrees; I don't know who, but we got an experienced man on the way. He'll be our new Three Six."

"As long as it isn't Dickson," Eward muttered.

"One last thing," Littnan added. "That pathfinder team will be here in a while. We've already talked about where they're going in. Bo, you'll secure the LZ site for them. While they're coming in, Marsh, I want you to take your people back up to the clearing. Do not, I repeat, *do not*, press the issue. Make contact, stay below that clearing, and bring pressure on them; keep them in those bunkers. But don't expose yourself, and stay the hell out of that clearing."

"Roger," Marsh said.

Littnan looked at his watch. "It's almost 1500. The engineers ought to be enroute by 1600. I'll let you both know. That's it."

Littnan called at 1630 to tell me that the pathfinder team from the 326th Engineers was en route. I was to take two squads and secure the area.

What we wanted to do was to blow an LZ, about 25 or 30 meters wide, just above the junction of the two trails at the foot of the ridge. This was the only place level enough to bring Hueys in. The slope here fell off into a shallow, sparsely-covered valley, about 100 meters to the south.

It might be asked why, with that large expanse of treeless slope just meters away, we were going to the trouble of blowing an LZ, or why we hadn't brought the medevacs in there the previous day. Then, Rairdon had hovered his LOH over the bare southern slope, as close as possible to the tree line.

The answer is twofold. First, because the southern slope was too steep to be really suitable for an LZ — we'd used it yesterday in an emergency, with Rairdon's LOH, when there had been too many casualties from Fourth Platoon to evacuate all of them by jungle penetrator, but it was not something that we could continue to count on. Huey pilots do not like the idea of backing out of an LZ, which they'd have to do if they came directly at the slope, and even less do they like the fact that their blades would be only a foot or so off the ground, which would be the case if they came in across the slope. To continue to rely on Rairdon's smaller, more maneuverable LOH was unrealistic; he could carry only two or three men at a time. Secondly, it would be impossible to secure the southern slope; it was too large an area, and there were too many hilltops and ridges overlooking it from which a sniper or trail watcher could shoot down at landing aircraft. I personally had had all I wanted of trying to bring helicopters into indefensible LZs back on Hill 1485. The LOH, of course, had been exposed the whole time the day before, but that had been, as I've said, an emergency, and anyway, that's why the pilot was known as Crazy Rairdon.

The spot Littnan picked for an LZ was also the point where the Engineer team would be inserted; there was a small patch of blue sky there, not large enough for any kind of helicopter to land, but large enough to allow for an easy rappelling maneuver. Eden's squad secured the area immediately around the insertion point; I sent Hyde's squad down to the trail junction, about 30 or 40 meters away, and had him secure that and the trail between us.

Less than a minute after we'd moved into place all hell let out for lunch. A tremendous burst of automatic weapons fire erupted to our east, from the top of the hill; Eward must have made a bit more contact than he'd intended. When I got the mike from Helms, however, I heard Marsh telling the CO that he was taking no casualties. The fire, he said, was coming from the hill above him, and also from the ravine to his south. That ravine, of course, was simply the head of the valley I was overlooking at the moment, but he was much farther up the ridge, just below the hilltop.

I waited until he was through talking and asked Littnan if the engineers were still on the way.

"Hell yes," he said, showing that he was distraught. (Hell and damn were the two strongest expletives he used. A frown, from him, was a raging tantrum. The contrast between him and Robison couldn't have been greater.) "Are they too good to be shot at? Darn right they're coming."

"Roger. I'm in place." I handed the mike back to Helms. The volume of fire from our east lessened; apparently Eward and the NVA were moving towards a mutual accommodation. A few minutes later, I heard the heavy whop-whop of a Huey. Helms picked up his mike; one of Littnan's RTOs was on the line, telling him that the pilot was on the net. It was our old friend Black Widow Four Two. Helms called the pilot; listened and answered, and then looked over at me.

"He wants some smoke," he said.

I nodded. A moment later, the bright chrome yellow smoke from one of my grenades was billowing and dancing through the trees. The hammer-sound of the Huey became louder as it approached. Helms spoke again into the mike, and then clipped it back onto his harness.

"He's here," he said, unnecessarily.

30. The Book of Myles Westman

YD322985; 12 May: 1700

The slick appeared through the treetops overhead. Black Widow Four Two chivvied his craft back and forth for a moment, placing himself directly over the small clearing. A rope snaked down from the starboard side, whipping back and forth in the prop blast; the last of the yellow smoke was torn into ephemeral fragments by the same fierce wind. A moment later, two black-and-green jungle boots appeared, followed by the rest of the engineer's body. He slid down the rope, holding on to it with his left hand, which was raised over his head; his other hand was holding a bight rope, with which he could, by tightening or loosening it, control his rate of descent. He was still only a few feet below the skids when his body jerked; his left hand let go of the rope. The engineer's right hand was looped around the bight cord; his left arm and shoulder fell back, but his body still hung from the rope, suspended by his right arm. His helmet fell off and landed almost at my feet. For a second I was stunned; we'd heard no shot, but then, we wouldn't have, with the noise that the Huey was making. Then I spun and moved quickly to Helms, but before I could grab the mike the pilot realized that he was being shot at. Possibly he might have thought that the engineer had already descended, but in any case, he had no choice. He pulled his craft up and to port, trying to escape. This pulled the engineer through the branches of a large ironwood tree; the rope wrapped itself around a heavy limb and tautened.

For a terrifying moment I thought the helicopter would be pulled back down by the rope, tilting its blades into the treetops and sending it crashing down on our heads. Overhead, Captain Tom Lough, CO of Bravo Company of the 326th, came to the same realization; with only a moment's hesitation, he pulled out his knife and cut the rope. The Huey swerved off with a roar; the engineer fell 30 feet to the ground. Doc Stenger raced to his side.

Littnan was already on the radio; he'd heard the Huey fly off and knew that it had left too soon.

"One Six, this is Six. What's going on?"

"Sniper fire from our south. He got that first engineer. Over."

There was a three or four second pause. "Roger. Was the bird hit?"

"I don't know for sure, but I think not. If it was, it wasn't hit bad. The engineer got it, though."

"Roger. What's his condition?"

I looked over to where Stenger, and now Schoch, were working on the man. Stenger was holding an IV bottle up over his head, while Schoch was bent over, possibly giving the man mouth-to-mouth; I couldn't tell because he was blocking my view. "He's alive," I said. "That's all I can tell you."

"Roger. Break. Black Widow Four Two, this is Bravo Six."

"Roger, Bravo Six."

"Were you hit, over?"

"Negative, Bravo Six."

"Can you hold up there while we try to secure the area, over?"

"Affirmative."

"Roger. Break. One Six, do you know where that shot come from, over?"

"Negative."

"Well, find out. Out."

I was beginning to understand that LZs and I just didn't mix.

Sergeant Wright had already moved among the men on the south side of the perimeter, checking to see if anyone had an idea where the sniper was—or, more probably, had been—shooting from. In the meantime, the volume of fire from us had increased again.

"Anybody see where it came from, Top?"

"No sir. No one saw it. Ulrich and Besak think it came from the bottom of the valley. In the tree line, along that trail."

"You mean down there, southwest?" I asked.

"That's what they say. Could be; they both heard it."

"Yeah." I stepped with him to the tree line and looked down to my right, where he was pointing. "That's a hell of an angle, Top. That bird was facing just about northeast; if that round came from down there, he was firing right at the tail ... well, no; I guess not. He was shooting at the engineer, wasn't he. Hell of a shot, though."

"Not really, Lieutenant. Three hundred meters—less, really. Not that tough a shot."

"Yeah." I didn't relish the idea of telling Littnan that I wasn't sure where the round had come from, and even less was I looking forward to telling him that I didn't think we could secure the area well enough to allow another chopper in. I called and gave him the news; he was noncommittal. A few minutes went by, during which he talked first to Eward, who was still taking heavy but ineffective fire, and then to Black Jack on the battalion net. While I was waiting, I had two or three of the men fire random single shots into the trees on the valley floor, just on the off-chance that we might flush the sniper. It wasn't much of an idea, I admit, but I couldn't think of anything else we could do at the moment. Ten minutes later, Littnan called back.

"Black Jack wants those engineers down there," he said. "They're on their way back. This time, as they make their approach, lay down suppressant fire into that valley."

I raised an eyebrow. The term "suppressant fire" sounds nice but it is, after all, only a phrase. With two squads and their organic weapons, which is what I had available, to cover an area two or three times larger than a football field, it would be no more than that. I repeated that I couldn't guarantee the chopper's safety.

Littnan allowed himself to become impatient, for the first time since he'd taken over. It's a gift I have. "I'm not asking you to guarantee anything, One Six; I'm telling you to cover the damn bird when it comes in. Out."

First Sergeant Murtiff came rolling down the trail a few minutes later. After a short conference, we decided to pull two four-man teams from the north side of the ridge and line them up along the south side. This gave us about 20 weapons, including Logan's M60. This was a bit better than before, but there was still an awful lot of valley to cover. Besides, there was no known rule of law or warfare which said that the sniper had to be in that valley; he, or another one or two just like him, could have set up on any one of the several knolls, ridges, or hilltops which overlooked our ridge.

Nonetheless, there we were, weapons trained and waiting, when the chopper returned. Poor Black Widow Four Two must have been wondering what the hell he'd done to deserve this. As soon as he banked and turned into the ridge, facing us, we began firing. I stood just behind Logan, watching his tracer rounds rip into the vegetation at the crest of the ridge to our south. I wasn't even looking at the chopper. Behind me, I heard the sharp snap! as Wright or Murtiff popped a smoke grenade. The wind was blowing from southwest to northeast, so I couldn't see, but I could visualize the smoke — green, or purple, or yellow — billowing out behind me.

The Huey was approaching fast, above me and slightly to my right. Then the noise level changed; he was about 10 or 15 meters out, his nose lifted, his tail swaying slightly as he maneuvered closer to the smoke. Suddenly, the engine noise changed again, from the heavy whup-whup to a runaway-washing-machine clatter. I looked away from Logan's tracers and snapped my jaws shut with a curse. His frame was shaking, his nose was down. I hadn't heard the shot — how could I, with all that noise? — but there was no doubt he'd been hit. I watched with a wretched sense of déjà vu as the Huey slowly tilted to port; a blade broke off from the shaft with a heavy sing-song snarl, and then the craft dropped like a stone. It hit the slope in front of us, bounced a few feet back into the air, and then rolled slowly down the hill, the remaining blades snapping off like brittle tree limbs; it came to rest on its back, awkwardly, like an upturned beetle. A second later flame gushed out of the rear of the fuselage, and we experienced a moment of horror, believing that the chopper would blow up with the survivors — if any — still inside. I had started to reach out a hand to Helms — by now, that gesture was automatic, a true Pavlovian reflex — but I jerked it back and ran down the slope. Several of the men had jumped from their position and were running toward the helicopter. I stopped, abruptly. Someone had to cover the men going to rescue the fliers; we were all exposed along that bare slope. But then I saw that Sergeant Wright was already directing fire, including Logan's M60, into a small wooded hilltop across the valley floor. He or one of the men might have spotted a muzzle flash; no one could possibly have heard anything.

Men had already reached the helicopter and were pulling the wounded out. That first burst of flame had subsided, but smoke still rose up from the rear housing. Two men — engineers, from their uniforms — had been thrown from the open-sided Huey as it rolled downhill; they lay only a few meters away. Kenzy and Mareniewski grabbed one of them by his arms and began dragging him up the slope. Samuel and Olson —

the two of them together couldn't have weighed 240 pounds—took the other one and somehow wrestled him up the hill. Within an unbelievably short time—I thought it was less than a minute although it may have been just a bit more—the crew and passengers had been evacuated and were on their way up to the ridge.

Just in time: The smoke suddenly thickened and slender yellow fangs of flame began biting the flanks of the fallen slick. I backpedaled up the slope, watching the fire build. Someone yelled from behind me—"There's one more! One more! There's a guy still down there!"

I swung around, staring. Gann, a few feet behind me, and I were the closest ones to the wreck. There was nothing for it but to go. Cursing as imaginatively as I could—which, all things considered, wasn't particularly imaginative at that; I am fairly certain I repeated myself several times—I ran down the hill, unlocking the safety of the weapon as I ran. Gann was right beside me and, with his longer legs, began to pull in front as we neared the chopper. The smoke was now thick and black; the flames were both larger and more intense, and I could feel the heat sear my unprotected skin as we got closer. I uttered a brief prayer that the explosion would hold off for just another minute. Or 30 seconds: *Half a minute, God. That's all I want from you.*

Upside down and canted as it was, I could see right into the interior of the Huey; nothing and no one was in it. Gann raced around the nose, peering down into the cockpit as he ran, and checked the other side, in case the man had been thrown clear. I leaned over to get a better look at the cockpit myself, just in case; as I did so, Logan's tracers flitted overhead, arcing into the tree line to my right rear. Gann and I stood and looked at each other, simultaneously shaking our heads. There was no one left.

Up slope, to my left, some others, Eden among them, were running down toward us; I also saw Wright standing on the ridge, waving emphatically for us to return, and in that instant began some really inspired and imaginative cursing.

"Gann!" I yelled to him. "Let's go!" I'm not sure he heard me, but he saw my gesture and needed no further encouragement. The two of us began to race up the hill; Eden had already stopped the others and reversed course; they were running up slope ahead of us, some 20 or 30 meters away. As we got closer, I could hear Sergeant Wright yelling that everyone was accounted for. I'd already—if somewhat belatedly—figured out what happened: Someone—crew, engineer or one of us—had forgotten, in counting the men off the Huey, to account for the engineer who'd been shot on the rope during the first approach. These things happen. It was an understandable error, one which had sent Gann and me racing across open terrain toward a burning and about-to-explode helicopter, but on the other hand, the worst that came from it was that I had had to run about 100 meters up a saw-grass covered slope in battle gear under a 100 degree sun. Things like that, I'm told, build character.

If this were a movie, the Huey would have blown up in a black-orange ball seconds after we left it, possibly knocking Gann and me to the ground. Since it was real, however, no such thing happened. Instead, the chopper continued to burn for another half hour or so, steadily, but without exploding, until it finally consumed all the fuel. That was okay with me. My nerves had had all they were ready for, by that point.

When I got back up to the tiny clearing, I found a sort of organized madhouse. Schoch and Stenger were treating the wounded, the most seriously hurt of whom were the engineer who'd fallen from the rope and Black Widow Four Two himself, a young black warrant officer, whose thin face was almost a dead grey from loss of blood: A ricochet had caught him in the stomach, and the deep red blood welled from the wound and turned his grey-green flight suit a shiny, dangerous black. I didn't know then—Schoch told me much later—that Muldoon, himself seriously wounded, had been commandeered into treating the wounded from the Huey; he worked on them for almost an hour, back at the Battalion CP. As a reward, however, he was medevaced out along with the pilot and the engineer as soon as they were both stabilized for the flight to the hospital.

Blowing the LZ took priority, of course, but it seemed no one could agree on how to go about doing it. Black Jack wanted to insert another engineer team, but Littnan doubted whether the engineers would be lined up in eager anticipation after what had happened. Even if we could find the engineers, we had to doubt that Black Widow would jump at the chance of delivering another Huey into the NVA's gun sights. Pilots are, by my definition, crazy, but they're not imbeciles. Littnan advised blowing the LZ ourselves; he and Black Jack discussed it at some length.

In the end, Littnan prevailed and we blew the new LZ at the base of the ridge, just above the trail junction; the terrain was only slightly sloped here and the nearest big-boled tree was a safe 50 meters or so away. I'd like to say we'd become expert at it, after Hill 1485 and all, but there were complaints. The Black Widow pilots expounded, loudly and pointedly, on the size, or lack of it, of the new LZ when we'd done. One of them compared it unfavorably to the patio behind his wife's home.

"Thank God for Westman."

Sergeant Wright nodded. He and I sat by the trail, watching while the platoon, under Nathan Hyde's direction—this would be Nate's last official duty before returning home—blew and cut the LZ. They were all working together, sweating heavily in the damp, hot air. Dickerson's squad, and a squad from Third Platoon, were deployed around the base of the shallow hill, facing south and west, as security. A second squad from Garza's group was facing north, guarding the trail we'd followed from the battalion CP area the previous morning. One of the fire teams was set up by the large mahogany tree, under the unexploded RPG. They weren't overly thrilled.

We watched and talked about the platoon. Muldoon was gone; he'd not return. We both felt his loss. It had been Sergeant Wright who had taken a rebellious and surly malcontent with a chip on his shoulder and a thirst for illicit alcohol and turned him into one of the best men in the platoon. There were many good men—Kenzy, Logan,

Gann, Helms, Snyder, and several others—but inevitably, when talking about good men, the conversation would have to turn to Westman.

"Best man I've ever seen, in or out of the Army. I wish we had more like 'im."

"Yeah." I hesitated. "Yeah," I repeated. It occurred to me that if only there were enough people like Westman in the world, there'd be no need for an army. But then I shrugged. There never has been, and there never will be. "How's the digging in going, Top? We done, do you think?"

"Okay. Just about. Went slow, you know. Damn tough roots. But they busted butt." He jerked his head in the direction of the hill behind us. "They seen enough of this area to know what'll happen if they don't dig deep."

"So what's up there, Top: What do you think?"

He shook his head, almost in anger. "Don't know, Lieutenant B. But they's more than some trail watchers. That's certain. *Best* we be diggin' deep."

I grinned. "Are you telling me that it's finally okay for me to get shook?"

He smiled at the old joke between us. "Lieutenant," he replied softly, "I reckon it's gonna be our *duty* to get shook."

I was determined that this afternoon, before it got dark, and for the first time on this operation, I would take my time preparing and eating a meal. I found a prize—a can of franks and beans, about the best that the C-rats had to offer—and, while that was bubbling over the stove and heat tab, ate some crackers, first with cheese and then with strawberry jam. After the main course, I finished it all up with pound cake and a Chuckles bar, washing it all down with a pint or so of warm, iodine-tainted water. Steak and French fries it was not, nor—I allowed my imagination and self-pity to get a little out of control—was it *risotto alla Milanese, vitello tonnato, saltimbocchi alla romana, prosciutto e melone, sole meuniere, pate de foie au compagne, zuppa di pesce, smoked Smithfield ham, Kansas City barbeque, Barolo, Chateau Barton or Napoleon*.... Every once in a while, I got a bad attack of the damn-it-alls.

The troops were a little more animated that night. That was understandable. The previous night, it had rained, we hadn't had a chance to dig in properly, nor to take our creature comforts—I doubt that there had been many, if any, hot meals the night before—and, most of all, the mauling of Bravo Four was fresh in everyone's mind. Tonight, we were dug in, we'd eaten and rested, there was no rain and Spooky—dear old ugly guardian angel Spooky—would be flying overhead. Most importantly, we'd probed the bunkers above three times—us once and Bravo Two twice—and killed anywhere from four to six NVA while suffering only one casualty between us. And that one—Muldoon—was probably grinning from ear to ear while on his way to a hospital ship somewhere.

And yet ... and yet, there was a sense of imminence, an unpleasantly resonating vibration just below the sensory threshold. I sensed it. The troops sensed it. This was nothing like what we'd felt on Hill 1485. There, we'd found ourselves, willy-nilly, in a firefight, surrounded and cut off. At no time during that period did we have a choice, nor were we in doubt. The enemy would attack us, and continue to attack us until we were overwhelmed or we proved ourselves capable of resisting. There had been fear, of course; you can't be surrounded by a numerically superior force without there being *some* fear, but there was little uncertainty. We knew what to expect. Tonight, things were different. Dong Ap Bia, the Mountain of the Crouching Beast, was already in dark shadow, proof against the faltering westerly light. We could only sit, speculate, talk and wonder.

31

Feeling Our Way

YC323984; 12–13 May 1969; 1800

Most of the troops were doing just that, as I made my rounds of the perimeter. Nelson sat with his back to a tree, a few feet from his freshly dug foxhole. Hernandez and Williams sat nearby; all three were eating dinner. Clifton, helmeted and holding his weapon, sat with his back to them, looking out across the north slope of the ridge. The other three paused momentarily to greet me as I walked up, and then resumed eating. After another moment, when it became obvious that I was just standing there and had nothing to say, Nelson resumed the conversation they'd evidently been having before I came.

"Yeah; Shit yeah. You just watch: They'll be gone tomorrow."

Hernandez, his broad, flat, sharp-nosed face creased by a slight frown, shook his head doubtfully. "I don't know, man. Maybe."

Nelson finished spooning the last of his spaghetti and meatballs into his mouth, laid the empty can carefully beside him, and picked up an already opened can of pears. "Uhhm," he said with his mouth full. "N-no way they're gonna be up there." He waved the can at the hill for emphasis. "Yesterday, ol' Four Six just walked into the shit, man. It'd been us, wouldn't never happen, you know? We was movin' slow, an' *careful*, man; careful. So, okay, Four Six gets their asses kicked, but we went up there today — an' Two Six did too — and whatta we get? Not a scratch. Nada, 'cept for Doc and you know that sonuvabitch prob'ly *jumped* into that RPG — didn't he, Lieutenant?"

I grinned. "I don't know, Nellie. He might have."

"Shit," Nelson snorted. "He was so fuckin' happy to get outta here...." Finished with his pears, he laid that can next to the other. He delved into his pack and brought out a couple of tropical bars. "Point is," he continued, stripping the wrapper from one of them, "we didn't take shit for casualties today. You watch; we'll go up there tomorrow mornin' and they won't be nothin' there."

Hernandez, his own meal finished, was scouring and rinsing his canteen cup. "Nellie, you're talkin' shit. You hear what they was puttin' out today? Didn't hit nobody 'cause nobody was dumb enough to move into that clearin'. What the hell you think they got up there? Couple of mouse-dick trail watchers?"

Nelson nodded. "Yeah. That's 'zactly what they got."

Hernandez snorted derisively. "Yeah? Well, you and Clif was sure movin' in a helluva hurry this mornin', comin' down off that hill and leavin' that Ninety of yours behind. You sure was movin' fast for nothing but no trail watchers."

Nelson shrugged angrily. "Hey, man; we had a fuckin' RPG go off right in our face. We wasn't runnin' down no hill. We was *blown* down that sonuvabitch. Ain't that right, Lieutenant?" Without waiting for my reply, he went on, aggressively hunching his shoulders and leaning in toward Hernandez. "And anyway, Two Six went up an' got the mother back — took it right away from 'em. They kicked ass and took names, too. So did Clif an' me. Be real, man. Them gooks is long gone. Spooky's gonna fly tonight." He waved at the sky above us. "Charley an' Delta's gonna move into them ridges 'long side of us — ain't that right, Lieutenant? There — see? Gooks'll have a whole battalion diggin' in their shit tomorrow. They'll be long gone. Long gone."

Williams, who'd been quietly smoking a cigarette, crushed the butt out on the sole of his boot and tossed it into the empty can. "Ain't never heard of no trail watcher got no fuckin' fifty caliber, man."

Nelson shrugged. "Yeah, well ... gooks ain't gonna fuck with no battalion." He looked up at me. "Whattya think, Lieutenant? What's up there?"

I gave a quick shrug of my own. "I don't know, Nellie. We'll see. Maybe when Charley and Delta start putting pressure on them tomorrow morning they'll take off. They usually do."

Hernandez slumped moodily against his pack. "I hope so, man. This is gettin' to be too much like combat."

After finishing my rounds, I returned to my CP. It seemed empty without the raspy tenor cursing of Muldoon's. There was just enough light left for me to read a few pages more of *Typhoon*. I'm normally a fast reader. But the afternoon had been one interruption after another, so I'd only made it to the end of Chapter Three. I pulled the book from its plastic bag, opened it and began reading. Conrad's prose stole over me like swift twilight.

> "...He was not scared; he knew this because, firmly believing he would never see another sunrise, he remained calm in that belief.
>
> "These are the moments of do-nothing heroics to which even good men surrender at times. Many officers of ships can no doubt recall a case in their experience when just such a trance of confounded stoicism would come all over a whole ship's company. Jukes, however, had no wide experience of men or storms. He conceived himself to be calm — inexorably calm; but as a matter of fact he was daunted; not abjectly, but only so far as a decent man may, without becoming loathsome to himself."

I let the book rest against my lap while I stared at the dark forest. I shut the book and put it back in its waterproof bag. It was too dark to read anymore.

Spooky came on station soon after that; the entire eastern sky was pitch-dark, and in the west only a thin band of purple remained as a relic of the lost daylight. I made one more round of the sector, to ensure that the men were alert and to remind them that Spooky would begin firing soon; most of them were already aware of it. Since Bravo Six would be controlling Spooky, there was nothing for me to do but sit back with my legs stretched out and my hands clasped behind my head, and watch the fireworks.

They began as a thin, continuous, slightly curved red line, bright and electric against the southern sky. Only one bullet in six was a tracer, but the six-barreled miniguns in the C47 put out so much fire that it seemed every round was outlined against the dark. A couple of seconds later, the sound came, barely audible over the drone of the engines: A faint, comical burp, prolonged and monotonous, like that of a man who'd drunk too much beer too quickly. There were no other sounds: The M60 rounds made no audible noise as they ripped through the leaves and branches. Most of the fire was being directed into the clearing and the bunker complex above it. I felt hungry: There was one last, treasured pack of Chuckles in my pack and I took it out, unwrapped it, and began eating them, slowly, trying to guess, in the dark, which flavor I was tasting. For some reason, the only one I could be sure of was licorice. A thought came to me, as I chewed away at the sticky, gummy stuff, that all this sugar couldn't be doing my teeth a whole lot of good, but then I shrugged. Tooth decay was not real high up on the list of things that threatened me at the moment.

Watching Spooky was not quite the soporific that I'd expected; for some reason my eyes wouldn't close. It was very late when they did, and the CO decided on a brutally early wake-up call; it was not yet 0500 when Helms shook me awake. I'd managed only an hour or less of sleep. My mouth tasted vile from the Chuckles, my muscles were stiff from lying on the exposed roots, and my mind sneered heartlessly at the rest of my body as it sent out whimpering demands for coffee. It was too dark for anyone to risk lighting a heat tab to heat water, so I would have to do without.

YD323984: 13 May: 0500

The three of us—Eward, Garza and I—joined the CO at his CP, stumbling and crashing our way through the trees. It was just past 0500, and the darkness surrounding us had not quite reached the tipping point, that mysterious moment when the dark grey shadows suddenly become recognizable shapes. Far off to the east, along the coast, dawn's first light would be tinging the ocean a ghostly silver, but here, under the shadow of the mountain, it was still deep night.

Littnan greeted us quietly, and then immediately got to business. Swiftly and tersely, as was his way, he laid out his plans for the morning. Two Six—Eward—would prepare to probe the hill again within the hour: Black Jack wanted them in place and ready before dawn. In the event of further determined resistance, Eward was to pinpoint the bunkers rimming the clearing and mark them with smoke grenades. He was especially enjoined to locate and mark, if possible, the .51 caliber gun. Three Six would

31. Feeling Our Way

back him up and secure the trail between the NDP and the clearing. First Platoon would secure the NDP, the LZ, such as it was, and the trail between them.

"I'll be up there with Three Six," Littnan continued. "Frank, I want you down by the LZ. Top will stay here at the NDP. Marsh, you've got 30 minutes to get your people ready." He paused; I still could barely see his face, but that didn't matter because he was almost always expressionless anyway. His voice, however, normally cool and even, contained just a hint of something unusual as he uttered the next sentences.

"By the way ... two things. The battalion CP group was shot up yesterday, if you haven't heard about it, by a couple of our own gunships. Nobody dead but a lot of wounded. There's no battalion staff left. And ... Firebase Airborne was hit last night, by the 6th NVA." He paused again, for a full three seconds. "Alpha Company, 2/501st lost over 25 dead and more than 60 wounded. The base was overrun."

There was a dead silence. None of us spoke, but I could feel then tension press on us all. "Overrun"—the filthiest word in an infantryman's vocabulary. But even as I knelt there, stunned, my mind began doing the math. The 6th NVA at Dong Ngai; the 29th here ... a regiment here, a regiment there ... what had we gotten ourselves into?

"Any questions?" Littnan finished up. Under the circumstances, that was almost hilarious. None of us said a word, however.

"Then let's go."

I stumbled back to my own CP in a fog, my mind almost paralyzed by so many competing thoughts. Jerry Wolosenko—had he been hit at the battalion CP? Was he one of the wounded? I would worry about that for the next several days, particularly when I found that no one could tell me anything. (In the event, Jerry had never made it out to the A Shau in the first place; Howard had left him behind at Blaze.) And Airborne—*my* Airborne—overrun. First the 2/17th, now the 2/501st ... and we were probing and attacking in that same deadly valley. My mind went back to that incredible stairwell winding its way down the massive slope of Dong Ngai. The enemy owned the A Shau.

Dawn was still little more than a light grey streak across the eastern horizon when Second Platoon assembled on the trail. They were still in a relatively light-hearted mood; the men were relaxed, joking and smiling. Only three men seemed not to join in the general careless banter: The point man and slack man — understandably — and Eward. This surprised me. Marsh Eward had by now firmly established himself as a resolute, methodical, straightforward man, undemonstrative and even unimaginative. He was not precisely grim, but his face showed none of the gleeful sardonicism of the previous day. Eward was not one to make up imaginary bogeymen, but neither was he one to ignore evidence simply because it was unpleasant.

A young, short blond trooper named Cowans took the point and the ubiquitous Sergeant Randolph was slack. At Eward's terse nod, they turned to face the hill and began moving up the trail, slowly. It took a while for Two Six to clear the NDP area; Eward had specified a larger than normal interval between the troops. His rear element had barely left the perimeter by the time Cowans reached the steep rise below the clearing. Three Six was still waiting in the NDP, bunched up; there was no place for them to go. For the first time, I think, I was struck by how precarious our position on that steep, narrow ridge actually was. We had no choice but to line up in single file, or, as Three Six was doing, bunch up in knots of men. Either way, we were vulnerable. I remembered reading about the battle of Stirling Bridge, when the English had been forced to cross a narrow bridge almost one-by-one, to be attacked and slaughtered by the Scots waiting for them on the other side. Things hadn't changed much in 700 years.

I saw Littnan frown as he looked at Three Six clustered together; he picked up the mike, shook his head and replaced it: There was no point in calling Eward. Littnan could hardly ask him to tighten up his file and bunch his men closer together when there existed the very real possibility of ambush or booby traps along the trail; that was why Eward had spread his people out in the first place. Like me, Littnan was coming to terms with the limits the geography was placing on us.

The line continued to inch forward. Marsh was deploying his men to the right and the left, as I had the previous day. The sun had just made it over the mountain crest, and it was filtering and streaming through the leaves overhead, in shafts and needles of golden light. Smokey blue-white mists still clung to the valley floor and the slopes south of us, half-glimpsed through the green tapestry around us. For the first time in three days, the artillery was totally silent; Bilk Two Three buzzed high over our heads, unseen, its tiny engine barely audible. To the northwest, behind the battalion CP, a pair of gunships circled, like metallic hawks, ready in case Eward needed them. Somewhere to the south, but high and far, a couple of F4s waited for Bilk Two Three's call to action; they were there, invisible and inaudible, far above the ground and the infantryman, where everything is a pale gelid blue and ice-white and the sun, so ponderous and grayish yellow to us below, was a white-hot needle stabbing the earth.

The forest animals were active, loud and insistent in their morning challenges to the world at large. At least, they were so in the immediate area surrounding the NDP, and that was reassuring. I saw Littnan, busy on both radios, give me a sidelong glance and that reminded me that I wasn't supposed to be here; the CO had said he wanted me down by the LZ. I don't know why; LZs and I just did not get along. Maybe he thought that, if I worked at it long enough, I'd get it right. Giving one last glance around the perimeter to make sure it was secure, I tapped Helms on the shoulder and made my way down the trail to the LZ.

The LZ was secured by First Squad; Logan and Westman were seated by the trail on the left, their M60 pointed down the bare southern slope. The others were scattered around the perimeter in good order; Sergeant Wright rose from his seat on a fallen log and joined us as we entered.

"Everything quiet, Top?" I asked.

He nodded. "Yes, sir. But this LZ's a mess. We must notta done much last night."

I glanced around. We'd had less than an hour of daylight to blow the LZ, and it showed. It was still barely large enough for an LOH; a Huey would have an extremely difficult time getting in, and even if it did touch down, the pilot would have to back up and drift blindly across the slope until he had enough room to turn his aircraft and move away from the clutching branches that rimmed three sides of the LZ. Even an LOH would have a delicate task of turning itself around. There were a few trees along the periphery, which had been blown or cut down but had left behind four and five foot-high stumps. These would have to come down, since pilots understandably hated landing near anything that high: a sudden shift in the wind or inadvertent move by the pilot could send a hovering Huey crabwise, to catch a skid against one of those stumps and tip over.

I gave a disgusted shrug. "I'll call the Old Man and tell him. He'll probably want to give us the job after Two Six gets back. By the way, were there any signs of a probe last night?" One of the things Littnan had worried about was that the LZ might have been booby-trapped against us, since we'd not been able to secure it last night. I wasn't all that worried: Spooky had flown almost all night, and while he'd concentrated on the bunkers above us, he'd also made several passes all around our positions, at irregular intervals. It would have taken a very dedicated or very foolhardy NVA sapper to creep up to the LZ and set up a significant booby trap. It takes a while to rig up a 100-pound bomb; while the NVA sappers were unquestionably very accomplished at their job, I was skeptical of just how cool and detached one of them could be while working on 100 pounds of explosives with Spooky lolling about, showering the ground below with enough M60 rounds to annihilate a small city. Hell, I thought, if he had that much *sang-froid*, he'd have dispensed with the bomb and walked right into our CP and just called on us to surrender. Nevertheless, Wright and Hyde would have checked, and since Littnan would ask me, I asked him.

"Not a thing," Wright was saying. "Nothin'. No tracks. No signs at all."

"Okay." I frowned. "Top...."

"Sir."

"How are the men?" It had been a long time since I had felt the need to ask that question, but the conversation between Hernandez and Nelson was on my mind.

Sergeant Wright shrugged, looking away over the valley to the south. "Anymore, you know them better than I do, Lieutenant. But since you ask ... they're okay."

I looked at my watch: 0645. Eward would have long since finished deploying his men by now. There were no sounds coming down from the hill to indicate that anything was happening. Helms had shrugged off his pack and was seated on a tree stump, holding the mike loosely in his hand. I opened my mouth to ask him if anything was going on but shut it with a sudden snap. Dennis would let me know instantly if anything was said that I needed to know. There was no need for me to badger him about it. Nerves, I thought. What I was waiting for was a transmission from Eward, in his casual, high-pitched east coast twang, with the announcement that he'd reached the bunker line and the NVA had pulled out, as expected. Wishful thinking.

Wright had gotten Westman to start cutting down a couple of the nearer, taller stumps, and the solid *thock*! of the hatchet pounding the wood spread across the valley. I turned and watched for a moment. Westman had stripped to his waist. The long ropy muscles rippled and bunched under the sweat already gleaming across his pale blond torso. Even using only the short-handled, clumsy army issue hatchet, Westman quickly chopped his way through the eight-inch stump. His tall body swayed in unconscious grace, slipping unthinkingly into the lumberjack's rhythmic strokes. I shook my head with a slight smile. There were times when Westman seemed to belong to another era, another world entirely. Logan, cross-legged behind his M60, was grinning and aiming ribald, sardonic comments at his assistant gunner.

"Stroke! ... stroke! ... stroke! Oh, how the mighty redwood falls! Go get 'em, Swede! Get that mouse-dick tree! Don't let the thing get away — chop it!"

Westman, I knew, would be grinning. He delighted in Logan's banter. It was an unlikely friendship, between the sweet-tempered, wide-eyed, enthusiastic, ingenuous farm boy and the sardonic, unflappable, cynical and urban Logan; I could never imagine Tim as being anything but a twentieth century American. Yet I never saw two closer friends than they.

I heard a harsh snap of static behind me; Helms had turned on the speaker. I continued to watch Westman for a moment or two, but then, at 0652, barely audible — Eward was keeping his voice low — Two Six finally called.

"Bravo Six, Two Six, over ... Bravo Six, this is Two Six, over...."

Hssss sssnap! "...Six, over."

"Roger. Two Six. I'm up here, ready to go, but there's no sign of them, over."

"Roger, Two Six. What's the visibility? Did those air strikes knock any of the vegetation down?"

"Negative. Still can't see a damn thing. Just those bunkers we knocked out yesterday, over."

"Roger. What's it look like to you, Two Six: They still up there?"

"Yeah, they're here all right. I haven't moved into the clearing yet, but I got the feeling that when I do, the party's gonna start."

"Okay. Be careful."

"You got my word on that."

"Good. Keep me informed. Out."

Helms glanced at me obliquely as he fiddled with the squelch adjustment on the set. "You reckon they're gone, sir?" he asked, casually.

"I don't know. We'll find out in a minute."

"Yeah, I reckon we will. Who's on point?"

"Cowans."

"Don't know him," Helms grunted.

Another couple of minutes of radio silence passed. Westman's hatchet was quiet too; he'd stopped for a rest. Then:

31. Feeling Our Way

"Six, this is Two Six."

"Roger, Two Six. Go ahead."

"Two Six. I don't like the idea of moving anybody into this clearing. I think I'm going to try some recon by fire, over."

"Roger, Two Six. Do that."

A moment later, some scattered but persistent M16 shots sounded from up above. They were joined a moment or so later by the heavier pounding of an M60, and then gradually, imperceptibly, the volume increased. At a certain point, the sound swelled with the addition of enemy weapons, AK-47s and DP machine guns and a claymore or two, until we were listening to a full-throated firefight. After a few minutes, when we thought it was as loud as it could get, the hard slam! of the RPGs and the obscene bass cursing of the .51 began to rock the hillside.

Eward was staying off the radio and Littnan, patient and cool as always, was leaving him alone, but sitting where I was, over 400 meters from the clearing, I was able to easily distinguish the heavy NVA fire. I felt a small shiver move down the back of my neck. The NVA was still there, in force, and willing to fight. These were no trail watchers.

The radio silence continued. I was beginning to wonder if Marsh and his RTO had been hit; surely even Marsh would have something to say by now. Finally, at 0711, his voice, barely audible through the thunderous roar of the shooting, called out the ritual:

"Bravo Six, this is Two Six. We're taking heavy incoming from our entire front, over."

"Roger, Two Six. Are you taking casualties?"

"Affirmative. It looks like they got claymores set up in the clearing — new ones. They weren't there yesterday. I'm afraid to move up against them. There are beaucoup."

"Roger, Two Six: Don't try. Can you spot the bunkers from where you are?"

"Wait one." There was a pause, during which the fire intensified. I stole glances at the men scattered around the perimeter; their faces were guarded and carefully inexpressive. They realized, as well as I did, the significance of the volume of fire the NVA was putting out.

"Six, this is Two Six. I got a man hit real bad — RPG. And I'm beginning to take hits on my right flank. I think the party's over, for the moment."

"Roger. You don't think you can hang in there and get close enough to mark a few of those bunkers?"

"Sure I can. I'd just never get back, over."

"Roger. How many casualties?"

There was a pause, while Eward figured out the code. "Sierra. I say again: Sierra. All Whiskey India Alpha, over."

I glanced at Helms. Like a dummy, I'd neglected to check with him about the day's key word. He permitted himself the slightest, politest, most gentle of smiles.

"Three," he said, with no hint of smugness.

"Okay, Two Six," Littnan was saying, "bring 'em back. I'll see you at the CP."

"Roger."

I felt Wright standing behind me. "Ol' pucker factor's goin' up, ain't it, sir?" he asked in a soft, absent voice.

I nodded agreement. "What's up there, Top?" I didn't expect an answer; this was the ultimate in rhetorical questions. Wright made no attempt to reply, not even by so much as a twitch of a facial muscle. He gazed, thoughtfully, at the hill. From the corner of my eye, I saw two or three of Hyde's squad members; they too were looking up the slope, as was I, for that matter. With each hour that passed, the mountain loomed larger.

Hyde was still there. Sergeant Nathan Daniel Hyde, E-5 squad leader of First Squad, First Platoon, Bravo Company. Instead of leaving, he chose to stay until it was over; he couldn't and wouldn't leave his men. He had been with me on Dong Ngai, Hill 1485, when we thought without doubt we would die; he'd walked with me along that harrowing trail from the battalion CP to the base of the ridge we stood on now, when death whispered at us with every step, and he would continue to stay with me and his men through the next 100 hours. I could only pray that death would leave the tall Louisiana boy behind, and seek other, less worthy prey. He was striding about the LZ, from one position to the next, checking on his men, briefly massaging Westman's shoulders, smacking Logan's helmet hard at some comment Tim made, pausing briefly to give Ray Carlton, the despised Short Round, a word of encouragement. Hyde was the perfect squad leader.

I had intended to stay at the LZ until Eward's three wounded — no; they were four now — were brought down and evacuated; Warrant Officer Bill Rairdon, Crazy Bill, was already bringing his fragile LOH into the LZ. But before the first of the wounded men was brought down, Littnan called and told me to join him and the others at the CP. On my way up the trail, I passed first Williams, who greeted me quietly, and then Hernandez. The fourth man on the trail was Nelson, and he greeted me with a nod, half rueful, half angry.

"Guess there's a mess o' trail watchers up there, Lieutenant," he grinned, in spite of himself.

I grinned back. "Guess there is, Nellie."

It was 0745 when I sat next to the others waiting at Littnan's CP. Garza, who was seated in his usual cross-legged, straight-backed Indian fashion, greeted me with a nod, his flat brown face as impassive as ever. Eward was still with his platoon, supervising the removal of the wounded from the ridge through the CP to the LZ below. Sergeant Murtiff crouched opposite Garza, frowning at the dirt by his scuffed boot. Russ Crenshaw, with nothing to do because the F4s were flying sorties and he had no artillery to call in, was leaning against a nearby tree, trying futilely, as always, to clean the lenses of his eyeglasses. That's why I had stopped wearing mine; perspiration, mist and dirt ensured that I could see less with them on than off. Conzoner stood by Littnan, with his radio, but Price had his off and on the ground beside him; he sat leaning against another tree, eyes closed, chest rising and falling slowly as he catnapped. The only sounds now were the familiar screech and crump of the jets.

Littnan finally handed the mike to Conzoner and joined us, kneeling down beside me. He removed his helmet, wiped his short black hair, slick with sweat and tossed the helmet down, crown first, to spin slowly, one partially loose strap flapping against the camouflage cover. The cover was no longer new and crisp; in just three days, the colors had faded and were smeared with dirt, sweat and much else. Just like ours.

Littnan had his battalion net on speaker; Black Jack was flying overhead, in his LOH. He shook his head at one particular exchange with Charlie Company:

"This is Black Jack. What is the problem down there?"

By some quirk of atmospherics—one I was ruefully familiar with—we couldn't hear Charlie Six's response, although he stood on a ridge a kilometer away. But we had no trouble hearing Black Jack's next transmission.

"I don't care how you do it. Get your asses moving up that hill. You're being paid to fight this war, not discuss it."

I raised an eyebrow. "About a 9.7 for style and content, I'd say."

Littnan allowed himself a quick smile and shrugged.

"How's the LZ?" he asked me.

I made a gesture with my right hand. "It's there. Some of the stumps were too high and Sergeant Wright took care of that. It's still not big enough, though. Not for a Huey, anyway."

Littnan shrugged. "It could be twice the size and I still wouldn't bring in a Huey unless it's an emergency. That slope is too bare and the tree line to the south is too close. They can sit there in those trees all day and blow us away." He rubbed his jaw, where a dark red cut showed where he'd cut himself shaving that morning. "Even a LOH is taking a chance. You got a gun down there, right?"

He meant an M60. "Yeah, I do. You want me to send another one down there?"

He thought about it a second. "No. Let's leave things as they are. Just tell Sergeant Wright to make sure he gets good fire out into that tree line."

We were interrupted by voices and the sound of thudding feet. Four men were hurrying down the trail, carrying a sagging poncho liner. Blood had seeped through the porous material and stained and stippled the mottled green and brown nylon. I caught a glimpse of a white, loose face, glazed eyes and an arm, torn and red. I glanced away. *RPGs. Fucking RPGs.*

A tired, strained Eward joined us a moment later. His other wounded, including a white-faced Cowans, holding a bloody arm gingerly as he walked, moved through the CP on their own—a good sign, in that they were ambulatory. But there were three of them, in addition to the boy in the liner.

Eward had little new to add. The first line of bunkers had in fact been destroyed, but there were many left, along the saddle and across the slopes of both knolls. The .51 was still at its old stand, dispensing large-caliber slugs and a healthy serving of fear. Spider holes, probably used by RPG gunners, were dotted across the entire area, and at least two DP positions had been spotted. And still, Marsh pointed out, they refused or neglected — take your pick — to mine the neck of the clearing, along that steep rise.

None of us believed it to be neglect. Littnan shook his head. "They're just about putting out a welcome mat. And the hell of it is, we have to go through that clearing if we're going to get anywhere. We can't flank it."

We shrugged. We'd known that within five seconds of seeing the clearing.

"Charlie Company," he continued, "is on that ridge to our south. 318977. They've already had contact this morning. It was light, just AK fire and a couple of RPGs, but the Air Force is hitting that ridge too, along with ours. Alpha has moved into the CP area and relieved Delta. They're on their way to another ridge, just north of ours. We can't see it from here but it's basically at coordinates 326988. They ought to be in position by 1000 hours: About two hours from now. First of the Oh Six is still about ten klicks south of us. They're not finding anything there, and I get the idea from Black Jack that Iron Raven will bring them up to join us if we haven't cracked this by today.

"One more thing: Sergeant Garza reports that his lead element took a couple of sniper rounds from the upper end of the valley there, to our south — above the LZ. That means the enemy may have a force down there between us and Charlie Company, and that the trail leading from our ridge to his might be infiltrated. In any case, that means that we'll have to worry about switching from offense to defense immediately, if they attack our flank while we're attacking the hill. We've got to be real careful about the trail leading from the CP to the LZ; that's where we'll be most vulnerable. And, oh by the way: The final numbers for Airborne are 26 killed and 82 wounded. And the CP had 35 wounded."

Eward stirred. "You got any good news?" he asked.

"No. Why?"

There wasn't anything Marsh could say to that.

We spent another half hour or so on routine business, until Littnan stood up. He glanced up at the sky. "More of that rain coming. We'll let the flyboys do their thing for a while, but be ready to move up. That means," he said to me with a slight smile, "don't start any long chapters."

"That's okay," I said, standing up in turn, and stretching cramped muscles, "I won't."

Marsh Eward and I walked a few steps together. "I guess it's time for me to get some breakfast," he said. "I figure getting killed on an empty stomach is bad for your health."

We paused for a moment. Both of us were thinking the same thing, but neither wanted to say it. It was the same question we'd been asking for the past three days, and no one had answered it yet. What were we facing? Neither of us wanted to ask the question, not because there would be no answer but because we didn't want to hear the answer when it came. It wasn't a case of showing fear. Admitting you felt fear in circumstances like ours was like admitting to being wet while swimming in the middle of the Pacific Ocean. Suddenly, Conrad's words returned to me. It wasn't fear; it was intimidation that we couldn't admit. Day by day, hour by hour, the mountain intimidated us more, and neither one of us could admit that to himself, much less his brother officer. Stolid, unimaginative Eward felt it as much as I. I was beginning to get angry.

32

Sanguis Agni

YC323984; 13 May 1969; 0900–2400

Early that morning Black Widow Four Three delivered a present: A new medic, named Hudson. Sergeant Wright and I let out simultaneous sighs. A greater contrast to Muldoon would have been hard to find. Hudson, from California, was laid back to the point of vacuity, with long black hair and dark eyes that seemed to be focused several planetary orbits away. Well, you make do with what you have, Wright and I agreed. Wright led him up to our platoon CP, while I smiled grimly at the thought of what Dennis would think. If Dennis and Muldoon had been polar opposites ... I wasn't sure if Helms and Hudson belonged to the same species.

The morning was more of the same: Waiting in place at the NDP, watching and listening to the artillery and air strikes pounding the mountain. Early in the afternoon, Conzoner told Helms that I was needed at the CP.

I found Littnan sitting on an upturned ammo crate at his Command Post. Dark circles under his eyes showed his fatigue. The strain of the last three days had ravaged his face that a week ago, when I'd first met him, had seemed so young and unlined. I'd not had much sleep during the last two nights, and I was exhausted, but I realized, on seeing him, that he'd not had any. He pinched the bridge of his nose between thumb and forefinger, holding himself still for a few seconds; then he looked at me, nodded, and indicated with a wave of his hand that I should sit on the ground to his right. Marsh Eward, with his inevitable cup of hot chocolate, joined us immediately. We exchanged a few noncommittal words while waiting for Sergeant Garza.

He strode up a minute or so later, shoulders straight, black eyes flashing, his face split by a thin, cold slash which those who didn't know him well might mistake for a smile. He squatted on the ground, Indian style, in front of Littnan, who nodded again, wearily.

"We're going back up," Littnan announced, softly.

We looked at him silently while he paused, staring with a concentrated frown at the ground. After a moment he shrugged, as if throwing off a weight, and raised his head. His voice and manner became brisk and businesslike, as they normally were.

"You'll lead, Frank," he said, looking at me. "Charlie Company is going to move up that ridge to our south; Delta will do the same to our north." His mouth tightened. "It's imperative"—he emphasized the word—"that we push on past the clearing this time. Charlie and Delta will be pushing hard. If we can't make our objective, they'll be split and exposed. We've been knocking on that door for three days now. It's time we kicked it in."

We exchanged looks. Littnan, seeing our expressions, nodded. "I know. I know what you mean. I'm beginning to wonder what's up there myself. Still, it's what we have to do. We've got to make it at least to that saddle, if not the top of the hill. Any ideas?"

Eward drained his cup with a backward toss of his head. "Sure. I still say we should send Bo on a CA."

Littnan ignored him. "Anything at all?" he asked, looking at each of us. "Ever hear of the Fake Bombing Run Trick? No? Well, it's not included in those courses on Tactics at Fort Benning. It's been tried before but we've added a few twists to it.

"The idea is this, Frank: You move up the ridge to just below that clearing. Just your lead element; leave the others about 50 meters behind, back at that bend in the trail. When you get there, give me a call. I want you all the way up there just to have a quick look around, in case there's something new they've done. On your call, I'll have Bilk Two Three drop a marking round into that clearing. While he's doing that, you and your lead element move fast and join the rest of your platoon down below. As soon as Bilk Two Three's done his thing, you guys hunker down and stay down, because a One Oh Five will make a good, noisy pass with 20mm, and he'll pull his release handle; the gooks will hear that click and hit their bunkers. Nothing will drop, but they will have to assume that it was just a mechanical problem, especially when they hear the second Oh Five start a run."

He fixed me with a look, leaning forward for emphasis. "As soon as that first plane clears, you get your people up and make it up the ridge, fast, into the clearing. Just do a sprint. The idea is, the gooks will all be in their bunkers, hunkered down, and you can get into the bunker line and start doing some damage. Be sure to bring plenty of grenades. All of them. Concussion, smoke, CS—anything we can get. While you're rushing the bunkers, Two Six will move right in behind you. If you can secure the saddle and at least one of the knolls, then Two Three can secure the clearing. The theory is that you'll find them sitting in their bunkers with their fingers in their ears. Got the picture?" He arched an eyebrow at me.

I stared back. "Yeah. Clear. What happens if we go up there and they aren't in those bunkers?"

Littnan shrugged and said nothing, eloquently.

"Your widow gets a nice letter and maybe a posthumous medal or two," Marsh chipped in.

"She won't be the only widow if those gooks aren't in their bunkers when I get up there," I pointed out. "You really think this will work?"

"Yeah, I do," Littnan responded. "Or I wouldn't be sending you up there. I *think* it will work. It ought to work. But it may not. If it doesn't ... well, that comes with the territory, Frank. You know that. Look," he added, in a more energetic tone, "nothing else we've tried has worked so far. We might as well try it."

"The way I see it," Eward added seriously, "the only difference is that you get clobbered all at once, instead of being sliced up a little bit at a time. Ain't no way we're gonna keep pounding away at those bunkers without losing men, one after another."

"I agree," Littnan nodded. "Frank, it all depends on your timing. I'm almost certain that they'll duck into those shelters and bunkers when they hear the One Oh Fives come in, but you'll have to be right there, right on top of them, within seconds of the time the second one makes his run. If it weren't too risky, I'd even have the first one drop a 500-pounder on them, just to make them think we're serious. But we can't take that chance. You'll have to be within 75 meters or less if you're going to have any chance of getting up that hill in time. Start running up as soon as the first one ends his 20mm run. You just can't afford to be late."

"Or too soon." Garza spoke for the first time. "Dey don't all get in dose bunkers right away; one, two, dey stay behin' and mek sure. Dey see you, it's all bad."

Littnan shrugged. "Timing," he repeated. "Timing is the key, and we can't practice this at all. You'll get one chance to do it right, Frank."

I shook my head. There was a small, icy lump in my stomach, small and dense, like an iron ball. The clearing loomed over me like a dark storm cloud on an eastern horizon. To ask my people to go rushing up there, blindly, into the killing zone ... if it worked.... Fine. If it didn't ... my mind fixed on the image of broken bodies flopping across the clearing, dancing to the music of that damned .51. I swallowed. There had been a time in my life when I had viewed a vivid imagination as being a good thing.

"What do you think?" Littnan was looking at me. He was asking my opinion, but this was a company commander in the airborne infantry asking one of his platoon leaders about an assigned mission, and it was also, rank aside, one officer of that unit — a proud, valorous unit, with a long history of heroic endeavor — challenging another, in the presence of his brother officers. I let my eyes fall to the ground, conscious that the others were looking at me. I sighed. There were only two possible answers: *Yes,* or, *No, I have a better idea.*

I had no better idea, unfortunately.

"Okay. How much time do I have?"

"An hour. We go at 1400. Get your people briefed thoroughly, Frank. I can't emphasize too much that the timing of this has to be right."

"Yeah. Me neither."

"Okay. By the way — your packs."

"What about 'em?"

"Take them with you but leave them down at your assembly point. I don't want them on your backs when you make that run up to the bunkers, but if you get to that saddle, I don't want to lose too much time getting them up to you."

"Right." I noticed that he'd said "if." Littnan was a realist.

Forty-five minutes later, I was finishing up the briefing. Eden and Dickerson were there, and Sergeant Hyde with his entire squad. They would be the point squad, and I wanted to be sure that they all understood what had to happen.

"Remember," I emphasized, "Remember that as soon as you hear that first One Oh Five fly over us, you move out. Don't worry about the second guy: He's not going to drop anything. Walk up to the clearing, as fast as you can walk; once you're in the clearing, sprint, fast. Logan and Westman will set up their M60 on the left flank of the clearing, to cover us. Get into those bunkers along the saddle and the knolls; it's about 40 meters or so, so it'll take you about ten seconds. That second One Oh Five will be just clearing the mountain by that point, if we time it right. Two men to a bunker, just like in training. One fires his 'sixteen on full automatic, the other drops an M1 or concussion grenade. Don't use CS or smoke until I tell you to. We don't want that stuff floating around the hill while we're looking for bunkers. We won't have time for prisoners, so if anyone comes out of those bunkers, wounded or not, you waste him right away. We can always take prisoners later, after we've taken the bunker line. Priority target is the .51, which is on the right-hand knoll.

"Second Squad will move up right behind First; you guys will concentrate on the left side of the clearing, and the left knoll. Third Squad, with Sergeant Wright and his RTO, will move up to the lip of the clearing, spread out, and hold in place until I signal. Even when I move you up, I want the 'sixty to stay at the clearing; make sure that Two Six is right there behind you. I don't want a gap between you and their lead element. Top, if you see that they're not there, get on the horn and do something about it." I stopped and looked around. "Any questions?"

There were none.

"Okay. We'll be moving out in a few minutes. Men, this is going to take speed. You two," I nodded at Dickerson and Eden, "make sure your men understand that. Speed. You see someone slowing down, you kick his ass and get him moving. We get up there fast enough, and it'll be a piece of cake. If we're too slow ... bad news. See you all in a few minutes."

Some 15 minutes later, while we sat in place, each with his own thoughts — there was no conversation I could hear — Littnan called and told me to start. Bilk Two Three was buzzing somewhere overhead, droning like a big, lazy housefly. I raised an eyebrow at Sergeant Wright, shouldered my harness, and nodded at Gann, Hyde's point man.

We went rather more quickly than usual, since Bilk was already on station. We covered the first 100 meters in less than two minutes, which was break-neck speed for us. But Gann slowed abruptly when he reached that part of the trail where the ridge narrowed and steepened; we were then about 125 meters below the clearing, and about 75 meters from the dog-leg where we would wait. We were still well below the clearing when we heard the sounds of rifle and automatic weapons fire to our south. Moments later, Littnan called.

"Charlie Six's run into something over there on his ridge. There's going to be a hold. They're asking Bilk Two Three to take a look. This'll take a while."

"Roger," I said. "Are we still going ahead with this or do you want me to move back?"

"Affirmative. This is still a go."

"Roger. I'd like to at least pull my point element back a bit; they're on that real steep razorback right now. If it's going to be a while I don't want them strung out that close to the gooks, over."

"Roger. Do that."

I spread the word and Gann began to backtrack down the hill, to an area where the ridge broadened and we could set up some semblance of a defensive posture. Hyde let Gann move past him and then fell in behind him, in the slack position. I had a momentary feeling of awe at the courage it took for him to walk a ridge in the A Shau, up with the point element, when his DEROS date was staring him in the face. I was beginning to understand Sergeant Novak better. The closer a man gets to his return home, the more crushing the pressure becomes. It's one thing to walk point when you've months to go; it's quite another to do so when you can count the days, the hours, the *heartbeats*, before you board a jet and suddenly, magically, as if by the wave of a wand, find yourself in The World; safe, free, remote from hardship and fear; you can actually feel the grasping claws slip away as you climb that stair into the 707.

I shook my head. Hyde was ... I had a moment of humility, as I thought about the men whose leader, by congressional authority and nothing else, I was. No officer can ever be good enough to deserve men like these.

YC325983: 1400

We settled down; the men's faces were blank and closed. They knew this wasn't over. To our south, somewhere overhead, unseen because of the dense tangle of branches above us, Bilk Two Three's steady drone was clearly heard as he circled over Charlie Company. A few minutes later, I heard the *whoosh-pop!* of the marking round slamming into the ridge above their position. Slowly, the sound of his motor dwindled; he was moving his slow, clumsy defenseless craft out of harm's way. In his wake would come another type of craft entirely: A sleek, deadly 25 ton jet, looking like a wizard's cross between a bird of prey and a shark. I wondered briefly what it would feel like to stare at one of those beasts head-on as it flew at you with a 1,000-pounder on its wing...

Helms stood a few feet away, back bent over to take the weight of his PRC25. Logan and Westman, inseparable, knelt a few feet beyond him, festooned with M60 ammunition, staring quietly to the south. Beyond them, I couldn't see, because of a slight bend in the trail. Above me, Hyde was standing still, looking down at Gann, who had dropped his pack. He was crouched, motionless, his rifle pointed back up the trail, his back rigid and tense. Hyde and I strained to see what he was looking at, but all I could see were the same trees and bushes we'd been inching past for the last few days. They'd assumed a marked familiarity, as buildings will when you pass them on your way to work. I thought about asking Gann what he was seeing or hearing, but decided against it. Gann was one of the best. When he had something to say, he'd say it.

Hyde and I looked at each other, expressionless. We waited. He might have started to say something, but if so he had to pause as the deep, ripping scream of an F4 split the sky overhead. We involuntarily crouched a little lower as we heard the click of the release mechanism. Seconds later, the CRUMP-WHUMP! of the explosion sounded loud and immediate, to our southeast. I frowned. I couldn't see it, but the explosion sounded much higher on Charlie's ridge than I expected. The bomb should have landed a kilometer or so away, to our south. It was hard to be sure in thickly forested, steep-walled terrain, but this sounded as if it had come from our east, almost directly ahead of us and a bit to my right as I faced the hill.

But I turned my attention to Hyde, who had whispered something to Gann. He leaned over to whisper in my ear in turn. "Thought he saw some bushes move, up ahead. But they're still now. Reckon it might 'a been the wind."

I nodded back. I was just turning to Helms when the second jet arrived; again, the ordnance seemed to land to our right front. I hesitated, considering, and then motioned for Helms to hand me the mike.

"Bravo Six, this is One Six, over."

There was a pause, and then Conzoner answered. "One Six, Six is on the other net, over."

"Roger. I need him."

"Roger. Wait one."

I fidgeted while I waited. Hyde, seeing that I would be a while, moved up to join Gann; together they knelt, several meters above me, gazing at the trail above us. I could hear Bilk Two Three's high-pitched engine as he moved back over the area, sniffing and prowling, trying to spot the damage. The jets returned to their circling orbit several miles away.

"Roger, One Six. What's up?" Littnan's voice filled the receiver.

I thumbed the mike. "Those runs Bilk's calling in; are they supposed to be going into Charlie's ridge, over?"

"That's affirmative, One Six." His voice sounded curt and hurried. I could bet he was talking to Black Jack on the battalion net, and was probably being asked why we hadn't overrun the hill yet.

"Roger. But they sound like they're going into the hill right above us, over."

"Negative. How far are you from the clearing?"

"Just about 150 meters. Maybe a bit more."

"Roger. Be ready to move as soon as Bilk Two Three's done with Charlie Company."

I handed the mike back to Helms and moved back up to crouch a few feet behind Gann and Hyde. Bilk Two Three circled above us for a moment, and then I heard the second marking rocket. I relaxed. This one was to our south, well away from the hill above.

The day was hot. Sweat streamed down our faces as we knelt or stood in place. I heard the approach of another of the F4s. I heard the click of the release and, in an absent-minded way, began to count the seconds. I'd gotten as far as four when the trees turned a flat, ugly white, as in a blinding lightning bolt. The noise, when it reached me a split second later, was not even sound: it was a *force*, a physical assault on not just my ears but my while body, as if some careless Titan was holding me in his hands and clapping heartily. I remained upright, but how, I don't know. Gann and Hyde were knocked to the ground. They lay there covered by branches that had been scythed from the trees above us as neatly as if that same Titan had taken a machete and casually swept the tops off of them. I could see the blue sky, where seconds before there had been only the dark silver-green leaves visible.

It took an effort to turn and hold out a hand to Helms, who was struggling to his feet, body pulled to earth by the weight of his pack. I wondered, as I helped him up, whether I would ever hear anything again. Facing west, I saw several men rush down the trail. My ears were okay, because I could now hear them calling for a medic. I moved down a bit, past the slight bend, to look straight along the ridge. Nelson, one hand clutched to his side, was staggering up the path; a broad splash of dark red stained his fatigue jacket. Clifton and Hernandez raced to his side, ripping open bandages from their first-aid pouches. I opened my mouth to ask how badly he was hit and froze.

Far off to the southwest, somewhere near Laos, I could see the sun glitter off the wings of another F4 as it wheeled and banked in the air. He was miles away, but miles mean nothing to a craft flying at nearly the speed of sound. I would never have seen him, had not the first bomb cleared away so much of the canopy above me. I watched in sick fascination as his wings winked silver and then disappeared as he completed his turn and leveled out. A second or two later I saw him, head on. I had the answer to my idle question from a few minutes ago. He was headed right at us.

At his speed, he would need less than 15 seconds before reaching his release point. My throat was dry as I motioned urgently for the mike. Two precious, agonizing seconds passed while he fumbled for the horn on its clip on his shoulder. I slapped the headpiece to my ear and then knew real fear. Helms had of course turned off his speaker so I was unaware until then that there was someone on the net. It was Garza, reaming out one of his squad leaders in a flat monotone for breaking contact with his main element. It is impossible to break into a radio transmission as long as someone else is holding down the talk button. Seconds and miles rushed away as Garza spoke. Terrifyingly close and rushing closer as I stared, the jet flew on, green-grey, shark-bodied, screaming like a monstrous bird of prey. The sound, I thought, the sound was the worst of all: Harsh, tearing, jagged, covering the gamut of pitch from a low, grating rumble to a thin, ripping screech; even more than the sight of it, the sound was the avatar of death.

Even as I desperately squeezed the button and tried to interrupt, I knew it was too late. Already, the pilot was lifting that sleek, flattened nose, exposing the dead-white underbelly and, fat and prominent under its wing, the black 500-pound bomb. The craft was close now, so close I could see, in that instant before the nose lifted, the pilot's helmeted head bent over his instruments. In that same instant, Garza stopped transmitting and I screamed into the mike, but too late; I knew it was far too late. I had no time to be calm. I had no power to remain calm; my voice screeched like an old woman's.

"Six! This is One Six. Abort! Abort! Abort!"

Even before I finished screaming, I heard the click of the bomb release and I looked up, helplessly, as does an exhausted rabbit when he hears the scream of the eagle. The roar increased until it seemed to shake the very mountain beneath us: Black and tumbling against the sky, the bomb began a lazy, heedless descent.

Oh, dear God, it's coming right at us.

"Hit it!" Someone yelled, and indeed there was no time for anything else. The noise dropped suddenly, ominously, in pitch and volume as the aircraft rushed by overhead. I fell to the ground, arms over my helmet, pressing it desperately to my head. *Any second now.*

The explosion, when it came, was loud but not the cataclysmic roar that the first had been. There was no blinding white glare, no body blow. There was an intense yellow flash somewhere behind me, up on the hill. Even before my ears stopped ringing, I had the mike to my mouth again, yelling into it.

"Six, this is One Six. One Six, over."

"One Six, this is Six. What's your problem, over?"

"This is One Six. Abort those runs. They're landing right on top of us."

There was a pause. "Negative, One Six. Bilk Two Three says they're not coming anywhere near you."

I swore. "Damnit to hell, two of those 500 pounders landed in our laps. You tell—"

I was interrupted by a hoarse cry behind me. "Oh, Goddamn. Goddamn! No! Goddamnit! No! NO NOHHH!" This last was a ragged cry torn from a man's throat, a shriek of despair hurled at some unfathomable wrong. I turned my head. Logan and Kenzy knelt by a still, prone figure. It had been Logan who had cried out.

He lifted his head and stared through me, without recognition; without, I think, awareness. Tears tracked down his freckled red cheeks, cutting their way through the encrusted dirt, spilling out over his chin and jaw. His mouth worked, but silently now, as if that last wretched cry had deprived him of speech. Kenzy bowed his head, one hand a fist held to his mouth, the other, palm down and rigid, held trembling in front of him, almost but not quite touching the shoulder of the fallen man. As if, held out like that, he could blot out the sight.

"Wait one!" I snapped into the mike, protocol forgotten. Kenzy's body hid the man's face from me and I had to step around his shoulder, getting between him and Logan. I knelt. I could see the blood welling slowly from the wound, a large ragged tear, two or three inches wide and almost five inches long, splitting the back of his head. Fair blond hair, matted with sweat and dirt and blood and shreds of brain tissue, framed the hidden face, but even before I gently removed Logan's big, rough red-haired hand from the cheek it covered, I knew who it was. The sight of that face, so white and bloodless, went through me like a spear of ice and iron.

"Oh my God," I whispered. "Oh my God. Oh — gaaaughh!" I couldn't finish the words. A mounting fury pushed its way through numbed vocal cords, to emerge ugly and evil. I stared. Beside me I could hear Kenzy's harsh weeping, Logan's muted gulping. I was dimly aware that silent, unbelieving men were gathering around us.

"Westman!" I heard someone say, in a hushed, shocked voice. "Westman! It's Westman!" The name was repeated, throughout the platoon, in the same hushed tone, like a prayer at vespers.

I held myself as rigid and unmoving as a statue as I called Littnan. "This is One Six," I said, quietly now. The time for screaming had passed. "I just took a KIA from that bomb that landed nowhere near us." I paused. "Over." A universe of rage filled that one word.

A second or two passed. "Roger, One Six. I'll tell Bilk Two Three to abort. Senior Medic's on his way up."

I made no reply. I looked up to see Sergeant Wright, hands on hip, standing over me.

"Get the platoon into a perimeter, Top," I said, tightly.

"Yes, sir." He glanced at the body, looked away, and began giving orders. Kenzy got up and moved, but Logan continued to kneel by Westman, his hand on his friend's shoulder now. Wright reached out a hand but pulled it back. He caught my eye, hesitated, nodded slowly and moved away. Logan's eyes never left Westman's head. He didn't look up even when Hudson, his own eyes dark and opaque with shock, knelt beside him.

Helms handed me the radio again. It was Littnan.

"Yeah?"

"I'm on my way up."

I handed the mike back to Helms with no reply. I could hear Bilk Two Three overhead. The jets had been called off, to return to their lair in the sky. He remained on station, circling. *You bastard, You stupid, stupid bastard.*

I heard pounding footsteps, boots against the earth. I looked down from the terrible sky to see Doc Schoch, bareheaded, long dark hair streaming behind him, kit bag flopping against his shoulder, running up the trail. Without pausing even to nod he flung himself at the body, roughly but unintentionally shouldering Hudson aside. Seconds later, Schoch's head jerked up.

"He's alive. He's breathing."

I ran over, but stayed behind him. There was no use in my getting any closer. Schoch's hands were a blur as he opened up his bag, pulled out a pair of IV bottles, flung the bag behind him, bouncing it off my legs, and carefully, precisely, inserted the needle into Westman's arm. He handed the bottle to a dazed Hudson to hold, while with quick, gentle fingers he examined and cleaned the wound.

I could hear it now; a soft, sighing snuffle. Westman's shoulder jerked imperceptibly with each sigh; his blue eyes were wide but unseeing, fixed on the earth inched from his face. Sob followed sob, deep, wide-spaced, but quietly, quietly, as might a child whimper, huddled in his room after a beating, quietly, afraid to cry out loud for fear that his father will hear.

I knelt down, "How is he?" I started to ask, but remained silent. Schoch's air of intense concentration was soundproof. After a few minutes, he settled back, his face grave. Slowly he took a trach tube, which he'd uncoiled, and wound it carefully back up. It was the last sign of the cross before the dirt begins to fall on the coffin. He looked over his shoulder at me, glanced back at Westman's head, and then looked away. He made a brief, almost imperceptible shake of his head.

Westman sobbed again. Each one was softer, quieter, than the last. Each was more desolate, more forlorn, as a child who knows there will be no comforting for his hurt. I became aware that I was pounding Schoch's kit bag with my fist; blow after unconscious blow. Faintly, as if over unimaginable distances, I heard the tinkle of broken glass. Remotely, as if through a thousand gauntlets, I felt the damp of spilt fluid. I continued to punch the bag. My eyes were on Westman's face.

He sniffled once more, and this time I could see the slight flaring of his nostril, but his eyes were already fixed and dull, opaque; painted-over windows in an abandoned building.

Schoch barked out a command: Someone laid a poncho down beside Westman. Slowly, tenderly, Hudson and Schoch lifted his body and placed it, still prone, on the poncho. Gently, reverently, they folded the sides over him. Logan, still kneeling by his friend, watched without comprehension, his eyes following their movements with an anxious puzzlement. Schoch, Hudson, Hyde and Kenzy lifted the poncho. Tears still ran down Logan's red, heavy face. His eyes dropped back down to the dull red splotch where Westman had lain. Mercifully, I don't think he'd ever heard Schoch call out that Westman was still breathing.

Westman's face was just visible; the back of his head, with that horrible gaping hole, was hidden. Two boots, muddied and scuffed, protruded, toes down, from the other end of the poncho. He was now altogether a child, lying huddled on his stomach, his arms folded underneath him, hugging his own chest, sighing over some unimaginable sorrow. As they lifted him, Myles Westman gave one final, barely audible sigh, long and hushed. His last breath ended in a faint, dry hiccup. Blood welled slowly out over the end of the poncho, then ran in tiny rivulets underneath, like water along a leaky pipe, until it reached the middle, where it formed a big, pulsing tear that dropped to the earth below, one after another, slowly; eternal tears shed by all the mothers of humanity. I followed the dull red trail with my eyes, past Helms, who stood with the mike in his hand, past Eden, past Captain Littnan and Conzoner, standing silently some 20 meters away. Logan knelt quietly, staring at the ground. He had finally run out of tears.

"Sweet!" I looked back. It was Wright. Sweet, looking confused and hesitant, was stumbling down the hill toward the LZ far below us. "Sweet! Come over here!" Wright repeated, pointing to a spot along the perimeter. Sweet looked at him, blankly, but continued his stumbling way downhill.

The rage and guilt inside me burst, like a lanced boil. "Damn you!" I yelled, getting to my feet and rushing at him. "Damn you, Sweet." I reached out and grabbed his thin, throbbing, sweat-dampened neck. "Move, you little bastard! Get over there." I pushed and jerked the youngster to where Wright was standing. "Move, you little son of a bitch." I gave him one last shove and delivered him to Wright.

I whirled and walked blindly past Littnan. He reached out with his hand, grabbed my arm and pulled me to a stop. I glared at him but said nothing. I couldn't speak. I couldn't think. I couldn't do anything but stand there and rage.

"Take it easy," he said in a cold, flat voice. He stared at me. "Are you okay?"

For another long moment I held his stare, hating him. Then I dropped my eyes. Something elemental went out of me, to leave me limp and dull. "Yeah," I said quietly. "Yeah, I'm okay."

"All right." He stared at me some more. "I'm going to have Three Six continue the attack, Frank. I think your people need to settle down a bit." He meant me, of course.

"Right."

"Anyone else hurt?"

"Yeah. Nelson. Got hit by shrapnel." I glanced around, looking for my gear. My eyes passed over Schoch's sodden kit bag. I had broken every IV in it.

"Okay," Littnan said. "Get your people together and move them back to the NDP area."

"Yes sir."

Littnan put out a hand as I started to move away. "Frank."

"Yeah."

He stared at me, expressionless. "You have to get over this. I need you."

I shook my head. "Okay. I'm fine."

We stumbled back to the NDP site. Along the way, I saw splotches and streaks of blood where it had dripped from the poncho. By the time we reached the NDP, Schoch and the other medics had already placed Westman in a body bag. It lay, zippered shut, to be taken to the LZ. Hudson stood over it, looking perplexed and mildly upset, like a man who's gotten off at the wrong bus stop. He said nothing as I walked up to him and looked at the bag. Situations where "Oh, wow!" or "Yeah, man!" wouldn't serve left him with nothing to say. I took a last look and walked away. I never saw them take the bag down to the LZ.

YC323984: 1530

Third Platoon, led by Sergeant Garza, went up, had two men wounded by RPG fire, and returned. The Fake Bomb Run was abandoned. They went up the conventional way and were repulsed the conventional way. Except for the first day, when Denholm's platoon had been allowed to move into the clearing before being annihilated, none of us had made it past the lip of the clearing. This had been Three Six's first attempt. Understandably, although Garza was an outstanding leader, his platoon, cabled together from two under strength platoons, was not going to be asked to do much as long as First and Second platoons were available. Marsh Eward and I would have to bear the brunt of it for a while. It was, as PFC Wright said, enough to make you so damn proud you'd puke.

Three Six wouldn't have had to go at all, had it not been for the bombing and my subsequent loss of self-control. I had to admit this to myself, as we sat at the NDP, listening to the firefight Garza's people were engaged in. Black Jack's words, from Dong Ngai—less than two weeks earlier, although it was an eon—came back to me and I at last had to acknowledge the justice of his criticism. I was not allowed, and less should I allow myself, the luxury of feelings. It was the worst excess of self-indulgence. While I had been venting my rage and sorrow, my platoon, the company, Charlie and Delta Companies, who had been moving up their own ridges, had all been jeopardized. Again, I could feel the impact of his cold blue eyes and the cutting edge of his voice: My responsibility lay not to one man but to everyone in the mission. Captains Jessup and Sanders had been told that Bravo Company would attack the middle ridge while they attacked theirs. They did not expect to be told that Bravo's assault would be held up while Bravo One Six threw a tantrum.

No one said anything, of course. Not even Littnan. But I felt it nonetheless. And yet … and yet I knew that I couldn't have acted any differently. It was not in me to watch a man die, uselessly, stupidly, grotesquely and not feel it. And—I was forced to admit—my rage and sorrow had not been for Westman alone. It had been for all of us, and of course for me above all. So much of our grief at another's death is for what that death whispers to us in the dark. On reading Donne's poem—for the first of a thousand times—I had thought that the words, "ask not for whom the bell tolls" express empathy and altruism. No. They are a celebration of self-absorption, a paean to a fearful narcissism.

What a wretched way for a man to die, I reflected. What a damned useless, stupid, almost clownish way to die. The rest of us could derive no profit from such a death; extract no moral, deduce no truth, realize no comfort. Westman was a martyr, not to any ideal, or nation, or cause or virtuous principle, but to the dogma of chance, to the chaos of Brownian movement. He had been butchered to satisfy an equation in some mad god's calculation of probabilities. This is what our universe had come to mean: It had no more moral sense than that. Calculate the odds, and then watch the wheel spin.

And I? I was a failed shaman, a defrocked, discredited priest, bearer of a dishonored talisman. Like the King of the Golden Bough, my life should have been forfeit. Had it not been my duty to ward off evil? What else were my incantations for? I was supposed to keep my people alive, and since skill or intelligence or bravery had no effect, why then, I should have called on all the demons and spirits: Goat's entrails. Newt's eyes. The sacrificial lamb. But the rituals failed, and the Great God of Chance had remained unappeased. A sliver, the size of my palm, had slithered and snuck and curved and darted its way through a thousand branches, past a hundred boles, to land on that one small spot of earth where Westman, his hands full of ammunition and gear, his helmet knocked from his head when its front rim struck the ground as he dove, lay with his head bared for the sacrificial blow. And so he died. One chance in a million? In a hundred million? And so we pray. And when the prayers fail — as fail they will — then the supplicant can only kneel, and despair.

I uttered one last, luciferan prayer. *God, how could you do this? Men must die — but Westman? He was what You wanted us all to be. You could have taken any of us, but You took the one man of us all who was most like Your Son. And now You demand worship and thanks? I owe You nothing.*

It was at this point in my thoughts that I became aware, with a consuming self-detestation, that I was despairing more for myself than for Westman or Logan.

Agnus Dei, qui tollis peccata mundi...

Bravo Six, this is One Six. Abort, for the love of God...

Third Platoon returned. Two wounded men were sent back to the LZ. The rest returned to their foxholes. We — the platoon sergeants and platoon leaders — gathered once more at the CP. Garza could add nothing to what we already knew about the clearing, except for one thing: The enemy may be placing snipers well up in the trees over the knolls and saddle, firing down on us. Also, he warned, some of his men reported heavy movement in the draws on either side as they descended the ridge after the attack. We shrugged at that; some of our men had reported movement, particularly at night, but that raised no alarm in us: Our position lay between the Laotian sanctuaries and Dong Ap Bia; it should be no surprise that the enemy moved past us on their way up or down the mountain.

Littnan grunted, and, after a pause, told us of what was happening with the rest of the battalion.

Delta Company, moving into position along the ridge a thousand meters to our north, had encountered heavy opposition, including RPG, heavy machine gun and intense small arms fire. They took some wounded, including Al Mattioli, their platoon leader, at the base of a steep, high ravine that split the ridge in a sharp V. Against the advice of Luther "Lee" Sanders, Delta's new CO, the medevac Huey approached the site. Since all the wounded were at the base of the ravine, alongside a small stream, the pilot had to descend into the gap, and then hover a hundred feet or so above the wounded. The first man had been placed in the wire basket, and was being winched up, when the NVA fired *down* on the chopper from the ridge. The RPG hit the tail rotor, the chopper plummeted instantly to the ground, crushing not only the man in the basket but the other wounded and the man directing the pickup. They rescued the pilot, but all the others were killed when the Huey exploded moments later. Including the men caught underneath, four crewmen and seven troopers died. Alpha Company had to send a platoon out to help Delta carry all the wounded out; no one was going to risk another medevac.

While that was going on, Charlie Company was running into severe problems of their own, to our south. After the initial contact, which had prompted them to call in the F4, Joel Trautman was ordered to take his First Platoon down to the base of the ridge and cut down and secure a PZ for evacuating the wounded. This he did, but then, realizing that there was no security between the PZ and the company CP, he pulled a squad out and took them up the trail. He'd been gone only a couple of minutes when the NVA assaulted the depleted platoon, killing two and wounding one, before being driven off by Trautman and the men of the other squad.

We absorbed all this in silence. That changed our thinking quickly. The first thing we saw, clearly — all of us — was that it was no longer a question of the NVA sitting back and waiting for us to hit them. As both Delta and Charlie could attest, they were coming out from their bunkers and hitting us first. What we also saw clearly now, was something that we had increasingly become aware of: This was no small force we were fighting. The idea of trail watchers had long been discredited, but now we had to face the reality that the enemy wasn't a couple of platoons or a company, scattered across the vast mountain. Bravo, Charlie and Delta had all been met with heavy resistance at approximately the same time and across three widely divergent ridgelines. Only a battalion, or more, could do that. By the time Littnan finished speaking that feathery tickling at the nape of our necks became a gaunt, icy hand clutching our bowels.

That night, we maintained a high state of alert, although our troops were bone-tired and none of us had much spare energy. Lack of sleep, and the constant build-up and release of adrenalin had brought us all to exhaustion.

I made my rounds that night, but with none of the usual quiet conversation with the troops, beyond the most basic necessities. Neither they nor I were in a mood for it. When I reached Logan's position, on the end of our sector, I nerved myself to say something to him, or at least to lay a hand on his shoulder, but when I saw him, huddled in his poncho, sitting alone to one side of the foxhole, staring out into the dark, I quailed. Either he had, with the miraculous but perilous facility of the young, put aside his memory of Westman's last moments, so that I would only bring them back, unbidden; or he was still seeing his friend die before his eyes, and nothing I could do or say would change that, ever.

The CP, when I returned, seemed as dark and impersonal as the forest. Sergeant Wright sat with his back against a tree, head slumped down to his chest, totally silent and unmoving. Dennis, one hand still on the receiver, was curled awkwardly against the radio, sleeping or at least resting with eyes shut. Hudson sat beside him, but in no way did he seem a part of the scene; he stared, with eyes vividly bright in the forest gloom, at something that only the Hudsons of the world can see. PFC Wright, on duty, tapped his chin repeatedly with the top of the receiver, and did not look my way as I lay down near him, with my head against my pack.

There could be no thoughts of home, tonight. I rarely brought them to mind, but tonight I knew, instinctively, that they would drive me insane. My beloved father, my wife, my still-unseen son; none of them could exist in this world, none of them had a place in it. A complete and rigid detachment from everything that I had ever known before was all that kept me sane. The forest; the smell of loam and mold, of rotting leaves and rotted flesh; the sounds of small life and great death; the dark that only promised a greater, blacker darkness: This forest was my world, and I wanted desperately then to escape it, but I had no where to go. This had nothing to do with fear; fear was an everyday companion. This was the iron grip of fate, and released its hold on no man.

And then a small light shone in the darkness. I had one memory, one only, that offered refuge. I had collected a series of scores, in the original German; small volumes bound in stiff yellow paper, each containing the full orchestral score of a Brahms symphony. The one I knew best was his Fourth, and the movement I loved most was the haunting second: I lay there and sounded, in my head, the opening bar, and as I did I fiercely willed myself to trace in my mind the notes as they lay on the page; the signature, the key, the ligatures, the staccato ... everything as Brahms had written it. The first bar, and then the second ... the sixth — no; back to the fifth: I'd missed the entrance of the strings ... I could not believe in God, but if He existed at all, then the great composers were His voice, and only something that transcendent could lift the dark around me. Home, family, friends, were all gone from me, and would endure no longer than I. But those horns would sound forever.

33

Logan's Run

YC323984; 14 May 1969; Morning

We awoke — rather, we arose — to a cool grey light; the inevitable clouds shadowed the dawn. I felt chilled, still clammy and damp. My shirt had an unpleasant, oily feel to it as I donned it. Helms had coffee ready — he'd had the last radio watch — and he offered me a steaming cup. I drank it gratefully. It tasted as wretched as ever, but the liquid warmth of it was what mattered. I rubbed my head and neck vigorously with a towel — as close to a shower as I would get — and then lit a cigarette. The blue-grey smoke from my Camel seemed to become one with the grey mist overhead. I was hungry, but not enough to really consider fixing anything. Maybe a cracker and peanut butter…

Price stood over me, leaning slightly toward me. "CO wants you, sir."

As soon as I arrived, only a moment later, Littnan began talking. "We're going after them this morning. No more probes, no more half-ass tries. We want a hard, aggressive push, all across the mountain. Delta's moving to our left, and Charlie's on our right.

"Punch it through, guys. We can't keep losing men like this. And this time, I want Two Six and Three Six moving up together. Frank, you're my reserve, and you'll secure the trail back down to the NDP. I want you," he nodded at Eward, "on the left and Third Platoon on the right. Move up together, platoons abreast, and stay together. Stay even, I mean. Fan out when you get to the clearing. Don't get bogged down. Have your men hit the front bunkers and then leapfrog — leave the mopping up to the rear squads. Push, push, push. Get up that damned hill, over the knolls and up on the crest."

He paused to look at us. "We can't see it from here, but the crest of Dong Ap Bia has been cleared. Daisy chains, artillery, all those bombing runs — the tree cover is gone. That means the enemy has no place to hide. Break through the bunker line and you'll be in the clear.

"Hopefully, all three companies will break through, but even if only one of us does, then that one will immediately move across the summit of the hill and start firing down on the enemy from behind, catching them between the company moving up and the elements on top. Everything they've got is oriented down-slope, so we should be able to move in behind them almost at will.

"Now remember this: Charlie and Delta are going to be pushing hard. They're going to depend on us. We're in the middle; we're the linchpin, the keystone. If we don't make it up there ... well, we will. And once we do, we've split the enemy force. It's all there for us: All you guys have to do is push.

"Keep radio contact. That's a must. Talk to each other. Talk to me. Let everyone know what's going on. When you break through past the tree line, pop smoke immediately. Call me, but pop smoke first. We want to have your position marked right away, in case we need to bring ARA or Bilk. The ARA is out of Eagle. Their call sign is Random Four Four. The password for the day is Granny Fork."

"Granny Fork?" Eward interjected. "Who the hell thinks up these things, anyway?"

Littnan shook his head, unsmiling. I realized he was extremely tense. Nothing else betrayed it: not his face, not his voice; it was as calm and level as always. But there was an unusual hint of impatience in that quick shake of his head. Well, we all were tense.

"The keyword for today is Bared Sting — that's Bravo Alpha Romeo Echo Delta. Price and Conzoner have already given your RTOs the main and backup frequencies to your RTOS."

He turned to me. "Remember — and remind your people — that Delta and Charlie were hit from the flanks. So was Garza. Tell them to keep alert and pay attention to their front, not to what's happening up on the hill above them. Recon Platoon has found beaucoup tracks on the trail between here and Battalion, and then on out towards Laos. They're moving pretty free around us, so keep your eyes open."

He glanced at his watch. "It's 0630. We move at 0900. Get your people fully prepared — ammo, water, aid kits — everything they need. Oh, I almost forgot. Frank — same time, around 0900; a resupply is coming in. So you'll have to secure the NDP, the trail and the LZ, for that few minutes. Any questions?"

Eward stood up, stretching in the early morning damp. "Arty prep?"

"Same stuff as usual. We'll be starting soon and we won't let up. The enemy isn't going to notice anything different. By the way — Eward, Garza: Tell your rear squads the same thing I just mentioned to Frank. Watch their flanks while they're on that hill. Okay."

He turned away with finality. The three of us did the same; Eward and I exchanged one look, a quirked eyebrow apiece, before walking to our CPs.

Within minutes of the platoon leaders returning to their own platoons, the mood in the company changed. There was a palpable tension, an electric atmosphere of anticipation. It was neither optimism nor despair; simply an expectant, roiling sense of imminence. For good or ill, we all felt, affairs were coming to a climax. For the first time, I noticed, amongst all the troops, signs of nervousness: Tapping fingers, jittery feet, quick, purposeless gestures, sudden, choked-off laughs. It wasn't fear. It was closer to impatience. They wanted this over with. We all hated waiting.

33. Logan's Run

The closer 0900 came, the more pronounced the mood became. Men, particularly from Second or Third Platoon, would rise suddenly from their seats and walk short distances with quick, impulsive steps. A high-pitched, choppy laugh would suddenly cut through the murmurs, as suddenly subside. One man, a heavy set trooper from Eward's platoon, named Little, sat on a tree stump and with intense if nonsensical concentration, snapped a magazine into his M16, pressed the release pin, and reloaded it, all in one continuous motion, over and over again. Another sat with his back against a tree, with his helmet lying upside down on the ground six feet in front of him, methodically flipping card after playing card into the target. I tried to remain as calm and detached as possible, but even so I could felt a pulsating tight constriction across my chest, squeezing and relaxing. I picked up the movement with my left hand, opening and closing it in time with it. A moment later, I was startled to notice that all three of us—Little, the trooper, and I—were moving to precisely the same rhythm.

Time passed slowly, but it passed. Eward and I met at the CP. We had no business there; our wanderings happened to take us to the same place at the same time. We looked at each other for the briefest moment, expressionless, then shrugged and turned away without a word. "Good luck" meant nothing. The finger already was moving along the wall.

AT 0845, I sent Hyde and Eden down to the LZ, to secure it while the Black Widow flight arrived. Dickerson set up his squad along the trail. Second and Third were already moving out, but it would take a while before their rear elements cleared the NDP. Artillery had been falling for some time now: 155s and 8-inchers from Currahee and Berchtesgaden. A series of explosions sounded above us: Crrump-Whump! Crrunp-Whump! Crrump-Whunp!! They sounded like insistent, monstrous heartbeats in a great beast's chest.

0900. Eward and Garza were well up the trail by now, their rear elements just beginning to clear the NDP. At 0905, Eward radioed back that his lead element was at the lip of the clearing. Two or three minutes later, Garza reported the same thing. Behind me, at the LZ, I could hear the heavy thrumming of the resupply ship's blades as the pilot settled it into the clearing down there. I called Wright to tell him to move as much ammo—the principal item of resupply—as Eden's squad could carry up to the NDP as soon as it arrived; Hyde's squad could remain behind, to secure the LZ for the ship's departure and then bring the rest up at their leisure.

By now the last elements of the platoons had moved out, and Littnan, with his entourage of RTOs, was moving up behind them. Russ Crenshaw, with his RTO, followed him. Russ was concentrating mightily. He was trying to walk the 155 fire up the hill, in front of the advancing troops, but it was useless. For one thing, there simply wasn't enough room between the clearing and the summit—maybe 100 meters, but probably less. For another, Russ wasn't working by sight; in these steep mountains and dense forests, he had to judge the fall of the rounds by sound, something he was trained for — *but*, after four days of continuous bombardment and firefights, his ears were shot. He could still hear, but with nothing like the fine discrimination he had — and needed — the first day. He confessed to me later that afternoon that he no longer had any idea where the rounds were dropping.

Eden's people arrived, huffing mightily under the strain of carrying the crates of ammo up the trail. I directed him to place them all in the center of the NDP. Glancing at my watch, I decided he had time to return to the LZ for another load. In the meantime, Littnan's CP group was well up the trail from us now. Gathering my CP group, minus Wright and his RTO, who were still down at the LZ, I moved up from the NDP to a point where I could see Crenshaw's RTO — the last man in the company CP group. Helms, Hudson, Brown and I had nothing to do right now; we might as well act as security for that section of trail until Hyde moved off the LZ.

The first scattered shots from M16s rang out, distantly. That had to be Eward's people. A few answering AK-47s could be heard. The 155s ceased; the 8-inch fire had lifted earlier. For the moment, it seemed as if little was to happen. But of course we knew that wasn't so. Gradually, the level built up; Third Platoon was now adding to the din. How Eward and Garza could fit all their people in that small space — no one had said they'd entered the clearing yet, and the little slope below the clearing's lip was hardly large enough for a squad — was an unanswerable question.

Wright and Murtiff decided to bring all the ammo and the rest of the supplies up, which really was a good idea. I didn't want to have to worry about securing both the NDP and the LZ and the trail in between. Once Hyde's and Eden's men had dumped the supplies and taken up positions, I was free to move up and join Littnan, now standing with a mike in his ear, a good 40 or 50 meters up the ridge from me.

Garza and Eward both called, on the company net, so I could hear that they thought they were in position.

"We're moving up," Eward called in.

A moment later, the whole mountain erupted in flame and sound.

To our left and right, Delta and Charlie Company were in contact — heavy, sustained contact. The fire coming from their two ridges was intense. But it was nothing compared to what was coming down to us from up above. The spitting barks of the M16s became one voice; the hammering of the M60s merged into a sheet of sound, a smothering curtain of noise. It seemed as if one could *walk* across the sound, as if it had, in fact, crystallized the very air into something ponderous.

Suddenly, convulsively, we rushed forward, further up the trail. Second and Third Platoons both had entered the clearing. The rate of fire — the enemy's as well as ours — intensified, if that were possible. Littnan and I advanced another 50 meters, and then knelt, side by side. An M60, off to my left front — we must have been much closer to the clearing than I'd thought — was sustaining an incredible rate of fire; the man was going to burn out the barrel. Dadadadadadaum ... dadadadadadaum ... dadadadadadaum. Heavy, insistent, demanding. Charlie and Delta were firing at the same rate. I couldn't hear them, but I knew they were, as a man swimming in the ocean knows he is surrounded by cubic miles of water, even if he can't see them.

My body was vibrating with the sound. It was willed forward by it, pushed and pulled by its orphean call. Dadadadadum ... dadadadadadum. I felt alive, and somehow powerful, and completely impervious. Littnan and I happened to glance at each other; spontaneously, we grinned. This was it, we felt. This was victory — this is what we expected, this is what we had been born to do. As if able to read my thoughts, Littnan nodded in affirmation. Dadadadadum ... dadadadaddum. A dragon's roar.

This dragon needed feeding. They were low on ammo up front. Eden's squad began shuttling ammo up. One of his troopers, Clark Besack, was tireless. Time after time he raced up the slope, carrying a case of M60 ammo under each arm. Mareniewski too carried huge loads, mouth turned in an inverted U from the strain of carrying the 50-pound boxes. But the most impressive of all was Eden. Eden was everywhere, directing his men, urging them forward, screaming at the slow and the hesitant, all while carrying one or two cases himself. After several trips up and down the ridge, he fell to his knees not far from me, hands on the top of his thighs, head bent, chest heaving in a mighty effort to suck more oxygen into his body. And then he started to struggle to his feet.

I stared, amazed and a little shamed. This was the man whom I'd relieved twice, whom I'd reinstated only with reluctance and out of extreme necessity. *You're a great judge of character, chump*. I moved over to him as he was still getting up, and laid a hand on his shoulder.

"John — I wanted to tell you you're doing a great job — just terrific. I couldn't ask any more from anyone."

He looked up at me. His breath was still coming in large gulps and gasps, and he couldn't speak, but his eyes shone with pride and he smiled. I turned away with another reminder of how blessed I was.

I was holding the radio mike hard against my ear; it was the only way I could hear anything. Even though Littnan knelt on the ground only a foot or so away, I could hear him only through the radio — and not very well then. By now the noise level passed limits beyond which I'd never experienced or imagined.

Eward was as laconic as ever while in contact, but Garza, moving across the right side of the clearing, called to tell Littnan that they had knocked out a bunker at the base of the right knoll. A moment later, he reported a second bunker destroyed, and that his Second Squad was at last moving up the face of the knoll itself. Then Eward called to report that RPGs were being fired down on his men from the north knoll, the one on the left. He couldn't risk moving up its slope until the RPG gunners were killed or neutralized.

Littnan leaned over to me, put his mouth an inch from my ear, and screamed into it; I could barely make out what he was saying: Delta Two Six reported breaking through the first bunker line; there was little word from Charlie but Second and Third Platoons were heavily engaged on their ridge south of us. A moment later, Garza called to say that his Third Squad was starting up the south knoll.

And then they set the mines off.

Even amidst the overwhelming fire, the heavy boom of the combined explosions could be heard clearly. They'd all been set off at once, with hardly a second of elapsed time. Eward called, and his voice was a shout that was barely audible.

"Six ... Two Six. Claymores ... all over.... Can't move...."

"Roger, Two Six." Littnan's mouth moved, inches away, but I could only hear his voice, tinny and distorted — Helms had cranked the volume up to the highest setting — through the radio. "Three Six is moving up that knoll. Can you support him, over?"

"I don't know. Can't see ... from where we are."

"Six, Six, this is Three Six. Taking 'eavy fire. Claymores knock us down. Can't hold. Can't stay here, over."

"Roger. Can you see Two Six from your position?'

"Negative."

"Roger. Can you hold your position while he moves up?"

"Negative, negative. We takin' bad hits, losin' men, over."

Littnan dropped the mike from his ear and hung his head down, concentrating. I could see a jaw muscle twitch. When he raised it back up to his ear, Eward was calling.

"...taking casualties. Can't stay...."

"Roger. Two Six, you hold in place. Break Three Six, can you get your wounded out?"

"That's affirm. But gotta move now, Six."

"Roger. Pull out, bring your men down. Break, Two Six, cover Three Six's withdrawal. Can you hold where you are?"

"Negative. Every time my ... head up ... world of shit."

"Then bring 'em back, after Three Six has cleared. Do you copy?"

"Roger."

Littnan's shoulders slumped. Then he motioned to Price for the other mike, the battalion net. While he spoke into it, reluctantly telling Black Jack of our withdrawal, I saw two shadows flit by; Besack and Eden, on their way back up the ridge to the clearing, each carrying two cases— more than 100 pounds— of ammo. And they were *running* up the slope.

I felt a tap on my shoulder: Helms was pointing to Dickerson, who was standing a few feet behind me, making urgent motions toward the NDP. At the same moment, Wright called.

"One Six, this is One Five. We're taking pretty heavy incoming from that area to our south; small arms and RPGs."

"Roger. Be right there." As I stood up, Dickerson leaned over and yelled in my ear. "We got incoming all along the trail between here and the NDP. Heavy."

I felt my mouth go dry. The enemy fire at the top of the hill had barely slackened, and we were getting hit with heavy fire at our NDP and along the trail, simultaneously.

And Charlie and Delta were still in heavy contact themselves. Jesus, what were we facing here?

Littnan caught my eye; he hadn't heard Wright, I knew, because he was still on the battalion net. Conzoner, though, had monitored Wright and was standing over Littnan, waiting for him to finish to pass on the word. Still ... I took two steps and knelt down by Littnan and shouted in his ear: "Taking fire at the NDP. Going down there now."

He looked up, momentarily startled, and then nodded and spoke into the mike again. Motioning to Helms, I began to run down the trail, alongside Dickerson. I was frankly worried. The broad, low LZ, with its open reed-covered slope, was relatively easy to cover; it was large enough to set up a full perimeter, and the south slope was a ready-made field of fire. But that's not where my people were. Instead, we were strung out along a relatively narrow ridge; the foxholes in the NDP formed a long, very thin oval, and nothing like a circle. A foxhole on the south side of the perimeter was only ten meters or so from one on the north. There could be no defense in depth; if the enemy broke through a single position they would effectively have broken our line. We stood an excellent chance of being overrun.

As I moved down the trail, the fire became louder and more intense. Dickerson had three positions, about 20 meters apart, but one facing north and the other two south. As I approached, First Sergeant Murtiff was pulling one man from each position and setting up a fourth, also facing south. He was also screaming at the men to stop firing indiscriminately.

"Look what you're shooting at, God damn you!" he bellowed with all the fury of his 18 years in the Army. "You're killing leaves, you sorry fuckers." Turning away, he saw me and moved up to meet me; we met half way and knelt down.

"Fire's coming from the south," he said. "All of it."

"Okay. Is the NDP getting hit bad?"

"No. No worse than here. Wright's got it under control."

"Okay. I'm going down there. We —"

I was interrupted by Helms, who stuck his head in between ours. "CO's pulling everyone back. Third Platoon's already moving. Charlie and Delta are pulling back too."

Murtiff opened his mouth to say something but closed it with a snap: An RPG went off against a tree, a few meters away. We sprawled face first on the ground, and then got up immediately. It was a useless thing to do — by the time the RPG exploded, it was far too late to duck, but it was reflex and nothing could be done about it. By that time, the first of the Third Platoon troopers came running down the trail.

"Aw, fuck it," Murtiff growled. He made a gesture with his hand, jumped up and grabbed the man, unceremoniously pushing him toward the south side of the perimeter. He then stood in the middle of the trail, oblivious to the AK rounds snapping and chipping the branches just above his head, and directed traffic, gradually forming Third Platoon into a semi-circle facing east, south and north.

Taking a deep breath, and hoping that the NVA wouldn't choose that moment to assault the trail, I ran down the path, followed by Helms and Brown. Hudson had been commandeered by Schoch, to help treat Eward's and Garza's wounded. It was only another 30 meters or so to the NDP site, but it seemed like one of those infinitely long corridors in a dream, the ones that never end. This one did: I could see Wright, crouched down by the pile of ammo; PFC Wright knelt by his side, and was passing out small boxes of ammo to runners from the front positions. My eyes took in all they could, before I crossed the space between me and Wright; almost all the fox holes were manned, at least, all that I could see from where I stood; the ones on the north side held one man each; the ones to the west and south held two. Logan, his M60 set up along the south side but facing back to the west, was clearly visible, with his red hair and knotted, bulging shoulders.

Dickerson's men, no longer needed because of Third Platoon's withdrawal, were streaming into the NDP; Wright and I both directed them into foxholes, mainly on the south and west sides. Wright and Hyde had been fighting off an attack with basically a squad, augmented by one or two of Eden's men.

The fire suddenly slackened considerably; both from us—there was much better fire discipline down here — and from the enemy. To my left, further up the trail, I could hear the same thing happening. Amazingly, almost all that Niagara of sound slowed to the smallest trickle; a few isolated shots from far up on top of the ridge, as Two Six disengaged, and an odd AK round or two.

There was a small fold of ground, not really big or deep enough to be called a draw, much less a ravine, leading off to the southeast at the east end of the NDP. I motioned for Hyde to pull Logan's gun and move it up to cover that draw, just in case. I was then standing in the middle of the perimeter, talking to Wright and Hyde, when Besack and Mareniewski came stumbling and gasping down the trail. Besack was soaked—literally drenched—with sweat, and his lungs were laboring to pull in air. They came to a stop, hands on knees, heads down, sobbing. Then Besack looked up and forced some words through his throat.

"Eden ... hit."

Damn! I felt an icy jolt clutch my stomach. Eden! Just when ... I broke the thought off. "How bad?" I asked.

Besack shook his head, slowly, but even so the sweat flew off his hair and neck and splattered over me. "Don't know. Ski 'n me were bringin' up some more ammo, jus' before they pulled back, and Eden was up front, ahead of us. I didn't..." he paused to take a breath. "I didn't see him get hit. But one second he was there n' next he wasn't. I had my hands full, or I'd gone lookin' right then." He paused again to take a few breaths. "He oughta be on his way down by now."

"Were there many guys hit?" I asked.

They both nodded. "Beaucoup. 'Specially those last coupla minutes."

Wright and I exchanged glances—another squad leader gone. "Kenzy?" I said.

He nodded, but before be could say anything Littnan called.

"Things quieted down back there?" He asked.

"Roger. I was just about to move out front here and look for signs of them."

"Negative. We've got some people hurt bad. We're going to need to open up that LZ again. I'm going to send Three Six down to secure it, so he'll be moving through your area pretty soon. I'm on my way down right now."

Almost immediately, Third Platoon began arriving, some of them carrying the wounded. Wright and I stepped aside to let them by. There were nine wounded, some of them seriously — RPGs, I thought, for the hundredth time. Fucking RPGs. I shook my head in mute and helpless rage at the sight of one soldier's arm. It was a stump; nothing was left from the elbow down.

The next few minutes were chaotic, as Sergeant Wright and I struggled to set up security around the LZ and some along the trail, while laying out the wounded in a shaded spot secure enough and yet close enough to the LZ. I was completely engrossed in this, so that I saw but paid no attention to a stir among the troops at one of the positions around the LZ; I vaguely noticed Besack and someone else talking and gesticulating.

It was a minute or so later that Sergeant Wright strode up to me.

"Sir, did you send Logan anywhere?"

I looked at him in surprise. "Logan? No. Why?"

Wright's lips thinned in his characteristic frown. "Him and Besack — just took off runnin' a moment ago. Back up the trail. Logan left his gun. What —"

Schoch interrupted us. "Guys, I need a count from you. We're trying to get the wounded out right away."

Sergeant Wright shrugged. "Nobody from our platoon, Doc."

I started to open my mouth but he suddenly remembered. "'Cept for Eden."

Schoch looked at the two us. "Eden? Was he hit bad?"

"I don't know," I said. "I haven't seen him yet, but Besack said he was..." I trailed off at the look on Doc's face.

"Eden's not down here," he said tersely. "All the others are."

Wright and I exchanged stricken looks. Cursing, I instinctively grabbed my rifle and began running up the trail, yelling back at Wright to stay at the LZ. I ran through the NDP area with only a glance, and was still running some 40 or 50 meters past it, when I saw several Second Platoon troopers coming down the hill. Eward stood a few meters away, waiting on them.

"Marsh!" I yelled. "Eden ... do you know where he is?"

Eward grimaced and pointed up the hill. Behind the troopers was Logan, cradling a loose body in his arms. Besack walked a few meters in front of him. Even with all the noise from the adjoining ridges, I could hear sobbing and cries of agony; Eden's right foot dangled loosely, attached to his leg by the remains of his boot and a few shreds of tissue and tendons. The troopers moved off the trail and stood, rifles ready, facing back up the hill as Logan walked through our position, red face a furnace of exertion and emotion, mostly, I could tell, anger.

A machine gun round almost severed Eden's ankle; he was standing just off the trail, with his right leg planted against the steep slope of the ravine, and when that leg was hit, he toppled into the ravine and slid a couple of meters before coming to a halt under a pair of small palm bushes. Second Platoon ran by him on the retreat back to the NDP. In fairness to Eward's people, most of them had been higher up the ridge, at or near the clearing, and hadn't seen him get shot. Only the few who remained down the ridge, closest to the NDP, were in a position to see him fall. One of these, already carrying a wounded comrade, saw Logan and told him that he'd seen Eden hit and thought he might still be up there.

Logan, six feet two inches and 180 pounds of rhinocerine fury, grabbed a bayonet and scabbard from the cover of his extra machine gun barrel and clumped up the slope, leaving an open-mouthed Eward in his wake. Marsh and his troopers ran back up after him, but stopped 20 or 30 meters below where Eden had been hit. They lay down a continuous burst of suppressive fire as Logan first pulled Eden up from the ravine, then splinted his wound, and finally, carrying him the way a father would a small child, ran down the hill back through Eward and his men.

Eward, Besack and I followed Logan; he paused at the NDP only long enough to loose a couple of furious curses at those members of Second Platoon he could see, but continued to jog down to the LZ. Eward stopped at the NDP. He grimaced again, and finally looked me in the eye.

"Sorry, Frank. Honest to God, I didn't know. No idea."

I nodded. "Yeah. I know that, Marsh. Not blaming you or your guys."

When Besack and I arrived at the collection point, Eden lay on the ground, still screaming in agony. Schoch stopped what he was doing and moved swiftly to Eden's side, calling Hudson over to help him. He immediately began working on the sobbing Eden. Only then did I notice what Eward had mentioned: A rough field-expedient splint on Eden's leg, strapped tightly to boot and upper calf.

By now some of the men from First Platoon had moved up and were crowded around Logan, patting him on the back and saying, with open and heart-felt admiration, "Atta boy, Tim. Way to go, man. Good man, Lo."

I pulled his arm and brought his head down to closer to my level. "You are a fucking idiot, Logan," I said in his ear, "and you just took ten years off my life. But thanks."

He grinned, his ill humor and rancor forgotten. "Eden owed me 50 bucks, Lieutenant. A man's gotta look out for his investments, ya know."

His eyes then fell on Schoch, still swiftly and competently working on Eden, who no longer groaned and writhed, but lay still, his eyes half-closed, breathing slowly. Shock, of course.

"What's taking you so long, Doc?" he cried out, his usual good humor fully restored. "I did your job for ya. I splinted the leg for ya. All you gotta do now is write up the damned tag."

Schoch of course paid no attention; as always, he was focused on the patient.

"Doc," Logan persisted, "tell me somethin'. Ain't that the best splint you ever seen? I mean, field expedient n' all? Whaddaya say, Doc?"

I almost laughed. Logan was obviously far prouder of the splint than he was of having run into a killing zone, alone and without weapon, to rescue a comrade. The latter was merely part of the daily drill, all in a day's work. The former, on the other hand, was a prodigy of skill. He continued to wheedle and prod Schoch, who ignored him for some time, until, finally, he dropped back on his heels and placed his hands in his lap, a signal that he was finished. Doc O'Keefe, the senior battalion medic, had in the meantime been fashioning a stretcher, and now at his direction Hudson and another medic gently lifted Eden and placed him in it.

"So, what about that splint, Doc?" Logan asked again.

Schoch glanced up, his face deadpan. Getting up in one swift motion, he turned to face Logan.

"It was a good splint," he agreed. "A fine splint. Congratulations. I'm glad you paid attention in first aid class. But there's one thing...."

He pointed to Eden, on the stretcher, as the medics began moving him down to the LZ. His left leg still had part of Logan's splint, the dirty white bandage visible against the green trouser leg. His lower right leg, with bloodstained tatters of fatigue material flapping in the breeze, was now encased in a tight, inflated plastic splint.

"The next time," Schoch continued, remorselessly, "remember to splint the broken leg, not the good one. It's better for the patient."

There was a moment's silence. Logan, who was almost completely unflappable, threatened to lose his cool for only the third or fourth time all year. First the rat, then the latrine, and now this ... his small eyes popped open and his mouth hung wide, but he recovered swiftly.

"Oh," he said, nodding in satisfaction, "that explains it. I was wondering what he was complaining about after I fixed him up."

34

The Bamboo Corridor

YC323984; 14 May 1969; 1300–1600

The rifle fire had ceased, completely now. The jets returned and began their sky-shattering runs, one after another. The ground shook with their coming. These were no longer the 250 or 500-pound bombs of the previous days, but the monster 1,000 and even 2,000-pound ordnance, the kind that scoured craters 15 or 20 feet deep and as many as 60 across. Trees the height of ten story buildings, seven or eight feet in diameter, simply disintegrated, and entire sections of forest disappeared, to be replaced by an ugly scar of burnt earth.

The evacuation of the wounded took a while; ten men were relayed back to the battalion LZ on Rairdon's LOH, including Eden. There were no dead, but an additional six men were wounded, lightly — mostly small fragments of shrapnel — and were treated there by Schoch, O'Keefe and the others.

Sergeant Wright and I met briefly, while this was going on. Kenzy now took over as squad leader — that was settled — but we had to shuffle men around, to even out the numbers. Then we made the rounds of the platoon sector, separately.

The men were shaken; there was little doubt of that. So, for that matter, was I. For the first time, the full reality of what we faced lay before us. If anything, it was even more evident to the platoon leaders and company commanders, for we knew what most of the troops, at that point, did not: Delta and Charley were as heavily engaged as we; the First of the Five Oh Six, advancing up the ridges to the south of the mountain, several kilometers from us, was facing extremely heavy resistance and, in the end, would take very heavy casualties. And, of course, Alpha Company of the Second of the Five Oh One had been brutalized up at Firebase Airborne. Three full battalions of infantry were being stiff-armed with almost contemptuous ease by the enemy.

The most devastating, fearsome sound in battle, from the times of the Assyrians, is the unexpected clamor of battle to one's rear. Man, like any other animal, no matter how ferocious or deadly, must know that there exists a path of retreat, a safe zone to the rear, a friendly presence at his back. Take that away, suddenly, and panic can and often does set in. The Romans, the finest soldiers in history, died like frightened sheep by the thousands at Cannae, for just that reason. Not only had the NVA withstood the combined assaults of three infantry companies, and the tons of ordnance we'd dropped, but they had gone on the offensive with a series of counterattacks that had, at one point, threatened to cut Bravo in two. Just how successful those counterattacks had been, how close we had come to our own Cannae, we didn't know even then, but we were soon to find out.

The men were subdued, quiet, introspective, even morose. There was little laughter. Even Logan's Run, as we came to call it, later, once the momentary euphoria of the event passed, was set aside, ignored now in the general silence. Part — a large part — of this was fear. It lay over all of us like a noxious fog, heavy and oppressive. Each man felt it, but worse, each man knew that his comrade could see it. One man, afraid and alone in his fear, can warm himself by the heat of his comrades' courage and resolve. Many men can do this; that is why the unit is so important. But there eventually comes a tipping point; like water molecules in arctic air, there comes a moment when there is no more heat to share, and all become ice, at once, suddenly.

So it happens in a platoon. The individual, afraid and alone, reaches out to hid comrade for warmth and finds nothing but lonely ice. Men who are afraid sit in silence, and avoid each other's eyes. First Platoon stared at the ground, and said nothing.

Sergeant Wright and I tried. I was afraid; I believe that he was too, but of course, we could not show it. Our rank demanded that we not show it. Our rank demanded more; I must not only master my own fear, but that of my men. Sergeant Wright and I, each in his own way, set about to do that.

What worked best, I found, was also the easiest. Talk. Break the silence; remove that deadly introspection, shatter the ice that covered each man's soul. Talk about nothing; the weather, baseball, C-rations we hated, the cloud shapes overhead, how many stoplights a man's hometown had … banish the silence, get the men to look up, at each other, and not at themselves. Fear, like ice, grows fastest when left alone.

We met — Wright and I — back at the platoon CP after we'd made the rounds. We exchanged a few sentences, and then sat. We'd done what we could. The rest was up to the men, and that extraordinary resilience that defines and shapes the human condition.

I tried reading, but the only thing I had left, unread, was some silly adventure novel by someone named F Vanwick Mason. He set the novel in Southeast Asia, in the early 1960s. After his first description of the tropical rainforest, in which he had his hero dress in a full length, sealed rubber "jungle suit" so he could survive the terrors of the killer jungle, I threw the book aside. Actually, I threw it away; the ultimate and most derogatory literary criticism at my disposal. I resolved then never to write about a locale or environment I had never actually visited.

But aside from the book itself, I was too tired to read. My eyes were heavy, my mind felt gritty and dull. Today was the 14th of May; since the night of the 8th, I'd managed less than four hours of sleep. I ended up laying my head up against my pack, and resting.

I might have dozed off, because everything seemed so nicely, refreshingly dark and quiet, when I opened my eyes to see PFC Wright kneeling by my side, shaking my shoulder.

"Old Man wants you, Lieutenant," he said.

I nodded, rose, stretched and, still heavy-limbed, walked up to Littnan's CP. Eward and Garza were already there.

Littnan was seated, but he stood up as I approached, and looked directly at me.

"Black Jack wants us to go back up," he said, as usual without preliminary.

I stared. "You're shitting me," I said, in reflex.

"No. You'll lead."

I dropped my eyes to the ground, hands fixed on hips. An ice shaft thrust itself through my stomach. I did not want to go back up that hill again.

"Any ideas?"

I thought for a moment. The morning's assault, with two platoons, had only reinforced what we already knew: No matter how many platoons we sent up, the razor thin ridge and the clearing itself limited the number of men who could enter it to no more than a squad. That's what kept defeating us. Having two platoons attack, as we had that morning, meant that we had twice the number of men strung out along the ridge as usual — that's one reason why the NVA counterattack had almost succeeded.

So what was I to do? My mind, that wonderful, self-satisfied precision instrument that I valued so highly, came up with nothing. A total blank. Nothing. My brain simply sat there, useless, sucking up an inordinate amount of oxygen and energy, and producing a big fat zero.

"Charlie Company's already in contact; they've been hammering at their own ridge all day," Littnan went on, without waiting for my reply. He could recognize a blank look when he saw one. "Delta's going to move back up, too. And the Oh Six is on their way, so you won't be alone. We'll have a lot of help."

I grunted. "Okay ... *you* have any ideas?"

Littnan's face, normally a stiff mask, momentarily dissolved into a flickering kaleidoscope of emotion: resolute, compassionate, angered, weary, despairing, baffled, sorrowing, impatient, amused. Then the shards coalesced and the mask was whole again. One side of his lips twitched in a brief smile.

"Yes," he said. "I do. I want you to move with all deliberate speed."

I had to laugh. "Deliberate speed. That'll get 'em every time. Okay, when?"

"Fifteen minutes. Two Six will be your backup."

On the way back to my platoon, I wondered — for the first time — how they would respond. They were tired and afraid, never a good combination. It is physical, you see. Courage requires energy. I stopped on the edge of the platoon sector, silently observing them. Jorgenson, Olson and Besack were playing a quiet, subdued game of blackjack; Hernandez and Ulrich sat together, smoking and talking in undertones. Carlton sat off by himself, by a tree, arms pressed tightly to his sides, as if cold. Kenzy, his face calm and pensive, was silently oiling his rifle.

The CP group was seated nearby. Helms looked up from his task of cleaning his radio; his placid oval face, with the corner of his right lip that always seemed to be on the verge of lifting into a smile, stiffened when he saw me. Helms had been my RTO less than two months, but it now seemed a lifetime, and he knew me very well by now. Sergeant Wright, too, knew me. He stood up and walked over to me, his face impassive.

"Get the troops together, Top," I said quietly.

Moments later, most of them were assembled on the path; only a few remained at their foxholes, but they were listening, I could tell, from the set of their shoulders. The men, by that point, knew very well what I was about to say.

"Saddle up. We're going back up," I said.

There was no immediate reaction; just a few blank stares. Then:

"That sonuvabitch is gonna get us all killed, man."

"Tell Black Jack to take the fuckin' hill his own damn self."

"That fuckin' glory hound—fuck him!"

"Why don't that yellow motherfucker walk up there with us, huh? Sittin' back there in the fuckin' rear."

I stood there and said nothing, just looked at them. Sergeant Wright, his gear buckled on, his rifle in his hand, did the same. After a moment, Kenzy shrugged, reached down, picked up his gear and began putting it on.

"Okay. Get your shit. Let's go. Lieutenant said move, so move."

Hyde, his dark-stubbled, gaunt face rigid, nodded and signaled his squad. My jaw twitched as I watched him. How much longer could that man go on? He had less than a week left in country.

Ten minutes later, they were ready, in file, weapons and ammo in place. Dickerson's squad would lead; I indicated this with a nod and a gesture. The men were silent now, expectant, angry and resigned. For a moment we all stood motionless on the ridge, waiting, and then Logan spoke up.

"Whatta we do when we get up there, Lieutenant?" he asked, in a conversational tone.

"We kick the fuckers off the hill," I said.

"Oh. Okay. It's good to have a plan, ya know?"

A ripple of silent laughter swept through the platoon. I turned and began moving up the path, smiling. God bless Timothy Logan.

Littnan was waiting for me at the east end of the NDP. "Everyone's ready," he said. "Garza says he thinks that right-hand knoll might be ripe for the plucking—*might*, I said. Be careful. Try to stay out of that clearing as much as possible."

"You can't get to either knoll without going through the clearing," I said tonelessly.

"Yeah. Good luck."

Bresina was Dickerson's point man. His grey GI glasses were misted with sweat as he walked slowly up the path, past the NDP, up along the same trail we always followed. There was no alternative, of course. To move into the ravines on either side would be witless, and fruitless as well. I initially kept an eye on Ulrich and Hernandez, the two most vocal in their reaction to the news of the renewed assault, but they moved along with the rest. Ulrich looked surly, but when did he not? It was his way, and he had never shirked before. In any case, none of that mattered anymore. The moment mattered, and the next step. That formed my mental horizon: Where to place my foot; when to turn and look behind me; how much pressure to exert with my thumb upon the safety latch; how long to hold my breath while listening. My choices were few and simple.

Nonetheless, we moved slowly, and had only gone less than 200 meters when Captain Littnan called. In some way I could not explain, I knew long before Helms handed me the receiver that the attack had been called off.

Littnan's voice was crisp and noncommittal. "Bring 'em back, One Six. Make sure there's no one on your tail."

"Roger." I called out to Bresina in a low voice; I set him, Ulrich, Dickerson and myself up just above and below a slight elbow in the trail, as rear security, and then called Wright and told him to reverse the column and return to the NDP. While we waited, I listened. To the south, where Charlie Company had been engaged all day, the volume of fire had risen and fallen, and risen again, throughout the day; now intense, now sporadic or silent all together. At the moment, it was moderate, or so it seemed. Delta was still in contact — I could hear the occasional bark of a rifle or the heavy pounding of the machine guns, but nothing like the miasma of sound that had spread across the mountain earlier.

We waited until the first two squads were reported in the NDP, and then the small security force backed down the hill. At a certain point, perhaps halfway, we turned our backs to the hill and walked normally. It wasn't dismissal. The beast had not done with us yet, I knew.

Littnan was standing by his radios, as usual. Eward, looking unusually tired, stood beside him. Garza sat, Indian fashion, on his other side.

Littnan hardly waited for me to join them. "Black Jack's called off the attack, Frank. Charlie Company's in trouble. He wants you to go over...." He hesitated, something so completely out of character with him that I almost stared in astonishment. "He needs someone to go over there and help them out. Help them bring back their gear.... And any other help you can give them."

I was silent while the implications of what he'd just said set in. Charlie Company did not have enough men to bring their own gear back. I would have to take my platoon — fewer than 30 men, now — across 1,000 meters of enemy-held ground to a ridge occupied by a decimated — a more than decimated; by deduction, Charlie was at less than half strength — company, and then bring everyone back along that same trail. It should be an indication of the size of the beast Dong Ap Bia had shown itself to be,

34. The Bamboo Corridor

that I greeted this mission with an almost light heart. A week earlier, I'd have labeled it a borderline suicide mission.

"Why me?" I asked. Actually, I didn't really ask; it was just a flippant comment, and I expected no answer, least of all from Littnan, who rarely joked, but he did answer. It wasn't a joke, however.

"Because," he said, "Black Jack requested it. His exact words were: 'Send that big-headed wop over there.'"

I raised an eyebrow. Eward snickered. Even Garza smiled, or something like that. Littnan was perfectly serious, however.

Time was critical, so we dropped our packs at the NDP, bringing along only water, ammo and extra medical supplies, and then moved down through the LZ, all the way to the trail junction at the base of the ridge. The RPG, I noted, still was stuck in the tree. The trail leading back to the battalion CP led off to the right, north. The other arm instead followed a path to the southwest, through low scrub country. I would follow this for a short distance, and then drop down a steep but relatively open and low bluff, leaving the trail. Charlie's ridge was due south, so the trail, even though it eventually threw another arm out to that ridge, would take us too far out of the way. Besides, following enemy trails while the area was crawling with enemy just wasn't very bright. Just to remind us of his presence, the burned-out Huey from the other day lay like a huge dead bug on the slope to our east.

We descended the bluff, and moved through low, single canopy growth, not too thick. The point man, Hernandez, put away his machete after a while; it wasn't needed. We followed this for a short while, and then broke out of the small growth into more open, scrub brush and reed-covered land. The terrain was a series of low rolling hills and broad saddles. For us, after the backbreaking ridge of the west slope, this was table-top flat. We came across several trails, crisscrossing the area; all the ones that ran roughly east to west showed recent heavy use. That made sense: The Laotian border, with all that it meant to the enemy, lay only a couple of kilometers to our west. Finally a path, a small but man-made trail through the brush, clearly marked, led almost directly south.

I hesitated only a second. The trail led straight to where we wanted to go, and I had already been told, twice, that time was critical. The most direct path to Charlie lay along the path, then. The terrain here was open, and relatively flat, so even if we moved off the trail, to one side to the other, we might just as well have been on it, for all the concealment that would afford us. The alternative was to turn sharply east or west and move well away from the trail, and then resume our southward advance. That was witless. First it would take too much time, and secondly, in this area, there was little guarantee there wouldn't be another trail leading south — in fact, there was every reason to believe that there would be.

So we ended up following a trail after all, but at least this one led to where we were going, and the terrain was open enough that the fear of ambush receded — not much, but a little. Despite the pressure of time, however, we moved slowly. I can ignore orders, tactics and common sense, but I could not ignore the memory of what had happened to Chuck's platoon. We took our time.

Still, it was no great period of time before we left the open scrub and entered another single canopy forest, similar to the one across the valley. After perhaps 50 meters, the path enlarged and split: The smaller arm broke sharply to the west, along the slopes of a small but steep hill we found rising up directly in front of us. The large path continued straight, up the hill, and in the direction we needed to go. Hernandez looked back at me, and I immediately indicated that he should continue south.

Before we could move, however, Helms tapped me on the shoulder. It was Black Jack.

"You gotten to Charlie yet?" he asked.

"This is Bravo One Six. Negative. I'm about Alpha Golf Golf meters, direction Golf, from them right now."

"Roger. Move it. I want you there ASAP. And Bo—you do what you have to, to take care of things. Understand?"

I almost dropped the receiver. Twice. "Bo?" Since when did Black Jack call me "Bo"? And that last sentence ... I shook my head.

We started up the hill; the trail here was about five feet across, huge by the standards of the area around Rakkasan, but average for the A Shau. It led up through typical heavy growth, but after 30 or 40 meters, Hernandez stopped. I moved up beside him and saw why; the trail continued, but it was now flanked by the same bamboo-vine combination we had come to grief over several times before. The bamboo was over ten feet high, so the trail led like a tunnel through it. I nodded and Hernandez resumed his slow advance.

He hadn't gone 20 more meters before he halted a second time; this time he sank to one knee, looked over his shoulder, and motioned me forward, holding his finger to his lips. I crept as quietly as I could and knelt by his side. After a moment, I heard what he'd heard: Low, indistinct voices. I turned myself and made a quick, emphatic gesture with my right hand, palm down, and then repeated Hernandez's finger-to-lips warning.

The voices were so low I couldn't recognize them, as either English or Vietnamese. They could have been Hungarian, for all that. But suddenly, several voices broke out, loud and shrill, followed immediately by the chatter of small arms fire and the gassy snap of an RPG being fired; moments later we heard the dull slam as it exploded some distance away.

Hernandez and I exchanged glances. The voices had been Vietnamese, and even if they hadn't been, the RPG spoke its own language. We were within a few meters of a North Vietnamese Army unit, of unknown size, shooting at Charlie Company from a small hill adjacent to their ridge. We crouched low, weapons ready, straining to hear more. Helms, who had of course long since turned off his speaker, handed me the mike. But before calling the CO, I took a moment to consider.

34. The Bamboo Corridor

The trail continued straight for another 10 or 15 meters, at which point it both leveled off—at the top of the hill—and curved to the left, the direction the voices had come from. The bamboo wall was impenetrable; it grew thickly clustered, interwoven with vines, thorns and small saplings. It wasn't as bad as The Wall—it lacked the saw grass—but it was just as unyielding. We could not move through it quickly or quietly, and so for our purposes we could not move through it at all.

When Helms handed me the radio, I'd whispered to him to send back for Nate Hyde, who was well back behind us. Moving as silently as only a woodsman like him can move, he suddenly materialized by my side only a moment or so later. I indicated the area to our left; he listened, and within a short time, low murmurs and other sounds could be heard. I let him listen for 10 or 15 seconds.

"How far away are they, Nate?" I asked, in a small whisper.

"Twenty. Maybe twenty-five meters."

I looked at Hernandez, still crouching nearby, and he nodded.

"Direction?"

Hyde shrugged. He and Hernandez both pointed to our left front, about 45° from the line of the path. I took out my compass and performed a quick check: The heading was 105°, or just a bit south of east. The path must have curved slightly to the west before curving back sharply east ahead of us.

Without looking at my map—and I didn't want to risk the crackle of stiff paper at the moment—I had a rough idea of where we were, and the map could only give that, anyway. We were a few feet from the crest of a low but relatively steep hill just north of the base of Charlie's ridgeline, and perhaps 800 meters from Bravo's. The southeast side of the hill, opposite our position, must offer both a view of and an open fire lane to Charlie Company positions. The nature of the weapons the enemy had just used—direct fire small arms and RPGs—told me that much. I deduced that the bamboo we crouched in right now must be an extensive growth; probably covering a good deal of the hill, or the trail would have skirted it to one side or another. No matter how dedicated the NVA might be—and they were just soldiers, after all, not supermen—no one in possession of his faculties would cut through the bamboo mix for the jolly-be-damned hell of it. But somewhere to our east, facing south, was a bare open spot, of unknown but presumably limited size, from which the enemy was firing down on Charlie.

That much I could confidently deduce. Unfortunately, the rest was conjecture. This trail: Did it lead down the opposite side of the hill, into a draw or saddle, and thence on up onto Charlie's ridge? Or did it continue to curve to the left and lead into the NVA's position? If it continued south, was it at any point exposed to the NVA position? How many NVA were there? Exactly where were they? Were they dug in, with overhead cover? Were they isolated or part of another, larger unit?

I had several choices. I could mount a direct attack, trying to punch through the bamboo. This was a non-starter: I could move neither quickly nor quietly, so that was out. I could launch a grenade attack immediately, or wait for them to talk loudly again, to get a better fix on direction and distance, and then throw grenades. This idea appealed to me; the havoc 25 grenades, launched simultaneously, could wreak was substantial, *but*—if the NVA were dug in, if they weren't exactly where we thought they might be, if they were not in an open space, as I surmised, but were instead firing through lanes cut into the bamboo forest, if ... and if they survived the attack, as they would if any of these conditions prevailed, then our own position would turn precarious, and even deadly. It would be like trying to fight in a hallway or concrete tunnel; there would be no room to maneuver, and only two or three of our weapons could be brought to bear at any given time. No—that spelled disaster.

I could move east or west and attempt to come at the NVA from another, safer direction—that was possible. But it would take time. What if I did so, found and killed a handful of trail watchers or a small RPG team, and in the meantime Charlie Company was overrun while I was playing around, less than 200 meters away but engaged in a nickel-and-dime firefight? I shook my head.

The fourth option was the safest and the most consistent with my orders: I would back the platoon up, skirt the entire hill by taking the trail around to the west, and as soon as we reached a suitable location I would call in artillery or ARA. I thought about it. This whole process took no more than 15 or 20 seconds at most, but they were a long, long time passing. It actually should have been an easy, split-second decision— follow orders and move away—but I had, for five days now, been shot at, bombed, repulsed and generally toyed with, as well as frightened into a scowling funk, and I was sick of it. For the first time in my life, I wanted to really kill somebody, and not in a clinical, detached manner by robotically calling in some far-away artillery shells, but to lead a screaming, cursing, bloody-minded assault on these miserable peckerheads who'd been making life difficult for me and my men. I amazed myself. The best part of me, as I'd been repeatedly told throughout my life, was my brain, and here it was just shrugging its shoulders and saying, to the raging hormone factory it was supposed to control, *hey, do what feels good.*

But I did check myself. I had felt the adrenalin start to rise, but I forced myself to do what was smart. I knew better, anyway. The rewards of an attack on an unknown size force were far outweighed by both the risks and the exigency of my orders it hand.

I gave the signal to move back; for the second time that day, the platoon reversed direction and moved back down a hill.

My first act, on reaching the bottom of the trail, was to pull out my map, get a fix on my current position, and then work out where the enemy was. I had pretty carefully counted the steps back down the trail, so I had a decent notion of how far the crest of the hill was. I called Littnan and asked for Russ Crenshaw, and gave him the coordinates of the NVA position.

"We're moving along the base of that hill," I told him, "following a trail to the west; from there we'll cut back south again. Give me five minutes and I'll clear this section of the hill. The bad guys are either on top of or on the south slope of the hill. Go get 'em."

I then told Littnan what was going on, while we moved along the trail westward. It was closer to ten minutes, not five, before the first of the 81mm mortar rounds started falling, but that was good enough.

In the event, I was wrong about westward trail skirting the base of the hill. In fact, the hill was much longer than I had thought, although not at all wide. It extended much further west than it originally appeared to, and so the second trail eventually turned south and climbed the same hill, only about 200 meters west of the bamboo trail. As we began climbing again, we could hear the heavy crump of our mortar fire impacting on the area we'd left 20 or 30 minutes earlier.

The north slope, which we climbed, was here moderate and somewhat open, in contrast to the steep, bamboo-shrouded trail further east. However, once we reached the crest and began descending, the slope became much steeper and the vegetation closed in on us again, so we could not see across the ravine that separated us from the ridge we were aiming for. Only at one point, as we followed the precipitous path down, did I look up to see, about 100 meters away, the leaves and limbs of trees that apparently covered the north flank of Charlie's ridge.

Dickerson had replaced Hernandez with Mareniewski on point, and Ulrich was slack man. I had to grin, suddenly, when I saw Ski trip over a root and almost fall. The thought of having Clumsy Carp walking point in the A Shau would have paralyzed me a few months back; now he was just one of the guys, and was as trusted as anyone else — except that we still wouldn't let him set claymores.

Ski and Ulrich came to a halt when they reached the base of the slope; I moved up beside them and saw that the trail was crossed here by another, one that led from west to east. The three of us knelt there and looked around. I didn't need Nate Hyde for this: Two arms of the trails, the one that headed west from the crossing, and the one that continued to lead south, across the ravine and up the slope of the ridge before us, were covered by innumerable tracks; not even the daily heavy rains had washed them out. But every one of them was of a GI boot. No tracks had been seen as we crossed over the hill behind us, so that led me to the inevitable conclusion that Charlie Company, when they'd moved up to this ridge, had in fact taken that first trail coming off Bravo's ridge, the one I'd rejected because I thought it would take us too far to the west and out of our way, and had followed it all the way around the open country we'd crossed, but further west, around the western tip of the hill we'd just descended, and then back east to this crossroads, where they had turned south again to mount the ridge.

So our path led directly ahead. But there was a problem. Directly ahead of us was a company that had been badly mauled, and they would be trigger-happy and inclined to sudden violence. They knew we were approaching — Black Jack had been in contact with them — but would they remember? And the fact was that my efforts to contact them had been, to this point, fruitless. I swallowed. Time was pressing. But I didn't want to risk moving up the trail until I had spoken to someone from Charlie and had let him know we were there, a few meters away.

I set up security along all four trails, and spent the next five minutes calling Charlie. No one answered. Finally, Black Jack broke in and asked what I was doing. I gave him a brief sitrep, and then mentioned why I was trying to call Charlie Company.

"Roger, but you need to move up there. The situation isn't getting any better and it isn't getting any earlier in the day. I've lost contact with Charlie Six but I did talk to his One Six a few minutes ago. Hurry it up."

I handed the receiver back to Helms and shrugged. There was no time left to ponder. I did retain the two elements securing the east and west-leading trails, and I put Jones on point, as the best of our remaining point men, but there was no point in further delay. We began to move across the ravine and up the other slope.

No more than 15 minutes later, an LOH flew low over our heads, to descend only a short distance away. Jones cleared a small fold, densely covered by high brush and small trees, and then, as he stepped out of it, there were the last few meters of the ridge's slope, clear and bare, directly in front of us. The remaining ascent was only about 40 meters, but it was very steep; it was at the very edge of the ridge that the LOH hovered as we approached. Actually, I noted in consternation, it was quivering in the air, balanced precariously on one skid, while the other hung out over the slope. The LZ was that tight.

But by the time we started up that last 40 meters, the LOH lifted and took off, flying directly overhead toward the battalion CP to the north of us.

35

Charlie's Ridge

YC318977; 14 May 1969; 1600–2200

I looked around in puzzlement. The LZ was here, within meters; the closer we approached, the more my bafflement grew. We were, by now, right on top of the LZ and I could see no one, nothing; not one bit of security anywhere. The trail angled now, to the left, bypassing the LZ itself, but I still could see nothing. Only when we mounted the last few meters and reached the ridge top did I see anyone. There were four or five men, huddled together, at the far side of the LZ, under a knot of small trees. They were weaponless, helmetless, and, I could now tell, wounded. These were men awaiting medevac. But where in hell was the security for them?

I blinked two or three times. I barely knew Captain Jessup, the Charlie Company CO, but I knew Jim Goff and Joel Trautman, two of the platoon leaders, and I couldn't believe they'd allow such a shambles. We moved along the trail, past the wounded and into a small tree-shaded clearing just past the LZ, and stopped, in shock.

My God. My God.... I stared around me in disbelief; Jones and Olson, standing silently beside me, did the same, mouths open and eyes widened.

Bodies lay everywhere. For that first mind-freezing moment, it had seemed as if the ground were literally covered with them. There were 20 or 30 of them. In that first, horrified glance, they'd all appeared dead. I now saw that only some were. The others lay on the ground, unmoving, staring straight up into the sky or off into the distance. Not a single one held a weapon, nor even facing out from the clearing. Not a single one, as far as I could see, had so much as looked our way as we filed up the ridge and into the clearing. For all they knew, or apparently cared, we could have been NVA.

There *were* bodies—a long line of them, stretched out along the bushes to my left. Some were whole, with deep, ragged reddish black shrapnel wounds. Some were in scattered, barely recognizable pieces. One, the last in line, lay staring at the sky with wide-open eyes. One single small hole, hardly more than a reddish bruise, at first glance, marred the fair blond hair above the boy's left ear. He gaped at the sky with mouth open, as if in vast surprise.

Brown, his tall, gangling form stooped under the weight of his radio, walked by me. He stopped in mid-stride, his mouth working. His eyes, crinkled in disgust and pity and fear, were fixed on the dead man's face. A fly, lured by the rich sweet incense of death, had settled on his face and was scurrying about, crawling ecstatically in and out of his mouth, like an acolyte preparing for the sacrament. I heard Brown gag.

"Move it," I shoved him. "Keep going!" I gave him a second rough shove, and he stumbled on, following the others.

I walked up to one trooper who lay with his back against a tree. His head was flopped loosely to one side, his hands lay still and relaxed alongside his legs, palms turned up, fingers curled slightly. He might have been asleep, or dead, but I saw his eyes were open and his chest rise and fall.

"Where's Captain Jessup?" I asked. He gave not the slightest flicker of a response or awareness. I repeated the question, but the man didn't move at all. I felt the hair on my neck stir; I stepped back with the same horror that Brown had felt a moment before. This man only needed the fly...

My mouth went dry. *What in the name of God had happened here?*

But before I did anything else, I had to do what I came for. The platoon was still strung out behind me, but I gave quick orders: Hyde's squad would secure the LZ; Dickerson's the area around us, and Kenzy's would move up the ridge and see if they could establish contact with some functioning element of Charlie Company.

"But," I warned Kenzy, "don't go too far. We don't know what happened here, and I sure as hell don't want you to get too far out. No more than 100 meters—then you come back—clear?"

He nodded. He had to wait for his squad to move up, but he was ready. In the meantime, I grabbed Hudson.

"The wounded need water and attention. It's all up to you. Grab who you need and start helping them."

He nodded, his large brown eyes empty and lost, but at least there was a spark in them, somewhere.

Finally, it struck me—I've said I'm not particularly quick-witted—that Crazy Rairdon, while probably clinically insane, wasn't an idiot. Even he wouldn't land on a ridge in the middle of the A Shau without some form of contact with the ground. Someone had to be talking to him. That someone hadn't been at the LZ—I was sure of that—but he had to be somewhere close by. I went looking for him.

I found Captain Jessup instead. A short distance up the ridge, was another, larger clearing. Several men lay about this one too. One, directly ahead of me, lay alongside a radio. I moved toward him, and then saw an older man, sitting nearby, with his back against a tree. By "older," I mean a man in his late twenties. This was Captain Jessup. I walked up to him, and for a moment I thought he would lie there, as had the other man, just staring off into nothing. This whole ridge, I thought, was just one great charnel, full of dead men and men who mimicked death. But as I approached he finally raised his eyes and looked at me. I grimaced and looked away. They had no more life in them than the man lying dead in the pile back at the LZ.

He nodded remotely, without emphasis, as if my appearing before him was the answer to some unimportant question he'd posed much earlier, and had lost interest in. Between him and the RTO stretched out before him, I saw, was the radio, and the black receiver, lying stark and abandoned on the ground. Finally, he spoke.

"Who're you?"

"One Six. Bravo One Six."

He looked away. He hadn't asked the question as if he cared about the answer.

"What would you like me to do, sir?"

I had to repeat it. The second time, he looked at me in puzzlement. "What?"

He continued to stare. I felt pressure building up inside me, a monstrous cauldron of rage, pity and disgust. I wanted to scream and plead with him at the same time: *Jesus! You're an officer ... an airborne infantry officer, in the United States Army. Do something. Get up. Get off your ass and do something. Jesus, will you stop looking like that!*

I heard someone moving behind me. Turning, I saw a man coming down the trail, without helmet, limping badly. His right leg, stained dark red with blood, dragged uselessly behind him. He wore glasses and had short, light brown hair. A lieutenant's bar showed black against his dirty fatigue shirt lapel. His name — Cray — was on his shirt, but I didn't recognize it. I realized he had to be the artillery FO. He limped past me, almost hopping, one legged, the last few feet, until he reached a tree against which he leaned. His face was white and bloodless.

"No use," he croaked, to no one in particular. "Can't do it." He closed his eyes for a moment, breathing hard. Then he looked at Jessup. "Jim's hit. So's Sully. Can't find Trautman."

Jessup, lost in his own thoughts, made no reply. But Cray went on. "Ten KIA, now. Don't know how many wounded. But I can't go on. This leg...."

I spoke to him instead. "Jim? Jim Goff? He's hit?"

Cray closed his eyes again. "Yeah. Earlier. Bad. Real bad."

"And Sullivan?"

Cray barely nodded now.

"He's hit bad too?" I persisted.

"I don't know. Maybe." Sweat dropped from his face in a persistent stream. It wasn't just the heat and exertion, I realized, but the pain. Shock wouldn't be far behind.

"Christ, I'm thirsty."

Grimacing — at myself, for being such a blockhead — I unscrewed the cap from my canteen and handed it to him. His throat worked noisily as he swallowed the warm iodine-tainted stuff. I looked around for Muldoon, and then realized with a pang that he wasn't there. Hudson.... But he was back at the LZ, where the other wounded were.

Sergeant Wright strode up, his face tight-lipped and glowering. He stood over Captain Jessup and glared at him. "Where's your first sergeant?"

I blinked. Sergeant Wright was usually the most punctilious of NCOs. Now he radiated anger and disgust. These were American troops, fighting men in a proud and tough division. And they lay about like so many rag dolls.

Jessup gazed up at him. If he was offended by Wright's tone, he gave no sign. "He's hit. Don't know how bad. Haven't seen him in an hour."

"Top." I took his rigid, tensed arm. For the briefest, maddest moment, I had the urge to look him in the eye and say, "Don't get shook 'til I get shook," but I decided not. There are times when my sense of humor simply loses perspective. "Are the LZ and this clearing secure? And has Kenzy reported back?"

He pulled his eyes from Jessup's face.

"We've got security. Kenzy's just up the ridge; Charlie One Six is up there too; he's pulling everyone back down."

"Do they have any medics? Hudson's all alone down there...."

He shook his head. "I don't know, Lieutenant."

"We got one, I think." It was Cray, seated now, on a fallen log, with his leg held out in front of him. "Don't know for sure."

"Senior medic's dead."

I jerked around; it was Jessup. He was still lying with his head back against the tree, but there was a small sheen of life on his face now.

"Senior medic, and two of the platoon medics," he continued. "Dead or wounded."

Three men came shuffling down the trail, carrying a fourth. The two in front held an arm each, while the other held up both feet. The fourth man was alive; he groaned and swore softly as he swayed in their grasps. A bandage, thin and pitiful looking, oozed blood around his thigh. They reached the clearing where the other wounded lay, and deposited the man with the others, quickly, without glancing about to see if they'd dropped him on stone or root or branch. They walked back up the hill, their faces closed and remote, not looking our way as they passed. The wounded still lay in the sun. One man walked among them, stopping to talk to each. He made no attempt at treating them. He was probably informing them of their status for evacuation, I thought. Then I did see Hudson, bareheaded, crouching by one of them, working on his wound. I shook my head. Hudson wasn't enough. Not even Muldoon — not even Schoch, would be enough by himself.

I looked back at Jessup. "Do you have any idea where your one medic is?"

He shook his head, but Cray answered. "I think it's Trautman's guy, so he's up there with him. Don't know. If he is, he's needed up there."

I felt my stomach flip. Jesus. Charlie Company had disintegrated. Now I understood Black Jack's words.... *You do what you have to, understand?*

"Deleone's hit." This was Jessup, speaking again. Deleone was his first sergeant. "Goff. Kent's hit, too. I don't know about Sullivan. I think he's hit. Haven't heard from him. Carson, Easley ... I don't have much in the way of NCOs."

His voice, so remote and empty, suddenly cracked and shook. "I don't have much in the way of a company."

I looked at him; his voice had cracked but his face remained stolid and unmoving. I hesitated ... "How many have you lost?" I asked.

He shrugged, almost nonchalantly. "Who knows? Forty. Fifty ... sixty?" He stared down at the ground and then squinted up at me. When he spoke this time, his voice was conversational and even careless, as if we were seated in a bar somewhere enjoying a casual drink.

"You know," he said, "I just lost my whole company and I don't even know what I did wrong."

He looked at me with a peculiar intense expectancy. He wasn't pleading or hoping ... he was waiting. He had confessed; now I had to absolve him.

Ego te absolve. Ite sine peccatum.

But I wouldn't. I glared at him with cold disgust.

The rains came, late — it was 1630. They came down hard and grey and cold, slanting across the ridge as if to sweep it clean. I saw someone — not one of mine, so it was someone from Charlie Company — moving down the line of bodies, covering each with a poncho. The wounded lay on the ground, lashed by the rain, but the dead ... he covered them, and perhaps he hoped that they would simply not be there when he lifted the ponchos again. I heard Wright, voice tight with suppressed anger, order some of the Charlie troopers to grab ponchos and cover the wounded.

I debated on whether it was worth the trouble to don my rain jacket, and then kicked myself mentally. My jacket was stuffed in my rucksack, which lay on the ridge back at the Bravo CP. I leaned back against the trunk of the tree, although it was no protection against the rain, or the wind either. Jessup seemed indifferent to the weather. The rain drummed on his helmet, ran down along the chinstraps dangling form each ear, and from them dripped in a steady stream onto his neck and shoulders.

Cray was hobbling down to the LZ, supported by Sergeant Wright. A couple of Charlie's men came down the trail; one held onto the other, who was trying to help his comrade along without aggravating the large tear in the man's chest. The rain was coming so hard now I couldn't see clearly enough to tell if the blood was frothing as it seeped from his wound. Probably not, I told myself. He'd hardly be walking with a punctured lung, would he?

I heard movement, a sloshing and sucking sound. It was Jessup, struggling to his feet, slipping in the mud. He made it though, turned to his RTO and tapped him gently on the head.

"C'mon, Masters. Up."

Masters got up slowly, mud and rain dripping from his arms. He reached over, grabbed the straps of his rucksack, grainy with sand and wet dirt, and pulled them over his shoulders. The mike still lay in the dirt behind him, and he almost stepped on it.

Jessup looked up at the sky, oblivious to the raindrops plastering themselves against his eyes. "Soon's this shit's stopped," he said, in that same mild, conversational tone as before, "we can get the rest of the wounded out." I wasn't sure if he was addressing me, or someone else.

It was 1705; the sun would set in a little over an hour, and darkness was never far behind. The rain stopped, leaving the forest smelling of mildew and rotted wood. Somehow, in this valley, it never seemed to cleanse.

Two more troopers came down the path, and then a steady stream of them, but these carried weapons, and moved more purposefully than the others. I saw the spare, dark-haired form of Joel Trautman, Charlie's First Platoon leader, trailing them. He saw me at the same moment and walked over to where I was standing.

"Frank."

"Joel. Damn.... How are you?"

He shrugged. He looked over my shoulder and his dark eyes flamed with anger. I turned; it was Jessup, standing there, holding his radio now. I could feel Trautman's body tremble with repressed emotion, and I was standing two feet away. I took his arm and half-turned him away from his CO.

"Is everyone back now?" I asked.

"Everyone who's coming back," he said in a flat voice. Then he shook his head. "Sully came down with what's left of Second Platoon; he's hurt, but he can walk. I'm the last man."

I shook my head; I hadn't even seen Sullivan move through the NDP; I must have been focused on Jessup. "What about gear? Anything left back up there?"

He grimaced. "Shit, Frank: There's stuff all over the place. But I'm not going to lose any more men trying to get it." He made a gesture. "There aren't any weapons left, anyway."

"Okay. Wounded? I've counted about 25, maybe a few more, and I think eight dead."

"That's 'cause we got a bunch of them out earlier."

I frowned; looking at the LZ, and the clearing...

"Joel ... how many men do you have?"

He looked at me squarely. I have 18."

I swallowed. "And Sullivan?"

"About six."

"Goff?"

"Maybe ten, eleven. I'm not sure anymore. We'll have to take a count."

Charlie had started with 135 men. If Trautman's numbers were   "Oh, my God," I whispered.

Helms handed me the mike. "Black Jack," he said.

"This is One Six." I kept forgetting to add the "Bravo," but hell, he knew who I was. I looked at my watch; it was now 1725.

"This is Black Jack." His voice, as ever, was sharp, high and incisive. "What's your situation now?"

"We've got the LZ and the ridge above it secured. All personnel and weapons are back from the contact point, and we're gathering the rest of the gear."

"What about casualties? You got a final count?"

"Negative. We're trying to get that now."

"Rairdon is on his way to you right now. He thinks he can carry four out at a time — he's got some kind of rig set up."

I raised an eyebrow. Four men at a time? An LOH was designed to hold two ... well, he didn't earn the name "Crazy" by sticking straw in his hair.

"Soon as you get all the wounded out, I want you to load up as much gear as you can, and then burn the rest. You copy?"

"Roger."

"Then move back to Bravo's NDP area. You tell Charlie Six I want him and the rest of Charlie with Bravo tonight."

"Roger." I understood, of course. I glanced at Jessup, to see if he was monitoring the radio, but he was not. Well, it made no difference anyway. Even before Black Jack's call, I had already made up my mind that I would move back to Bravo's ridge, even if it meant moving throughout the night. Now, with Black Jack's explicit instructions ... I shook my head again. It promised to be a rat fuck even Robison would be proud of.

Joel was looking at me. He had only overheard my end of the conversation, of course, but he must have sensed something, perhaps in the way I'd looked at Jessup.

"We're joining the rest of Bravo tonight?"

I nodded.

"We got time to get there?"

"We'll make time." I looked at my watch; it would be dark very soon.

Kenzy and some others, from Bravo and Charlie, were setting up a pile of gear in the middle of the clearing. We would take with us what we could, including, of course, all the radios, weapons, starlight scopes and other sensitive gear, and each man would carry at least one if not two packs, but that still left a sizeable amount of gear we would have to destroy: Rucksacks, clothing, ponchos, personal items. Canteens and C-ration cans were punctured to make them unusable; from somewhere up the hill came the dull boom of excess grenades being thrown down the ridge's flank to explode. Ammo was distributed — the bulk of what we would carry out with us in the rucksacks was to be ammo and magazines — and what couldn't be carried was piled into the middle of the other gear, to explode once we set fire to it all. We decided, at the last minute, to add the few extra PRC25 batteries to the conflagration; they were heavy, and the men had enough to carry. By the time the men finished, the pile was six or seven feet high and about ten across.

We moved everyone down to the LZ area; Sergeant Wright and Kenzy stood by the pile with several thermite grenades. A moment later, the unnaturally white searing flame of the phosphorous began hissing and spitting amongst the gear. Several large branches and small trunks had been laid as a base, and when these caught fire, the flames turned a pale yellow. We cleared the area: The ammo would start cooking off, and the fumes from the burning batteries would do no one any good.

In the meantime, Rairdon made his runs; he was shuttling the men to the LZ at battalion, which was only, on a straight line, about three kilometers away, so his flights weren't taking long. He had evacuated all the wounded, and was coming back now for the heavy gear — the M60s, radios, large canisters of 7.62 ammo, and so on — that he could carry. Trautman and I were standing by the LZ; Rairdon was hovering several meters away from us, balanced on one skid, aligned with the ridge, as he had done all day. This meant that on his port side the tips of whirling blades were only about five feet from the ground. Starboard, because of the steep slope, they were 15 or even 20 feet up.

Afterwards we all agreed that what happened next was so surreal, so bizarre, that we watched it unfold before our eyes in total disbelief, unable to act until it was too late. A new replacement, just arrived on this flight, had exited on the down-slope side of the craft; he was now making his way up the steep ridge to the LZ, helmeted head down and dragging his M16 behind him. We watched him idly, several of us, and then realized that he was aiming to walk directly behind the hovering LOH. As I said, we were simply unable to react. The whole event had an aura of fate about it; it was inevitable, and nothing we could do would prevent it, even as we all began, too late, to shout warnings.

The man took one more step, oblivious of the LOH's tail, of the sound of its engine, and of the whipping swish of its blades. That last step raised his head to the level of the blade. A heavy, meaty thunk! sounded amidst the high-pitched roar of the motor, and the craft swayed slightly as Rairdon fought to overcome the sudden imbalance. The trooper simply collapsed, face forward, as if he was a marionette and all the strings were loosened.

A collective, sickened groan was heard all over the LZ. Rairdon, still not sure exactly what had happened, did the only thing he could do: Throttle up and lift his little ship up in the air, bank and fly off. The man lay face down, crumpled like a used-up rag, and motionless.

I turned away, sick. I had to take several deep breaths, because I was about to throw up. Besides, I didn't want to look. I had already seen enough of death in all its forms. I was reminded, sharply, of Ted Billings' words from that day back on Rakkasan, when the lightning had set off all the claymores: *Jesus, there are more damn ways to get killed around here.*

Then I heard a shout, and several more. I whirled, utterly shocked. The man was alive after all. The medic was kneeling by his side, trying to decide if his neck was broken, whether he could be moved, when the man raised his head, shook it, and rolled over to a sitting position. All he would suffer was a massive headache. Months later, when I talked to Rairdon about it, the pilot suggested that the man had had the incredible luck of walking into the blade's path at the precise point where his height intercepted the plane of the blade; he received a glancing blow on the very top of his helmet. A split-second later, and the blade would have caught him flush on the back of his head, and either decapitated him or have broken his neck.

He was lucky, then, but he also caused us some major problems. By the time he'd been attended to and Rairdon returned, we'd lost a precious quarter of an hour; darkness was fast approaching, and Rairdon could make no more flights, which meant that we'd have to carry some of the heavy gear we'd expected him to fly out. It was too late to add the stuff to the fire, and anyway, an M60 doesn't burn particularly well. There was nothing for it but to add the weapons to our load.

Charlie Company had 41 men left. Eighty-eight troopers had been killed or wounded in two days. Several more were wounded but made the trek back with us that night. I stood in consternation as the numbers were relayed to me and then to Black Jack. I stared at Jessup, who was still standing passively off to the side, with his RTO and no one else, and then looked at Trautman. I asked no question, of course, but he understood.

"There's a clearing up there," he said tiredly. "Up along the top of the ridge. It looks like maybe they cleared out the underbrush, cut a few small trees down. They put bunkers all along the back end of the clearing, and more up on the hill behind it. They loaded it up with claymores, and had two machine guns sighted on it."

"Yeah," I nodded. "We've got one just like that over our way. I know what you mean."

His eyes flickered. *No you don't. You can't possibly know what I mean*. But he went on in the same tired, even voice. "Jim Goff took his platoon up into one side of the clearing this morning. For a while, it looked like he was going to push through, take out some bunkers. Sully moved in on the other side, about 50 meters away. I was down here, securing the LZ. Jessup ... anyway, things changed in a hurry. The gooks started pouring shit down on Goff and Sully, a whole world of it. Around 1000, I went up there with my platoon. Goff's platoon sergeant got hit up there. Lost his eyes, I think. Both of them. He can't see, anyhow. Jim got hit, bad, in the back. Broke his spine, I guess. I know he was screaming all the way down the ridge, when we evacuated him later. I mean, Jim's a big man, you know — you remember. We couldn't lift him, had to drag him ... God, he screamed.

"Sully was hit too, not that bad, but he was hit, and then the squad leaders, all of them. They were all just pinned down. Couldn't move. The more guys got hit, the harder it got to pull them back. I didn't have many guys. Had to leave the LZ almost bare — just a few guys there and ... no one in between. No one at the NDP."

Instinctively, we both looked at Jessup, a few feet away; we were speaking in low voices, however, and he couldn't hear us. Besides, I thought, he still hasn't returned from wherever he'd been for the past few hours.

"They slipped some people down into the ravine over there — the one south of us, not this one. Caught a lot of the wounded coming down. Killed a bunch of them. That's when we lost our medics, I guess. I got Goff's platoon disengaged, and then started trying to bring Sully back—we were trying to pull everyone back, then. But...." He shook his head. "They were all over the place. Damn it, they were all over us."

He stared in silence at the ground for a long moment, then suddenly looked up, as if awaking. "Well," he said, in a brisker, harder voice. "That was it. Bad day at the office, man."

"Yeah." I had nothing to say to him — what *could* I say? Better luck next time?

"I got to get my guys ready to move. I'll be bringing up the rear; Jessup'll be between me and you."

"Okay. We'll be moving soon."

"How far is it?"

"Took us about two hours."

He nodded and moved off. I watched him go, thinking: He's held Charlie Company together for almost the whole day. I avoided looking at Jessup.

I did call Littnan, to tell him we were on the way, and to ask if he had any word back on the effectiveness of the 81mm fire on that NVA position we'd run into earlier.

"Negative, can't say. But Black Jack or someone called in some ARA on that same hill about an hour ago. Maybe that'll keep their heads down, over."

"Roger. We'll keep our eyes open."

"Be careful. There are beaucoup NVA units in the area."

"Roger." Thanks for the tip.

It was a nightmare.

The sun had set, and the heavy rain clouds made the brief twilight even shorter. We were all burdened. Each of us carried at least one pack, with as much ammo and other important gear stuffed into it as possible. Many of the M16s had been flown out by Rairdon, but many remained, and some men had to carry as many as four or five of them. Some of the bigger men in my platoon, like Mareniewski, Snyder and Clifton, carried two packs. Logan was terribly laden: In addition to his own M60 and ammo, he carried a pack, several bandoliers of M60 ammo from Charlie Company, an M16, and several rounds of 90mm ammunition. It's safe to say that we all carried at least 100 pounds that night, and some of us closer to 120.

The burden of the gear was one thing. Then there was the added burden of fear. It was no use trying to deny it. Fear fastened itself to Charlie Company like a remora, not just clinging but grinding away, drilling deeper into everyone's vitals. Nor were my men immune. Fear spreads. And, events of the day aside, we had reason to fear. We were 70 men — two platoons — walking through a valley that belonged to the enemy.

The Charlie Company men were exhausted. My men were tired, but they were on the verge of collapse. It began about 1730, as we slogged our way slowly along the narrow trail I'd followed that afternoon. Jessup called, demanding that we stop and set up an NDP. I had already thought this out. Even if I could trust Charlie Company —

and I did not — to set up an NDP here, in a low valley, with multiple regiments of NVA known to be in the area, in the middle of one of their known resupply and reinforcement routes, was madness. Between the two ridges, there was no appreciable high ground, and little concealment. Bravo Company was still too far away to come to our aid, and we would be overrun by morning.

From that moment on, Jessup kept up an increasingly strident series of calls, wanting to know our location, how much longer it would be, demanding a rest and, constantly, wanting to set up the NDP. I developed an automatic, non-thinking response: *We're almost there. Just around the bend. Next hill we climb. Just a few minutes more.* I didn't even consider reasoning with him, or laying out the facts. Parents who've faced a long road trip with small children know exactly what went on that night, except for the fear.

It kept multiplying, in everybody. Fear not so much of the enemy, or possible attack, or even of death. It was just fear, blind, visceral, unfocused fear. I could sense it all around me. Fatigue makes cowards of men — I'd noted that before. The extreme fatigue Charlie Company experienced that day and night led to extreme fear. Fear grows in the dark — it is instinctual — and that night was also the darkest I could recall; heavy moisture-filled clouds blocked the moon and all starlight, and absorbed any ambient light as a sponge does water. We couldn't see two meters, and many, especially in Charlie Company, walked holding the shoulder of the man in front of them. There were moments when I thought they would not go on, that they would simply fall to the ground and refuse to move. If that had happened ... my mind refused to deal with that.

It almost happened. It was much later, at around 2000, and we were still several hundred meters from Bravo. Jessup called again. This time, he said, he wasn't asking. He was ordering me to turn around and join him; he'd stopped at a small hill — it was really nothing more than a slight elevation; we'd crossed it several minutes earlier — and was setting up an NDP. He reminded me that he as the senior officer, and demanded that I turn back.

I stood there for a moment, mike in hand, debating on what to do. Aside from Black Jack's order, I wasn't about to spend the night with Jessup. I had three choices: Leave him — and the rest of Charlie Company — behind and rejoin Bravo with just my own platoon. Unacceptable. Or, directly confront Jessup, which would bring about the very thing that Black Jack wanted to avoid, that he had made very clear was to be avoided: A circumstance where he would have to broadcast the fact that I had relieved Jessup. The only other option was to walk back, convince Trautman to summarily incorporate the rest of Charlie into his own platoon, give them the order to move, and then help me deal with Jessup and the two or three surviving members of Jessup's CP. I didn't care for any of them. Or ... there was a fourth...

"Roger, Charlie Six." There are lies, and then there are damned lies. I decided that what I was about to say was merely a lie, and I wouldn't be damned for it. "My lead element's almost at the perimeter now. I think they're in sight, already. We'll be there in a minute or two, over." Well, maybe it was a damned lie at that.

"This is Charlie Six. You've been telling me that for the last hour. I'm not moving any farther in the dark. I'm ordering you to stop, over."

"This is Bravo One Six, " I replied. I didn't stress the "Bravo" but I made sure he could hear it. "Negative. We're almost there. We'll all be better off if we can get to Bravo's perimeter. Break. Break. Bravo Six, this is One Six."

Littnan's voice sounded immediately, telling me he'd monitored Jessup's call. We were all on the same frequency tonight. "This is Bravo Six. Go."

Jessup was still on the radio, and I knew he was listening. "This is One Six. My lead element is moving up a slope right now. I think we're close enough for you to see us. Please alert the perimeter that we'll be entering shortly, over."

"Roger, One Six. I think I can hear you now."

That's my beautiful, beamish boy, Captain! Bless your heart.

"Roger, Bravo Six. Break. Charlie Six, this is Bravo One Six. Bravo Six says he has us in sight, over." Actually, Littnan had said no such thing, but, if you're going to lie, make it thorough.

"This is Charlie Six." Jessup's voice mingled anger and bafflement. "I'm stopping right here, over."

I hadn't been married long, but I had had time to learn one valuable lesson: The best way to win an argument is to say nothing. My wife had taught me that within a week. I handed the mike back to Helms and just kept moving.

Jessup really had no choice. Not only did he have fewer than 50 men, but he had no real idea of where he was. And it was much more than even money that his own One Six would disregard any order coming from Jessup.

I couldn't tell Helms to turn off the radio—that would have been idiotic, under the circumstances—but I did tell him to ignore all calls from Jessup from that point on. I was, by this time, so angry with the man that whatever sympathy I had for him — and his losses had been truly staggering—was swept away by my disgust at his panic and lack of leadership. I was a lieutenant with less than a year in country, and he was a seasoned captain; the tactical situation should have been clearer to him than to me, but his fear overcame his common sense.

The final 100 meters were worthy of Dante. Everyone, by this time, was beyond exhaustion; we'd reached that point of numb automation, when one leg followed the other not through an effort of will or resolve but merely because the mind was too tired to think of anything else to do. Logan was in front of me, and he was worn out. He was carrying too much weight, even for his powerful frame, and, in common with other big, strong men, he couldn't understand why his body was no longer responding. Powerful as he was—I'd seen him pick up a machine gun by the tip of the barrel and hold it out with arm extended—he couldn't understand why his legs no longer could lift themselves up the slope, or his torso was cracking under the weight of the pack. I felt bad for him, but especially now, with Jessup ready to drop down at the first opportunity, I couldn't afford to let anyone stop.

I cursed and wheedled and abused him the rest of the way. At first, he responded with tired jokes; then offended grunts, and then mutinous muttering, followed by a weary cursing of his own and, at the end, the last 100 meters, a sullen, exhausted silence. Every few meters he would stop, unable to move. I would take my hand and give him a stiff push in the small of his back. At first I was encouraging; then mildly demanding, and in the end vilely abusive.

"Move, you red-headed son of a bitch. Move that lard-assed body of yours, damn you. Get up this hill, you pizza-faced moron. Get up there or I'll cut your balls off and stuff 'em up your fat ass. Move, Logan. Move, you fat-ass. You stop one more time, you useless piece of shit, and I'll leave you here for the fucking leeches."

Logan was one of the two or three best men in the platoon, a man I admired greatly, and he had reached his physical limit, but I couldn't afford to let him stop. And in fairness to Charlie Company, who were all strung out behind us, we had to reach the Bravo perimeter as soon as possible.

It was 2130 when we straggled up the last few meters, past the overturned Huey, up that last slope to the LZ. Logan, grunting and panting harshly, made one last effort and finally stumbled onto the top of the ridge. The light here was marginally better; I could see, outlined against the night sky, black on black, the helmets of the men of Eward's platoon as they stood or sat in their foxholes. We pushed our way past them, to the center of the LZ. Logan dropped his burden and fell to the ground, where he lay blowing and sputtering like a spent bullock. I knelt by his side, my own chest heaving from the exertion of that last climb.

"You okay?" I huffed.

He opened his eyes. "Yeah. I'm fine. I don't feel a damned thing."

"I'm sorry I had to push you like that, Lo. But we had to keep moving." I paused for a breath. "I wanted to get you back here with Bravo."

Logan closed his eyes, groaning. "So you did all this for me?" he finally whispered.

"Just for you, Lo."

"Yeah. Well, thanks for thinkin' of me, Lieutenant. I'll never forget this."

I grinned. Logan was fine.

Leaving Sergeant Wright to move our platoon into our sector, I went to the CP in search of Captain Littnan. I found him standing by his radios, a cup of hot chocolate in his hand. When he saw me, he called something over his shoulder, to Conzoner, and a moment later he took another cupful from him and handed it to me.

"Here. You look like you could use some."

I took it gratefully, swallowed a mouthful and closed my eyes momentarily in bliss. My muscles creaked and twitched, but at least they were free of the weight, and the need to take one more agonizing step.

"What a helluva way to make a living," I muttered for perhaps the hundredth time.

Littnan nodded. I could see his helmet move in the dark, "Looks like these clouds are here to stay tonight. Feels like more rain," he added, after a moment.

"Yeah. Is Charlie going to move into our perimeter?"

"No, we're already too crowded, with Recon Platoon moving in for the night — that's Howard's idea. But they won't have to go too far. Just on the other side of the LZ, between it and the trail. They can't come to too much grief there. And Alpha will be moving through us; they're going to take over Charlie's ridge."

I nodded. I'd have to warn my people ... then I remembered that it was Eward, not me, who was covering the LZ. Jesus, I was tired.

"You really didn't want to spend the night out there, did you?" Littnan's voice broke into my thoughts, such as they were.

"No." I hesitated. Littnan was pretty straight and by the book. And this concerned another company commander. "I've never seen anything like what I found on that ridge today," I said, finally.

Littnan raised the tin cup to his mouth and swallowed some more hot chocolate. "Yeah," he said grimly. "I know. He ... they were in bad shape. But before you think too badly of them, remember what they went through."

"Oh, I know." I nodded. "Shit, I'm not condemning anyone." *Well, yes I am.* "I probably would be a basket case if it happened to me — 70% losses. I understand that. But I still didn't want to be out there with them."

"Men react differently. We all do — and we don't know how we'll react until we get there." He drained the last of his drink and laid the cup carefully on the top of his rucksack beside him. I thought he was through; Littnan was one of those rare people who, when they'd said all there was to say, simply stopped talking. It was unsettling, sometimes. But after a moment, he went on.

"You never know. Everyone breaks, sooner or later. Everyone. Most of us are just lucky enough not to be in Jessup's position. If we ever get there.... Don't judge Jessup until you've been there."

36

Fratricide

YC323984; 15 May 1969; 0600–1200

As tired as we were, no one got much sleep that night. If the enemy was going to hit us during the day, might they not try at night? We all had to face the fact that we were no longer the hunters running down an elusive fox, as we had been throughout our time in the AO. We were now two lions facing each other across a territorial boundary, and we had to accept the fact that the other one might very well have the larger claws and the deeper bite. And, more importantly, it was his territory.

But dawn arrived without incident, and with it the sixth day. The early morning quiet was torn by the banshee shrieking of the F105s, this time bringing the huge bunker-shattering 2000-pound bombs that pulverized almost 2,000 cubic meters of forest in one cataclysmic roar. Again and again they came; a second flight bore napalm, and its greasy yellow flame boiled into the sky along the beast's head and shoulders. Finally, at 0700, they stopped. Even from here, 500, 600 meters below the impact point, we could smell the sickly-sweet and bitter odors of burnt sap and charred earth.

Breakfast was a makeshift affair, but I found myself ravenously hungry; along with sleep, meals had been hard to come by over the previous few days. It wasn't, this time, lack of food, but lack of time to eat it. Water, too, was in short supply. There was none anywhere close—the Rao Trang was two or three kilometers away—and bringing in enough water for a battalion strained the resources of even Division Logistics. Helms and I decided that we had enough for one canteen cup of coffee, and I used that to wash down the dry, sticky fruitcake that cemented itself to my teeth and gums. One full canteen, I kept for later. We all did. Another definition of Hell is to be wounded and have no water.

Littnan called us together soon after that. The artillery had taken over where the Air Force had left off, and the constant booming above our heads punctuated his short, terse sentences. We would begin our next assault at 0900. Garza would go, supported by Eward. I would secure the NDP and, if needed, the LZ. As always, Littnan was cool, even-toned and professional. I have never seen a calmer and more competent officer.

When the briefing ended, we stood up but remained there, hands on hips, silently staring at the ground. Then Eward and I glanced up at the same time. Our faces were motionless and utterly opaque. He finally quirked an eyebrow and gave a small shrug. I nodded. We had, after all, expected no less. Garza left to prepare his people. Marsh and I went our separate ways.

At 0845, we began to collect along the ridge trail, something that had become an almost tribal ritual. The men were quiet, with no more jokes or even low-voiced muttering. They wouldn't have heard each other anyway: The sound of the artillery increased in volume and frequency, and to our south, there came the heavy droning of the air assets—Cobras, ARA, gunships. A grim, stoic purposefulness was all that the young faces around me showed.

At the CO's nod, they began moving. The thunder from the hill increased to a level I had not heard before, and I would have thought that impossible. How much ordnance could they possibly throw at the beast? Huge waves of sound came crashing like a monster surf over the valleys and ridges. I saw Crenshaw grimace, shake his head and hand his mike back to his RTO, and then shout something in Littnan's ear: By now, Crenshaw's ears were thoroughly incapable of picking up any one sound out of the constant roar.

But then there *was* one sound that dwarfed the rest. Incredibly, I could hear the thing approach, almost as loud as an F105, and its impact shook the ground and the very air. Then another ... I walked up to Crenshaw, removed my helmet so I could push my mouth right up against his ear, and yelled.

"What's *that*?" I thought I knew the sound of every type of ordnance we had, but this...

He shouted back. "...New Jersey."

"I didn't ask *where*; I asked *what*?"

He shook his head and tried again. "Battleship *New Jersey*. Sixteen inch guns."

The battleship New Jersey?

He grinned. "Sounds like the end of the world, doesn't it?" He nodded at the hill. "And that's going into the east side of the mountain, about 500 meters away. Think what it sounds like there." (This was reported at the time, and by several people. But the facts are that the *New Jersey* left Vietnamese waters for Korea in late April, weeks before Dong Ap Bia, and so could not have been present then. To this day, I have no idea what those sounds were. The *New Jersey* did fire in support of 101st Airborne operations, but earlier in the war, in 1967.)

A few minutes later Littnan heard from Garza: The lead element was now at the clearing. By now, all three companies had reached the ridge tops. Most of the fire, especially the huge rounds Crenshaw attributed to the *New Jersey*, had been plastering the top or east slope anyway.

Now, the deluge of artillery stopped, leaving behind only the patter of light rifle fire and the overhead buzzing of the Hueys and Cobras. A week before, what we were hearing would have been considered significant fire; now, after that stupendous racket, it was an almost pastoral quiet. Littnan motioned me forward. I joined him in his crowded CP area. Three radios, not including Crenshaw's, were on the ground by his feet; Conzoner turned up the speaker on his, the Battalion net, while Littnan kept the receiver from Price's radio stuck in his ear, listening for Garza. The third radio, tuned to the Brigade Liaison's net, was currently being taken up by the S3.

Slowly the volume of fire picked up as the lead elements of the companies began to engage the enemy. Delta Company in particular seemed to be in heavy contact; we could hear the hammering of M60s clearly over the thousand meters of distance. Littnan was listening to Garza's transmission, nodded in agreement, and then replied.

"Keep pushing it. Keep the pressure on 'em. They're catching it from all sides now."

He handed Price the receiver, looked my way and smiled briefly. "Well, this may be it, Frank. Finally. Garza's telling me he isn't getting much resistance from those knolls. Maybe those One Oh Fives blew them out of there this morning." His voice was at once detached and pitched with satisfaction.

I nodded, filled with the same conflicting thoughts reflected in Littnan's voice: A muted elation and a distant skepticism. Neither of us could forget that just 24 hours ago we had exchanged a grin of victory, only to see it all unravel. We waited.

We spent the next 20 minutes listening to the transmissions, and they all spoke of hope: Harkins reported that the lead platoon of his Alpha Company had pushed up to and was now engaging the enemy at the clearing that had devastated Goff and Sullivan's platoons yesterday. Sanders pushed his units hard, and told Black Jack a few minutes later that one of his squads appeared to be within sight of the summit. The best news, for us, came some time after that: Garza's first squad had at last cleared the bunkers and was now in possession of the right-hand knoll, the one through which the trail to the summit of Hill 937 ran. He had three lightly wounded, he told us, but was bringing up his second squad.

The small arms fire picked up. I briefly etched out in my mind what would happen next: With that one knoll secured, Garza would bring up his M60 and start laying down suppressant fire on the saddle and the knoll on the left side. It wouldn't even be necessary to capture that knoll, since he now had a clear path to the summit. All he had to do was neutralize the fire from there. Once he broke through to the top, Second Platoon could move up while Third Platoon secured a foothold on the summit of Hill 937 itself. Then both platoons could take the knoll, one from the flank and the other from the rear, while we moved up to block the enemy's front. It would be all over in minutes, if all went well.

Littnan's thoughts must have been similar to mine, because he leaned over and asked if my lead element, securing the trail above, was in contact with Eward's rear squad.

"I'll check," I said, and took off. I found Clifton, my point man, kneeling on the trail less than ten meters from Eward's last squad, but there was a gap of about 20 meters between Clifton and the next man down — too much. I returned to Littnan's CP area, went through it, and sent three men to tighten up the gaps above us.

Littnan watched them run by. "Everything okay?" he asked.

I nodded. "Yeah. We've got enough people up there now — I think Eward's pulling his guys up a bit, getting ready. Unless you disagree, I'm going to leave one squad back at the NDP and bring the other two up when Eward moves up."

He thought about that for a moment. I could sense his reluctance. "That'll leave a gap between the NDP and you."

"Yeah, I know. If we leave the NDP, though, we leave our gear unsecured." Garza and Eward's platoons had left their rucksacks and other heavy gear behind, of course. That might not have mattered, but the pile of extra ammo did. We couldn't leave it behind, unsecured. That meant we'd have to take it with us.

Littnan's response was interrupted by a heavy, thunderous burst of fire from our left. Delta had run into something. But the net remained empty of traffic; Harkins reported a bunker taken, and that was it.

But a few minutes later, the net became active. There were several transmissions, back and forth, from an unidentifiable caller in Delta. Apparently the lead squad had bogged down within meters of the summit; we could hear them arrange for ARA. While I listened to that, Garza called Littnan. The CO spoke briefly, listened, and spoke again. Then he turned to me.

"Garza's got some more wounded, including a couple of guys who might need evacuation. Looks like we'll have to secure that LZ again. Go down there and make sure the trail between us and the LZ is secure."

"Roger." I started to turn away. I heard the captain call out to First Sergeant Murtiff, telling him to prepare the LZ for medevacs. As I stood and began walking away, I could hear the broken transmissions over the Battalion net.

"Roger, I see your smoke, over."

"Affir ... you ... on three one five, over."

"Roger, I copy.... One ... five."

I was ten meters from Littnan, with Murtiff right behind me, when for the second time that week the entire world was washed out in a glare of dead white.

There was a harsh, flat crack, not at all loud, and an acrid smell of smoke and scorched, white-hot metal and an impression, just below the level of consciousness, of bright red lines of fire streaking through the air past me. Yells and screams tore through the air. I whirled to find a scene of carnage: Bodies lay everywhere. Littnan was down. So were Conzoner, Price, Peters and Crenshaw, who lay with his right leg twisted underneath him. Jorgenson, Sweet, Murtiff.... My mouth went dry, and all I could do was stare for a long moment.

Snyder was one of the men I had moved up; he was still in the CP area but had escaped unhurt. Schoch apparently was unscathed also, because I saw him move quickly to Littnan's side, pause briefly, and then turn to Crenshaw. He yelled something to Snyder, who grabbed one of the radios. I looked up and down the trail; from where I stood, I could see almost no security around us; Jorgenson and Sweet, who had been securing the area immediately around the CP itself, were both down. I looked over my shoulder; Helms, who was standing several feet away, having already started to move down toward the LZ ahead of me, was unhurt.

"Tell Wright to bring a squad up here, now," I yelled. When I turned back, I saw Snyder holding out the radio; it was the battalion net. I ran forward and took it from him.

"Black Jack, this is Bravo One Six, over." By now, it was habit. I kept my voice flat and low-pitched.

"This is Black Jack. What have you got down there?"

"One Six. We just took a round, maybe two. I don't know what it was; it didn't sound like RPGs, over."

"This is Black Jack. It wasn't RPG. It was that goddamned ARA. You just took four 2.75s in your column."

"Roger." I was too stunned to be angry. "Bravo Six is down. So's Bravo Five. And a lot more."

"Roger. How's your Three Six element doing?"

"They were okay, the last time I heard, a couple of minutes ago."

"Tell 'em to keep up the pressure. I want those objectives secured."

"Affirmative."

"You got any FOs down there?"

"Crenshaw's down. So's his RTO. I just got mine, over."

"Keep Three Six moving up. We'll lift the mortar and arty."

"Roger," I replied. "I'm going to check on Three Six now."

"Roger. Out."

Marsh Eward was running down the ridge through the CP; he dropped to his knees beside me.

"You just finish talking to Black Jack?" he asked.

"Yeah. Marsh, we got a mess."

"Yeah. I was just getting ready to get on the horn myself when I heard you pick it up. Where's Littnan?"

"He's over there. I don't know how bad it is but he's not moving. Look, Black Jack says keep pushing. How about you move back up and take care of things there, and I'll try to get things straightened out down here? We need a casualty report and I guess we'll have to open up that LZ."

"Yeah. Hey — what the hell hit us?"

"ARA. Two Seven Fives."

"Bastards." Eward stood up, shook his head, and began running back up the ridge toward Three Six and the clearing.

Six bodies lay scattered about the radio I was using. One of them was Price. He was unquestionably dead, with half his head torn off by shrapnel; the ground under him was literally red with his blood. Conzoner was sitting up, with his right hand pressed to his chest. His face was white, and he seemed not to see me, but he was breathing normally, so I judged that his lungs weren't perforated. Crenshaw and his RTO lay side by side, next to their radio. Russ's leg was split open, from thigh to knee; his face was twisted in agony, but he remained silent. His RTO lay with eyes open, a trickle of blood seeping from his mouth. Jorgenson was off the trail, his head hidden by a bush; he lay unmoving.

Littnan, his arm and shoulder drenched in blood, lay next to Price's body. I saw him struggle to get up, and quickly moved to his side.

"Don't move, Captain," I said, gently pushing him back to the ground. His face was white, and his eyes dull. He stared at me without recognition for a moment, then nodded and rested his head back against the dark earth.

"How bad ... is it?" He winced. He was asking about the company, not himself, but I deliberately misunderstood him..

"Bad enough. You've been hit in the arm. You hurt anyplace else?"

He shook his head slowly. "Arm is ... numb. Wh ... what hit us?"

I gritted my teeth. "ARA."

Anger and disbelief flashed through his eyes. "Christ!" It was the strongest swear word I'd heard him use. He closed his eyes, mouth white and tightlipped.

The medics were frantically working on Peters, Crenshaw's RTO. Hudson was wrapping bandages around Crenshaw's leg. As fast as he wrapped, the bandage turned red. I turned my attention back to Littnan.

"Do you want some water?"

"No. B ... Black Jack.... Call...."

"I already have. Three Six is continuing the attack. Marsh is up there right now."

"Okay." He closed his eyes, and for a moment I thought he'd finally passed out, but he opened them again. "How many ... hit?"

I hesitated, but decided he had a right to know. "Ten, twelve."

"CP?"

"Everyone in the CP's hit, sir."

He grunted softly. "Top?"

"Him too."

"Got ... the whole ... crew, huh?"

"Yes, sir."

"Okay. You're in charge ... take ... care of 'em."

"Yes, sir. Just lie back.. I'm getting you a medic."

"No. Others ... first. I'm ... not bad."

The firefight, which had been steady up to that moment, suddenly erupted in a heavy wave of sound. Suddenly I realized that most of it was NVA.

"Two Six, this is One Six. What's going on, over?"

There was nothing, at first, just more and more intense fire from above. And then, behind me, I heard a few shots coming from down the trail. I looked around; there was no one now between the CP group—which now consisted of the casualties and the medics working on them, and no one else—and the trail below us, leading to the LZ. I made a rapid calculation in my head: There was no way to secure the entire ridge anymore, not with Garza's Three Six element near the summit and Eward's platoon already entering the clearing. There was simply too much space and not enough men. The specter of Charlie Company grinned savagely at me.

"One, this is Two. Go." Eward's voice interrupted my thoughts.

"What's going on?"

"Damn if I know. Something's got these little mothers all stirred up. They're all over the place, all of a sudden. Sons of bitches must think there's a war going on."

"Roger. I'm hearing fire from my right rear. Anything off to your flanks?"

"Affirm. All over the compass."

"Do you and Three Six have a way out?"

"Affirm. For now. But if they pinch off that knoll there, between me and Garza, he'll be in a world of shit."

I looked around me. Helms was standing behind me, having returned from delivering my message to Wright. He had his radio tuned to the company net, so I dropped the receiver and took his. Just then, a trooper from Eward's platoon walked by; he was one of a pair who'd brought back a wounded man from Three Six. I didn't know his name, although I recognized his face. Reaching out, I grabbed his arm and pointed to the battalion net radio lying at my feet.

"Put that on," I yelled.

He looked at me slack jawed. "I ain't no RTO," he said.

"You are now. Put it on."

As he reluctantly put it on, I picked up the receiver, holding it to my ear with one hand and its cord up in the air with the other, to keep it from getting tangled up as the man struggled with the harness. Black Jack was already on the horn.

"...going on, over?"

"This is Bravo One Six," I replied. "Two Six and Three Six are taking heavy incoming, from all sides. I've also got fire coming from my right rear, along that south slope."

"Roger. How bad is that?"

"Don't know. Just started up. I've got Two Six on the line and he's telling me he's still got a way out, but it may be closing, over."

"Roger. Delta and Alpha are getting heavy fire too. Are you up at the FEBA?"

"Negative. I'm on my way up, soon as I find out what's happening behind me, over."

"Roger. Don't take all day at it. Is your LZ secure?"

"That's what I have to find out. I sent word down to secure it just before the ARA hit, over."

"Well, you're gonna need the son of a bitch, so make sure it's secure. I got a new Six and a new Three Six on the way to you, when you can secure the LZ. And you'll have to bring the wounded out. You got a count yet?"

I had to concentrate to remember the day's keyword: Formal Ring. "I got a partial. KIA: Oscar. WIA from the ARA hit: Foxtrot Golf. And at least Mike WIA from the Three Six element, over."

"Can Three Six keep up his attack?"

"Wait one." I thumbed the switch on the other receiver. "Two Six, this is One Six. How are things now?"

Eward's voice was barely audible; the level of fire around him had ratcheted up enormously in the past minute. "This is Two Six. We're catching some real shit up here. Are you on your way up?"

"Roger, in a moment." I wasn't panicked, but I was deeply worried. I still had no idea what was going on behind me, and I had no one near me whom I could send to find out ... except for Helms. I looked down; Conzoner's radio, the one tuned to the company net, the same as Helms', lay on the other side of Price's body. I made a quick decision. "Wait one," I called to Eward.

I stepped over Price, reached down and picked up the receiver, handing the other back to Helms. I shouted in his ear: "Call One Five: Find out what's happening down there. ASAP."

He nodded and put the mike to his lips.

"Black Jack, this is One Six. I'm moving up now. Three Six and Two Six are still heavily engaged. I've got someone checking on the LZ right now."

"Roger. Are you up there yet?"

"Moving."

I had to push the trooper with the radio forward; he wasn't so much afraid as confused. I nodded at Helms, who blew out his cheeks and nodded back. We had made about 50 meters or so when Helms tapped me on the shoulder.

"Two Six is on the line. He needs to talk to you. And Sergeant Wright says they're getting harassing fire from the south. He's not sure how many of 'em."

I nodded and took the line. I was walking almost crab-like, with one radio cord stretched out in front and the other behind me. I thumbed the receiver.

"Roger, Two Six. What's happening?"

"They got snipers all over the place. Watch yourself. Wait one.... Bo, things are bad. We're taking heavy fire, and now some of it's coming from behind us, from where Delta's ridge is."

I blinked. That was very worrisome. Up to now, we'd received fire only from the east — the knolls and clearing — and the south. Now he was getting it from the north. I looked up the trail ahead of me, but could see little; this part of the ridge was the very narrow, steep razorback just before the clearing.

Before I could reply to Eward, however, Wright broke in. Simultaneously, I heard a burst of heavy fire from below. "One Six, this is One Five. We are taking heavy incoming, from our south and west. They are probin' us pretty good, over."

My mouth went dry. That completed the circle. We were surrounded.

36. Fratricide

"Bravo One Six, this is Black Jack."

"Roger. This is One Six."

"Alpha may have to withdraw. What's your sitrep?"

"This is One Six. We're in trouble. Two Six is reporting very heavy fire from his east, north and south, and my One Five down at the LZ says he's got enemy units to his south and west."

"Roger. Delta's taking heavy casualties. Bring them back down, *now*. And stay on this damn radio."

"Roger." I shifted to the other radio. "Two Six, can you withdraw? You and Three?"

"Roger. If we hurry. Three will have to clear, and then we can move down."

My mind raced. Things were as bad as they could be. "Roger. Look, let's do this. I gotta move back to the NDP and the LZ. I'm worried about that. You take charge up here, and bring everyone down ASAP: We'll consolidate around the NDP and the LZ."

"Yeah. Sounds good."

I shouted to Helms and Garvey — the reluctant RTO — to follow me.

When I got to the NDP, things were even worse than I'd feared. Snyder and the other two with him had left the trail and moved back down to rejoin First Platoon at the LZ. Only a few Two Six troopers, those who, like my unfortunate RTO, had brought the wounded down, were anywhere near the NDP. Leaderless, they still had at least secured the immediate area — but they were all on the south side, of course. Between them and my First Platoon was a gap of about 100 meters. This was precisely what had happened to Charlie Company. But I couldn't move the CP group — the medics and wounded — so I had to bring at least a squad up to secure the trail. Once Eward brought back the other two platoons, we could cover everything, but in the meantime we were vulnerable.

I bent over to yell into Schoch's ear; he was now working on Littnan. I wanted him to know what we were doing, but he barely nodded. He was concentrating on his job.

Moving down the trail, at a run, I could hear the fire in front of me; it was getting heavier, but at the moment it seemed to be M16 and M60. Snyder and two or three others were kneeling along the trail just above the LZ, facing south. Beyond them was the LZ itself. I covered the last 30 or 40 meters in a crouching sprint. I could hear the heavy thumping of Helms' boots behind me, and hoped that Garvey was behind him. I didn't have time to turn around to look.

Hyde was the first one to see me. I ran over to him. "Nate: Take your squad, move it up the ridge to the NDP. We got a gap between us and the NDP right now. You copy?"

He nodded and moved off immediately, gathering his men. I saw Wright kneeling by his radio at the edge of the LZ.

"Top: I'm sending Hyde up to secure the trail. We're bringing everyone back down from the clearing. Alpha and Delta are getting hit too. Soon as Eward's back, we'll consolidate around the NDP and the LZ."

"Yes, sir. We got ammo on the way?"

"Not now. But we have a couple of crates back up there."

"Okay, sir. They're movin' in behind us, along that trail leadin' back to the battalion."

"Yeah, I know. Eward says he's taking fire from the north."

He nodded. "We'll hold 'em here."

I began running back up the hill. I knew Dennis would keep up. Garvey would just have to suck it up.

I found Hyde setting his men up along the trail; his last man was Carlton, looking scared and wide-eyed, but at least responsive this time; he was covering the area between himself and the NDP, a gap of about 15 meters, with his M79. Logan, with his M60, was set up in the middle of the squad, facing southwest along a partially clear draw that led up to the trail.

"Two Six, this is One Six. How're you coming?"

"Three Six just cleared; Garza's gonna set up along the east side of the NDP. I'm on my way."

I never responded. All hell let out for lunch.

Months later, at Bien Hoa, I would break out in a sweat, thinking about how close we came to being overrun. The NVA had infiltrated down the ravines to our south, and up from the Laotian border to the west, and launched an all-out assault on us in that moment. One minute — no more — after Hyde's squad plugged the gap, they hit us. If they'd been 65 seconds sooner.

"Bravo One Six, this is Black Jack. Is your new Six in place, over?"

I blinked in astonishment. Couldn't he see? Then I realized he probably couldn't; he was probably over at Delta right now. "Negative. The LZ is not secure. We're under attack from three sides right now."

"Roger. I have mortars if you need 'em."

"I got Two Six and Three Six still moving. When we consolidate, I'll let you know, over."

"Roger. Stay in touch with me. Out."

The AK rounds were snapping leaves and twigs from the trees overhead; I still hadn't heard the sound I feared most, however — there was no RPG fire. I decided that I would wear Helms and Garvey to a frazzle if I had them follow me up and down the ridge, so I tapped Dennis on the helmet. "Stay here. Switch radios with this guy here. I want you to monitor the Battalion net. I won't be far."

He nodded, wide-eyed himself. In all the time he'd been my RTO, I had never seen Helms flinch, and he didn't now, but I could see the fear deep in his eyes. He was smart enough to know that this was even worse than Dong Ngai.

I ran crouching past Hyde's squad, to where Dickerson's squad lay stretched out. The incoming fire there was more intense, but at the moment, the NVA seemed content to pour small arms fire in. But on my way back up, I heard shouts and a sudden burst from Logan's gun: They were coming up that small draw to his front. I ran past him, with just a pause to look down the draw; I could see movement but nothing else. Logan was sighting carefully, loosing bursts of 10 or 15 rounds, not indiscriminately but in measured fire.

"Two Six, this is One Six. We're under assault. Watch yourself, over."

"I'm back down where you are. I can see you. Garza says he's taking fire from directly above us, and they're moving up that ravine to his south. I've filled in around the NDP."

"Roger." I picked up the other receiver. "Black Jack, One Six, over."

A new voice answered; Black Jack's RTO. "Black Jack's on the other net, One Six."

"Roger. Tell him we're being attacked from south and east, and we're receiving fire from all directions, over."

"Roger. Delta's getting hit too."

The next few minutes were simply chaotic. Fire was coming in from everywhere, and shouts and yells indicated where first one and then another position reported NVA moving in their front. I was crouched over, running up the ridge, and almost ran into Eward coming the other way. Our eyes locked. Neither of us said anything, but later we agreed that our reactions were simultaneous and immediate. We both straightened up. No more scuttling like a crab. Call it pride, or duty, or the sobering understanding of what fear could do, we stood together in the middle of the trail and looked at each other grimly.

"They're coming up from the ravine and down from the clearing," he said.

"Yeah. They're trying to break through the middle of the trail, cutting off the LZ."

"That's what I thought. How are we for ammo?"

"Okay. It's all up here with you, at the NDP."

"Good. I'll stay up top, keep an eye on things up there."

I knelt down once, alongside Logan: The men around him were yelling that the NVA were coming up the hill; for a moment, I saw nothing, and then, for the only time in all that period of combat, including at Dong Ngai, I saw the live enemy: Five of them were running up the slope, but not at Logan. They were assaulting Dickerson's positions just above the LZ. Logan's shoulders tensed as he brought the muzzle of the machine gun around, and then the gun bellowed, and the five went down, one after another, in quick succession. I stood up and walked down toward the LZ. I carried my rifle, but afterwards found that I'd not even loaded it; the magazine was locked, but I'd never chambered the round. It didn't matter. I wasn't supposed to be a rifleman.

The LZ was holding; the enemy had tried to move across the lower saddle, at the trail junction, but had been repulsed by machine gun and rifle fire. Farther up, Snyder and his team had used grenades to clear the area in front of them. The next ten minutes were just a repetition, a sort of boring but necessary ostinato. Move up the ridge, look, move back down. Get on the radio, talk, put it down. And move up or down the ridge again.

It ended, finally. The enemy broke off the attack, up and down the ridge. Almost at once, the firing slacked and petered out. A few calls rang out, mostly in question; I heard someone cry for a medic. Eward and I met a second time, in the NDP. There was no exultation on our faces. Nor even relief. A file clerk, putting away the last piece of correspondence, might have felt as much.

I had no emotion, but I understood this: The troopers of Bravo Company, in dire circumstances, had withstood a serious and determined enemy counterattack. Exhausted, at half-strength and battered as they were, they held. That Eagle on their shoulders means something.

37

The Number Seventeen

YC323984; 15 May 1969; 1200–1800

Half an hour later, two men jumped out of an LOH at the LZ. Our new company commander had arrived, along with a platoon leader.

His name was Chappel; a tall, somewhat gangly man with light sand-colored hair, slightly receding across the top. He came up to the NDP, saw the radios and came over to where we — Eward and I — were standing.

"I'm Butch Chappel," he said, holding out his hand.

"Frank Boccia." I gave his hand a quick shake.

"I've heard of you. You must be Eward." He said, reaching out to Marsh. "Heard of you too. This is Lou Charles."

Charles was a couple of inches taller than I, stocky, with a dark-visaged face that was almost oriental in appearance. He nodded to the two of us. As we were to find out, he was a man of few words.

"Where are my RTOs?" Chappel asked.

"They're hit. You'll need some new ones. For right now, your best bet is to grab a pair of warm bodies and stick 'em in the harness."

"Well, that's what I expected. Charles here is going to take over Third Platoon. Who's that?" he nodded at a figure standing nearby, with a sergeant's chevron on his sleeve. I turned and blinked in surprise. It was Leanahan, the commo sergeant. Until that moment, I hadn't realized he was with us, although I did recall that we had stripped the rear of all personnel.

"Sergeant Leanahan."

"Oh. Where's Garza?"

Someone was sent to grab Garza — he was still up at the far eastern end of the perimeter, making sure that the enemy didn't simply roll down the ridge onto us. Garza became the company first sergeant again, since Charles was taking his platoon. Fourth Platoon was by now defunct: We didn't have enough men left to field four platoons. As a matter of fact, we had barely enough for two.

Doc O'Keefe, from Battalion, was flown in a little while later, to help with the casualties; our medics were overwhelmed. Rairdon's shuttle started at that point; Pitre, a rifleman in Garza's platoon, his head peppered with deep red holes from shrapnel but still clinging to life, was the first one evacuated. He would die two days later. The medics worked to stabilize the rest. I walked down to the LZ after briefing the new CO. O'Keefe looked up as I walked by and called out.

"Hey, Lieutenant: Let's take a look."

I frowned in puzzlement. "Look at what?"

"Your leg." He pointed down. I looked; a small patch of blood stained the right outside trouser leg, just below my knee. I hadn't felt anything. A moment later, with my trouser leg rolled up, he took a thin tweezers-like instrument and plucked something from my leg; I could feel my skin pull out a bit along with the tiny — and it *was* tiny — piece of shrapnel. He looked at the wound critically and daubed it with a stinging liquid.

"Lemme get a bandage," he muttered, but I shook my head and rolled my pants back down.

"Get serious, Doc. I've had paper cuts that hurt more."

He nodded. "Well, it wasn't much at that." He pulled out a yellow cardboard tag. "I'll write you up...."

"What for?"

"If you want. You get a Purple Heart with that tag."

I looked him in the eye. O'Keefe, like Schoch a Conscientious Objector, was a decent man. "Doc...."

He nodded. "Well, I was just asking."

A moment later, I saw Sergeant Wright moving in my direction, his face set in a dark bronze mask.

"Top," I nodded, as he reached me.

"Got a count, Lieutenant."

"What have we got?" I had a hollow feeling in my midriff.

"Clifton's down. Took some RPG frags just now." He took a deep breath. "That leaves us with seventeen, Lieutenant."

Seventeen: a number. A prime number; my mind went through the series: One, two, three, five, seven, eleven, thirteen, seventeen, nineteen, twenty-three ... I stared into the formless blur of trees on the north side of the perimeter for a long moment, and then, with the force of a blow, it hit me.

"Seventeen?" I whispered. "That's all? We have seventeen men left?"

"Yes, sir. That's it."

I turned away. What in God's name had happened to my platoon? Where had they gone? I tried to puzzle it out, to go back over the last six days and find the flaw in Wright's number ... half my platoon, gone? How? When? How could I have...

"Seventeen?" I asked again.

He nodded, without looking at me; he was staring out over the ridge, toward the distant mountains in the west, hazy in the noon sun.

37. The Number Seventeen

I felt a rising nausea, a physical reaction. I was afraid I was going to be sick. Seventeen? I had left Blaze, on April 25, with 34 men. And then the names started confronting me, etched in fiery red, like tracer rounds in the dark: St. Onge, Evans, Vandenburg, Brown, Sweet, Jorgenson, Westman, Nelson, Muldoon, Hannah, Eden, Gann, Clifton, Jones, Williams, and even Novak.

I waited while Rairdon's LOH settled into the clearing, picked up another of the badly wounded, and took off again. The rest were lined up along the trail, just off the LZ. For an unsettling moment, the scene reminded me of Charlie Company from the day before, but there were obvious differences. Our troops were in place, on guard, looking grim. The medics were there, working on the wounded. The dead were already in the dark green body bags—Price, Jorgenson and Peters, Crenshaw's RTO.

There were still over 20 men waiting to go. I wandered through the group, unsure of why I had come down here in the first place. First Sergeant Murtiff lay with his back against a tree, his hard little eyes still bright and wrathful, like a wounded boar's. There was Conzoner, a white bandage wrapped around his chest, and Micheaux, arm bloody and limp. Crenshaw, his bluff and hearty face twisted with pain, lay with his leg still thrust out before him, a mass of red and black and bone-white. Littnan lay still, his chest barely rising and falling. Sabatini, one of Garza's men, with a ragged red stump of a bandage where his right hand had been: Clark, the man who wanted to play centerfield, in a friend's arms, with his right leg missing below the knee; he would chase no more fly balls: Lance, with his left cheek ripped open: Barber, quiet and still with an AK round through his chest.

And there were more. After a moment, I abruptly turned to go. As I did so, a hoarse cry of pain stabbed at me. It was Crenshaw; in turning I'd accidentally kicked his leg. I started to blurt out an apology but his eyes were closed and he was looking away. Schoch had pumped him full of morphine long since.

Alongside the trail, lying on his back, was Gann. His blond head was dark with sweat; blood covered his left shoulder and spotted his left leg. His eyes were closed, but when I knelt down beside him, he opened them, saw me, and gave a slow, close-mouthed smile. I shook my head: I had no words for him or myself. He smiled again, nodded his head slowly, in understanding of what I wanted to but could not say. Sweat, in large tear-shaped drops, stippled his face and neck. Painfully, he raised his right arm and fumbled for my hand. He smiled once more, locking his eye on mine. I could see the pain in them, and some fear, but also trust and affection, or even love, but above all, forgiveness. He squeezed my hand weakly, as if to comfort me.

I could bear no more. I bent my head, covered my eyes, and wept.

Exhaustion lay over us like a comforting blanket, dulling our pain, blurring the images of the past hour. There was no sleep, of course, no real rest, but I lay there, back against a tree, basking in silence and the comforting absence of will or purpose, save for a remote and fitful pinprick of conscience: Get up, check the platoon, get a count, check your ammo ... something resembling duty kept prodding my languor, and I wished Duty in hell.

"Lieutenant."

My eyes were wide open, because I could see, on a leaf of a bush only a few feet away, a small fly struggling in the sticky sap that coated the surface ... or was it drying blood? I was lying not far from the rockets' impact. I hadn't seen Helms kneel beside me. He repeated my name.

I finally left the fly to its fate, and looked up.

"CO wants to see you, sir."

I was too tired for anger. A small part of my brain, the older, reptilian part, immediately knew: We were going back up. That's why he wanted to see me. The pitiful little homo sapiens brain scoffed in derision. It wasn't possible.

It was 1300. Eward and Charles were there, seated across an upturned ammo crate from Chappel. I knelt on the ground, next to Marsh.

Chappel shared this much with Littnan: He moved right to the point.

"Delta Company lost several men this morning; they're down in a ravine right now, trying to extract the dead and wounded. They can't attack, but us and Alpha are ordered to press on against the enemy positions. Take the pressure off of Delta, see if we can finally break through."

Eward made a sound. It might have been a grunt, or a softly phrased expletive.

Chappel frowned. "I won't have time to learn the tactical situation up there. I haven't had time for much of anything. I know they have bunkers, and we haven't rooted them all out. The question is, can we do it now?"

Neither Eward nor I responded. My head was hanging down, focusing on the scuffed, muddy beige of the toe of my left boot. Charles spoke up.

"My guys say they've reached the knoll twice, about half way up from the clearing. This might be the time."

"Frank? Marsh? You on board with that?"

Eward said nothing. I opened my mouth, closed it, opened it again. Fear swelled inside me, fear as I'd not known it before. It wasn't the fear of death—death was a minor affair—but the fear of what I would see in my men's eyes when I told them they would have to face the beast again.

"They came within a minute or so of overrunning us this morning, Captain. Going back up may just leave us open to another attack from those ravines to the south."

"Well, we don't have a choice."

Then why the fuck did you ask, damn you!

We talked for a while longer, about tactics, communication and contingencies, but if my mind recorded any of it, it was wiped clean within seconds. None of that mattered.

Eward and I stood up together, when we were done, and our eyes met once again. There was in his, and probably mine, a tiny shrug, an oriental acceptance of what was to happen. My mind, tired as it was, reached out for but could not quite grasp that line from the *Rubaiyat*: *and when the cup is passed, shrink not*. We had 20 minutes.

I reached the platoon sector. The men lay or sat upon the ground, resting, or grieving, or ... Helms was the first to see me; his eyes widened. I stood silently by my gear, looking down the ridge: Snyder, Logan, Hernandez, Samuel, Kenzy, Hyde, Ulrich, Dickerson ... there were more, but not as many as before.

I was supposed to give the order — the crossed rifles and black bar on my lapel said so. But not even their weight could force open my throat. I could not bring myself to speak. Sergeant Wright, who was leaning against his pack, near the center of the perimeter, with his back to me, sensed something, as so often he did: Turning his head to face me, he looked directly into my eyes for several seconds. Then he gave a quick, crisp nod.

One of the others — I don't remember who — looked up at the same time, and stood up. Gradually, the conversation, the low murmuring and soft whispering that had filled the air when I walked up, died away. One by one, the men lying or sitting before me twisted their heads to look, first in question, then doubt, realization, anger, and, at the end, a dull acceptance, so much like mine that it stabbed me, a self-inflicted wound.

There was stillness, now, a complete cessation of movement, such that for a moment I had an impression of looking at a painting, or rather, a monument, with the lean rigid figures sculpted in greened, rusty bronze. The afternoon sun peeked and winked through the leaves above us in tiny shafts of light. As in a domed cathedral, when a fugitive sunbeam slips through a chink in the heavy stained glass windows and cleaves the gloom with a searing white blade, it left the surrounding shadows darker and more impenetrable.

The stillness was broken by the boom of artillery, landing in a preliminary patter of death on the hill behind me. Each boom meant another square meter of forest shattered and shredded; another patch of skin ripped from the beast's frame. But it still stood, snarling its defiance, challenging us with its carrion-choked claws, furious, ready to rend us again. As if awakened by the roar, the bronze statues stirred.

One by one, then, they got up, to stand, uncertain only of the minor question of what exactly to do next. One by one, they began silent, almost furtive motions: Bending over to pick up their gear, looking at and clearing their rifles, shrugging on a harness, swishing a canteen to see if it still held water...

Kenzy, his square, hard face grey with fatigue, was the first to stand and move to the trail, his rifle unconsciously held at a perfectly correct military port arms position. Then Snyder, his chinstrap characteristically dangling from his helmet; Hernandez, Abbot, Logan ... one after another, in silence, they moved to the trail and stood there, waiting, looking not at me, nor the mountain, but steadily and resolutely at the man in front of them.

I had not — and could not have — spoken a word. Finally, I reached down and took up my own gear and rifle, and placed my helmet on my head.

Chappel appeared at the head of the trail; the artillery barrage had intensified. It was time. He looked at the men behind me, and then at me. "Are you ready?" he called out.

I felt a surge of conflicting emotions: Pride, sadness, humility, anger, utter desolation.

"Yes," I answered.

The assault — the 11th by our company — began immediately. Alpha Company was pushing up the ridge to our south, its lead elements entering the same deadly clearings that had destroyed two platoons of Charlie Company the day before. Delta was grimly trying to hold off the NVA while retrieving their people from the ravine they were in. And we moved up the ridge once again. I wondered if I could ever be whole again, ever free, unless this writhing, blasted, smoking ruin of a beast, this golem of seared dirt and splintered rock, was utterly, completely, eternally wiped from the map, from the very Earth. The men shooting down at me were merely men, and unimportant. It was the mountain I hated.

We could hear the .51 caliber — it was still there — and its mind-chilling, deep-throated bark. RPGs began to slam against the trees above and behind the clearing; stripped now of limbs, they offered poor targets, and many of the deadly rounds went over our heads to explode harmlessly in the ravines to either side. Rifle fire began to surge in volume. The bunkers were destroyed, many of them, but the enemy had dug new fighting holes along the knolls and the saddle.

Eward's platoon moved across the clearing, attempting to get to the left-hand knoll. First Platoon moved to the right; I set up a machine gun there, directing its fire into the knoll, trying to suppress the fire from there as Second Platoon moved up. Samuel was firing his M79, dropping his rounds into the right-hand knoll, where the .51 was hammering at Eward's people, pinned down now by its heavy fire at the base of the north knoll. But the trees on the south side of the clearing, or rather the ones on the upper slope of the steep ravine to the south, still were relatively unharmed, and many of Samuel's grenades exploded harmlessly in their upper branches.

My platoon had not, at this point, been hit hard. The enemy, seeing that it was the north knoll that was the more vulnerable, concentrated their fire against Eward's people. Chappel called then, to tell me that Alpha had pushed through their clearings and were within a few meters of the summit. Eward, pinned down by the heavy gun and the RPG fire, tried a desperation move: A squad, led by Sergeant Randolph, tried to maneuver along the slope of the ravine on the north side of the ridge; at that point it was even steeper and narrower than the ravine to the south, along whose upper edge we were perched. If they could make it, then they might be able to approach the knoll from its north side, protected from the .51 fire.

We began to inch our way up into and through the right side of the clearing; the .51 was almost certainly bunkered, but the riflemen supporting it might be in open spider holes, vulnerable to our own grenades. There was the chance, then, that we might finally silence the heavy gun.

And then the claymores and shape charges went off. Once again, the enemy had moved down into the clearing between artillery and air assaults and laid down yet another belt of claymore mines. They caught Eward's men while they were moving, scything them down with the unexpected hail of pellets. A moment later, Eward was calling me, asking if I could send a squad to the left, to support him while he pulled his men back. I grabbed Dickerson and told him to move along the lip of the clearing to the left side, to that small hump where, six days before, Snyder had made his solitary stand.

Chappel called then, alerted by the transmissions between me and Eward. I returned to Helms from sending Dickerson out just in time to hear the tail end of Chappel's call.

"...Six, this is Six." I didn't hear the first part, so I was unsure whom he was calling, but Eward answered a moment later.

"This is Two Six."

"Roger. Are you making any progress, over?"

"Negative." Eward's voice was noncommittal.

"Alpha's made it to the top, or close to it. When they do, they'll be pushing across the hill toward your location, so look out for them, over."

"Well, they better hurry it up, because my people are getting shot up pretty good."

"Have you reached that little hill yet, the one you're supposed to secure?"

"Negative."

"What's the problem?"

I could almost hear Marsh snort in disgust before he thumbed the mike. "The problem is they've got claymores set up, along with that .51, and they got me pinned down."

"Roger. Break. One Six, where are you?"

"On the right side of the clearing."

"Can you advance? Take the pressure off Two Six?"

"Same story here. The claymores are set up along the base of the south knoll, and that's where the gun is. Plus they got new positions dug into the saddle, where they can fire on us or on Two Six."

"Well, Alpha Company is moving."

There's no telling what I would have said in response, because before I could reply several RPGs went off, all at once, some landing across the clearing where Eward's people were, and some in the trees behind me. I heard a cry and a yell for the medic, from my right, so I knew one of my men had been hit.

Eward was saying something—I couldn't quite make it out—when fire broke out behind me, down the ridge. A moment later, when Eward finished speaking, Lou Charles broke in to say his platoon, strung out along the ridge behind us, was taking fire from the south ravine. Once again, the NVA had maneuvered men down the ridge and were firing at our flank.

By now, the situation at the clearing was untenable. Eward was pinned down by the heavy machine gun and the RPG fire; I could only maneuver around the edge of the clearing, not through it, and the longer I stayed where I was, the more men I would lose to RPGs. To take my men across the clearing, in the teeth of the claymores and the machine gun fire, was not even to be considered. It couldn't be done. And Eward was losing men as we sat.

It was Eward who radioed Chappel. "Six, this is Two Six. I've got beaucoup casualties, and I got no chance of moving up. Longer I stay here, the more I'll get hurt. I'm pulling back, over."

"This is Six. Wait one. Let me see if Black Jack concurs."

"This is Two Six. I'm pulling back."

"This is One Six. I agree with Two Six. The fire's just as heavy today as it was a week ago, over."

"Roger. Out."

"One Six, this is Two Six. Can you hold while I pull back, over?"

"Roger. "

Fifteen minutes later, Marsh and I stood together at the lip of the clearing, facing back up the hill. Gear lay heaped and scattered across the clearing above us; lost and discarded equipment, some of it whole, some of it torn and shredded by the inanimate fury of trinotrol and gunpowder. Shell casings, IV bottles, empty magazines, bandages and first aid cases, helmets, packs, fatigue shirts, ponchos; here and there an empty boot, a shard of plastic from a shattered rifle stock, and, incongruously, a few feet from me, a book. To our right, at the base of the knoll, I could see the twisted leg of an NVA soldier, dead alongside his spider hole.

Eward and I examined the scene clinically. The platoons, with our wounded, were wearily trudging down the hill behind us. It was time to withdraw.

"Hey, Lieutenant! You comin'?"

I looked over my shoulder. Andersen, one of Eward's men, was crouched by the trail, beckoning. The battle was not quite over; there were still shots coming from our right rear, where Lou Charles was fighting off the NVA there; a few shots rang out from our left front, from the knoll. We looked at each other. Any moment now, the NVA could come down from the saddle and knolls, to press on our column, catching us between them and the fire to our rear.

We needed a rear guard, someone to hold them back if they came ... our eyes met once again; an unspoken challenge and agreement rang out between us. It was the strangest fact of all, that between Eward, a man with whom I had almost nothing in common, and me there existed an almost perfect bond of understanding. I had never been much of a believer in ESP and all that nonsense, yet he and I understood each other perfectly, time and again, without ever speaking a word.

To each other, that is. Eward did speak to Andersen. "Move back," he yelled. "Keep your eyes open along the sides, and get 'em movin'. We'll bring up the rear."

Andersen gave us a blurred, scared look and ran crouching down the trail. Eward and I faced to the front; we edged away from each other until we were about two meters apart. Then we began a slow, deliberate movement down the hill, one foot at a time, backing up while our heads moved constantly from side to side. Every few seconds, one of us would fire a short burst up the ridge, and then continue our slow movement rearward.

We were past the clearing and the steep slope leading to it; step, squeeze, step ... suddenly I looked at Marsh and grinned, and he responded with a smile and a shake of his head. I was unsure then whom we were mocking — ourselves or what lay above us.

We reached the perimeter, and the men who stood there, in a knot, waiting for us. The firing from the south had ceased, and an uneasy silence lay over all of them. We turned our backs on the ridge behind us. Impulsively, I held out my hand; Eward took it and we shook, firmly, with only the briefest of eye contact. Then we separated and went to our platoons.

A pile of gear lay in the middle of the NDP. I was reminded sharply of Littnan's words, only the previous evening, although that seemed an age past: Now we were where Charlie Company had been yesterday. Sergeant Hyde stood by with some thermite grenades, and in a moment the flames would tear at the rucksacks, fatigue shirts, poncho liners, harnesses and red-stained bandages. Hyde placed his grenades carefully, and the white flame and dirty smoke began to consume the pile.

38

The Stain

YC315993; 15 May 1969; 1700–2400

We moved out soon after that. Delta Company, as battered as they were, took our place on the ridge. They would be reinforced a day or so later by a unit from the 502nd. It was already twilight when we started filing down the trail to the battalion CP. The company column was much shorter returning than it had been a week ago.

First Platoon was in the lead, and Sergeant Dickerson, who'd been down this trail twice already, walked the point. He knew it well, and maintained a good pace for the first several hundred meters. We were burdened with extra gear and weapons. But we had no food, little ammo and almost no water, so our load was light, and the path was well worn and smooth. Night had almost completely fallen by the time Dickerson began leading us up the base of the hill from which the NVA had hit Eward's people on the night of the 10th. After a moment's discussion, Captain Chappel decided to push on over the hill and down the other side, to that small valley below the bluff on which the Battalion CP was located. It would be safer, he felt, to move in the dark than to set up 400 or 500 meters from the battalion, low on ammo as we were.

There were two trails now, where before there had been one: The one trail led up the hill; this was the one we'd followed, going the other way of course, a week earlier. The second branched off to the west, our left, and skirted the hill. This had been used over the past week by the units moving back and forth between the ridges to the south and the battalion. Dickerson would have taken that trail—indeed, it was he who had first blazed it, the night of the 11th, when Littnan had dispatched his squad for more ammo. But Chappel decided to have us go straight up the hill, across the top and back down, following our original and since unused trail.

It was a short and not particularly steep climb to the crest; the trail turned to the west and began to descend. We soon reached the place where the bamboo stalks had been knocked down, and we began crawling. Dickerson still led, followed by Logan and then me.

The stench wafted across the path almost as soon as we crouched down. It was worse, far worse, than anything I'd endured to date. It was a gagging, heavy, putrid smell, with none of that tinge of sweet foulness of fresh carrion. As we advanced, on our hands and knees, it got worse, until I began to think we would have to back our way out; it became difficult to breathe.

"Oh, no! Goddamnit!"

Logan lost his balance, and fell back and to one side. He was only a foot or so in front of me. I tried to avoid his fall but couldn't, and got entangled with his gear. My right hand reached out; the barrel of my M16 struck the stock of his M60 and that knocked me off balance, and I fell, instinctively putting out my left hand to break my fall. Instead of earth, it plunged into something cold, damp, yielding, and indescribably rotted. It was the open chest cavity of the dead NVA soldier.

"Oh, Christ!" I heard Logan say, in a thick, wretched voice.

We struggled upright, trying not to touch each other or ourselves. I was glad of the darkness; I could not see what was on my hand. Logan was making small, childish gagging sounds, but I remained silent, willing myself to keep my jaws clamped so tight they hurt. I was afraid that if I opened my mouth even a tiny bit, all the vomit in hell would pour out.

At least the smell was no worse; of course, it couldn't be. I saw Logan as a dark shadow in front of me; he had struggled to his knees, and was staring at the ground.

"You okay, sir?" Helms asked from behind me.

"Shut the fuck up!" I snarled. Then, sheepishly, I said, "Yeah, Dennis. Sorry. I just stumbled. C'mon, Logan. Move."

"Christ Almighty," Logan said.

"Go." With my right hand, I unscrewed the cap to my canteen and then removed it from the harness. "Reach into my pack, will you Dennis?" My towel should be right on top."

I poured water over my left hand, and a little on the towel, and then vigorously rubbed my left hand and wrist. From the corner of my eye I could see Logan doing the same. When I finished, I threw the towel away. I shuddered at the thought of forgetting and wiping my face with it later on. I then made a careful detour of the foul mess in front of me and warned Dennis, telling him to pass the message down the line. As we cleared the area, and my left hand pressed against the damp, loamy soil, I continued to compulsively rub it in the dirt.

We set up not far from our first night's NDP, at the base of the bluff, across the valley from the hill. It was completely dark by then, and we made little effort to be tactically sound; we had a full company above our heads, with the CP. By chance, First Platoon ended up on the southwestern side of the perimeter, the only part of the small valley that had any significant tree cover, scant and shrub-like as it was. We settled in with only four positions of three men each, and the CP group, but in reality we were all fairly close to one another.

There was little conversation. Sergeant Wright sat off to one side, totally silent and introspective. John Wright and Helms murmured occasionally to each other, but soon fell silent. Hudson was at the company CP, talking to Schoch. No one slept, as tired as we all were. I could hear the low-pitched voices of the platoon all around me.

Hudson returned an hour or so later, and with him Schoch. They exchanged a last word or two, and then Hudson rolled out his poncho liner. I thought Schoch would return to the company CP, but instead he walked to where I was sitting, a few feet away, and sat heavily down beside me. Schoch was not close to anyone, except for O'Keefe, but if he did want to talk it was often me he would choose. I was never quite sure why.

The silence deepened; even the low murmuring had died away. I picked up a small twig lying at my feet and snapped it in two; the *crack* clove the soundless night.

"You a churchgoer, Frank?"

If he'd begun reciting *Gungha Din* in Urdish, I couldn't have been more surprised. It wasn't the use of my given name: It was the question itself. He had never before shown an interest in religion, one way or another. Schoch had told me, casually, as we discussed dog tags and what was written on them, that he was an agnostic, an adherent of the religion of None, as he'd dryly pointed out.

"No," I said briefly.

"No. Me neither." Schoch's head drooped to his chest. For a moment, I thought he'd finally fallen asleep. But he raised it again, to stare out past the few trees and into the long dark beyond them. "Do you believe in Hell? I mean, in punishment?"

I was vaguely irritated. I was tired, bone-tired, and the memory of a hundred beer-fueled, maudlin nights during my high school and college days jarred me. It was sophomoric and pretentious, I thought to have left this sort of thing behind along with all the other academic impedimenta.

"I don't know." I finally replied, since he seemed to expect an answer. "Dante's inferno ... it's vivid; you can picture it. His paradise is a vague blur. I've seen what hell must look like; the closest to heaven I ever got was sitting on the Via Veneto sipping Campari and watching the Italian girls go by."

Schoch shook his head. "You really believe that?"

I shrugged impatiently. "It's not important, Doc."

I couldn't have answered anyway, even if I wanted to. I simply didn't know. Of all the poetry I had read, in English, Italian or French, or in translations from the Greek, the Roman, Russian, German, Japanese — all of the world's great literature — I could remember only one complete poem, and it wasn't written by Shakespeare, or Keats, or Browning or Dante or Yeats or Schiller or Lorcas. It was written by a man with no name that I knew, and may not have been written by one man at all, although I believe it was. Whatever his name, he was a barefoot, illiterate hunter-gatherer from Africa, a member of a tribe whose name I forgot and could never recall. But one day, late in the afternoon, as the sun fell, or perhaps during the deep, fearful night, or in that grey, chill moment before dawn, this man had looked into his soul, and mine:

At Day's end, the Sun dies, and is no more
But in the morning, he comes again.

38. The Stain

At Night's end, the Moon dies, and is no more
But in the evening, he comes again.
At Life's end, man dies, and is no more
And he comes never again.

How could Schoch expect an answer? It was Forster, I remembered, who said we move between two darknesses. Why would we expect that the journey between the darknesses should be lit?

"I believe that I am hungry, and will have breakfast soon," I said. I was hoping that Schoch would go away, or at least leave me alone. For a moment, he did, staring out at the same darkness as I. But then he turned to me again.

"There is a hell, isn't there? I don't think there's a heaven. But hell...."

"Maybe. I don't know."

He shook his head forcefully, petulantly. "You're Catholic. Hell, I mean: You're Italian, and they're Catholics, aren't they? They believe in Heaven and Hell, don't they?"

I decided not to tell him that Italians were still the most pagan people on earth. "Well, some do."

"So? If there's Hell, who ends up there? I mean — who does the choosing?"

"You're asking the wrong guy. I spent 16 years in Catholic schools, mostly run by the Jesuits, and they're all Irish. Irish Catholics recognize only two sins: Fornication and masturbation. All the rest is okay."

"I'm trying to be serious."

"So am I. You have no idea what serious means until you've knelt in the confessional and told Father O'Malley that you put your hand on Mary Alice Foley's tit."

Schoch grinned in spite of himself, but then his face straightened again, quickly. I forestalled him, almost in a panic. I knew now what he wanted: Like Jessup a couple of days earlier, he wanted to confess, and I was no Sacerdote. I babbled hurriedly, before he could speak.

"A tit is good for 20 Hail Marys, 20 Our Fathers and at least a dozen complete Stations of the Cross. Father Burns was even worse: Fifty rosaries and extra Stations of the Cross. Get caught looking at a girl during religion class — well, the nuns didn't believe in that namby-pamby redemption stuff, so they'd just pound you with a ruler. Sex in any form was pretty damned painful."

I thought for a moment that this had quieted him, because he sat in silence, carefully stripping a dead fern of its curled brown fronds. After a minute or so, he threw it away with a quick flip of his wrist, and then placed his palms against the flat, squared cheeks of his face. He sat like that, very still, for several more moments before speaking.

"I can't sleep, you know?"

I was stubbornly determined not to respond to him, except in light-hearted jest. First Jessup, and now him. I'd felt pity and anger for Jessup, but nothing more; forgiveness was not mine to give. I felt the same pity and anger for Schoch. It would be an act of charity — one of the cardinal virtues— to listen to him, I knew; Christ would have listened. Well, no one has ever mistaken me for the Savior.

"Yeah. None of us is getting enough sleep," I replied. "I don't think I've slept at all these past few nights." In the dark three faces looked down at me: St. Onge, Westman, Jorgenson.

That poor, lost, uncertain part of me — the one with all the answers, with the superior smile so easily removed — whispered insistently that I had done nothing wrong. I had not fucked up. I had not screwed the pooch. I had been careful. I had been painstaking. I had been calm and level headed and professional and not once had I made a mistake that had cost lives. *It isn't my fault that you three died.*

So my modern, rational brain screamed in indignant protest. But the other part, the smaller, older, dumber, wiser part; the part that had grown up in the ancient plains and had watched the sun and the moon die; the part that had seen the harsh red sunset and ragged brown clouds blot out the day, and had heard the growl of The Beast across the night plains— that part muttered, in its primitive, visceral, marrow-fed way, of Original Sin. It was with you, the ancient voices whispered, when the Roman Legions with their sturdy legs and pitiless swords crossed the fields of Gaul. It was with you when the first farmer ploughed the rich soil of the Euphrates. It was with you when Homo Erectus chipped his pebble tools, and it was with you even when tiny Australopithecus peeped fearfully around the bole of a solitary acacia. Westman died to cleanse you of it, as others have died before him, as did that poor, sorrowing carpenter in Judea, but — and here the voices lowered, the chant slowed, and the words were spoken not in anger or triumph or derision, but in a bleak and desolate lament: *you will never be rid of it.*

I knew what Schoch wanted. I had heard the story. Not all at once, but in muttered bits and pieces; a word or two here and there. Briefly, I went over it in my mind, while he sat beside me, burdened with the weight of the Beast.

> *It was at the base of Dong Ngai, while I was on Hill 1485, and Sergeant Novak crouched despairing behind a tree. Contact was heavy, and there were wounded. Several of them lay hidden in a small fold, near the LZ, while a firefight raged a short distance away. The men guarding the LZ were pulled forward, leaving it empty, with only Schoch left behind with the wounded. He was standing apart from them, fortuitously hidden behind a small bush. In his hand he held an M16, belonging to one of the wounded men; it was one of several left in a pile by the LZ. Now that the security force was further up the hill, Evans, one of the wounded, had asked Schoch to grab his weapon.*
>
> *And as Doc stepped around the bush, he found two NVA standing before him, weapons raised, ready to fire on the knot of unarmed, wounded soldiers. Doc Schoch, a conscientious objector from California, was suddenly all that stood between five American soldiers and death. He had no time to think; he had no time to call for help. He had no time. And so, in a series of movements that he had never performed before, that he had never expected to perform, that he would not have performed for all the world and salvation itself, he raised the alien thing in his hands, and flicked off the safety, and fired directly into the backs of the NVA, ten, twelve, fourteen unending rounds, and he watched them topple and fall, slumped forward, to lie at the base of the small fold in death.*

38. The Stain

By now I was terrified; Schoch wanted to confess that sin, binding me to those wretched moments, so he had someone to share his guilt. I wanted no part of it. I had enough of my own. St. Onge, Westman, Jorgenson. Driven by that fear, I stood abruptly and walked away, a good five meters or so. Then I stopped; I could not see but I knew his eyes were fixed on my back, just another black shadow in the darkness. I sighed and returned to where he was seated, still staring into the darkness. I laid my hand on his shoulder for a brief moment. "I'm sorry, Doc," I said. And I was, but there was nothing I could do.

I made a quick round of the sector before returning to the CP. Helms sat with his back against a tree; even in the dark I could see his oval face and the small, boyish smile. But his eyes weren't boyish anymore; They were weary, inexpressibly weary, as no 20-year-old's should have been.

"Where you been, Lieutenant?" he asked.

"Here and there. Talking to Schoch. Why? Something going on?"

"Nah. Old Man called a while ago but it wasn't anything important. How's the Doc?"

"Okay," I lied. "Tired."

"Yeah. Me too." Dennis yawned suddenly. "Good man, Doc Schoch."

"Yes, he is." I looked around me. The night was cloudy, with the heavy feel of rain, but for some reason it was well lit; I could see fairly well. Sergeant Wright sat up against another tree, asleep, or at least with eyes closed. PFC Wright lay on the ground a few feet away, head resting on his pack, eyes open and glinting in the strange cloudy light. Brown was no longer there—evacuated with the other wounded; he had re-injured his wrenched shoulder. And Hudson ... I had no idea where he was. Perhaps he didn't either, I thought. But that was unfair, and I reproached myself for it. Hudson was no Schoch or O'Keefe or Muldoon, but he'd done his job. The CP looked so empty now, with or without his presence.

Helms must have sensed what I was thinking, for he said, "Things are too quiet without Doc Muldoon, aren't they."

"Yeah. I wonder how he's taking to Japanese beer?"

Helms smiled. "I don't reckon it'll make any difference to him, sir. Alcohol's alcohol."

I grinned back. "Yeah. Probably. The dumb shit's going to try to make up for the last six months all at once, I'll bet."

"Is that where he is, by the way? In Japan?"

I shrugged. "I don't know for sure, Dennis. Doc O'Keefe told me that's where most of our guys are going—Evans, then a hospital ship, and if it's long term, Japan. But I don't know for sure."

Wright woke up, or at least opened his eyes. "That's where they always end up," he said.

Helms nodded, yawned and stretched out his arms. His head was bare and his light brown hair was tousled and matted; he looked like a high school freshman, except for the thin wisp of beard along his jaw. I felt my own jaw: My stubble, after seven days, felt neither thin nor wispy. I fingered the thick, prickly hairs along my upper lip. God knows what I looked like.

The night was not only cloudy and damp, it felt oppressively hot. We'd been shivering the night before; now we sweated in the dark. Helms leaned over and grabbed a canteen from his gear. "Thirsty, Lieutenant?" he asked, unscrewing the top.

"A bit," I admitted. "You go ahead and drink first."

He nodded, tilted the canteen up and took a swallow. In the dark, I saw the sudden white as his eyes popped open, and he gagged convulsively, bringing the canteen down with a jerk. "Whoooeee," he gasped.

I raised an eyebrow. "What's wrong?"

Helms shook his head, eyeing the canteen speculatively, and then grinned. He handed me the container. "See for yourself, sir."

I took it from him, eyed both Wrights—the other had lifted his head up at Helms' snort—and sniffed. I raised both eyebrows. "Hmm." I took a swallow. "Holy shit," I said. "Where'd you get this stuff?" It was bourbon—harsh, rotgut, fiery stuff, that had never seen the inside of an oak barrel, but bourbon.

"I don't know," Helms said. "It was one of the ones we brought back with us, somebody else's gear. I thought it was water; this is the first time I tasted it."

I glanced over at Wright. There came a memory, from eons ago, of a young and earnest officer's feelings of outrage at his CO's drinking in the field. I liked that young lieutenant—he seemed such a nice, naïve fellow: I wondered where he'd gotten to.

"Well, whoever it is," I said, "here's to him." I took another swallow and passed the canteen to Sergeant Wright.

Top nodded, held up the canteen in a salute, and drank. He passed it on to PFC Wright and wiped his lips.

"Little rough on the throat, ain't it?" he grinned.

"Here's to 'em all," PFC Wright said. He raised it up, lowered it to his lips, and drank. Helms got it back and took another swallow.

"I didn't know you drank, Helms," I said, as he lowered the canteen.

"I don't, sir. Want some more?"

"No. But pass it on down the line. I guess everyone can use some tonight."

And it wasn't as if it had to go that far, I thought bitterly. There's only half a platoon left anyway.

The canteen made it all the way through the platoon, and was buried with full military honors at about 0400.

YC317988; Battalion CP; 16–17 May 1969

The morning came, as had almost all the mornings in the A Shau, cool and grey, with moisture dripping from the trees and brush, and in our hair. We rose stiffly, moving

38. The Stain

cramped or numbed limbs to get the circulation moving faster. Delta Company had already assembled on the bluff overhead; by 0700, they were moving through our positions, on their way to the mountain. We began moving up almost before they were through. There was no exchange of banter or even casual remarks; they moved through us in complete silence, and we stood and watched them without a word.

Reaching the Battalion CP, I gave a quick look around. Holes had been dug around the big perimeter, but not particularly elaborate or deep holes, considering how much time they'd had to work on them. A TOC had been set up, partially dug into the ground, partially built up with sandbags, and so had a couple of other structures inside the perimeter: A commo hut, a medic's hutch, and an S2 shop. Several staff officers were visible, standing around the TOC. I recognized few of them — most of the ones I knew had been wounded, or had been sent to replace line officers who'd been killed or wounded. I looked eagerly but in vain for Jerry Wolosenko. I found out later that he'd been flown in on the 15th but sent back to Camp Evans that very morning.

To my left was a strange-looking group; it took me a few seconds to realize that these were the war correspondents we'd been hearing about. There were about 10 or 12 of them, dressed in jungle fatigues but bareheaded and weaponless, and possessed of that detached insouciance that even more than their press badges identified them as media. One, a bearded tall man, took out a camera and began snapping pictures. I heard him say something to a companion, in French. The others watched us with disinterest and speculation both. I turned away. The camera kept clicking.

We moved through the CP area, and found our sectors. Captain Chappel's CP was a rude lean-to a few meters behind Black Jack's TOC. My own turned out to be a pair of adjacent foxholes, halfway up the barren shallow northeastern slope. From where I stood, I could only see more low ridges and hills; the A Shau itself lay behind them. But dominating the northern horizon was the awesome, shark-toothed Dong So, with its massive black shoulders and sharp, needle-tipped peaks. Behind me, but seen only as a dim, indistinct mass, lay the Beast.

We were given responsibil-

The author in the early hours of May 16, having just arrived at the battalion CP after Bravo had been pulled from our ridge the previous night.

ity for five positions, and each position consisted of a pair of two-man foxholes. It was impossible to man them; we simply didn't have enough people. Even with the CP group, we didn't have 20 men. But Sergeant Wright and I made the rounds, doing the best we could. We were promised replacements that day, or the next.

We lost another man even as we walked the perimeter. An unexpected Huey arrived, and left moments later, with Sergeant Hyde aboard. He took with him my undying but unspoken gratitude and admiration. It all happened so quickly that I had no time to say goodbye. It was probably just as well, I thought, when I heard the news a few minutes later. How could I have expressed what I felt without embarrassing us both?

I was glad — inexpressibly glad — that he was gone, and safely, but that meant that once again we were left with nothing at the squad leader level. Hyde was gone, Eden, who had blossomed so magnificently in just those few days, was gone, never to return — he would spend the next two years on crutches — and many of my most experienced men were dead or wounded.

Fifteen replacements were flown out to us later that day; we split them evenly across the company, five to each platoon. This brought our total to 21 — still grossly under strength, but at least we had enough to man the perimeter. There were 17 line troops, which meant that three of our positions were manned by three men and not four, but that couldn't be helped. We spent the day cleaning weapons, relaxing and watching the two shows someone provided for us.

The first of these was familiar enough; the Air Force was pounding the hill with 1,000 pound bombs. As I watched the mottled sleek shapes I was struck once again by their appearance. A modern warplane approaches the ultimate in functional design. The damned thing *looks* deadly, even standing still. When it's hurtling through the air with a 1,000-pounder under a wing it's the stuff nightmares are made of.

The second, more entertaining show was unaccustomed and unexpected: The news correspondents. By actual count, we tallied 17 different dives for cover during the afternoon, and we took not one incoming round. Almost any sound was enough to set them off. I imagined they would take their cue from us, and watch to see what we did. A few of them, to be fair, did that, or were veteran enough to understand what they were hearing. But some of them.... Once, a machine gun crew in Second Platoon test-fired their weapon, sending a heavy, sustained burst into the shallow valley below, and four newsmen standing nearby turned dead white. But a moment or two later, after almost peeing their pants, one of them walked up to a trooper and asked banal questions in the most condescending and offensive manner imaginable. It really was quite a performance.

It may have been this, or it may have been that I have never held newsmen in general in high regard — I'd read Colonel Lindbergh's account of the sleazy creeps who broke into his home to take pictures of his dead child — or it may be that some minor devil, undetected by the Sisters of Mercy, who otherwise had striven earnestly to bludgeon away all the little demons in me, whispered persuasively in my ear, but I got an idea while walking by their sleeping area late that afternoon. A few of them were industriously, if ineffectually, setting up their ponchos as tents for the night. I halted and watched them for a moment. One of them, a tall, blond fellow with — I swear — dimples, stopped what he was doing and gave me a nod. That was probably the trigger.

"Hi," I nodded back. "Mind if I make a suggestion?"

He spread his hands winningly. "Sure. Anything." I wondered if he was a TV correspondent. He had a nice, resonant baritone voice, and there *were* the dimples.

"Well," I said, "it's late afternoon and it hasn't rained. Generally, if it hasn't rained by now, it won't. I'd suggest you not put up your ponchos."

"Oh? Why not?"

I took an extra second to make sure my face stayed straight. "Well, there'll be a bright moon tonight, when these clouds pass by, and those ponchos of yours are new, and real shiny. NVA'll spot the moonlight off the top of your hutches a klick or two away. They've got positions all over these hills around us, and they'll triangulate and plot your position within ten meters. Then they call in their 82mm mortars, and...." I made a gesture.

The man's eyes widened fractionally. "Is that right? Sure. Oh. Thanks."

I waved negligently. "Not at all. It's as much for my safety as for yours. They don't always hit what they aim at, and it might be my hutch they hit. Take care."

I gave him a friendly smile and walked on. I could see him whispering to his friends, and as I moved down the hill, I saw them taking one of the ponchos down. I spent a good deal of the rest of the afternoon praying for rain. It stayed dry, though. Damn.

The Battalion CP remained near the original LZ, which was a broad, low, flat, grass-covered hilltop. Under normal circumstances, our company, even with the 15 replacements well under strength, could not have covered its broad expanse. The hill and its slopes were so bare and smooth, however, that we were able to space our positions out at twice the normal distance. Even so, several positions on the southeast side of the perimeters had to be manned by HHC soldiers who were given a rifle and thrown into the foxholes. The reason they were on the southeast side was that this was, in the estimation of the S3, the most vulnerable and the side most likely to be attacked, and according to Major Howard, this motley gaggle of wide-eyed, nervous cooks, clerks, typists, chaplain's assistants, maintenance crews and jeep drivers were the finest fighting men in the battalion. This imbecility was passed on at the S3's briefing later that evening. On hearing it, Captain Chappel, who had up to that moment retained a reticent and poker-faced calm, turned to me with arched eyebrows and pursed lips. I made a gesture with my hand. He had obviously not had prior contact with Howard. I did have a passing thought, as we listened to his drivel, about how Black Jack could possibly tolerate Howard and his nonsense, but I filed it away under the great unsolved mysteries of the universe. Honeycutt was a hard-ass SOB and all that, but he was a very competent and demanding commander. Maybe he kept Howard around as a sort of court jester.

After the briefing, Marsh Eward and I stood by the TOC and looked out over the hills and valleys around us. The sun was setting — it was not quite 1830 — but a bank of heavy dirty gray clouds over Laos leached it of most of its color; only a pale rose stain below and a deep mauve tint above the cloud bank marked the sun's presence. The sky over our heads was clear, but dull grey and dirty blue from the high haze; off to the east, above the high peaks, it was already a deep charcoal. The hills, never colorful even in the brightest sunshine, were clad in somber and funereal green. Even the rough grass at our feet seemed barren of life and color; brittle griseous stalks lying flat against the stippled ground.

Eward and I gave a slow look around the compass: West to Laos, north to the black Dong So; east to the A Shau, unseen behind the low ridges between us, and lastly south. I realized with a shock that this marked the first time all day I'd looked in the direction of Dong Ap Bia. Had I been avoiding its view? I recalled how many of us, in those last two or three days, sat with our backs to the mountain, like little children refusing to turn and look, for fear of the unseen beast. I started to say something about this to Eward but snapped my mouth shut quickly. Marsh, the most prosaic of men, would have merely stared at me and, possibly, taken my temperature. There was little to see up there anyway. We were facing the north slope, which was still thickly wooded.

"Those damn foxholes aren't dug deep enough," Eward said, after a moment.

"Hmm? Oh. No, I guess not. You'd think Delta or Charlie — especially Charlie — would have dug deeper."

"If we get mortared, we're in a world of shit."

"Yeah. Well, maybe not. At least there aren't any trees around us. No airbursts."

He shrugged. "It'll be assholes and elbows, anyway. I'm going into Evans tomorrow."

"No!" I said in surprise. "R&R at a time like this?"

"They're putting me aboard Bilk Two Three; I'm going to fly a recon with him, to see if I can spot some of those damned bunkers from the air." Eward nodded in satisfaction. "That ought to be fun. I've never flown in one of those things before."

"Good for you." I felt a vague disappointment. "How come you got picked to go? I'm smarter and better-looking than you."

"Because," he replied gravely, "at least I know what I'm looking for. I didn't hide behind a tree with my eyes closed the whole time."

We chatted a few more minutes before heading for our separate platoons. I'd made light of the matter with Marsh, but the truth was it did rankle a bit that I hadn't been asked. I'd never flown in one of those things either.

It was well past dark when we were called back up to the TOC for another briefing. Grumbling and snorting, the four of us, Chappel, Charles, Eward and I, joined the staff and liaison officers — about 15 of us in total — in the crowded TOC. Black Jack had just landed; he'd been up in his LOH all day, reconning the hill, as he did almost every day. Howard had begun the meeting before the colonel joined us, strutting about like Reepicheep on Benzedrine, but as soon as Black Jack stepped into the TOC Howard disappeared before our very eyes. He may even have kept on talking, but certainly no one was paying him any attention. Black Jack stood up on a small platform — an empty ammo box — looking the same as ever: Short, wiry, cocky, glacier-eyed and belligerent. I shook my head. Like him or not — and it was impossible to like him — he was the paradigm of a battlefield commander. If you wouldn't follow him, you wouldn't follow anybody.

His performance that night was typical: scathing impatience, icy contempt, corrosive belligerence, unbridled pugnacity. It occurred to me as I listened that this was a man to whom it would never occur to cease attacking. There are plenty of men — I'd like to believe that I am one of them — who never stop fighting as long as they're under attack, who will never give up; that's commonplace enough. Black Jack simply never stopped fighting. Odds meant nothing, one way or the other: A hundred against one or one against a hundred, his instinct was to attack, and keep attacking until the enemy was destroyed. All in all, I admitted grudgingly, I was glad he and I were on the same side.

39

The Storm

Battalion CP; YC317998; 18 May 1969

The 18th began as a hot, overcast day, with the certainty of another thunderstorm before the day was done. Once again the jets came in, sortie after sortie. Always, there was the scream and the tearing rumble, the smoky red flash, the dust cloud and, seconds later, the heavy crump. We were too far away to hear the other, deadlier sounds: the click of the release mechanism, the patter of dirt, the heavy chunk! of falling casing, the tortured whistling of shrapnel. There was an odd, disjointed feel to all this; we were spectators now, in a way that we could not be just two days earlier. These sorties were remote events, momentary flashes in a dull green landscape, distant cloudbursts in a far off sky.

After finishing our morning chores, such as they were, we filtered up to the company CP, where the radios were set to the various frequencies. Chappel, his helmet off, revealing a prematurely balding blond head, sat amidst the RTOs—unfamiliar faces, all; not one of those who'd come in with us a week ago was left—listening on the mikes, but as more and more people arrived—Eward and Charles were there, of course, and Sergeant Garza, and even Sergeant Wright and Sergeant Stempin, now Lou Charles's platoon sergeant—he had the RTOs turn up the volume on the radios, so we could all listen in.

Eward's flight with Bilk had been postponed. We stood or knelt alongside each other during a good part of the morning, listening and commenting. Unlike the time at Brick, when we'd monitored the CAs, however, we weren't very vocal. Back in March, never having seen combat, we were all experts, eager to point out a deficiency or mistake. Now, we listened, and said little beyond a soft expletive or a word or two and a glance.

As the morning went on, and the volume of sound from the mountain increased, we quieted even more and listened tensely. At 1100, Bilk Two Three called in to sign off; he and his big brothers were done for the day. Now the companies began moving up the ridges. Delta was on the center ridge—our ridge. Dave Lipscomb was another OCS classmate of mine, and I had spoken briefly with him on the radio, warning him about the clearing, the knolls and the interlocking fields of fire.

39. The Storm

Most of the traffic came over the Battalion Net — Black Jack, as usual, was in his LOH over the battlefield, and the transmissions came through clearly. Delta called in first: They killed two NVA along the trail just above our NDP. Eward and I exchanged glances. That meant they were still well below the clearing. Alpha, moving along the southernmost ridge, the one on which Charlie had been devastated a few days before, met nothing — no resistance at all. Perhaps, we commented, the enemy had finally pulled back. Laos was only a couple of kilometers away.

There was no sign of the 1/506th; they were moving up from the south, along the far southern slopes of Hill 900, the companion to Hill 973. In theory, their lead elements should have been within a kilometer or less of Alpha's column; the ridge they were on led up to the saddle between Hill 900 and Hill 973. But nothing was seen or heard to indicate that the Currahees were anywhere near the hill.

The next hour was more of the same: Cautious, slow advances, brief exchanges of small arms fire, few if any casualties and no sign of a determined enemy resistance. By now, 1300, the two companies were well up their respective ridgelines, almost to the top. Garza returned from a check of the perimeter to point out the heavy, blackish cloud barrier to our west: The daily thunderstorm would come early. We hurriedly covered the radios with ponchos, to keep the rain off of them. Nothing, we knew, would keep us dry.

It was shortly after that, around 1330, that the rifle fire, which had been light and sporadic, suddenly increased in volume. I was back at my platoon sector, checking on something, and at the noise I looked up to see a decided stir in the group around the radios. A couple of newsmen, who'd been standing nearby, looking out over the hills to the north, began running toward the TOC, where the correspondents were listening to the radio. I jogged up to the company CP.

"What's up?" I asked Lou Charles, but he made a shushing motion with his hand.

"Something's going on with Delta," he muttered in a low voice. One of our RTOs switched his radio to the Delta Company net. There was a sputter and crackle of static, made worse by the approaching storm, and then a voice, clear but too loud, broke through the static.

"...real heavy fire from our north. I'm going to try to take this knoll to my right, over."

"Roger. I've got ARA on the way. Keep pushing."

"Who is it?" I whispered to Eward.

"Don't know. One of the Delta guys."

"That bit about the right-hand hill — you think he's up in the clearing?"

Eward nodded. "Sounds like it." He shook his head. "Also sounds like he's taking casualties."

"This is Three Six," the voice sounded again. "I'm going to need more ammo. My Mike Sixty ammo is running low, over."

"Who's Three Six?" Charles asked.

"Lipscomb," I muttered. "Dave Lipscomb. Damnit, I warned him about that clearing."

"Three Six, this is Delta Six," the other voice responded. There was a long silence — on the radio, that is. On the ground, the noise level continued to increase; by now the firefight had reached almost the same level of intensity as the 14th and 15th.

"Three Six, this is Six," the CO repeated. And, a moment later: "Three Six, Three Six, this is Six. Do you copy, over?"

Eward and I exchanged cold, grim looks. Three Six had been on the horn only seconds before...

"Three Six, goddamnit, get on the horn! Three Six, Three Six. This is Six."

Black Jack's hard-edged tenor broke in. "Delta Six, this is Black Jack. What's going on?"

"This is Delta Six. I can't raise my Three Six all of a sudden. He was taking fire, but he said he thought he could take this hill to his right, just above the clearing. I better go up there and see what's going on."

"This is Black Jack. Keep pushing. Don't stop. If he's on that hill, get the rest of your unit up there *now*. Don't give them a chance to throw him off of it, do you copy?"

"Roger."

I had a sick feeling in my stomach. Dave had gone through the clearing, but the NVA had had the better part of two days to rebuild his defenses there. Then a new voice came over the company net.

"Delta Six, this is Three Five, over."

"Roger, Three Five. Where's Three Six."

"Three Six is down. He's gone. So are two of my squad leaders. We need some help up here."

"Roger. Did you take that hill Three Six was talking about?"

"Negative. We're on this saddle between two hills, taking some real heavy fire. I can't move my —" The voice broke off; we could distinguish the RPG explosions even from a kilometer away.

"We're on our way," Delta Six was saying.

I turned my back on the radio for a moment. Dave Lipscomb — short, dark-haired, wiry, intense. I had known him only casually at OCS — Personnel hadn't put a whole lot of thought into splitting up the candidates into the various platoons: It was all done alphabetically, and First Platoon's roster ranged from A to E. Dave had been in Third Platoon, as I recalled. And our paths hadn't crossed much here; by chance, our contact with Delta Company had been limited. I hadn't gotten to know Lipscomb very well. I never would, now.

We listened to the two nets for the next ten minutes. Alpha Company, moving along the ridge south of Delta, had suddenly run into increased resistance and were engaged in firefights of their own, not as intense as what Delta was facing but enough to slow their progress to a virtual halt. Delta Three Five — Lipscomb's platoon sergeant, a tough old World War II vet named Carlisle — had gathered up the remnants of Delta's Third Platoon on the saddle between the two hills, those two damned, terrible knolls guarding that butcher block of a clearing. Lipscomb had assaulted the right-hand knoll, as we had tried to do for seven days — it was the nearer of the two, and appeared to lead directly up to the summit of Dong Ap Bia itself. Apparently, he had succeeded in making it up to the top of the knoll with two squads, but there, caught in the crossfire from the north (or left-hand) knoll and the summit before him, had been annihilated. Carlisle, with the platoon's First Squad, had fought his way up to the saddle, where he gathered the remnants of the other squads, but he was now cut off from the rest of Delta. Jerry Walden, Delta One Six, was trying to bring his platoon across the clearing to link up with Carlisle.

Sergeant Carlisle, with incredible skill, fought his way back up the slopes of the south knoll and reached the summit, where he found the bodies of Lipscomb, his RTO and several others. The rest of the company tried to link up with him. Lee Sanders, the Delta CO, was hit and turned command of Delta over to the only officer left, Walden, who'd been with the company only since late April. He too was wounded moments later, and with him his platoon sergeant. The entire company was trapped, and their casualties mounted, threatening to overwhelm them, as they had Charlie Company three days before.

Alpha Company was steadily pushing up the south ridge, but encountering more and more resistance. Frank McGreevy was hit while his platoon was still below the clearings where Charlie Company had been ripped up in days before; Dan Bresnahan's Third Platoon was moved up and took over the assault. It was hard going; tough, bunker-by-bunker advances, at close quarters, fought as much with grenades as with rifle fire — the same stuff we had faced over the past week. But Harkins was reporting his lead elements were within sight of the summit; another hundred meters of fighting would bring them to the top of the hill. Walden, before he was knocked out of the fight, had reported the same thing — but of course, as we subsequently found out, he'd mistaken the knoll, on which Lipscomb's body still lay, as the summit. It was an easy thing to do, if you were lying or kneeling at its base.

So hopes were high at that moment, despite the losses. And then it all started to fall apart. The first blow was the loss of Walden and Stearns, his platoon sergeant. Not long after that, we listened incredulously to the exchange between Black Jack and Harkins: Alpha was taking fire from their right flank, from a ridgeline near the summit of Hill 900.

"Bullshit!" Black Jack responded. "That can't be. That's where the Five Oh Six is."

Bowers, the battalion Commander of the 1/506th, had reported that his lead company was on the south crest of Hill 900, the southern peak of Dong Ap Bia, and about 500 meters from Hill 937. In other words, they were hard on Alpha's flank, no more than 100 meters from them.

After a minute or so of should-be and can't-be, Honeycutt concluded that Bravo

Company, 1/506th, was inadvertently firing on Alpha 3/187th's advance. He was flying that day with Crazy Rairdon, and the two of them took the fragile LOH and buzzed over the ridge on which the 506th supposedly was, and drew immediate fire—from AK-47s.

A few moments later, he radioed Bowers to tell the CO of the 506th that his lead company was 300 or 400 meters southwest of where they thought they were—on a ridge to the west and well away from Alpha's ridge. The ridge supposedly occupied by friendly troops was instead crawling with NVA, firing down on Alpha.

In the meantime, Charlie Company, reinforced by a squad from our own Third Platoon, was moving along the trail between the Battalion CP and Bravo's ridge—we always thought of it that way—up which Delta was advancing. They were bringing ammo for the seriously depleted Delta troops, and were also to serve as a reserve. Even before they reached the trail junction that marked the beginning of the ridge, the company began receiving fire from both flanks—the north draw and the area west of the trail. No one was killed, but a few were wounded and the resupply column ground to a halt, several hundred meters short of our old NDP, which Delta was using as a CP and collection point for the wounded.

To cap a miserable week's performance, our air support struck again: A Cobra, flying unauthorized in the area, fired on Charlie Company's column, wounding several troopers. An apoplectic Black Jack ordered the Cobras and gunships out of the area. In addition to wounding several, this deprived us of genuine air support: How could we trust these guys? In the end, a staggering 30 percent of our casualties were to come from friendly fire.

Delta was by now hanging on by their fingernails; seriously shorthanded, almost depleted of ammo, and facing an increasingly aggressive enemy pressure from the south ravine—the same one from which they'd launched the attack against us. Black Jack was screaming at Jessup to move his company up

Lt. Col. Weldon "Black Jack" Honeycutt yells orders over a field radio to a company working its way up the ridgeline toward Dong Ap Bia (AP Photo/Hugh Van Es).

39. The Storm

through the fire and up the ridge to link up with Delta. Finally, at about 1430, they did so. But by that time, the situation, so promising an hour before, had deteriorated to the point of disaster. Delta simply didn't have enough people left to bring back their own dead and wounded, much less continue the assault.

Jessup was ordered to send a platoon up the ridge to link up with Delta's lead elements. The job fell to Joel Trautman, naturally enough — he was the sole remaining veteran platoon leader. Joel began moving his platoon up the ridge, past the NDP, up to the razorback section below the clearing, and there got pinned down. While Delta's remaining troopers in the clearing began to maneuver their way around the base of the knolls, Trautman urged his men up through the clearing to their aid. He'd taken perhaps two steps before he was hit by machine gun fire, and knocked off his feet into the draw along the trail.

As he lay there bleeding heavily from his wounded leg, the rest of his platoon, and the men of Delta, remained pinned down by increasingly intense fire. By now, further assault was the last thing on their minds. Their survival was in question.

At the base of the ridge, Honeycutt landed at Bravo's old LZ and moved up to the NDP a hundred meters up the ridge. He talked to a few of the wounded, and was on the radio when the NVA came boiling out of the same draw in the south ravine from which they'd hit us two days earlier. For a moment, it appeared that we'd lose a battalion commander, as well as the better part of two companies, because if the NVA succeeded in overrunning the NDP, they would cut off Delta and Trautman's platoon from the LZ and trap them in the clearing and the narrow, indefensible razorback trail. The attack was beaten off, but just barely.

And then the storm broke.

We'd seen something similar, that second day, but this was even worse. This wasn't rain: It was as if the sky had opened up and dropped the Red Sea on our heads. But it was far worse for another reason. Days of constant bombing, intense artillery and maneuvering had stripped the upper slopes of both ridges bare of all vegetation; trees were reduced to blackened sticks; the brush, vines and ground cover was wiped from the ground — and the dirt had been pounded and pulverized into a grayish powder. When the heavy rain came, there was nowhere for it to go, nothing left to absorb it. A mountain forest is a huge, efficient sponge, easily absorbing the tons of rainwater dumped on its slopes. But not today: There was no forest left up there.

Way back in February and early March, we'd encountered a similar problem on a much smaller scale, when, during the rains of the monsoons, we followed trails muddied and torn by a hundred or more booted men up a steep slope. But then, it had just been a narrow trail surface, and the mud had been compacted; the top one or two inches were slippery, but below that remained the still-firm ground.

Not on these slopes. This wasn't just a trail surface; this was an entire mountainside that had been stripped bare. The water, tons of it, penetrated the loosened soil, turning it quickly into a liquid, slurry-like wave. Gravity took care of the rest.

Men were literally washed down the slopes, absolutely powerless to stop their descent. There was nothing to grab onto, nothing to stop them as they were carried down by the flowing mud and water. This wasn't a case of someone slipping and sliding, as we'd experienced: Soldiers were simply scoured off the face of the mountain as if by a fire hose. Those few troopers with Carlisle, on the south knoll, found themselves in a muddy heap at its base moments after the rain began. Alpha's advance was stopped dead for the same reason; men who'd fought and labored to advance 20 or 30 feet in the teeth of enemy fire suddenly found themselves 15 or 20 meters down the slope, unable even to see where the ridge was anymore.

Fortunately, the rain took no side in the battle. It reduced visibility for the NVA equally; they couldn't see to fire down on the suddenly helpless Americans any more than the troopers could see to shoot at them. Also fortunately, Bravo and Alpha companies of the 506th were able to advance far enough to take some of the pressure off the beleaguered Rakkasans. Since their slopes, south of Hill 900, had not been hit by bombs and artillery, the trees and ground cover remained in place, and sucked up the downpour. They, at least, could move.

But it was also evident that they couldn't move fast enough or far enough to secure Hill 900, and if they couldn't do that, then our battalion, by now decimated and unable to advance in the teeth of the storm, could not hope to win back the ground they'd paid so dearly for over the morning hours. At 1530, Honeycutt reluctantly ordered Charlie and Delta to withdraw; Alpha was told to hold in place until her battered sister companies could remove their dead and wounded. They had to do so: The area south of Alpha's ridge, instead of being in control of the 1/506th, as planned, was swarming with NVA. If Alpha had moved back prematurely, the enemy could have followed right on their heels and caught all three companies at the base of the center ridge. Alpha had to fight off a couple of more assaults along its flanks before finally, late in the afternoon, pulling back from their ridge.

The final blow came when Alpha linked up with Delta. Charlie and Delta had managed to retrieve all their wounded — Joel Trautman, lying helpless on the side of the upper ridge, was among the last rescued, and it took a determined assault by several Delta troopers to do that — but Delta's dead, including Dave Lipscomb, were still on the knoll, left behind; it had been impossible to move up the mudslide to get to them. First Alpha tried, while it was still raining, and then, late that night, after the rains ceased, Charlie and some men from Delta moved back up to the clearing and up the still-muddied slope to bring the last of them down, somewhere around midnight.

The mood in the battalion that night was one of bitter exhaustion. It wouldn't be an exaggeration to say that many of the troops, even the unwounded ones, were in shock that night. Later, perhaps, we would understand how close we came that day to breaking the enemy's back — all elements, including the Currahee's lead companies, had been within 100 meters of the summit of the hill, and the 29th had by this point already suffered over a thousand casualties—but in the late afternoon hours of the 18th, while we stood chilled by the day's rain, such things seemed remote.

Bravo's CP was deathly quiet as the transmissions over the various radio nets slowed to an occasional rasp of static. The storm, easily the worst we'd experienced, instead of moving through the valley rapidly, as its previous brethren had, remained glowering overhead, with occasional flashes of lightning and low rumbles of thunder. A fine grey haze covered the eastern sky, that portion of it that the heavier slate-grey clouds did not; to the west, the sun was visible only as a faint, indistinct smear of light grey, tinged with dirty orange, on the featureless horizon. The air, as usual, smelled of damp mold and rotting leaves; it blew from the southwest.

Word of the debacle spread quickly. The men sat around their foxholes, quiet and with heads hung. The newcomers were apprehensive and nervous; the veterans despondent and surly. I walked around the perimeter alone, slowly, hands on hips, head bent, depressed, angry and numb. I reached the southeast corner of the perimeter and immediately turned around. I stopped, furious with myself, and brought my head up with a jerk. Once again, I was avoiding looking at the Hill. I turned back, lips pressed into a tight snarl. There it lay, grey and motionless in the sunless light, sprawled across the earth like the demonic beast that it was.

Damn you; you know I fear you, don't you! You know I'm praying to a God that I don't even think exists that I never have to set foot on your flanks again. Is there blood enough on this earth to satisfy you?

I returned to the platoon, stone-faced. Helms, his face stained with mud, looked up as I approached, opened his mouth to say something, and, seeing my expression, shut it. No one else even looked my way.

Battalion CP; Waiting; YC317998; 19 May 1969

The next morning, the 19th, Eward left early for Camp Evans, to board that spotter plane. Sometime later a polished, hatched Huey—a command helicopter—landed, and Zais, the Division Commander, alighted, along with his staff. What none of us knew then was that an intense but behind-the-scenes debate, reaching up to the highest levels of MACV and beyond, to the Secretary of State, was held to determine the final decision on what to do next. Only much later would we learn, for example, that the 2/506th was already airborne—Lt Col Sherron, their Battalion Commander, was in his command helicopter, hovering over the LZ, ready to drop down on the battalion LZ and relieve us. Black Jack, unaware of this until Sherron landed, convinced Zais to give him one last chance at the hill; all he needed, he told the CG, was one company in direct support and for the other units—the 1/506th, the 2/3rd ARVNs, the 2/501st—to perform their part of the mission. Honeycutt insisted to the CG, with some justification, that the Rakkasans had not yet been thrown off the hill by the NVA; our two main assaults had been stopped by our own incompetent ARA and the ill-timed and extraordinary rainstorm.

We knew nothing of this, but we did know that Alpha Company, 2/506th, landed on the LZ on the 19th, to back up Delta on the center ridge—*our* ridge. I was on the LZ when they arrived, and the first platoon off the Hueys was led by Len Maher, another OCS classmate of mine. Alpha wouldn't linger long—they were moved out to join Delta almost immediately—but Len and I did have a chance for a brief word or two.

"You've been on the hill, haven't you?" he asked, after an exchange of greetings.

"Yeah. We got pulled out day before yesterday."

"Yeah. You're with Bravo, then?"

"Yeah."

"Jim Goff—he's with Bravo, right?"

"No. Jim was with Charlie."

Maher shook his head slightly and frowned. "Was?"

"He was hit a few days ago. Wounded. So was Joel Trautman. And..." I hesitated.

"Yeah?"

"Dave Lipscomb's dead. He bought it yesterday."

Maher lowered his head for a moment and then raised it, his face expressionless. He and Lipscomb had been in the same training platoon in 55th Company at OCS, and were good friends. He looked over my shoulder in the direction of the hill. The beast couldn't quite be seen from where we stood.

"That thing must be a motherfucker," he said. A few minutes later, we shook hands, wished each other luck, and he and the rest of his company began that trek to the base of the ridge.

There was little to do at this point. I wrote some letters home, the first in over a week, and cleaned my rifle and a .45 that I'd somehow picked up on the hill. I made the rounds of the platoon sector just after noon; I was struck, and vaguely bothered, by the lassitude and indifference of the troops. It wasn't hard to understand. These men had been on an adrenalin high for seven days and nights, without sleep. Not even 20-year-olds in prime condition can recover from that overnight.

The rest of the day was spent in maneuvering the battalions. The ARVNs were relocated to the east side of the mountain, below the peak of Hill 900. The 2/501st was brought in to a small bare ridge north of Hill 937, and began to cross the intervening ridges that lay athwart their path to the hill. The 1/506th continued their advance, slow as it was, from the south. And of course, our companies, reinforced by Alpha of the 506th, gathered at the base of the two ridges to the west. The third ridge, the one farthest north, was abandoned. The terrain there was simply too difficult.

At 1400 of the 19th, the mortars came. We heard the dull, hollow thump and heads jerked up all around, in a vain and somewhat witless attempt to spot the mortar round and its launcher. A few seconds later, a cloud of dust spurted up from a ravine some 800 or 900 meters to the northwest; a little more than three seconds later, we heard the dull, low crump of the explosion. The next thump sounded a few seconds later; this round landed a bit closer, about 500 meters out.

I walked up to the CP, where Captain Chappel was already on his radio. Around us, the men were making their way to the foxholes, but slowly, almost leisurely. There was no hurry at that: The NVA gunner was walking his rounds up to us, and was taking his time doing it. His performance so far hadn't been any too impressive. I waited until Chappel got off the horn and, when he looked my way, quirked an eyebrow at him.

"Radar's on it," he nodded. "There's some ARA on station for when we find 'em."

"Shit," I said distinctly. "I'm a lot more afraid of the fucking ARA than I am of the gook mortars."

Chappel frowned but said nothing. Well, he hadn't been on the receiving end of 2.75 rockets.

As I returned to my own CP, I smiled at the sight of the newsmen, crouching uncertainly behind their sandbagged sleeping area. They knew the mortars were aimed at us, but were unsure what to do; they saw little evidence, from our reaction, that we thought there was any danger. As a matter of fact, however, I was something less than totally carefree as I approached the perimeter. Too many of the troops were still wandering around, helmetless and even weaponless. I wasn't worried about the mortars, but there wasn't any law that prevented the NVA from launching a ground attack, however unlikely such an attack might be.

A few moments later, however, all the perimeter positions were manned. The CP group — except for Sergeant Wright, who was in a position up front — stayed out for a while, looking over the area in front of our sector, until two rounds landed about 100 meters away. We all jumped in then, crouching and waiting. The next two, however, landed even farther away.

"Christ," PFC Wright muttered in disgust. This guy must be smokin' somethin'. Tell him to quit wasting our time."

"It's bad shooting," I agreed. So far, none of the rounds had landed anywhere close to the LZ, and that was one big target. The phrase "couldn't hit the ocean if he was standing in it" came to mind. PFC Wright was right; it was a waste of everyone's time.

The ARA came around a few minutes later, raking the hills and valleys to our northwest with white-streaked rockets. Whether they hit the enemy mortar position, or merely scared it off, or if the NVA just gave up in humiliation, we couldn't tell, but within a few minutes of the ARA's arrival the shelling ceased. Gradually we relaxed. There had been the possibility, however slight, that the mortars had merely been cover or prep for a sapper or infantry attack. Mind you, none of us really thought it was so: The NVA had been doing some very strange and unsettling things up here but a frontal assault on a dug-in position covered by air and artillery would have been more than strange: It would have been downright imbecilic.

We maintained full alert status for another half-hour anyway, but then we returned to normal. There was a stir among the newsmen and staff a short while after that. A recently captured NVA prisoner was brought in to await a Huey ride back to Camp Eagle for interrogation and a POW camp. He had been part of a trail watching team that had been ambushed by a patrol from Alpha Company. I walked by the TOC, where he was being kept, a little while later. He sat huddled on the ground, his arms tied behind him, his khaki uniform stained and torn. His eyes were dull and glassy, as if he were in shock, and he very well may have been. I felt a brief stab of pity; he seemed child-like, tiny, miserable. But then I recalled that his might have been the hand that fired the RPG. I tightened my lips and moved on. As I walked away, I saw, from the corner of my eye, Howard standing by the prisoner, posturing and pontificating to the assembled newsmen. This pleased me greatly. Howard had had nothing at all to do with his capture and would have nothing to do with his interrogation, but he would have disappointed me cruelly had he acted otherwise.

I sat down at my own CP and listened to a low-voiced, dispute between the two RTOs; Helms, as always, calm and measured, PFC Wright intense and emphatic. My mind was somewhere else, and couldn't quite register the meaning of their words.

Pack! Pack!

We cast startled looks at each other. AK-47 rounds, unmistakably. And they'd come from the northeast sector — Second Platoon's. Automatically, Helms held out the mike as we twisted about and flopped onto our stomachs, our free hands grabbing for our weapons. There was nothing on the net; no one was speaking at all. I saw several men, Eward — returned from Evans and the Bilk flight — among them, running in the direction of the perimeter, and a moment later a heavy burst of fire — outgoing M16 and M60 — ripped through the air. I got to my knees and took a quick look at my sector. Everything was okay except for two of the newcomers who were standing, rubbernecking, trying to glimpse what was happening in Second Platoon. I pursed my lips in wrath and had already taken two or three angry steps when Sergeant Wright's large bulk materialized alongside them. Seconds later they were in their foxholes, looking chastened and looking out.

ARA was gone, but a brace of Cobras was on station, and the sky over the east perimeter was streaked orange and white by their tracers as they laced the area from which the shots had come. While the sleek dark gunships made their runs, four men, carrying a stretcher, hurried up the slope, past the company CP and up to the LZ, on which, fortuitously, a Huey was sitting, waiting to return to Evans. A moment later the wounded man was on his way to the hospital. The Cobras, like a pair of angry foxhounds, still sniffed and snarled and spat.

Nothing was said over the radio, and we were still on alert so I couldn't leave my CP area, so it wasn't until Sergeant Wright returned to the CP that we found out what had happened. His normally calm, unruffled expression was the same, but there was a hint of angry satisfaction in the set of his mouth and jaw. He sat down beside me, ripped the helmet from his head, dropped it to the ground, and ran a hand through his heavy, crinkly hair.

"You hear what happened?" he asked, after lighting a cigarette.

"No. Nothing's come over the horn."

He nodded, and blew out a stream of smoke. "Second Platoon trooper went outside the perimeter to take a crap. Didn't take nobody with 'im. He got 30, 40 meters out and a gook sniper got him. In the back, and through the chest."

PFC Wright shook his head. "He went out by himself? Nobody with him? The dumb shit."

Sergeant Wright nodded. He gave a flick of a half-smile and looked at me. "Guess who it was?"

"I don't know," I said, but even before I finished saying it I realized that I *did* know.

"Morris."

I nodded. Of course. "Yeah. If anyone would do something like that...."

"*That* ain't no surprise," he agreed. "But you shoulda seen 'im when they went out an got 'im." Wright allowed that hint of satisfaction to show once more. "He was blubberin' like a baby, Lieutenant. Cryin' and sayin' 'Thank you! Thank you!' over an' over. Kept holdin' on to Doc Schoch's hand. Couldn't believe they'd gone out there to get 'im."

John Wright snorted. "Well, what the fuck did the sonuvabitch expect? That'd they'd just leave 'im there?"

"That's exactly what he expected," I said.

"Oh, bullshit!" he answered.

I grinned. PFC Wright was filling the void left by Muldoon. "The proper way to disagree with a superior officer," I said mildly, "is to say something like: 'Are you sure that's the case, sir?'"

PFC Wright nodded, thoughtfully. "Right. Are you fuckin' well sure that's the case, sir?"

"You didn't know Morris, did you?" Helms interjected, surprisingly.

"No. I mean, yeah, I'd seen him around, an' all, but I was here only about a week before he got transferred."

"He really thought that. Believe it," Helms said.

Wright scowled at all of us in turn. "Well, he's the dumbest sonuvabitch I ever heard of, then."

I looked at Sergeant Wright. "Do you think he finally gets it now, Top?"

He shook his heavy brown head. "I don't know, Lieutenant. Maybe. Maybe not. One minute ain't gonna change a lifetime."

I nodded. I despised Morris and his self-destructive anger, but then, I told myself sharply, I had to remember that I had been raised in privilege and comfort. I had no idea — none — of what it meant to grow up poor and black in the American South of the 1950s.

Twilight of the 19th was now upon us. The western sky over the Laotian mountains was, for once, clear of clouds, and a spectacular sunset was the result. The entire western sky was a sheet of intense rose, streaked with scarlet, amber, gold, pale yellow, green and mauve. The air felt almost liquid; heavy, clear, silent as an ocean deep. The men were subdued. Hardly a sound marred the evening stillness. Even the animals, usually at their most active at this time of night, were quiet. It was a scene of peace and beauty, but it was a watchful peace, a peace of tension and anticipation, and it was a disquieting beauty: The sunset mirrored the red shield of Mars, the harbinger of a darker, more terrible red in the morning.

The silence was shattered by a sudden, unexpected yell. Heads snapped around. A single figure stood, outlined against the sky, bare headed, shirtless, hands on hips. My eyes widened in disbelief. It was Grump Ulrich, and he stood facing, not the sunset, but the darkening eastern sky, the sky over the Crouching Beast.

"Hey! HO Chi Minh! We're comin' over there tomorrow and we're gonna stomp your skinny yellow ass off that mountain! DO YOU HEAR ME?"

With that, he turned and slouched past us back to his position, his face set in its perpetual scowl. It ought to have been comic, or even pathetic. And yet it wasn't. I felt my heart lift as it had not since the first day of the battle.

I bowed my head, so the others could not see the tears in my eyes. Perhaps I was wrong about God. Perhaps He did exist after all. A cold and mechanical evolution could not explain Grump Ulrich, or Hyde and Westman and Helms ... *Thank you. Thank you, if You do exist, for allowing me the privilege of knowing these men.*

Sometime during the day, or perhaps earlier, during the night, Abrams, Stillwell and Zais made the decision to continue the attack.

40

The Naked Beast

Dong Ap Bia; YC327982; 20–21 May 1969

Marsh Eward and I settled in an out-of-the-way corner of the TOC the next morning, early—it was not yet 0630. Marsh had been asked there, since he'd made the flight with Bilk on the 19th, it was thought that perhaps he might be of use if questions about bunker emplacements arose. I had no business there at all, but the communications were far better there than at our own CP, and I was determined to hear what happened.

Eward had told me, the previous night, of his recon flight. Seen from the air, he said, the hill was almost completely bare all along the top; what few trees remained standing were solitary posts stripped of branches. Craters pockmarked the slopes and in some places had obliterated the terrain feature entirely. And still, the bunkers were hardly visible. New fighting positions—nothing more than foxholes—had been hastily dug into the slopes of the two knolls overlooking our clearing—to Eward and me, it would always be remembered thus. The bodies of several NVA were plainly visible in the draw to the south of the knolls, Marsh added; the enemy had lacked the time and perhaps the men to crawl down and retrieve them. The entire hilltop, he said, was blasted into desert.

The sun was well up in the sky when, at 0730, the assault began. From early dawn to just moments before, the 8-inch and 175 artillery from Berchtesgaden and Currahee pounded the hill. We went outside to observe some of it. Dust and smoke lay over the mountain, obscuring the crests and upper slopes. There was nothing to see. Eward and I returned to the TOC and sat.

The first half-hour seemed to be a repetition of the previous ten days: The lead platoons pushed up the ridges without significant opposition until they reached the bunkers in and around the clearings, and then got pinned down. We could hear the small arms fire swell in volume from where we sat, almost two kilometers from Alpha's ridge. It seemed the same, but in reality it was not. This time the attacks were coordinated. Repeatedly, we heard references to the 2/3rd—the ARVN force—progressing up the steep eastern ridges. At one point, indeed, Captain Remington, a Brigade S3 officer, whom we knew slightly, made the comment that Iron Raven was spending a good deal of his time trying to get the ARVNs to slow their advance.

"What for?" Eward snorted. "It's their war, ain't it?"

Remington laughed but explained: Conmy was worried that the ARVNs would reach the top, move across the hill and run into the fire of the advancing U.S. troops.

The 506th was finally breaking through the bunkers on the south slopes, and had advanced up to Hill 900; they were slowed there by intense RPG fire from the bunkers on the crest, but at least Alpha's flank was no longer threatened. Delta, with Alpha of the 2/506th in close support, had already re-taken the south knoll; minutes later, a platoon from the 2/506th — I wondered if it was Len Maher's—finally took the left-hand, or north, knoll and the saddle in between. Now they were within 75 meters of the crest, and no longer had to face the withering crossfire of the knolls.

But it was Alpha Company that struck the biggest, or at least the most spectacular blow. Pinned down, unable to advance in the face of the still-heavy fire from the crest, Harkins tried to rally his troops for one last surge forward — they were within sight of the crest. He was wounded moments later, when an AK round took off part of his ear; blinded by the blood and unable to hear well, he continued to urge his men on, but they were hugging the ground, trying to avoid the intense small arms fire from the bunkers.

And that's when Spec4 Johnny Jackson decided enough was enough.

Jackson, in Alpha's Third Platoon, was one of the oddest physical specimens I'd ever seen. A football player in high school, he seemed to be put together from two completely different bodies: From the chest down he was blade-thin and wiry, with narrow hips and stick legs. But his neck and shoulders belonged on an NFL linebacker. That's one reason that, as thin as he was, he carried his squad's M60. Lying in a small crater, hearing the M16 fire around him sputter to a halt as more and more troops hugged the ground, he suddenly got angry. Besides, he said later, he was already so far up the ridge that if he tried to retreat he'd just get shot in the back. And lying where he was huddled into a ball, waiting for the first NVA with a grenade to blow him away, didn't appeal to him either.

So, in the tradition of American soldiers from the days of Concord on, he said, "fuck this," jumped to his feet and started running *up* the hill, straight at the nearest bunker, firing his machine gun as he moved.

How he survived the first few seconds is cause for wonder, but one thing to keep in mind is that by now the trees were all either knocked down or stripped bare, and the riflemen who'd sat concealed in their upper branches during earlier assaults were no longer able to fire down on the advancing troops.

He made the first bunker, stuck the barrel of the machine gun into its slit opening, sprayed the interior, withdrew the smoking barrel and ran up to the next bunker to his right. Repeating that process, he zigzagged up the slope, silencing bunker after bunker, until he looked around him for another bunker and realized two things: First, there were no more bunkers and, secondly, he was standing on top of the hill. The time was 1230.

40. The Naked Beast

At first, the other troopers of Alpha simply lay in place, watching in amazement as Jackson cleaned out the first few bunkers. But then, one by one, they got to their feet and moved up after him, grenading and shooting up the odd bunker or foxhole Jackson had left untouched. A few minutes later, they stood on the hill alongside him, and began moving to their left, or north, toward the ridge that Delta still was assaulting. Not long after that, a spurt of purple smoke far across the hill marked the presence of the 2/3rd, and by then the 1/506th had cleaned out the bunkers on the south slopes of Hill 900.

The messages coming into the TOC changed dramatically. They were the harsh, pitiless songs of victory.

"This is Bravo Six. We're on top of Hill 900. Dozens of bodies here, no live enemy. I'm sending a platoon off to the east to check out that draw over there. Be advised."

"Goddamn! Look at 'em! They're running! They're running! This is Charlie Six; get me some arty here. There're hundreds of them, running down that draw to the west! Fire for effect; they're in the open! *Goddamn.*"

"Roger, my guys just found a trench here, just off the north knoll. Got about a hundred bodies here, 'bout two, three days old. Man, this place is bad news. We'll need gas masks. Nobody else home."

"Iron Raven, got the enemy on the run, moving down the hill, toward the north. Get me some ARA over here, quick. I'm popping smoke...."

"Just fire for effect; they're all over the place, runnin'...."

"Catch 'em in the open, they're taking off for Laos...."

"This is Crazy Otto Seven. Just fired a marking round. Fire for effect...."

"This is Random Two Four. Can't fire over there, Black Jack. Too close to the ARVN unit."

There was more, but Eward and I turned away. For a moment, we stood in the darkened TOC, looking, not at each other, but at the muddy PCP flooring. Then Eward finally spoke.

"Best get back to the platoon," he said. "Still a lot of work to do."

The troops had already gotten the word — they'd seen the smoke, of course — but for the most part they sat in their holes, eating, smoking, writing letters or playing cards. There was little conversation, and none of it concerned the taking of the hill.

Robert Kenzy looked up as I walked by.

"All over now, Lieutenant?"

"Yeah, Kenz. All over."

"I hear Delta still had a tough time on our ridge. Lost some more people today. You know how many?"

"No. Haven't heard."

"Yeah, well ... that was a tough nut. Got any idea how many gooks we got?"

"No. Haven't heard that either."

"Yeah." He shook his head. "You know what, Lieutenant? A hot shower and a night's sleep — reckon we earned it, sir."

I smiled. "We just might let you clean up a bit."

I was surprised to find that I felt nothing. When I reached the CP, I found Helms sprawled out beside his radio, asleep. He awoke as I sat down, and reached out with his hand.

"Want the radio on, sir? Just shut it off a minute ago."

"No." I held a hand up. "No, just leave it off, Dennis."

"Yes, sir." Helms nodded. I closed my eyes and sat back.

Twenty-four hours later, we were ready to leave. Replacements had been flown in, particularly for the fallen officers. Delta Company did not have a single officer left. Charlie had lost all of them except Jessup. Alpha had lost two, and we three. Every Company Commander except for Jessup was wounded, two of them seriously. Three of the four FOs were down. The only original platoon leaders to make it through the fight were Gordie Atcheson and Dan Bresnahan of Alpha, Eward and I. Black Jack had been wounded twice; even Howard had been hit lightly by shrapnel from the ARA, as had several of the staff officers.

We lifted off, and as the pilot turned eastward, the beast lay before me, naked and blood-ugly in the grey afternoon light. I stared at it without really understanding the emotions I felt: Anger, yes, and hatred, for the hill itself, for the uncaring mass of rock and clay, this beast lying sprawled below me, baneful even in death. I hated the beast not simply because of the guilt and grief I felt for the death of my men, not just because the 11 days prostrated before it had made me confront myself, see things in myself that I would rather not have seen, dredged up fears and weaknesses and selfishness and ignobility: It was much more than that. I hated the thing because, in the end, it had so effortlessly demanded everything of me and taken it, without my consent, without my volition, without even my understanding. I had been sucked dry, stripped bare and cast away as a fly, snared, bound, and eaten by a voracious spider is discarded into the hellish midden. Everything I had, every resource, all my strength, all my life's blood, had been taken from me, used, and discarded. It was the final sacrifice, the final mortification, the final angelus in this the blackest of masses. But the worst of it was the knowledge that I was no hapless fly. None of us were. Jessup, Schoch and I; we were men, and had within us what the fly struggling in the web has not: Moral choice. That was what the beast had done to us, ultimately, and why I hated it so. Father, how can you forsake me, and bring me to face an evil I had no hope of avoiding? You left me to confront The Beast with no other weapon than my will, and no armor except my humanity. In the end, it hardly noticed its victory.

Epilogue

The battle ended on the May 20, but the Rakkasans took a month or more to recover. In almost any other war, we would have been disbanded as a unit, our casualties were so high. But the Rakkasans were not, and have served valiantly in Afghanistan and Iraq, the most highly decorated battalion in the U.S. Army.

Bravo was taken immediately to an in-country R&R facility, actually a U.S. Navy oil pumping station on the beaches of the South China Sea, not far from Hue, where we spent a week. After absorbing several replacements, we ran some routine patrols in the area around Camp Evans, in the surrounding plains and the first ridgeline—the one that held Firebases Long and Helen, then being dismantled. At this point, I was made XO, and had no argument to make against it. We returned to the pumping station in late June, this time as a security force, but in reality it was simply a second R&R. I left for my own R&R, in Hawaii, where I met my wife, on July 2, returned and was given an unimportant assignment on the battalion staff.

By that time, Honeycutt was gone; he'd been replaced prematurely. Gone too were all the company commanders, either wounded or, like Captain Harkins, given staff jobs. Black Jack's staff was gone, for the most part, but Major Howard remained, inexplicably. Marsh Eward, Gordie Atcheson and I were the three remaining veteran platoon leaders, and none of us received a worthwhile assignment. Dan Bresnahan, the other surviving platoon leader, returned to the States where he entered rotary wing flight school.

It became apparent that the incoming battalion commander wanted his own people, and we weren't among them. So be it. The most pernicious and most costly Pentagon policy of the Viet Nam war was the imbecilic decision to rotate battlefield commanders, and particularly battalion commanders, the ones who actually fought the war, on a six-month basis. I have no hesitation in stating that this one decision cost the lives of thousands of U.S. soldiers. When you add the horrific political decision, made by Lyndon Johnson, to restrict the ground war to South Viet Nam, thus giving the North Vietnamese the luxury of unlimited and untouched sanctuaries in Laos, Cambodia and North Viet Nam, you have a recipe for what took place.

The Rakkasans returned to the A Shau in August, and the casualties mounted again. Two more of my men died there: Jayson "Grump" Ulrich, on an anonymous hill not far from Dong Ap Bia, in August, along with a replacement named Bowman; and, late in November, the medic Hudson, killed by a mortar attack on a firebase. Lou Charles was wounded on his last night in the field, in October, and with him Paul Samuels.

In October, I was notified that I was to have a second R&R — an unheard of event. I had not asked for one, nor did I particularly desire it. I was married, after all, and the expense of flying my wife out a second time from the East Coast to Hawaii was considerable, and then too she had our new baby to attend to. But a few days before I was to go, I was finally told why. I was going to Honolulu to take part in a ceremony bestowing American citizenship on some 300 non-citizens currently serving in Viet Nam. And so, on that day, I stood with my hand raised and took an oath swearing fealty to the greatest country on earth.

Of those who made it home...

Dennis Helms returned to his beloved Beverly in early 1970; he went to college, got his degree — and a commission in the North Carolina National Guard — and then became an ordained minister; he and his wife continue to live in North Carolina, in a small town not far from Charlotte, and they remain two of this country's most decent people. I see them frequently.

Francis Doc Muldoon, after recovering from his wounds, was mustered out of the Army and returned to Wilmington, where I visited him later. Doc's demons still lived, but he remained as I knew him: Fiercely independent, and unafraid. He never blamed anyone else for his troubles, and he was one of the most loyal men I ever knew.

Sergeant Samuel Wright finished his career in the Army and retired, with his wife, to Columbia, South Carolina. There he started a second career as a bus driver for the city. I saw him at several of the reunions at Fort Campbell. After more than 40 years, I retain an enormous affection and respect for this man, the model of a professional NCO.

Jerema Wolosenko began a software engineering firm in the Boston area, where I visited him and his still-lovely wife. Chuck Denholm survived his wounds and returned, first to Iowa, but eventually moving to Appleton, Wisconsin, where he was president of an executive search firm. In what must be a coincidence, Chuck, Jerry and I, although out of touch for the first decade or so after the war, each fathered a son during that time; when we all met later on, we were astonished to find out that we had all named our sons Alex. Great minds, guys.

John Snyder and his wife are still active dairy farmers in Pennsylvania. John and I appeared together in Oliver North's War Stories episode on Hamburger Hill, having been flown to New York for the interviews. He and Linda faithfully attend the reunions, and just as faithfully have kept in touch, particularly during my illness.

Nathan Hyde lived in Monroe, Louisiana; I corresponded with him for a while. Alas, Nathan died a couple of years ago, but I will never forget him.

John Eden went back to live in Martins Ferry, Ohio, where, despite his lifelong limp, he worked for the Post Office. John died young, of cancer.

I visited Phil Nelson, still bluff and forthright, in a very small town in central Virginia, home to many of his tribe. To this day, Nelson maintains that had First Platoon been in the lead on that afternoon of May 11, and he at point, we would never have walked into the ambush.

I went to see Tim Logan in Indianapolis, a dozen or so years after the war. I recall driving sown a suburban street, looking for his address, and then seeing four or five children with bright red hair, running about a yard. I had no need for the address, at that point. Tim and I sat up all night, talking. He is a great talker still.

Over the years, I've seen a few of the others, at the Fort Campbell reunions: Steven Conzoner, still living in Milwaukee; Wayne Olson, in northern Michigan, not far from Tom St. Onge's parents; Paul Samuels. Ray Carlton — Short Round — now a mature and confident man, called me several times, although I missed seeing him at the reunions.

After retiring, I drove up to Hermansville, Michigan, a small town near Iron City, where I visited with Tom St. Onge's parents; the town has built a small museum in Tom's honor. His nephew has provided me with several photographs Tom had sent home.

I never made it to Thief River Falls, the home of Myles Westman, but I have been in touch with his relatives. I told them how much we thought of Myles.

At the last reunion, in May 2012, Charles Littnan attended. We spent many hours discussing what took place on Dong Ap Bia. He was my CO for only a little over three weeks, but he was a thorough professional and I admired him greatly. Despite his wounds — it took him years to fully recover — he remained in the army but is now retired, living in Arizona.

Finally, I have spent some time with General Honeycutt (now long since retired, of course). He hasn't changed much. He did let me in on a secret: The fact that First Platoon got the tough assignments — Dong Ngai, rescuing Charlie Company — was no accident. I never heard a word of praise from the man, but he trusted me. Well, as I said, he wasn't paid to be my buddy. And he still swells with pride at the job his Rakkasans did, in those ten days in May.

Glossary

90mm Vietnam era version of the bazooka, served by a two-man team, firing HE, armor-piercing or flechette rounds.

105mm Smallest of the standard army artillery pieces. Spoken as One Oh Five. The 105 refers to the diameter of the barrel in millimeters.

155mm One Five Five. Medium artillery.

175mm One Seven Five. Heavy artillery.

8 Inch Eight inch. Another standard army artillery piece, close to the 175 in size, but a howitzer; the barrel is measured in inches, not millimeters.

ACL Aircraft Load — the number of non-crew allowed on a flight. In a Huey, the usual number was 5 or 6; with 4 crew, that meant 9 or 10 people max.

AK-47 The Kalashnikov. The principal infantry rifle used by the NVA, firing a 7.62 round. Heavier than the M16 (more than 9 pounds) but more robust.

AO Area of Operations.

APC Armored Personnel Carrier.

ARA Aerial Rocket Artillery. Usually 2.75 rockets carried by a modified Huey.

Arc Light A B52 strike against ground targets in Viet Nam.

B52 The Air Force strategic heavy bomber, used both against North Vietnamese targets and in South Viet Nam.

Base Camp Large, semi-permanent headquarters and logistics center for a brigade and division.

CA Combat Assault.

Canister Round An artillery (or M79) round loaded with balls or pellets instead of HE.

CG Commanding General.

Claymore M18A1 anti-personnel mine; it is manually operated on command through a pair of wires leading to a hand-held generator. Convex in shape, containing a C4 explosive band in the back fronted by hundreds of small steel balls, it is held in place by a pair of simple tripods stuck into the ground.

CO Commanding Officer.

Cobra Vietnam-era attack helicopter Bell AH-1.

Glossary of Terms

CP   Command Post.

Crane   CH54 Skycrane, a huge 6-bladed helicopter capable of lifting 50,000 pounds.

DEROS   Date Eligible for Return from Overseas Service — the day you go home.

DOR   Date of Rank.

Drag Man   The last man in a unit file, responsible for covering the rear of the unit.

Ell Tee   The initials LT — a lieutenant.

F4   A single-seat fighter-bomber used by both the Navy and the Air Force in Viet Nam.

F105   A two-seater fighter-bomber used in various roles, including infantry support, in Viet Nam. Also referred to as a One Oh Five.

FDC   Fire Direction Center. On a firebase, the command and communication post where the artillery plotted their fire missions.

FEBA   Forward Edge of the Battle Area: That sector of a unit's position closest to the enemy.

Firebase   Usually isolated posts for artillery, guarded by an infantry detachment.

Flechette   Barbed, angular metal packed in canister rounds. Lethal at close range.

FO   Forward Observer. At the company level this was a commissioned artillery officer, usually a first lieutenant. Each platoon also had an enlisted FO.

G1   See S1 below

G2   See S2 below

G3   See S3 below

G4   See S4 below

G5   See S5 below

Gunship   Modified Huey helicopter armed with 7.62 caliber machine guns mounted in pods of 6.

HE   High Explosive.

Hill nnn   Hills or mountains on a military map are referenced by their height above sea level in meters; thus the summit of Hill 937 was 937 meters high.

Hook   Short for Chinook, the CH51, a large cargo and personnel helicopter still in use.

Huey   The Bell UH-1 all-purpose utility helicopter, ubiquitous in Viet Nam. Also referred to as ship, slick, chopper, aircraft and taxi.

Key Word   A simple substitution code, changed daily, wherein the digits one through zero are sequentially represented by the letters of two unrelated words. E.g. "Alvin Comet": 1 is A, 2 is L, 3 is V, and so on through 0 is T.

Klick   Kilometer.

LOH   Light Observation Helicopter. The OH6A Cayuse. A small two-seater, unarmed and armorless. Very maneuverable but very vulnerable.

LP   Listening Post.

M16A1   The M16; standard army infantry weapon in Viet Nam. It fired a 5.56 round carried in a ten-shot magazine; later versions accepted both a 20 and a 30-round magazine. Only 39" long and weighing just over 7 pounds loaded, it was ideal for the densely vegetated mountain rainforest we operated in.

Glossary of Terms

M79 A shotgun-like weapon designed to shoot grenade rounds at relatively short range. It could also shoot flechette canisters.

Mad Minute A tactic used on firebases and base camps, wherein at a specified time all weapons were fired into the night, along the entire perimeter, to disrupt or discourage a potential sapper or ground attack. Despised by the troops.

Medevac Medical Evacuation helicopter (a modified Huey), or the evacuation itself.

Mike 60 An M60 7.62 caliber machine gun, weighing about 23 pounds, standard equipment for an infantry unit.

NDP Night Defensive Position. A defensive perimeter, roughly circular, designed to defend against attack from all directions. In Viet Nam, for a variety of reasons, NDPs were rarely dug out; almost always they were changed daily.

NVA North Vietnamese Army. Not a guerrilla unit but the fourth-largest standing army in the world, with a company TOE more formidable than ours.

OCS Officer Candidate School—for the infantry, at Fort Benning, Ga.: An intensive six-month course at the end of which the successful candidate receives a commission as a second lieutenant in the US Army Reserve and is assigned to active duty.

OP Observation Post

OPCON Operational Control

Password A two-word phrase used in a challenge-and-response in order to establish the identity of an approaching individual.

Point Man The first man in a patrol file, responsible for leading the way and spotting the enemy, mines, booby traps or other dangers. A job of great responsibility and considerable personal danger.

PRC10 The older field radio in use in the army, weighing almost 26 pounds and not always reliable. Replaced by the PRC25.

PRC25 A portable field radio, weighing about 18 pounds; solid-state FM with an effective range (in the mountains) of between 15 and 30 kms; equipped with both a transmitter and a hand held microphone that looked like a civilian handset of the era.

PZ Pickup Zone.

RIF Reconnaissance in Force. A platoon or company-sized patrol.

RPG Ubiquitous and deadly: Rocket Propelled Grenade; ostensibly a hand-held anti-tank weapon but used by the NVA in an anti-personnel role.

RTO Radio-Telephone Operator. Refers to the individual who carried a PRC25 radio on his back. Each platoon leader and platoon sergeant had an RTO; so did the company commander (who had two) and company first sergeant; and the commissioned FO.

S1 The staff officer and organization responsible for administration and personnel for the brigade and battalion. A G1 would have the same duties but for a division or higher level.

S2 The staff officer and organization responsible for intelligence at the brigade and battalion level as the G2 did at division or higher.

S3 The staff officer and organization responsible for operations and planning for the brigade or battalion. G3 had the same duties at division or higher.

S4 The staff officer and organization responsible for supply and logistics for the brigade or battalion. The G4 did the same for the division or higher.

S5 The staff officer and organization responsible for psychological operations for the brigade or battalion. G5 did the same for division or higher. In Viet Nam, the S5 had almost no meaningful function.

Slack Man The second man in a unit file, supporting the point man; placed usually five to ten meters behind him.

Slick A stripped-down Huey, the workhorse of an airmobile unit. So named because side doors, interior seats and dividing bulkheads are removed, leaving the interior bare and open.

Stand To A specified time, usually just before dawn, when everyone dons weapons and gear and stands ready to fire in their bunkers or foxholes.

Spooky Modified C47 carrying three miniguns, one firing from the rear and the other two from the port side, each consisting of six M60 barrels firing standard 7.62 rounds. Also called Puff the Magic Dragon. Absolutely lethal against exposed infantry.

Spooky The second version: A modified C130 carrying a single 40mm cannon and two 20mm Vulcan cannons, and, later, a 105 artillery piece.

TDY Temporary Duty

TOC Tactical Operations Center; a command and communications center.

TOE Table of Organization and Equipment.

Index

1st Cavalry Division 15, 84, 158
1st Platoon B Co., Bravo One 14, 16, 17, 51, 55, 57, 60, 76, 78, 87, 88, 93, 104, 116, 118, 122, 137, 139, 144, 165, 167, 249, 258, 270, 274, 276, 281, 311, 314, 325, 326, 341, 361, 374, 377, 409, 418, 422, 423
1/502nd Battalion 278, 422
1/506th Battalion Curahees 278, 348, 376, 378, 435, 437, 438, 440–442, 448, 449
173rd Regiment 159
2nd Platoon B Co., Bravo Two 17, 48, 50, 58, 78, 91, 104, 118, 132, 142, 169, 196, 253, 258, 280, 281, 321, 326, 336, 339–343, 361, 365, 367, 368, 371–374, 378, 403, 408–410, 418, 419, 430, 444, 445
2/3rd ARVN Battalion 278, 441, 442, 447, 449
2/17th Cavalry Battalion 173, 174, 186, 199, 219, 248, 276, 341
2/326th Engineers 23, 321, 329, 331
2/501st Battalion 99, 167, 341, 376, 441, 442
2/506th Battalion 278, 283, 304, 441, 442
22nd Field Hospital 95, 106, 136, 139, 267, 269
29th NVA Regiment 309, 341, 440
3rd Brigade 101st 9, 28, 173
3rd Platoon B Co., Bravo Three 17, 31, 48, 51, 96, 104, 109, 129, 132, 136, 149, 155, 167, 169, 193, 258, 266, 280, 302, 304, 305, 310, 314, 329, 335, 360–362, 365, 367, 368, 371–373, 403, 405–410, 412–414
3/187th Battalion Rakkasans 9, 186, 199, 276, 278, 341, 366, 440
312th Arty Battery 20
4th Infantry Division 116
4th Platoon B Co., Bravo Four 159, 196, 258, 282, 297–300, 302, 304, 305, 307, 311, 316, 325, 326, 329, 336, 338, 413
42nd Maintenance Co. 270
5th NVA Regiment 99
6th NVA Regiment 199, 341
64th NVA Regiment 81

A Luoi 157, 176
A Shau 90, 99, 109, 110, 116, 144, 154, 156–158, 160, 164, 167, 170, 171, 173, 176, 249, 257, 273, 280, 298, 341, 354, 382, 388, 428, 429, 432
Abbot, PFC Edward 44, 45, 46, 47, 66, 70, 88, 97, 111–115, 149, 417
Abrams, Gen. Creighton 446
Alpha Co. 2/506th 341, 376, 400, 442, 448
Alpha Co. 3/187th 56, 60, 61, 79, 80, 101, 117, 118, 122, 124, 131, 154, 212, 213, 217, 218, 238, 275, 279, 283, 348, 363, 403, 407, 409, 416, 418, 419, 435, 436, 438, 440, 444, 448–450
Andersen, PFC 87, 420, 421
Apache Snow 270, 272, 273
Area 54 219
Area 82 279
ARVN 85–87, 90–92
Atcheson, 1st Lt. Gordon (Alpha 3 6) 218, 227, 233, 234, 236, 237, 241, 450

B52 strike arc light 52, 288
Ba Long 84
Battalion CP incident 341, 348
Bennet, 1st Lt. George (Bravo 3 6) 14, 15, 16, 17, 20, 22, 49, 50, 56, 57, 67, 68, 74, 77, 78, 80–82, 85, 87, 98
Besack, PFC Clark 141, 332, 369, 370, 372–374, 378
Bien Hoa 14, 81, 82, 88, 93, 104, 239, 251, 267, 268, 292, 410
Bilk Two Three 282, 283, 219, 282, 283, 302, 308, 314, 319–321, 342, 351–358, 432, 434, 441, 444, 447
Bilk Two Two 169
Billings, 1st Lt. Ted 148, 153, 394
Black Widow 4 2 330–333, 335
Black Widow 4 3 350
Black Widow 4 4 28, 88, 165
Black Widow Squadron 90, 92, 94, 165, 335, 367
Bowers, Lt. Col. John 437, 438
Bravo Co. 1/506th 438, 440
Bravo Co. 3/187th 9, 66, 95, 96, 100, 107, 122, 130, 138, 159, 207, 217, 227, 238, 272, 275, 276, 280, 361, 363, 377, 383, 385, 393, 397–400, 412, 441
Bravo CP Incident 404–407
Bresina, PFC Anthony 76, 166, 249, 294, 309, 310, 380
Bresnahan, 1st Lt. Dan (Alpha 1 6) 214, 217–220, 222, 223, 225, 229, 233, 234, 236, 238, 240, 257, 437, 450
Brinkman, Spec4 201, 202, 205
Brown, Spec4 Charles 20, 24, 35, 63, 89, 166, 175, , 193, 196, 201–204, 242, 252, 259, 277, 289, 302, 323, 368, 372, 387, 388, 415, 427
Burnetta, Sgt. Greg 141, 148, 149

459

Camp Eagle, 101st Division Headquarters 9, 139, 270, 366
Camp Evans, 3rd Brigade Headquarters 9, 11, 13, 18, 19, 28, 31, 48, 67, 82, 88, 94, 95, 104, 106, 109, 133, 139, 141, 148, 149, 150, 154, 156, 163, 170, 173, 235, 255, 267, 268, 277, 329, 427, 429, 432, 441, 444
Carlisle, Plt. Sgt. (Delta 3 5) 436, 437, 440
Carlson, SSgt. O.B. 210
Carlton, PFC Raymond 128, 175–177, 184–187, 192, 197, 198, 327, 328, 346, 378, 410
Carter, Spec4 (Bravo 6 Romeo) 11, 12, 13, 17, 22, 34, 52, 55, 76
Chappel, Capt. Butch (Bravo 6) 413, 416, 418–420, 422, 427, 429, 431, 432, 434, 443
Charles, 1st Lt. Lou (Bravo 3 6) 413, 416, 419, 420, 432, 434, 435
Charlie Co. 3/187th 48, 54, 57, 60, 67, 75, 81, 101, 173, 227, 279, 282, 283, 304, 329, 339, 347, 348, 351, 354–356, 361, 363, 365, 366, 368, 371, 376, 378, 380–400, 407, 409, 415, 418, 421, 432, 435, 436, 438, 440, 450
Chieu Hoi 117, 118
China Sea 13
Clark, PFC 124, 415
Clary, PFC Steven 51, 53, 149
"The Clearing" 304, 305, 308–370, 434–440, 448
Clifton, PFC James 159, 249, 250, 315, 317–319, 321, 322, 338, 339, 356, 378, 396, 403, 414
Co Trang 13
Cobra Incident, Charlie Company 438
Coc A Bo 13
Coc Muen 13
Conmy, Col. Joseph (Iron Raven) 77, 81, 137, 138–140, 186, 198, 199, 219, 229, 236, 258, 262, 273, 348, 447–449
Conzoner, Spec4 Steve (Bravo 6 Romeo) 20, 22, 32, 34, 37, 40, 53, 58, 61, 63, 64, 67–70, 75, 76, 79, 82, 89, 90, 129, 287, 297, 347, 350, 355, 360, 366, 371, 399, 403–405, 408, 415
Cowans, PFC 341, 342, 344, 347

Cray, 1st Lt. 389–391
Crazy Otto One Eight 173
Crazy Otto One Seven 173, 449
Crenshaw, 1st Lt. Russ 92, 296, 302, 315, 346, 367, 368, 384, 402–406, 415
Cu Chi 15, 16

Da Krong River 84
DaNang 81, 154
Dandridge, 1st Lt. Mike (Charlie 2 6) 49, 50
Deleone, 1st Sgt. (Charlie 5) 390
DeLorean, Spec4 (Bravo 2 5 Romeo) 196
Delta Co. 3/187th 20, 54, 57, 60, 101, 167, 173, 174, 204, 205, 207–209, 214, 217, 227, 238, 279, 280, 283, 304, 329, 339, 348, 351, 361–363, 365, 366, 368, 371, 376, 378, 380, 403, 404, 407–411, 416, 418, 422, 429, 432, 434, 435, 438–440, 442, 448–450
Denholm, 1st Lt. Charles (Bravo 4 6) 81, 82, 93, 98, 103–105, 107, 108, 138, 141, 149, 152–156, 159, 164, 166–170, 173, 189, 232, 250, 260, 261, 266, 267, 272–274, 277, 279–281, 293, 296–307, 310, 314, 316, 361, 382
Dewey Canyon 84, 158
Dickerson, Sgt. 141, 159, 160, 191, 197, 256, 260, 293, 294, 301, 302, 306, 309, 335, 353, 367, 370–372, 379, 380, 385, 388, 410, 411, 417, 419, 422
Dickson, 1st Lt. Lenville (Bravo 3 6) 93, 103, 104, 108, 126–130, 133, 135, 136, 138, 140, 142, 150, 152–156, 164, 166–170, 173, 189–191, 196, 197, 201, 218, 219, 228–231, 236, 239–241, 244, 250, 260, 261, 266, 267, 295, 296, 302, 329
Dong Ap Bia, Hamburger Hill 13, 279, 280, 287, 299, 305, 308, 316, 317, 325, 337, 362, 365, 380, 402, 403, 432, 437, 448, 449
Dong Ngai 13, 257, 273, 341, 346, 361, 410, 411, 426
Dong So 13, 429, 432
Dong Tien Con 13
Dougherty, Maj. Maurice 181, 182, 193, 210
Dragon's Tooth 13
Drozd, Sgt. Edward 141, 149
Dufresne, Capt. Tyler 204, 205, 225, 266

Eden, Sgt. John 83, 109, 111, 113, 115, 117, 127, 141, 159, 160, 191, 193, 196, 197, 201, 205, 249, 256, 281, 282, 293, 294, 302, 310, 315, 317, 319, 320, 330, 334, 353, 360, 367–370, 372–374, 376, 415, 430
Edwards, Mark 280, 311, 312, 317, 323
Evans, Sgt. Lloyd 141, 159, 253–256, 415, 426
Eward, 1st Lt. Marshall (Bravo 2 6) 315, 320, 325–329, 332, 340–342, 344–352, 361, 365–370, 372–374, 378, 380, 381, 399–413, 416, 418–422, 432, 441
Ewell, Maj. Gen. Julian 151

F4 Incident, Bravo Company 380–384
Firebase Airborne 257, 268, 273, 274, 341, 348
Firebase Barbara 84, 85, 94, 100, 122, 123, 158
Firebase Bastogne 155
Firebase Berchtesgaden 169, 202, 205, 260, 262, 325, 367, 447
Firebase Blaze 47, 145, 164, 168, 171, 176, 177, 235, 269, 270, 273, 275–277, 279, 341, 415
Firebase Brick 94, 100, 106, 434
Firebase Currahee 367, 447
Firebase Eagle's Nest 13, 155
Firebase Helen 9, 10, 11, 13, 16, 17, 23, 28, 30, 33, 41, 60, 66, 67, 74, 75, 81, 94, 103, 137, 154–156, 160, 161
Firebase Jack 154, 156
Firebase Long 13, 23, 60, 67, 81, 98, 103, 154, 157
Firebase Rakkasan 9, 13, 16, 17, 21, 27, 60–62, 66, 103, 109, 115, 117, 133, 136, 142, 143, 147, 149, 154–156, 160, 161, 164, 165, 170, 203, 257, 258, 382
Firebase Strike 131, 155, 157
Fleagane, PFC Jon 180, 182, 183

G2 Division Intelligence 81
G4 Division Logistics 401
Gann, Spec4 Terry 159, 191, 196, 249, 256, 288–292, 294, 334, 336, 353–356, 415
Garvey, Spec4 407–410
Garza, Plt. Sgt. Luis (Bravo 5) 12, 22, 28, 29, 58, 60, 61, 67,

Index

73, 78, 80, 82, 86, 87, 92, 93, 134, 136–140, 150, 153, 159, 174, 280, 302, 304–308, 312–314, 316, 328, 340, 346, 348, 350, 352, 356, 357, 361, 362, 366–370, 372, 378, 379, 380, 381, 401–404, 407, 409–411, 413, 414, 434, 435
Genna, CWO2 Chris 194–196, 213, 219, 223
Ghost Rider Squadron 189–215
Goff, 1st Lt. Jim (Charlie 2 6) 81, 387, 389, 390, 392, 395, 396, 403, 442
Gouch, Capt. Mike 193–195, 211, 212

Haney, Maj. Gerald (chaplain) 137, 138
Hannah, PFC Andrew 124, 149, 415
Hansen, Maj. Carl (XO) 96
Harkins, Capt. Bob (Alpha 6) 136, 214, 215, 216, 217–222, 224–234, 236–238, 240, 275, 403, 404, 437, 448
Hash, PFC 20, 24
Hathaway, PFC Thomas 20, 22, 63, 67–70, 82
Helms, PFC Dennis (Bravo 1 6 Romeo) 141–143, 153, 160, 166, 175–187, 189, 194, 196, 198–200, 203, 207, 208, 211, 212, 222, 224–227, 235, 239, 248, 249, 254, 259, 262–265, 277, 278, 281, 284, 285, 289–291, 294, 295, 297, 299, 302, 311, 315, 317–320, 323, 330, 331, 333, 336, 340, 342–346, 350, 354–356, 358, 360, 364, 365, 368, 370–372, 379, 380, 382, 383, 386, 392, 398, 401, 405, 407–410, 416, 417, 419, 423, 427, 428, 441, 444–46, 450
Hernandez, PFC John 38, 76, 260, 296, 297, 338, 339, 343, 346, 356, 378, 379, 381, 382, 385, 417
HHC 3/187th 99, 100, 431
Highway 547 99, 157
Highway 548 (Yellow Brick Road) 157, 167
Highway 601 67
Hill 105 154
Hill 142 74
Hill 150 131
Hill 154 117, 131, 154, 247
Hill 178 154
Hill 504 48
Hill 674 see FB Helen

Hill 770 165, 168, 276
Hill 900 435, 437, 440, 442, 448, 449
Hill 937 see Dong Ap Bia
Hill 990 164
Hill 1485 174, 176, 178, 185, 223, 235, 250, 255, 257, 262, 298, 301, 303, 310, 317, 330, 335, 336, 346
Ho Chi Minh Trail 157
Honeycutt, Lt. Col. Weldon "Black Jack" 76, 77, 85, 86, 95, 96, 99, 100, 101, 104, 106, 136, 137, 141, 142, 144, 145, 147, 150, 152, 153, 155, 156, 160–164, 166, 169, 174, 179, 181, 183, 187, 189, 190, 192, 198, 201, 202, 204, 205, 207–212, 214, 217–221, 225, 227, 233–240, 243, 250, 261, 262, 269, 272–274, 279, 280, 283, 287, 288, 293, 296–300, 302, 308, 309, 320, 329, 332, 335, 340, 347, 348, 355, 361, 370, 378–382, 385, 386, 390, 392, 395–397, 403, 405–407, 409–411, 420, 424, 431–439, 441, 449, 450
Howard, Maj. John (Sierra 3) 205, 237, 238–240, 242, 262, 264, 269, 273, 274, 341, 403, 431–433, 444, 450
Hudson, Spec4 350, 358, 359, 361, 364, 368, 372, 374, 375, 388–390, 406, 424, 427
Hue 9, 13, 15, 76, 90, 99, 156, 157
Hyde, Sgt. Nathaniel 28, 37, 40, 41, 42, 62, 63, 70–72, 77, 83, 118, 119, 123, 128, 132, 141, 153, 159, 166, 167, 172, 175, 177, 184–187, 189, 191, 192, 196, 197, 201–208, 213, 246, 255, 256, 290, 292–294, 302, 319, 320, 330, 335, 343, 346, 353–356, 359, 367, 368, 372, 379, 383, 385, 388, 409, 410, 417, 421, 430, 446

Jackson, Spec4 John 448, 449
Jackson, PFC William 311, 312, 323
Jacobs, Spec4 Demar 149
Jefferson, Spec4 Alton 50
Jessup, Capt. Paul (Charlie 6) 347, 361, 386–393, 395–400, 425, 438, 439, 450
Jones, 1st Lt. Albert (Bravo 2 6) 12, 16, 17, 18, 21, 49, 50, 57, 74, 75, 77, 81
Jones, PFC Lewis 37, 61, 76, 124, 159, 387, 415

Jorgenson, PFC Jerome 255, 315–317, 378, 404, 406, 415, 426, 427
Joubert, 1st Sgt. Donald (Alpha 5) 215, 234

Kaminski, PFC Doug 25, 26, 109, 121, 124, 128, 129, 141, 142, 149
Kenzy, PFC Robert 70–72, 74, 123, 159, 191, 193, 196, 197, 207, 256, 333, 335, 357–359, 372, 376, 379, 388, 390, 393, 417, 449
Khe San 157
Khe Tre 157

Laird, Melvin 107
Laos 13, 156, 157, 176, 279, 280, 291, 299, 309, 327, 356, 362, 366, 410, 432, 435
Larson, Spec4 Terry (Bravo 4 6 Romeo) 303, 306, 310
Leanahan, Sgt. Reggie 134, 135, 137, 138, 140, 273, 413
Leech Island 99, 100
Lipscomb, 1st Lt. Dave (Delta 3 6) 434–437, 440, 442
Littnan, Capt. Charles (Bravo 6) 271–274, 277, 280–283, 287–291, 293–297, 300, 301, 304, 308–315, 318–321, 325, 326, 328, 330, 331, 335, 340–348, 350–358, 360–363, 365–371, 373, 378–381, 384, 385, 396, 398–400, 402–406, 409, 415, 416, 421, 422
Logan, PFC Tim 65, 66, 79, 119, 124, 128, 142, 143, 166, 175–183, 185, 186, 197, 198, 201, 204, 222, 249, 250, 271, 314, 315, 327, 328, 333–335, 342, 344, 346, 353, 354, 357–360, 362–364, 372–373, 379, 396, 398, 399, 410, 411, 417, 422, 423
Lough, Capt. Tom 331
LZ2 Battalion CP 279, 280, 376, 394, 422, 429, 431, 438

Maher, 1st Lt. Len (Alpha 2 6) 442, 448
Marines 84, 158
Mareniewski, Spec4 Edward 41, 42, 47, 69, 79, 118, 124, 125, 132, 253, 311, 317, 320, 323, 333, 369, 372, 385, 396
Mattioli, 1st Lt. Al (Delta 2 6) 209, 210, 219, 363
McCarrell, Spec4 196, 197, 298, 303, 305, 306, 310, 312, 318

Index

McGreevy, 1st Lt. Frank (Alpha 2 6) 217, 218, 219, 222, 229, 233, 437
Meehan, Sgt. Maj. 239, 243, 268, 270
Meyers, Spec4 19, 20
Micheaux, Plt. Sgt. 173, 192, 194, 196, 197, 200, 304, 415
Mills, Spec4 305, 306
Molinar, WO Luis 193, 210
Moran, 1st Sgt. (Delta 5) 268, 269, 270
Morris, PFC Alvin 25, 26, 83, 90, 91, 109, 121, 149, 445
Mot, Col. (5th NVA) 99, 101, 105, 106, 147, 242
Muldoon, PFC Frances 20, 23, 24, 30, 39, 63, 64, 66, 68–72, 88, 89, 91, 105, 109, 111, 121, 124, 142, 160, 166, 174, 175, 252–255, 258, 259, 262, 263, 277, 278, 281, 282, 284–286, 290, 301, 302, 315, 317, 319, 321, 323, 324, 335, 336, 338, 339, 350, 389, 390, 415, 427, 445
Murtiff, 1st Sgt. William (Bravo 5) 159, 172–174, 255, 256, 260, 267, 271–273, 301, 302, 312, 328, 329, 333, 341, 346, 368, 371, 404–406, 415

Nelson, Spec4 Phillip 27, 141, 145, 159, 249, 250, 255, 256, 288–290, 292–294, 315, 317–319, 321, 322, 338, 339, 343, 346, 356, 360, 415
USS *New Jersey* 402
Nolan, Spec4 Daniel 190, 191, 196
Novak, Sgt. Mike 159, 253–256, 354, 415, 426
Nui Khe Thai 131, 132
Nuoc Ke Trai 81, 131

Ogle, Capt. S1 James 99, 100, 104
O'Keefe, Spec6 322, 375, 376, 413, 414, 424, 427
Olson, PFC Wayne 124, 309, 333, 378, 387

Pacoh Tribe 13
Parson, CWO2 Bill 209, 210, 212
Perfume River 13, 99
Peters, Spec4 296, 404–406, 415
Phou Reck 13
Pitre, Spec4 Jordy 414
Powell, Spec4 Richard 191, 206, 207, 217, 226, 227

Price, Spec4 Joseph (Bravo 6 Romeo) 58, 287, 297, 302, 347, 365, 366, 370, 403–405, 408, 415

Quan Aim Hoa 279
Quang Tri 81, 84, 90, 154

Raffaelle, Maj. Gene (S3) 9, 10, 15, 58, 62, 94, 109, 132, 141, 145, 147, 148, 155, 161–163, 205, 235
Rairdon, CWO2 "Crazy" Bill 303, 304, 329, 330, 346, 376, 388, 393–396, 414, 415, 438
Randolph, Plt. Sgt. (Bravo 2 5) 196, 197, 201, 224, 312, 313, 341
Random 2 4 449
Random 4 4 366
Rao Lao 176
Rao Nai 276, 277
Rao Trang 158, 168, 169, 401
Recon Platoon 3/187th 258, 366, 400
Robertson, Spec5 220, 221, 227
Robison, Capt. Barry (Bravo 6) 9, 11, 14, 16, 17, 20–22, 26, 28, 29, 32, 34, 42, 45, 48–52, 55–60, 67, 68, 72–76, 78–82, 85–87, 92, 93, 96, 99, 103, 104, 105, 107, 109, 118, 120, 121, 122, 126–140, 147–155, 160, 161, 164, 166–174, 227, 229, 235, 242, 249, 250, 251, 253, 257, 259, 260, 262, 264, 267–68, 271, 272, 330, 393
Rosenstreich, Sgt. Aaron 303, 305, 306, 310, 318

S1 Admin & Personnel 141
S2 Intelligence 81, 108, 156, 260, 291, 429
S3 Operations 16, 23, 77, 80, 108, 141, 142, 156, 235
S4 Logistics 63
St. Onge, PFC Thomas (Bravo 1 5 Romeo) 124, 142, 160, 166, 175, 176, 184, 186, 193, 197, 206, 207, 226, 227, 252, 257, 415, 426, 427
Samuel, Spec4 Paul 27, 39, 127, 153, 261, 315, 317, 319, 333, 417, 418
Sanders, Capt. Luther (Delta 6) 218, 236, 238, 280, 361, 363, 403, 436
Sandler, Sgt. Webord 18, 19
Savoy, PFC 86, 92
Schoch, Spec5 Nicholas 67, 86, 92, 256, 301, 302, 307, 322,
323, 331, 335, 358, 360, 372–376, 390, 404, 409, 414, 415, 424–427, 445
Searcy, WO2 Elton 194, 212, 215, 219, 223
Sheets, Lt. Col. Barracuda 15, 16, 23, 27, 55, 75
Sherron, Lt. Col. 441
Simpson, Plt. Sgt. 268, 270
Skinner, Spec4 Russ 37, 38, 44, 77, 82, 83, 109
Snyder, Spec4 John 79, 153, 159, 160, 253–256, 310–312, 315–320, 323, 336, 396, 404, 405, 409, 411, 417, 419
Song Bo 13, 14, 17, 37, 39, 40, 42, 74, 76, 78, 80, 82, 84, 109, 117, 131, 132, 154, 168
Song Hou Trach 99
Song Ta Trach 99
Song Trach 154
Spooky C147 198–200, 310, 336, 339, 340, 343
Stearns, Plt. Sgt. (Delta 1 5) 437
Stempin, SSgt. Paul 21, 24, 27, 39, 43, 44, 45, 75, 77, 82, 83, 87, 88, 434
Stenger, Spec4 Norman 190, 196, 198, 206, 207, 217, 220, 223, 224, 226, 227, 282, 301, 302, 331, 335
Stewart, Jimmy 81, 82, 98
Stillwell, Gen. Richard 446
Strobe 198, 199, 201
Sullivan, 1st Lt. Donald (Charlie 3 6) 389, 390, 392, 395, 396, 403
Sweet, Spec4 Floyd 360, 404, 415

Tanaka, Spec4 273, 275
Tet Offensive 15, 76, 99, 157
Thomas, 1st Lt. Gene (Bravo 2 6) 85, 86, 92
Towson, PFC Mike 86–88, 92, 149
Trangh, Capt. 91
Trautman, 1st Lt. Joel (Charlie 1 6) 81, 363, 387, 389, 390, 392, 394, 395, 397, 398, 439, 440, 442
Tunney, Spec4 191, 196, 302, 306, 310, 324

Ulrich, Spec4 Jayson 76, 159, 249, 296, 297, 309, 310, 327, 328, 332, 378, 379, 385, 417, 446
USO 120

Vandenburg, PFC Robert 119, 193, 196, 198, 415

Index

Walden, 1st Lt. Jerry (Delta 1 6) 236–238, 437
The Wall 78, 117, 126, 383
Watson, Capt. David 181, 187, 193, 206, 303
Westman, PFC Myles 128, 166, 196, 199, 271, 314, 328, 335, 336, 342, 344, 346, 353, 354, 358–362, 415, 426, 427, 446
Williams, PFC Wesley 338, 339, 346, 415
Wolosenko, 1st Lt. Jerema (Bravo 2 6) 93, 97–99, 103, 104, 105, 107, 108, 117–120, 122, 126, 127, 129, 130, 132–141, 142, 145, 146, 153, 156, 160, 163, 203, 235, 242, 247, 341, 429
Wright, PFC John (Bravo 1 5 Romeo) 141, 259, 262, 263, 277, 323, 361, 364, 368, 372, 378, 423, 427, 428, 443–445

Wright, Plt. Sgt. Samuel (Bravo 1 5) 16, 18, 19, 20, 22, 23, 26, 28, 30, 34, 35, 36, 37, 39, 40, 42, 44, 47, 53, 54, 55, 58, 61–69, 78, 79, 82, 83, 85, 88, 91, 109, 111, 113, 116, 130, 141, 142, 152, 153, 159, 166, 171–175, 249, 251, 253–256, 259–263, 268, 270, 274, 277, 281, 282, 284, 290, 300, 302, 309–312, 317, 323, 327, 328, 332–335, 342–344, 346, 347, 350, 353, 358, 360, 364, 367, 368, 370–373, 376, 377, 379, 380, 389–391, 393, 399, 405, 408, 409, 414, 417, 427, 428, 430, 434, 443–445

Zais, Maj. Gen. Melvin 77, 102, 258, 441, 446